MW01106750

AS ONE WHO SERVES

Dear Joe!
May you have a wonderful
birthday. Good reading!
Love, Anna

As One Who Serves

THE MAKING OF THE UNIVERSITY OF REGINA

James M. Pitsula

McGILL-QUEEN'S UNIVERSITY PRESS
MONTREAL & KINGSTON | LONDON | ITHACA

ISBN-13 978-07735-3055-3
ISBN-10 0-7735-3055-x

Legal deposit second quarter 2006
Bibliothèque nationale du Québec

Printed in Canada on acid-free paper that is 100% ancient forest free (100% post-consumer recycled), processed chlorine free

This book has been published with the help of grants from the University of Regina and the Humanities Research Institute at the university.

McGill-Queen's University Press acknowledges the support of the Canada Council for the Arts for our publishing program. We also acknowledge the financial support of the Government of Canada through the Book Publishing Industry Development Program (BPIDP) for our publishing activities.

LIBRARY AND ARCHIVES CANADA
CATALOGUING IN PUBLICATION

Pitsula, James Michael
As one who serves : the making of the University of Regina / James M. Pitsula.

Includes bibliographical references and index.
ISBN-13: 978-0-7735-3055-3
ISBN-10: 0-7735-3055-X

1. University of Regina – History. 2. Nineteen sixties. 3. Regina (Sask.) – Social conditions – 20th century. 4. Saskatchewan – Social conditions – 1945–1991. I. Title.

LE3.R4P583 2006 378.7124'45
C2005-907127-3

Set in 10.5/13 Electra with Helvetica Neue
Book design and typesetting by zijn digital

Contents

Acknowledgments

This book is a work of personal scholarship that represents my interpretation of the history of the University of Regina. Neither the university nor any other body commissioned it or exercised editorial control. This has been a self-assigned project, not an official history, and I have approached it as I would any other scholarly undertaking. At the same time I am aware that, as a member of the Department of History at the University of Regina, I am not an unbiased teller of this story. While I have tried to be detached and objective in my use of evidence, human beings are never completely detached and objective. I have told a story that seems to me to be both true and compelling. It will be up to the reader to judge.

I would like to thank Mark Vajcner, the archivist of the University of Regina, and archives staff members Selina Coward, Elizabeth Seitz, and Chris Eirich for their co-operation and assistance. In addition, I am grateful for the help provided by Myfanwy Truscott and Nancy McNeill at the Campion College Archives and Library and Judith Halliday at Luther College Library. My thanks go to Cheryl Avery, archivist at the University of Saskatchewan, and Trevor Powell, Chris Gebhard, Tim Novak, Cari Schwartz, Ted Sheard, Catherine Holmes, Bill Wagner, Susan Millen, Kathryn Burianyk, Fay Johnsen, Sandra Miller, and the other members of the staff of the Saskatchewan Archives Board, all of whom have dealt considerately with my requests. Marilyn Bickford, secretary of the University of Regina's Department of History, helped greatly with the electronic formatting of the manuscript. I benefited immensely from the expertise of editors Mary Williams and Joan McGilvray, and the careful attention Agnes Bray gave to the page proofs. Thanks are also due to Frances and Pat Pitsula for their personal support.

Several people – Evelyn Jonescu, Cam Blachford, Otto Driedger, Jack Ito, Robert McLaren, Ernie Nicholls, Allan Blakeney, Lloyd Barber, Tommy McLeod, David Barnard, Kathy Heinrich, Jim Tomkins, Stephen McLatchie, Reid Robinson, H. Bruce Lobaugh, John Griffiths, Dave Button, Ken McGovern, Richard Hordern, Mary Jesse, and Bryan Hillis – have read the manuscript, or portions of it, and I am grateful for their comments and suggestions. I of course take full responsibility for the contents of the book.

As I was applying the finishing touches to the manuscript, there was a knock at my office door. It was a student offering to shine my shoes in exchange for a donation to the annual Shinerama cystic fibrosis fundraising campaign. I felt a bit awkward, but he said, "That's the university motto, isn't it? ... Something about serving." This book is dedicated to the students of the University of Regina – past, present, and future.

AS ONE WHO SERVES

Introduction

This book is a sequel to *An Act of Faith: The Early Years of Regina College*, which told the story of Regina College from its founding in 1911 to the outbreak of World War II in 1939. The present volume carries the narrative forward to 1974, when the University of Regina was established by an act of the Legislature of Saskatchewan. I use the word *narrative* advisedly, because it aptly expresses the approach I have taken. History, for all the analysis, conceptualization, and theory that it requires, is fundamentally a story with a beginning, middle, and end. It describes human interactions through the passage of time, or as Donald Creighton once said, it is about character and circumstance. History explains what happens to people when they are confronted with opportunities and adversities, and it reveals how they bend or fail to bend to their purposes what fate has doled out.

The basic premise of this book is that a university is both an institution dedicated to teaching, research, and public service and a community of students, faculty, administrators, support staff, alumni, and others who share a common identity and sense of purpose. A community has a life, and every life has a story. This book is about how a college became a university or, more specifically, how Regina College, a junior college of the University of Saskatchewan, became in 1961 the University of Saskatchewan, Regina Campus, and then in 1974 the University of Regina.

It begins with Regina College handing over its buildings and campus to the Department of Defence for use as an air training school during World War II and taking up temporary quarters in a downtown office building. After the war, veterans arrived in great numbers, causing an upsurge in enrolment, and then when they left, an equally rapid decline. After a near-death experience in 1949–50, the college gained a new lease on life mainly as a provider of a wide range of semi-professional courses and through a reinvigorated art and music program. The turning point was in 1959, when the University of Saskatchewan, under the pressure of baby boom enrolments, decided to establish a full arts degree in Regina. This led to the rapid development of the Regina campus from fewer than 300 students in 1959 to more than 4,000 ten years later. A new campus was built on a barren plain at the edge of the city, buildings were constructed, faculty hired, and programs in arts and science, education, administration, engineering, graduate studies and research, and social work put in place. The story is about how students, faculty, administrators, and others made the University of Regina – that is, how they worked out what kind of university it was going to be.

The organization is partly chronological and partly thematic. Although the book begins in 1939 and carries forward to 1974, there are chapters devoted to specific subject areas such as art and music, athletics, professional colleges, federated colleges, the student movement, and so on. This results in a certain amount of moving forward and backward in time as individual themes are dealt with. To assist the reader in keeping track of the order of events, I have included a timeline in the appendix that provides a chronological list of significant developments mentioned in the text.

Leo Tolstoy wrote, "Happy families are all alike; every unhappy family is unhappy in its own way." I hope this is not true of universities, because the University of Regina has, I believe, a history with many distinctive features: roots as a Methodist Church college, location in the capital city of a province with a well-defined political culture, a complex relationship with the University of Saskatchewan, and a prairie tradition of pragmatic idealism encapsulated in the motto "As One Who Serves."

In addition, and of utmost importance to the story, is the fact that the university took shape in the crucible of the 1960s, a time of social change, political unrest, and cultural transformation that began in the late 1950s, peaked about 1968, and subsided in the early 1970s. The University of Regina was, in a manner of speaking, a child of the 1960s. This fact lies at the very centre of the story. It is inescapable, whether one considers the Regina Beach Statement, which defined the philosophy of liberal education at the Regina campus, the work of the painters in the School of Art who gained national recognition as the Regina Five, the new teacher education program introduced in the Faculty of Education, the emphasis in the Faculty of Administration on conceptual learning over skills training, the systems approach in the Faculty of Engineering, the debate in the Department of Physical Education about the goals of the athletics program, the perspectives on university education offered by Campion College and Luther College, the establishment of the Women's Centre, the partnership with the Saskatchewan Indian Federated College in 1976, and last, but not least, the student power movement.

During the 1960s traditional institutions, established authorities, and cultural norms were called into question. The civil rights movement in the United States challenged the segregationist laws and practices that had made African Americans second-class citizens. The drive for equality and social justice extended to Canada, where French-speaking Quebeckers asserted themselves to bring about a fundamental political, economic, social, and cultural transformation known as the Quiet Revolution. Aboriginal Canadians rejected the paternalism of the Department of Indian Affairs and claimed treaty rights, land entitlements, and the right to self-government. In the latter part of the decade, the women's liberation movement came to the fore and began to change the role of women in Canadian society.

Historian Doug Owram suggests that the symbolic starting point of the 1960s in Canada can be traced to Christmas Day 1959, when a small group of professors and students who belonged to the Combined Universities Campaign for Nuclear Disarmament marched through the deserted streets of Ottawa to lay a wreath at the National War Memorial.[1] They were protesting against the Cold War arms race, condemning both the Soviet Union and the United States for what seemed to be a heedless rush to nuclear war and global destruction. The Vietnam War further energized the peace movement, especially after 1965, when the United States escalated its military involvement. It is difficult to do justice to the enormous impact of the Vietnam War on the political turmoil of the 1960s. As Canadian philosopher George Grant observed, for many people it represented the first major catastrophe of the twentieth century that seemed to emerge not from an enemy of liberal democracy, such as Naziism or Communism, but from liberal democracy itself.[2] As far as the opponents of the war were concerned, the United States and her allies (including passive allies such as Canada) were destroying Vietnam under the pretext of liberating it.

The protest movements of the 1960s had an intergenerational dimension. The baby-boomers born at the end of World War II came of age in the 1960s. It was their historical moment, their time to make a mark on the world, and they took full advantage of the opportunity. University undergraduate enrolment in Canada increased from 96,690 in 1959 to 276,297 in 1970.[3] Universities scrambled to keep up with the demand, hiring faculty, constructing buildings, and developing new campuses. In western Canada the University of Victoria, Simon Fraser University, the University of Calgary, the University of Lethbridge, Brandon University, the University of Winnipeg, and the University of Regina all attained university status in the 1960s or shortly thereafter.

Many, though by no means all, of the students found much to criticize in the education they received and in the institutions that offered it. The student power activists, often supported by a substantial portion of the student body, asserted the right to control their own affairs without the quasi-parental interference of university administrators. They also demanded a say in running the institution through representation on university decision-making bodies. By the end of the decade both points had been conceded. The more radical students and their allies among the faculty questioned the basic goals and values of the university. They argued that the academy served the interests of the "power elite" and "military-industrial complex" more than it met the needs of the vast majority of people. The university, the critics said, was not a neutral institution engaged in teaching and the pursuit of truth for its own sake, but rather a complicit partner in an iniquitous political and economic system. They pointed to military research linked to the Vietnam War, technology supplied to big business, and young people educated – or, more accurately, processed – to conform to the requirements of the corporate world.

The radical critique of university education had another dimension linked to the counterculture's rejection of what was perceived as the excessive rationalism and individualism of technocratic, capitalistic Western society.[4] Dr William E. Hordern, president of Lutheran Theological Seminary at Saskatoon, touched on this theme in his dedicatory address at the official opening of Luther College, a federated college of the Regina campus, in October 1971. He said that many young people had become disillusioned with science and reason because they seemed not to address "the deeper mysteries of life, the things that make life worth living." Youth had "charged that the rational and scientific mind has to deny the existence of anything it cannot control within its own methods, and that means ultimately if you can't see it, you can't feel it, or touch it or smell it or weigh it, if you can't make a profit out of if, and you can't kill somebody with it, then it doesn't exist." According to Hordern, this was why young people were turning to Eastern religions and even to LSD-induced visions; they were in search of "a faith that will be open to the mysteries of life that transcend what reason and science can capture."[5]

The questioning of science, technology, and what the Western world calls "progress" lay at the heart of the sixties counterculture. Hordern, citing C.S. Lewis, observed, "The statement that science gives man control over nature hides the truth that science gives a few men control over nature and over other men. It puts into the hands of a few who have the knowledge and the power the ability to control the future of us all." Hordern's reply to the student critics of university education was "Don't throw out the baby with the bathwater." The answer to the misuse of reason is not irrationalism. The great need of our time, he said, is to put "the powers of education, science, and knowledge at the service of men," rather than putting men at the service of science and technology. University education should not be a means for the elite "to lord it over all men," but rather it should be made "more truly the servant of all. Instead of forcing upon men the future the experts think will be good for them, the experts must help the man to achieve the future he chooses for himself." "If this were a sermon," Hordern continued, "I would have chosen for my text Jesus' words: 'You know that those who are supposed to rule over the Gentiles lord it over them and their great men exercise authority over them, but it shall not be so among you, for whoever will be great among you must be your servant and whoever will be first among you must be slave of all. For the Son of Man came not to be served, but to serve, to give his life as ransom for many.'"[6]

The biblical passage Hordern quoted (Mark 10:42–5) was similar to the text that had inspired the Methodist founders of Regina College. They had selected in 1912 "Ut Qui Ministrat," or "As One Who Serves" (Luke 22:27), as the college motto.[7] The Methodist Church, like other Protestant denominations in Canada in the late nineteenth and early twentieth centuries, embraced the social gospel movement, which emphasized the application of Christian principles to the solution of social problems. Its goal was "to build the Kingdom of Heaven on earth."[8] Reverend J.S. Woodsworth, a Methodist minister from Winnipeg, preached a sermon at Regina's Methodist Metropolitan Church (the home church of Regina College) in May 1913 that began, "Thy Kingdom come, as in Heaven, so in Regina and Moose Jaw, Saskatoon and Winnipeg." He said that for a long time the church had "spent its time telling people how to die and how to get into Heaven, away from this wicked world. I am glad that the new thought is how to live so that Heaven may be brought to earth. We are learning that religion is not a form, not a creed, but a life."[9] Woodsworth's path led him away from theology to sociology and eventually to politics, where he achieved prominence as the first leader of the Cooperative Commonwealth Federation (CCF).

The social gospel spirit animated Regina College in its early years. The first president, Reverend Wilbur W. Andrews, former dean of applied science at Mount Allison University and an ordained Methodist minister, attended the Social Service Congress in Ottawa in 1914, where he delivered a speech titled "Political Corruption and Its Cure." He endorsed a number of progressive causes, including the vote for women, Chinese immigration to Canada, and "socialistic" legislation along the lines of the reforms introduced in Germany and Great Britain. His wife, Nellie Greenwood Andrews, campaigned for women's suffrage, served as president of the Saskatchewan Women's Christian Temperance Union, and had the distinction of being the first woman elected to the Regina Collegiate Board.[10]

President Andrews believed that the Bible should be read, not as a "sectarian theological textbook," but rather as a great work of literature whose truth should be "permitted to shine in its own light and make its own appeal." He introduced a human relations course in which the students' "duties to each other will be discussed by themselves with their teacher, and also their duties and privileges to the State, the methods of our government, the responsibilities of the various classes in the community towards each other and so forth, so that they may see the reason why public spiritedness and unselfish aims are demanded by the very conditions of our social and national life."[11] The teacher of the course was Reverend Hugh Dobson, who was later appointed western field secretary for the Department of Evangelism and Social Service of the Methodist Church. The first part of the course dealt with anatomy, the functioning of the human body, and the rules of good health; the second covered the "causes that have preceded our social problems, inventions and discoveries, effects of machinery, immigration, and causes of the growth of cities and the decrease in rural population, problems of town and country, public spirit, suggested reforms." Part three examined the duties of citizenship and the principles of democracy, while the fourth and final segment encouraged students to think about moral decisions and "religion as the basis of all moral life."[12] Guest speakers were brought in to acquaint the students with the latest social developments. J.S. Woodsworth discussed the impact of immigration, industrialization, and urbanization, Nellie Forman of the Regina Settlement House described her work with the immigrant poor, and Emmeline Pankhurst, the celebrated British suffragist, gave an account of her recent visit to Soviet Russia.[13]

When Reverend Ernest W. Stapleford took over as president in 1915, a position he held until 1934, the spirit of the college altered slightly – or perhaps, more accurately, it was projected differently. Stapleford, who excelled as a fundraiser, had excellent connections with members of the business community, not only in Regina but also in eastern Canada and, to some extent, the United States. Swinging his cane with a flourish, he cut quite a figure as he strolled down Scarth Street, exuding a booster spirit. He criticized "snobbish magazine writers" who took "pot shots" at businessmen. As he reminded the Regina Kiwanis Club, "Nearly all the finer things of life – art, colleges, and hospitals – had been made possible through the gifts of men who had made their money in commerce."[14] The truth of the matter was that President Andrews, for all his academic qualifications and progressive views, had been a failure as an administrator, especially on the financial side. If it had not been for Stapleford, the college would have descended into bankruptcy.

The social gospel aspect of Regina College did not disappear. It was upheld through the influence of Maude Stapleford, wife of the president. The couple worked as a team: he raised the money and she nurtured the spirit. This relationship, typical of gender roles at the time (male breadwinner/female nurturer), was transposed onto the larger life of the college. It was the perfect combination. Thanks to President Stapleford, the college was financially viable; thanks to his wife, the social gospel ethos survived.

A graduate of Victoria College, Maude Stapleford was active in community affairs, serving for six years as president of the Regina Local Council of Women. As chair of the council's Standing Committee on Laws for Women and Children, she spearheaded a number of important legislative reforms, including the establishment of the right of a mother to equal guardianship and custody of her children and the right of a wife to a more equitable share in her husband's estate. A story was told about how formidable an advocate Maude Stapleford could be. The Staplefords lived in a suite in the girls' residence of the college, across Wascana Lake from the Legislative Building. It was said that when the premier looked out his office window in the wintertime and saw Mrs Stapleford trudging across the frozen lake on her way to an interview with him, he "trembled in his boots."[15]

Her community involvement included the Babies' Welfare Home, a shelter for dependent children under the age of three; the Everywoman's Fund, which raised $50,000 to pay for sanatorium care for mothers with tuberculosis and their babies; the Victorian Order of Nurses; the women's auxiliary of the Institute for the Blind; and the Regina General Hospital. In addition, she served on the executive of the Imperial Order of the Daughters of the Empire, the auxiliary of the Regina Symphony Orchestra, the Women's Canadian Club, the Women's Educational Club, and the University Women's Club. Although this is not a complete list, it is sufficient to make the point. The Staplefords were a team. Together they accomplished what neither alone would have been able to achieve. They represented a college that was both financially sound and rooted in its social gospel tradition.

The Regina College ideal was based on social service and good citizenship, as well as academic excellence. It anticipated the 1960s debate about the value and purpose of liberal education, a debate in which radicals and activists at the Regina campus criticized the educational status quo for its narrow focus on technical training and its failure to relate the curriculum to the urgent problems facing humanity. Although social gospel discourse differed from that of sixties activism, the essential spirit was similar. Both regarded education as something more than specialized training; the goal was to prepare the student for responsible citizenship and service to an ideal greater than oneself. Hence the double significance of "As One Who Serves," which was both the motto chosen for Regina College in 1911 and the one selected for the University of Regina in 1974.

The liberal arts debate in the 1960s focused on the "Educational Policy for the Liberal Arts," better known as the Regina Beach Statement, which the faculty adopted in 1964. Although the document was a compromise formulation, as is usually the case with mission statements, it emphasized the need for the university to make itself relevant to current social concerns and to serve as "an important part of the critical intelligence of society, examining institutions, seeking to penetrate the future, sensitive to change, aware of the past, and of the manifold problems and dangers of the present." This critique was to be "sustained by constant reference to essential human values, which demands a deliberate renewal of the study of the nature of love, of justice, freedom, beauty, science: in fact, all those values which give meaning and substance to life."[16]

As time went on, "Regina Beach" became a battleground. It acquired significance far beyond what a literal reading of the text could justify and became a symbol for the various debates that were underway. These debates, while brought into sharp focus in the 1960s, were not unique to that decade. They are inherent in the very nature of a university. Is the goal of university education to train students to make a living or to teach them how to live? Is the purpose of a university to pursue knowledge for its own sake or to apply knowledge to the solution of society's problems? Is the role of a university to promote the values that sustain our civilization or to criticize the flaws in the established order? Is the aim of the university to promote individualism or to build community? Should the university emphasize teaching or research and publication? The answer is that the university must do all of these things. Such tensions will never be resolved, nor should they be, for if they were settled categorically in favour of one side or another, something good would be lost and the university would cease to be what it is supposed to be.

The Regina Beach Statement did not capture fully the complexity of these tensions. It failed to affirm that truth is worth pursuing whether it is socially useful or not. It had more to say about undergraduate teaching than about graduate studies and scholarly research. It left the impression that criticizing the existing social order and serving the best interests of society are always one and the same thing. At the same time, the statement should not be completely dismissed or relegated to the dustbin of history. A manifestation of sixties idealism, it expressed values that are as relevant today as they were in 1971, when Reverend Hordern asked, Do science and technology serve humanity or does humanity serve science and technology? Is knowledge used to control others or to set them free?

Students play a large part in the story of the making of the University of Regina, and, as a result, they figure prominently in this volume. Students in most university histories are an anonymous cast of thousands, the extras on the set, before whom administrators and faculty members perform their star turns. I have set out to write a different kind of history, one in which the role of students in the life of the university community is fully presented. Four of the seventeen chapters deal exclusively with the activities of students, three chapters have long sections about them, and they have a presence in many of the other chapters. This is as it should be. The students of the sixties reinvented what it means to be a student. They created the "citizen-student," the student who both participates fully in the life of the university, including its governance, and engages the wider issues of society, indeed of the globe. Students of the sixties reflected and shaped the trends of the times and in so doing helped define the University of Regina.

However, one cannot deny the decisive influence of senior administrators such as the deans of Regina College, William Ramsay, Steward Basterfield, and William A. Riddell; the principals, Riddell and John Archer; and the presidents of the University of Saskatchewan, J.S. Thomson, W.P. Thompson, and John Spinks. I have tried to put the reader in the shoes of these people, to chronicle their achievements, the difficulties they faced, and how they dealt with them. I have not been uncritical. When tact and truth came into collision, I have generally erred on the side of truth.

Occasionally, lower-level administrators or faculty members make a dramatic appearance and contribute to the storyline. Dallas Smythe comes to mind, as do Alwyn Berland, Allan B. Van Cleave, Tommy McLeod, Reid Robinson, Ray Harvey, Wes Bolstad, Robert N. Anderson, Ernie Nicholls, Don Clark, John Mantle, Cam Blachford, Fred Anderson, Les Crossman, Ernest Thackeray, Duncan Blewett, Joseph Wolfson, Howard Leyton-Brown, H. Bruce Lobaugh, Ken Lochhead, Art McKay, Ronald Bloore, Charles Lightbody, Peter Nash, Morris Anderson, Milnor Alexander, Evelyn Jonescu, and many others. The women in this list are few and far between. This was one of the things the 1960s would change.

Before beginning the story of the making of the University of Regina, it is necessary to provide some background information. The university is part of a larger community, sharing the life of the city and province to which it belongs. The roots of the University of Regina go back to 1911, when the prairie west was still in its pioneer stage. At the turn of the twentieth century, the population of the portion of the Northwest Territories that in 1905 became Saskatchewan stood at approximately 100,000.[17] Spurred by the federal government's "Last Best West" immigration policy, the number soared to 492,432 in 1911, and 921,785 in 1931.[18] Agriculture was the main foundation of the economy, so much so that when provincial treasurer Charles A. Dunning announced in 1920 that the total value of Saskatchewan's agricultural production exceeded $370 million, he had to admit, somewhat apologetically, that his department had no information about the extent of manufacturing in the province. The next year he corrected the omission, informing the legislature that manufacturing output totalled $50 million per year. The figure must be taken with a grain of salt, since "manufacturing" was defined to include the output of everything from creameries and flour mills to printing offices and garages.[19]

Though narrowly based on agriculture, the Saskatchewan economy boomed. The number of farms increased from 119,451 in 1921 to 136,472 in 1931, while average farm size grew from 368.5 to 407.9 acres. The number of tractors rose in the same period from 19,243 to 43,308, the number of automobiles from 36,093 to 65,094, and railway mileage from 6,296 to 8,268.[20] The late 1920s was a time of buoyant prosperity. The Regina *Leader*, celebrating Canada's Diamond Jubilee on 1 July 1927, published a full-page advertisement titled "Saskatchewan, Its Place in, and Contribution to the Canadian Confederation." It boasted that Saskatchewan was the:

> FIRST Province in Canada in per capita wealth.
> FIRST in production of wheat.
> FIRST in production of oats.
> FIRST in production of rye.
> FIRST in production of flax.
> FIRST in the breeding of horses.
> FIRST in quantity of commercial clays.
> FIRST in production of sodium sulphate.
> FIRST by reason of the lowest death rate.
> FIRST in number of rural telephones per capita.
> SECOND in railway mileage.
> SECOND in number of telegraph offices.
> SECOND in egg production.
> SECOND in production of barley.
> THIRD in population.
> THIRD in reserves of coal.
> THIRD in poultry values.
> THIRD in aggregate wealth.[21]

A cartoon on the front page of the *Leader* on 22 December 1920 captured the spirit of the era. Two muscle-bound figures, their heads depicted, respectively, as a sheaf of wheat and a sheaf of oats, pose cockily next to trophies they have won. The caption reads: "At the International Livestock Fair at Chicago Canadian wheat and oats took the sweepstakes grand championship of America, also Durum championship. Canada also took livestock championship and lesser prizes too numerous to mention."[22] Saskatchewan was the home of champions.

On the political front, the Liberal Party was dominant. It held office continuously from 1905 to 1944, except for a five-year interval (1929–34) when a coalition of Conservatives, Progressives, and independents formed a one-term government. Thus it was the Liberals, not the Conservatives, who put their stamp on the province during its formative years. They governed with a mixture of calculating pragmatism, mild reformism, and ruthless machine politics.[23] Ideologically, they were free-enterprisers, but not obsessively so. Successive governments intervened directly in the economic development of the province, establishing public utilities through the Department of Telephones and the Saskatchewan Power Commission[24] and extending generous loans to the Saskatchewan Cooperative Elevator Company and Saskatchewan Cooperative Creameries.[25] In the realm of social policy, the Liberals were cautiously progressive. Premier Walter Scott gave the vote to women in March 1916, Saskatchewan being the second province in Canada to do so.[26] The government passed the Workmen's Compensation Act and set up a bureau of labour "to monitor working conditions and labour standards."[27] The Mothers' Allowance Act provided pensions to mothers raising children without the support of a male breadwinner, juvenile courts kept young offenders out of jails, and the Minimum Wage Board protected female employees.

Public education received a high priority, in part because it was considered necessary for the conversion of the large non-English-speaking population to Anglo-Saxon norms. The government in 1916 commissioned H.W. Fogt, a specialist in rural schools from Washington, DC, to conduct a survey of educational conditions in the province. He reported that only 129,439 of the 165,176 young people in Saskatchewan between the ages of six and eighteen were attending school. According to Fogt, the gap between the elementary and secondary schools was "needlessly wide and difficult to span," and high schools were "rather exclusive and aristocratic in [their] tendencies."[28] The province in 1916 had only twenty-two high schools; a mere 17.4 per cent of children aged fourteen to eighteen were exposed to secondary education. The shortage was most acute in rural areas, a problem that Regina College, as a residential school, sought to address.

While the Liberal government focused attention on upgrading education at the primary and secondary levels, it was equally concerned with post-secondary training. Walter Scott had only a grade 8 diploma, but he nonetheless firmly believed in the value of higher learning.[29] His government in 1907 introduced the University Act, which created the University of Saskatchewan and gave it monopoly degree-granting powers (except in theology) in the province. By the terms of the act, the nine-man Board of Governors was responsible for selecting the university site. The board met on the evening of 7 April 1909 to make its decision. It came down in the end to a contest between Regina and Saskatoon, with Saskatoon at last emerging the winner. The margin of victory was not made public; nor was any information given out as to how individual board members voted or why they voted as they did. The board decided to say as little as possible to avoid fuelling speculation or controversy – a futile hope, as it turned out.

Four members of the board came from the northern part of Saskatchewan (that is, the northern part of the main settled area, which is geographically in the lower third of the province), and four hailed from the south (the Regina area to the American border). The ninth member was Walter Murray, a philosophy professor from Dalhousie University, who on 20 August 1908 had been named the first president of the University of Saskatchewan. Murray voted for Regina because he saw advantages to having the university located in the capital city, where he felt it could be of greater service to the state.[30] It follows that at least one of the board members from the south voted for Saskatoon, because if all the southern votes had been cast for Regina, the outcome would have been 5 to 4 for Regina. Levi Thomson, a board member from Wolseley, a town 100 kilometres directly east of Regina, confessed in a letter to Walter Murray on 12 April 1909 that he had voted for Saskatoon: "I am the guilty party in the eyes of my Regina friends. I don't feel at all guilty, but I can understand that they can feel they have a serious grievance against the man who gave a South vote in favour of Saskatoon."[31] Thomson was a staunch Liberal, having run as the party's candidate in the 1904 federal and the 1905 provincial elections. He dispensed political patronage in the Wolseley area and was himself the beneficiary of government favours.[32]

It was immediately assumed that the government had influenced Thomson's vote. Premier Scott had appointed three of the board members, the senate elected five, and President Murray served ex officio. Two of Scott's appointees were from the north and therefore expected to vote for Saskatoon; his sole appointee from the south was Thomson, the only southerner known not to have voted for Regina. Walter Murray had warned the government not to interfere with the process. He wrote to Scott on 8 October 1908 that party politics was the "great bane" of universities and that meddling in the location decision would set a bad precedent for other university matters – the appointment and dismissal of professors, the letting of contracts, and "the dozen and one things men wish to use to their own advantage." The university, he feared, would become "a prey to the schemes of designing men."[33] He went on to say that the government could interfere in the site selection in one of two ways: amendment of the University Act to take the decision out of the hands of the Board of Governors, or employment of "secret influence." The former, he said, had at least the merit of openness, frankness, and courage; the latter was "just as injurious and [would] beget suspicion."[34]

When Murray learned the result of the board vote, his first instinct was to resign.[35] The very thing he had warned Scott against had come to pass. Only after consulting with university chancellor E.L. Wetmore and Robert Falconer, a close friend and president of the University of Toronto, did Murray decide to stay. He worried that a resignation would throw the university into an even worse political crisis. Thereafter, Murray always insisted in public that politics had never entered into any aspect of the life of the university. Privately, he admitted to W.P. Thompson, president of the university from 1949 to 1959, that "he [Murray] was certain that the choice of Saskatoon over

Regina for the site of the university was arranged through the appointment of certain members of the board and pressure brought to bear on them."[36]

The Regina *Leader*, a Liberal Party organ, tried to smooth over the difficulty the dispute had caused. An editorial on 9 April 1909 stated:

> Now that the question has been settled it should be regarded by all as settled, and settled wisely and well. There should be no heart-burnings, no fault-findings. The residents of each of the several aspiring cities may still be as profoundly convinced as ever that the University would have attained to a greater measure of success and more rapidly, if located in their midst, but there is no longer anything to be gained by urging such views. There is one common duty now devolving upon each and all as loyal citizens of Saskatchewan, and that is to accept the decision reached … although the Parliament Buildings of Saskatchewan are at Regina, our pride in them should be equaled by Saskatoon, and Saskatoon's pride in the stately structure, which will soon arise on the banks of the noble Saskatchewan River should be equaled by Regina. Both institutions belong to both and to all, and are created and maintained for the benefit of all.[37]

Arthur S. Morton, a member of the history department at the University of Saskatchewan and author of *Saskatchewan: The Making of a University*, maintained that the editorial "turned out to be a very accurate reflection of the opinion not only in Regina but also in the province at large." He added, "the Board's decision was accepted by the public with remarkable acquiescence, and attention turned almost at once to considerations of getting the University started."[38] Jean E. Murray, another member of the University of Saskatchewan history department in Saskatoon and also the daughter of Walter Murray, cited the editorial to similar effect in her 1959 article "The Contest for the University of Saskatchewan." She intimated, without actually saying so, that while Premier Scott was tempted to interfere in the location decision, he did not.

The Conservative *Daily Standard* did not accept the Liberal newspaper's contention that politics had not played a role in the decision to give the university to Saskatoon: the Liberals were "vipers" who "gamble[d] with loaded dice and gave pointers to gamblers." The new university, the paper predicted, would never be anything more than the "University of Saskatoon," and a true University of Saskatchewan would yet arise.[39] *The West*, another Conservative publication, stated bluntly, "The governors were selected by the government with the end in view that has been attained. Does anyone deny that the university location was not decided [*sic*] some time ago?"[40] If Conservatives did not believe the *Leader*'s version of events, neither, apparently, did Regina Liberals. Enraged, they held an emergency meeting, which Premier Scott's secretary characterized as "one of the warmest which has taken place in

Regina for many moons." Norman MacKenzie, a Liberal stalwart and future benefactor of the MacKenzie Art Gallery, "paced his office all one day very much after the manner of a caged tiger while the air was positively blue in his vicinity."[41] Regina alderman F.N. Darke proposed in a letter to the *Leader* on 12 April 1909 that an additional storey be added to the collegiate building then under construction. The third storey, he suggested, could be used to house a medical college and a law school. "These are institutions," he said, "which belong to the city for which we will have to provide and which cannot be taken from us, if our citizens are true to their own best interests."[42]

In June 1909, a mere two months after the decision to locate the university in Saskatoon, the Saskatchewan Methodist Conference discussed the possibility of establishing a residential college in Regina. While the immediate goal was to provide secondary education for the youth of the city and surrounding area, long-term plans included first-year university courses. The General Conference of the Methodist Church approved the project, and the provincial government granted the charter of incorporation on 23 April 1911.[43] It was to have been called Saskatchewan College, but when Walter Murray objected, the name was changed to Regina College. Murray also intervened behind the scenes to make sure that the college did not receive any government funding, subsequently commenting to Robert Falconer, "Why then should we fear though the Methodists rage and Regina imagines vain things?"[44]

Despite Murray's reservations about the project, he offered words of congratulation at the cornerstone-laying ceremony on 25 October 1911. "The forces of education in this new land were as yet all too few," he said, "and the task too great to waste useful time in idle controversy. Each had its work to do ... the two [the college and the university] would go hand in hand in the upbuilding of the youthful mind of the province."[45] The honour of laying the cornerstone belonged to Lieutenant-Governor George W. Brown, Norman MacKenzie's law partner and a member of the Regina College Board of Governors: "Slowly and ponderously the stone was lifted and swung into the waiting bed of mortar which had been carefully spread by the hand of the Lieutenant Governor. A moment sufficed for the test, and then, with heads bared, the watching throng were given the assurance: 'In the name of Christ and for the service of man I declare this stone to be well and truly laid as the chief stone in a building dedicated to the training of young people to intellectual mastery and in the principles of Christian citizenship.'"[46]

Though the main college building was not yet completed, classes had already begun in temporary quarters in the old hospital building at 2240 Hamilton Street. Twenty-seven students enrolled on the first day. Most were in their teens, but there were also a few Methodist Church probationers who had preached on circuits in the Regina area. Long after classes had started, letters continued to come in from farm workers who wondered whether it was possible to register for classes after the harvest was done. One aspiring student wrote: "Many years ago me and my brother went to school for a few years, but when we came out here we all had to work and leave school. Now we have made some money and feel that we cannot make the best of things without more training. Have you any course which will fit us for the life which we have open to us here. We want to have a good start in English and be able to get something out of life. When should we come in? We are ready now."[47] Here was a natural constituency for Regina College – young people (and some not so young) from rural Saskatchewan who did not have access to high school education where they lived.

The home town of the college was, in 1911, a thriving city of just over 30,000 people. Those of British origin formed the majority (20,960), followed by Russian (a rather strange census category that included Austrian, Bulgarian, Hungarian, and Rumanian) (3,352), German (2,758), French (520), Ukrainian (299), and lesser numbers of various other groups. The 1911 census identified only six Aboriginal persons living in Regina, which suggests that most First Nations people were still living on reserves, though census undercounting may also have been a factor. By religion, Anglicans came first (7,372), then Presbyterians (6,875), Methodists (4,969), Roman Catholics (4,750), Greek Orthodox (2,312), Baptists (1,416), Lutherans (1,255), and Jews (860).[48] Regina College, while unapologetically Methodist in orientation, was open to students of all denominations. Religious conformity was not required, but students were strongly encouraged to attend a church or synagogue at least once a week.

Regina during these years was a hopeful, growing community, its economy based on its role as a service centre and distribution point for the surrounding hinterland. Thirty of the sixty-seven wholesale firms operating in the province in 1913 were located in the city, not to mention the provincial head offices of several banks, trust companies, and insurance firms.[49] Real estate speculation was rife and potentially very lucrative. Even Walter Scott participated in land deals, advising his business partner at one point not to sell any property unless he could realize a profit of 50 per cent or more on the transaction.[50] However, economic growth was not always smooth; fortunes were lost as well as gained. A severe pre–World War I recession jolted the city, real estate values crashed, and the population fell by 1916 to 26,000. The economy rebounded during the war, and after a post-war readjustment it moved on to greater strength during the mid- and late 1920s. Imperial Oil built a refinery, and General Motors in 1928 opened an automobile assembly plant. By 1931, the population exceeded 53,000.

The college prospered with the city. Under the leadership of Reverend Ernest W. Stapleford, the campus, attractively situated between College

Avenue to the north and Wascana Lake to the south, acquired four new buildings: a girls' residence, a gymnasium, a central heating plant, and a music and art building (Darke Hall). The number of academic students increased from 136 in 1922 to 239 in 1929, while enrolment in the music conservatory rose from 387 in 1921 to 662 in 1929.[51] The college in 1925 acquired the status of a junior college in affiliation with the University of Saskatchewan. This meant that students could take the first year of the three-year Bachelor of Arts program in Regina before proceeding to Saskatoon to complete the degree.

Walter Murray agreed to this arrangement, but only to forestall what he considered a worse development. As he explained in a letter to H.M. Tory, the president of the University of Alberta, "The Junior College movement here was advocated for the simple reason that I did not see any other way to head off a very serious and dangerous attack which would have gathered behind it the strength of the Capital, the largest city in the province, and would have been promoted by the leaders of at least two churches [Methodist and Roman Catholic], one of them exceedingly powerful and well-entrenched. I have reason to believe that they would have succeeded in securing at least degree-conferring power."[52] The list of junior colleges included three other Regina institutions – Campion College (Catholic), Sacred Heart College (Catholic), Luther College (Lutheran) – as well as Outlook College (Lutheran) in Outlook, St Peter's College (Catholic) in Muenster, and Moose Jaw Central Collegiate. All the colleges were allowed to appoint their own staff to teach first-year university courses, but university faculty set the examination papers and assigned the grades.

Stapleford increasingly came to believe that Regina College had to introduce a degree program or else it would stagnate. With the extension of high schools in rural Saskatchewan, it was not as necessary as it had been in the pioneer era for young people from small towns to come to Regina to continue their secondary education. Enrolment figures showed a growing proportion of students concentrated in the higher grades. In 1922, 82 per cent were enrolled in the lower high-school grades up to and including grade 11; by 1929 this number had fallen to 52 per cent.[53] The high school constituency of Regina College was disappearing. The future, if there was a future, lay in university work.

The Regina College Board of Governors in May 1929 decided to open negotiations with the university, and a written proposal reached President Murray in November 1930. Regina suggested a federation agreement, by which the college would offer courses leading to a BA, but the university would set the standards and confer the degree. The university rejected the proposal on the grounds that it would result in the diversion of provincial government funds from Saskatoon to Regina: "We are of the opinion that neither the needs of the province, nor its financial ability justify any division of the University's resources or equipment."[54] Premier J.T.M. Anderson, speaking at the Regina College commencement exercises in June 1931, predicted that the smaller colleges in the province would eventually receive degree-granting privileges. Murray immediately fired off a letter to the premier, presenting the contrary arguments. Anderson replied that the newspapers had distorted his remarks, but he did not back down from the position that small colleges might in future offer a full arts course, even if they did not grant degrees.[55]

Murray then invited the Carnegie Foundation for the Advancement of Teaching to carry out an investigation and prepare a report on higher education in Saskatchewan. Heading the inquiry were W.S. Learned, who had worked with Murray in 1923 on a Royal Commission on education in Manitoba, and E.W. Wallace, principal of Victoria University, a federated college of the University of Toronto. Victoria, like Regina College, owed its existence to the Methodist Church. The report, *Local Provision for Higher Education in Saskatchewan*, stated that Regina's plan for a degree course was unaffordable without a sizeable private endowment, which the college did not have. Learned, the main author of the report, acknowledged that since 1909 less than half as many University of Saskatchewan graduates with a Bachelor of Arts or Bachelor of Science degree had come from Regina as compared with Saskatoon, even though Regina had a larger population (53,000 compared with 43,000 in 1931). He said the solution to this problem was not to offer a degree course in Regina, but rather to provide loans to enable students from outside Saskatoon to finance their university education. This recommendation was not implemented.

The Learned Report suggested that Regina College evolve "outward" as a community college, teaching technical and vocational courses and providing adult education and general education for those not capable of, or interested in, university studies. It could also provide cultural enrichment to the community, such as was already being done through the Conservatory of Music. The report urged the four junior colleges (Regina, Luther, Campion, and Sacred Heart) to coordinate their activities and work with the high schools to make efficient use of the educational resources in the city.[56] Murray, of course, expressed delight with the report, which he termed a "masterpiece … admitted by all those who agreed and those who were disappointed to be unanswerable. I believe it has disposed of the problem for at least twenty years."[57] Stapleford thought that Learned and Wallace had overlooked the advantages of a small college over what Stapleford called "the Henry Ford method of education" – the mass production of graduates on the academic assembly line.[58] However one looked at it, Walter Murray had scored a coup, effectively blocking the expansion of Regina College to a degree program.

The times, in any case, were not propitious. The city and province were experiencing an economic depression of catastrophic proportions. Net farm income, which had stood at $184,665,000 in 1928, fell to minus $31,117,000 in 1931.[59] Two-thirds of the rural population depended on relief, and there were medical reports of malnutrition, even scurvy, in some parts of the province.[60] Twenty-three per cent of adult male wage earners in Regina were out of work in June 1931, a number that declined only slightly to 19.7 per cent in June 1936.[61] The relief quota in 1932 was sixteen dollars per month for a family of four, with 15 per cent more for each additional person and a corresponding deduction for fewer persons.[62] One distraught citizen wrote to the mayor of Regina on 12 December 1932, "I am a married man with two small children out of work and on relief for the last month. Thanks God I get just enough to eat, but children are without shoes and clothing also my wife needs shoes and overshoes and not saying anything of myself ... God only knows that I am telling you the truth and I haven't got a cent to my name now. I did not apply for relief until my last dollar went, as I did not believe in charity as long as I am able to work, but as I can not get any work, so I was forced to apply for relief."[63]

The prevailing economic gloom extended to Regina College, where academic enrolment declined from 239 in 1929 to 134 in 1932. Although the Board of Governors reduced tuition and residence fees and allowed payment in farm and garden produce, it was to no avail. Even scholarship winners turned down awards because they could not afford to come to college.[64] The student newspaper resorted to black humour: "Have you heard the story of the farmer down south who fainted when it began to rain? The only way the family could revive him was to throw a couple of buckets of dust in his face."[65]

President Stapleford put on a brave front and travelled to eastern Canada to beg for money. He addressed the Toronto Board of Trade on the theme "The West Will Come Back," and in his private diary he invoked Walt Whitman:

> Do the feasters gluttonous feast,
> Do the corpulent sleepers sleep,
> Have they locked and bolted the doors?
> Still be ours the diet hard and the blanket on the ground,
> Pioneers! O pioneers![66]

The cold reality was that the college was losing between $25,000 and $30,000 a year and tottered on the brink of financial ruin.[67]

Walter Murray saw an opportunity. Representatives of the University of Saskatchewan Board of Governors met with their Regina College counterparts on 19 December 1933. The college was willing to turn over all of its buildings and property, valued at more than $800,000, if the university agreed to provide, in the not too distant future, a full BA program in Regina.

The university declined the offer. Negotiations resumed, and the university spelled out is terms on 13 January 1934. It promised "to continue and maintain Regina College conserving the best of the past and seeking to realize the ideals of culture and character which inspired its founders." Further, it would "continue the staff of the Conservatory of Music"; "appoint to the University staff such members of the academic and administrative staff of the College as have given long and excellent service"; and "appoint an Advisory Committee of the University Board of Governors and four of the Board of Regina College to have oversight of the work of the College, to make expenditures within the amounts authorized by the University Board, to certify accounts for payment and to make such recommendations as they see fit."[68] The university also agreed to "maintain the high standard of excellence of the Conservatory of Music and enlarge its sphere of usefulness," and, as soon as financial conditions permitted, "include a School of Art which would make a contribution to the life of the community comparable with that made by the Conservatory of Music."[69]

The members of the Regina College board were not altogether satisfied with these terms. They requested an additional sentence, which would read, "The question of expansion to a University college shall be an open question for determination for the future." This the university accepted, since it was obvious that the clause imposed no definite obligation. The Regina board, bowing to the inevitable, agreed to the deal on 22 January 1934. Stapleford was sure that a mistake was being made. As a gesture of symbolic protest, he insisted on entering into the minutes an alternative plan by which the college would retain its autonomy and expand to a degree course.[70] The official transfer took place on 1 July 1934. Regina College was no longer a church college in affiliation with the University of Saskatchewan; it was now an integral part of the university. Control had shifted from an independent board to the Board of Governors of the University of Saskatchewan. This meant that for all practical purposes, Walter Murray, through his appointed dean, was now running the college. Despite the expense to the university – the total debt of the college as of 1 July 1934 was close to $100,000 – Murray was sure that he had done the right thing: "Great as was the operating loss of 1934–35, it is more than offset by the advantages from the attainment of the University's great objective – to be the one recipient of state aid for University purposes and the sole degree conferring power in the province."[71]

Stapleford continued as a member of the academic staff and "principal of the administrative staff," a meaningless title, since real authority rested with the new dean, who reported directly to Murray. The university dropped instruction in grades 9, 10, and 11 and offered only grade 12 (or what was then known as "senior matriculation") and first-year arts. Enrolment fell to 121 students in 1936–37 (99 of whom were in first-year arts) and 84 in 1939–40 (78 in first-year arts). The residences were almost vacant – twenty-two occupants in 1937 and sixteen in 1938. Stapleford could only lament, "The buildings at Saskatoon are overcrowded and the magnificent plant here is half empty."[72] When the director of the music conservatory resigned in 1935, the university delayed finding a replacement. Finally, in 1939, one of the current members of the staff was elevated to the post. In 1936 Norman MacKenzie, a former member of the Regina College Board of Governors, died, leaving to the university his art collection and money for the construction of an art gallery in Regina. An architect was commissioned and tenders were called for, but Murray did not think there was enough money in the estate to build the gallery, and he made no attempt to raise additional funds.[73] For Stapleford, this was the last straw. He despaired at what was happening to the college he had built, and, feeling powerless to do anything about it, he submitted his resignation in 1937 and moved to Toronto.

These developments set the stage for the story that is told in this book. Many of the themes of the evolution of Regina College to independent university status in 1974 can be traced to events that occurred during the formative years of the province. The 1909 decision to give the university to Saskatoon acquired a mythic significance, captured in the symmetrical phrase "Regina got the capital and Saskatoon got the university."[74] The one-university concept exerted a powerful influence, not only among those who embraced it, but also among those who resisted it. It was a fixed idea that both framed the debate and added an emotional element. Walter Murray was not alone in thinking that the notion of a degree course in Regina was "dangerous heresy."[75]

The Methodist Church founded Regina College in 1911 for "the training of young people to intellectual mastery and in the principles of Christian citizenship." The college grew and prospered during the 1920s, but it met with disaster in the economic collapse of the Great Depression, which hit Saskatchewan harder than it did any other province. President Stapleford tried desperately to save the school through expansion to a full BA course that would have attracted Regina students for whom university studies were unaffordable unless they could live at home. His plan failed, partly because of the adverse economic conditions and partly because of Walter Murray's shrewd academic statesmanship. The University of Saskatchewan took over ownership and control of the college in 1934, rescuing it from its financial problems, not entirely for altruistic reasons, but rather to prevent the development of a degree course in Regina. By 1939 the college was ready to enter a new chapter of its history. Having weathered the 1930s Depression at the sacrifice of its autonomy, it was now ready to face the challenges of World War II.

1 Regina College in World War II

William Ramsay, dean of Regina College and occupant of the dean's suite, was not happy at the prospect of having to leave his home. It was March 1940, eight months into World War II, and the University of Saskatchewan had decided to place Regina College at the disposal of the Royal Canadian Air Force for use as an air training centre. Ramsay would have to vacate his comfortable apartment, with its south veranda and fine view of Wascana Park and the Legislative Building.[1] He regretted the disruption of the academic life of the college, which he had nurtured carefully since assuming the deanship in 1934. But what bothered him even more was the suspicion that the move was entirely unnecessary, and that some other building could have been found to accommodate the needs of the air force.

William Ramsay was an exceptionally fine teacher – "teacher extraordinary" had been the description applied to him when he received an honorary degree from the University of Saskatchewan in 1961.[2] He believed that the essential purpose of education was to lead students out of their small, confined worlds into the realm of universal truth and to help them distinguish "what is mere show" from "what is real and worthwhile."[3] Although his subjects were Latin and Greek, his lectures ranged over broad areas of learning and were spiced with quotations from Shakespeare, Milton, Tennyson, and "the great chorus of dedicated minds expressing thought and judgment in ways never equaled before or since." He was apt to say that "the most modern writer in the world is Plato, except for the New Testament."[4]

Ramsay had a gift for communicating with his students. When asked for the secret of his success as a teacher, he replied, "I didn't do anything different from anyone else except try to associate with the pupils and find out what they thought about things. Identifying yourself with your pupils – that's the great thing in teaching."[5] A student in the class of 1937 at Regina College recalled that he was "fond of informing us often that Apollo was the god of 'light, healing, and forgiveness.' After we had, presumably, assimilated this fact, it went something like this: Dr. Ramsay shut his eyes tightly and described rapid circles in the air with his forefinger, all the while saying, 'Apollo is the god of light, healing, and – .' At this point the eyes flew open, the finger stopped, and the person to whom it pointed was expected to finish the statement – 'forgiveness.'"[6]

J. Francis Leddy studied Greek and Latin under Ramsay, when the latter was on the teaching staff at the Saskatoon campus prior to his appointment as dean of Regina College. Leddy later served as a senior administrator at the University of Saskatchewan and then as president of the University of Windsor. In 1956 he reminisced that Ramsay "is still remembered here in Saskatoon as perhaps the most outstanding teacher of language we have ever had. His methods were unorthodox but exceedingly effective, and neither in Oxford nor in Chicago did I meet anyone of comparable skill in teaching language."[7] Leddy reminisced, "he came into our classroom seeming to be much vexed, and in three short sentences he gave us the scenario: 'Boys, I think a man should be able to practice his golf swing in his own front parlor if he wants to.' We kept a wary silence. 'What if I did break the chandelier – I have to pay for it, don't I?' We maintained our silence. 'And how did I know that she was having a Tea this afternoon?' The quizzical good humor displayed in such sallies never left him and somehow much expedited his major objective in imparting a knowledge and love of Greek language and literature."[8]

Born in Ontario in 1876, Ramsay graduated from Queen's University in Kingston in 1902 with a BA in classics. He came to Saskatchewan in 1910, when he accepted a position at Central Collegiate in Regina. His reputation caught the attention of Walter Murray, president of the University of Saskatchewan, who invited him to join the academic staff in Saskatoon. He taught courses in Latin and Greek during the regular term and spent his summers at the University of Chicago taking classes towards his PhD degree.[9] His doctoral thesis was titled "Propaganda in the Plays of Aristophanes," and he confessed that by the time he finished it, in 1927, he was able to detect propaganda in almost everything Aristophanes wrote.[10]

When Ramsay was appointed dean of Regina College in 1934, he inherited a prickly situation. He had to deal with Ernest Stapleford, who was greatly disheartened at having been ousted from the presidency and some-

Regina Central Collegiate staff, circa 1915. William Ramsay, who served as dean of Regina College from 1934 to 1940, is second from the right in the back row.

what resentful at the turn of events. In addition, some staff members had to be let go, while others wondered what to expect under the new regime.[11] Ramsay's fatherly manner and kindly concern smoothed over the difficulties and eased the transition. Stapleford left the college in 1937, and the other faculty members adapted to their new roles. Ramsay's method may be glimpsed in an incident involving biology professor Jake Rempel. Shortly after Rempel, a conscientious teacher and first-rate scholar, left for his summer vacation, he was informed that his laboratory had been broken into and supplies had been taken. Ramsay wrote to assure him that everything had been taken care of. The locks on the doors of the laboratories and offices had been changed, and the microscopes and slides securely stored in the safe. Ramsay then added a personal note: "Don't worry about it and try to get some flesh on your bones. A little practice in golf and contract [bridge] might not be amiss."[12]

His technique with students was the same. If a student was doing badly in his classes, Ramsay made an effort to discover the reason. He talked to students, learned what they were thinking, and tried to be of help. The faculty and students became his extended family, and the college his home, not only because he lived there, but in the psychological and emotional sense as well – all the more so because his wife had died in 1934, the year he came to the college, and, at the age of 58, he had been forced to reconstruct his personal life.[13] Little wonder he was disappointed in 1940 when he learned that he would have to move, and the college life he loved so well would be disrupted for the duration of the war.

The first inkling that something was afoot came in October 1939. J.L. Deering, chairman of the Regina Municipal Air Board, suggested that the University of Saskatchewan make the college available to the air force. The RCAF had not made a firm commitment to come to Regina, but the municipal authorities hoped to lure it, using the college buildings and property as bait. After discussing the matter, the college's Advisory Board (which consisted of three members of the university's Board of Governors and four members of the former Regina College Board of Governors)[14] resolved that since the dominion government had not approached the university concerning the use of the buildings, action on the matter was premature.[15] A Regina *Leader-Post* editorial threw cold water on the idea. "It is apparent," the paper claimed, "that there would be not a little opposition to the use of Regina College for this purpose, at least, unless or until it might be established that there was no other suitable building in the community available." It recommended that the air force consider leasing "one of the older yet serviceable hotel buildings in the city" or erecting a temporary building.[16]

On 2 March 1940, Colonel Goodwin Gibson, real estate advisor to the Department of National Defence, appeared before the Advisory Board and stated that the college buildings, together with the adjacent normal school, were "absolutely required" if Regina were to have an air training centre. The Advisory Board, on the basis of this information, recommended that the Board of Governors accede to the request, provided that every effort were made to retain Darke Hall (the concert hall and home of the Conservatory of Music) for the use of the college.[17] University president James S. Thomson reported that Colonel Gibson had been "much impressed" by the work of the conservatory and did not insist on having the hall.[18] The Board of Governors on 16 March 1940 agreed to place the college at the disposal of the Department of National Defence, on the understanding that the department would reimburse the university for expenses incurred in relocating the college and renting alternative accommodation.[19]

Ramsay could not understand why the members of the Advisory Board did not fight harder to keep the college from being dispossessed of its home. He was especially baffled by the attitude taken by Douglas J. Thom, who had been a member, first of the Regina College Board of Governors and then of the Advisory Board, since 1910. "I do not mind his differing in opinion," Ramsay wrote on 4 March 1940, "but his whole attitude this morning seemed

At the left is the main Regina College building (two cars parked in front), which is connected to the tower and to the girls' residence on the right side of the tower. The Regina College buildings were handed over to the air force for use as a training centre during World War II.

to me to convey the notion that we should be satisfied to start up again with very rudimentary conditions ... If Mr. Thom, Mr. Deering and Mr. McNiven (Liberal M.P. for Regina), and it should be added, Mr. Thom ably assisted by his wife, had spent as much time and energy on keeping the College for us by getting other quarters for the flying forces, the College would not have been lost to us."[20]

Ramsay called a meeting of the academic faculty to inform them of the impending move. They reacted with keen disappointment, one staff member openly questioning whether there was any point in trying to keep the college going. Another suggested that the faculty attempt to recruit an "extra committee of citizens" to support the college through the difficult times it was experiencing. Ramsay asked President Thomson to issue a statement to reassure the staff that the university was not abandoning them or the college.[21] Thomson did so, taking the opportunity to appeal to their sense of patriotism: "I think the only kind of consolation that we can extract from the whole situation consists in the reflection that such inconveniences as those to which we are exposed are minor incidents in a colossal struggle. They are

Regina College viewed across Wascana Lake from the Legislative Building. The campus is on the right, the buildings set back slightly from the shoreline. At the extreme right is the normal school. Just to the left is the flat-topped drill hall that the air force constructed during World War II, and further to the left is the main college building (with the tower clearly visible), separated by a small space from Darke Hall.

as nothing compared with the dreadful sufferings to which those who are engaged in education are exposed in countries where the enemy we fight has had his way."[22]

Thomson was then in the third year of his presidency. Born in Scotland in 1892, he arrived in Canada in 1930 and became a professor of systematic theology and the philosophy of religion at Pine Hill Divinity College in Halifax. He remained there until 1937, when the University of Saskatchewan chose him to fill the retiring Walter Murray's oversized shoes. Thomson had limited administrative experience, a considerable handicap for the job he had undertaken. As University of Saskatchewan historian Michael Hayden observes, "Bit by bit it became evident that Thomson did not understand. More and more the executive of the board ran things."[23]

The president was an ordained minister of both the Church of Scotland and the United Church of Canada, and something of a "warrior cleric."[24] As a young man, during World War I, he had interrupted his studies at the University of Glasgow to serve for three-and-a-half years in the British army. He had never doubted the righteousness of the cause,[25] and his patriotic enthusiasm for World War II was equally ardent.[26] He spent hours in his office talking with students who claimed to be conscientious objectors, trying to point out to them the error of their ways. "I have used every method open to me from something approaching abuse to long, drawn out arguments," he admitted, "and in the main, I find them invincible."[27] Not surprisingly, Thomson believed that it was both appropriate and necessary for the university to lend Regina College to the air force.

Faced with the necessity of finding new quarters, Ramsay scouted a number of properties in the city, among them St Mary's School, the Regina Trading Company Building, the Darke Building, and the Hotel Saskatchewan. The one he thought most suitable was the Regina Trading Company Building, at the northeast corner of Scarth Street and 12th Avenue. It had a spacious interior, excellent lighting, and well-constructed floors and walls. He wrote with enthusiasm to Thomson, "The building is really attractive."[28] The president, however, had other ideas. He sent university business manager F.E. Riches, a voluble, brusque Englishman with an eye for cutting costs, to have a look.[29] Riches advised in favour of Benson Elementary School, which was located in the northwest part of the city close to Luther College and the RCMP barracks.[30] Following Riches's recommendation, Thomson pronounced Benson School "the best prospect" for a new home for the college.[31]

Ramsay was appalled. He invited the faculty to make a tour of the school, and they were uniformly of the opinion that it would not do. There was no space for staff offices and no facilities for physical education. The science laboratories would have to be located in the basement, where the fumes could not be ventilated. The basement was so damp that portions of it were completely unusable. Worst of all, there was no definite separation between the part of the building designated for the college and the area the schoolchildren would continue to occupy. Regina College students would have to share washroom facilities with seven year olds.[32]

The one advantage of Benson School was its location, only a few blocks away from Luther College. This meant that Regina College students could live in the Luther dormitory and take some of their classes at Luther. The proposal might also have been part of a long-term strategy. "I have a pretty strong idea," Thomson wrote in 1941, "that when this wretched war is over and we get back into our own premises, the time will be ripe for a complete reorganization of facilities for Junior College education in the city of Regina." He predicted that "There will be such a state of financial stringency that probably voluntary institutions such as Luther College, and probably even Campion, will be glad to fall in with some kind of new idea for the provision of Junior College education."[33]

It is not clear exactly what Thomson had in mind, but his comments echoed the 1932 Learned Report. As mentioned earlier, the report recommended that Regina College develop as a community college offering first-year university courses, music and art, and technical and vocational training. It further proposed the coordination of the resources of the four junior colleges in the city (Regina, Campion, Luther, and Sacred Heart) and the collegiates to create a superior junior college, giving a sound preparation for university training and a full range of non-academic courses.[34] The Benson School plan, by bringing Regina College and Luther College closer together, conformed to the general thrust of the Learned Report.

The fact was that Regina College presented something of a problem for the university. It was neither fish nor fowl, neither high school nor university. It offered only senior matriculation (basically the same as grade 12) and first-year university instruction. The senior matriculation enrolment would inevitably shrink as more students attended high schools where they did not have to pay tuition. This meant that Regina College had a dubious future as a one-year institution, with almost no continuity in the student body from one year to the next. In the long run, it was not a sustainable operation. Perhaps this was why Thomson mused about reorganizing the junior college system after the war and hoped as a preliminary measure to bring Regina College into closer association with Luther College.

Dean Ramsay, for his part, feared "the loss of identity for Regina College." "I feel, too," he told the president, "that we and Luther stand for different things, and that there could be no fusion. In stating this, I am not making an adverse criticism of Luther College."[35] Moreover, Ramsay did not agree with the conclusions of the Learned Report. He believed rather that Regina College should expand its academic offerings beyond the first-year level. In 1938 he supported a petition to the university from a group of public school teachers asking that they be allowed to take more than five courses for credit at the college (five courses constituting one year's work towards a three-year degree).

Saskatoon rejected the proposal, President Thomson citing "limitations of staff, equipment, library and laboratory facilities" at Regina.[36] He claimed that allowing anything beyond the first year would create a situation where a degree earned at Regina College would have less value than one taken at Saskatoon.[37] Thus the difference of opinion between Ramsay and the president on the Benson School issue may have been linked to a more fundamental disagreement concerning the future of the college. Ironically, Ramsay, who had been sent to Regina College to replace Stapleford, whose plan for expansion to a degree program had been defeated in 1934, ended up endorsing what the former Regina College president had tried to do.

Unofficial word that the Department of Defence intended to take over Regina College first leaked out to the general public on 6 March 1940, following a comment made by Alderman T.G. McNall at a meeting of Regina City Council. Alderwoman Mrs Ashley Walker expressed the opinion that the city would suffer major damage if Regina College were handed over to the military authorities. "The college," she said, "was of great importance to education in Regina and its loss would be regretted by the citizens generally."[38] Although the defence department declined to comment on the reports, the city was rife with rumours. Regina College art instructor Gus Kenderdine, speaking at the opening of an exhibition of paintings on 6 March 1940, bluntly informed the audience, "We are losing the college for the duration of the war." He emphasized that a place would have to be found to house the college's large art collection: "At no time before have we been so much in need of a gallery ... it would be a refuge for tired souls."[39]

As news of the imminent takeover spread, other groups voiced their concerns. The Regina Youth Council, meeting at the YWCA, passed a motion stating that "on the American continent we must preserve the values for which the war is being fought, and one of the chief of these values is education." They sent copies of the resolution to the minister of defence, the premier of Saskatchewan, and Dean Ramsay.[40] J.O. Probe, the CCF candidate for Regina in the upcoming federal election, to be held 26 March 1940, made the fate of Regina College a campaign issue. He declared that more suitable accommodation could have been found for the men coming to Regina under the air training plan, mentioning in particular the Hotel Saskatchewan: "We have in this city one of the finest quarters that could be offered to the military authorities. I refer to the magnificent structure on Victoria Avenue. Why not turn over one floor, two floors or the whole dashed building?"[41] While congratulating the Board of Trade for bringing the air training centre to Regina, he said he did not think it should have been done at the expense of the "scholastic welfare of the boys and girls of the city."[42]

President Thomson tried to calm the controversy with a public statement on 16 March 1940 in which he assured Reginans that "the work of the college in its entirety will be continued." He made it clear that the decision to give up the college had been made on the recommendation of the Advisory Board, a group of men, he said, "who had been interested in the work of the college before it became part of the university, and some of whom had taken an active share in its life from its very inception." These men, the president emphasized, had not been "exposed to any pressure either by the representative of the ministry of national defence or by any local parties, but the request was made with such cogency that they became persuaded of their duty to entertain the proposal very seriously." Thomson said he welcomed the expressions of "widespread concern" and hoped the university could count on "a continuance of this public interest and loyalty to the college during this period of temporary disarrangement."[43]

At the annual college banquet on 16 March 1940, the president reminded students and faculty of the plight of their counterparts in Czechoslovakia and Poland. "It was not the buildings that made the college," he declared, "but the students and teachers."[44] The opposition in Regina to the dislocation of the college indicated a high level of support for the institution. It reflected, too, the fact that in March 1940 the war had not yet entered its most serious phase. France was still expected to put up a strong fight, and prospects for the victory of the allies appeared reasonably good. The sudden and unanticipated defeat of France in June 1940 made the situation much more dangerous and had a sobering effect on public opinion, but in March 1940 it was harder to convince Reginans that the college should be given up. The *Leader-Post* on 19 March published an article titled "Regina College's Gift to War." Signed by a "Regina College Student," it portrayed the removal as a noble sacrifice: "Today we hear the tramp of soldiers' boots and the throb of the war drums, but when peace comes Regina College will resume its rightful place in the community, happy that it has done of its best in a time of national crisis." During the war, the article continued, the college would have to "mark time," but, when peace returned, it could anticipate attaining "the status of a complete university institution."[45] This hinted at a quid pro quo, a degree program as compensation for wartime sacrifice, but there is no evidence that the university contemplated such a trade-off.

The *Leader-Post* offered its own editorial opinion. It acknowledged that while relocation was undeniably a setback, Regina College was not without resources and support: "The institution is less than three decades old, but in this relatively short space of time memory and achievement of cherished form have been written into its walls and classrooms. Regina College has splendid builders and ably are its traditions being maintained."[46] The newspaper promised that the gesture the college had made would not be forgotten. When the war was over, it predicted, the public would respond with "warmth and alacrity" to the needs of the institution.

Despite all the public discussion of the impending move, there was still no announcement of a new home for the college. President Thomson wrote to Colonel Gibson on 18 March 1940 that the university wanted to lease premises in the Regina Trading Company Building,[47] and Gibson replied on 25 March, asking for an estimate of the cost of the move. Thomson said it would be at least $17,000, including the expenses involved in making the necessary alterations to provide for classrooms and laboratories. He added in a telegram, "Cost of transferring equipment back to Regina College at conclusion of your occupancy is not included and will be raised when College is handed back."[48]

On 14 April 1940 F.E. Riches, university business manager, cabled President Thomson: "Payment costs involved transfer to Trading Co. definitely refused ... Gibson arranged discussion accommodation with Premier and Minister of Education ... As a result met School Board offered part Lakeview school which can be partially cut off ... Tentative arrangement proceeding."[49] This was followed by a second communication, from university chancellor P.E. Mackenzie to Thomson on 16 April 1940, which read, "Gibson definitely declines to make Defence Department responsible for Trading Company rent. Provincial Government requires Lakeview School for Normal [school]. Benson only left."[50] It looked as if the college was headed to Benson School and not the Regina Trading Company Building.

Dean Ramsay told the *Leader-Post* on 19 April 1940 that "things are even less definite than they were five weeks ago."[51] An article in the paper on 6 May hinted darkly that classes might have to be cancelled for the duration of the war and all students transferred to Saskatoon.[52] The next day Regina City Council appealed to the university's Board of Governors to "do all in their power to continue teaching facilities of the college and not make a definite decision for the time being." A delegation of United Church ministers, consisting of Reverend Dr A.D. Mackenzie, Reverend F. Milligan, and Reverend Dr R.J. MacDonald, appeared before City Council on 7 May 1940 and urged that the college be kept open.[53] Although the church no longer had any formal connection with the college, many members of the clergy remained loyal and were solicitous of its welfare. It is possible, too, that Ramsay was orchestrating the agitation to put pressure on the university.

What happened behind the scenes is not clear, but on 13 May 1940 President Thomson announced that the college was moving to the Regina Trading Company Building.[54] Under the terms of the lease, the Department of National Defence would give $20,000 as compensation to the university, which meant that the university had to pay most of the cost of renting the temporary space and moving back to the college buildings at the end of the war. The Department of Defence agreed to keep the premises in good shape and restore them to their original condition, except for "wear and tear to the extent which would have been reasonable had the said premises continued in use and occupation as heretofore."[55]

On 20 May 1940, one week after it had been confirmed publicly that Regina College was moving to the Regina Trading Company Building and not Benson School, William Ramsay submitted his resignation as dean. Although at sixty-four he had not reached normal retirement age, he felt that one more year in harness might impair his health.[56] As it turned out, he managed to enjoy a lengthy retirement, playing golf and reading Plato until his death at the age of eighty-nine.[57] But there was more to Ramsay's resignation than was given out in the official story. He had come to believe that Regina

William Ramsay in advanced years (date unknown). At age sixty-four he resigned as dean of Regina College. In retirement he said that his favourite pastimes were playing golf and reading Plato. He died in 1965.

College was not getting a fair deal from the university. In a parting letter to President Thomson, he expressed himself freely:

> The one-year course in Regina College and the failure of the University Council to appreciate its obligations to Regina College tend to make the best efforts of the Arts staff here futile. It is not that I wish a change in our status at the present time; I do not wish either the spending of much time on the consideration of our College problems in wartime. I do wish, however, the negative attitude on the part of the University Council to cease. The staff here and I have given, I think, loyal service. The University Council should be loyal to us. An Advisory Board here, altered to represent the educational interests of Regina and Southern Saskatchewan, with which you, as President, could discuss the educational issues, which concern Regina College, would do much to secure a feeling of support for the University including Regina College.[58]

Thomson replied cautiously, "I cannot express in a letter the kind of sentiments that I would wish. They are largely sentiments of sympathy that the question of moving out from Regina College should have affected you so deeply that you have felt compelled to take this step."[59] We can only guess at Thomson's private thoughts. Chancellor P.E. Mackenzie vaguely alluded to the situation in a letter he wrote to Thomson on 10 July 1940. Referring to the choice of a successor to Ramsay, Mackenzie commented, "I expect that while [the successor] will seek to maintain the advancement of the college, he will not do so by attempting to impair the integrity of the university, which in the light of past experience, tends to add to one's peace of mind. I am sure that this matter must have given you considerable worry. It pleases me to think of the relief you must feel, in having settled it in a way which affords a brighter outlook."[60] "Impairing the integrity of the university" was a euphemism for allowing a degree course in Regina.

Moving day was Saturday, 31 May 1940. William Ramsay packed up his belongings and vacated his suite, faculty members cleaned out their offices, and movers transported filing cabinets, desks, and books to the new quarters. Carpenters at the Regina Trading Company Building put up partitions for the library and assembly hall on the second floor and made modifications for staff offices, classrooms, and laboratories on the third floor. There was enough room to accommodate 150 students. The Conservatory of Music continued its operations at Darke Hall, which had not been turned over to the air force. The normal school occupied rooms in Lakeview Public School, and the Regina College art collection as well as the provincial museum exhibits, previously housed in the normal school, were moved to the top floor of the General Motors Building at the corner of 8th Avenue and Quebec Street.[61]

Two trainloads of RCAF recruits rolled into Regina from Toronto on the morning of Monday, 30 June 1940. Greeting them at the station were Lieutenant-Governor Archibald P. McNab, Mayor James Grassick, and the officers of No. 2 Initial Training School (the official name of the training centre at Regina College) and No. 4 Training Command, which controlled RCAF operations in the district. The recruits formed ranks and marched south down Scarth Street to the skirl of the Regina Boys' Pipe Band. Arriving at the normal school, which was to serve as their barracks, they stowed their kit bags and headed to the college dining room for a meal of roast beef and mashed potatoes. They relaxed for the rest of the day, playing softball and volleyball with equipment donated by the YMCA. Classes began bright and early the next morning, with instruction in mathematics, hygiene, law, discipline, and the history and traditions of the air force. There were also drill, physical training, and practice on the Link Trainer, a device with controls and instruments that simulated airplane flight.[62] After four weeks at the initial training school, the men proceeded, according to their progress and abilities, to more specialized training as pilots, observers, wireless operators, or gunners. Each month 500 recruits passed through the school, for a total of 6,000 a year.[63]

Regina College, meanwhile, settled into its new quarters in the Regina Trading Company Building, just five blocks north of the College Avenue campus. Designed by architects Story and Van Egmond and constructed in 1920, the building had four storeys, a full basement, and frontage of 75 feet

The Regina Trading Company Building, at the northeast corner of Scarth Street and 12th Avenue, home to Regina College from 1940 to the end of 1944.

on Scarth and 125 feet on 12th Avenue.[64] The owners were a group of local shareholders, including C. Morley Willoughby and George Barr, friends and supporters of Regina College.[65] This must have been helpful in obtaining the lease, and Willoughby was added to the Advisory Board at about this time.[66] The other tenants in the building were a motley lot – the Princess Beauty Shop, the Arcade Coffee Shop, Capitol Shoe Repair, the Accordion Academy, the Union Electric Company, T.W. Wilson (tailor), Pearl Derby (shorthand teacher), and Mrs J. Stevens (corsets).[67]

To find a new dean to replace Ramsay, President Thomson first approached D.H. Russell of the College of Education at the Saskatoon campus. "Quite frankly," Thomson wrote to Russell, "ever since coming here I have wanted a man who would worthily represent the University in the city of Regina, and I feel assured that you could do so. I am more persuaded of this since you have taken to yourself a wife."[68] Unfortunately, Russell accepted a position at the University of British Columbia, and Thomson had to look elsewhere. He finally chose Steward Basterfield, who had taught chemistry at the Saskatoon campus since 1913.

Basterfield had received a Bachelor of Science degree from the University of London in 1908, and, like Ramsay, had earned a PhD at the University of Chicago during summer sessions and while on sabbatical leave from his regular teaching duties. His publications ranged over many topics, from the chemistry of organic sulphur compounds to the rivalry between Newton and Leibnitz, and his scholarly achievements were recognized in his election to the Royal Society of Canada in 1933. One of his special interests was the problem of reconciling the natural sciences with the humanities in "a new system of knowledge, a weaving together of the main strands of thought that have been spun by busy workers in so many intellectual mills."[69] As a youth, he had trained for the Methodist ministry and served in the mission fields of northwest Saskatchewan, and, while he chose science as his profession, he retained a lifelong interest in spiritual and religious matters. Indeed, he contended that science belonged ultimately to the world of the spirit, as did literature, art, and music.[70]

Basterfield spent his spare hours writing a history of science from ancient Greece to the modern age, a project he never completed. President Thomson was also interested in the history and philosophy of science, and the two men mulled over the subject in long, rambling conversations. They travelled, as Thomson phrased it, down the centuries "in a happy surrender to the enchantments of philosophical thought."[71] Thomson held a dim view of narrow, overspecialized education, which he described as "going on endlessly, adding credit to credit, and then completing the process by digging down a very deep, narrow and dark hole which is called research for the Ph.D."[72] He found a soulmate in Basterfield, with whom he reported having a "closer intellectual affinity" than with any other member of the university faculty.[73] The two happily whiled away the hours in philosophical discussion, vaguely and uncomfortably aware that the ideal of the gentleman scholar who knew a little bit about everything was rapidly becoming obsolete in an age of departmentalization and specialization.

Basterfield had a warm, friendly manner, and he "understood the therapeutic value of a cup of coffee or a pot of hot chocolate and unrelated discussion between teacher and student before the final coming to grips with the problem itself."[74] His soft English accent and dignified old-country air put visitors at their ease. A faculty member who came to his office on a matter of business might leave an hour later having listened to "a lucid, delightful and quite impromptu discourse on the beauties of Chinese pottery, the satiric wit of Bertrand Russell or the theory and practice of the Jacobins."[75] Cliff Blight, registrar and instructor in mathematics, remembered long conversations with Basterfield as they drove up and down the dusty roads of southern Saskatchewan recruiting high school students to attend the college. A simple

Steward Basterfield, dean of Regina College from 1940 to 1950. He said of the wartime move of the college to the Regina Trading Company Building, "We regret having to vacate our own delightful halls, but we are still a community of scholars, and can, in the ardent pursuit of knowledge, easily forget the small inconveniences imposed on us by the exigencies of war."

question, Blight recalled, could set off a learned lecture that carried the travellers to the next town.[76] It was like listening to the radio.

Basterfield's weakness was administration. His filing system consisted of "a pile of letters and copies in a basket, unorganized and incomplete."[77] He transacted business informally, often without leaving a written record of what had been done. This led to a certain amount of confusion and made it difficult for others to pick up the threads. Basterfield's greatest strength was his optimism and determination to place the best possible face on the move to the Regina Trading Company Building. The local community supported him, turning out in large numbers for a reception on 17 September 1940 to mark the opening of the new quarters. As the *Leader-Post* reported, "a handsome arrangement of palms and ferns graced corridors, reception and tearooms, and flame-colored gladioli offered further adornment." The 600 guests in attendance represented the civic, educational, and business elite of the city, including the lieutenant-governor, the chief justice, the chancellor of the university, senior RCAF officers, the mayor of Regina, and several members of City Council. The consensus was that the college had found "exceptionally favorable quarters" for its temporary home.[78]

The new location had its drawbacks, especially the lack of campus grounds, but there were compensations in being in the heart of the shopping and business district, such as "a coffee shop in the basement, a beauty parlour on the mezzanine floor, and a cinema across the road."[79] Basterfield beamed that the spirit of academic life was something unique, created by students and teachers independent of time and space: "We regret having to vacate our own delightful halls, but we are still a community of scholars, and can, in the ardent pursuit of knowledge, easily forget the small inconveniences imposed on us by the exigencies of war."[80]

The students took advantage of the downtown amenities. The student newspaper, the *College Record*, carried ads that read, "Between Classes. Park Billiards, Basement McCallum Hill Building; National Billiards, Basement Mitchell Building,"[81]and the Arcade Coffee Shop promised "Hot Lunches Cold. Meet Your College Pals Here." After the graduation ceremonies at Darke Hall in May 1942, Mrs Palmer, proprietor of the coffee shop, handed over the soda fountain to the students. "What a soda it was that Don had to drink!" the student newspaper declared – "two other victims risked their constitutions on two very chocolatey chocolate milk shakes 'shaken' by Joan's 'own little hands.' Yum! Yum!"[82]

The new location was a good deal noisier than the old had been. The honking of car horns, the screech of brakes, and the cries of newsboys interrupted the drone of the lecturer. The Voice of Prophecy Hall rented space in the building adjoining the college library, moving one student to complain, "I love singing, I enjoy church music, I like sermons and I relish prophecies, but somehow they don't mix with differential calculus and nineteenth century French."[83] The building had other disadvantages. The laboratories were smaller than those in the college building, the hallways more crowded, and there was no gymnasium. Physical activities were arranged for the students at the YMCA and YWCA, including "floor gymnastics, other organized recreation, and swimming."[84] In addition, students and faculty took up bowling, competing in a Thursday afternoon mixed league.[85] A faculty member captained each team, ex officio, as one professor hastened to explain, and "not from merit."[86] Ernest "Red" Thackeray (so nicknamed because of his red hair), who taught physics and mathematics, was known for laying down "a smokescreen with his old faithful pipe when he bowls so that his word must be taken for the score." The women participated as well as the men, sometimes outdoing their male competitors: "Well, hang your heads boys, a member of the Weaker Sex, that chick from Matric, Jean Cardiff, has pulled off a 310 game."[87]

Oddly enough, the inadequate facilities did not depress school spirit. The *College Record* encouraged students to display the college colours (green and gold) and promoted the purchase of sweatshirts, sweaters, and other items bearing the college insignia.[88] Student president Ralph Foster composed a song titled "A Salute to Regina College," which was performed at the annual banquet on 15 March 1941.[89]

> Hail to Regina College, her glory we extol.
> Hail to our Alma Mater, her honor we uphold.

The green and gold of her sons of old bring a gallant picture near,
These days to me will always be filled with mem'ries rare and dear.
Drink to her fame and fortune, let her banners proudly wave.
A salute, a toast we offer to you our loyal and brave.[90]

According to Government of Canada regulations, all male university students who were of military age and physically fit were required to take military training with the Canadian Officers' Training Corps (COTC) or the comparable naval or air force training units. A Regina platoon of the University of Saskatchewan COTC was organized under the command of Sam E. Stewart, the Latin and Greek instructor who had been hired to replace Ramsay. It comprised all male students of military age from Luther, Campion, and Regina Colleges. The initial group of seventeen drilled in the Regina College gymnasium Tuesday and Thursday evenings from 7:30 to 9:30.[91] By 1943–44 the platoon had grown to forty-five men. Also in that year a squadron of the University Air Training Corps was organized, with nineteen men participating.[92]

National Selective Service regulations designated certain university courses as having special importance to the war effort. They included engineering, medicine, dentistry, pharmacy, agriculture, and science. Students enrolled in these programs were permitted to continue their studies until graduation, provided their grades were satisfactory. Indeed, they were not allowed to enlist in the armed forces without the approval of the Wartime Bureau of Technical Personnel. The government regarded sciences and engineering as vital to the prosecution of the war effort, and it did not want higher education in those areas to suffer a decline. Students in fields that were deemed non-essential, such as the liberal arts and humanities, could continue to attend university only if they ranked in the upper half of the class, as determined by standard examinations.[93]

In one case, which came to the attention of Dean Basterfield in July 1942, a young man who had enrolled in pre-medical studies at Regina College was called up for military training. He came to the dean for advice and assistance. Basterfield's opinion was that the student should be allowed to register in the university and continue his academic program. "He is an excellent student," the dean wrote. "I am convinced he is not a shirker, though his conscience baulks at the idea of slaughter. However, he is anxious to do his duty and he feels he can do it best in medical service towards which he has a long-standing ambition."[94] Basterfield asked President Thomson to support an appeal on behalf of the student to the National War Services Board, but Thomson declined. He said that "with the getting abroad of the news that medical students would not be called up, we have been rather plagued with senior men who have taken a rather sudden desire to enter upon the study of

TABLE 1: Regina College Enrolment, 1939–40 to 1944–45

	MATRICULATION	FIRST YEAR	SPECIAL	AUDITORS	TOTAL
1939–40	6	78	58	47	189
1940–41	9	60	47	10	126
1941–42	15	47	21	20	103
1942–43	26	59	51	29	165
1943–44	23	64	46	31	164
1944–45	70	57	43	45	215

Source: University of Saskatchewan, *Annual Report of the President*, 1939–40 to 1944–45.

Medicine. In one or two of the cases the applications have seemed so suspicious that one can hardly avoid the conclusion that the study of Medicine was being used as a means of avoiding military service."[95] Nor did Thomson think that religious scruples should enter into the question. He pointed out that under War Services Board regulations conscientious objectors of military age were to be sent to labour camps and under no circumstances were to be allowed to continue at the university.

Table 1 shows the enrolment at Regina College during the war. The number of first-year students declined from seventy-eight in 1939–40 to a low of forty-seven in 1941–42, before reaching a level of fifty-seven in 1944–45. The number of matriculation (grade 12) students, by contrast, increased from six in 1939–40 to seventy in 1944–45.

"Special" students were those taking only one or two courses for credit (as distinct from full-time students, who took three or more courses), and "auditors" were those attending classes but not taking examinations for credit.[96] Dean Basterfield attributed the drop in enrolment in 1940–41 to the enlistment of young men in the armed services and to the lack of residence facilities, the latter having been turned over to the air force when the college moved to the Regina Trading Company Building.[97]

As the war continued, the military continued to draw off students. The dean recorded in 1941–42 that eleven students joined the RCAF, and in 1942-43 another fourteen enlisted in the army.[98] By the following year the Regina College honour roll bore the names of 205 men and women. Of these, eleven had fallen in action or in the line of duty.[99] When the veterans started to return to civilian life, the pattern was reversed and enrolment began to climb again. They were eligible for Government of Canada educational allowances, and many of them took the opportunity to resume their schooling. The first to arrive, in 1943, were discharged aircrew and soldiers who had

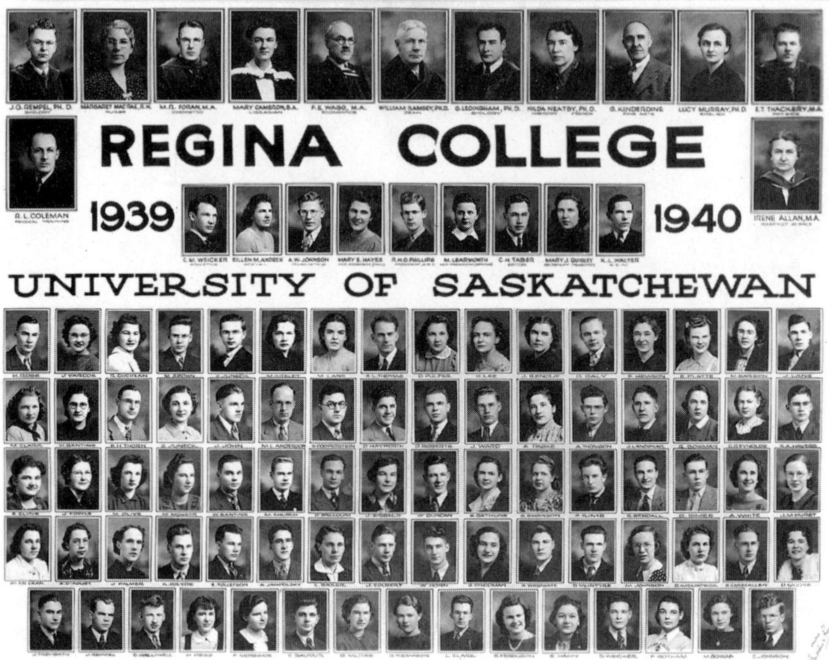

The faculty and full-time matriculation and first-year arts and science students at Regina College in 1939–40. The enrolment of full-time students was only eighty-four.

been wounded, sick, or disabled.[100] In January 1945 Regina College inaugurated special matriculation courses for demobilized servicemen, supplementing the courses scheduled for the fall. The special classes continued through the summer so that students could complete a five-class matriculation program by August 15 and enter university courses in September. This cut a full year from the time required for veterans to prepare for university entrance.[101] The special courses accounted for the jump in the number of matriculation students from twenty-three in 1943–45 to seventy in 1944–45. The influx of veterans not only increased the size of the student body but also altered its composition. As table 2 indicates, the gender balance among matriculation students tilted in favour of males.

The world crisis caused by the war made a deep impression on young people, engendering a spirit of patriotism and sacrifice. Saskatchewan's minister of education, Hubert Staines, warned the students attending the annual college banquet in March 1942 that they were living at a time when the fate of civilization hung in the balance. "For those whose destiny was to be young at this juncture," he said, "there was before them unparalleled enterprise both

TABLE 2: Regina College Enrolment by Sex, 1941–42 to 1944–45

YEAR		MATRICULATION	FIRST YEAR
1941–42	males	11	22
	females	4	25
1942–43	males	19	36
	females	7	23
1943–44	males	13	32
	females	10	32
1944–45	males	52	19
	females	18	38

Source: University of Saskatchewan, *Annual Report of the President*, 1941–42 to 1944–45.

in winning victory and in rebuilding the world." Other speakers developed the same theme. Sam Stewart, in the toast to the students, reminded them that it was the "duty of each of them, and the duty of every Canadian, in time of war to avail himself of the opportunity of taking training for specific usefulness." Chancellor P.E. Mackenzie recalled with pride the sacrifice the college had made in placing its buildings at the service of the RCAF, and President Thomson expounded on the valuable role that science was playing in winning the war. He told the students that any young man who had enrolled in a science course should not feel guilty if he hadn't enlisted in the armed forces. "To be in a position to offer leadership in medicine, chemistry, engineering or any form of applied science was the finest contribution he could make to Canada." (Arts students, presumably, were expected to feel guilty.) The war theme extended even to the souvenir place cards on the tables, which represented the flags of the twenty-six allied nations. At the front of the hall the British and American flags were displayed, and the musical entertainment for the evening featured songs identified with the nations united in the struggle against the Axis Powers.[102]

The students absorbed these messages of patriotism, responsibility, and duty. Their attitudes were also shaped by the recent experience of the Depression of the 1930s. Since many of them came from families that had known hardship, they did not take educational opportunities for granted. Frank Wagg, the registrar, noticed in September 1939 that two female students had been awarded Dominion Youth Training scholarships. The difficulty was that their families were on relief. This meant that if the girls accepted the scholarship money, an equivalent amount would have to be deducted from the relief payments. Wagg's solution was to arrange for a portion of the scholarship to be sent directly to the college to cover tuition fees and to have the balance released to the girls in small amounts so that the subsidy did not come to the attention of the relief authorities. "This is not, as it may appear, a mere subterfuge," Wagg unapologetically observed, "but it is a means of securing that the prime purpose of this scholarship itself is not defeated."[103]

Even middle-class families felt the pinch of the Depression and were careful how they spent their money. A female student from a fairly well-off family asked her mother for a new winter coat because the old one had gone out of style. Her mother replied that the coat would have to last her another year. The student rebelled, refusing to wear the coat, choosing instead to shiver all winter in a sweater and light jacket. The lesson was clear: money was not something to throw around wastefully; every penny counted.[104] It is important to remember that the Depression did not end as soon as the war started. It dragged on well into 1941 as the economy recovered completely and entered the zone of full employment. The students who came of age in the early 1940s had a serious, dutiful outlook. With the world in ruins, they were not disposed to complain too much or cause trouble. Rebellion for them meant refusing to wear an unfashionable coat. As Dean Basterfield remarked in his 1941 report, the students had shown "a splendid college spirit," had "cooperated willingly in maintaining good discipline and their relations with staff have been consistently marked by the utmost courtesy and friendliness." In 1942 he added, "Every phase of student life has been marked by friendly feeling and willingness to cooperate."[105]

The *College Record* on 4 December 1939 reported the death of Flying Officer "Pete" Johnstone. A brilliant student and an outstanding athlete, Johnstone was the first college alumnus killed in action.[106] Student Grant Carscallen wrote an article in which he imagined a bombing raid on Regina. A veneer of humour masked a sober message – the war was coming close to home:

Looking up I perceived a score or more planes circling the city. They were huge, almost ungainly craft, painted silver. On the wings and fuselage the black cross was clearly visible, while on the tail the all-too-familiar swastika could be discerned. They were flying ridiculously low, seemingly in contempt of our pitifully weak anti-aircraft defences. If any pursuit planes had engaged them beforehand, they certainly must have been destroyed, for not one could be seen up there. The Germans were simply bombing with impunity wherever and whatever they liked.

Crash! There goes the top of the Parliament Building. Oh well, the T.C.A. pilots were always complaining about it anyway. Bang! Well, I guess Dr. Rempel will have to postpone that Biology test we were to have on Tuesday. The Science Theatre is taking a trip to the country ... "Come with Me," said an RAMC [Royal Army Medical Corps] sergeant, his arms loaded with bandages. We ran after him as he rushed along Hamilton Street towards Victoria Avenue, where bombs had just fallen. When we had safely crossed Twelfth Avenue, a bomb struck the *Leader-Post* building and wrecked it completely. "I guess we'll have to rely on the *College Record* tonight," I heard a soldier remark as he passed us. "Yes, and Red Ryder was just pounding the daylights out of Lucky Drake, too," his companion replied.[107]

A letter to the editor of the *College Record* demanded to know why there was no Union Jack flying over the college.[108] Another extolled the fine qualities of "our leader," Winston Churchill, ignoring Canada's own prime minister, the dull and uninspiring William Lyon Mackenzie King.[109] An editorial urged that all male students, not just those of military age, be obliged to join the COTC and that all female students enrol in a first-aid, ambulance-driving, and/or other war-related course.[110] This drew a response from Bob Ellis, a student who opposed compulsory military training. He pointed out that those who worked in war industries also performed a vital service, and that university-trained men had special skills to contribute to the war effort. Such skills would be wasted if everyone were forced into the army: "In this war the production of war materials is going to be as important a factor in determining the outcome as the building of our armed forces."[111]

A notice appearing in the *College Record* on 20 March 1941 urged students to discard tinfoil in special boxes placed in the common rooms.[112] The paper also suggested that corsages not be worn at formal dances, "because it is a useless waste of money during a war," but, since "the ladies must have flowers," small bouquets of "fragrant sweet peas" were sold for twenty-five cents.[113] Student Mae King pondered the moral dilemma "Should Girls Wear Silk Stockings to School?"

Shouldn't the money spent on sheer hose be used instead for war purposes? This can best be decided by the girls themselves. "If we're going to be patriotic, what are we to wear on our legs?" they wail. "No cotton or lisle for us!" Well, what about crepe stockings? They look alright. Or, if you object to the feel of them, why not wear rayon stockings? They look the same as pure silk stockings – but they are not as expensive. I strongly suspect that most girls wear rayon stockings anyway. If you are boycotting silk, give yourself a thrill by trying Nylon stockings – the ones made out of coal and water. These aren't all the possibilities. Why not knit woolen stockings? Make them in bright colors (your school colors) with fancy stitches. Put on your thinking caps, girls, and start a fashion feature.[114]

The toll on the home front was not only economic, but also emotional and psychological. Students worried about the safety of family members and friends serving overseas in the armed forces. Mae King, in November 1940, reflected on the burden of anxiety for "The Unknown Legions":

Those who cannot sail the seas,
Who cannot soar,
Who never know the roar of guns,
Fight their battle too.
Those who see their dear ones go,
Who stay their tears,
And patiently allay the fears of others,
Know a fighting too.[115]

Students meditated on the ideals for which the war was being fought and on the world they were about to inherit. An editorial in January 1942 decried the fact that before the war Canadians had paid only lip service to their "shabby democracy." Politicians had been held in low esteem, and public office regarded as a "dirty profession." The war, terrible as it was, had at least awakened Canadians to the value of what they had previously taken for granted. Students had an obligation, the editorial said, to "do more than just believe in democracy. *We must make it work* ... ALL OF US MUST BECOME POLITICIANS."[116]

Student Alice Goodfellow elaborated on this theme in an article titled "Tomorrow," published in November 1940. She began with the assertion that the older generation had been tested and, in at least some respects, found wanting. After all, she reasoned, if they had been above reproach, "the world would not have plunged into its present state." It was up to the younger generation to improve upon the tarnished ideals of the old, "to substitute new ones for the worn out, and perfect, to the best of our ability, those with hope." As daunting as this task might seem, there was no excuse for weakness or despair: "Youth! What a glorious task we have – the building of a new world! We should be proud that some day we shall live in the new world order that will arise out of the chaos." Their first responsibility was to study hard and equip themselves for the job ahead. "If we leave our present tasks for tomorrow," she wrote, "we will be too late ... Let us prepare!"[117]

Towards the end of the war, there were signs among the students of a new spirit of Canadian nationalism. Frances Hyland, who attended Regina College in 1944–45, recorded her thoughts upon viewing an exhibition of Canadian paintings in May 1945. She noted that Canadians had a tendency to downgrade their own achievements – "if it's Canadian, it can't be that good." Hyland rejected this type of thinking: "Canada is no longer an outpost of Empire, a struggling colony. [It] is a country firmly established in the eyes of the world, having her own traditions and evolving a national identity. Let us not be afraid to grant our own talent its due."[118] It was time for Canadians to overcome their inferiority complex and assert themselves. Heeding her own advice, Hyland embarked on a career in the theatre, winning international recognition for her talents as an actor.

With end of the war in sight, in late 1944, the RCAF cut back on the intake of aircrew and closed down No. 2 Initial Training School. The move back to the old campus took place over the Christmas break of 1944–45. Although the college had endured a difficult time, it emerged from the war in fairly good shape. This might not have been so had it been relocated to Benson School rather than the Regina Trading Company Building. Being situated in a well-appointed office building in the heart of the business district carried a prestige that would have been totally lacking if the college had been banished to a remote elementary school, out of sight and out of mind. Ramsay had served the college well in refusing to accept inferior quarters.

Shortly before the move back to College Avenue, a reporter for the *College Record* asked students what they thought about the return. Some grew serious because they realized that the war was coming to an end. Others looked forward to going back to their old stomping grounds. "Just think," one said, "how you can go roaming over the campus; or sit by the lakeshore during that spare. And won't it be nice to be able to gather a crowd in the halls and hold a gossip session. We won't have to go around on tip-toe either." But there were aspects of the Regina Trading Company Building location they would miss: shopping during spares, visiting the nearby poolrooms, seeing the girls at the lunch counter and Marion, the elevator operator: "Just think – never again to hear her cheery voice as we sleepwalk into the elevator at 8:29. We should take her with us. All we'd have to do then is install an elevator." Then the question was asked: "Do you think moving back to the campus will improve school spirit?" Instantly the answer came back, "I think it's pretty high now."[119]

2 Post-war Bulge and Bust, 1945–49

"You couldn't always pick them out in the halls or in the classroom. Most of them had discarded their blue and their khaki in favour of worsted or tweed. Just when you took it for granted that one of these had come to college straight from high school, a chance remark about the Ardennes Bulge or the gaggle formation over Leipzig made you reassess his years. And his experience."[1] Thus English professor Les Crossman described the new type of student who arrived at Regina College after the war. The veterans had an enormous impact, both in their coming and in their going. When they arrived, they strained the capacity of the college to the breaking point. When they left, the once-crowded classrooms suddenly looked empty.

Under the terms of the Veterans Rehabilitation Act, the Government of Canada paid tuition fees and living allowances for ex-servicemen and women attending university or enrolled in pre-matriculation courses.[2] The subsidy continued for a period equal to the length of the veteran's service in the armed forces, but those who did well in their studies were eligible to have their benefits extended beyond their service entitlement. In order to qualify for assistance, a returned soldier had to "commence or resume training within fifteen months after discharge, except for good reason shown to the satisfaction of the Minister [of Veterans Affairs]." A married veteran received a living allowance of eighty dollars per month and a single veteran received sixty dollars. Allowances for dependent children were twelve dollars for each of the first two children, ten for the third, and eight each for the fourth, fifth, and sixth. Veterans could also earn up to seventy-five dollars a month in other income without incurring a reduction in their living allowance, except for wages paid in connection with their training, in which case the limit was forty dollars per month. Wives of veterans could earn as much as seventy-five dollars per month without financial penalty.[3]

The influx of veterans made a huge impression on Canadian universities. In 1946, the high point of veteran enrolment, there were 35,000 registrations of ex-servicemen and women. This compared with a total full-time undergraduate enrolment in Canadian universities and colleges of 35,164 in 1939.[4] At Regina College the number of full-time matriculation and first-year students jumped from 127 in 1944–45 to 417 in 1945–46. The college offered first-year engineering courses for the first time, largely to handle the overflow from Saskatoon, where facilities were strained to the limit. There were eighty-eight engineering students in 1945–46, all of them men. Overall, the full-time student population consisted of 349 men and 68 women, a huge shift in the male/female ratio as compared with the war and pre-war periods.[5] The *College Record* hinted at the implications for social life: "The influx of returned men to the college in January was hailed with delight by all the student body, though it was noticed that certain parties were having much more trouble keeping up their harems than formerly."[6]

The increased numbers of students all but overwhelmed the administrative and academic staff. The registrar "could not quite understand why he was no longer able to call every student by name. And Professor Thackeray understood too well why his physics lab seemed suddenly under-equipped and under-staffed."[7] The chemistry lab was also cramped, and the top floors of the tower on the west side of the main college building had to be converted into drafting rooms for the engineers.[8] Despite the difficulties, the college made the necessary adjustments. As Les Crossman recalled, "Nobody shouted 'Go home, Vet.' Here and there they broke the seams of a tight little college, but they also gave it something of the atmosphere of a university."[9]

New instructors were appointed in chemistry, mathematics, biology, English, French, Latin, descriptive geometry and drawing, and physical training, as were laboratory demonstrators in chemistry, physics, drawing, and biology. Among those hired were Les Crossman in English and George Ledingham in biology, the latter replacing Jake Rempel, who was transferred to Saskatoon.[10] Historian Hilda Neatby also left for Saskatoon in 1946. She had been a particular favourite of the veterans, who liked the fact that she did not pull rank. If a student offered an opinion different from her own, she considered it respectfully, provided he could back it up with evidence and logic.[11]

Initially, there were concerns that the veterans would not perform well academically. Many of them had been out of school for a long time and had forgotten much of what they had previously learned. There were doubts as to whether they were ready to settle down to serious study and fears that

TABLE 3: Comparison of Academic Performance of Veterans and Civilians, Regina College, Christmas Examinations 1942

Engineering	veterans	186 classes	31 failures	16.7%
	civilians	212 classes	53 failures	25.0%
Arts and science	veterans	241 classes	51 failures	21.2%
	civilians	427 classes	97 failures	22.7%
Matriculation	veterans	118 classes	55 failures	46.6%
	civilians	139 classes	58 failures	41.7%

Source: Archives of the University of Saskatchewan, President's Office Records, series 2, B151, Regina College, 1946–47, F.E. Wagg to J.S. Thomson, 29 January 1946.

they would be tempted to break loose after years of strict military discipline. Another worry was that the older and worldly wise veterans would not fit in well with younger students, "who had never smelt the smoke of battle."[12] Such fears were for the most part unfounded. The veterans, as a group, applied themselves more diligently to their studies than did many of their civilian counterparts. Because of their greater maturity, they were on the whole more focused and definite in their aims. Many of them had families to support and needed to be able to earn a living as soon as possible.

Academically, they performed better on the average than other students (see table 3). Registrar Frank Wagg compared the results achieved by veterans and civilians in the Christmas examinations in 1942. He noted that the veterans had a lower failure rate in first-year engineering and arts and science courses and a higher failure rate in the matriculation program. For many of the demobilized men the matriculation course was the first exposure to formal schooling for some time. Wagg anticipated that as they became more accustomed to the academic routine, their grades would improve. Dean Basterfield was equally optimistic, observing in his 1945–46 annual report that veterans showed "a definite superiority in academic attainment and they have given excellent leadership in student life."[13]

The veterans blended fairly smoothly into the life of the institution. The college did not set up separate sections for them, but rather mixed them in with the younger students, who in some cases became their tutors.[14] Student president Bob Fuller extended a special greeting in the *College Record* of 4 December 1944. "I am quite sure," he wrote, "that I speak for all the council when I say that we will be glad to help in any way we can to make the transition back to college life as easy and pleasant as possible for you."[15] The college put on a reception for the newcomers in January 1945. Dean Basterfield gave a speech, the students held a dance, and "our active social director, Jim, endeavored to teach the college yells to those unfortunates who as yet haven't learned them."[16] The teachers tried to be helpful and met the veterans at least halfway. Registrar Cliff Blight, himself a veteran, knew how to bend, or even "fracture" the rules, if he thought that doing so was in the best interests of the students.[17]

Even so, the veterans did not have it easy. The *College Record* in May 1945 published the poem of an ex-airman bored with earthbound civilian life:

> Weary, the road I walked with eyes cast down;
> The way is dusty and my step is slow.
> A laggard pace for one who loved
>   to show Heels to the wind, and called the sky
>   his own.
> But now, what magic frees the troubled frown
> That knits my brow? – Though faint,
>   that sound I know –
> Beats now my heart turned to each throb; I glow!
> I search the sky, until against the crown
>   Of yonder cloud the flash of sun on wings
> My vision meets; I soar, away, away
> To laugh and know the fellowship of things
> I knew, unfettered and unbound by clay.
>   Oh Fates that mock! The distant murmurings
>   Die – Endless before extends the dusty way.[18]

A disturbance involving veterans occurred at a local hotel in May 1947. The details are hazy, but it seems the ex-soldiers thought that the police had treated them unfairly. They appealed to the college Advisory Board for a remedy, but on the advice of the chairman, Mr Justice H.Y. MacDonald, the board stayed out of the dispute.[19]

Veterans showed signs of having a political consciousness not shared by the other students. In an article titled "What Price Education?" J.D. Herbert pointed to the irony of the government's paying for a man's university education only on the condition that he was willing to lay down his life for his country. "Isn't it paradoxical," he asked, "that boys should be forced to know the stench of death, the cacophony of the battlefield, cold strain and exhaustion before they know the good things of life?"[20] To protect and advance their interests, veterans from across Canada organized the National Conference of Student Veterans in Montreal in December 1945.[21] The Regina College branch held its first meeting on 13 December 1947, when it authorized the delegates from Saskatoon to represent them at the upcoming national conference in Toronto. The most important issue was the fight for increased

World War II veterans enrolled at Regina College in 1945. As English professor Les Crossman wrote, "Here and there they broke the seams of a tight little college, but they also gave it something of the atmosphere of a university."

benefits. The organization, through persistent lobbying, was able to secure an increase on 1 January 1948 of ten dollars per month in the basic allowance and six dollars per month for each of the first two children.

The Regina branch subsequently invited J. Probe, the CCF member of Parliament for Regina, and Clarence Fines, the provincial treasurer, to attend one of their meetings. The politicians encouraged them to keep up their campaign for increased allowances.[22] The veterans were proud of what they had accomplished as soldiers, citizens, and students. As G.K. Piller, himself a veteran, wrote in 1948, "Although this group of students represents the older portion of the College student body it has, in the past year, shown a remarkable sense of understanding and cooperation with the remaining younger generation." He added, poignantly, "We as veterans can be proud of the fact that we have, if nothing else, at least learned and proven that we are human beings and can adjust ourselves to any type of civilian life including college life."[23]

Many of the veterans came to Regina College without a high school diploma. They registered in the matriculation program, which qualified them for first-year university studies. Matriculation and grade 12 were not exactly the same thing, since the former comprised a select group of six grade 12 subjects: English (literature and composition); history; either French, Latin, German, Greek, Icelandic, or Norwegian; Latin or mathematics (algebra, trigonometry, and geometry); a science; and either biology, chemistry, physics, geology, agricultural economics, music, or one of the foreign languages listed. To make the program more manageable for the veterans, the university reduced the number of courses needed for matriculation from six to five. In addition, specific requirements varied depending on the university program the student intended to enter. Latin, for example, was needed for type A arts (literary), and mathematics was compulsory for type C arts (natural sciences), medicine, or household science. The basic intention of the matriculation course was to provide the student with a solid foundation in the fundamental subjects. As Dean Basterfield explained, "It [was] not to be treated as a conglomeration of subjects which a student may happen to fancy."[24]

The first-year programs, like the matriculation program, were structured in a rigid manner and allowed few options or electives. The requirements for first-year arts and science and first-year engineering were as follows:

FIRST YEAR ARTS AND SCIENCE

Type A – Literary Course

1. English 2
2. Political Economy A
3. Biological Sciences A

4&5. Two from French 2, German 2, Greek 2, Latin 2

Type B – Social Sciences

1. English 2
2. Biological Sciences A

3&4. Two from Economics 2, History 25, Philosophy 5

5. One from French 2, German 2, Greek 2, Latin 2

Type C – Natural Sciences

1. English 2
2. Political Economy A
3. One from French 1, French 2, German 1, German 2

4&5. Two from Chemistry 1 or 2, Physics 1 or 2, Biology 1, Mathematics 7

FIRST YEAR ENGINEERING

1. English 3
2. Mathematics 7
3. Chemistry 4
4. Drawing 1
5. Descriptive Geometry
6. Physics 3[25]

It was a meat-and-potatoes, no-nonsense curriculum. The newer social science disciplines, such as psychology, sociology, and anthropology, were absent, and the fine arts were nowhere to be seen.

For those students who did not intend to pursue a university degree the college offered a Certificate of Associate in arts, which signified the completion of junior college work. It was granted to students who had completed matriculation, English 2, and either four classes in arts and science or two classes in arts and science and courses in music, household science, or accounting. The latter options were not accepted for the Bachelor of Arts degree. The certificate had a more vocational bent, and it required only one year of study after matriculation, as compared with the three years needed for the BA.[26]

The members of the Regina College faculty were also members of their corresponding university departments, and their names appeared with those of their Saskatoon colleagues in the university calendar. They had equal authority with respect to conducting classes, setting examinations, and disciplining students.[27] Hilda Neatby titled her brief reminiscence of the years (1934–46) she spent at Regina College "So Much for the Mind,"[28] a pointed reference to her 1953 book *So Little for the Mind*, a scathing indictment of declining standards in public education. For Neatby, Regina College exemplified the traditional system, which demanded hard work, sound preparation, and intellectual rigour. As one Regina student commented in 1955, with mingled pride and chagrin, "It's common knowledge that if you can get through here, you can get through anywhere. The problem is to get through."[29] Or, as Dean Basterfield put it, the college offered "no snap courses or easy backdoor admission to the university." The matriculation course, he boasted, "is no sanctuary for spivs, drones, or deadbeats."[30] Academic studies formed the core of Regina College. Everything else – athletics, social clubs, and extracurricular activities – took second place. It can be described, with only slight exaggeration, as an intellectual boot camp cranking out scholarship winners. In 1950 five of the previous nine Rhodes Scholars from Saskatchewan had attended the college.[31]

The academic year began in September and came to a close with final examinations in mid-April. The high school year, by comparison, extended from September to June. The matriculation students, who followed essentially the same curriculum as their counterparts in grade 12, had to cover the material in less time. As one student remarked in an article in the college newspaper in May 1945, "We have to go much faster and therefore can only cover the work once so you either get it the first time, or you don't get it. This makes for intensive study outside of school on your part." "If you have an assignment to do and don't get it in on time," the article continued, "that's your lookout. The prof doesn't say anything to you and, on the other hand, if you get a low mark you don't ask the prof about it because you know you did not hand the exercise in on time."[32]

As long as they got their work done, students were accorded a measure of freedom to do what they liked during their spares. They could leave the building, drop in at Scotty's for a Coke, or wander around downtown. If they remained on campus, they had the option of socializing in the common room or studying in the library. Smoking was permitted in the common rooms, though not in the halls, although even this rule was "blissfully ignored by the male population." Student Bob Ellis summed up the main difference from high school: "In College we alone are responsible for our studies. The classes are held; the rest depends on us." He said that he liked being addressed as "Mr Ellis." At first he thought the professors were being sarcastic, but gradually he came to the realization that "the faculty must consider us being adults."[33]

Mid-term examinations were held in late October and Christmas examinations in mid-December. After the papers had been graded, the faculty met as a group to discuss the progress achieved by each student. Assessments, conducted behind closed doors, were brutally frank:

> Student A: see the Dean
> Student B: not working, missing classes in Latin
> Student C: good worker
> Student D: very weak
> Student E: advised to drop French 2
> Student F: nebulous
> Student G: lazy!!
> Student H: "happy-go-lucky"
> Student I: attitude in lab is poor. needs too much prodding
> Student J: no ability
> Student K: working but no results
> Student L: sloppy[34]

A student who failed more than two subjects in either the mid-term or Christmas examinations was deemed ineligible to participate in extracurricular activities.[35]

Discipline was assumed as much as it was enforced. Students who misbehaved in class were asked to leave on the understanding that they were not to come back until called for. Those who missed classes had to supply, upon their return, "a letter from their parents or guardian or from a doctor." If a student was absent for more than 10 per cent of the lectures in a given course, he or she could be barred from writing the final examination. This rule was later relaxed to a certain degree, but the principle was still maintained that "willful and persistent absence" from class would result in disciplinary measures.[36] "Habitual neglect of work" could lead to expulsion, and students who conducted themselves in an "improper manner" were liable, on recommendation of the Faculty Committee on Discipline, to be "reprimanded, fined, suspended or expelled." One offence was sufficiently serious to receive special mention in the calendar: "The use of liquor at any time within the College premises is strictly forbidden, under penalty of expulsion and forfeiture of fees."[37]

Despite this rather fearsome and forbidding regime, Hilda Neatby characterized relations between faculty and students as "easy and friendly."[38] Bob Ellis remembered the faculty as "sympathetic and understanding, and always ready to extend a guiding hand."[39] The small size of the college afforded many opportunities for interaction both inside and outside of the classroom, a happy contrast, said Dean Basterfield, to the "enormous classes" and "mechanical processing of students by assembly-line methods" typical of large universities.[40] George Robinson, the student who proposed the toast to the college at the annual banquet in 1946, went out of his way to say how much he appreciated the opportunity to get to know the professors and to engage in "an interchange of ideas and outlooks that forms a lasting basis for broader human understanding."[41]

Students and faculty interacted with each other in intramural sports, which resumed after the war, when the college regained access to its gymnasium. The faculty entered a team in the basketball league, winning the championship in 1949 with a 37 to 29 victory over the engineering students. The *College Record* congratulated the "scarred veterans ... who had shown for once and all that they could beat the pants off the younger generation any time."[42] Physics professor Ernest Thackeray refereed college basketball games, keeping the crowd entertained at halftime with demonstrations of ball-handling skills, including trick shots that involved throwing the ball over the rafters and into the hoop.[43] Sam Stewart, who coached basketball, was "Mr Stewart" in the classroom, but "Sammy" on the court.[44]

Faculty and students came together on two formal occasions, one at the beginning and the other at the end of the school year. The faculty reception, typically held in late September or early October, was an official welcome for the students. The dean gave a speech extolling the benefits of college life, and members of faculty and their wives were introduced. There was instruction in the college yells ("15-40-23, Regina College, who are we, Tyro, Pigskin, zig-boom-bah, Regina College, RAH, RAH, RAH"),[45] as well as music, dancing, and refreshments.[46] One of the goals was to mix students from different high schools and begin the formation of a Regina College group identity. The *College Record* in 1948 reported that the event "would have been much better had the students forgotten that they were from Luther, Scott, Central or wherever and realized that they were all Regina Collegians and as such should be friendly to each other ... I'm sure that as they get to know each other better in class and through participation in extracurricular activities, the social functions will be bigger and better all the time."[47] However, most students attended the college for only one year. A sense of community had to develop quickly, if it developed at all, and once established, it could not last very long.

The annual college banquet, held on a Saturday evening in mid-March, marked the end of all extracurricular activities; the students then had a full month to concentrate solely on academic work and prepare for final examinations. A day or two before the banquet, the Students' Representative Council gave out awards for participation in extracurricular activities at an event known as "colour night." The SRC came up with the idea in 1936, and they, not the faculty, selected the winners according to a point system of their own devising. The awards, crests in the shape of the letter *R*, were divided into three orders of merit – major, medium, and minor – depending on the student's level of contribution.[48] After the prizes were handed out, the students held a dance in the college dining room. The *Leader-Post* on 15 March 1940 described the scene: "For the dance the dining rooms were gaily decorated in the college colors, green and yellow, with college pennants adorning each pillar in the room. The orchestra stand was set off with green and yellow pennants also."[49]

The banquet was the central and defining ritual in the life of the college. In 1945 it was held in the basement of Westminster United Church, with 175 guests in attendance.[50] The dignitaries seated at the head table included Chancellor P.E. Mackenzie; President J.S. Thomson; members of the Regina College Advisory Board (Chief Justice J.T. Brown, Honourable Mr Justice H.Y. MacDonald, David M. Balfour, D.J. Thom, and Morley Willoughby); Dean Basterfield, who was master of ceremonies; Premier T.C. Douglas, the guest speaker; Dr Rex Schneider, president of Luther College; and Dan Cameron, director of the Conservatory of Music. The after-dinner program consisted of a series of toasts, always the same ones in the same order, interspersed with musical performances and sessions of "community singing."[51]

In 1945 Dean Basterfield opened with a toast to the king. The guests sang university and college songs, including "clever parodies on 'Solomon Levi' and 'She'll Be Coming Round the Mountain.'" Erica Zentner performed a violin solo, and Helen Lamont sang "Lindy Lou" and "Without a Song." Student Margaret Cumming proposed a toast to the college, and Morley Willoughby gave the reply. He surveyed the thirty-five-year history of the institution, pausing over the highlights and praising the quality and dedication of the faculty, the industriousness and talent of the students, and, last but not least, "our connection with the university." Dr Jake Rempel gave the toast to the students, touching on the main features of college life: the academic program, music and art courses, "splendid" library, sports, dramatic productions, debating club, and social activities. His sly jokes at the expense of faculty members were "a big hit with students." Bob Fuller, president of the SRC, delivered the final toast of the evening, a tribute to the university, to which

President Thomson responded. Thomson took as his theme the contribution Canadian universities had made to the war effort and his pleasure at seeing so many veterans in attendance at the college.[52]

The toasts completed, Premier T.C. Douglas, the invited speaker, gave the main address. He was still in his first year of office, having been elected in June 1944 as head of the first socialist government in North America. His Cooperative Commonwealth Federation (CCF) won 53 per cent of the popular vote and forty-seven of the fifty-two seats in the legislature. The long reign of the Liberals, who had dominated Saskatchewan politics since 1905, was over. Having endured the Depression and World War II, people were ready for change. They wanted government to take responsibility for the economy, to ensure full employment and a basic standard of health, education, and social services. These things the CCF set out to do, embarking on an ambitious program that transformed Saskatchewan and, to a certain extent, served as a model for the rest of Canada. It created eleven new Crown corporations, introduced hospital insurance, reorganized the school system through the implementation of the larger school unit plan, passed a new trade union act, brought in compulsory no-fault automobile insurance, established the Department of Social Welfare (Saskatchewan had never had one), increased old-age pensions and mothers' allowances, and introduced Canada's first Bill of Rights.[53] And it did all of this in its first term in office.

Douglas tried to convey something of his spirit of reform-minded idealism to the Regina College graduates. He said that schooling by itself produced neither virtue nor happiness. To be truly effective, it had to be combined with another ingredient. "One could point to men," Douglas said, "who were educated devils, men whose genius was turned to destruction of mankind. Knowledge could be a diabolical thing in the hands of the unmoral and the unscrupulous." True happiness, he maintained, was not something that one sought; it was a by-product of service and of losing oneself in a great task that transcended personal ego. There were many opportunities for service in the post-war world, and many challenges for those who wanted to make a contribution to the betterment of society. He encouraged the students to answer the call to help others and, in so doing, to secure personal fulfillment. The entire address was lightened, according to the *College Record*, with humorous stories; for instance, a joke about King Arthur that "gave a new twist to an old legend and brought forth hearty applause and laughter from the entire assembly."[54]

The annual banquet affirmed and strengthened the Regina College community. It gave students, faculty, and board members a feeling for what the college was, what it was trying to achieve, where it had come from, and where it was going. Every year the same series of toasts was given and the same things were said. The history of the college was reviewed – the humble Methodist beginnings, the expansion in the 1920s, the hardships of the 1930s, the sacrifice of the college buildings during the war – and the promise of the future was invoked. Many banquet guests had heard it all time and time again. The point, however, was not so much to communicate information as to perform a ritual and to repeat the well-worn phrases that bound the community together.

It was significant, too, that there was no toast to the faculty; rather, the teachers were the ones who put on the event for the students. It was an opportunity for the members of the faculty to make a symbolic gesture of service, showing respect for the students and honouring their achievements. As Hilda Neatby recalled, "The spring banquet regularly reduced the faculty to frustration, if not despair, but always – somehow – 'came off' superbly."[55] In addition, the banquet gave the college an opportunity to present itself to the larger community. Prominent citizens sat at the head table, the guest speaker was a person of distinction, and the event was always written up in the *Leader-Post*. The college, in effect, announced to the world, "Here we are, we have been here for a long time, and we continue to do good work. We are proud of our accomplishments, we have a promising future before us, and we deserve your support."

The banquet was always held on a Saturday evening, and the next day was designated "college Sunday." Students attended, on a voluntary basis, a non-denominational church service at Darke Hall, where they sang hymns and heard a suitably uplifting sermon. President Thomson, a United Church minister, especially enjoyed college Sunday. He took great pains with the details of the service, helping to select the Bible lessons, advising on the choice of hymns and where the choir should stand. He even had ideas about what should be done with the proceeds from the collection. "My own suggestion to [the students]," he wrote in 1939, "would be that they should give it for the relief of students in China at the present time. However, they should have the opportunity to decide for themselves."[56] His sermon in 1940 expounded on a text from the Gospel of Matthew: "... and Jesus said, 'Follow Me.'" He maintained that while the youth of Germany, Italy, and Russia had been misled into thinking that their political leaders were almost gods, young people in Canada and other democratic countries chose Jesus Christ as their spiritual leader. Although faith had been sorely tested by all the strife and suffering that existed in the world, Thomson held to his belief that where there was darkness there was also light: "Jesus comes and shows us what life may be, and even pain, sorrow, darkness and death is an instrument of life."[57]

Both the church service and the annual banquet were held about one month prior to final examinations. This meant that there were no closing exercises to acknowledge that students had successfully passed their exams and completed their course of studies. In 1938 Dean William Ramsay and the faculty decided that there was a need for such a ceremony to be held early in May. The university administration resisted the idea because examination results from Luther and Campion Colleges were not available as soon as those from Regina College, and the university wanted to release all the results at once. Both Campion and Luther were junior colleges affiliated with the University of Saskatchewan, as Regina College had been before 1934, when it became part of the university. This was why Ramsay took offence at being told that Regina College grades could not be given out in advance of the Luther and Campion grades. He felt that the status of the college was being downgraded. Moreover, the delay meant the closing exercises would have to be postponed until the latter part of May, by which time most of the out-of-town students would already have left the city. Although it took a full year of wrangling, Ramsay eventually won the point. On 1 May 1939 Regina College held its first closing exercises since the university had taken it over. President Thomson instructed Ramsay not to call the ceremony "convocation," with its connotations of university status, and Ramsay replied that he had no intention of doing so.[58]

While the fall reception and the closing exercises bracketed the school year, the time in between was filled with a diverse range of extracurricular activities. Social life centred on dances of various kinds. The Christmas formal on 21 December 1949 featured "music to the styling of Doug Painter, with smooth waltzes and fox-trots." Dean Basterfield, members of the faculty, and the SRC president formed a receiving line to greet students and alumni.[59] As befit the formality of the occasion, the women wore evening gowns – "those heavenly creations of mankind" – some conservative and others daring, "a fact in itself adding colourful excitement to the party."[60] "Judging by the number of 'tuxes' owned by the boys," the college newspaper acknowledged, "the formality will mostly be confined to the distaff side, but it is imperative that at least 'second best' suits be worn."[61]

Informal dances were held after basketball games, the players from the visiting team attending as guests. "Glenn Miller and many other famous bands," with coach Sam Stewart at the controls of the record player, provided the music.[62] On 4 November 1944, students gathered at Darke Hall and went as a group to the YMCA gym to watch the "overworked college team" compete against the RCAF squad from the training school. After the game, they "mobbed the kitchen" and "gorged themselves on 'dogs and cokes.'" "Due to unforeseen circumstances, the 'jukebox' decided to take the night off and Mr. Johnson (bless him) came across beautifully with his streamline version of a 'Platter Twister.'" Since "nothing short of an amplified foghorn can be heard above stampeding students, talent was drafted to pound the ivories for the Alma Mater." The session closed with "the blending of voices in school yells, followed by God Save the King."[63]

Student taste in music extended to modern jazz. A record club was formed in 1949, the members gathering in each other's homes to listen to the latest releases. "Platter-chatter was mainly confined to 'le jazz hot' and blues."[64] The *College Record* kept track of new arrivals at the local record stores so that students could rush out and buy them as soon as they came in. The talk in November 1948 was of that "new form of music, Be-Bop." The student music columnist enthused, "Dizzy Gillespie is the one who is now setting the pace in modern music. The big band field this issue is dominated by Woody Herman's new release, 'Four Brothers.'"[65]

In accordance with college regulations, patrons and patronesses, selected from the faculty and administrative staff, attended all the dances.[66] They sometimes took to the dance floor, as when, after a student jitterbug demonstration, Mr Foran (chemistry) and Mr Coleman (physical training) "tore in and strutted their stuff." Dr Ramsay, Miss MacRae, and Mr and Mrs Wagg meanwhile occupied themselves the entire evening "in a stiff game of bridge." "The part we really liked," one student said, "was the refreshments." "Nobody can think of calories when ice cream, cake and Coca-Cola are in the air." There were also hints that something stronger than Coca-Cola was consumed: "Tinkle, tinkle / Do you think / A little drink'll / Do us any harm?"[67]

The Sadie Hawkins dance in the last week of February reversed gender roles. The girl invited the boy, paid the admission price, bought the refreshments, and escorted her date home at the end of the evening. Inspired by the comic strip "Li'l Abner," students dressed in Dogpatch garb. The boys wore corsages made of cabbage leaves, radish roots, celery stalks, and onions coated with red nail polish. "Sadie," in charge of the guest book, was a "tall red-haired lad in flowing evening gown." The "coke bar" did a booming business, since "the damsels footed the bills." Couples let loose with the "Kickaboo Kick, Weakeyes Stumble, Wolf Gal Gait, and the Salomie's Bounce."[68]

The Sadie Hawkins dance temporarily overturned the dating code. Boys normally took the initiative, while girls waited by the telephone. The standard dating culture mimicked the conventions of middle-class married life in which men were the breadwinners and decision makers, while women were the homemakers and caregivers. Sadie Hawkins turned things upside down for one night. It did not challenge the rules governing gender relations in any serious way; it merely offered an ironic commentary.

Another activity that defined gender roles was the tea. The *College Record* in the fall of 1939 complimented the girls for having "entertained charmingly" at a "tea hour" to which were invited the girls from Luther College.[69] Dean Basterfield and his wife regularly hosted teas, as on Sunday, 7 March 1948, when the tea table was "adorned with yellow tapers and a bowl of golden tulips." Mrs Basterfield presented "a charming appearance gowned in cherry

The 1948–49 Regina College Cougars basketball team. Coach Sam Stewart (back row, middle) called it the best team the college had ever produced. In the back row furthest to the right stands Wes Bolstad, who in 1966 became the first director of the School of Administration at the Regina campus.

red with a triple strand of pearls." Lucy Murray (PhD in English literature) appeared "most stylishly attired in a figured gown, which was the last word in 'the new look.'" French teacher Gertrude Friedman was "très chique" in a powder-blue frock and matching hat.[70]

The mother and son tea in November 1948 subtly delineated the boundaries of masculinity. Gender roles were reversed, as with the Sadie Hawkins dance, and, again, supposedly it was "all in fun." The boys received the guests, poured the tea, and served the crumpets. "Can't you just see a great big, tough engineer carrying a tea cup across the room," asked the *College Record*, "chewing the corner of his lip, concentrating like mad on trying not to spill. Then a relieved expression replaces the worried one as some kind mother takes the cup from his vice-like grip. If you want to see all this happen, make a point of attending the 'Mothers and Sons Tea.'"[71] There were no female students enrolled in engineering at this time. It was an all-male group. The effect of this curious tableau was to reinforce the masculine identity of the profession by dramatizing the absurdity of a male engineer trying to perform a female task.

Gender differences were also manifested in sports, with male athletics taking pride of place over female athletics. "Basketball is the leading sport in the college," the *College Record* announced in November 1947, "so everybody get out and support your teams." The 1940 men's team competed in a

The 1948–49 Regina College Cougettes basketball team, which defeated Central Collegiate 8 to 3. Neither team scored a basket until the third quarter, when Doris "Ding Dong" Bell (third player from the right in the back row) "twined in a long corner shot."

league that included Luther College, Campion College, the normal school, Central Collegiate, Scott Collegiate, and Balfour Technical Collegiate. The team missed first place with a 30 to 29 loss to the normal school in the last game of the season. The gym was packed and the crowd intense: "The lusty cheers greatly added to the excitement of the game. The students are really giving the team great support. Many of the old college yells were used by the enthusiastic audience and also new ones made up on the spur of the moment."[72]

The name "Cougars" was adopted in the 1944–45 season.[73] With the enrolment of the veterans at the end of the war, the basketball team included older and more experienced players who overmatched their high school and junior college opponents.[74] As a result, the team entered the senior men's city basketball league, playing against the likes of the Canadian Legion Juniors, the Mounties, and the Bill and Fred Toilers. The highlight of the season was the annual exhibition classic against the Orphans, the University of Saskatchewan (Saskatoon) junior team. It was a two-game, total-point series, one game played in Regina and the other in Saskatoon.[75] The Cougars dominated from 1945 to 1949. The 1948–49 squad was especially successful, winning twenty-four games in twenty-eight starts and losing none of their games by more than five points. Coach Sam Stewart called it the best team the college had ever produced.[76] In addition to the senior basketball team, there was also a

The 1948–49 Regina College hockey team. Although basketball was the premier sport at the college, hockey kindled a fierce rivalry, especially with Campion College and Luther College, both of which later entered into a federation with the University of Regina.

junior team (the Cubs), which played in the city intercollegiate league, and a third team, the Matric Juniors, which competed at the junior intercollegiate level.[77]

Girls' basketball developed more slowly because it was assumed there was something unladylike about girls playing sports. The *College Record* in February 1940 gave an account of a game against the team from the normal school in which "numerous times our players were amazed to see the ball taken right out of their hands as they gracefully pose to shoot a basket. However, they soon realized that the basketball floor was no place for gentle, dignified co-eds, and began to give as well as take." The newspaper advised the girls to "learn the rules of the game."[78] Although the team had greatly improved by its next outing, the players "were still in somewhat of a daze when someone in black and red [the normal school colours] came and took the ball from them while they looked for a fellow player."[79] The Cougettes, as they were called, managed a victory against Central Collegiate in February 1949 with the astonishingly low score of 8 to 3. Neither team scored a basket until three-quarters of the way into the game, when Doris "Ding-Dong" Bell of Regina College finally "twined in a long corner shot."[80] The Cougettes captured the intercollegiate championship in 1948, defeating Central 21 to 17 in "a fast,

The 1948–49 Regina College debating club. Margot Moffat (fourth from left) and Don Fraser (third from right) captured the J. Alex Mackenzie Debating Cup in competition against the University of Saskatchewan.

aggressive contest" that saw them "take the lead from the starting whistle and hold it throughout the entire game."[81] The junior girls, the Cubettes, posted losses in the 1948–49 season of 60 to 1 against Balfour Tech and 79 to 11 against Sacred Heart Academy. They finally claimed a "moral victory" by losing to Central by only 19 to 17.[82]

Although basketball was the premier sport at the college, the men's hockey team had an intense rivalry with Central, Luther, Campion, Balfour, the normal school, and Scott. Games were played in the 6,500-seat Queen City Gardens, which had "an ice surface of 192 feet by 84 feet, with a goal at each end, yeah! and red spots, blue lines, whistles, peanuts and popcorn!" Tempers flared in a game against Campion in February 1940, with "the smaller college lads handing out stiff body checks to Campion forwards." Regina College scored a goal in the first period, Campion tied it up with four minutes left to play, and two minutes later they notched the winner.[83] In 1948 the college had wins against Scott, Luther, Balfour, a tie with Central, and a 6 to 1 loss to Campion.[84] Sports were an important part of building a sense of community at Regina College and at the other colleges in the city. Reportedly, when Luther played Campion (the Catholic college) there were no atheists in the audience.

Students also participated in extracurricular activities such as drama and debating. The J. Alex Mackenzie Debating Cup was awarded in an annual competition between Regina College first-year students and their counterparts in Saskatoon. After Margot Moffat and Don Fraser represented Regina in the 1949 contest, Moffat gave an account of the experience in the *College Record*. The pair toured the Saskatoon campus, gazing enviously at the modern equipment in the *Sheaf* (the Saskatoon student newspaper) office:

"Do you know that there were three standard model typewriters in that office? Yes. And in use a lot too or they couldn't afford to keep them." But the students were not willing to concede overall superiority to Saskatoon. Convocation Hall, they thought, was nothing special – "nothing compared with our own Darke Hall."[85] By the time they reached the cafeteria, a crowd of Regina College alumni had gathered around them. According to Moffat, they told the debaters "they'd better take the cup back to the College where it belonged and they were really enthusiastic, much to the disturbance of the Saskatonians. Well, with that spirit behind them, what could the team do but win for the Dear Old Alma Mater? ... This is what the College has done for people. It has made them into one big happy family." Finally, it was time for the debate. Moffat and Fraser carried the day, successfully arguing the negative of the resolution "that American culture is beneficial to Canada and should be encouraged."[86]

Regina College after the war was a growing, vibrant place. Academic programs expanded, extracurricular activities flourished, and, thanks to the veterans, enrolment increased substantially. The peak year was 1945–46, when there were 417 full-time students. Enrolment fell in successive years to 320, 244, and 190, hitting a low of 188 in 1949–50.[87] The college, in an effort to check the decline, introduced a first-year commerce program in 1947–48, which attracted thirty students.[88] The trend still continued downward, and Dean Basterfield was forced to admit in 1949 that the college faced an "anxious period" in its history.[89] Although the institution could easily accommodate 300 students, enrolment was less than 200. Heavy overhead costs led to annual deficits.

The executive committee of the Board of Governors in February 1949 recommended a number of cost-saving measures, including staff reductions, cancellation of first-year courses in engineering and commerce, and closure of the residences and cafeteria.[90] The freed-up space was to be used for the Natural History Museum, the provincial archives, and the offices of the correspondence school.[91] In addition, tuition fees for the arts and science course at Regina College were to be doubled to bring them in line with Saskatoon rates. The central problem was the decline in enrolment caused by the departure of the veterans. The college, not for the first time in its history, faced a crisis of survival. Post-war boom had turned into bust. Clearly, a new strategy was needed to resuscitate the college and place it once more at the centre of the educational life of the community.

3 A New Lease on Life: Regina College in the 1950s

The Regina College Advisory Board met on 12 March 1949 to discuss the problems caused by the shrinking enrolment and financial shortfall. Its members expressed opposition to the university's proposal to cancel the first-year courses in engineering and commerce. If the goal was to attract more students, they argued, it made no sense to eliminate programs that were popular. In addition, they asked for the resumption of courses in the School of Art, which had fallen on hard times because of the failure to appoint a successor to director Gus Kenderdine after his death in 1947. The board also suggested that the college conduct a special recruiting drive for students in the spring of 1949, and, further, that the principals of the city's three collegiates (Central, Scott, and Balfour) be added to the board so that they might encourage some of their graduates to do first-year university work at the college.[1]

A *Leader-Post* editorial on 11 March 1949 took note of an unusual proposal emanating from the student newspaper in Saskatoon. The *Sheaf* recommended that the medical school be transferred to Regina and the new medical facility under construction in Saskatoon be converted into an arts building. The medical school would then have access to the superior hospitals in Regina, and Regina College would be filled with students.[2] The *Leader-Post* congratulated the students on the bold originality of their plan, adding, however, that it was "not entirely lacking in impertinence."[3]

Rumours circulated in Regina that the college was about to close. City Council passed a resolution on 15 March 1949 advocating the continuation of the existing academic program and the re-establishment of classes in fine arts and drama. A group calling itself the Regina Art Center Association made the point that when the university had taken over the college, in 1934, it had promised to open and maintain an art school. By allowing the art school to lapse, the university was in breach of its obligation.[4] The United Church, as it was apt to do when Regina College was in trouble, entered the discussion. The executive of the Saskatchewan Conference appointed a committee composed of Justice H.F. Thomson[5] (chairman), Reverend J.S. Leith, and Reverend H.R. Lane "to hold a watching brief over the interests of the United Church in Regina College."[6]

University chancellor F.H. (Hedley) Auld made a surprising announcement on 26 March 1949.[7] He admitted that the size of the Regina College deficit had been miscalculated. University officials had failed to credit to the college a share of the provincial government grant to the university. They had assumed that all the money given to the university was for the Saskatoon campus, and Regina College had to pay for itself. When the correction was made, the college showed a surplus of $20,000 in 1945–46.[8] The serious financial problems began in 1946–47, when the deficit was $67,148 ($30,148 if the Regina College share of the provincial grant to the university was taken into account). It was $94,181 in 1947–48 (corrected to $64,181) and $91,051 in 1948–49 (corrected to $65,051).[9] Since this was unsustainable, a solution had to be found. Auld did not think that low enrolment, which was the underlying cause of the financial difficulties, could be attributed solely to the departure of the veterans. He said that he had heard "on credible authority" that the general opinion throughout the province was that the first-year courses were more difficult at Regina than at Saskatoon, and this discouraged students from enrolling at the college.[10]

Auld laid out a plan to restore Regina College to solvency. He did not agree that first-year courses in engineering and commerce should be cancelled. If the classes were not offered, he noted, some of the students might go to Saskatoon, but others would leave the province, and "some would not go anywhere." The result would be a net loss to the university. He had five positive suggestions: resume teaching in the School of Art; retain the college residences; aggressively recruit students in Regina and tributary areas; inform the people of Regina that the future of the college depended on their support; and enlarge the Advisory Board of Regina College to increase community interest in the institution. He warned, however, that if these measures did not cause a turnaround, "more drastic alternatives" would have to be contemplated.[11]

The university Board of Governors spent the better part of a day discussing the situation. At the close of their deliberations, President Thomson issued a lengthy statement, which the *Leader-Post* published in full on 9 April 1949.

He began by thanking the Regina City Council, the United Church, and the Regina Art Center Association for the interest they had shown in the welfare of the college. The university, he acknowledged, had an obligation under the terms of the 1934 agreement to develop Regina College as an educational centre that would "conserve the best features of the traditional course," maintain a high standard of excellence of the Conservatory of Music, establish a school of art, and "offer to students who did not intend to proceed to a university degree opportunities to study in those branches of the sciences and the humanities which make for good citizenship and success in their chosen vocations." Thomson gave his assurance that the promises would be kept. He then appealed to parents in Regina and the surrounding area to send their children to the college. The quality of instruction, he emphasized, was as good or better than what was provided in Saskatoon: "The illusion that because Regina College is rated as a junior institution therefore its instruction must be of lesser quality ought to be dispelled. On the contrary, it should be understood that because classes are smaller and intimacy with members of the faculty more readily available, the educational opportunity at Regina College is even better than at the university."[12]

Thomson made one other announcement. He said that the university would revive the teaching of art at the college and build an art gallery using the money that Norman MacKenzie, a Regina lawyer and art collector, had left for the purpose when he died in 1936. Thomson's statement was well received in Regina, so much so that when he left the presidency at the end of June 1949, it was rumoured that he had been pushed out because of his pro-Regina sympathies.[13] In reality, he resigned for reasons unrelated to Regina College. As a non-scientist with little interest in specialized research, he was out of step with the ethos of a modern university.[14] Moreover, as historian Michael Hayden makes clear, he had fallen out of favour with the provincial government, which did not have complete confidence in his ability as an administrator.[15]

The choice of a successor was virtually automatic. Walter P. Thompson (or W.P., as he was usually called) had served as acting president in 1942–43, when Thomson had filled in as general manager of the Canadian Broadcasting Corporation, and for shorter stretches at other times. He had been the president's right-hand man. "There was almost a beaten path between his office and mine," Thomson wrote; "hardly a day passed on which I did not break in upon his smoke-encompassed presence to seek his counsel."[16] W.P. Thompson had come to the University of Saskatchewan as a biology professor in 1913. A graduate of Toronto and Harvard, he had an active research career and published numerous papers on the genetics and cytology of cereal plants.[17] He was appointed dean of junior colleges in 1933, became dean of arts and science in 1939, and rose to the presidency in 1949.[18]

While the changing of the guard was taking place in Saskatoon, Regina College struggled to reverse its enrolment decline. In May and June of 1949 five members of the faculty hit the dusty roads of southern Saskatchewan in an attempt to recruit students. Each traveled 500 to 600 miles, visiting high schools, meeting with students, and distributing calendars.[19] As a result, the enrolment of rural students increased to eighty-five in 1949–50, compared with seventy-five the previous year. The bad news was that the number of students from Regina fell from 115 to 103, for an overall decline from 190 to 188. Dean Basterfield glumly concluded that high school students in Regina had "not yet realized the advantages of taking their first year in their own city college, an integral part of the provincial University, but prefer to seek the well-known but mostly illusory greener pastures elsewhere."[20] The 1949–50 enrolment of 188 fell far short of the 300 students needed for the college to break even.[21]

Dean Basterfield reached retirement age in 1949, and W.P. Thompson began to look for a suitable replacement. One day the president was working in his office when biology professor Jake Rempel happened to walk by. Thompson called him in and pointed to a list of six candidates for dean of Regina College, which he was going to present at a meeting of the Board of Governors that afternoon. Rempel, who had taught at the college in the 1930s and early 1940s, ran through the list and eliminated the candidates one by one, giving his reasons in each case. After Rempel had rejected everyone, Thompson looked at him and said, "You are not much help." It was now fifteen minutes before the Board of Governors meeting. Rempel quickly described the situation at Regina College, outlined the necessary qualifications of the new dean, mentioned the sort of wife he needed to have, and concluded by saying that Dr William A. Riddell would be ideal for the job.[22]

A few days later, in October 1949, Chancellor F.H. Auld called on Riddell at home. Riddell, who held the post of director of provincial laboratories for the Department of Health, assumed the visit had something to do with the building of the new United Church in the Lakeview area of Regina, since both he and Auld were on the planning committee. Instead, the chancellor asked if he would consider accepting the deanship of Regina College.[23] Riddell wrote to W.P. Thompson on 1 December 1949 to say that he was "definitely interested" in the job.[24]

The prospective dean was born in 1905 on a pioneer farm in western Manitoba. He completed a Bachelor of Science degree at the University of Manitoba in 1926, majoring in both chemistry and botany, and went on to the University of Saskatchewan for a master's degree in 1928; there his thesis supervisor had been Steward Basterfield. He earned a PhD in synthetic organic chemistry from Stanford in 1931 and then landed a job as instructor in chemistry at Regina College. He and his wife returned to Saskatchewan at

William A. Riddell, who resigned his position as director of Provincial Laboratories to become dean of Regina College on 1 July 1950. He wrote to his parents, "It was a very difficult decision to make as I have mentioned in previous letters ... However, I think that the field of opportunity for service to the community is greater at the college."

the worst possible time. As they "crossed the prairies on the train no golden fields appeared before [them], only mile after dreary mile of dust-blown areas, fences buried in dust or piled high with Russian thistle."[25]

They remained at the college until 1935, when Riddell accepted a position as research chemist for the Fisheries Research Board of Canada at Prince Rupert, British Columbia. Three years later he was back in Regina, this time as an analyst with the provincial Department of Health laboratory. The principal function of the laboratory was to assist in the control of communicable diseases, but it also performed autopsies, investigated cases of food poisoning, and conducted clinical blood analysis.[26] Riddell enjoyed the work, rising to the top job as lab director in 1942.

When he indicated to President Thompson that he was interested in assuming the deanship of Regina College, he did so on the understanding that certain conditions would be met. First, he wanted to report directly to the president or the president and the Board of Governors, not to some intermediary body or administrator. Second, the university had to promise to develop the School of Art along the same lines as the Conservatory of Music, including the construction of an art gallery to house the Norman MacKenzie collection and other works. Finally, the university had to make a "serious effort" to allow Regina College to function "as a real educational force in the community." This included an unbiased examination of the question of the extension of academic work at the college beyond the level of first-year classes.[27]

An unexpected hitch occurred in early December 1949. In the course of the annual budget discussions between senior university officials and the Cabinet, the government asked the university "to consider carefully the desirability of continuing Regina College." Thompson told Riddell that this did not necessarily mean that the college would be closed, since the university, not the government, was responsible for the internal allocation of the university budget. Nonetheless, Thompson candidly admitted that a suggestion of this kind coming from the government "must be carefully considered."[28] Riddell replied on 9 December 1949 that he had received the same information from sources in Regina. He was prepared to let the matter rest until the university authorities had decided what they wanted to do. He added, however, that he did not want the deanship unless he had an assurance that the college would be allowed to exist for at least another five years. He did not think that it was possible to restore the college to solvency in less time than that, and he did not want to have the rug pulled out from under him after only one or two years.[29]

The Board of Governors appointed a committee to decide the fate of Regina College. It consisted of Chancellor Auld; President Thompson; Arthur Moxon, chairman of the Board of Governors; A. McCallum, deputy minister of education; and Colb McEown, the president's executive assistant, who acted as secretary. The committee met at Regina's Hotel Saskatchewan on 25 January 1950. In the morning they interviewed Dean Basterfield, who told them about the spring recruiting drive and the failure to increase the enrolment in 1949–50. They asked him why the performance of Luther College grade 12 students was superior to that of Regina College matriculation students. Basterfield answered that the college had a number of repeaters – students who had failed to obtain their high school diploma elsewhere. Besides, he said, the academic term at Regina College was shorter than Luther's by two months. Committee members also inquired about the first-year university courses. They noted that while the dropout rate was high, the failure rate was no higher than Saskatoon's. Reports were received from the deans of arts and science, engineering, and commerce at Saskatoon, all of whom testified to the fact that there was no significant difference between the academic performance of students who took their first year at Regina College and those who completed their entire degree at Saskatoon. The deans interpreted this to mean that academic standards at the college were sound.[30]

The committee reconvened in the afternoon for an interview with the Regina College Advisory Board. They discussed a proposal to discontinue the teaching of academic courses at Regina College and to use the facilities to continue the Conservatory of Music, establish a college of art, house the Norman MacKenzie art collection, and provide a home for the Provincial Museum of Natural History. In support of this recommendation, Auld cited the fact that the college deficit for 1949–50 was approximately $54,000. D.J. Thom and C.T. Darke, two members of the Advisory Board, strongly opposed the elimination of the academic courses. They argued that not only should the existing courses be maintained, but also that new courses leading to a degree in music should be added.

Clarence Darke was the son of Francis N. Darke, a long-time member of the Board of Governors of Regina College who had donated the money to build Darke Hall in 1929. D.J. Thom had been a member of the original board in 1910 and had served continuously, first on the Board of Governors and then the Advisory Board, for forty years. He called attention to the fact that under the terms of the 1934 takeover agreement, if the university closed the college, then the buildings and property would revert to the original owners. One can imagine the scene. A cold winter day in January, the afternoon sun filtering through the tall windows of the Hotel Saskatchewan, the crusty old lawyer leaning back in his chair and calmly reminding the visitors from Saskatoon of the contents of the document he had helped draw up sixteen years earlier.

Thom's case rested on the fact that prior to 1934 Regina College was the registered owner under the Land Titles Act of the main college site. The title was subject to restrictions contained in an Order-in-Council dated 7 August 1915, which stated that Regina College could not at any time lease, sell, or otherwise dispose of the land without the approval of the Lieutenant-Governor-in-Council. When the land was transferred by the college to the university, the approval of the Lieutenant-Governor-in-Council was obtained by an Order-in-Council dated 29 June 1934. This Order-in-Council approved the transfer on certain terms and conditions, attached as schedule A. The latter consisted of five communications passing between representatives of the university and the college dated from 13 January to 24 January 1934.[31] Included was the promise on the part of the university to "continue and maintain Regina College as a Junior College conserving the best of the past and seeking to realize the ideals of culture and character which inspired the founders."[32] Therefore, if the university closed down the academic program of the college, the property transfer of 1934 would be rendered invalid.

The committee adjourned until the evening, when it met with W.A. Riddell, the incoming dean. He proposed maintaining the existing academic courses and adding "terminal courses at the sub-professional level," such as a course to train hospital laboratory technicians. Specifically, Riddell recommended the continuance of first-year arts, commerce, and engineering; an examination of the feasibility of providing two years of pre-medical arts; the expansion of the services of the Conservatory of Music and possibly a degree course in music; the resumption of instruction in art; and the promotion of terminal courses to serve young people who did not plan to attend university.

He suggested that the latter might include vocational programs for lab techs, library assistants, psychiatric aides, and medical and dental secretaries.[33]

The committee endorsed Riddell's plan. It also acknowledged that the 1934 agreement imposed "a very real obligation" on the university: "If the University finds itself unable to continue the College in accordance with the conditions under which the College was acquired, it would seem that the College should be returned to its original owners, unless the Governors of Regina College would consent to an amendment of them." Thom's legal argument had apparently carried the day. Thus, the committee recommended keeping the college open, but on a different basis than before. It envisaged the development of "a genuine community college in Regina with courses far outranging University preparatory work and touching the community in other ways."[34]

This was both a blueprint for a new lease on life and a reversion to the Learned Report of 1932, which had recommended that Regina College evolve outward as a community college rather than upward as a university. Such had been the policy of President Walter Murray in the 1920s and 1930s, J.S. Thomson in the 1940s, and now W.P. Thompson in the 1950s. All that was new was a more specific enumeration of the terminal courses Regina College could offer to young people who would not go on to university.

The university took the recommendations to the provincial Cabinet. After some close questioning from the provincial treasurer, Clarence Fines, the government gave its consent. The university was allowed a grace period of five years to implement the strategy. Riddell thought this would be sufficient, because he assumed that in five years the increase in the number of students graduating from high school would ensure the viability of the college.[35] The faculty and staff at Regina College breathed a sigh of relief. The rumour that the college would be shut down had taken a toll on morale; now they knew their jobs were safe, at least for a while.

On 1 March 1950 Riddell took the plunge, leaving the provincial laboratories to become dean of Regina College. He explained to his parents that "It was a very difficult decision to make as I have mentioned in previous letters, particularly leaving the group that I had at the lab here. However, I think that the field of opportunity for service to the community is greater at the college."[36] If for some reason his plan to put the college back on its feet did not work, he had a fallback position. As dean he carried the rank of full professor of chemistry in the university. If Regina College went under, he could exercise the option of joining the teaching staff in Saskatoon.

When Riddell officially took over as dean on 1 July 1950, he inherited an administrative mess. As the wife of physics professor E.R. Thackeray pointedly remarked, "Poor Dr. Basterfield disliked the administrative angle so much and the college needed a pulling together after the debacle of the war years. It had to wait until W.A. Riddell got going!"[37] The accountant, J.P. Ross Brown, made it clear that he took his instructions from the bursar in Saskatoon and would brook no interference from the new dean. Riddell managed, with great difficulty, to obtain a copy of the budget, and when he saw it he was appalled. Some items were set too high, while others, such as the cost of heating the buildings, were implausibly low. Riddell wanted to revise it, but he faced opposition from university officials who were reluctant to alter the amounts allocated for various expenditures. They were afraid that the government, which had accepted the previous figures, would raise awkward questions if the sums were suddenly changed.

Riddell discovered that "in general the attitude of University people in Saskatoon was one of indifference." Indeed, it was obvious to him "that some people in Saskatoon looked on Regina College as an unwarranted drain upon the resources of the University; others hoped that it would just disappear."[38] He exempted Thompson from this attitude. The president, Riddell believed, saw the college as performing a useful public relations function. It was tangible proof that the university was doing something in Regina and gave residents of the city an additional reason to contribute to university fundraising campaigns. Thompson in 1954 credited Regina with having given over a million dollars to the university's endowment.[39]

Riddell had on the whole a good working relationship with Thompson. The president was always available for consultation and advice, but he never dictated to the dean what he should or should not do. Thompson communicated his wishes in more subtle ways, and Riddell quickly learned to read the signals. The key was the angle of Thompson's pipe. "When relaxed," Riddell noted, "his pipe drooped at a comfortable angle but as his concern mounted the pipe would cock upward and I would expect some word of caution, disagreement or, on rare occasions, mild criticism."[40]

One of Riddell's first initiatives in 1950–51 was to launch a two-year training course for hospital laboratory technicians. This required the introduction of a new course in bacteriology and two half-courses in chemistry. A federal health grant of over $19,000 paid for the construction of the necessary laboratory facilities, while a continuing grant from the same source covered the cost of hiring instructors. The program was modified in 1952–53 from two years of classwork followed by six months of training in a hospital laboratory to eleven months of continuous training at Regina College followed by twelve months in a hospital lab.[41] It was altered again in 1956–57 to provide for two years of instruction at the college, interspersed with three months of practical training in the hospital between the first and second years and a period of six months after the second year.[42] Since technicians were in great demand, the program was popular. Enrolment grew from ten in 1950–51 to forty-three in 1958–59. In addition, a centralized lecture program for nurses

Laboratory technician students at Regina College in 1954. The program was introduced in 1950 as part of W.A. Riddell's effort to revitalize the flagging college.

was introduced in February 1953, duplicating the program offered in Saskatoon. In 1956–57 a total of 193 nurses received part of their training at Regina College.

Beginning in 1951–52 the college inaugurated a non-credit extension course for accountants. One night a week was devoted to accounting and one night to business mathematics. The courses were reorganized in 1954–55 into four certificate programs: accounting, business administration, public administration, and secretarial administration. Provincial civil servants and municipal government employees jumped at the opportunity to upgrade their accounting and managerial skills. Senior government bureaucrats – such as the deputy provincial treasurer, A.W. Johnson, and the deputy minister of municipal affairs, Meyer Brownstone – agreed to serve as instructors.[43] The program attracted fifty-nine students in 1956–57.

In addition to the certificate programs in accounting and administration, nurses' training, and hospital laboratory technician courses, the college offered numerous short-term adult education classes. A course on investment planning, given in 1951–52 in co-operation with the Investment Dealers Association of Regina, attracted over one hundred participants. A series of lec-

Student nurses at Regina College attending an anatomy lecture in the science theatre in 1954.

tures on atomic energy, a topic of great interest in the 1950s, drew audiences ranging in size from 78 to 155 people. In 1953–54 short courses were offered in oil geology and electronics, the latter assisting 238 students to upgrade their skills in radio and TV repair and servicing.[44] The college seemed endlessly inventive in mounting courses that appealed to the public. Chief Justice J.T. Brown, a member of the Advisory Board, even suggested a "two-year finishing course for girls."[45] The judge, apparently, was not impressed with the deportment of young ladies in Regina. His course proposal was one of the few not taken up.

Riddell succeeded through his abundant energy and administrative skill in diversifying the vocational and adult education courses available at the college. He could rightly claim that the school was now "much more than an Arts college."[46] It had a lively atmosphere and the buildings were full of people at all hours of the day and night. Staff members had a renewed sense of purpose. There was a general feeling that the college was going somewhere and making a valuable and growing contribution to the community.

If there was disappointment, it arose from the fact that enrolment in the matriculation and first-year university programs continued to slump. The total in 1950–51 was 152, down from 188 the previous year. Riddell attributed the decline to two factors: the downward trend in the number of students graduating from high school and unexpected crop damage caused by a late frost. The poor harvest led to a decrease in registration of rural students from eighty-three to fifty-three. Academic enrolment dropped again in 1951–52 to the perilously low figure of 120. Riddell again blamed a bad harvest, but he pointed optimistically to demographic trends that showed an expected increase in the number of high school students.

The impact of the post-war baby boom was beginning to be felt. The birth rate in Regina rose from 19.4 per thousand of population in 1943 to 28.4 per thousand in 1953, while the population of the city grew from 58,000 to 73,000 over the same period. The superintendent of public schools for Regina predicted that there would be 11,500 children in the public schools by 1958, a gain of over 28 per cent compared with 1954. It was only a matter of time before the baby boomers graduated from high school and headed to university.[47] The year 1952–53 marked the beginning of the turnaround. Full-time academic enrolment at Regina College increased to 172 students, 52 more than the previous year. Half the increase was attributable to first-year engineering students, whose numbers rose from twenty-two to forty-eight. Academic enrolment in 1955–56 exceeded 200 for the first time since the departure of the veterans, and in 1958–59 it reached a decade high of 327, a figure that represented 18 per cent of the total first-year registration of the University of Saskatchewan.[48] Table 4 sets out the distribution by type of program. The high enrolment of engineering students was especially striking. At sixty-six, they were second in number only to arts and science, with eighty-eight students.

Fifty students were enrolled in matriculation in 1958–59. The program had evolved somewhat over the course of the decade. In 1954 the number of required courses was reduced from six to five. Initially, the lighter load had been put in place to ease the burden of the veterans, but now it applied to everybody. The university decided that a six-course load was too heavy, especially when first-year students had to take only five courses.[49] To improve the quality of students and their chances for success, the minimum grade 11 average required for admission to the matriculation program was increased in 1956 from 60 to 65 per cent. The regulation did not apply to adults (twenty-one years of age or older), who were admitted even if they did not have grade 11 standing. The rationale for this exception was to give older applicants who had not completed high school an opportunity to further their education. If they managed to complete the matriculation program, they could go on to university. If not, they had to drop out.

There were, generally speaking, three types of matriculation students: younger students with grade 11 or partial grade 12 standing, adult students

TABLE 4: Regina College Full-Time Academic Enrolment by Category, 1958–59

TYPE OF PROGRAM	NUMBER
Arts and science	88
Agriculture	1
Commerce	27
Education	38
Engineering	66
Home economics	1
Pharmacy	9
Matriculation	50
Hospital laboratory technician	43
Fine art	4
Total	327

Source: University of Saskatchewan, *Annual Report of the President*, 1958–59.

from Canada, and foreign students. Adult students preferred Regina College to high school because the other students were closer to their own age. In addition, they could, through the matriculation course, qualify for university admission in less time. The high schools demanded that a student complete grade 11 before entering grade 12. The college imposed no such requirement for entrance to the matriculation program, provided the student was at least twenty-one. In addition, the shorter college term gave students more time to work and earn money before entering university in the fall.

The foreign students who enrolled in the matriculation course came from countries such as Poland, Liberia, Nigeria, and Trinidad, where academic accreditation did not conform to the Canadian system. The college allowed them to upgrade their standing in a relatively short time in order to qualify for university entrance. In 1956–57, for example, the college had forty-nine matriculation students: eleven under the age of twenty-one, twenty-three Canadian adults, and fifteen foreign students. Eight in the first category, six in the second category, and fifteen in the third completed the course. The low success rate was attributed to the poor academic background of the incoming students and the difficulty of covering a large amount of material in a short time.[50] It was not easy for the college to attract younger students to the matriculation program. Regina high school principals did not like to lose their best students; they wanted to hold on to the scholarship winners, who brought prestige to their schools.[51] As a result, the younger students who entered the matriculation program tended to be problem cases – the ones who, for one reason or another, did not fit in at high school or who had failed grade 12 the first time around. This helped account for the high failure and dropout rate.

Despite these difficulties, enrolment in the matriculation and first-year university courses continued to rise through the mid- and late 1950s. This, combined with increasing numbers of students in non-credit courses, placed pressure on classroom and laboratory space. Overcrowding and the need for expanded facilities were constant themes in Dean Riddell's annual reports from 1954 onward. The Conservatory of Music overflowed with students, and it desperately needed more practice studios. The science laboratories served almost double the number of students they had been designed to accommodate. The gymnasium was in such heavy use that intramural sports had to be restricted, and all casual, unscheduled recreational activity was prohibited.[52]

During World War II a temporary medical inspection building and a drill hall had been constructed on campus. They were poorly built structures with an expected life span of fifteen to twenty years. After the war the RCAF turned them over to the college as compensation for the expenses the university incurred in restoring the main buildings to their pre-war condition.[53] In February 1945 John Sturdy, the minister of reconstruction and rehabilitation in the provincial government, asked the university for permission to convert the medical inspection building into a twelve-unit apartment block for emergency housing for demobilized men and their families. Sturdy promised to return the building, which was renamed the Happy Landing Apartments, for use as a university dormitory in September 1945.[54] When the time came for the transfer, the government reneged on the agreement. The housing shortage in Regina was still acute, and the lease was extended for five years. The drill hall, meanwhile, was used as a garage and machine shop for government vehicles.[55]

The college Advisory Board in May 1950 asked the Board of Governors to terminate the leases on the two buildings so that they would become available for college use. Sturdy, now the minister of social welfare, opposed the idea, suggesting instead that the leases be extended for another five years. He said the welfare clients who occupied the Happy Landing Apartments would have a hard time finding other accommodation. The Board of Governors turned down the request for a five-year extension, but it agreed to renew the lease on a year-by-year basis.[56] In November 1951 the Advisory Board again asked for the return of the RCAF buildings, a request that was repeated in October 1952 and February 1953.[57]

Finally, in May 1953, President Thompson announced that the Happy Landing Apartments – but not the drill hall – would be given back to the college. A debate ensued as to whether the building was fit for use or should be torn down. The university decided, on the basis of an engineer's report, to convert it into a combination biochemistry lab, bacteriology lab, and ballet studio. The college finally gained full possession of the building in 1955, when the families who had been living there were evicted.[58] The acquisition alleviated the overcrowding to some degree but did not solve all the college's space problems. Riddell in 1954–55 called particular attention to the cramped quarters of the nursing program and the urgent need to enlarge the Conservatory of Music. The tone of his reports became increasingly impatient as he struggled to maintain programs with grossly inadequate facilities.

The provincial government, to the considerable annoyance of the college, continued to use the former drill hall as a garage and machine shop. Riddell called it an eyesore and a nuisance "that would not be tolerated in a corresponding situation on the Saskatoon campus." Traffic was blocked, roadways were a "sea of mud" in wet weather, and the long line of wrecked cars outside the college buildings gave the appearance of a junkyard.[59] Equally galling to Riddell was the derisory one-dollar-a-year rent the government paid for the drill hall. The property was easily worth $8,000 a year as warehouse space.[60] The deputy minister of public works also wanted to move the garage, but as long as the university did not press for it, he could not secure the funds to do so. The deputy minister, according to Riddell, had been "somewhat profane in his comments" on the subject.[61] The dean, on the authority of the Advisory Board, in May 1958 asked the Department of Public Works to close down the garage. He pointed out that "the government has been asked to vacate this building several times during the past seven years since the emergency which made it necessary of the government to use this building has now passed."[62] The reply came back from the minister of public works that he had not been able to convince his colleagues in Cabinet that 1958 was the year to move.[63] The garage was not closed down until 1965, when the government transferred light-vehicle repair work to the private sector.[64]

The university did, however, fulfill its obligation to construct an art gallery in accordance with the terms of the Norman MacKenzie bequest. The small structure attached to the girls' residence in 1953 cost only $68,779 and did not harmonize at all with the adjoining red-brick college buildings. George Barr, who was to lead the campaign for a full degree program at Regina College, referred to it as a "lean-to faced with stucco which is a blot on the landscape."[65] President Thompson acknowledged that after the building had been completed $120,000 remained in the MacKenzie estate, but he said that at the time the gallery was planned and started, the money had been tied up in unsold properties. He noted also that the terms of the bequest obliged the university to pay an annuity of $3,000 to Norman MacKenzie's widow.[66]

The accumulation of grievances led Riddell to compose a stiff memo in April 1954. Headed "not submitted to everyone," it consisted of a long list of complaints. He pointed out that the university had allocated nothing for capital expenditures for Regina College since the college had been taken over in

The Norman MacKenzie Art Gallery, built by the University of Saskatchewan in 1953 with funds from the MacKenzie estate. George Herbert Barr, leader of the campaign for a degree program at Regina College, described it as "a lean-to faced with stucco which is a blot on the landscape."

1934, with the exception of the costs involved in reconverting the buildings after the war and in rebuilding the collapsed west wall of the gymnasium. All of the funds for the construction of the art gallery and the remodelling of the library and art school had come from private donations and bequests. Even the replacement of musical instruments had been charged to a college endowment fund. The university in the post-war period had received large capital grants from the federal government, as had all Canadian universities, but none of this money had found its way to Regina College.[67] Riddell also questioned some of the accounting practices of the university. The college, he argued, was entitled to an annual rental payment of $8,000 for the drill hall, but it received nothing. All the revenue from the summer school classes held at the college, which amounted to about $10,000 a year, was credited to Saskatoon, even though the college provided janitorial services, administrative support, and library facilities.

It was unusual for Riddell to be so forthright and demanding. He was at heart a team player and a loyal supporter of the university administration. Besides, he knew what it meant when W.P. Thompson's pipe was cocked in an upright position. But by 1954 the problems were so severe that he could not keep silent. In November 1954, one year after the completion of the "stucco lean-to," the college Advisory Board asked the Board of Governors to spend what remained of the MacKenzie estate to build an extension to the art gallery.[68] The architectural firm of Izumi, Arnott, and Sugiyama submitted drawings in February 1955 for an extension that would accommodate both the gallery and the art school.[69] The Advisory Board approved the plans in September 1955 and urged the Board of Governors to proceed with construction "at the earliest possible time."[70] The extension was officially opened on 17 October 1957, an event described in the *Leader-Post* as "a long-term dream come magnificently and usefully true."[71]

The Conservatory of Music, not having a bequest to draw upon, did not fare as well. The Advisory Board discussed in 1953 the need for an extension to Darke Hall,[72] and in 1955 architect H.K. Black was asked to prepare a preliminary cost estimate.[73] A detailed requirements study was completed in 1958 and placed in the hands of the university superintendent of buildings with the understanding that the architect would begin work on plans in the fall.[74] But nothing was done, and the overcrowding only grew worse. In 1959 over 900 conservatory students occupied a space that was adequate for 400.[75]

The gymnasium was the same story. The Advisory Board talked about the need for an improved facility in 1955.[76] By 1958 the situation had reached crisis proportions. The floor was not large enough to accommodate more than ten to twelve students at a time for the type of instruction recommended in the university program. Since university regulations required all first-year students to take two hours of physical education each week and anticipated enrolment for 1958–59 was estimated at 315 to 350, the gym had to be booked for classes about sixty hours per week. In addition, it was used for intramural sports, team practices, and intercollegiate competition. The Advisory Board recommended the construction of a new, larger gymnasium and the conversion of the existing structure into a physics laboratory.[77] They passed a resolution on 2 May 1958 asking the university to do something to alleviate the problem "at the earliest possible date."[78] In October the situation had deteriorated to the point where the physical education program was described as "completely ineffective."[79] Early in 1959 it was discovered that, owing to the settlement of the soil, the foundations of the gymnasium were so badly damaged that it had to be closed while repairs were made.[80]

By 1959, college classrooms were booked for 80 per cent of available hours. Class scheduling was difficult, and it was almost impossible to book a room for a meeting or special seminar.[81] The library, which had grown to 25,000 volumes, had enough shelf space for two more years of acquisitions, but there was not enough room for students to read and study. Although the biology laboratories were adequate, the chemistry labs were crowded and the physics lab "badly crowded." The physical sciences laboratory, located in the basement, lacked proper ventilation and was overheated by ceiling steam pipes. The laboratory annex (the former Happy Landing Apartments), which had been considered for demolition in 1956,[82] was still in use as the bacteriology

Students studying in the Regina College library. By the end of the 1950s the college facilities – the library, classrooms, laboratories, gymnasium, and Conservatory of Music – were overcrowded.

and hematology lab, the biochemistry lab, the ballet studio, and the sculpture studio. Students performed their laboratory experiments to the accompaniment of a thumping piano.

According to Riddell's assessment in 1959, every aspect of college activity, except the art school, suffered for want of space. Classrooms, laboratories, library, gymnasium, and music studios were all overcrowded.[83] The only new buildings constructed in the 1950s – or since 1934, for that matter – were the art gallery, in 1953, and its extension, in 1957. Both were paid for with private funds. There were plans in 1959 to build "at the earliest possible date" an extension to Darke Hall, a new gymnasium, and a new arts building. The latter was to provide a dozen classrooms, eight or ten offices, and "a library of adequate size for many years of increase in the number of books as well as students."[84] No architectural drawings were approved, and no ground was broken. Everything was in the planning stage.

The Saskatoon campus, by contrast, experienced a building boom in the 1940s and 1950s.[85] Ironically, the relative neglect of Regina College during this period proved in the long run to be of great advantage to the development of the University of Regina. If a new gymnasium and a new arts building had been constructed on College Avenue in the 1950s, it would have been much harder to establish a new campus in the 1960s. The university in Regina would have been committed to a downtown site that was too small to accommodate growth on the scale that was later required. Thus the failure to develop the old campus inadvertently paved the way for the full-scale emergence of the new university.

Regina College came out of the 1950s with good prospects, especially considering that at the beginning of the decade it had been on the brink of closing down. William Riddell rescued the institution and gave it a new lease on life. Under his leadership, the college introduced a hospital laboratory technician course, a nursing program, and evening classes in accounting and administration. The School of Art was revived and the Conservatory of Music reinvigorated. The college was once again an interesting place where people gathered for art exhibitions, concerts, courses on radio and television repair, and lectures on atomic energy. The vitality and sense of purpose that had been absent in the 1940s, when the college had drifted slowly downward into inactivity and irrelevance, was restored.

Riddell's plan in 1950 had been premised on expansion of vocational and cultural courses, as distinct from academic programs. Although the matriculation and first-year university courses were maintained, they were not regarded as the primary area of growth. This reflected the decline in enrolment that had occurred with the departure of the World War II veterans. But then the trend started to reverse. Beginning in 1952 the number of first-year university students increased, slowly at first and then more rapidly. By 1959 classrooms at Regina College were filled to bursting, not only with vocational students, but also with students working towards a university degree. It turned out that Riddell's plan had been a detour rather than a permanent change in direction. Regina College was on the road to becoming not a community college but a university.

4 Obeying the Rules: Student Life in the 1950s

Control, restraint, and obedience to authority were the hallmarks of Regina College student culture in the 1950s, but here and there, just below the surface, were traces of subversion foreshadowing the upheavals of the 1960s. Academic studies and faculty-supervised extracurricular activities dominated student life. Students showed limited interest in the affairs of the wider world and almost no desire for active political involvement. Their horizons did not extend much beyond the campus, where they saw themselves as in training for "real" life, not yet ready to assume the rights and responsibilities of citizenship. Their lives, by later standards, were sheltered and insular. Regina's first television station did not begin broadcasting until 1954,[1] and air travel was still an exotic adventure. Students in the 1950s were, on the whole, disinclined to challenge the status quo; earnest and somewhat naive, they took pleasure in simple things. Even their vices and misconduct, judged from the perspective of the present day, had an aura of innocence about them.

The rituals of campus life had not changed significantly since the 1940s. The fall term began with a reception hosted by the dean and his wife. The *College Record* described the event in 1951:

> Dr. Riddell greeted us warmly and requested us to construct paper hats with the emphasis to be placed on novelty. While many of the creations looked like gaudy lampshades, some were truly startling. The best of these were awarded prizes in the fashion show that followed. Next, three teams were chosen and contests were held, the best of which was the jelly bean hunt. The idea of this effort was to notify the

team captain, the only one who could collect the beans. The winner, it was later learned, had pocketed most of the beans earlier, with the idea of eating them later no doubt. Later, one of the lads, anticipating a waist judging contest, removed his belt. Since it was a balloon-breaking contest, instead – severe muscular contortions were required to avoid a rather embarrassing exposé. Several other games were run off, points were totaled and winners announced. By this time most of us were quite ready to relax over excellent refreshments. After a few rounds of songs and jokes, the party broke up. Grateful for the company, good food and high entertainment, we bid our hosts goodnight.[2]

The party had the wholesomeness of a church social, and the account of it in the newspaper bears no trace of irony.

The 1954 fall reception followed a slightly different format. Guests were given name tags and divided into groups according to their month of birth. They learned college cheers, sang songs, played games, and performed a snake dance through the halls.[3] Snake dances, also known as conga lines, can have disruptive effects in busy public areas. The students at the Saskatoon campus in the 1950s and early 1960s had a tradition in the fall term of invading the downtown business district, breaking up traffic, and causing mild mayhem.[4] It was a way for them to call attention to themselves, display their power, and temporarily disturb the peace.

Students in a real sense were and are a subject people. They follow a course of studies that others have prescribed, and they obey rules that others have devised. The snake dance – which involved taking control of the streets, if only for a short time – represented for the Saskatoon students a symbolic overturning of the power structure. It was not a serious rebellion because it was well understood that everything would quickly return to normal. Such hijinks were regarded as effusions of youthful high spirits, not expressions of student power as the term was later understood. The students of the 1950s who engaged in temporary outbursts of mild lawlessness – snake dances, panty raids, and so on – were, more or less unconsciously, just blowing off steam and making a symbolic statement about their subordinated status within the educational system.

However, the students at Regina College in 1954 were not ready to go that far. They held their snake dance safely within the confines of the college under the watchful eye of the faculty members who presided over the fall reception. Later, as we shall see, they took to the streets, but in the 1950s such bold acts of rowdiness were unthinkable. Rule breaking was still a matter of individual deviance or non-conformity. There was as yet no pattern of collective student misbehaviour.

The traditions of the annual banquet and college Sunday continued through the 1950s. The guest speaker at the banquet in 1958 was Dr Leon

Katz, a physics professor at the University of Saskatchewan in Saskatoon, who had just returned from a visit to the Soviet Union. He spoke of the progress the Soviets were making in science, technology, and education. The college newspaper, which had been renamed the *Sheet* in 1956, gave a favourable account of the speech. It said that Professor Katz had "cleared away much of the fog" of biased reports about the Soviet Union in the Western media and that he had presented "a very clear picture of the power and vitality of the Russian education system."[5] Katz's speech came on the heels of the successful Soviet launch of the first man-made satellite into space in October 1957. The launch had caused a panic in the West because it seemed to indicate that the Soviets were winning the race for technological supremacy. Hence the timeliness of Katz's speech and the positive reaction to his praise of the Soviet Union, even at the height of the Cold War.

College Sunday still attracted a good student turnout. The service in 1958 was led by Reverend W. McArthur of the Canadian Bible College, who took for his theme "discipleship's discipline." The college's Singing Parsons performed "The Lord's Prayer" and "I'll Walk with God." Dean Riddell assisted at the service, as did Students' Representative Council (SRC) president Del Warren.[6] Both college Sunday and the annual banquet died out in the early 1960s, victims in part of the huge increase in enrolment, which made intimate gatherings impossible and weakened the close community feeling of the old college.[7] The decline of college Sunday can also be attributed to the spirit of the sixties, which was hostile to established institutions and organized religion.

The Student Christian Movement (SCM) had been established as a national organization in 1920,[8] and the Regina College branch continued to operate with modest success through the 1950s. It sponsored in 1949–50 a Sunday evening discussion series on the theme of marriage, which sparked a vigorous debate on the pros and cons of going steady. A feature of the 1950s dating culture, the practice was admired for its almost obsessive imitation of the monogamous marriage ideal, but some were concerned that it could lead to a greater degree of intimacy than was considered desirable for an unmarried couple.[9] The marriage seminars were so popular that they were repeated the following year.[10]

Dean Riddell in 1954 gave a series of three lectures on the topic of God and evolution. According to the student newspaper, he "showed clearly how science could explain things satisfactorily only up to a certain point – then we must depend on faith."[11] Also that year, the SCM hosted a program called "This Is Our Faith," which featured representatives of different denominations talking about their beliefs.[12] The chapel service, a holdover from the days of the old Methodist college, was still a part of campus life. Services were held from 10:20 to 10:40 three mornings a week.

Members of the Student Christian Movement, 1950–51. While continuing to function in the 1950s, the organization had only modest success.

Despite the roster of activities, the SCM was not always successful in addressing the spiritual needs of students. Earle Hawkesworth, the SCM secretary in Saskatoon who oversaw the activities of the Regina branch, expressed concern in April 1951 that the chapel service, which in his opinion ought to have been "central in the life of the SCM," was not fulfilling its function.[13] Reverend Glynn Firth, who succeeded Hawkesworth as secretary in 1952, had an even gloomier assessment. He wrote to Riddell in March 1952, "I am forced to face the painful fact that the Movement accomplished little or nothing among the members of your student body this year."[14]

The SCM in the 1950s focused almost exclusively on matters of personal faith rather than social action or social justice. In that sense, it had broken with the social gospel tradition of the early days of Regina College. Reverend Firth defined his mission as helping young people achieve "greater personal integration and an understanding of the Christian way."[15] The topics selected for discussion, such as Bible study, doctrinal differences among denominations, marriage, and the theory of evolution, did not have a political or social service dimension. The conservatism of the organization was further revealed in an incident that occurred in 1953. A female member of the SCM in Saska-

Regina College students at the prom, 1952–53. Dances, both formal and informal, occupied a central place in student social life in the 1950s.

toon married a man who had run as a candidate for the Labour Progressive (Communist) Party in the federal election that year. This caused a bit of a scandal. Riddell reported to Firth that a number of people did not think it was proper for a woman married to someone "with such political tendencies" to continue as a member of the SCM.[16] This mindset explains why the SCM was not a breeding ground for the 1960s student movement. It had lost touch with the political activists who wanted to take on issues like the Cold War and the arms race.

In the 1950s dances, formal and informal, continued to occupy a central place in the life of the college. At the fall initiation dance in 1951 students waltzed, jived, and danced a Paul Jones to the accompaniment of Ross Reibling and his orchestra. The highlight of the evening was Jim Wightman's "How High the Moon" drum solo.[17] Later in the fall the social committee sponsored a Moulin Rouge cabaret. Men wearing berets and turtleneck sweaters and girls in slit skirts danced to what the college newspaper characterized as "French music," including such tunes as "La Vie en Rose," "Madame," and "Allons à Ma Maison" ("Come on-a My House").[18] "Three golden-clad cigarette girls" brightened the intermission at a dance in 1952, their supply of Export cigarettes and chocolate bars selling out in fifteen minutes. Faculty

Two Regina College students, 1952–53. The world was their oyster.

members glided through a "few safe waltzes" before giving over the floor to "jiving Jacks and Jills."[19] Sock dances after basketball games were still popular. In December 1954 the visiting team from Miles City, Montana, joined in the bunny hop, jive, and rumba: "The joint was really jumpin!"[20]

Faculty patrons and patronesses were in attendance at all social events. According to 1955 regulations, they were met at the door by representatives of the SRC and escorted to an area that had been reserved for them. The students were supposed to ensure that the patrons had an enjoyable time. "These functions are more a duty than a pleasure to patrons," the rules stated, "but without patrons there are no functions." Faculty members were not expected to police the function. If they decided that the dance was not being conducted with proper decorum, they simply withdrew, at which point, "*THAT FUNCTION ENDS IMMEDIATELY.*"[21] The shrill tone of this pronouncement hinted that there might have been some recurring discipline problems. Beneath the veneer of conformity and obedience, an incipient challenge to adult authority was stirring.

But there were no signs of rebellion in the French club, organized by Professor Margaret Belcher for the stated purpose of helping students "get more from the study of French." At a meeting in January 1958 the members solved a crossword puzzle in French and sang a "hearty round of 'Frère Jacques.'" Other activities included performing comic French skits, listening to "a very interesting talk on French-Canadian life," and viewing Miss Belcher's coloured slides of her trip to France.[22] French culture was considered some-

The French club, 1950–51. Professor Margaret Belcher, the club's guiding spirit, is in the middle of the front row.

Students at Regina College, 1952–53, wearing berets and affecting French airs.

thing exotic – listening to a recording of "La Vie en Rose" or contemplating a picture of the Eiffel Tower was a rare treat, not to be missed. The students at Regina College in the 1950s had little direct experience of the wider world. The student newspaper published articles about riding on a subway, flying in an airplane, and spending Christmas in Vancouver. It was assumed that these were novel and exciting adventures that other students would want to read about.[23]

Sports continued to figure prominently in student life, even though it was difficult for the athletic teams to find suitable competition. The men's basketball team, the Cougars, was too good for the high school league, and the senior men's league scheduled games in the middle of the week, which interfered with academic work. As a compromise, the Cougars competed in the senior men's league before Christmas and restricted themselves to exhibition games after that. In 1954–55 they played exhibition games only against junior college teams from Glendive and Miles City, Montana, and an annual series against the University of Saskatchewan junior team.[24] The Cubs, the second-tier Regina College men's basketball team, composed of younger athletes, played in the intercollegiate league. They lost only one game in the 1957–58 season, and, as result, they were deemed too good for the league and disqualified from the playoffs in 1958–59.[25] The awkward status of Regina College, situated as it was in a no man's land between high school and university, caused problems for the athletic program. The college could not easily find a comfortable niche.

Girls' basketball was still influenced by the perceived tension between lady-like behaviour and athleticism. According to a newspaper report of a December 1949 game, the girls "showed good form that night, playing a consistent game, but were unable to find the range. Being a little short on reserve strength, the girls were played to their utmost, but it's one way of reducing, eh, girls?"[26] The Cougettes lost 40 to 4 to Central Collegiate in January 1950, prompting the reporter to comment, "They have been too lady-like in their playing, lacking the drive that earns a win."[27] By 1958–59 the team was more competitive, ending the season with eleven wins and one tie; they scored 387 points, and had 171 points scored against them.[28] "It's funny how things change," Coach Arnie Lowenberger mused in January 1959, "usually there is a shortage of girl players and a plenitude of boys. But this is not only the first year I haven't had to use a girl who hasn't played before, but there are a lot of good players not on the teams." The team was poised to win the Regina city championship when high school officials stepped in and ruled it ineligible for the playoffs.[29]

Intramural sports continued through the 1950s. Students participated in basketball, badminton, bowling, curling, volleyball, and ping-pong. In 1957–58 nine teams, including one faculty team, entered the noon-hour basketball league. Fourteen teams, which included students and professors, curled once a week and competed in a bonspiel at the Regina Curling Club.[30] The bowlers gathered at Vic Alleys on Saturday afternoons, "the studes mowing down the mahogany [and setting] some highly enviable scores."[31] The swim club met sporadically, depending on whether pool time could be booked at the Y,[32] while Sam Stewart's rifle club had regular Thursday evening practice sessions. Although rifles were provided, students had to purchase their own ammunition – "65 cents for 22-calibre longs." "Young ladies interested in the club or the large male preponderance" were invited to "join in the fun."[33]

The students of the 1950s tended to be conformist in behaviour and pragmatic in outlook. Their attitude to college education was captured in English professor Les Crossman's "Lines Written upon Revisiting Regina College in Midsummer." A parody of Wordsworth's "Lines Written above Tintern Abbey," the poem is about a young man pondering his future after having failed his first-year English course. Should he quit school and get married or should he study for the supplemental exam in September in the hope of obtaining "the cherished D?"

Comrades, leave me here a little, while as yet 'tis early morn;
Leave me here, and when you want me, sound upon the Buick's horn.
'Tis the place; and all around, I seem to hear professors drone
Of the long result of Time in soporific monotone.
Many a morn by yonder icy casement ere I went to dine
Did I look on great Wascana, snow-bright in the crisp sunshine;
Many a morn I sat in lecture – drowsy, yawning – unimpressed
With platitudes of wisdom from the pundit – thumbs in vest.
"Tennyson: consummate craftsman!" "Keats: 'twas he that died so young."
"Oh! Do read Fitzgerald's *Omar*!" (Must be time the bell was rung.)
"Hardy's theme was resignation." "Browning: shameless optimist!"
"Housman's scholarship – amazing!" (I peek slyly at my wrist.)
In the Spring the snow on Scarth Street melts – then freezes, forming ice;
In the Spring the young collegian toys with thoughts of shoes and rice.

Then her look was pallid, colder than should be for one in love,
And I pleaded, "Amy dearest, try to understand, my Dove."
O my cousin, shallow-hearted! O my Amy, mine no more!
Faithless girl to say your lover dated others by the score.
I shall burst all links of habit; I shall wander far away –
Off to Pense, or Dilke, or Rouleau: curse the city's hectic fray!
There, the passions cramped no longer, I may do as Nature bids:
I will take some country maiden, wed her, raise a dozen kids.
Iron-jointed, mutton-headed, they shall romp the prairie dell –

Plough the furrow, clout the baseball: some may make the N.H.L.
Fool, again the dream, the fancy! But I know my words are wild,
For I count the gray bucolic lower than the urban child.
I, forsake my native city – vacant of our glorious gains?
I, a heavy-booted rustic tramping o'er Balcarres plains?
Never! I could not endure 't! My *Omnibus*! I'll bone it up;
Read my Browning: come September, who knows? – I may pass the supp.
Then to other halls of learning: some years hence, an L.L.B.,
Then return to fleece my townsmen. Brother, that's the life for me!
I'll become a city father – live in comfort, live in style:
Better fifty years of Scarth Street than a cycle in Delisle.
But the Buick's horn is sounding, and my comrades wait for me;
So farewell, beloved College – grant me but the cherished D.[34]

In Crossman's poem, student and professor occupy separate worlds. The professor drones on about Tennyson and Keats, while the student has thoughts only for the LLB. The depiction is, of course, incomplete, since student culture in the 1950s did not function autonomously, but rather under the supervision of faculty. The activities of the Students' Representative Council, for example, were closely monitored. Elected by the students, the SRC consisted of a president, vice-president, secretary, treasurer, director of athletics, director of debating, director of music and drama, director of social activities, the editor of the newspaper, and the editor of the yearbook. Each director was partnered with one or more "faculty advisors," who offered guidance and supervision.[35] The SRC constitution stated that the student president was "responsible to the Dean of the College for the conduct of the SRC and of the Students' Assembly and for the general oversight of all student activities."[36] In addition, the dean or a member of faculty had to co-sign all the cheques for SRC expenditures.[37] Thus, student government did not draw authority and legitimacy solely from the students who elected it; it was responsible to the dean and operated as an extension of the college administration.

The students for the most part accepted this arrangement. The only hint of mild resistance related to the management of the college newspaper. William Kinsman, the faculty advisor in 1950–51, encountered the editor in the hall near the beginning of the fall term and asked him to come to his office to talk over plans for the year. Kinsman asked specifically for the names of the staff, their positions, publication dates, and the budget. Although the editor did not show up at the faculty advisor's office, he assured him in casual hallway conversation that everything was proceeding satisfactorily. Kinsman later read and approved the galley proofs of the first issue. At the end of November he asked the editor how things were progressing and was told that the Christmas issue was ready to be sent to the printers. However, the issue

Members of the Regina College faculty in March 1952. English professor Les Crossman is standing at the door.

did not appear, and when the editor was confronted in the hallway about this, he said that he was no longer eligible to serve as editor because he had failed too many mid-term examinations. Kinsman suggested to Dean Riddell that he, Kinsman, be allowed to start up the paper in the fall, working with the students and assisting in the selection of the editor.[38]

A second incident occurred in December 1955, when the paper carried the announcement, "The articles in this publication were subject to CENSORSHIP!! Was it good reading?" The word *censored* was stamped over a large blank space on the front page, and below it appeared the editor's letter of resignation. The faculty advisor gave his reason for the intervention: "You may wonder why a censor stepped in at this point. You have freedom of the press, haven't you? You must remember, however, that along with the privilege of the press goes the responsibility of printing only the truth (and even then a newspaper is subject to libel action). The truth of the article is often difficult to establish but the editorial board is still responsible for it. If an article unjustly damns a person or a situation, a retraction may be printed, but a retraction never completely erases the hard feelings or vicious rumors about the situation."[39] The editor's resignation did not spark a protest. There were no demonstrations, boycotts, or strident claims that students had the right to control their own newspaper without faculty interference. Students basically accepted the fact that the faculty was in charge.

An unofficial ideology governed extracurricular activities in the 1950s. They were regarded as a component of the student's overall education, not something that students created for themselves or an autonomous culture that they controlled. Extracurricular activities were a planned aspect of the educational program; they were meant to train students to be sociable and get along with others – to cultivate a "good personality." During his dispute with the editor of the *College Record*, Kinsman said that his goal was to give students with a common interest "an opportunity to work together, and by working together to grow in ability, to enlarge mental horizons, and to improve personality."[40] Although extracurricular activities were supposed to be fun, they were not frivolous. Their purpose, according to Dean Riddell, was to provide young people with "experience that will assist them in taking a constructive part in the life of their community."[41]

Students endorsed and internalized these values. Student Margot Moffat wrote in 1948, "If you have come to college to further your education, try not to neglect the other part of your education, which is, very naturally, learning to get along with other people."[42] A letter to the editor in February 1955 explained that students were "tomorrow's leaders," not only at the national level, but also in their local communities, where they were expected to take positions of leadership in service clubs and church organizations: "We will be responsible for leading the people in many types of projects and this will require a great deal of talent that can only be learned here and now when we have the opportunity to do so."[43] Extracurricular activities were seen as a rehearsal for real life, a training ground for service clubs and women's auxiliaries. It was assumed that existing social and political arrangements were more or less satisfactory, and that all a student needed to do was find a slot and occupy it.

The post-war emphasis on the vital importance of democracy reinforced this idea. World War II had been fought to defend "the democratic way of life," and the Cold War was waged to preserve it. As SRC president Bert Promislow pointed out in an article titled "Presenting True Democracy," the college gave students an opportunity to learn about democracy through participating in student government, "thereby preparing themselves for their future role as citizens."[44] The keyword was "preparing." Students in the 1950s, unlike their counterparts in the 1960s, did not see themselves as full citizens in the university or in the world at large. They were citizens in training.

The student newspaper in the 1950s rarely mentioned the issues that students would have to deal with as full citizens. Its faculty advisor stated in 1951 that the *College Record* did not "pretend to be a newspaper" but was, rather, a record of school events.[45] This signalled a change from the immediate post-war period, when veterans had attended the college in large numbers. The paper at that time had covered topics of wider political significance. G.K. Piller in 1948 discussed the issue of nuclear energy. He noted that when the atomic bombs had been dropped on Hiroshima and Nagasaki in 1945, there had been a good deal of talk about using nuclear power for peaceful purposes. The public had been offered visions of "horseless buggies" propelled by atomic energy, better ways to cook food, and beneficial climate changes. Piller wondered what had become of all these ideas and why governments were concentrating exclusively on the production of weapons of mass destruction.[46]

I. Kreel's "A Real Education," which also appeared in 1948, reviewed a series of guest lectures that had been given at the college over the course of the academic term. The topics included the role of the university in the modern world, the operation of the United Nations, and "the situation in China today." Over 70 per cent of the students had attended, and the lectures had given rise to a great deal of discussion and debate. Kreel said that this was "real education," because, unlike the material found in textbooks, the lectures dealt with contemporary problems that had to be solved. He asked the SRC to organize more events of this kind: "If these are held frequently, and are strongly backed by a students' council, I feel it will go a long way in developing an aware, conscious student body. *How about it?*"[47]

When the veterans left the college, the political content of the newspaper largely disappeared. Apart from a brief reference to "hot debates" during study breaks in the men's residence at the time of the 1958 federal election,[48] no mention was made of national or provincial politics. At the municipal level, the SRC petitioned Regina City Council in 1955 for reduced student rates on city buses.[49] The request was turned down, and the SRC reapplied in 1956, again unsuccessfully.[50] Twice rebuffed, the students gave up and quietly submitted to the edict of the civic authorities.

Colleges and universities in the 1950s functioned *in loco parentis*.[51] This was evident at Regina College in the faculty's supervision of the SRC and the imposition of regulations concerning dances. It was obvious, too, in the rules governing the residences, especially the women's residence. The external doors were locked each night at 11:00, at which time the girls were expected to be in their rooms. They could apply to the warden for late leaves until 12:30 a.m. on Wednesday, Thursday, and Friday; and until 2 a.m. on Saturday. In addition, the warden could authorize overnight and weekend leaves at her discretion, provided the student's parent or guardian had signed a form indicating where the girl was allowed to stay. Only a limited number of leaves was granted, and the girls had to sign a register upon leaving the residence and again when they returned. During evening study hours, from 7:00 to

10:00, the residence was supposed to be quiet, and students were not allowed to visit in one another's rooms. After 11:00 p.m., talking, typing, and listening to the radio were forbidden. Unauthorized visitors were strictly prohibited – any breach of this rule was referred to the faculty discipline committee.[52]

The regulations for men were less stringent, probably because of the sexual double standard that prevailed in the 1950s. It was considered more important for unmarried girls than for unmarried men to preserve their virginity.[53] But men, too, were subject to a strict disciplinary code, the severity of which was evident in an incident that occurred in 1950. On the weekend of 11 November a group of boys had a party in the residence. They consumed liquor and threw empty bottles out the window onto the pavement below. During the ensuing investigation, the culprits were asked whether they had committed the offence as charged.[54] Three boys confessed and were expelled from the residence, but they were allowed to continue attending classes on a probationary basis. This meant that if they kept their records clean, they would be eligible for readmission to the residence at the beginning of January 1951. The main condition of their probation was that they were not to set foot in the residence, which was located on the third floor of the main college building.

All three boys were found in the residence on Friday, 24 November 1950. One of them said that he had been sitting on the stairs of the main building when someone told him there was going to be a residence fire drill. Joining the other students, he went up to the residence and participated in the drill. Later, when he was asked whether he had understood that he was not supposed to go into the residence, he replied that he had understood, "but did not think about it then." The second boy also participated in the fire drill, and his explanation was similar to that of the first boy.

The third boy, a Chinese Canadian, had a different story. A first-year engineering student, he had been working in the drafting room, which was located on the top floor of the tower on the west side of the main college building. To gain access to the room it was necessary to pass through a portion of the corridor of the men's residence and then go up a flight of stairs. The student had been told when he was placed on probation that although he was allowed to use that section of the corridor, he was not to enter any of the rooms. He obeyed the rule, except in one particular. He began leaving his coat in the residence room at the bottom of the staircase leading to the drafting room. He could have kept his coat in the boys' common room, but it was inconveniently located in the basement at the opposite end of the building. He finished his work in the drafting room at 5:45 p.m. on Friday, 24 November. When he went to retrieve his coat, he found that the door to the room was locked. He walked down the corridor and entered another friend's room, where he sharpened his drawing pen. The occupants of the room warned him that he was going to get into trouble, but he seemed unconcerned. As he left the room, the warden of the men's residence saw him and demanded to know what he was doing there.

The faculty discipline committee adjudicated all three cases on 27 November 1950. It decided that there was reasonable doubt as to whether the first two boys had deliberately violated the terms of their probation. They were given a severe reprimand, and warned that they "had placed themselves in a precarious position as far as their probation [was] concerned." The third boy, the Chinese Canadian, was expelled from the college. The committee ruled that he had wilfully broken the terms of his probation.[55]

This was not the end of the matter. The boy's landlord wrote a letter to President Thompson protesting against the expulsion. He said that he had spoken with several students who believed that the boy had been given "a dirty deal." The landlord also reported a conversation with one of the members of the discipline committee, who claimed that the faculty had been very considerate towards the Chinese Canadian boy. They had spoken to him very slowly to be sure that he understood what they were saying. But, as the landlord remarked to President Thompson, this was a strange approach to take given the fact that the boy had been born and raised in Canada and spoke perfect English. As for the charge that the boy had intentionally flouted the authority of the discipline committee, the landlord said that such an idea had "never entered the boy's mind as he is not that kind of person." He added, "Why should a person's whole life be changed and all his future plans shattered because he had made one mistake himself and then was misunderstood by the very people who should be helping him?" The boy was "very broken up" over the incident and, in the words of the landlord, might "turn bitter." One thing was certain, he said. If the boy had come from a prominent Regina family and had not been the son of a Chinese café owner, the case would have been handled much differently.[56]

President Thompson asked Dean Riddell to review the incident and the procedures that had been followed. The crucial factor for Riddell was that the student had apparently broken the rules deliberately. "It was the feeling of the Discipline Committee," he wrote to Thompson, that this was a case of "flagrant refusal to abide by the rules of the Discipline Committee and, since, in the first instance, the case had been a serious one which the university cannot tolerate, the Committee felt that they would be left without any further authority if this matter was not dealt with immediately and in a drastic manner."[57] Thompson did not overturn the decision. He merely remarked on the discrepancy between this boy's punishment and that meted out to the other two.[58] The latter were readmitted to the residence after one month. The Chinese Canadian boy left the school and did not return.

The case revealed the vulnerability of students in the 1950s to the exercise of power by college authorities. The discipline committee did not have any student representatives, and there was no formal process for appealing its decisions. The boy was expelled not so much because of what he had done, but because of his alleged attitude. According to the administration and faculty, he had defied authority every time he put his coat where he had been told not to put his coat. The offence was more symbolic than real. The student had not done anything to disrupt the learning environment. Indeed, troublemakers are not usually found doing schoolwork at five o'clock on a Friday afternoon. Clearly, the issue was one of control and of establishing who was in charge.

As a final irony, it turned out that the Chinese Canadian boy had not even been at the college when the drinking incident that led to the probation had taken place – his roommate had used their room for the party while he was at home for the weekend. During the investigation, the three boys had been asked whether they had ever brought liquor into the residence. The Chinese Canadian boy had confessed that on a previous occasion he had done so: "At the first dance, four of us boys wanted something to drink at the dance, so I went down town and brought up some beer. As far as this weekend goes, I wasn't there."[59]

The issue of racial prejudice hung over the whole case, though it was not explicitly addressed, except in the letter from the landlord to the university president. In another case, it was discovered that a Black student living in the men's residence had broken into the girl's dormitory. The men's warden was horrified at the possibility that news of the incident might leak out to the general public. The student was expelled and everything kept quiet. As these incidents reveal, racial discrimination was not much talked about in the 1950s. The *College Record* made scant reference to it. The student newspaper in the 1960s, by contrast, was full of articles about the civil rights movement, Aboriginal issues, and various forms of racism.

Gender inequality was not totally ignored in the 1940s and 1950s. The *College Record* in 1940 congratulated the Government of Quebec for finally having granted the provincial vote to women.[60] On the other hand, a male reader took strong exception to the expansion of women's rights. In a letter to the editor in February 1941, he pronounced chivalry dead, the victim of the masculine pretensions of feminists: "They have ousted many a good man from his job so they should be expected to open doors, remove their hats when in a room because they have lowered themselves to the status of men." You could not expect a man, the writer continued, to respect a woman who "drinks, smokes and swears," or "lets fly a cackle that would put any hyena to shame."[61] A 1948 article declared that the day of the liberated woman had arrived. It was now accepted as a matter of course that "women wear silk stockings, short skirts, low shoes, no corsets, an ounce of underwear, have bobbed hair, smoke, paint and powder, drink cocktails, play bridge, drive cars, have pet dogs and go in for politics."[62]

In the 1950s women's issues were at low ebb. The SRC constitution at Regina College required that the president be male, and the vice-president female. Student Joan Hart protested against this in February 1960: "This year the female enrolment far outnumbers that of the male. Why don't these women insist on their democratic rights and have the constitution amended in accordance with the times? In unity there is strength, so unite, girls, if you want equal status in the presidential race."[63] Her suggestion was taken up, and shortly thereafter the students voted to eliminate the discriminatory provision in the constitution.

Gender issues formed the subtext of a conflict between the engineering students, who were all men, and the hospital laboratory technician students, the great majority of whom were women. The former were on a career path to relatively well-paid professional jobs; the latter could expect to earn modest incomes as semi-professionals working within the male-dominated health profession. The engineers savoured their macho image, carried themselves with a certain swagger, and projected a sense of self-importance. They referred to themselves as "royal fellows" and the "rulers" of the school. They boasted of entering the largest number of candidates in student elections and of supporting college activities with more enthusiasm than anyone else.[64] An engineering student bragged that half of those who attended the Valentine's dance in 1950 were engineers and their dates,[65] and that nine engineers were playing on college basketball teams in 1958.[66] Sharing a male camaraderie that set them apart from other students, they organized their own "smokers" and dances.[67] According to engineering student G.L. Parrott, a "young lady from residence" had asked, "What makes the engineers think they are so d_ smart?" "There is only one answer," he replied. "We are prouder and more spirited because we stick together. We stick together because we have a class of square guys. In a solid male class we are all judged on one criterion, the criterion of a regular fellow."[68]

This drew the retort, "[Parrott] was not fooling there – what a bunch of squares ... As for supporting college functions, how can you fellows do that when usually you are so full of alcohol you cannot support yourselves?"[69] The capacity for imbibing large quantities of alcohol was part of the masculine mystique. The engineers' school song celebrated their prowess at downing "forty beers" at a sitting. Other students scoffed: "Perhaps they enjoy making fools of themselves, but the way they take over a dance is no fun for anyone else who is interested in dancing and not in seeing how much liquor they can stow away. Liquor has its place (there is a place for the engineers, too, but it has not been dug yet), but the engineers overdo it in their attempt to appear big shots ... We do wish they would grow up. They act like little boys who think they have a reputation to live up to."[70]

Although the engineers and the lab techs pursued different programs of study, they had some classes, such as chemistry, in common. The girls complained that the boys were too domineering and had inflated opinions of their own abilities. A 1955 letter to the editor signed "the lab techs" stated that "Between classes they set the halls into a mad uproar and in their spare periods, of which they seem to have an abundance, they invade the library where they make general nuisances of themselves disturbing students who are trying in vain to study." Further, the engineers allegedly lowered the intellectual level of the college: "We [the lab techs] try exceedingly hard to maintain a high average in the chem labs while the engineers insist on dragging it down with their measly 10's and 20's." The low marks did nothing to curb their "habit of boasting endlessly about their so-called accomplishments. Who wants to 'demolish forty beers,' anyhow?" Worst of all, the engineers were discourteous towards women: "These would-be plumbers and bridge-builders have proven beyond a doubt that they are extremely impolite. In their eyes, the age of chivalry is certainly dead. As soon as the class is over, they bolt for the door, heedless of any weaker individuals whom they happen to be trampling."[71] The lab techs sent a mixed message. While they resented the overbearing engineers, whose pretensions exceeded their abilities, they wanted to be treated like "ladies."

"Frustration," a poem that appeared in the April 1959 edition of the student newspaper, recounted the story of Horace, an engineer who killed himself when he discovered that an arts student could drink forty–one bottles of beer. The poem portrays engineers as conformist, anti-intellectual, and unhip.

I give you
Horace
Horace was a conformist –
Pity
He hated intellectuals
Mainly because he
Wasn't
He hated beards
Mainly because he
Hadn't
He hated abstract art
In public
In private he –
Wondered ...

It was at this
Party.
Horace was the only
Engineer
There.
So he had a
Tradition
To fulfill.
It seems that engineers
Have to
Embarrass all the girls,
Tell the sexiest stories,
And drink the most
Liquor.

Seems they usually
Lose at first,
Too
Well, like, Horace
Tried
He told stories that
Would make
The Dean of Engineering
Abdicate.
He embarrassed the girls
Excruciatingly.
But who drove him
Goo-goo
Was some slob
From arts and science
Who –
Before Horace's blurred,
Horrified
Eyes
Drank forty-one beer[72]

A *Sheet* article in January 1959 brought a political perspective to the discussion. It characterized engineers as boosters of technology, cogs in the military-industrial complex, builders of bombs, and quintessentially "corporate men." The high point in an engineer's career was the moment he had "a control panel installed in his back which can be controlled from a central authority known as 'boss,' 'chief,' or 'big brother.'" It was even rumoured that engineers reproduced themselves through technological processes: "The fairy tale of Cinderella might easily be changed to have as its hero a woman engineer at Ford, whose fairy godmother changed her into a gigantic slide rule with units for horsepower conversion and who subsequently marries an IBM electronic calculator."[73] The article anticipated the countercultural themes of the 1960s: suspicion of technology, antipathy to large business corporations, and rejection of the Cold War.

Regina College students held a beatnik party in November 1960. Bill Taylor played the bongos, and Miriam Promislow "recited poetry to the accompaniment of wailing jazz." "Traditional Beatnik candles in wine bottles added to the effect by their mysterious flickering light." One guest came to the party "costumed as a conformist, but the Beatnik crowd soon turned him into a cool cat with disheveled hair and a black shoe polish beard."[74] "On Chianti," published in the student newspaper in 1961, breathed a countercultural spirit:

Chianti is hot, still summer days, warm, laughter-sprinkled nights, girls with unfettered breasts, and bright skirts, men with sweaty backs, and flashing teeth, old men, placed in a park, and mountain rivers rushing to the bosom of a lazy, sparkling sea.

Corn! You say?

Quite right! We must be realistic. We must forget this sentimental crap and speak of more important things: Detroit's last bloated offerings, pastel toilet paper, and togetherness and television programs that always end happily, and never ever offend minority groups, but which always manage to offend everybody else with their commercials,

– of more important men, 'cause after all, anyone of importance today subscribes to the Great Doctrine of Planned Obsolescence, as applied to the human race.

– of more important times, let's say the founding of the great WASP Utopia, whose motto will be – "TOGETHERNESS, SECURITY, CONFORMITY."

But what about Chianti? Oh it also will be infinitely superior, made in tanks of stainless steel, and packaged in unbreakable plastic bottles, and much more safe to drink because, as the labels will say – "UNTOUCHED BY HUMAN FEET"[75]

Another sign of a shift in student attitudes was evident in a January 1959 *Sheet* editorial condemning authoritarian teaching methods. A student had been severely reprimanded for a comment he had made in English class concerning "the integrity of Cleopatra." The professor made repeated references to the allegedly "licentious nature" of the student's character and his supposedly inferior intelligence. "In high school this would be considered unjust," the editorial declared, "in a university, it is an outrage." Students, it continued, had the right to think for themselves and to question the professor's opinions. The purpose of a university was "to teach reasoning, to gradually unfold the power of the mind, and to point the road ahead, not to snap rings in noses and drag people down the path the instructor has traveled." Students were entitled to the freedom "to develop individually, in their own way, using the reason that was substituted for authority in the Renaissance." "Mass-produced ideas and stereotyped opinions" were contrary to the true spirit of education.[76] The point was later reinforced in a cartoon that depicted a student with his head in a vice, grimacing in pain, while a professor stood over him asking "Anybody else disagree?"[77]

Despite the signs of opposition to authority, the incidents of student disobedience were still mainly individualistic and hedonistic. On the night of 26 February 1953 four boys entered the girls' residence reception room at about 10:30 in the evening. They became rowdy, "singing boisterous songs to such an extent that two of the residence girls and their escorts left the room to visit elsewhere." At 11:20 p.m., after the residence lock-up, the warden found two male students on the girls' residence floor. One said he had gone up to borrow a book, while the other gave the excuse that he had tried to find his friend to tell him it was time to leave the building. After they were evicted the men continued their "boisterous singing" outside the girls' residence until 12:45 a.m. According to the disciplinary report, it had been quite obvious "that some of the group at least had been drinking and that at least one unidentified person had been drinking in the common room during the rowdy behavior."[78]

On another occasion, in November 1956, three boys were found drinking in the men's common room.[79] As we have seen, students sometimes smuggled alcohol into dances, and the engineers' boast of drinking forty beers at a sitting was not entirely without foundation. The severity and elaborate nature of the college's disciplinary regulations, which were written as though every possible breach of decorum had to be anticipated and explicitly forbidden, suggested that the authorities feared a breakdown of discipline and order. Constant vigilance was needed to keep bad behaviour in check. Under the tranquil surface of obedience, discontent simmered, but it was apolitical and without a coherent philosophical justification.

Student culture at Regina College in the 1950s was in this respect not dissimilar from that found at other colleges and universities. There was, however, a specific malaise rooted in the fact that the college was stranded in an intermediate position between high school and university. This malaise was often discussed in terms of a lack of "school spirit." The student elections in the fall of 1954 aroused so little interest that three positions were filled by acclamation and the others remained vacant.[80] Dean Riddell called a special meeting of the student body to rustle up enough candidates to allow the SRC to perform its duties. Student Gwen Ellis in January 1950 expressed her feelings in "J'accuse": "In brief, to get to the gist of the matter (and gist in time, too) we have no appreciation of the finer things in life – namely, ourselves!"[81] An editorial in November 1953 asked, "What's wrong with the College? Why don't we ever have any fun? Why don't we get to know the other students? What has happened to all the dances, the parties and the pranks which we thought went with university life?"[82]

A letter to the editor in February 1955 put the case strongly: "This is my first year as a student at Regina College and I am almost glad to say that it is my last ... Never yet have I seen a group of students with as much lack of spirit as the students in Regina College." Students, the writer said, complained of being too busy to get involved in college activities, but the same students had time for playing bridge and going to movies, dances, and "beer gardens."[83] The letter drew a reply from another student, who made the obvious point that most students attended Regina College for only one year, and it was difficult to build school spirit in such a short time. At the Saskatoon campus elections for the SRC were held in the spring so that student activities could be planned over the summer and commence as soon as the fall term started. This was not possible at Regina College because there was no continuity in the student body from year to year. By the time students got to know one another, it was time for them to go their separate ways.[84]

This was the nub of the problem. As enrolment in the matriculation program declined in proportion to the total student body, Regina College became increasingly a one-year college, a way station for those in transition from high school to university – or, as one student put it, an "orphaned waif on the University of Saskatchewan's doorstep."[85] Dean Basterfield had identified the issue as early as 1948: "most students spend only one year in the College and there is consequently a lack of continuity in our work and a sense of instability in our academic life. Students are continually moving on; they pass through as pilgrims of a day, and we scarcely get to know one another."[86]

The status of the college posed a problem for faculty as well. It was difficult to attract highly qualified personnel, except on a temporary basis, because research-oriented scholars inevitably moved on to a degree-granting university, where they could be part of a large department and have the opportunity to teach senior courses.[87] Historian Hilda Neatby and biologist Jake Rempel left for Saskatoon in 1946; historian Roger Graham followed in 1956. Riddell even encouraged Graham to go because he thought he would leave the college at some point anyway, and if he transferred to Saskatoon he would at least stay in Saskatchewan.[88] It was to no avail, however, for a few years later Graham left the University of Saskatchewan to take up an appointment at Queen's University.

The case of physicist E.R. Thackeray illustrated how the junior college environment could frustrate the career aspirations of the ambitious scholar. Thackeray complained to President Thomson in April 1945 that he put in thirty-two hours of teaching per week, not including the time required for preparing lectures, setting up apparatus for laboratory demonstrations, and marking assignments. "I have found it necessary," Thackeray wrote, "to return nearly every Saturday and Sunday during the school term. Even with that I feel I have not done justice to the courses or to the students. There are not enough hours in the week."[89] In 1946 he left for two years to pursue doctoral studies at Madison, Wisconsin. In order to raise the necessary funds, he and his wife depleted their savings and sold their house and most of their furniture. Back at Regina College in 1948 with his freshly minted PhD, Thackeray found himself once again teaching nothing but elementary courses and with no opportunity to conduct research.[90] He asked President Thomson in May 1949 for a transfer to Saskatoon, adding that he had an offer of an appointment as associate professor at the University of Akron, in Ohio, at a starting salary of $4,500 per year.[91] By comparison, Riddell's salary as dean of Regina College in 1950 was $5,000.[92] Thomson replied that while he sympathized with Thackeray's plight, admired the sacrifices he had made to earn the PhD, and applauded his desire to remain in Canada, there were no vacancies in the physics department at Saskatoon.[93] Thackeray left for Akron, where he was soon promoted to the position of department head.

From the point of view of both faculty and students, the one-year status of Regina College left much to be desired. Faculty members were not able to develop to their full potential as scholars, and students were deprived of the best teachers. Nor was it easy for the college to build a sense of community when the composition of the student body was constantly changing.

But perhaps the difficulties should not be exaggerated. Students were able to rise above the adverse circumstances. The last word on student life in the 1950s belongs to the author of "Valediction," an engineering student, who described the feelings of his classmates as they left the college at the end of the 1958 academic year:

> [Leaving] is not without sadness, though! They will surely miss the mischievous pranks they played by building chair-castles, knotting lamp cords, hiding drawing boards, etc. Struggling hard to forget old memories, they start to leave their "Ivory Tower" – leaving the pigeons to look after it till next year. Descending several storeys of stairs, a familiar aroma attracts their olfactory senses. Undoubtedly H_2S. They are captured by the odor and stop. However, they soon turn away – cringing, only to have their eyes travel in the direction of the Science Theatre. At this sight their fingers twitch – recalling the many days of writer's cramp.
>
> Down another flight of stairs. Here we recall many days where we spent the first hour in English, the second in Math. If the first one didn't get us, the second one did! Still as confused and illiterate as the day we entered, we quickly continue, giving it up as a lost cause ... 10:20 and the periodic visit to the cafeteria to see if the doughnuts are still as greasy as ever and to see if our skill at throwing "serviette balls" into coffee cups is up to par. The five-minute bell (i.e., the bell of 5 minutes duration) rings, and we decide to continue the unhappy journey homeward. The library – ah yes, wonder what it looks like? Might as well drop in now and see what's there. This completed, we make a last-minute dash to the gymnasium where the Engineers suffered defeat in most competitions – but graciously!
>
> At last we leave, and a great sigh of relief can be heard coming from where the staff had assembled. The building itself takes on a calm and peaceful look of solitude now that we have left. But then, wait till next year – we might be back again to raise the roof.
>
> Earnestly, though, we have enjoyed our year at Regina College, and we know that it will always be a year to recall, for having met a great number of good friends and having had a wonderful time.[94]

5 The Campaign for a Full Degree Program

The question of whether a student should be allowed to take more than five university courses at Regina College had been discussed intermittently for more than three decades. President Ernest Stapleford raised it in the 1920s, Dean William Ramsay brought it up in 1938, and Dean Steward Basterfield revived it in 1946 and 1950.[1] Dean William Riddell broached the matter again in April 1951. He pointed out in a letter to President W.P. Thompson that the five-course limit had been imposed prior to 1934, when the university had assumed ownership and control of the college. Since the college was now part of the university, the rule was, in Riddell's opinion, "definitely discrimination against this portion of the staff." He said there was "continuous demand" on the part of teachers in the city who wanted to take more than five courses at the college as they worked towards their BA degree. Noting that "a number of staff here feel quite strongly about this matter," he asked for Thompson's advice as to the proper procedure to follow in reopening the question.[2]

Thompson answered that the appeal should be directed to the University Council. He referred the matter to J. Francis Leddy, dean of arts and science in Saskatoon, who informed Riddell on 18 April 1951 that "whether Regina College should be more than a junior college involves more than the qualifications of those who are now on the staff. Any significant extension of the range of work offered at Regina College would undoubtedly raise a number of related questions concerning the validity of a further duplication of university work in this province."[3] The Regina College faculty prepared a brief, which they presented to a special committee of the University Council composed of G.E. Britnell, W. Roger Graham, R.N.H. Haslam, S.R. Laycock, Hilda Neatby, J.G. Rempel, W.A. Riddell, G.W. Simpson, J.W.T. Spinks, J.H. Thompson, W.P. Thompson, with J.F. Leddy as chair. Only Riddell and Graham were faculty members at Regina College. Neatby and Rempel had been transferred to Saskatoon in 1946.

The committee deliberated through the morning and afternoon of 4 May 1951, weighing arguments for and against Regina's request. Riddell and Graham emphasized that since Regina College was not in the same category as the other junior colleges, the extension of the five-course rule would not set a precedent. They pointed out that the college was already offering enough classes to fill a second year, and that it was difficult to explain to people in Regina why they were not permitted to register for them. Those defending the existing restrictions said that if the concession were granted, then other junior colleges, particularly in Regina, would consider themselves entitled to look for similar privileges; raising the limit from five to ten courses would lead inevitably to a request for an extension to fifteen; Regina College would end up asking for more staff members; and students admitted to a second year at the college would not have as wide a selection of courses as their counterparts in Saskatoon. As the meeting wore on, it became obvious that unanimity would not be reached. A vote was taken, and the committee decided "by a substantial majority" to leave things as they were.[4]

Riddell was disappointed, and Frank Wagg, a United Church minister and the former registrar at Regina College, uncharitably remarked that the university's policy was not likely to change until there had been "a few funerals in Saskatoon."[5] By 1954 the college was offering thirty university courses, but no one was allowed to take more than five for credit. It was possible for a student to take five courses at Regina College or by correspondence and five additional courses at summer school and complete his or her degree with one year's residence at the Saskatoon campus. The summer school courses were deemed, as Riddell put it, "in some mysterious way" superior to the courses offered at Regina College during the regular term, even though some of the summer school courses were actually taught at the college. "This regulation," Riddell observed, "in effect makes the College program and the academic staff second rate and even implies lesser importance than Summer School staff although in many instances Summer School staff is recruited from those not on the permanent staff of the University."[6]

Beginning in 1952, a group of citizens outside the college began to agitate for a full degree program. The driving force behind the movement was Regina lawyer George Herbert Barr. Born in Ontario in 1878, Barr moved to Regina in 1898, where he articled in the law office of his uncle, George W. Brown, a future lieutenant-governor of Saskatchewan and the first chairman of the

George Herbert Barr, who in 1952 took up the campaign for a full degree program at Regina College.

Board of Governors of Regina College. Barr travelled east to complete his law studies at Osgoode Hall in Toronto, graduating in 1907. When he returned to Regina, he set up a practice and acquired expertise in constitutional law. He was one of the lawyers who argued Saskatchewan's case for provincial control of natural resources before the Privy Council in London. He was also a strong believer in co-operatives, which he regarded as the answer to many of western Canada's economic problems. For a number of years he acted as solicitor for the Saskatchewan Grain Growers' Association, and he obtained the charters and prepared bylaws for the Saskatchewan Livestock Pool, Saskatchewan Poultry Pool, and Consumers' Cooperative Oil Refinery. He successfully defended the wheat pool when private grain companies attacked the legality of co-operative marketing practices on the grounds that they were in restraint of trade.

Barr also contributed to several community organizations. He was a member of City Council in 1915, one of the first members of the Public Library Board, a member of the council of the Board of Trade for ten years, president of the Canadian Club, a member of Knox Presbyterian (later Knox-

Ethel Laureen Barr, wife of George Barr. Their home, just three blocks up the street from Regina College, was a focal point for the cultural and social life of the city.

Metropolitan United) Church, a founding member of the Regina YMCA, president of the Saskatchewan Boy Scouts Association, and a charter member of the Children's Aid Society.[7] In 1906 he married Ethel Laureen Dawson, whose involvement in community activities rivalled his own. Her parents had arrived in Regina in February 1883, and her mother had been a strong supporter of the arts in the pioneer community. Ethel Barr followed in the family tradition, helping to organize the Orpheus Club, the Regina Women's Musical Club, the arts and letters committee of the Local Council of Women, and the Regina Art Center Association. She had a hand in preparing a brief to City Council in 1949 lobbying for the reintroduction of the teaching of art at Regina College and the construction of an art gallery.

The Barr home, a solid brick structure at 2102 Scarth Street, just three blocks up the street from Regina College, served for forty-nine years as a focal point of cultural and social life in the city. Many community organizations had their founding meeting in its "high-ceilinged, pillared living room," and there was seldom an evening when a group of some kind did not convene there — the Women's Canadian Club, a United Church association, the Local Council of Women, the Chamber of Commerce, the Canadian Bar Association, or one of the other organizations to which either George or Ethel Barr belonged. The couple hosted the Saturday Night Club, an informal group of businessmen and professionals who came together for no purpose other than good conversation. It included the editor of the *Leader-Post*, the manager of the local branch of the Bank of Montreal, the manager of the wheat pool, the director of the Conservatory of Music, and the head of the Regina Public Library. The Barr home was a hub of cultural, intellectual, and educational activity in the community, and after 1952 it became the unofficial headquarters of the campaign for a full degree program at Regina College.[8]

Before launching the campaign, Barr wrote to E.W. Stapleford, the former president of the college, then retired and living in Toronto. Dated 15 January 1952 and marked "private and confidential," the letter stated: "What I have in mind is the chance which the coming generation of the youth of this city should have to get a university education leading to a degree while living in their own homes here. It is a long story and I imagine no person in Regina knows more about it than I do as I was present at the meetings of prominent supporters of the Scott government when the facts were disclosed showing that we had been betrayed by the politicians and that the youth of our city and this part of the province were sacrificed on the alter of political expediency."[9]

The meeting to which Barr referred took place shortly after the university Board of Governors voted 5 to 4 on 7 April 1909 to locate the university in Saskatoon rather than Regina.[10] It was widely believed at the time that the Liberal government led by Premier Walter Scott had intervened to determine the outcome, and Reginans were both disappointed and resentful. According to J.W. McLeod, private secretary to Premier Scott, "quite a number of prominent Grits [were] vowing summary vengeance upon all and sundry connected with the Government. A hurry-up meeting of about 20 or so of the workers was held and I believe the gathering was one of the warmest which has taken place in Regina for many moons."[11] The person who chaired this meeting of irate Liberals was thirty-one-year-old George Herbert Barr.

Forty-three years later, Barr resumed his campaign for a university in Regina. Aged seventy-four and stricken with arthritis, he was an unlikely champion for the youth of the city. He explained his motivation in a letter to Premier Douglas in 1954: "I am a product of the very thing which I am advocating for the young people of this city."[12] Growing up on an Ontario farm, Barr had made the daily trek to the local country schoolhouse. Among his classmates were a future minister of defence, two future members of Parliament, three medical doctors, a high school principal, and a missionary. His teacher, C.B. Corless, later trained as an engineer and became general manager of the Mond Nickel Company (which merged with Inco Limited in 1929). Barr always said that his life had been entirely altered through the influence of this teacher, and the two men kept in touch until Corless died, at the age of eighty-four.[13] For Barr, education was the magic elixir that had transformed him from a boy milking cows into a lawyer arguing a case before the highest court in the British Empire. He wanted other young people to have the same chance to make something of their lives. "You can well understand," he wrote to Premier Douglas, "that with that background I am interested in seeing that the young people of this city and the surrounding country, for generations to come, get their fair start in life."[14]

Barr outlined his strategy in his letter to Stapleford in January 1952. He planned to ask the mayor of Regina to call a public meeting to discuss the possibility of establishing a university program in the city.[15] As a first step he set up a meeting with the mayor and the chairmen of the public and separate school boards. He feared, however, that the *Leader-Post* would not support the campaign, since it seemed "reluctant to do anything which would not be acceptable to the university authorities."[16] Stapleford offered words of encouragement: "My heart is still with Regina College and I do hope that your efforts will be crowned with success"; but, he cautioned, "The University will fight every step of the way."[17]

Dean William Riddell learned of Barr's project and immediately dissociated himself from it. He assured President Thompson that the college was not giving the campaign either open or covert support.[18] The Regina College Advisory Board at a special meeting on 28 February 1952 passed a resolution affirming that "Present efforts to extend the work of Regina College in the areas of art, music and community service should be continued and intensified, but no plan for extension to degree work [should] be entertained at this time."[19] At this stage Barr was at odds not only with the university but also Regina's civic and educational elite. He was considered a crank, a Don Quixote tilting at windmills.

Undeterred, he managed to persuade Mayor Gordon B. Grant to set up a committee to examine the Regina College issue. Composed of Stewart Young (chair), Dr Rex Schneider, Mrs A.L. Hall, W.N. McGillivrary, R.A. Milliken, W.E. Murray, and M.J. Spratt, it held ten meetings, collected information, and conducted surveys. It presented a report in February 1953 recommending against Regina College's expansion to a full degree program. Alderman H.G.R. Walker protested that while establishing a degree course would be expensive, the cost was justified if it improved access to higher education for young people in the southern part of the province. Council member Mrs F.S. Rawlinson agreed, noting that, from her observation, many young people in Regina went to work directly from high school with the intention of saving money for a university education, but once in the workforce most of them remained there, never realizing their goal of obtaining a university degree. Alderman L. Robinson, who was a member of the university senate, sided with the committee. "It would be a splendid thing," he said, "if we could have a degree granting institution in Regina, but ... I think it would be financially unsound to have what would be, in effect, two universities." He thought that Regina should consider itself fortunate to have a junior college.[20]

The *Leader-Post* supported the committee's recommendation, with the proviso that the question might be reopened at a later date.[21] Barr dismissed the report out of hand, while Stapleford called it "mere piffle." His letter to Barr was tinged with resignation: "Unfortunately, Saskatoon is in the saddle as far as university work is concerned. The people of Saskatoon naturally look upon the university as its greatest asset. They are not broadminded enough to be willing to share it with Regina, even though their selfish attitude is robbing thousands of boys and girls of Regina and the South of university privileges." Stapleford saw more reason for optimism over the long term: "Before long Regina will have a population of 100,000. Surely the people of the South will arise in their might and demand university privileges for their children. Time is on your side Mr. Barr, but I wish you were twenty years younger so that you could carry this fight to a finish."[22]

Barr took up the campaign again February 1954, contributing two articles to the *Leader-Post*. This time he had the newspaper in his corner. An editorial, "Let Regina College Grow," praised his articles as "most timely" and endorsed the idea of a full degree program. The paper called upon Regina's three MLAs and two provincial Cabinet ministers to apply pressure on the provincial government to expand the college.[23] Three weeks later a delegation including Duncan Grosch, president of the Regina Chamber of Commerce, V.R. Metheral, chairman of the Regina Trades and Labour Council, and A.E. Wilson, president of the Central Council of Regina Home and School Associations, appeared before City Council to request that a public meeting be held to discuss the question.[24]

The mayor called the meeting, which took place on 19 March 1954 at City Hall auditorium with about 150 people in attendance. Barr spoke for a full hour, and then there were several shorter speeches, some supporting and others opposing the proposed degree program. F.G. England, a former alderman who had arrived in Regina in 1887, claimed that the residents of the city would be breaking faith with the pioneers if they did not build a university in Regina. A.E. Wilson declared, "It is a serious matter when a youngster with a brilliant public and high school record cannot go to higher education because his parents have not sufficient funds to send him out of the city." D.J. Thom, however, thought that "too much attention is being given today to the importance of a degree." Saskatchewan, he believed, should have one university of standing rather than a multiplicity of small colleges. R.A. Milliken, a graduate of the University of Saskatchewan College of Law, supported Thom's position. He claimed that in other cities where junior colleges had been built up into universities enrolment had declined, but where they had evolved into vocational colleges it had increased.[25]

At the end of the discussion Barr moved and Metheral seconded a resolution, which was voted on and approved:

Whereas there is an ever-increasing number of young people in the City of Regina, qualifying for a University course, whose parents cannot afford to send them away from home for such a course, and

Whereas Regina has the largest school population in the Province, and

Whereas it is in the public interest that they should be given the opportunity to develop their latent talents and thus be fully equipped to take their rightful place as useful citizens, and

Whereas the Citizens of Regina, in addition to contributing their fair share of taxes to equip and maintain the Provincial University at Saskatoon, have provided at Regina College buildings and equipment worth approximately a million dollars, for the higher education of our youth, and,

Whereas Regina College was taken over in 1934 and became an integral part or branch of the State University of the Province as a public institution,

Now therefore be it resolved that we, a representative meeting of the Citizens of Regina hereby request the government of the Province of Saskatchewan to take the necessary steps to give Regina College its rightful status, in fact, as a branch of the Provincial University, by empowering it to give our students a four-year course [including the matriculation year] leading to a Bachelor of Arts degree, and further, that in the annual appropriation of public funds for higher education, a sufficient portion thereof be earmarked for such purpose, and that a copy of this resolution be sent to every member of the Legislative Assembly of this Province, in the hope that our youth will receive justice at their hands, and thus be enabled to make the greatest possible contribution to human welfare.[26]

The Regina College Citizens' Committee was set up to work for the implementation of the resolution. It had three subcommittees (finance, research, and publicity) whose members belonged to a broad spectrum of community organizations. Most had modest middle-class or working-class backgrounds. Among them were four managers, two lawyers, two teachers, a medical doctor, a farmer, an engineer, a jeweller, a hardware store owner, the general secretary of the YMCA, the wife of a dentist, the wife of a teacher, a printer, and a unionized employee from the Department of Highways.[27] The finance subcommittee was composed of V.R. Metheral, chairman (employee of the Saskatchewan Department of Highways and president of the Regina Trades and Labour Council); D. Duncan Grosch (manager of the Montreal Trust Company and president of the Regina Chamber of Commerce); G.N. Menzies (compositor at Commercial Printers and a former alderman); and G.H. Barr (lawyer). The members of the research subcommittee were J.E.R. Doxsee, chairman (teacher for the Collegiate Institute Board); Dr George

Walton (medical health officer for the City of Regina); Alex Aitken (manager of the Regina Chamber of Commerce); Mrs J.R. Hoag (wife of a dentist and past president of the Regina Local Council of Women); Mrs F.S. Rawlinson (a former alderwoman and wife of a teacher at Balfour Technical School); Leslie C. Sherman (an alderman and teacher for the Collegiate Institute Board); J.W. Peart (president of T.W. Peart Ltd hardware store and chairman of the Public School Board); James Grassick (farmer); P.F. Groome (assistant chief engineer at City Light and Power); and V.E. Nordlund (retired). The publicity subcommittee included: J.J. McLean, chairman (manager of City Dairy and past president of the Regina branch of the Canadian Legion); George Bothwell (manager of an advertising agency); A.E. Wilson (president of the Central Council of Regina Home and School Associations); E.H.M. Knowles (lawyer); F.G. England (proprietor of England's Jewellers, Regina pioneer, and a former alderman); W.A. Wellband (general secretary of the YMCA); and A. Swartzfield (occupation unknown).

It is worth noting that the members of the Regina College Citizens' Committee did not represent the wealthiest segment of the population. The rich had always been able to afford to send their children to the University of Saskatchewan, or to McGill University, the University of Toronto, or some other out-of-province institution.[28] The main impetus for the establishment of a university in Regina came from community-minded people of modest means for whom university education represented a heavy expense. George Barr was not a wealthy man. When he and his wife sold their Scarth Street home in 1956, they moved into a small bungalow in Hillsdale.[29] Their son Robert, also a lawyer, had nine children, many of whom doubtless aspired to a university education. It is possible that George Barr had them in mind when he launched his campaign for a university in Regina.[30]

The Regina College Citizens' Committee did not receive support from the principals of the city collegiates. T.W. Hunt, principal of Central Collegiate, said in March 1954 that he was satisfied with Regina College's status as a junior college. He thought it unlikely that there would be a sufficient number of students in the immediate future to warrant the additional expenditure of a degree program. T.W. Cowburn, principal of Balfour Technical School, held the opinion that while there might be an argument for second-year arts in Regina, a full course was not advisable until the city had grown considerably larger. A third principal took the view that if a boy or girl were truly determined to acquire a university degree, "there is nothing in the world to stop them." Why he knew of many students who had worked their way through university, "at great personal sacrifice no doubt," and had succeeded beyond their wildest expectations. The deputy chairman of the Public School Board predicted that in time Regina would have a full university, but that day was a long way off.[31]

Father Athol Murray, president of Notre Dame College in Wilcox, a small town near Regina, took a different view of the matter. He thought that Regina needed not merely a degree course but "a full-fledged, chartered UNIVERSITY OF REGINA." Very much in harmony with George Barr, Father Murray demanded that society give higher priority to the needs of youth: "When one considers the implications of this all-important question of our youth, the broken lives, the defeated hopes and the national frustrations and failures which result from the frivolous inertia with which it is treated, it is difficult to restrain within oneself a savage rage." Canada was a wealthy country, he said, and it could afford to spend more money on education: "Not all your love for sport, not all your fine cars and new houses, not all your financial success, can ever move back the finger of fate. Tomorrow science and Saskatchewan, and Canada, will have moved forward one more step, and there will be no appeal on the judgment which will then be pronounced on an uneducated Saskatchewan."[32]

E.C. Leslie, a Regina lawyer and a member of the university Board of Governors, attended the public meeting on 19 March 1954 that had launched the campaign of the Regina College Citizens' Committee. He submitted a private report to President Thompson about what Barr had said and the reaction to his speech. Scanning the audience, Leslie noticed that Barr's supporters "were mostly people who have children coming along to an age where if they want a University education they will have to leave Regina, and they were naturally prejudiced in favour of establishing Regina College on a full Arts degree basis." Leslie did not see much of a threat to the university in the agitation. He advised Thompson to remain calm and avoid a public statement. "Sometimes," Leslie wrote, "a reply to statements which one does not like serves only to prolong a controversy which would otherwise die down." Leslie did not regard Barr as a serious opponent. On the contrary, he dismissed him as "a smouldering volcano of ancient hates and grudges."[33]

When Woodrow Lloyd, the minister of education, received the Regina College Citizens' Committee resolution, he forwarded it to President Thompson and asked him to provide "the official point of view of the University."[34] In advancing the request, Lloyd said that he did not think the movement had "any very wide-spread support."[35] A joint committee of the Board of Governors and senate prepared a report, which was duly submitted to Lloyd on 25 May 1954.[36] Divided into three sections, it comprehensively set forth the university's position.[37] Part 1 attempted to refute the charge that Regina College had been neglected and underfunded. According to the university's calculations, it had spent $315,400 on the institution since 1934, above and beyond the college's share of provincial and federal government grants based on the ratio of full-time degree students at Regina to those at Saskatoon.

Part 2 presented the case against establishing a degree course in Regina. It began with the warning that "if the Government were to take the action requested in the resolution, it would mean direct governmental interference in University affairs." This implied that it was up to the university, not the government, to decide whether Regina should have a degree program. Secondly, the university maintained that the youth of Saskatchewan were better served by a single strong university than by a number of weak colleges dispersed throughout the province. If Regina were to have a full arts course, then Moose Jaw, Prince Albert, and North Battleford would want one, too. The concept of one first-class university in Saskatchewan would be destroyed.

The report added up the average cost for a student enrolled in an academic term of seven and a half months in the College of Arts and Science in Saskatoon:

Tuition	$175.00
Incidental fees (including health services	$37.50
Board and room (two students per residence room	$400.00
Clothes, laundry, entertainment, transportation	$250.00
Total	$862.50

A student living at home, the report estimated, would save only $250 per year. It was suggested that out-of-town students could easily borrow this sum. As to the claim of the Regina College Citizens' Committee that young people in Regina were being denied a university education, the report conceded that "in many cases some degree of sacrifice will be necessary to enable a boy or girl to attend university." Rather than seeking to ease the burden on Regina students by making a degree course available at Regina College, the report argued that "it would seem better to undergo an even greater measure of sacrifice in order to enable students to have the benefit of the much greater opportunity which a strong central institution affords."

According to the university, the cost of providing an arts course in Regina would be substantial. A large capital outlay would be needed to expand laboratories, classrooms, and the library, not to mention an additional annual expenditure of $90,000 to maintain a larger staff. Since it was not expected that many students would enrol in the Regina degree program, the expenditures would be out of all proportion to the returns. The university said that it had other needs that were far more pressing, including a veterinary college, a dental college, a course in physiotherapy, a "school for rural girls like the School of Vocational Agriculture for boys," and departments in sociology, geography, anthropology, and archaeology.

Part 3 laid out a vision for the development of Regina College. According to the report, the residents of Regina would be best served by a community college offering first-year university courses, terminal courses of a vocational and semi-professional type, and an assortment of classes in music and art. It was obvious that the university had made no concessions to the demands of the Regina College Citizens' Committee. The 1954 report, which received the unanimous approval of the Board of Governors and senate, was essentially a dusted-off version of the 1932 Learned Report. The message was the same: no university in Regina.[38] The capital city reacted with sharp disappointment, and the *Leader-Post* published a cartoon depicting the education system in Regina as an uncompleted building that was missing its capstone.[39]

In June 1954, following the release of the university's report, the committee asked for an interview with the provincial Cabinet.[40] The government put off the meeting until 2 December 1954, at which time the committee presented a brief that attempted to refute the report.[41] The brief had the endorsement of seven home and school clubs, the Regina Trades and Labour Council, the women's auxiliary of the Regina branch of the Canadian Legion, and the Zion United Church Women's Association. It challenged the university's statement that the province could afford to support only one university. According to the brief, the Maritime provinces, with a population of 642,584, had one college for every 91,798 people. Ontario, with 4,797,542 people, had eight universities and colleges, or one for every 599,692 people. In Manitoba the ratio was one for every 388,271 people. Saskatchewan was out of line with the rest of Canada — it had only one university for 843,000 people.

As for the contention that there were not enough students in Regina to support a degree course, the brief stated that such an argument "comes with poor grace from those who have themselves created this situation by discouraging attendance at Regina College." Many students chose not to enrol at the college because they knew they would have to leave after one year. "It is a principle very well established at common law," Barr argued, "that no person can take advantage of the non-fulfillment of a condition the performance of which has been hindered by himself." The brief also rejected the idea that the government did not have the right to force the university to establish a degree course in Regina. Barr maintained that it was a fundamental rule of interpretation that "wherever any body appointed by the state is given a monopoly, the section granting such monopoly must be most strictly construed and the parties given such monopoly should be limited to the powers so granted." The University Act of 1907 gave to the University of Saskatchewan monopoly degree-granting power (except for theology), but "to extend that power to enable the governing body to deprive any branch of the University except those situated at Saskatoon of the right to give a course leading to a degree would in effect change the Act and enable the governing body of the University to encroach upon the jurisdiction of the legislature." If a degree program were introduced in Regina, the University of Saskatchewan would still control the content of courses, the standard of scholarship, and the granting of degrees. This, the Regina Citizens' Committee asserted, would not detract from the university, but add to its usefulness.

Although the brief did not have short-term results, Barr kept up the pressure. He addressed a meeting of the Regina Trades and Labour Council in February 1955, urging its members to support a call for an amendment to the University Act to provide for the establishment and maintenance of a full arts course in Regina. "The time has come," he declared, "for a showdown with the university authorities to see that Regina College is given its true status." He added that it was fitting for him to place the proposal before the labour council, since it had been the first organization in Regina to come out wholeheartedly in support of the degree program and the first to make a "substantial monetary contribution" to the Regina Citizens' Committee. Barr was gratified also to have encouragement from Ross Thatcher, then the CCF member of Parliament for Moose Jaw-Lake Center (before he switched over to the Liberal Party), who came out strongly for a degree course at Regina College.[42]

A *Leader-Post* editorial, "Perseverance Will Be Rewarded," published on 28 March 1955, underlined the fact that high school enrolment was increasing at a rapid pace. Other provinces had seen the writing on the wall and were taking action to expand opportunities for university education. The Ontario government had recently announced an expansion of post-secondary education facilities at Lakehead College in Port Arthur (now Lakehead University), and British Columbia was in the process of enlarging Victoria College (now the University of Victoria) and affiliating it with the University of British Columbia. The lessons for Saskatchewan were obvious: "The time will come, and it is not far away, when the university and government will have to yield to the strong case which is being presented on behalf of the extension of Regina College — a case that is growing stronger daily."[43]

J. Francis Leddy, the dean of arts and science in Saskatoon, claimed in June 1955 that the increase in university enrolment in Saskatchewan was not expected to exceed 25 per cent in the next ten years, a rate of growth that he said was "quite manageable with our present university capacity."[44] President Thompson delivered the same erroneous message to the university senate in November 1955. He stated that while Canadian universities as a whole could expect an increase in student population of 55 per cent by 1961–62, the University of Saskatchewan could expect growth of only 18 per cent over the same period. The main reason for the difference was the loss of population Saskatchewan had experienced in the 1930s and early 1940s. A secondary factor was the relatively small percentage of Saskatchewan high school graduates who attended university: 4.1 per cent in 1951 as compared with the national average of 7.2 per cent.[45] What actually happened was quite different from what Leddy and Thompson predicted. University enrolment in Saskatchewan grew from 3,156 in 1955 to 11,192 in 1965, an increase of over 250 per cent.[46]

The League of Women Voters in Regina sponsored a public debate on Regina College expansion on 28 April 1955. Duncan Grosch, past president of the Regina Chamber of Commerce and secretary-treasurer of the Regina College Citizens' Committee, remarked that, with a provincial election looming, the topic was likely to emerge as a "red hot political issue." Dean Leddy, who argued the university's case in the debate, criticized what he termed the "reckless and irresponsible" statements and "muddled thinking" of Regina College supporters.[47] He mentioned in the course of his remarks that in 1954–55 492 students from Saskatoon and 274 from Regina had been enrolled at the Saskatoon campus.[48] J. Foster, secretary of the Regina Trades and Labour Council, seized on these figures as proof that about 500 Regina young people were being denied a university education. He said that if Saskatoon, with a population of 53,000, sent 492 students to the University of Saskatchewan, then Regina, with a population of 75,000, ought to have supplied at least 750. (Foster's population figures for Saskatoon and Regina were out of date. The correct number for Saskatoon in 1955 was 61,167; for Regina, 83,216.)

Foster estimated the total cost of a year at university at the Saskatoon campus for a Regina student at about $1,500. If a university program were available in Regina, the cost would be $300 to $400 — a saving of about $1,100 per year.[49] Leddy disputed these calculations. According to him, the total cost of a university year at Saskatoon for an out-of-town student was only $825, and therefore the savings to a Regina student, if the degree course had been offered in his or her hometown, would be in the order of $400 per year, far less than Foster's estimate of $1,100. Leddy also pointed out that in counting up the number of Regina students attending university, Foster had failed to include Regina students who had enrolled in out-of-province universities.[50]

E.C. Leslie kept President Thompson apprised of developments in Regina. He reported that only about 125 people had attended the debate and that "there [was] no great public demand in Regina for the establishment of a full arts course at the College." His advice to Thompson was that the university "remain silent." Leslie thought that it had been a mistake for Leddy to participate in the debate because it just kept the pot boiling.[51] Thompson agreed. The debate, he believed, had served no useful purpose and had only made trouble for the university.

Riddell's assessment of the state of public opinion differed substantially from that of Leslie. The dean considered it significant that the Trades and Labour Councils of both Regina and Moose Jaw supported the establishment of a degree program in Regina. These were the very groups whose opinion counted with the CCF government. As Riddell wrote in a memo to Thompson, "Since this group represents a section of the population where financial barriers to education are the most evident, these representations are certain to carry a lot of weight with the government." The debate, Riddell added, had "stirred up some of the older and influential people in Regina," and "continuation of the dispute through the local press [had] not helped in any way." He was encountering increasing numbers of people, not only in Regina but throughout the southern part of the province, who were "outspokenly in favor of extending the work as proposed by Mr. Barr." Moreover, Riddell detected "an increasing body of antagonism developing toward the University," and this was found "not only among the uneducated or uninformed but includes many who are university graduates and hold positions of some importance in their communities." He thought that the university had made a mistake in formulating its own response to the report of the Regina College Citizens' Committee. From a public relations point of view, it would have been better to refer the matter to an independent (or seemingly independent) commission, as Walter Murray had done when faced with a similar situation in 1932.[52] Thompson replied that he had approached the Carnegie Corporation to carry out a study, but it had turned him down.[53]

The Regina Trades and Labour Council (TLC) in June 1955 sent a brief to the premier, the Regina representatives in the provincial Cabinet, and the Regina members of the university Board of Governors. It placed the issue of educational opportunities in the context of the Cold War, claiming that Russia had one university student for every 150 of population compared to one for every 250 in Canada. "At the present rate," the brief stated, "by 1960, Russia will be training more scientists and engineers than all the NATO countries combined, something we can ill afford to have happen!" The brief took note of demographic trends projecting enrolment increases in Canada by 1961 of 42 per cent in elementary schools and 51 per cent in secondary schools: "The time has arrived for proper planning for the future educational needs of the people, not only of Regina and the southern part of the province, but all of Saskatchewan and all of Canada."

Premier T.C. Douglas underlined this sentence in his copy of the brief, as well as the statements "The paying for board away from home means many children are not able to receive university training" and "There are some who will try to make out that it costs very little more to feed and cloth [*sic*] a youth away from home. We have only to examine the income of some parents and the size of their families to ask ourselves if it would be possible to board them all out on his income. Then, too, a youth when at home, while going to University can help and aid the family in many ways — this is lost when they are away, making the problem more difficult for the parents." The Regina TLC acknowledged the argument made by university officials that centralizing facilities enhanced opportunities for the students who attended the Saskatoon campus. Their counter-argument was that the benefits of centralization did nothing for the students who could not afford to go there.[54] Both the Moose Jaw TLC and Regina Local 1867 of the United Brotherhood of Carpenters and Joiners of America endorsed the brief.[55]

Regina City Council sent a petition to the members of the legislature in February 1956. The council members had wanted to present it in person to the Cabinet, but they were told that the Cabinet ministers were too busy to receive the delegation. The brief repeated the by-now-familiar arguments and introduced a few new ones. It emphasized that Saskatchewan was the only province in Canada whose largest city did not offer its young people a degree course, and Regina was "the only city in Canada of comparable size without degree-granting facilities." The council also claimed that the cost of expansion had been greatly exaggerated. With a small addition to the facilities and staff already in place in Regina, a full degree course could be given.[56]

The issue flared up in the 1956 provincial election campaign. A.H. McDonald, leader of the Liberal Party and of the official opposition, made public his support for a degree course at Regina College. Woodrow Lloyd asked, "Has the Liberal Party thought it through? Or is it just one more addition to the price of votes in Regina?" He accused the Liberals of turning the university into a "political football."[57] Marjorie Cooper, a CCF candidate in Regina, declared in a radio broadcast, "The decision regarding an arts course for Regina College is one that must be made by the university authorities, not by the government." It was a "real tragedy," she added, that the Liberals had brought the matter into the political arena. The Liberal government in 1907 had drawn up the University Act with the express purpose of insulating the university from political interference. This was a wise policy, she said, and ought to be respected.[58]

The Liberal candidates in Regina in the 20 June 1956 election, all of whom supported the expansion of Regina College,[59] went down in defeat. Cooper and her CCF colleagues were re-elected, and the government returned to power. The issue had been handled quite differently in Alberta. There the legislature unanimously approved a motion supporting the expansion of university facilities in Calgary and Lethbridge. No one had charged the opposition Liberals, who had introduced the resolution, with interfering in the affairs of the Edmonton-based University of Alberta. It was considered normal in Alberta for elected officials to talk openly about the extension of university opportunities, but in Saskatchewan politicians who broached the issue were attacked.[60] The one-university concept was deeply entrenched, rooted as it was in the early days of the formation of the province, when "Regina got the capital and Saskatoon got the university."

George Barr returned to the fight in December 1956, issuing a pamphlet titled "Wake Up, Regina! A Call to Action." Now seventy-eight years old, he had lost none of his enthusiasm for the cause. He recounted that when the TLC delegation had appeared before the Cabinet, they were told that they should be more interested in a technical institute than a university. Barr thundered that "this was certainly no compliment to the working people of this City. Are not their children just as much entitled to a liberal education as any other people in the City?" He appealed to the higher aims of the people of Regina: "The greatness of a City does not depend on bricks and mortar, but rather on the character, ideals and aspirations of its citizens." Barr recalled that on the afternoon of 30 June 1912 he had stood at the window of his home and watched as two blocks away a cyclone levelled the houses along Lorne Street: "How did our citizens react in the face of that disaster? In a space of hours I think every able-bodied man and woman joined in a great community effort to overcome that calamity and never ceased in their efforts until the City was re-built. That is the spirit of Regina. We are now facing another challenge involving the lives and welfare of our children – a situation which is artificial and man-made. I am confident with the same community spirit and united effort we can successfully meet this challenge."[61] Boasting that the Regina TLC, the Regina local of the wheat pool, the alumni association of Moose Jaw Teachers College, and the home and school clubs of Regina all supported a degree course for Regina College, he urged these and other organizations to circulate petitions for presentation to the legislature at the next session.

In the broader context, the provincial economy was booming, the grim legacy of the 1930s Depression now left behind. Farm income rose steadily, and average farm size increased from 551 acres in 1951 to 686 acres in 1961. Even more important, the economy became more diversified and therefore more stable. In 1945 agriculture had accounted for 78 per cent of commodity output; by 1959 this figure had fallen to about 40 per cent.[62] Oil production, which had been a meagre 1,019 barrels per day in 1944–45, rose to 145,000 barrels in 1960, 28 per cent of total Canadian output.[63] Natural gas production soared from one billion cubic feet per year to over 15.5 billion in the period 1951–60, the value of uranium production reached nearly $60 million in 1958, and the province's first potash mine went into full-scale production in 1962. Provincial finances were robust, revenues rising from $63.5 million in 1950–51 to $143 million in 1958-59, resulting in an unbroken string of surplus budgets.[64] The strong economy led to an increase in the population of the province from 831,728 to 925,181 in 1961 (an increase of 93,453). Close to 41,100 of this increase was attributable to Regina, whose share of the total provincial population grew from 8.6 to 12.1 per cent.[65] From an economic perspective, the time seemed ripe for university expansion.

The pressures of the baby boom made opposition to a degree program in Regina increasingly untenable. By the mid-1950s it was evident from elementary and secondary school enrolments that universities had to prepare for a flood of students. Edward Sheffield, a federal government consultant, predicted in 1955 that owing to demographic pressure alone university enrolment would double by 1965.[66] But demography was not the only factor. In the 1950s business, government, and individual citizens began to attach a higher value to university education. As mentioned previously, the 1957 launch of the Soviet satellite Sputnik spread fear that the West was losing the race for supremacy in science and technology. Many concluded that more money had to be invested in university training of scientists and engineers. Equally significant from the 1950s to the 1970s was an expansion of white-collar employment in administration, finance, and the public sector.[67] Because advanced levels of education were required for these white-collar positions, university education was in high demand. It was considered the ticket to a middle-class standard of living. In 1951, only one in twenty Canadian eighteen year olds went to university. By the mid-1960s, it was one in ten; and by the early 1970s, one in six.[68]

The University of Saskatchewan was feeling the pressure. In 1958 the decision was made to restrict enrolment in first-year engineering to 400 (Saskatoon and Regina combined), because the university did not have the capacity to handle more than this number in the second, third, and fourth years.[69] This was not good public relations for the Saskatoon campus, especially at a time when government and society placed such a high premium on the applied sciences. The minister of education, Woodrow Lloyd, intimated in a memo to Premier Douglas on 30 December 1958 that the time had come to consider expansion of university facilities in Regina:

> It seems to me that one point which should be considered when thinking of our next term's program is the extension of University facilities. I am not thinking just of additional buildings but rather of possible developments in Regina. You may recall that I have stated that there was no argument on my part against the development of more extensive facilities here once the enrolment at Saskatoon had developed to the point at which extension became desirable from the point of view of finances and also of educational returns. I don't know what size the University ought to achieve before thoughts are given to a second institution. Without any real reason I have always thought in terms of about 6,000 students as a reasonable size. I believe Dr. Thomp-

son said a few weeks ago he had thought in terms of 7,000. At any rate, it seems likely that the enrolment of Saskatoon will reach the 6,000 level within the next few years. Even with possible expansion at Regina it is certain I think that the enrolment at Saskatoon would continue to increase.

I wonder, then, if we should not be giving this matter some serious thought and if we ought to be discussing it at least with the President. I have not put this idea forth to anyone else. Perhaps we could talk about it some time.[70]

President Thompson, addressing the alumni banquet in Saskatoon on 7 May 1959, hinted that a change of policy was in the offing. He said that since enrolment at the University of Saskatchewan had doubled in the past six years, it might now be desirable to "develop branches in other centers." He acknowledged that there were differences of opinion as to how large a university should grow. The University of British Columbia had 10,000 students; the University of Toronto had 14,000. In his judgment the optimum number was "below either of those figures."[71]

A forward planning committee reported to the university Board of Governors in June 1959 that the upper limit on enrolment at Saskatoon should be set at "approximately double the present number," or about 8,000 students.[72] According to projections, full-time enrolment at Saskatoon was expected to reach 7,250 in 1964–65. The report went on to say that a limit on enrolment at the Saskatoon campus implied "the development of facilities for university education elsewhere in the Province." It recommended to the board "that the first step in such a development be the establishment at Regina of a three-year course leading to a Bachelor of Arts degree." Specifically, the recommendation was "that the second-year of the course be instituted in 1961–1962 and the final year as soon as staff and buildings are available and that this expansion be completed before considering other programs."[73]

This was a pivotal development because it led eventually to the establishment of a separate University of Regina. The decision was directly related to the anticipated large increase in student numbers and the need for new buildings and facilities at the Saskatoon campus. To pay for the expansion, the university considered mounting a major fundraising campaign. It hired a consulting firm, G.A. Brakeley and Company of Montreal, which had conducted campaigns for a number of other universities, to prepare a preliminary study. The firm reported that there was a reasonable chance for a successful campaign to raise $2.5 million, provided certain conditions were met. One of the conditions, which the firm "stressed very strongly," was that the university make "a clear statement regarding the policy for Regina College."[74] John Spinks, who succeeded W.P. Thompson as president of the university in October 1959, succinctly summarized the consulting firm's message: "no

Regina, no money."[75] There was little chance the fundraising campaign could achieve its objective without the support of Regina and southern Saskatchewan, and there was no hope of obtaining that support without expansion of university facilities in Regina.

The report of the forward planning committee went to the Board of Governors on 17 June 1959. The board, after discussing the matter, voted to submit the following resolution to senate: "Whereas the estimated enrolment on the Saskatoon campus will be 7,500 by 1964–65 and whereas when that number is reached it appears desirable to offer a three-year degree course in Arts and Science at Regina as soon as possible, be it resolved that the University gradually develop a three-year program in Arts and Science at Regina leading to a Bachelor of Arts degree by providing a second-year course in the year 1961–62 and the final year as soon as staff and accommodation are available, and that for the purpose of implementing this expansion the necessary study and planning be undertaken immediately to ensure the provision of adequate staff, buildings and campus area." The board agreed at the same time to "proceed with a fund solicitation campaign with an objective of $2,500,000 and that G.A. Brakeley and Company be employed as professional counsel."[76]

Before the senate dealt with the resolution, it received a report from the University Council. At a meeting of council on 6 July 1959, a number of faculty members expressed opposition to expansion in Regina on the grounds that it would result in unnecessary duplication of programs and weaken the quality of the work done in Saskatoon.[77] As the discussion dragged on, people left the meeting, until finally someone asked whether there was a quorum. President Thompson, who was chairing the meeting, stated that while the University Act required that senate receive the advice of council on academic matters, it did not have to follow that advice. He said he would "record that the vote was taken without quorum, but he meant to have the vote."[78] The council, "by a large majority,"[79] approved in principle the board's resolution of 17 June for a degree program in Regina.[80]

The senate considered the resolution on 8 July 1959. R.H. Macdonald, a Saskatoon faculty member, brought up the fact that in the past President Thompson had always opposed expansion of the work at Regina College beyond first-year arts and science. Why, he wondered, had the president reversed his position? According to W.A. Riddell, when Thompson heard this, his "pipe cocked up to the highest point possible and he quietly but very firmly pointed out that when new information or new needs arose, he could and would change his position and hoped it would always be so."[81] In reply to a question about whether the degree course at Regina College would create a rivalry between the two institutions, Thompson answered that the college would still be part of the university, not a separate entity. In the end the senate voted unanimously to approve the resolution.[82]

President Thompson took full responsibility for the decision and never sought to shift blame or credit to the provincial government.[83] It was fairly clear from Woodrow Lloyd's letter to Premier Douglas on 30 December 1958 that the government wanted the expansion to occur. Lloyd's conversion was significant. Throughout the 1950s he had defended the university's policy concerning development in Regina, so much so that George Barr referred to him as the "bête noire of his dreams."[84] There is no evidence that Lloyd told Thompson what to do. It seems more likely that both men came to the same conclusion at about the same time. However, it is quite possible that Thompson was influenced by what he knew to be the drift of government opinion. His parting words of advice to his successor, John Spinks, were, "But don't forget where the money comes from."[85]

When, in July 1959, the university announced its intention to establish a full degree course in Regina, the Saskatoon *Star-Phoenix* was not unfriendly. The paper emphasized that the university had acted "independently of any government or political pressure."[86] Regina City Council approved a motion addressed to the president of the university that read, "On behalf of the citizens of Regina we would like to express our delight and appreciation, through you to the university council, the senate, and the Board of Governors regarding today's announcement about the future plans for Regina College. Parents and young people in Regina and throughout southern Saskatchewan rejoice at this decision, as well as future generations yet unborn." Alderman M.V. Matthews paid special tribute to George Barr and his wife. "They carried the torch," he said, "even in the darkest hours."[87]

There was a good deal of truth to this. Barr had supported the cause even when it had not been popular to do so. When the Regina College Advisory Board in 1952 said a degree program was not necessary and when the high school principals of Regina mused about how good it was for young people to make sacrifices in order to have the privilege of attending university, he persisted in his quest. He was not afraid to make a spectacle of himself for what he considered to be a good cause. Finally, in 1959, he had the satisfaction of seeing his goal realized. Ironically, the strongest advocate for the youth of Regina was eighty-one years old.

6 Laying the Foundations

Once the decision had been made to establish a full degree program in Regina, attention turned to the work that needed to be done. What would be the nature of the academic program, which courses would be taught, and who would be hired to teach them? Would the new campus be restricted to arts and science or would there also be professional colleges, and, if so, which ones, and in what sequence would they be developed? What new buildings would be required, how large should they be, and in what order should they be built? Even more basic were the questions of who would be responsible for making these decisions, how would the Regina campus be organized, and what procedures would be followed in formulating and implementing policies. Was the development of the campus to be directed from Saskatoon, or would faculty and administrators in Regina take the leading role?

To answer at least some of these questions, the University Council, senate, and Board of Governors established in November 1959 the Special Joint Committee on Regina College Expansion and Administration Procedures. Its report, which was presented to council on 29 April 1960, recommended "that the objective for Regina be full status as a campus." The council modified this to read, "it is recommended that the objective for Regina be an institution having a large measure of autonomy." The report noted that the second year of arts and science had already been approved, and "the third year and full degree program will be offered as enrolment warrants it." "In the long range planning, as enrolment increases," the report continued, it is quite possible that other colleges and courses at the degree level, with the exception of Agriculture and Medicine, would be developed at Regina. It is difficult, at present, to determine how far this development will go and how fast this development would take place, but the present decisions should be such that they do not impose any undue limitations. The question of developing other colleges at Regina would be determined when the plateau or optimum size for the colleges at Saskatoon had been reached, and the college should then be divided and another branch developed at Regina. It was suggested that possibly one of the smaller colleges should be transferred to Regina in the early stages of development. The development of colleges and courses at Regina should provide for diversity and coordination between the two campuses. The general pattern of courses should be similar and provision should be made for uniformity in standards, examination procedures, treatment of students, etc. consistent with the general objective of a campus enjoying a large measure of autonomy and one which might usefully introduce some diversity in course offerings.[1]

With respect to organizational structure, the report suggested one board of governors, one senate, and one president for both campuses. Eventually each campus would have its own council responsible for academic programs and policies reporting directly to the senate, with the president serving as chairman of both councils. The council of the Regina campus would be formed "when the faculty was strong enough and sufficiently diversified to warrant this change." This might take place between 1962 and 1964, but "no later than the introduction of the third year of the B.A. course." A joint committee of the two councils was to be established as a coordinating body to deal with issues affecting both campuses. The joint committee would report to both councils, and either council could report to the senate. However, when one of the councils did so on a matter affecting both campuses, it would have to indicate whether or not the joint committee had approved the recommendation.

The report stated that colleges and departments at the new campus should be patterned on those of Saskatoon. The heads of the corresponding departments at the two campuses were to meet periodically – at least once a year. It was further recommended that in the interim period, until the Regina departments were larger, chairmen of groups of departments, to be known as chairmen of divisions, were to be appointed in Regina – one for each of the natural sciences, social sciences, humanities, and fine arts. Appointments at the Regina campus were to be handled by an appointments committee consisting of the president, the head of the Regina campus, the dean of arts and science (Saskatoon), the head of the department (Saskatoon), a member of the Board of Governors, and the division chairman in Regina. Later, when Regina had advanced to a full arts program, the head of the department in

Regina was to take the place of the head of the department in Saskatoon on the appointments committee. The appointments committee for chairmen of the divisions comprised the president, two deans (Saskatoon), two heads of related departments (Saskatoon), a member of the Board of Governors, and the head of the Regina campus. The report envisaged that a dean of arts and science for Regina would be appointed by the time a full degree course had been established. It further advised that the head of the Regina campus have the title "principal and vice-president of the University of Saskatchewan at Regina."

After having been debated and approved by council, the report received approval from the Board of Governors on 4 May 1960 and from senate on 11 May. The document set forth a process of development in Regina that was closely controlled by Saskatoon. Saskatoon-dominated committees were responsible for making recommendations for appointments of faculty, and the Saskatoon-dominated University Council was responsible for setting academic policy until some vaguely specified time ("between 1962 and 1964, but no later than the introduction of the third year of the B.A. course"), when a council was to be established in Regina. The report also made clear that the "general pattern and structure of courses, academic standards, and examination procedures" were to follow the Saskatoon model. The only indication of possible deviation related to the chairmen of divisions at Regina, for whom there was no counterpart in Saskatoon. The report assumed that the divisions were merely an interim measure made necessary by the small size of departments in the early phase of the development of the campus. However, Colb McEown, assistant to the president, noted in the course of the senate discussion that "it [was] possible that the divisional approach and not the departmental approach might develop."[2] This was the only hint that Regina might set out on a path of its own.

One of the key issues was the appointment of an executive officer for the Regina campus. A.W. Johnson, deputy provincial treasurer and a member of the Board of Governors, advised President Thompson in September 1959 that it would be necessary to appoint "an Assistant President or Associate President" to take charge of developments in Regina.[3] Thompson, as we have seen, retired at the end of October 1959, leaving to his successor, John W.T. Spinks, the task of creating a second campus and making the one-university/two-campus system work. Born the son of a livestock seller in 1908 in a small village in Norfolk, England, Spinks won a series of scholarships that led eventually to a doctorate in chemistry at King's College, University of London. He joined the Department of Chemistry at the University of Saskatchewan in 1930 and quickly gained a reputation as a research scientist of the first rank. He ascended the academic ladder, becoming head of the chemistry department, dean of the graduate school, and, finally, president in 1959.[4]

Riddell told Spinks in October 1960 that the failure to appoint a principal for the new campus was hampering progress. As dean of Regina College, and nothing more than that, he did not have sufficient authority to take charge of planning and development. The disgruntled Riddell added, "The Principal, when appointed, should have a clear understanding of the responsibilities he must assume and authority that he is given to meet these responsibilities. At the present time the authority appears to rest with the heads of the subject departments and I have had no clear direction about the action I should take, the responsibilities that I have and the authority there may be to take action."[5] Riddell thought it important to begin recruiting senior professors in Regina as chairmen of divisions so that they could provide leadership in hiring new faculty and shaping the academic program. Spinks did not see the urgency. Riddell, he suggested, could rely on advice from senior faculty in Saskatoon. The trouble was that they had their own problems to deal with in managing the rapid expansion in Saskatoon and had little time to spare for Regina.[6]

Riddell worried, too, about the difficulty he was having in hiring librarians. He had attempted to recruit staff at the annual convention of the Canadian Librarians' Association in Montreal, but to no avail. Since practically every university in the country was trying to obtain librarians, the market was very competitive. Regina had to find a way to purchase and catalogue the books needed to support the introduction of the second-year arts and science program in the fall of 1961. Adding to the problem was the requirement that department heads in Saskatoon approve the lists of books to be acquired. Most of them did not have time for this task, and in a few cases the lists that had been sent to Saskatoon for approval were not even acknowledged.[7]

Riddell was also concerned that no announcement had been made of the site of the new campus. Nor was there any campus plan – or, as he advised Spinks in October 1960, "If there is, I have not been consulted nor have I seen one." Riddell said he had been told that the first building could be planned and built by the beginning of the 1962 fall term, but to him that did not seem very likely. "The impression is abroad here," the dean complained, "that no serious effort is being made, nor will be made to give the faculty of the College an opportunity to be involved with the planning. I have been holding them in check until now, but the concern has reached a level that has caused the members of the Faculty Association here to make representations to the Executive of the Association. It is the feeling of the group here, and I agree with them, that in the planning of the campus and the buildings every effort should be made to have the new institution something to be proud of, rather than one that was conceived in haste as seems to be the likelihood at this stage."[8]

Faculty members in Regina decided to do some planning on their own. They initiated discussions in the fall of 1959 concerning the purpose and content of the arts and science curriculum. As one of the participants wrote, "The philosophy of liberal arts was on the anvil."[9] None of the faculty members involved in these debates, and that included the dean, had any experience in designing or administering a full degree program. When Riddell pointed this out, some of them interpreted it as "an insult to the ability of the faculty." The incident, Riddell later admitted, drove "a small wedge" between him and the staff.[10]

The faculty produced a report, which was in some ways critical of the existing university curriculum. The latter had been in place, with minor modifications, since 1941. The Regina faculty called for a fresh, innovative approach with a view to providing liberal arts students with a well-rounded education. "From its very nature," the report asserted, "a comprehensive general education demands flexible, and to some degree experimental, curricular requirements and teaching methods. It must be able to incorporate new philosophical insights and the products of interdisciplinary studies." Two courses in particular were identified as inadequate. One was Physical Sciences 100, which was said to be deficient because it did not have a laboratory component. The other was History and Philosophy 200, which allegedly lacked "an integrated analysis of a common theme."[11]

A more general failure of the existing program of studies, in the opinion of the Regina faculty, was over-specialization. The report recommended the addition of two required classes outside the student's field of concentration. It also favoured a compulsory fine arts course, noting in this regard that "in view of the special resources of Regina College in this field" – namely, the Conservatory of Music and the School of Art – students should "be permitted to choose a class in one of the following: History and Appreciation of Music; a corresponding class in Art and Architecture; or in Drama." Finally, the report appealed for a spirit of freedom and innovation in curriculum planning and an adequate budget to support "experimentation with teaching methods, testing, texts, etc." in the early stages of the development of the Regina campus.[12]

The dean of arts, J. Francis Leddy, did not think much of these proposals. He said the notion of a mandatory course for liberal arts students in fine arts was "interesting," but he doubted that the Saskatoon faculty would accept the idea. While conceding that some variations might be allowed between Regina and Saskatoon, it would be better "not to have too many such differences."[13] The university's Regina Campus Expansion Committee on Course Content and Staff tersely concurred that "no radical experiments should be attempted at Regina for the time being, and the development there should be, as far as facilities permit, similar to that at Saskatoon."[14] As Riddell put it, Regina was free to do anything it liked, as long as "we did it the same as in Saskatoon."[15] The Regina Faculty Association complained to Spinks on 14 October 1960 that development was stalled and that they felt excluded from meaningful participation in the planning process. They said that they did not expect to have complete control, but rather "that the Regina staff, strengthened by the appointment of able and experienced persons and by the appointment of an executive head of this institution, should be participating more actively in a development which concerns us more than any other section of the University community."[16]

The feistiness of the Regina faculty was evident in the spirited debate over the name for the new campus. They voted on 11 April 1960 by a margin of 9 to 8 to call it the University of the Plains rather than the University of Saskatchewan at Regina.[17] Because of the close vote, the issue was tabled for consideration at another meeting. Physicist Len Greenberg and art instructors Ron Bloore and Art McKay[18] composed a joint memo in support of the name University of the Plains, which they thought expressed "the broad, free and expansive character of our environment."[19] Greenberg added, "An education is not complete unless it has breadth. Our plains have breadth. Education reaches out in all directions, it is not to be directed inwards. Our aim, to give a broad education, is well presented by the feature, the Plains."[20] The problem with the name University of Saskatchewan at Regina, he said, was that it reminded people of the older campus. It implied that Regina was an appendage of Saskatoon rather than an institution with an identity of its own.[21]

At the next meeting, on 25 April 1960, the faculty voted 18 to 7 for a name that did not include the words "University of Saskatchewan." The final ballot presented two choices: Regina University or University of the Plains. The former won by a vote of 15 to 5.[22] The Regina College Advisory Board, whose members were older and had been associated with the college for many years, did not agree with this decision. They thought, as did Riddell, that it was important to preserve the link with the University of Saskatchewan. Riddell believed that since it would be several years before Regina established its own reputation for academic excellence, it was necessary in the early years to lean on the prestige of the parent university. His personal preference was for the name University of Saskatchewan in Regina, but he told President Spinks that he would not object to either the University of Saskatchewan *at* Regina or the University of Saskatchewan, Regina Campus.[23]

The Board of Governors on 3 March 1961 approved a motion creating two campuses: the University of Saskatchewan, Saskatoon Campus, and the University of Saskatchewan, Regina Campus.[24] The senate endorsed the new designation for the Regina campus, but not the change of name for Saskatoon. The campus in Saskatoon was still to be known as the University of Saskatchewan. On 1 July 1961 Regina College officially passed out of existence,

The crest of the University of Saskatchewan, Regina Campus, signifying the new status acquired by Regina College on 1 July 1961.

fifty years after it had been founded as a Methodist college and twenty-seven years after it had become part of the University of Saskatchewan. It was now the University of Saskatchewan, Regina Campus.[25]

The Saskatoon *Star-Phoenix* marked the occasion with a tongue-in-cheek editorial suggesting that the name did not go far enough. The new campus should have been called the "University of Saskatchewan, Regina Campus (adopted)," the designation "adopted" signifying the parental relationship between the main university and the southern branch. The newspaper said it regretted that Regina had no means of acquiring prestige other than borrowing the nomenclature of the older and more respected institution. The "treeless waste of the Regina plains" made it impossible to lay claim to "a leafy-bowered, ivy-covered campus." And as for "rich cultural tradition," about the only names that sprang to mind were "Pile-o'-Bones U" or "Palliser's Prairie Paradise College of Knowledge." In the end, the newspaper concluded that the attempt to find a suitable name for the new campus was doomed, since Regina's drinking water atrophied the brain cells and put an end to intellectual progress on the Regina plain.[26]

Coincident with the name change, Riddell was appointed dean of the College of Arts and Science at Regina (as distinct from dean of Regina College) and acting principal of the University of Saskatchewan, Regina Campus.[27] Although the Joint Committee of the Board of Governors, Senate, and Council on Regina College Expansion and Administration Procedures had in April 1960 recommended that the head of the Regina campus be designated "principal and vice-president of the University of Saskatchewan at Regina," the title "vice-president" was withheld. Moreover, Riddell was made

The installation on 4 May 1963 at Knox-Metropolitan United Church of William A. Riddell (left) as principal of the University of Saskatchewan, Regina Campus. Shaking his hand is university president John Spinks.

"acting principal" rather than principal. His first reaction was to reject the appointment "on the grounds that either I was a suitable person as Principal or I was not."[28] President Spinks assured him that it was very likely he would be made principal, but the Board of Governors needed more time to consider the situation, an argument that Riddell did not find convincing. Nevertheless, he swallowed his pride and accepted the offer. Ten months later, on 8 April 1962, he was appointed principal; on 4 May 1963 he was installed in office at a function held at Knox-Metropolitan United Church in Regina. There was no robing ceremony, and the formalities were less elaborate than those for the installation of a president. As Riddell noted, "President Spinks made it very clear that there was a distinction."[29]

When Riddell was appointed principal he was informed that he should consult with the president on points of major policy; with J. Francis Leddy, vice-president (academic), on academic matters such as appointments; and with Colb McEown, vice-president (administration) on administrative matters.[30] Riddell protested that as the head of the Regina campus he wanted to report directly to the president.[31] A vital principle was at stake. If Riddell had to go through the vice-presidents to get to the president, then the Regina campus was in effect subordinated to the senior administrative hierarchy in Saskatoon. If Riddell were given direct access to the president and made a vice-president of the same rank as Leddy and McEown, then Regina campus would have something closer to equality with the Saskatoon campus.

Spinks deflected Riddell's request, explaining that since he was in the habit of talking over major issues with his vice-presidents, it would expedite matters if Riddell were to deal with them first.[32] Riddell accepted this arrangement.[33] There was little else he could have done, short of resigning, but his failure to take a firm stand later created no end of difficulties for him. In Regina, he was perceived as too weak to defend the interests of the campus; in Saskatoon, he was perceived as unable to keep the restive Regina faculty in check. Riddell tried to keep everybody happy. He genuinely believed in the one-university/two-campus model and did his best to make it work, but it was a thankless and, in the end, impossible task.

The Board of Governors in December 1961 had debated whether to make Riddell a vice-president. Chancellor Hedley Auld was in favour of granting the title. He pointed out that "if an outsider – *any* outsider – were made head of the Regina Campus, he would undoubtedly be made Principal and Vice-President forthwith on appointment. The only outsiders whom we deemed eligible were disinterested [*sic*]." Failure to make Riddell vice-president "would imply further indecision on our part or perhaps inadequacy on his part. To delay recognition could create misunderstanding detrimental to the University." Leddy protested that his relationship with Riddell would be made more difficult if the Regina campus principal had the rank of vice-president. Spinks took Leddy's side over Auld's. He wrote in the margin of Auld's memo, "I am quite clear that Vice-President implies a degree of development in Regina which has not yet been reached." Spinks assumed that Regina had to develop to a certain point before it could claim more responsibility for running its own affairs. Riddell believed that Regina could not develop properly unless there was strong leadership on site. Spinks made his decision, Auld retreated, and Riddell was not made vice-president. The chancellor remarked in the course of the debate that he was worried "lest factions develop within the board on a regional basis."[34] It seemed they already had.

In addition to the belated appointment of a head for the campus, steps were taken to formulate the aims and philosophy of the new institution.[35] At the suggestion of McEown, Riddell prepared in October 1961 a document setting forth his vision for the development of the campus. He estimated an enrolment of 5,000 in twenty-five to thirty years (the actual figure was 4,345 full-time students by 1969), with an ultimate student population of about 8,000. This would mean that in addition to the arts and science program, a number of professional colleges would eventually be established. In the short term, however, the emphasis was to be on the liberal arts. "The primary objective for the Regina Campus," Riddell wrote, "is to establish a first rate Liberal Arts College providing as much opportunity as possible for the student to gain an understanding of the inter-relationships existing among the various disciplines. Only when this has reached a significant stage of maturity should Colleges be introduced on this campus."[36]

The fact that Regina was the capital city and home to government departments, agencies, and Crown corporations pointed to a prominent role for the social sciences. The Regina campus would be a natural counterpart to the Saskatoon campus, which emphasized natural and applied sciences. In addition, Regina had the Conservatory of Music, the MacKenzie Art Gallery, and the School of Art, all of which could be used to enrich the liberal arts and to support a degree program in fine arts. Riddell hastened to add, however, that while the greatest strength of the Regina campus was in the social sciences and fine arts, a well-rounded liberal arts program also required science departments of good quality. In a technologically advanced age, he said, no truly liberal program could be effective without "a deep understanding of the sciences and such understanding can only be attained when the students come in contact with senior science professors."

With respect to the professional colleges that were to be established after the liberal arts core was firmly in place, Riddell recommended that they have an emphasis not found in corresponding colleges in Saskatoon. The College of Commerce in Regina could develop as a school of administration, taking full advantage of the proximity to government and the specialization in the social sciences. The College of Education might concentrate on training teachers in the social sciences and specialists in art, music, and drama. Engineering could introduce a phase of study not already offered in Saskatoon. The basic aim of Regina campus, Riddell argued, should be to develop programs that complemented rather than duplicated those of Saskatoon, thereby providing students in the province with a more diverse array of programs. While some duplication was inevitable, since all universities had to offer certain basic programs, it should be kept to a minimum.[37]

McEown took Riddell's statement, together with some other materials, and prepared a document outlining the aims and philosophy of the Regina campus. University Council and the Board of Governors approved it in April 1962.[38] The basic aim was "to develop a fully autonomous academic group on the Regina Campus, capable of giving courses leading to degrees." The emphasis in the immediate future was on the "establishment of a strong liberal arts college." If the enrolment in Saskatoon were limited to 8,000, it was estimated that by 1975 there would be a need for a university in Regina to serve 5,000 students. The statement continued: "Such an enrolment will undoubtedly be reached ultimately and must be planned for. This means that a number of professional colleges will develop on the campus. The only present decision is not to establish Colleges of Agriculture and Medicine at Regina."[39] McEown thought it probable that a college of education would be the first to be developed, a prediction that proved correct.

In addition to the statement on basic aims, council on 11 April 1962 received and approved a report titled "Organization at Regina." It affirmed that assistant, associate, and full professors at Regina were voting members of University Council. Also, the members of the Regina faculty were formally constituted as the College of Arts and Science, Regina campus. As such, they had the right to discuss academic matters – scholarships, student discipline, the library – but matters of academic policy were to be referred to University Council and senate for discussion and approval.[40] Council was, of course, overwhelmingly dominated by Saskatoon. "Organization at Regina" further stated that matters of general university policy came under the control of the University Council, the senate, and the Board of Governors and were handled by various committees, such as the Forward Planning Committee, committees on buildings and grounds, and so on. These did not come under the jurisdiction of any one faculty and were therefore "beyond the authority of the College of Arts and Science (Regina Campus)."[41]

The Regina faculty appointed in April 1962 the Forward Planning Committee (Regina), which consisted of W.A. Riddell (chair), President Spinks, Professors Fred W. Anderson, Margaret Belcher, Harry Jack, A.B. Van Cleave, W.C. Blight, and A.A. McKinnon.[42] It was a subcommittee of the Forward Planning Committee, which reported to the Executive Committee of Council. All the members of the university Forward Planning Committee, with the exception of Riddell, were from Saskatoon, as were sixteen of the eighteen Executive Committee of Council members. The Forward Planning Committee, among its other duties, reviewed requests for staff increases in arts and science at Saskatoon and Regina and established priorities for the Budget Advisory Committee of Council. The latter body had no members from Regina. Thus, two key university committees that exerted influence over hiring priorities and the allocation of financial resources had in total only one Regina representative.[43] Ultimate authority over the running of the university rested with the Board of Governors (on the budgetary and administrative side) and the senate (on the academic policy side). Both bodies were weighted in favour of Saskatoon, as would be expected, since Saskatoon was by far the larger campus.

As mentioned earlier, Regina campus in the early years did not have formally recognized academic departments, but rather clusters of departments organized as the Divisions of Natural Sciences, Social Sciences, Humanities, and Fine Arts. The relationship between Regina faculty members and their corresponding academic departments in Saskatoon was not altogether clear. In January 1963 Cecil French, professor of sociology at Regina campus, proposed a new course titled Social Class in Modern Society, but he was uncertain about the procedure to follow to have the class formally approved. Principal Riddell consulted the head of the Department of Sociology in Saskatoon, who advised him that rather than trying to obtain approval for a new class, Professor French should simply teach the course under the heading of a class that was already on the books – namely, Sociology 205: Social Organizations. As a result, the class was taught under a somewhat misleading title.[44]

Another area of confusion was the appointment of faculty members. Riddell discovered that while some Saskatoon department heads tried to be helpful by making suggestions and examining applicant files, others gave the impression that they would prefer not to be involved in the affairs of the Regina campus. Some felt they were encroaching upon the territory of Regina division chairmen. Riddell came to believe it would be better if the department heads in Saskatoon were left out of the picture entirely.[45] The procedure for granting promotions and merit increases was another source of friction. Riddell met with the division chair to review the performance of Regina faculty members and make recommendations as to how they should be dealt with. He discussed the recommendations with the vice-president (academic) and vice-president (administration) in Saskatoon, who took them to the General Promotions Committee of Council. The latter did not have any Regina representatives, and it functioned remotely from the day-to-day operations of the Regina campus. This led Regina faculty members to question whether the committee could make even-handed decisions relating to a campus they knew little about.[46]

The discontent led the Regina faculty to request on 26 February 1963 that "appropriate steps be taken to set up a Council of this Campus." This had been promised in a senate resolution of 11 May 1960, but the date of the council's formation had not been clearly specified. The Regina faculty demanded prompt action. They said that it was inconvenient and time-consuming for them to attend council meetings in Saskatoon, and that they were thus prevented from participating effectively in decision making.[47] The University Council responded with a resolution on 11 April 1963 to establish a council at Regina campus effective 1 July 1964.

The dramatic resignation of history professor Charles Lightbody in July 1963 highlighted and galvanized the dissatisfaction of the Regina faculty. Lightbody, author of *Judgments of Joan*, an acclaimed study of the cultural significance of Joan of Arc, was the kind of professor around whom both students and legends gather. "His classroom," said former student James McConica (later a distinguished historian in his own right), "was a fertile delta, regularly inundated by the lavish outpourings of his mind."[48] Stories of Lightbody's absent-mindedness were legion, including an account, repeated with endless variations, of how he had stopped his car to help an elderly lady cross the street and then, forgetting about the car, had taken the bus home. Lightbody grew up in small-town Saskatchewan, attended university in Saskatoon, won a Rhodes Scholarship to Oxford, and, after studying and teaching for a time in the United States, returned to Saskatoon in 1948 as a professor in the Department of History. He became embroiled in various conflicts arising out of what he considered to be infringements of his academic freedom. He complained about restrictions on the classes he wanted to teach and limits to his right to order books for the library. Finding the atmosphere in Saskatoon intolerable, he sought and obtained a transfer to the Regina campus in 1962, where he stayed for only one year. Believing that Saskatoon exercised too much control over Regina, he resigned and accepted a teaching position at Brandon College.

Lightbody took the unusual step on 10 July 1963 of calling a press conference to announce and explain the reasons for his resignation. He declared that the time had come to sever "the continuing umbilical cord which ties the Regina Campus to the University at Saskatoon." Praising what he called the liberal and democratic atmosphere prevailing in Regina, he described the new campus as "a most noble experiment, superior in many respects, and very distinctive." He declared that "it should not be at the mercy of the vagaries of any other educational authority!" In order to achieve its full potential, the Regina campus needed to have "complete independence of outside control." Otherwise, its growth and development would be "stunted."[49]

A press release went out to all the television and radio stations in the province and to newspapers in towns and cities with a population of 2,000 or more. Lightbody called it his "21-gun farewell salute to Alma Mater!"[50] The release, while strongly worded, was mild in comparison to a private memorandum he sent to Premier Woodrow Lloyd (Lloyd had succeeded Tommy Douglas as premier in late 1961). The Regina campus, Lightbody claimed, represented "the newer spirit in the province," a breath of fresh air in comparison with Saskatoon. "It is strange," Lightbody quoted a colleague as saying, "that the most progressive province in Canada should have one of the most reactionary universities in the country."[51] Lloyd confined his response to praise for Lightbody's qualities as a teacher (the premier's daughter had been one of his students) and expressions of regret that he had found it necessary to leave Saskatchewan.

The Regina *Leader-Post* published Lightbody's press release in full and supported his call for an independent university in Regina. An editorial noted that while Regina campus remained an "appendage of the parent university," other fledgling universities in Canada were being granted the freedom to develop as they saw fit. Victoria College had obtained its independence from the University of British Columbia, Brandon College was on the path to autonomy from the University of Manitoba, and the new campuses springing up in Ontario had been given self-governing authority. According to the *Leader-Post*, only in Saskatchewan did an emerging university have to operate under the tight control of the parent institution. The paper described Lightbody as "an outstanding scholar and an inspiring educational leader" and expressed the hope that he would return to the province "at some future date when the Regina campus achieves its independence."[52]

Since President Spinks was out of the country, acting president Balfour Currie gave the university's official response. Currie dismissed Lightbody's charges as "hogwash," a comment that only added fuel to the flames. The executive of the Faculty Association at Regina campus (O.G. Holmes, L.H. Thomas, F.W. Anderson, and Miss M.E.P. Henderson) decried the use of the term "hogwash." They said that such language would "only enhance rather than allay public uneasiness about the academic well being of the University." The Faculty Association pointed out that no plan had yet been developed for Regina campus to achieve its autonomy, and they hoped that "action on this matter [would] be given immediate consideration."[53]

Regina campus SRC president Bob Gaudry issued a statement supporting Lightbody. He said the professor had voiced a feeling shared by "many professors and most students at Regina Campus" and pledged that the students would "continually fight for the goal of independence from the other Campus."[54] Regina alderman Vince Matthews also entered the controversy, criticizing what he perceived as Saskatoon's "opposition to too rapid development of the Regina Campus." He declared himself in favour of "complete autonomy" for the university in Regina in the "not too distant future."[55] The Saskatoon *Star-Phoenix* strongly defended the status quo: "We reaffirm that this is the seat of the parent university, while the newborn campus at the Regina end is an appendage. Emotion at the Regina end cannot change this fact of history." The editorial went on to assert that the people of Saskatoon were more literate than those of Regina: "Saskatoon, seat of the provincial university for more than half a century, not only has many more readers, but also has many more prolific writers than the southern city."[56] Clearly, Lightbody had touched a raw nerve, and now the debate was spinning out of control. Douglas Cherry, the chairman of the Faculty Association in Saskatoon, interjected a note of sanity, saying that in his opinion, the majority of faculty members in Saskatoon were not opposed to autonomy for the Regina campus. On the contrary – they desired it as soon as possible.[57]

Lightbody was delighted with the hornet's nest he had stirred up. "I have always looked for a sense of camaraderie," he confided to fellow historian Lewis H. Thomas, "and have it at Regina as nowhere else except in the army. It does my soul good."[58] He believed that if public pressure were kept up, independence for Regina could be quickly achieved. University officials, he remarked, feared publicity "as a wild animal dreads fire"; they would retreat if faced with a sustained campaign for an autonomous campus. But Lightbody, fired up by the tumult he had caused, exaggerated its significance. The University of Regina would not emerge as a separate institution for another eleven years.

There was, however, a more immediate sequel. In July 1963 a group of Regina faculty members organized a revolt against the campus administration and Saskatoon control. The insurgents were senior faculty members from a broad spectrum of academic disciplines, including Les Crossman (English), Len Greenberg (physics), Owen Holmes (chemistry), Marino Kristjanson (chemistry), George Ledingham (biology), Ken Lochhead (art), Lewis Thomas (history), Jack Boan (economics), Duncan Blewett (psychology), and Cecil French (sociology). On the evening of 29 July 1963, in the faculty lounge at the main college building, they confronted Principal Riddell. Their first demand was the appointment of a full-time dean of arts and science. Riddell had been serving as both principal and dean, a load that was too heavy for one man to carry. They nominated Fred Anderson, professor of economics at Regina campus, for the position, describing him as "a member of our present staff with a proven record of administrative and intellectual attainment, who has a deep affection for this institution, who has given much thought to the problem of a distinctive liberal arts development here, and who has the confidence and respect of his colleagues."[59]

The second demand was a change in the title of the head of the campus from "principal" to "principal of the Regina campus and vice-president of the University of Saskatchewan." This would give the principal more authority and allow him to assume a stronger and more effective leadership role. Other demands included the assignment of interim powers of council to the Regina faculty, the appointment of a forward planning committee responsible to the interim council, the vesting of responsibility for the appointment of Regina faculty and staff in the Regina campus (except for the participation of the president[60]), the removal of the requirement that division chairmen report to or consult with officers of the Saskatoon campus (again, the president excepted), and complete autonomy for Regina campus with respect to the submission of the budget to the Board of Governors and in matters of faculty promotions and merit increases.[61] The overall theme was the need for the Regina campus to take responsibility for its own growth and development.

Four days after this confrontation, Riddell took the demands to Spinks and McEown. They were somewhat sympathetic but not prepared to give the Regina faculty everything they wanted. The president agreed that a dean of arts and science for Regina should be appointed as soon as possible. The committee for the selection of a dean usually consisted of the president, two Saskatoon deans, and a member of the Board of Governors. In this case the composition of the committee was modified to include the president, Principal Riddell, a member of the board, a Saskatoon dean, and a member of the Regina campus faculty. The inclusion of a faculty member seemed designed to mollify Regina, but the faculty's nomination of Fred Anderson for the deanship was ignored.

Spinks and McEown also agreed that Regina campus budget estimates would no longer be channelled through the University Council Budget Committee but rather sent directly to the budget committee of the Board of Governors. Further, division chairmen were no longer required to consult with heads of departments in Saskatoon, and the appointment of Regina faculty members was to proceed without the participation of Saskatoon department heads. Merit and promotion were to be dealt with by the president and a committee of the Regina campus named by him, without the involvement of other Saskatoon personnel. Finally, the members of the Regina faculty were to assume de facto the duties and responsibilities of Campus Council in anticipation of that body becoming a legal entity.[62] On one point Spinks held firm. Principal Riddell was not to be made a vice-president of the university.[63]

Vice-President Leddy, who had been absent from the university at the time of the revolt, was not altogether pleased with the developments that had occurred. He informed Principal Riddell on 12 September 1963 that "the events of the summer" had given rise to some "pertinent questions." "Many of us were astonished," he wrote, "to read the criticisms of the policy and of the procedures of the University published in the newspapers by persons who had never raised these matters, to our knowledge, in any of the appropriate meetings of committees, faculties, or of the Council." He was referring to the statement made by the executive of the Regina campus Faculty Association in the aftermath of the Lightbody resignation. Leddy considered this behaviour "most irresponsible." It raised questions in his mind as to whether some of the Regina colleagues "understand that at least a minimum of good will is essential for cooperation in the work of so complex an institution as a university." "The recent publicity in Regina," he continued, "most certainly unfairly damaged the reputation of the University, quite needlessly and through shockingly casual irresponsibility." Leddy asked Riddell to convey this rebuke to the offending faculty members as soon as possible.[64]

The faculty revolt had revealed the weakness and ambiguity of Riddell's position. He was caught between a faculty demanding stronger leadership for the autonomous development of Regina campus and superiors in Saskatoon who did not want to relinquish control. Spinks was in a difficult position, too. Many members of the Saskatoon faculty had not been enthusiastic supporters of the 1959 decision to initiate a full degree program in Regina. He was condemned in Regina for not doing enough for the new campus and in Saskatoon for doing too much. Spinks's style of administration further complicated matters. He was reported to have told Regina Campus Council in 1964, as paraphrased by a faculty member, "Think of us as if we were a Scottish clan. I, as your leader, will take care of you, and you will support me."[65] This paternalistic attitude clashed with the democratic atmosphere that prevailed at Regina campus and the sixties spirit of demanding accountability from those in authority.

Even Riddell, who agreed with Spinks on fundamental university policy, sometimes chafed under his leadership. In February 1964 he asked Spinks to give him more authority over the hiring of faculty. As principal, he was responsible for recruiting new staff in the tough, competitive market of the early 1960s when the demand for academics exceeded the supply. Riddell wanted to be able to take quick action and make a job offer to a promising candidate without having to wait for the approval of the president. Riddell also wanted more control over building projects. He complained that once plans had been agreed upon he was powerless to make changes, even in matters of direct concern to faculty, such as the selection of furniture for offices and classrooms. Riddell told Spinks that if the best results were to be achieved, one of two things had to happen. Spinks had either to become more involved or less involved in day-to-day decision making. If the former, then he would have to spend more time in Regina attending planning meetings, convening appointments committees, and making himself available for discussions with faculty. If the latter, then he would have to delegate more authority to the principal. Riddell insisted that half-measures were not working. The campus was growing too fast to be administered by remote control. It needed effective leadership and sufficient planning capacity. Nor could the job be left to the faculty, who were occupied with their own teaching and research. As Riddell noted in a memo to Spinks, "Building from bottom will *not* work and has not worked."[66] Riddell proposed in 1964 that the principal be given "all the powers necessary to properly discharge the broad responsibilities he has been given. This might be achieved by establishing that there shall be a Principal with wide powers on each campus responsible to the President and that the President shall function as the Principal on the campus when he is in residence."[67] Reorganization along these lines eventually did occur, but not until another three years had passed.

While these organizational matters were being worked through, debate continued on the aims and philosophy of the new campus. The two issues were interrelated. If the Regina campus had a distinctive educational mission to fulfill, then it needed the appropriate administrative powers to make the dream a reality. Conversely, if Regina campus was empowered to make decisions about its own development, then such decisions had to be informed by an understanding of what the campus was supposed to accomplish. Premier Woodrow Lloyd contributed to this discussion in a speech he gave on 26

Premier Woodrow S. Lloyd laying the cornerstone of the first buildings at the new Regina campus on 26 September 1963. The speech he gave on that occasion reverberated through the campus in the 1960s and early 1970s.

September 1963 on the occasion of the cornerstone-laying ceremony of the new campus's first buildings. The speech reverberated through the campus as officials, administrators, faculty, and students tried to come to grips with what kind of university they were trying to create in Regina. Lloyd asserted that Regina should not merely duplicate what was being done in Saskatoon: "We in Saskatchewan have here an opportunity. If our need had just been more classrooms and laboratories this might well have been achieved elsewhere with greater ease and good effect. But something different can be done here – different and worthwhile and needed. So let me express the hope that this will not be just a small-scale model of that which has been done on the Saskatoon Campus."[68]

He went on to specify how the Regina campus might be "different and worthwhile and needed." He rejected the "ivory tower" concept of a university – the notion that it should be detached or insulated from the concerns of the world around it. "There may indeed be justification for some ivory towers," he said, "but not too many." He believed it was important that the university be "on the cutting edge not merely observing from a safe distance the scene which has passed by. It and its graduates will do this only if it is properly immersed in the lives of those who make it possible." The campus, to give but one example, could become involved in social policy research and in training graduates for work in public administration. He quoted lines from a poem titled "A University Goes to the People":

> What is my campus? Not the spired array
> of Edifice and pile in granite gray;
> But rather the free hillside, furrow-spread,
> Where wholesome labor flings the seed of bread.
> Or this my campus? Not the tranquil lane
> Where knowledge echoes knowledge back again;
> But rather the dim depths where miners creep
> To wrest black riches from the dayless deep.
> This is my campus. Not the playing field,
> Nor cloistered close, nor fountain court revealed;
> Nay rather where green chasms rip and rave,
> Our fishers ply their nets athwart the wave.[69]

The speech concluded with the hope "that those who at some future date, satisfy their curiosity of what we really did, will know, because of history, that the best hopes of Saskatchewan people were advanced by the fact of this institution."[70]

The speech, for those who were familiar with the social gospel traditions of Regina College, touched on familiar themes: social service, community involvement, and the application of ivory-tower knowledge to real-world problems. This was not surprising coming from Lloyd, whose CCF philosophy was partly rooted in the social gospel. His father had been a supporter of the radical farmers' movement and his mother "a very religious woman who instilled in her children a strong social gospel vision of a Christian's responsibility for the welfare of their fellow man."[71] What was especially interesting about Lloyd, however, was his strong support for the youth protest movement of the sixties. He saw the student movement as "the best hope to carry on the goal of creating a just society which was fostered by the farmers' movement and the labour movement a generation before."[72]

Woodrow Lloyd bridged the old and the new, making the link between the old social gospel tradition and the new sixties social activism that was such a distinctive feature of the emerging Regina university. This was why his cornerstone speech struck such a chord. The flaw in the speech was its easy dismissal of the ivory tower, which, ideally interpreted, is a metaphor for the pursuit of knowledge for its own sake. The university that tries always to be relevant is at risk of being irrelevant. By catering to the trendy, it becomes trapped in the mindset of the moment. A tension must be maintained between the search for Truth (with a capital *T*, and not in quotation marks) and the attempt to address immediate needs. Lloyd understood this – otherwise he would not have said, "there may indeed be justification for some ivory towers, but not too many"– but his speech tilted too far in one direction. Nonetheless, he spoke important truths. A university must be "on the cutting edge not merely observing from a safe distance the scene which has passed by," and it must be "properly immersed in the lives of those who make it possible." His message was inspiring, especially when he said, "something different can be done here – different and worthwhile and needed." But what exactly did this mean, and how could these ideals be implemented in the development of Regina campus?

7 Defining a Liberal Education

After the university made the decision in July 1959 to establish a full degree program at Regina College, the Regina faculty gave a great deal of thought to the nature and purposes of the academic program and how it might differ from the one offered in Saskatoon. Their discussions, while stimulating, did not produce tangible results. There was no policy statement to which the faculty could point and say, "This is what we believe in, and this is what we want to achieve." Such a document was produced at the end of 1963. The "Education Policy for the Liberal Arts," or the Regina Beach Statement, as it was more commonly known, summed up the aims and aspirations of the arts and science faculty and defined what they meant by the term "liberal education." While the statement never achieved broad consensus, it served as a rallying point and guide for the development of the campus.

A milestone on the road to Regina Beach was the hiring in March 1963 of Dallas W. Smythe as the chairman of the social sciences division. Though born in Regina, he had at an early age moved with his family to California. He attended the University of California, Berkeley, where he received an undergraduate degree and then a PhD in economics in 1937. He found work in Washington, DC, as associate economist with the Central Statistical Board. In his off hours he was involved with the American League for Peace and Democracy (ALPD), a left-wing group that was engaged in a campaign to assist the Republican forces in the Spanish Civil War. The House Un-American Activities Committee labelled it a "communist front" organization, and the FBI placed it under surveillance. The outbreak of World War

Dallas Smythe, appointed chairman of the Division of Social Sciences in 1963. He was a staunch defender of the vision of liberal education embodied in the Regina Beach Statement.

II led to the breakup of the ALPD, with the leftists splitting from the social democrats to form the Washington Committee for Democratic Action. This organization, too, was tagged a "communist front." Although it had but a short life, those who participated in it were branded as having "followed the party line." Smythe was affiliated with the leftists, but when interrogated by the FBI in March 1941 he could honestly say that he had not been active in the Committee for Democratic Action by virtue of the serendipitous fact that he had entered hospital for a gall bladder operation just as the organization came together.[1]

Smythe secured work as the chief economist for the Federal Communications Commission, a position he held from 1943 to 1948. As the Cold War took hold, the US government implemented a "loyalty program" to root out suspected communists. Smythe maintained that while he had attended one or two public meetings sponsored by the Communist Party and had friends who were members, he had never joined the party. Nevertheless, his past associations and activities were such that he was at risk during Senator McCarthy's witch hunt. He came to the conclusion that his days in government service were numbered, and he began to look for other employment.

He learned in 1948 that the University of Illinois at Champaign-Urbana was planning to establish an institute of communications research. He applied for a professorship, but when the appointment came before the Board of Trustees, one trustee produced a letter from the House Un-American Activities Committee denouncing him as a disloyal citizen. Only after the university had performed more security checks, including a phone call to the Attorney General of the United States, did the appointment go through.[2] At Urbana, Smythe carried out innovative research in the field of broadcasting and taught one of the first courses given at a university in the political economy of mass communications. He and his wife, Jenny, were active in the peace movement, and the FBI continued to monitor their activities. The couple felt increasingly uncomfortable living in the United States and began to consider the possibility of moving to another country. The Cuban Missile Crisis of October 1962 brought matters to a head. "If we and our two children were to die in a nuclear war," Dallas Smythe wrote, "we didn't want to do it as Americans."[3]

In November 1962 he wrote to J.F. Leddy, dean of arts and science and vice-president (academic) at the University of Saskatchewan, to ask if the university had a position for someone with his experience and expertise.[4] Leddy answered that he was "not at all sure about the opportunities which may be available for someone of your very unusual qualifications," but he passed the letter along to A.E. Safarian, head of the Department of Economics and Political Science.[5] Safarian informed Smythe that the Regina campus was looking for a chairman of the Division of Social Sciences, and that Smythe's interdisciplinary background made him a suitable candidate.[6] Riddell interviewed him and offered him the job; thus, on a hot sunny day in late August 1963, Smythe and his family arrived in their station wagon to start a new life in Regina. As he later recalled, "We had rejected the United States as a country to respect or to live in and looked forward eagerly to a better life in Canada."[7]

When Smythe took up his duties, he found a faculty lacking a clear sense of direction. It was recognized that the liberal arts would be an important feature of the new university,[8] but there was no consensus on the specific aims of the program or the means of implementing them. Even at this early stage pressures were developing for the establishment of professional colleges. The Regina faculty Forward Planning Committee in October 1963 agreed to the introduction of a diploma course in education, adding that "the structure of the university should be carefully worked out, so that the College of Arts and Science will remain its central *core*, so that all other programs presented for consideration can be seen in relation to it."[9] This made it all the more necessary for the faculty to work out what they considered to be the basic principles of arts and science education.

Smythe suggested that they invite Dr Robert Hutchins to spend a weekend with the planning group and act as a catalyst for the discussions.[10] Hutchins, president of the University of Chicago from 1929 to 1951, was well known for his unorthodox views on higher education. In *The Higher Learning in America*, first published in 1936 and reissued in 1961, he criticized the curriculum of the modern university, which he said had become fragmented, overly specialized, and disordered. It was like an encyclopedia that contained many pieces of information but no overarching truth. It lacked coherence, other than that provided by alphabetical arrangement. The university had departments running from art to zoology, but neither professors nor students fully understood the relation of one department to another. There was no attempt to present a "hierarchy of truths" or to help the students gain insight into the fundamental problems of life and society.[11]

In 1930 Hutchins had reorganized the academic departments at the University of Chicago into four divisions: humanities, social sciences, biological sciences, and physical sciences. He also established a "college" that offered an integrated curriculum in the freshman and sophomore years. At the conclusion of their studies, students sat for five required comprehensive examinations, one for each of the divisional fields and one in English composition. Hutchins helped design and teach a "great books" course, which was intended to engage students in reading and discussing the classic texts of Western civilization, to expose them to the "great conversation" about the nature of man and the meaning of life.[12] He was convinced that the modern university had lost its way. It offered students a grab bag of specialized and semi-professional courses to enable them to make a living, but it gave them nothing that would help them learn how to live. The university had turned into a bureaucracy focused on technique, a place where the important questions were never asked.

After leaving the University of Chicago, Hutchins became president of the Fund for the Republic, which had been founded by the Ford Foundation to support civil liberties and civil rights projects. The fund combatted McCarthyism and worked to eliminate racial discrimination in voter registration, housing, education, and employment. Hutchins reorganized the fund's operations in 1959, transforming it from an agency that dispensed grants to one that subsidized the Center for the Study of Democratic Institutions at Santa Barbara, California. Hutchins became the president of the centre, which he envisioned as an alternative university where prominent thinkers could engage in dialogue to clarify the issues and problems of democracy. It held seminars on a wide variety of topics, such as the role of technology, the responsibility of the media, the civil rights movement, the women's movement, student unrest, world peace, and economic policy.[13] All of these issues were of interest to Smythe. He regarded Hutchins as an intellectual mentor who offered penetrating insights into the problems of contemporary society and the modern university.

Although Hutchins declined the invitation to come to Regina, he invited the faculty of Regina campus to California to spend some time at the centre. This, Smythe noted, caused the professors to "prick up their ears," but the trip proved too difficult to arrange.[14] As it turned out, the retreat, held in December 1963, was not in a marble-floored villa set in "sun-dappled, eucalyptus-covered hills, with a broad view of the Pacific"[15] but in a freezing hotel at Regina Beach, about thirty miles northwest of Regina. The guest of honour was not Hutchins, but his associate, W.H. ("Ping") Ferry, who had worked with him for several years, first as vice-president of the Fund for the Republic and then as a member of the core group at the Center for the Study of Democratic Institutions.

Ferry was, in the words of Victor Navasky, who profiled him in the *Atlantic Monthly*, a "happy heretic."[16] Among his not entirely facetious proposals were the conversion of the New York Stock Exchange into a gambling casino, the restriction of the military draft to senior citizens "who had already had a chance to live," and a requirement that the president of the United States and the premier of the USSR each shoot fifty children before being allowed to push the button to start a nuclear war.[17] Despite his gadfly reputation, Ferry had a patrician background. The son of the former chairman of the board of the Packard Motor Company, he had taught at Choate (John F. Kennedy was one of his students) and had worked as a speechwriter for Henry Ford II. His employment history included a stint as public relations officer for the Political Action Committee of the Congress of Industrial Organizations and a partnership in Earl Newsom Associates, a PR firm whose clients included Ford, Standard Oil, Campbell Soup, and CBS.[18]

Ferry outlined his views on education in "Why the College Is Failing," a speech delivered to the American Association for Higher Education in July 1963. He claimed that universities were not dealing with the urgent problems facing society. Their graduates were "able perhaps to make a living, but unable to make a world." Ferry asserted that the "Smithian formulation," the notion that the pursuit of self-interest led in some miraculous fashion to the common good, was "absurd in the conditions of modern industrial life." "Horatio Alger is dead," he quipped, "but he still controls the curriculum." He thought that American universities evaded this basic truth because they were still traumatized at the thought of being labelled communist. McCarthyism had not been extinguished, merely "housebroken." Universities, as a result, were timid, docile, conformist, and afraid to do anything to rock the boat or challenge the status quo. They trained students for individual career success but had nothing to say about injustice, war, poverty, pollution, and the responsibilities of citizenship.[19]

Ferry was essentially a sixties student radical, except that he wasn't a student. Though not a socialist, he believed that collectivist solutions were necessary because policies based solely on individualism and the free market did not work anymore. For him, the university was not just a place where students went for professional training or even a place where they engaged in a random, open-ended search for truth. Like Hutchins, he believed that there were certain truths or moral imperatives that students needed to absorb in order to participate effectively as citizens in a democratic society.

Ferry developed these themes in his keynote speech at the Regina Beach retreat on 14 December 1963. He said that universities had fallen into the trap of equating technological change with progress, ignoring the fact that advances in technology had also brought a polluted environment, nuclear bombs, "cultural depravity and spiritual degeneration." The job of educators was to strip away the illusions that concealed this reality and expose the viciousness of the economic and social system. This meant clearing away "the rubbish produced by the status quo and by its confederates in the mass media for their own protection and enrichment." The goal of liberal arts education was to develop in the minds of students a "critical intelligence" and "political openness for human betterment, however radical or varnished over by epithets they may be." The key question, he said, was whether mankind would place its technical achievements under the control of a higher wisdom or whether technology would control mankind.[20] Thus Ferry took a position somewhere between questioning the status quo and denouncing it; searching for the truth and preaching it; fostering free inquiry and promoting a political agenda.

The essay Dallas Smythe wrote for the Regina Beach discussions ran along similar lines. He began with an overview of the general "state of the world." The pace of change was accelerating, science and technology were developing rapidly, industry was being automated, and many new nations were emerging from colonial status and achieving independence. Most significant of all, the threat of nuclear war was hanging over the planet. Smythe believed that if war were to be averted, "mankind will have to change its attitudes and institutions more in the next fifteen years than it did in the last 10,000 years." He placed his concept of liberal education in the context of this apocalyptic scenario. The purpose of the university was to extend and to transmit knowledge, and the function of knowledge was to "provide ways of finding solutions to man's problems." The pursuit of truth for its own sake was not sufficient; the truth being sought had to have an application. It had to be "relevant" – a favourite word of the 1960s – to the social, political, and economic crises afflicting humankind.

According to Smythe purely technical and vocational studies had no place in a community of scholars. Like Hutchins, he wanted to banish from the university all such courses of study, including "all instruction in routine accountancy, in all marketing, in all advertising, in all management courses."

Instruction in such subjects was to be transferred to "private schools or to industry to provide the on-the-job training where the ostensible purpose of such programs can be competently and relevantly achieved." Smythe also followed Hutchins in opposing a liberal arts curriculum that allowed students too much freedom to choose the courses they wanted to take – he dismissed this as "cafeteria-style education." In order for general education to be coherent, students had to be guided through the main areas of knowledge and given an understanding of how these areas were connected to one another.

Smythe's insistence on "relevance" led him to attack the concept of academic freedom, as it was conventionally understood. He argued that academic freedom was a luxury that a world in crisis and under threat of nuclear annihilation could not afford. "Too often," he said, "academic bureaucrats and professors act as though 'academic freedom' is a sufficient shield to protect them in the enjoyment of sinecures in which petty academic busywork, laziness, and a 'rear-view mirror view of the world' substitute for intellectual activity in either the pursuit or the application of knowledge. Unfortunately, it is a sufficient shield, unless revision of the curriculum is used to shake them loose from their socially-irrelevant stances." This was Smythe's radical statement, a clear departure from the liberal view that the purpose of a university is to facilitate the unconstrained pursuit of truth for its own sake.

Echoing Ferry, he declared that he favoured a liberal arts curriculum that rejected the "Smithian notion that an invisible hand would by some alchemy transform the results of individual selfishness into social welfare." He thought universities in the past had paid too much attention to the "individual as the object of education" and not enough to raising awareness that "institutions ... must be brought within the critical function of the educational process." Universities had to recognize the "crucial role of education in forming men's attitudes toward the institutions which provide not only men's consumer goods but his intake of cultural materials of all kinds." Students should be encouraged not merely to accept but also to evaluate critically existing political and economic structures and arrangements.

Smythe believed that this educational goal was entirely compatible with what he called Saskatchewan's tradition of "institutional experimentalism." By this he meant such innovative measures as progressive labour laws, social programs, medicare, and publicly owned enterprises. He had fled a country where he and his wife had been persecuted because of their left-wing political views. He thought that they had found in Saskatchewan a place where they could feel safe and at home. Premier Woodrow Lloyd's cornerstone-laying speech in September 1963 must have been music to Smythe's ears, especially the lines, "But something different can be done here – different and worthwhile and needed ... [the university must be] on the cutting edge not merely observing from a safe distance the scene which has passed by. It and its graduates will do this only if it is properly immersed in the lives of those who make it possible."[21]

Psychology professor Duncan Blewett wrote an essay for the Regina Beach retreat that dealt with some of the same issues Smythe and Ferry had covered. Like Smythe, Blewett began with the assumption that the world was in a perilous state and humanity beset on all sides with "deadly political and social problems and serious and unpredictable consequences of kaleidoscopic technological change." From this he deduced that existing programs and policies had failed and new ideas and solutions were needed. It was time to abandon the concept of the educated man as "an ambulatory encyclopedia" crammed with irrelevant and useless knowledge. Students had to learn how to think, to question authority, and to challenge the status quo. The most menacing threat to the university was the idea that it was supposed to operate like a business corporation and a bastion of "right thinking, respectability, lack of controversy, social docility, and ... whatever propaganda most suits those who supply the funds." Students must not, "as they do now, sigh for graduation so that they could begin to become educated." Blewett even suggested abolishing examinations and terminating "the vicious practice of granting degrees." This would send the clear message that the university was not "a vocational selection and trades training center," but rather a centre for independent and creative thought.[22]

Ken Lochhead, the director of the School of Art, shared this radical experimental spirit. He opened his discussion with the Zen Buddhist quotation "A drop of water has the tastes of the water of the seven seas; there is no need to experience all the ways of worldly life. The reflections of the moon on one thousand rivers are from the same moon; the mind must be full of light." He argued that a liberal arts college must be lively and creative, full "of romanticism, of individualism, of personal trust, of feeling for the informal, of the wild; with the acceptance of the simple and the real, with a sense of the importance of immediacy, with an insistence on judging life and art by the quality of experience, with a love of innovation and experiment." Students should be led to break up patterns of stereotyped thinking and discover "the sense of the vast alternatives which can replace the safe traditions of conventional thought." "Systematized knowledge and bureaucracy" paralyzed creative work. This was a little unsettling for Principal Riddell. On his copy of Lochhead's paper he underlined the words "systematized knowledge" and wrote in the margin, "a strength not a danger."[23]

English professor Alywn Berland occupied a middle ground between the radical ideas of Smythe, Blewett, and Lochhead and Riddell's more traditional views. Berland worried that liberal education was being driven to the margins of the university and was "fighting for its life." He accepted that professional training was part of the mission of the university, but he felt that

English professor Alwyn Berland, the main drafter of the Regina Beach Statement and dean of arts and science (1967–68).

it was necessary, more than ever, to affirm "the value of the liberal arts, of a liberal education, of those subjects to which every student must be given access not for the sake of his job, or even the immediate use of society, but for the sake of his growth as a man." A student was not just a budding professional or a "social unit," but a person with a right to live "in the fullness of his humanity."

Berland contended that society was overly fascinated with "technique" and assumed that technology could solve all its problems. The true strength of a civilization lay elsewhere. "The Greeks," he said, "could not broadcast the Aeschylean trilogy, but they could write it." Berland was not convinced that the ivory tower concept of a university was such a bad thing. It all depended on what you meant by the term. It could be taken as a synonym for irrelevant and disconnected from life, or it could signify "a traditional concern for human values and human knowledge ... a primary curiosity about man's history and man's art and man's scientific explorations ... a devotion to the monuments and treasures of the past along with concern for the achievements and perplexities of the present (all of which implies a concern for the future as well)." If one accepted the latter interpretation, then the more ivory towers the better.[24]

Berland, Lochhead, Blewett, and Smythe were all uneasy with the status quo in university education. They sensed that human values were under siege in modern society and that technology was out of control. They believed that the humanity of the student was the foremost concern of liberal education, and that technological progress, in and of itself, did not represent the highest ideals of human civilization. Despite their differences – Smythe emphasized radical approaches to political economy, Lochhead was more interested in new forms of artistic expression, and Berland expressed a deep appreciation of the Western cultural heritage – they shared the belief that true liberal arts education was liberating insofar as it helped the student to realize his or her full potential as a human being. It opened up new ways of seeing, feeling, and thinking rather than merely reinforcing the belief systems of the past.

Other members of the Regina campus faculty were more orthodox in their approach to curriculum planning and development. The leading exponent of what might be called the traditional point of view was Allan B. Van Cleave, who in 1962 had been appointed chairman of the natural sciences division. A graduate of the University of Saskatchewan, he held PhD degrees from both McGill and Cambridge. He joined the Department of Chemistry in Saskatoon in 1937, where he met Spinks.[25] The Spinks connection and the fact that the two chemists shared views on university issues lent a Saskatoon-versus-Regina dimension to the liberal arts debate. Spinks was out of sympathy with the spirit of Regina Beach. He later referred to the retreat as "the famous weekend discussion on the future of the Regina campus – led, I believe by a professor from California. It had, I think, a bad effect in that it supported the woolliness of some woolly thinkers."[26] Thus the debate over the principles of Regina Beach became entangled with the effort to secure the autonomy of the Regina campus. Van Cleave, in the minds of Smythe and his followers, was a surrogate for Saskatoon and an obstacle to Regina's fulfillment of its true mission as a university. Smythe, in the opinion of Van Cleave and his followers, was a false prophet who did not understand the proper role of a university. The conflict between Smythe and Van Cleave for control of the Faculty of Arts and Science and the direction of liberal arts education epitomized the battle for the heart and soul of the Regina university.

The paper that Van Cleave prepared for the Regina Beach retreat emphasized that while it was important to build a strong liberal arts college, it was unrealistic to think that the establishment of professional colleges could be delayed for long. He observed that "the majority of our students attend the university with the view of training themselves for entry into some profession. It is sheer 'ivory towerism' to think that they do not." Van Cleave did not think that the addition of professional courses would in any way weaken or detract from liberal arts studies. On the contrary, courses in engineering physics, geological engineering, or chemical engineering were, in his opinion, just as broad and comprehensive in their approach to basic scientific training as honours courses in the pure sciences.

Allan B. Van Cleave, appointed chairman of the Division of Natural Sciences in 1962. He upheld the traditional ideals of the university and opposed radical influences at the Regina campus.

Van Cleave opposed radical changes to the curriculum, warning that major departures from the existing model would cause difficulties for students who wished to transfer from one campus to the other. In his view change for the sake of change was not a good thing. "We must be reasonably certain," he cautioned, "that the changes proposed have real merit." Furthermore, changes were best carried out "in a spirit of cooperation with rather than of opposition to those who have designed the present requirements." In Van Cleave's judgment, the Regina campus would be well advised to concentrate its efforts on establishing as quickly as possible a reputation for high standards and academic excellence. This would entail, among other things, the development of honours and graduate programs in the sciences, as well as the acquisition of "first rate up-to-date scientific equipment ... so that a healthy spirit of investigation of the unexplored regions of science may be fostered."[27]

Van Cleave wanted the Regina campus to develop as a university engaged in liberal arts education, professional training, and specialized research. He assumed that scientific investigation and technological progress were desirable. Smythe, Blewett, and Berland were not so sure. Subjecting science and technology to critical scrutiny, they asked such questions as: What was the ultimate aim of research? Who did it help and whose purposes did it serve? Was humanity really better off because of it? To Van Cleave and many other members of the faculty, both in and outside the natural sciences, the answers were obvious and straightforward. To Smythe and his supporters, they were not.

It would be a mistake to oversimplify Van Cleave's understanding of the university. He did not see it merely as a research institute cranking out new technology and training the next generation of scientists to take their place in the technocratic social order. "Although the University is a public institution," he said, "it must be itself. It can do much for the province and the public and it is highly desirable that it do so. But it can't be all things to all people and allow peripheral functions to displace main ones and still be a University. We must be allowed to play our own role first and well."[28] For Van Cleave the mission of the university, that which made it what it was and not some other kind of institution, was the pursuit of truth for its own sake. To him this was the truly liberating aspect of liberal education. The practical applications of scientific discoveries were important but secondary benefits. Smythe, by contrast, believed that the quest for truth, based on academic freedom and devoid of social responsibility, had produced a technological juggernaut that was anything but liberating. This paradox – Van Cleave's support for academic freedom and the status quo versus Smythe's rejection of academic freedom (at least in the pure liberal sense of the term) and desire for societal transformation – lay at the heart of the liberal arts debate at Regina campus in the 1960s.

These ideas formed the intellectual backdrop when thirty faculty members gathered at Regina Beach on the weekend of 13–15 December 1963. At the conclusion of the deliberations, Alwyn Berland summed up the key points in a document titled "Educational Policy for the Liberal Arts," commonly referred to as the Regina Beach Statement (or sometimes the Regina Beach Manifesto). It began with a quotation attributed to Socrates – "The unexamined life is not worth living" – and continued in five parts.

I. The university has traditionally undertaken the role of preserving, transmitting, and increasing the intellectual heritage of man. We reaffirm our acceptance of this task.

II. This affirmation cannot be taken to mean that a university is a mausoleum of possibly interesting but irrelevant and impractical ideas, a repository of the past. No. There must also be an affirmation that the university is an important part of the critical intelligence of society, examining institutions, seeking to penetrate the future, sensitive to change, aware of the past, and of the manifold problems and dangers of the present.

III. Above all, the role of critic, of examiner of institutions and ideas, belongs to the modern university functioning as a community of scholars. Its criticism should be sustained by constant reference to essential human values, which demands a deliberate renewal of the study of the nature of love, of justice, freedom, beauty, science: in fact, all those values which give meaning and substance to life. This implies a de-emphasis of mere topicality in the subject matter of the liberal arts curriculum. Further, this examination requires that all liberal arts students should be involved with a wide range of subject matter, so presented that the student may be able to synthesize his total experience in the liberal arts college. Such a program will frequently call for a kind of intellectual slum-clearance, a breaking up of those conventional myths which are frequently identified with reality. This constant critique must be applied first to the structure and function of the university itself.

IV. The implication for educational philosophy is that above all the idea, the general context, the point of view is what should be transmitted to the student. The professor is charged with the responsibility of opening and of sustaining a dialogue with the student: the student must be encouraged to see that his relationship to the educational process, and to the dialogue, is not that of exposure merely, but of involvement. An exceedingly careful choice of basic material has to be made in order to achieve depth of appreciation in a given subject. Material will be continually re-assessed for its relevance and value. The development of critical intelligence in the student calls for considerable attention by the professor to the basic critical assumptions of his discipline. The "mindless counting" approach to knowledge finds scant welcome in the framework; and methodological hobby-horses and peculiarities become secondary.

V. Professors and students must be free to express themselves on all issues, controversial or not, but are responsible to the academic community.[29]

Parts I and V were fairly standard restatements of the traditional goals of the university: the preservation, transmission, and expansion of knowledge and respect for freedom of expression. Parts II, III, and IV related more specifically to the historical context of the 1960s and the concerns of those who were challenging the status quo. Part II asserted the importance of relating university activities to the life of the wider community. The university was not "a mausoleum of possibly interesting but irrelevant and impractical ideas," but rather an institution that was sensitive to "the manifold problems and dangers of the present." Part III affirmed the goal of not simply observing the passing scene but acting in "the role of critic," examining ideas and institutions, including the university itself. This critical examination was to be based on "essential human values" and a "deliberate renewal of the study of the nature of love, of justice, freedom, beauty, and science: in fact, all those values which give meaning and substance to life."

The ramifications of this idea were developed in the remainder of part III. Liberal arts students required a broad exposure to the many branches of knowledge. They needed to see information in a coherent framework rather than as isolated and disconnected fragments. Part IV emphasized the importance of "dialogue" in achieving this aim. Students should not learn passively, memorizing the required material. They must become actively involved in the educational process, seeking answers, formulating ideas, and finding an intellectual ground to stand on and call their own.

The Regina Beach Statement, while in keeping with mainstream university tradition, had a distinct philosophy and tone. It highlighted the importance of contemporary issues, general knowledge, conceptual understandings, and "essential human values." All of these items were interrelated and mutually supportive. A focus on basic human values helped students to organize the vast and bewildering array of knowledge they would draw from various disciplines into a pattern of meaningful generalizations, and this in turn would provide them with a foundation on which to make the kinds of decisions citizens are called upon to make – decisions about the kind of society they wanted to live in. The Regina Beach Statement was also notable for what it did not say. It did not say that the purpose of liberal education was the pursuit of truth for its own sake. The point of pursuing truth was to find it, and having found it, to do something with it – not just make a living but build a better world.

The Regina Beach Statement was taken up at a special faculty meeting held on 10–11 February 1964. Classes were cancelled for two days so that all faculty members could attend. Jack Mitchell, acting student president, asked permission for SRC representatives to sit in on the discussions, since the students were "very interested in future developments which would affect them" and felt that they "might be able to contribute something of value at the meeting."[30] Four students were invited and given speaking privileges equal to those of faculty, but they were not granted the right to vote. The student newspaper, renamed the *Carillon* in the fall of 1962, hailed the decision and expressed the hope that it would set a precedent for giving students "a permanent voice in the direction of university policy." The paper proclaimed that a breach had been made "in the traditional wall opposed to a student voice in university government."[31]

The Faculty of Arts and Science formally adopted the Regina Beach Statement and passed a number of resolutions intended to make it operational. The faculty recommended that a semester system be instituted so that the first year of liberal arts would consist of eight courses, four taught in the first semester (September to December) and four in the second semester (January to April), each class meeting for a total of four hours per week. This format would differentiate Regina from Saskatoon, where students took five classes (three hours per week) over the entire academic year, from September to April. The goal was to expose first-year students to a broad range of disciplines rather than forcing them to focus on a select group of subjects too early in their university careers. Another motion recommended that students be required to pass an examination "on a body of literature or other relevant data representative of the basic knowledge of one of the Divisions in which the student is registered." If the student failed the exam, he or she would not be allowed to graduate. This resolution, apparently modelled on Robert Hutchins's program at the University of Chicago, was tabled and not acted upon. It was considered too impractical a departure from conventional practice.[32]

In the immediate aftermath of Regina Beach there was a glow over the campus. Riddell sensed "a feeling of confidence that was not evident before."[33] Ferry, who had been sent a copy of the statement, bestowed compliments from California: "I congratulate you on it, and wish you the best of luck in fighting off the marauders from Saskatoon and elsewhere who look on such things as the pieties of a long-gone age."[34] The glow quickly faded. In March 1964 the Regina Campus Planning Committee sent a questionnaire to faculty members seeking their opinions on the administrative organization of the campus in general and the division system in particular. Responses ranged far beyond the specific questions that had been asked to reveal a widespread mood of "despair, frustration, and even bitterness" concerning the state of the campus.[35] Rumours abounded of faculty resignations and threats of resignation.[36]

The malaise arose from the feeling that while the Regina Beach Statement had been formally approved, nothing concrete had been done about it. Much of the uncertainty hinged on the fate of the division system. Divisions had been introduced initially because academic departments were too small to be viable units. The traditionalists had assumed that as departments grew in size they would be formally recognized as the fundamental components of the administrative structure, and the divisional structure would disappear. But there had always been those who regarded the divisions not as temporary expedients but as necessary and permanent features of campus organization. According to them, the divisional organization was inextricably bound up with the idea of a general, comprehensive, and well-integrated liberal arts education. Regina Beach reinforced this point of view. If you favoured what Regina Beach stood for, you supported the division system; if you championed the division system, you were a friend of Regina Beach.

Dallas Smythe, chairman of the social sciences division, was a strong believer in the division system. He went so far as to say that faculty members had an *obligation* to support it: "If you were hired to teach at 'The College' at the University of Chicago under Hutchins, you expected to live with its policy and structure, and if you found it uncomfortable you expected and you were expected to depart gracefully." Similarly, if you were hired at the Regina campus but preferred to work within a conventional departmental structure in a traditional educational policy framework, you were in conscience bound to hand in your resignation and look for another job. According to Smythe, faculty members who wanted to criticize the division system had to do so within its basic assumptions and not from the "atomistic, Adam Smithian point of view." He claimed that the system deserved a fair trial: "Five, ten or twenty years would not be an unreasonable expectation of its life."[37]

The Forward Planning Committee of the Faculty of Arts and Science (Regina) on 5 May 1964 set up a subcommittee to study the divisional organization.[38] This evolved into a special committee, which finally reported to Campus Council on 17 February 1965. The report recognized that the divisional structure represented an experiment in university government, and, as such, was attended by a number of uncertainties. The committee recommended that its proposals be adopted for a trial period of three years beginning 1 April 1965 and that at the end of that period the faculty undertake a re-evaluation. Each division (natural sciences, social sciences, humanities, and fine arts) was to have a chairman elected by faculty members, with the exception of the first chairman, who would be appointed by the Board of Governors for a five-year term. The chairman was responsible for coordinating the resources of the division with the purpose of developing a well-integrated liberal arts program. He would also represent the division in recommending to the president appointments and promotions of faculty members within his jurisdictional area.

The basic subunit of the division was the disciplinary committee, composed of all the faculty members belonging to a particular discipline (economics, psychology, history, and so on). The word *department* was not used, even though the disciplinary committees performed many of the same functions as departments. Since the division system was intended to be something new and departments were not supposed to have much power, the conventional nomenclature was avoided. The executive officer of the disciplinary committee was known as the chairman. In the original draft of the special committee's report, the position was designated as "secretary," but this term was dropped because it was already being used to describe those who did the clerical work in the departments. The chairman was to be elected by the faculty members of the disciplinary committee. His or her duties included preparing the committee's annual budget, controlling expenditures within the approved budget, representing the committee in the recruitment of new faculty members, as well as assigning teaching duties, coordinating library requisitions, arranging student advisory services, estimating textbook requirements, and coordinating student examinations. Each division was to have an executive committee made up of the chairman of the division and the chairmen of the disciplinary committees within the division. Its job was to look after program planning and matters of academic policy for the division.[39]

A notable feature of the committee's report on divisional organization was the proposal to elect chairmen of divisions and disciplinary committees. This was typical of the democratizing trend in university governance in the 1960s; faculty members across Canada and elsewhere demanded and received more say in the way universities were run.[40] Principal Riddell pointed out, however, that the election of officers such as the chairmen of disciplinary committees contravened the terms of the University Act, which assigned to the Board of Governors the duty of appointing "all such officers, clerks, employees and servants as it deems necessary for the purpose of the university, fix[ing] their salaries or remuneration and defin[ing] their duties and terms of office."[41] In the end, a compromise was reached. It was agreed that the president, in making his recommendation to the Board of Governors for the appointment of disciplinary chairmen, would give first consideration to the nomination put forward by the members of the disciplinary committee who had full academic tenure. In forwarding his recommendation to the president, the principal was to indicate whether or not he concurred with the nomination. The existing procedure for making appointments was formally upheld, but in reality a new and more egalitarian process was allowed to develop. The principal and the president, while preserving their power to recommend nominees to the Board of Governors, took into account the democratically expressed views of faculty members.

The Board of Governors on 24 June 1965 approved the proposals for the organization of the division system. They made only one slight change, replacing the term "disciplinary committee" with "subject committee."[42] The board thought that disciplinary committees would be confused with discipline committees, which were responsible for enforcing regulations and punishing misconduct. As it turned out, the subject committees in everyday conversation were referred to as "committees of instruction" or even "departments." In all other respects, the Board of Governors ratified the division system, although not all university officials were fully convinced of its merits. President Spinks advised the Regina Campus Council in October 1965 that strong departments were a must for the development of research and scholarly activity in a given field. There was nothing wrong with interdisciplinary studies, but their effectiveness depended upon the "excellence of the inter-acting bodies." "Putting the latter in mathematical terms," he said, "the cross-product of two interacting terms is zero, if one of the terms is zero, no matter how high the multiplying factor."[43] However, as Smythe would have said, the main purpose of the division system was not to foster research but to make the liberal arts program more integrated, conceptual, and broad-based than was possible under the existing departmental structure.

Parallel to the articulation of the division system, work proceeded on a new arts and science curriculum. The most innovative aspect was the first-year program. Students had to select their eight first-year courses from six different disciplines, and they had to take at least one class in each of the four divisions. Mathematics or logic and English literature were compulsory. The curriculum planners paid a great deal of attention to the structure and content of the introductory courses. These courses were supposed to delineate "the *boundaries* of the *discipline*," cover "the fundamental propositions and statements of the *corpus*;" and give an exposition of "the *methods* of the given discipline." In keeping with the Regina Beach Statement, they were to be based on "the broad, fundamental, organizing groups of ideas from which all special studies spring."[44]

Students were allowed to take no more than ten introductory classes (a maximum of forty credit hours out of a total of ninety-six) towards a BA degree. At least forty-eight credit hours had to be taken in one division – referred to as the major division – and a minimum of thirty-two hours outside the major division, with sixteen hours of electives. Each student selected a major from one of four types: a departmental major, involving study in one discipline (English, chemistry, history, and so on); a divisional major, involving study in more than one discipline (social sciences, humanities); a group major, involving study in more than one division (social sciences/humanities, humanities/fine arts); or an individual major, involving a program of study tailored to the needs and interests of the individual student. The program was designed to encourage faculty and students to think in broad, interdisciplinary terms.

The departmental major required a minimum of twenty-four hours in the major department. Of the remaining twenty-four divisional hours, no fewer than twelve had to be distributed between at least two disciplines within the major division. Each committee of instruction (or department) had a core program, which consisted of four to six classes that all majors in that discipline were required to take. In addition, each subject committee (that is, department) was limited to offering a maximum of fourteen different courses, excluding interdisciplinary courses.[45] The purpose of this regulation was to curb departmental empire building and to prevent the proliferation of classes based on the specialized research interests of professors rather than the overall goals of the liberal arts curriculum. The new BA program and the semester system met some resistance in Saskatoon, partly because of concerns that it would make it more difficult for students to transfer from one campus to the other, or from the Regina campus to another university, but it was finally approved and implemented in the fall of 1966.

The Division of Social Sciences was the division most committed to the broad interdisciplinary objectives of the new curriculum. It introduced three streams of courses (social theory, social structure, and social development) as vehicles for divisional majors. It also created a social studies committee of instruction to offer centralized introductory classes in statistics and methodology for all students in the division, regardless of subject major, and to act as an incubator for classes of a cross-disciplinary character. It established a sample survey and data bank unit to provide faculty, employees of government departments, and other researchers with access to up-to-date techniques for data gathering and analysis. The Canadian Plains Program, attached to the Canadian Plains Research Center, was later created as a focus for regional interdisciplinary studies.

The division system and the emphasis on interdisciplinary studies at Regina campus were departures from the Saskatoon model, but they were by no means unique in the wider Canadian context. As Paul Axelrod has demonstrated, the academic philosophy of "general education" had a significant impact on Ontario universities in the 1960s. All first-year students at York University were required to take interdisciplinary courses in the social sciences, humanities, and natural science. The University of Western Ontario in 1964 abandoned its traditional practice of offering separate courses for science and arts students in favour of a new "common first year program" that included subjects from "four divisions of Humanities, Social Sciences, Mathematics, Natural Sciences, and Miscellaneous, within certain specified limits." The University of Windsor pioneered combined programs in sociology and economics, sociology and anthropology, and sociology and political science. The common goal of such curricular innovations was the promotion of general education ("that part of a student's whole education which looks first of all to his life as a responsible human being and citizen") over specialized education ("that part which looks at the student's competence in some occupation").[46]

The general education theme surfaces in historian Patricia Jasen's analysis of the Canadian student movement in the 1960s. Student-power activists were critical of the traditional liberal arts program because, in their opinion, it failed to communicate "human values." Its social function, they said, was to train students "for jobs they did not want" and indoctrinate them "to be passive workers and consumers instead of politically active citizens." Student radicals demanded that the curriculum be "relevant," by which they meant that it should prepare them for "a life of effective action." Condemning the fragmentation of knowledge through the proliferation of disciplines and sub-disciplines, they called for a more integrated approach to learning. Overspecialization was viewed as serving the career interests of academics rather than the educational needs of students. Radicals said that they wanted a liberal arts program that enabled them to understand what was going on in society so that they could work to bring about meaningful change.[47]

Such ideas circulated widely in the 1960s, but their appeal was especially compelling at Regina campus. A new institution experiencing rapid growth,

T.H. (Tommy) McLeod, dean of arts and science (1964–67) and vice-principal (1965–69). He brought organizational expertise and academic leadership to the campus, helping to implement such innovations as the semester system, the division structure, and the new BA curriculum.

it had no well-established traditions to fall back on. In addition, it did not have a large number of professional schools, which tend to have a stabilizing effect because their mission is to prepare students for the workforce. In Regina, at least in the early years, the focus of development centred on the liberals arts. Moreover, the Regina campus was engaged in the process of establishing its identity, and the natural tendency was to try to differentiate the new campus from the parent university. Simply put, Regina wanted to be whatever Saskatoon was not. In the context of the sixties, this meant that since Saskatoon was traditional and conservative, Regina defined itself as innovative and free-spirited.

By the mid-1960s the Regina campus had put in place the divisional structure, the semester system, and the new BA curriculum. It had found a sense of direction and was moving purposefully to achieve its goals. Much of the credit for converting talk into action belonged to T.H. (Tommy) McLeod, who was appointed dean of arts and science at Regina in May 1964. He came to the campus with a Harvard PhD and a wealth of administrative experience. When the CCF formed the government in Saskatchewan in 1944, he served as economic advisor to the premier. Later, as secretary of the Economic Advisory and Planning Board, he was responsible for the coordination of economic development strategy and the evaluation of government programs in the context of a comprehensive planning framework. He carried out a study of the operations of the US Bureau of the Budget, which enabled him

TABLE 5: Enrolment of Full-Time Students at Regina Campus, 1959–60 to 1969–70

YEAR	NUMBER OF FULL-TIME STUDENTS
1959–60	295
1960–61	397
1961–62	643
1962–63	822
1963–64	934
1964–65	1,788
1965–66	2,255
1966–67 (fall)	2,705
1967–68 (fall)	3,308
1968–69 (fall)	3,794
1969–70 (fall)	4,345

Source: University of Saskatchewan, *Annual Report of the President*, 1959–60 to 1969–70.

to adapt the practices of that agency to the operations of the Saskatchewan bureaucracy. This resulted in better control of expenditures, more efficient use of resources, and an overall improvement in the administration of government departments. It amounted to a major innovation in the machinery of government. McLeod capped his career as a public servant by acting as director of the budget bureau and then as deputy provincial treasurer. He left government in 1952 to accept an appointment as dean of commerce at the University of Saskatchewan.

With this background McLeod was well equipped to take charge of organizational matters at the Regina campus, and he soon became Riddell's right-hand man.[48] Initially his Saskatoon background was held against him,[49] at least among the supporters of Regina Beach, but his good will and managerial competence won over the doubters. He worked for practical results and eschewed unnecessary confrontations. In this way he avoided becoming a lightning rod for discontent. Gradually the Faculty of Arts and Science came to a consensus on the key issues arising from Regina Beach. McLeod then took the plan to Saskatoon, where the university authorities were chronically suspicious of what was going on in Regina. McLeod, more than anyone else, was responsible for winning approval for the semester system, the divisional structure, and the other reforms. This led to his appointment as vice-principal of the Regina campus in 1965, a position he held along with the deanship until 1967, when he was made full-time vice-principal.

Enrolment of full-time students reached 1,788 in 1964–65, the year that marked the introduction of the third-year course. It was now possible, forty

Prime Minister Lester B. Pearson, who received an honorary degree at the first Regina campus convocation, held at Darke Hall on 17 May 1965. The theme of his convocation address was, appropriately, the value of a liberal education.

years after Regina College president Ernest Stapleford had broached the idea, to take a full degree program in Regina. The first person to receive a degree was Prime Minister Lester B. Pearson, who accepted an honorary doctorate at a ceremony held in Darke Hall on 17 May 1965. Appropriately, he chose for the theme of his convocation address the purpose and benefits of a liberal arts education.[50] He told the audience, which included the first seventy-two graduates of the Regina campus, that the hope of humanity lay not in technology but in the proper use of technology. "There are times," he said, "when one thinks ... that we will blow up this planet before we are able to take advantage of the knowledge that makes it possible for us to visit another one." For Pearson the idea of the sciences operating in isolation from the humanities was "something fearful to contemplate."[51] Uncannily, the prime minister put his finger on one of the major debates roiling the campus in the early years, confirming in the minds of his listeners the importance of defining a liberal education.

The convocation dance in May 1965 was held at the Trianon Ball Room in downtown Regina. Baskets of pink and white carnations hung from the balconies, and in the centre of the floor "a fountain raised on a dais reflected red, gold, blue and mauve lights in its playing waters. Coloured lights at the foot of the wide fountain highlighted the University of Saskatchewan crest placed at the base. Tables arranged in cabaret style were centred with the Hawaiian candles."[52] The celebration reflected the optimism of a growing campus. Student enrolment increased year by year, confounding even the boldest projections. The number of full-time students grew from 295 in 1959–60 to 2,255 in 1965–66. "History will record," the *Leader-Post* exulted in May 1965, that "the coming of the university ranks in importance with the arrival of the railway in the early eighties and the designation of Regina as the provincial capital in 1905 in shaping the destiny of the Queen City of the Plains."[53] The heightened rhetoric was understandable. Regina campus had 4,345 students in 1969–70. By comparison, Saskatoon, which began offering classes in 1909, reached an enrolment of 4,114 students in 1958–59.[54] In terms of student numbers, Regina had grown more in ten years than Saskatoon had in fifty.

But even at this moment of hopeful expectation, the *Leader-Post* fretted that something was missing. It worried that the university administration in Saskatoon showed "a complete lack of appreciation of the tremendous growth, with accompanying planning and administrative requirements." The 1960 recommendation to make the principal of the Regina campus a vice-president of the university had still not been implemented. Moreover, according to the newspaper, there had been a regrettable lack of "adequate planning and administrative leadership right on the campus with autonomous power to make decisions not subject to Saskatoon's approval and veto." The *Leader-Post* believed that the university in Regina required complete autonomy in order to develop normally and fulfill its purpose.[55] President Spinks strongly disagreed, and he took the opportunity of his 1965 convocation speech to rebut the newspaper's claims. In his judgment, one university with two campuses served the educational needs of the province more effectively than two separate universities could ever do. He said that a divided system "in which each campus competed with the other for limited funds by backdoor techniques would spell the doom of a first-class higher education system in the province."[56]

The students, too, became involved in the controversy. An editorial in the *Carillon* in March 1963 announced that it was time to sever "the mother-daughter relationship with that northern city."[57] In March 1964 about 200 students participated in a demonstration demanding "an autonomous, independent, and democratic university."[58] They marched to the Legislative Building and presented the minister of education with a petition bearing two requests: a rollback of the recently announced increase in tuition fees and the appointment of a Royal Commission on the organization and structure of university education in the province.[59] Although a few faculty members, including Ken

Students marching to the legislature in March 1964 to protest against projected tuition fee increases and demand autonomy for the university in Regina.

Lochhead and Len Greenberg,[60] encouraged the students, the star agitator was Charles Lightbody, who travelled from Brandon to lend his support. The Saskatoon *Star-Phoenix* published a cartoon depicting him as "Bonnie Prince Charlie" clad in a kilt and brandishing a sword, while leading the students in a charge on the legislature.[61] The protest attracted some attention but produced no concrete results. As one of the students put it, "We were patted on the head like good little boys and told to mind our own business."[62]

Principal Riddell privately rebuked Lightbody for his involvement in the march: "Your address to the students from the front steps [of the college building] appeared to be more concerned with an attack on the University of Saskatchewan than with the welfare and development of this campus."[63] Lightbody replied that he considered the principal's scolding "unsurpassed for sheer effrontery." He advised Riddell not to be deluded into thinking that minor devolutions of authority from Saskatoon to Regina would be sufficient to meet the needs of the Regina campus. Nothing short of a separate board of governors and president would provide the necessary degree of independence. As a parting shot Lightbody added, "I think that you might well prefer, even from a worldly point of view, to display some solidarity with your students and faculty."[64]

Riddell continued to believe in the fundamental soundness of the one-university/two-campus system. He pointed to the formation of the Regina Campus Council in April 1964, which increased the authority of the Regina faculty over academic matters pertaining to the campus. The hitch was that academic proposals from either campus that impinged on the sphere of the other required joint consultation, and final authority rested with the senate.

Budget issues had to be referred, in the last analysis, to the Board of Governors. Both bodies were Saskatoon-dominated. The top university administrators had built their careers in Saskatoon, where they lived and worked. There was no doubt that the larger campus was in the driver's seat.

At the first meeting of the Regina Campus Council, on 28 April 1964, a resolution was passed calling for the appointment of a Royal Commission on Higher Education.[65] According to the subcommittee report on the resolution,

> The University Act of 1907 deliberately created a monopoly of degree-granting powers, except in theology, for the provincial University. To many the concept of *one* provincial University has become a cherished concept, and it is indisputable that, in the past, the concentration of limited financial resources in support of one institution has had notable advantages. But after 60 years, a re-examination of this concept can be usefully undertaken in the light of current and anticipated trends in higher education in Saskatchewan. This may, or may not, have made this "ancient good uncouth." Responsible re-evaluation of the concept would be a service to all concerned with higher education in Saskatchewan and would make a constructive contribution to the public debate which has occurred during the past year.[66]

The resolution challenged the one-university concept, which had been part of the provincial psyche since 1907. It was the old Walter Murray notion that Saskatchewan was too small to support more than one university worthy of the name. Now this "cherished concept" had come under direct attack. The supporters of the resolution argued that "ad hoc decisions, hasty planning, a sense of pressure, and the feeling that vital decisions are being taken without adequate information and specialist advice" had hindered the development of the new campus. This had produced a "sense of frustration and a serious decline in morale."[67] The Regina Campus Council passed the motion and forwarded it to the university senate. There it died, because Saskatoon was not yet ready to give serious consideration to overhauling the one-university concept.[68]

The *Carillon* revisited the autonomy question in October 1964. It envisioned for Regina a "new kind of university," one that departed from the standard pattern of "overcrowded mass production factories for the assemblage of walking, talking creatures with a diploma in one hand and a bankbook in the other," institutions that churned out "technicians to supply society with the means of controlling its health, governments, businesses and machines." According to the *Carillon* Regina had the opportunity to build a true liberal arts college, but the dream could not be realized as long as Saskatoon was in control. Without autonomy Regina "would remain the branch office dispensing the same services as the main office."[69]

In September 1965 the student paper published the full text of the Regina Beach Statement on the front page.[70] It did so again at the beginning of the 1966 fall semester, together with a commendatory editorial.[71] Thus, student activists joined forces with Dallas Smythe, Alwyn Berland, and the other faculty supporters of the Regina Beach Statement. The manifesto became the rallying cry for an independent university. Without independence, there could be no Regina Beach, and without Regina Beach, independence was a hollow exercise. However, not everybody endorsed the Regina Beach Statement. The university authorities in Saskatoon saw it as a flawed document ("woolly," Spinks said), and not even in Regina did it have universal approval. There were many on the southern campus who wanted a well-rounded university, complete with professional colleges, and not just an experimental liberal arts college.

Regina Beach left an ambiguous legacy. It gave the Regina campus a much-needed sense of direction and a program for action: a divisional organization of the Faculty of Arts and Science in place of the conventional departmental structure, the semester system, a new BA degree program, and an emphasis on interdisciplinary studies. It nourished a spirit of independence and accelerated the drive for autonomy. But it also fed an internal conflict between those who supported radical innovations and those who favoured more conventional approaches to university teaching and scholarship. Regina Beach failed to acknowledge adequately the goals of the professional programs that began to emerge on the campus after 1964 – education, engineering, administration, and social work. It did not sufficiently recognize the importance of graduate studies, research, and scholarly publication in the life of a university. At times, it was used as a stalking horse for a left-wing political agenda. Nevertheless, it made a powerful statement of lasting value. It rightly emphasized that the aim of liberal education is not to train specialists and technicians but to provide a general, well-integrated education to help students grow as human beings and citizens. It summoned the university to its true vocation – upholder of essential human values and not-uncritical booster of science and technology.

8 Building a Campus

While the faculty worked at developing the academic philosophy and organization of the university, planning proceeded on the physical aspects of the new campus. The university administration at first assumed that the Regina College site on College Avenue would be adequate for the anticipated expansion. The plans for the Golden Jubilee fundraising campaign announced in August 1959 called for capital expenditures of $11,275,000 in Saskatoon and $2,650,000 in Regina.[1] The latter included an addition to Darke Hall; a combined classroom, laboratory, and library building; a physical education centre; and the conversion of the gymnasium into a physics building, all at the downtown campus.[2] The Regina faculty opposed these plans. They passed a resolution on 1 September 1959 affirming that "in view of the many inadequacies of the present College grounds as a site for the development of the University in Regina, the University authorities be requested to plan immediately for the selection and acquisition of a suitable site."[3]

The Board of Governors hired Toronto consulting firm Shore and Moffat to choose between two potential sites: the existing College Avenue location plus adjacent properties (totalling sixty-two acres), or the Dominion Experimental Farm situated on land leased from the provincial government at the southeast edge of the city (186 acres). The latter site was bounded on the west by Winnipeg Street, on the north and east by Wascana Creek, and on the south by the Trans-Canada Highway and a municipal road allowance. The building and grounds department of the university prepared a study in March 1960 setting forth the requirements for the site. It was to provide space for a campus with a potential enrolment by 1985 of 5,000 to 6,000 students. It had been agreed, the study indicated, that there were no limitations on the programs that might be offered in Regina, with the exception of medicine and agriculture, which were reserved for Saskatoon. The first colleges likely to be developed in Regina were arts and science, education, law, and commerce, with home economics, pharmacy, and engineering possibly coming later.

The requirements for physical education included a hockey and skating rink, twelve sheets of curling ice, six tennis courts, one regulation and one small swimming pool, four large gyms, five smaller floors and courts, one major playing field, five minor fields, two small practice fields, and a field house, as well as offices, dressing rooms, showers, and equipment storage rooms. The library was to have space for 150,000 to 175,000 books. The residences had to be large enough to accommodate 30 per cent of the total number of students who came from outside Regina. Since it was expected that about one-fifth of registered students would come from Regina, residential accommodation was required for 24 per cent of the total student body (that is, 30 per cent of 80 per cent). These numbers were based on calculations that had been used in planning the Saskatoon campus.[4]

Having assessed the two sites in the light of the requirements study, Shore and Moffat strongly recommended the 186-acre experimental farm site, suggesting also the acquisition of an adjoining eighty-three acres. The Board of Governors did not accept the recommendation and asked the consultants to make a second evaluation of the College Avenue location. This time Shore and Moffat took into consideration every piece of available land in the vicinity, including the property east of Broad Street owned by the Anglican diocese of Qu'Appelle and a three-acre island in Wascana Lake. The report of 11 June 1960 observed that in order to secure the gross square footage stipulated in the requirements study, it would be necessary to build four ten-storey towers. It added that positioning high-rise buildings near major traffic arteries did not make for a good academic environment. Moreover, the transportation of large numbers of students by elevator presented logistical problems. Elevators were costly to build and maintain, and congestion in the lobbies would slow pedestrian traffic. Future expansion would have to be at the expense of the limited open space and playing fields that remained after the initial development. Very soon the new university would be cramped and have no room to grow. The consultants' second report reached the same conclusion as the first: the College Avenue site would not provide "a pleasant university environment."[5] This time the Board of Governors accepted the recommendation.[6]

The Government of Saskatchewan also endorsed the selection of the experimental farm, and the Department of Public Works sought to obtain a release from the federal government's lease on the property. Adjacent prop-

The Dominion Experimental Farm, at the southeast edge of the city, which was selected in 1960 as the site of the new Regina campus.

erties were also to be acquired: seventy-seven acres owned by the Deerhorn Realty Company and fifty-seven acres owned by the Regina Land Development Company (the latter property was known as the Mackenzie farm). This increased the total size to about 320 acres. At this point the plan for the new campus linked up with a broader scheme for the development of the approximately one thousand acres of land surrounding Wascana Lake. The provincial deputy treasurer, Al Johnson, on 22 June 1960 wrote a memo to Woodrow Lloyd, then minister of education, recommending a master plan encompassing the legislative grounds, the new campus, lands dedicated to the arts and cultural projects, and park area for sports and recreation.[7] Others immediately saw merit in the plan, and the provincial Cabinet on 2 August 1960 established a committee to proceed with planning what became in 1962 the Wascana Centre Authority, a joint effort of the Government of Saskatchewan, the City of Regina, and the University of Saskatchewan.[8]

The public announcement of the campus site selection was delayed to avoid complicating the negotiations for the purchase of the properties the government did not already own. The strategy was not altogether successful. When the real estate agents acting for the provincial government approached the legal counsel for the owner of the Deerhorn property, his first words were, "Oh, you want this land for the new university campus?"[9] Eventually the transactions were completed, and on 24 January 1961 President Spinks officially announced the site selection. A *Leader-Post* editorial titled "A Long

An aerial view of the Dominion Experimental Farm. The small cluster of farm buildings near the centre of the photograph occupies what would later become the northwest corner of the campus. Planner Minoru Yamasaki truly had a blank slate on which to work.

Fight Won" reported that southern Saskatchewan was "jubilant" over the news. The only regrettable aspect of the matter, the paper said, was that George Barr, "stout champion for decades of the south's cause," had died in February 1960 and had missed out on seeing the full realization of his dream.[10]

Minister of Education Allan Blakeney in March 1961 spoke glowingly of the day when "a great new university will arise in Regina." He indicated that the development of the campus would start with a college of arts and science, and in due course professional colleges, such as commerce and law, might be established, either as new entities or as transplants from the Saskatoon campus.[11] R.H. (Rusty) Macdonald, a faculty member in Saskatoon and a member of the university senate, protested that such judgments were for the university to make, not the government.[12] Blakeney responded that he was merely repeating what President Spinks had announced – namely, that the university planned first to set up a college of arts and science and then to "examine the possibility of establishing colleges of commerce and law, either by transfer of those facilities from the campus of Saskatoon or by the establishment of second colleges here in Regina."[13]

Minoru Yamasaki, master planner of Wascana Centre and the Regina campus, arriving in the city in 1962. Behind him is Cass Wakowski, a senior member of the architectural firm Minoru Yamasaki and Associates.

One of the first tasks was to select a master planner for the entire area surrounding Wascana Lake. A committee of Colb McEown, Jim Wedgwood, Al Johnson, J.A. Langford, and Ken Lochhead considered various candidates.[14] Lochhead, the director of the School of Art at Regina campus, urged that the planner be a person of international reputation who would "bring a broad, new view to Regina."[15] Minoru Yamasaki of Birmingham, Michigan (near Detroit), seemed to fit the bill. Although not yet fifty years old, Yamasaki already had a number of prominent buildings to his credit, including the award-winning St Louis air terminal, the United States pavilion at the world agricultural fair in New Delhi, the McGregor Memorial Conference Center at Wayne State University, and the Oberlin Conservatory of Music.[16] Riddell was greatly impressed with Yamasaki's work, which he described as "exciting since it blends traditional Gothic, Romanesque etc. with strictly contemporary treatments. He gets dignity without heaviness, lightness without unsubstantiality [*sic*], and delicacy without fussiness." Riddell hoped that hiring someone of Yamasaki's stature would accelerate the "go-slow, take-it-easy" approach that Saskatoon, in his opinion, had adopted with respect to Regina campus. "There should be no looking back now," he exulted in July 1961, "until we have our Liberal Arts college established and are ready for the addition of the first professional college."[17]

Yamasaki invited Thomas Church, a landscape architect from San Francisco, to work with him on the Wascana Centre plan. They both believed that the overall concept was "a truly magnificent one": "This green centre bounding the shores of Wascana Lake in the Heart of the Capital City of Regina will become a vivid oasis made even more dramatic by the bareness of the Midwestern Canadian prairie; and in this verdant setting will be placed many of the aspirations of the people of Saskatchewan in physical form – the Government Centre symbolic of the Province and the working and living together of its citizens, the University and the aspirations of man for knowledge, and in its parks the reaching of man for beauty." The plan called for the construction of a new mall south of the Legislative Building along which government buildings would eventually be placed. The mall was to have a pool extending along its entire length, culminating in a large fountain, which would be transformed into an ice fountain in winter. All parking in the immediate vicinity of the mall would be in a large underground garage, eliminating unsightly vehicles from view.[18]

The park area around the lake would be designed to produce "the widest variety of emotional and recreational experiences within its borders, and none will come to the park without finding more than enough to satisfy their needs and desires." Across the lake from the Legislative Building, Yamasaki envisaged a large-scale overlook that "should have the much the same quality of the Piazza Michael Angelo in Florence." Further along the shore would be a major boathouse and the "Picnic Islands," with the "irregular shoreline, bays and inlets, evergreens and small structures reminiscent of the Inland Sea in Japan." The first quarter mile of the area across the future parkway was to be preserved as a quiet, wooded area, its only a feature a fine restaurant where Reginans could dine in "suitably elegant surroundings" with "waterside terraces, lights in the trees, chamber music and an excellent wine list." Next – and just as "charmingly done" – there would be an amusement and playground centre, having "some of the quality of Tivoli Gardens in Copenhagen, and perhaps some of Jones Beach. It could in spots have Disneyland overtones." Amusements could include miniature golf and softball, a shooting range, food concessions (but not "cheap" ones), hurdy-gurdy music, a small children's zoo, or at least a monkey village. Further down the shoreline would be constructed an artificial mountain, a hundred or so feet high. The park in this section would have a "wilderness" look, in contrast to the more intensive landscaping of the other areas.

A species of flowering tree, such as almond or crabapple, would be planted in great profusion and serve as the symbol of Wascana Centre, perhaps providing the theme for an annual festival – much like cherry blossoms in Washington, tulips in Holland, or camellias in Mobile, Alabama. In addition to the spring blossom festival, there would be a summer festival emphasizing "the flower beds at their most glorious color, trees in full leaf, band concerts, ballet and musical events at the water theatre and music basin, swimming, diving and boating competitions on the lake and in the pools." A September or October celebration, when the trees displayed their glorious autumn colors, might incorporate music, ballet, art, amateur theatre, sports-car racing, hobby shows, and a film festival. Rounding out the seasons, a winter carnival could feature iceboat and dog-team races, speed skating, figure skating, and "beautifully formed ice palaces."

One can imagine Yamasaki's visionary flourishes captivating the board members of the Wascana Centre Authority. They probably wondered what city he was talking about. Over forty years later there are no signs of the Tivoli Gardens, Piazza Michael Angelo, the Inland Sea of Japan, or the flowering crabapple festival, and no one in his right mind swims in Wascana Lake (Yamasaki apparently did not know about algae). Nevertheless, the rudiments of the plan and its essential inspiration have been realized – the overlook, picnic island, boathouse, fine restaurant, artificial mountain, wilderness area, concerts, winter carnival, and so on. Wascana Centre has become, as Yamasaki said it would, "the green heart of Regina."

As the master planner of the campus, he had a blank slate to work on, since there were no existing buildings or roads to interfere with the development of whatever concept he might devise. He based his conceptual approach on the belief that the university was "symbolic of the highest aspirations of man, and the physical environment which is built for its activities must strive to attain the nobility of these aspirations. It must have great dignity and yet not be pompous – just be warm and friendly and yet must give the kind of atmosphere which is conducive to study and to research."[19] The master plan located the academic buildings on the north side of the campus facing the lake and placed the dormitories and dining facilities to the south, close to Wascana Parkway. A residence for faculty and married students was situated south of the parkway, where there would be easy access to schools and shopping. At the northeast corner, land was set aside for research facilities. Athletic fields were to the east, and service buildings near the central area. A perimeter road circled the campus, and parking lots were strategically positioned near the entrances to athletic facilities and dormitories. The main entry to the campus was from Wascana Parkway (formerly Winnipeg Street) at the northwest corner of the site. The plan called for a platform that would extend from the building closest to the entryway and cross over the road.

Minoru Yamasaki presenting his master plan for the Regina campus to members of the Board of Governors. University president John Spinks, seated at the right, looks on skeptically.

On top of the platform a bell tower was to be constructed that would stand at least 160 feet high and be visible from across the lake and anywhere on campus. Although the tower was never built, the concept inspired the students in October 1962 to rename their newspaper the *Carillon*.

Yamasaki felt that the main problem with the site was the openness and barrenness of the surrounding prairie. To counteract this feature – or, more precisely, this lack of feature – he clustered the buildings to create a sense of intimacy and security. In the academic complex, the buildings were to sit on platforms or podiums that were larger than the buildings themselves; the podiums would link together to connect all the individual units. The podiums served several additional purposes: they made it possible for students to walk from building to building without going outside in severe weather; they raised the buildings above the grade, lending them an air of "dignity and pride"; and they acted as a unifying architectural element. With their continuous base, the buildings had a coherence that enhanced the overall aesthetic quality. To emphasize this sense of unity, the podiums were to be uniformly clad with Imperial gravel aggregate. The architects for the indi-

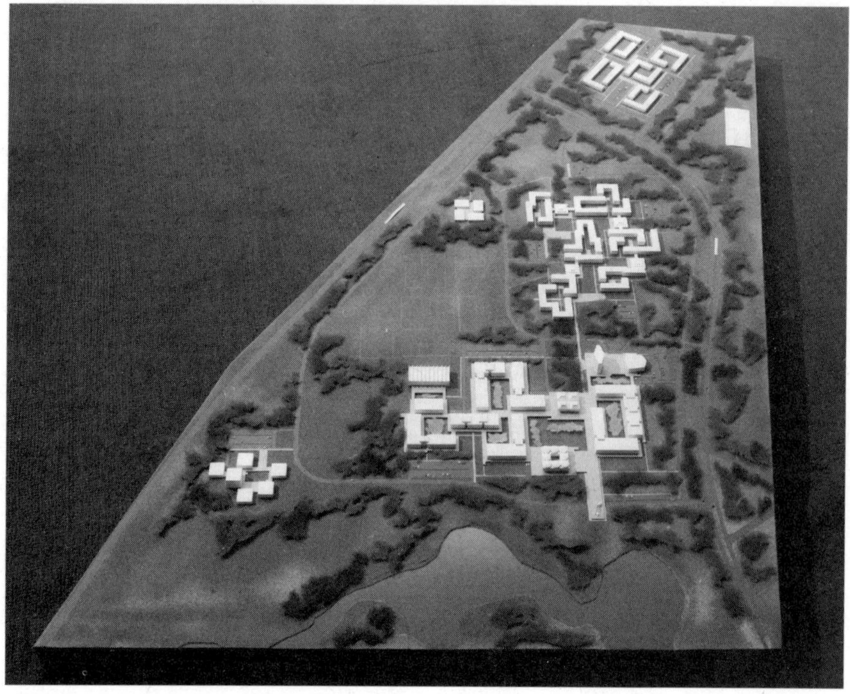

Minoru Yamasaki's model of the master plan for Regina campus. The cluster of buildings at the bottom constitutes the academic complex, the individual units connecting with one another to form courtyards. The middle buildings are student residences and dining facilities, and the smaller grouping at the top is housing for married students. The campus that eventually emerged departed significantly from this model.

vidual buildings were to be given as much freedom as possible, including freedom to choose materials, providing that their buildings conformed to the architectural theme of the entire complex.[20]

The podiums were to be about seven or eight feet above the grade on their exterior face and, on the interior court side, a full storey above grade. Around the courts were corridors that connected the buildings and lounges that opened into the courtyards so that students could enjoy the outdoors in warm weather. The top surfaces of the podiums were to be used for connecting walkways and outdoor space, but, here, it must be said, there was a flaw in Yamasaki's plan: the podium tops had a barren, cemented look, and they were unsuitable for pedestrian traffic in winter. A more fundamental defect of his basic approach was the attempt, in his own words, to "lose the sense of the prairie."[21] Instead of working with the environment he fought against it.

He failed to understand that the prairie was not just flat land; it was also sky, wind, and the curved shoreline of the lake.

Yamasaki presented his model and a master plan to the Building and Grounds Committee (Regina Campus) of the Board of Governors on 3 January 1962. The committee awarded Yamasaki the commission to design the first building project.[22] Known as Project I, it consisted of a classroom building and a laboratory building, both mounted on podiums, with space for 2,000 students.[23] It was to be ready for occupancy at the beginning of the 1964 fall term.[24] The size was later scaled back, and the project could finally accommodate only 1,200 students; this proved to be a major mistake, since the buildings were overcrowded from the day they opened.[25]

Cass Wakowski of Minoru Yamasaki and Associates presented the plans and models for Project I in October 1962.[26] Although the building committee approved the designs, President Spinks thought the buildings were a little too square in appearance.[27] Yamasaki replied that they were intended to be "elegant, dignified, aesthetically pleasing, but relatively quiet" and "secondary symbolically to such buildings as the Library. If you are fortunate enough to have a 'Taj Mahal,' that should be the Library. If all the buildings attempted to be monumentally outstanding, then the general impression of the campus would be that of chaos."[28] The classroom and laboratory buildings were intended in the short term to serve a double purpose. They not only provided space for teaching and research but also temporary accommodation for administration offices, the library, and a cafeteria. Later, when other buildings were completed, the released space would be converted into additional classrooms and laboratories to form the nucleus of the science group. Construction did not proceed as rapidly as Riddell wanted. Frustrated, he wrote on 10 December 1962 to Jim Wedgwood, the superintendent of buildings in Saskatoon, to say that he had driven by the experimental farm and had seen no sign of work being done.[29] His concern was justified. The scheduled completion date for the buildings had to be pushed back from September to December 1964,[30] and then to the summer of 1965.

Riddell was even more worried about what he considered inadequate provision in the university capital budget for the expansion in Regina. He advised Spinks on 3 November 1964, "I wish to stress once more the vulnerable position this campus would find itself in at this early stage if there should be any marked restriction in the development. There is already some uneasiness both here and in Saskatoon arising from the current austerity pronouncements and I believe it would take very little to begin an exodus that would be hard to stem. It is quite evident that the faculty is prepared to put up with difficult conditions as long as there are signs of development ... If, however, it became necessary to postpone essential buildings very far into the future in relationship to the demands for student places, I believe many would consider there were better prospects elsewhere." Spinks jotted in the margin alongside this comment, "Incredible that a senior officer should think this."[31] The president, it seems, thought that Riddell's panic was unwarranted.

Riddell grumbled that a committee of the Board of Governors had in late October 1964 revised the capital budget without consulting the Regina campus and without taking into consideration Regina's special needs. He cited a letter from Vice-President McEown stating that enrolment in Saskatoon "would become static by 1968." This implied that from 1968 onward the overflow students would go to Regina, which meant that there would have to be adequate space to accommodate them. "When the implications of this situation are taken into consideration," Riddell warned, "along with our projected expansion of existing programs and the less precise but no less real projections for new colleges within the next few years it is obvious that we are faced with a serious prospect. No provision for this situation appears in the capital budget presented to the Cabinet."[32]

Completed in 1965, the classroom and laboratory buildings were constructed of reinforced concrete with three different facings – the podium clad in an aggregate of crushed rock, the second floor with Tyndall stone, and the third and fourth floors with precast concrete panels covered in white quartz. The podium featured a series of arched windows and doorways facing an interior court.[33] The total effect was the clean and pure appearance that Yamasaki had been striving for, but the buildings in the bright sunshine were perhaps a little too gleaming and white. And there was far too much cement, especially in the courtyard in front of the classroom building. It was later dug out and trees were planted. About 400 students picked their way across muddy fields to attend summer classes in July 1965.[34] Poor weather delayed the completion of access roads and parking lots. There were no chairs in the library, many offices lacked furniture, and keys in many instances did not fit the locks they were supposed to fit. The principal's private washroom had a floor-to-ceiling clear glass window offering a full view to passersby on the podium.

The *Carillon* panned the buildings, describing the colour scheme as consisting of "off-white walls, off-white floors, and colourfully interspersed black furniture. In tasteful contrast to this the stairwells are decorated with off-white ceilings, off-white walls, off-white steps and colourful black risers."[35] A student poet mused:

> Walking through hallways of
> solid glass
> One wonders what totalitarian
> impulses

Created this landscape of void
This vacuum of invention.[36]

The buildings were also very crowded. The original design had made almost no allowance for lounge space, except the limited area available in the podium corridors. The cafeteria was too small to accommodate the number of people who wanted to use it, and patrons spilled out into the adjacent hallway.[37]

But at least the move to the new campus had begun. Premier Ross Thatcher, whose Liberals had defeated the Lloyd government in the 1964 election, snipped the ribbon at the official opening ceremony on 8 October 1965. The 400 guests could hear in the background the distant rumble of bulldozers excavating the sites for the next buildings on the construction schedule.[38] The requirements study for the library called for a building large enough to accommodate 500,000 books and 1,600 readers. Space not needed in the short run for library purposes was to be used for offices, classrooms, and the provincial archives.[39] Yamasaki considered the library the "Taj Mahal" building, and he said it deserved "better finishes outside and inside, a fine monumental lobby, a grand entrance, and a significantly more important approach."[40] As a result, the structure, with its sweeping arches and high-ceilinged ground floor, was the most impressive of the early buildings on the campus.

The official opening was held on 14 October 1967.[41] John Archer, archivist and professor of history at Queen's University and subsequently the principal and first president of the University of Regina, gave the main address. He echoed Yamasaki's belief that the library was the "spiritual heart of the university": "Let there be information retrieval, surely, but let there also be value retrieval. You must supply the resources. You must also give the service. Open the doors and let in all mankind who seek answers. Let in the old and the young – the scholar and the stripling, the bearded and the longhaired, the mod and mini. Above all, let in youth. Help those to interpret the call of the trumpet notes that sound faint in their ears. Our ears have grown dull. Help the young with their clear-eyed candor find fulfillment of those same dreams that lie unfulfilled and broken in our cupboards. Help the earnest and the hurried find sure standing in our society for the time comes when they must reach for the stars."[42] The building, now called the Dr John H. Archer Library, was the last Yamasaki designed for the campus. From then on the commissions went to local architects.

Joseph Pettick's plan for the Physical Education Centre had two stages, which together were to provide the facilities required by 1973. The first consisted of two gymnasiums, a swimming pool, three handball courts, a training room, team rooms, sports equipment storage rooms, lockers, a laundry room,

Premier Ross Thatcher snipping the ribbon at the official opening of the classroom and laboratory buildings on 8 October 1965.

faculty offices, student athletic offices, a general office, a conference-lounge room, and service spaces. The second stage, which never left the drawing board, was to include an exercise gymnasium, a "combatives" room, a dancing and fencing room, two handball courts and one squash court, a curling rink, and a classroom. The projected third stage, also not realized, included a skating rink, extra locker and shower room capacity, a classroom, a research laboratory and an archery range.[43] According to the plans laid down by the Board of Governors in February 1963, phase one was to have been completed in 1965.[44] Owing to delays, the facilities were not available until late 1966, and the official opening took place on 18 February 1967.[45]

Next was the education building. The Board of Governors in October 1964 gave the go-ahead to start the planning,[46] and in March 1965 it appointed Stock Keith and Associates (later the D.H. Stock Partnership) as the architect.[47] Vice-President Colb McEown in May 1965 outlined a schedule for the construction of the building. The requirements study was to be completed by 30 June 1965, tenders closed by 15 July 1966, and the building ready for occupancy by September 1968. Faculty members of the College of Education were asked to supply information for the requirements study, which they did, and the material was sent to the office of the superintendent of buildings and grounds at the Saskatoon campus for technical review. When the dean

The first three buildings constructed at the new campus, as viewed from the west. Clockwise from the top are the library, the laboratory building, and the classroom building.

of education, Lester Bates, spoke with the architect, Tom Ferguson of Stock Keith, in October 1965, he was disconcerted to learn that Ferguson had not heard anything from the superintendent of buildings and grounds and had therefore turned his attention to other projects. The planners in Saskatoon were still working on the requirements study more than three months after the deadline.

Bates inquired of Riddell, "Are our buildings being deliberately bypassed in order that there will be assurance that enough money will be able [*sic*] to complete those projects in progress, or projected, for the Saskatoon Campus? ... Unless I have real assurance that our building needs receive the kind of attention which a project such as this requires, I shall ask your permission to write directly to the Board of Governors to lay the matter before the body that created the Committee."[48] Riddell passed the letter along to President Spinks, who replied that Dean Bates was out of line in speaking directly with the architect. The proper procedure was to channel all communications through McEown, the chairman of the building committee. Spinks added that Bates's "comments about the people in Saskatoon and the Saskatoon authorities are in the worst possible taste, if not downright libelous."[49] The architect on 18 August 1966 presented a model of the proposed structure to the building committee.[50] The building was sized for an ultimate enrolment

left: The main floor of the library building, the high ceiling and sweeping arches reflecting architect Minoru Yamasaki's belief that the library should be the most impressive structure on campus.

right: William Riddell, John Archer, and Minoru Yamasaki in conversation at the official opening of the library on 14 October 1967.

of 3,000 in the College of Education. Although the number of education students was well below that level, the excess capacity was justified because of the general shortage of classroom space and faculty offices at the campus. The building opened at the beginning of the 1969 fall semester, one year behind schedule.[51]

According to the priorities set by the Forward Planning Committee in 1963, the first unit of residences at Regina campus was to have been completed in 1966. Thomas McLeod, dean of arts and science, suggested in November 1964 that planning commence for three units, each with a capacity of 600, and he added that construction of the first unit could not begin too soon.[52] The Principal's Planning Committee on 30 April 1965 expressed "grave concern" about the delay in the planning of the residences.[53] Campus Council shared the concern and pressed the Board of Governors to establish a project committee for student residences and to appoint a dean of residences as soon as possible.[54] The committee was finally appointed in June 1965.[55]

Residence planning took a sharp change of direction in July 1965 when Dean McLeod presented a proposal to the Principal's Planning Commit-

tee in favour of building residences within a "collegiate" structure. In his "Proposal for Organization of the University," McLeod suggested that a residence policy concerned exclusively with providing dormitory facilities did nothing to achieve "a more integrated and substantially enriched learning experience." He argued that a better approach was to conceive the campus as a system of residential colleges, each with the facilities needed to create a viable academic entity. A residence unit providing accommodation for 150 students would serve as the nucleus of a college of up to 500 students, resident and non-resident combined.[56]

According to the plan, each college would have offices for dons, tutors, and a complement of ten to twelve faculty members. There would be a few seminar rooms, one large classroom, a reading room/library, food services, a lounge area, and recreation facilities. Each college would be self-contained to a degree, but at the same time integrated with the service core of specialized facilities such as the main library, laboratories, major classrooms, lecture theatres, the Physical Education Centre, and the bookstore. The college would have a presiding officer, known as the master, who would have no administrative responsibilities other than to ensure that some type of meaningful and integrated academic, cultural, and social life developed within the college. To avoid nomenclature confusion, the existing academic colleges, such as arts and science and education, were to be renamed faculties. The latter would continue to have responsibility for developing and approving academic programs and recruiting teaching staff.

McLeod saw three distinct advantages to the college system. First, it countered the bureaucratizing tendencies of the modern multiversity, which consisted of a number of highly specialized and compartmentalized research and teaching units, each having little to do with the other. The colleges were a means of restoring, at least partially, a sense of unity and cohesion among different branches of knowledge. Chemistry and engineering students would rub shoulders with philosophy and fine arts majors, giving everyone an opportunity to learn from one another in informal settings. Second, the system would help bridge the gap between students and faculty. Although professors would not live in the college, they would have offices there, which would facilitate more interaction with students than was possible in the normal office building environment. Finally, McLeod hoped that identification with the college community would help dispel the feelings of alienation and anonymity that arose in the larger university environment. The sixties slogan "I am a student. Do not fold, bend, mutilate, or spindle" expressed widespread dissatisfaction with the dehumanizing effects of mass education. It was hoped that the college system would provide an intimate and friendly atmosphere, thereby helping to allay student unrest.[57]

Riddell and McLeod in July 1965 visited a number of institutions, including the newly founded York University and the University of Western Ontario, where the college system was either in place or in the planning stage. The trip confirmed their belief in the basic soundness of the concept. They decided, however, that the size of each college should be increased to 600 or 750 students (one-quarter to one-third of whom would live in residence) rather than the 500 previously contemplated. They also became more aware of the vital importance of the physical layout of the college to the success of the project.[58]

The proposal received enthusiastic support from the Principal's Planning Committee and the Executive Committee of Council. Regina Campus Council approved it in principle in October 1965 and requested that the necessary work begin at once.[59] The Board of Governors in June 1966 authorized planning for the first unit of the residential colleges, the project building committee to consist of President Spinks, Vice-President McEown, Principal Riddell, Vice-Principal McLeod, D.A. Larmour, and Professors Eric Stanley, Robin Swales, and Ruth Godwin.[60] The adoption of the college concept made necessary a major revision of Yamasaki's master plan, which had been premised on a clear separation of the academic buildings from the dormitory complex. Now the two were being fused in the same buildings.[61] The collegiate structure also threw a wrench into previous planning with respect to what would be necessary by way of faculty offices and classrooms in the non-college academic buildings and the sort of facilities that would be required in the planned students' union building.

When Yamasaki submitted a revised master plan, he insisted that the podium concept for the academic complex, which for him was the distinctive and unifying feature of the campus design, not be compromised. The building committee members were not happy with his revisions, because, in their opinion, he had placed the college units too far away from the other buildings.[62] Riddell offered a suggestion: "While we do not want the Colleges to be fully integrated into the podium, it is desirable that there be some connection with it in order to provide easy traffic flow from College to University facility and return. It is possible that a podium corridor might go along one side of the complex of Colleges."[63] Yamasaki sent a second revised plan, which was also deemed unsatisfactory.[64]

In November 1968 Yamasaki resigned from his posts as university master planner, master planner for Wascana Centre, and member of the Wascana Centre Architectural Advisory Committee. He informed President Spinks that he was too busy with other commissions to continue the work at Regina campus. He had also resigned from the National Council on the Arts in Washington and was in the process of disengaging himself from various other projects.[65] Moreover, the Regina work demanded a large portion of his staff's time, a commitment made more onerous by extensive travel to and from the head office in Michigan. Jim Wedgwood, superintendent of buildings and grounds in Saskatoon, suspected that there was more to the story. He confided to Riddell, "As we know, there is more involved than the two reasons he gives. Further, he resigned before and Mr. McEown talked him out of it."[66] It is possible that Yamasaki thought the Regina campus was straying too far from his original master plan.

Meanwhile, planning continued on the college residences. The idea was to build four residential units on a single podium base. Some facilities would be specific to each college, while others were to be shared by the complex as a whole. The latter included a centralized kitchen and serving area, two tennis courts, a squash court, a handball court, and a large lecture theatre for 250 students. The requirements study for the colleges reflected the buoyant optimism of the mid-1960s, when enrolment increases were exceeding all expectations and opportunities for expansion seemed unlimited. Each college was to have its own master's office and suite, dons' offices and suites (two faculty members, one male and one female, lived in and supervised the residences), secretarial offices, a counsellor's office, a main lounge (2,000 square feet), a music listening area of 1,000 square feet acoustically designed for listening to "high quality reproduction music" with "comfortable but not luxurious chairs" for fifty to one hundred listeners (next to this item Spinks jotted, "how boring!"), a TV lounge (500 square feet), a table tennis room, a craft room complete with pottery kiln, three individual music practice rooms, one group music practice room, a typing room, a library, twenty faculty offices, two fifty-six-seat classrooms, two forty-seat classrooms, and seven twenty-five-seat seminar rooms.

The residence proper was to have accommodation for 250 students, equally divided between men and women. Clusters of six, eight, or twelve students would be grouped together in a unit that consisted of a living room, a bathroom, and a kitchenette; each student had his or her own bedroom. There would also be a space set aside for "formal entertaining" by individual students: "The sitting room area should have two seven-foot sectional sofas with centre and end tables. Lamps would be placed on these tables for more intimate illumination. In addition to the sofas there should be three lounge chairs. There should also be paintings, drapes and a carpeted floor. The dining table should seat eight and should have an overhead lamp above it." There was also to be an apartment for the use of the president when he was in town, a place where he could entertain and hold receptions for up to thirty people.[67]

Premier Thatcher quickly brought the planners down to Earth. He had read a description of the projected facilities in the newspaper and was none too pleased. He sent an abrupt letter to President Spinks in December 1966 concerning what he called the "Regina dormitory" and asked why it did not provide rooms for a larger number of students.[68] "It seems to me," he grumbled in a letter he wrote a month later, "that some of the facilities that are being suggested in the newspaper should be curtailed and more specific accommodation provided. Since we are putting up most of the money, the Government would like to be consulted. The prompt cooperation of the people involved would be appreciated." The premier asked that the building committee contact him "at the earliest possible moment."[69]

Principal Riddell explained to Thatcher that "planning was well advanced" on the first units of the residential colleges and an architect had been appointed. It was hoped that construction could begin later in 1967 so that the first students could be accommodated in 1969. Riddell emphasized that there was a desperate shortage of space on campus, including "places for the students to go for studying or lounging when they are not in class."[70] The non-residential components of the colleges would go a long way towards addressing these needs. This upset the premier even further. He wanted to know how the project could have proceeded to such an advanced stage without the government having any knowledge of it.

Spinks wrote Thatcher on 28 January 1967 outlining the procedures followed in a university building project. First, a requirements study was drawn up listing the various rooms, offices, and facilities that were needed in the building. This was submitted to the building committee and the Board of Governors for consideration and possible revision. When they were satisfied, they passed it along to the Treasury Board (the financial committee of Cabinet) for endorsement. When this was secured, architectural drawings and plans were prepared and a cost estimate obtained, both of which were presented to the government for approval.

Spinks tried to mollify Thatcher by explaining that when Riddell had said, "planning is well advanced," he had meant only that the requirements study was nearly complete. When it was ready, it would be submitted to the government in accordance with established procedures.[71] Riddell telephoned Thatcher on 2 February 1967 to confirm what Spinks had written. Planning of the colleges was merely at the stage of assembling information about the space required and had only reached the point where the building committee could "talk intelligently about the matter." The premier made his wishes very clear. He wanted "residence accommodation, not a lot of other rooms and space."[72] Furthermore, he expected to be consulted about all buildings at the university in future.[73]

After university officials met with the Cabinet in January 1968 a new protocol was set up for capital projects exceeding $50,000. A senior member of the provincial Department of Public Works was to be a member of each building project committee; the minister of public works was to approve requirements studies, the architect's preliminary plans, cost estimates, and working drawings and specifications; and the Department of Public Works would henceforth call for tenders and award contracts for university buildings.[74] Increased government involvement in university building projects made the procedures more time-consuming and complicated. There were now seven steps: approval had to be obtained from the Regina campus building committee, the Board of Governors Building and Grounds Committee, the Board of Governors, the Department of Public Works, the Treasury Board, the Wascana Centre Architectural Advisory Committee, and the Wascana Centre Authority. Riddell, well aware that building projects were already behind schedule, dreaded the additional delays.[75]

By February 1968 the requirements study for the first college residential units had received the approval of the Board of Governors and was awaiting a go-ahead from the Department of Public Works.[76] The minister, Allan Guy, raised an objection in April 1968. He said he wanted a higher priority given to classroom space because if there were not enough classrooms, then enrolment might have to be restricted, which would create political problems for the government.[77] Whatever merit Guy's proposal might have had, it contradicted the major assumption of the planning process to that point – namely, that residential space was in urgent demand. Nonetheless, the university, in response to Guy's criticism, revised its long-term capital program to increase academic space in eight colleges, only three of which would have residences.[78]

It was becoming obvious that the government did not like the college concept. Guy said as much on 21 February 1969: "we contend that a standard non-College concept with the further opportunity for combined use of space and resources could achieve additional overall economies."[79] Jack Long, who had replaced Yamasaki as master planner, divided the projected four-unit college cluster into two separate entities – College West and College North. College West, which the university planned to build first, was designed to provide residence accommodation for 380 to 440 students as well as substantial non-residential space, for a total area of about 250,000 square feet.

There was some urgency in the summer of 1970 to start construction. The original plan had anticipated completion of the first residence in 1966. Four years had passed, and still no ground had been broken. The government, facing an election in the spring of 1971, wanted to get a construction project underway that would put people to work and boost the Liberal Party's chances of winning Regina seats. The campus was told in no uncertain terms that it had to spend $300,000 on capital construction for a student residence in the fiscal year 1970–71. Because of the need for prompt action, the Poole Construction Company was hired for a fee of $175,000 to take charge of the project.[80] This advanced the building schedule by about a year compared to what would have been possible if the university had handled it. Poole selected the architectural firm of Black, Larson, McMillan and Partners to help with the design of the building.[81] The result was an uninspiring structure that did not harmonize with the other buildings on the campus and was far removed from the original college concept as envisaged in the 1967 requirements study.

With College West ten months away from scheduled completion, Ray Harvey, who had succeeded Tommy McLeod as vice-principal in 1970, asked the fundamental question, "What is College West to be?" The original plan had called for three colleges in the first phase, each with 200 resident and 600 non-resident students. By 1972, there were supposed to have been seven colleges with residence accommodation for 1,400 students, and by 1975, ten colleges with 2,000 resident students. The total enrolment forecast had been 6,000 students in 1972 and 8,000 in 1975. The reality was that in 1972 only College West was completed, and it had residence capacity for 400 students out of a total campus enrolment of about 4,000 full-time students. A huge gap had opened between what had been planned and what had actually happened.

Quite apart from these compelling practical considerations, Harvey wondered whether the original college concept was not in itself flawed. Each college was to have had 800 students, only one-quarter of whom would live in residence. Would the non-resident students ever have developed a sense of belonging to the college? Would allegiances to the colleges have transcended loyalties to departments and faculties? Did an engineering student, an administration student, or a drama student really want to identify with a college rather than the academic unit in which he or she was studying? As for professors, did they want to leave their home departments and their colleagues and scatter into ten undifferentiated units? Finally, there was the issue of cost. Residential colleges were inherently more expensive than other types of university buildings because of the duplication of facilities and the need for a larger support staff. In the context of the budget restraints of the early 1970s, it was hard to justify the extra expenditures.[82]

In light of these arguments, Harvey asked whether the college system was still relevant or whether College West should be consigned to other purposes. The Long-Range Planning Committee on 29 November 1971 gave him an answer. It recommended that the non-residence part of College West be used for programs and services that, ideally, met three criteria: they must fulfill a university function, have an interdisciplinary dimension, and relate to the residential aspect of College West "as far as possible."[83] The building became the home, in the first instance, of the Bilingual Centre, the Canadian Plains Research Centre, the chaplain/student affairs adviser, the medical clinic, retail stores, general recreation facilities, and offices and classrooms for engineering, social work, mathematics, and geology.[84] College West became a grab bag of university activities with a dormitory attached, not at all a college in the sense originally conceived. It later served as an incubator for new programs, a place where innovative projects could be housed until they found a permanent home. An example was the Saskatchewan Indian Federated College, which occupied space in College West until it moved into its new building in 2003.

The original residential college plan might have had a better chance of succeeding had it been agreed upon at the very start of planning for the new campus. The decision to adopt the college system was made in midstream in 1965, when the classroom and laboratory buildings had already been completed. It was awkward to change direction at such a late date. The problems were exacerbated by delays in planning and constructing the first college units. The master plan had to be revised, the provincial government raised objections, and the Wascana Centre Authority vetoed the first designs because they were deemed cumbersome and incompatible with the master plan. The first unit, which was supposed to have been ready by 1968, did not open until 1972. By that time the campus climate had changed from one of optimism and growth to one of retrenchment and scaled-down expectations. What had been perceived as rational planning in the heady days of the mid-1960s turned out to be a wild goose chase. As a result, the Board of Governors officially rescinded the college concept for Regina campus on 7 September 1972.[85]

College West, for all its problems, did eventually see the light of day. The same could not be said of various phantom structures that were planned but never built, notably the ill-fated engineering building. In accordance with senate approval of programs in chemical, civil, electrical, and mechanical engineering at the Regina campus, the Board of Governors set up a building committee in October 1966.[86] The first draft of the requirements study, issued in June 1967, assumed an engineering student enrolment of 342 in 1971, 989 in 1975, and 1,247 in 1980, with a corresponding complement of professors and lecturers of thirty-four, sixty, and seventy-seven.[87] The plan was revised in March 1968 to provide for the amalgamation of the engineering building with a proposed physics building. The original intention had been for physics eventually to take over the entire classroom building, but, with lower than anticipated enrolments, it was decided that physics did not need that much space. It could share accommodation with engineering.

At the same time, campus planners revised downward the projected enrolment of engineering students. The 1969 requirements study for the engineering-physics complex was based on an estimate of 800 engineering undergraduates in 1975–80. The plan called for a building of 178,786 net square feet (304,000 gross square feet) that would cost an estimated $8,664,000.[88] The building committee appointed the team of Gordon R. Arnott and Clifford Wiens to design the structure. Arnott was with the architectural firm of Izumi, Arnott, and Sugiyama, and Wiens had designed the award-winning central heating and cooling plant on campus.[89]

Members of the Faculty of Engineering complained in March 1969 about the project delays. The original target date for occupancy of the building had been September 1970, but now it appeared that nothing more than design work was contemplated for 1969–70. The postponement meant that there were no facilities for conducting research and very limited opportunities to teach higher-level classes with a research component. The dean of engineering warned that if construction did not begin before September 1970 it would be difficult to hold the faculty together because professors would start looking for jobs elsewhere in order to reactivate their stalled research careers.[90]

The Department of Public Works in January 1970 vetoed the revised requirements study for the engineering/physics building. It accepted the estimate of 178,000 net square feet, but insisted the gross area be reduced from 304,000 to 286,000 square feet. It also demanded a cost reduction from $28.50 to $26.00 per square foot. Jim Wedgwood, who now had the title of director of planning for the university, thought the department's numbers were unrealistic, especially the target for gross square footage. Nor could he agree to any reduction in the total project budget.[91] Arnott and Wiens submitted an original and impressive plan for the building, on a par with Wiens's creative design of the heating plant, but it was all for naught. The provincial government on 3 March 1972 instructed the university to halt design work on the project.[92] No further funds were to be expended until a complete review had been carried out of the engineering program.

The cancellation of the engineering building was not the only disappointment. A biology/geology building, planned since 1968, was also deleted,[93] as were a fine arts building,[94] a principal's residence,[95] an arts/administration building, a humanities/social sciences building, the second stage of the Physical Education Centre, and additions to the heating plant.[96] The only building salvaged from this group was the combined administration/humanities building, which was completed in the spring of 1973. Principal Archer described it as "a bright, cheerful building" that "gives the lie to the assertion that moderate priced buildings cannot be attractive."[97] This was the last building – apart from the maintenance building, completed in 1974 – in the spate of construction at the Regina campus in the 1960s and early 1970s. There would not be another building erected until the Language Institute, completed in 1991, was constructed.

One can well imagine the psychological impact of these developments. Regina campus was truly on a roller coaster during these years. The prevailing attitude changed overnight from "The sky is the limit!" to "What do we do now?" First, enrolment had been severely underestimated, and then it was greatly overestimated. Planning under such conditions was fraught with difficulty, if not impossible. The mood swings were disorienting – from cautious optimism to heady boosterism to anxious despair, all in one decade.

One of the casualties of the downturn was the students' union building. The *Carillon* as early as January 1963 noted the lack of adequate facilities for extracurricular activities: "We have no gymnasium around which athletic activity and enthusiasm can centre. Also lacking are the facilities which on other campuses are supplied by fraternity houses and Student Union Buildings." The students took matters into their own hands, voting in 1963 to increase student activity fees from $15.00 to $23.25 per year; $2.00 of this was allocated to a students' union building fund.[98] They decided in 1965 on a further increase to $33.25, with $10.00 going to the fund.[99]

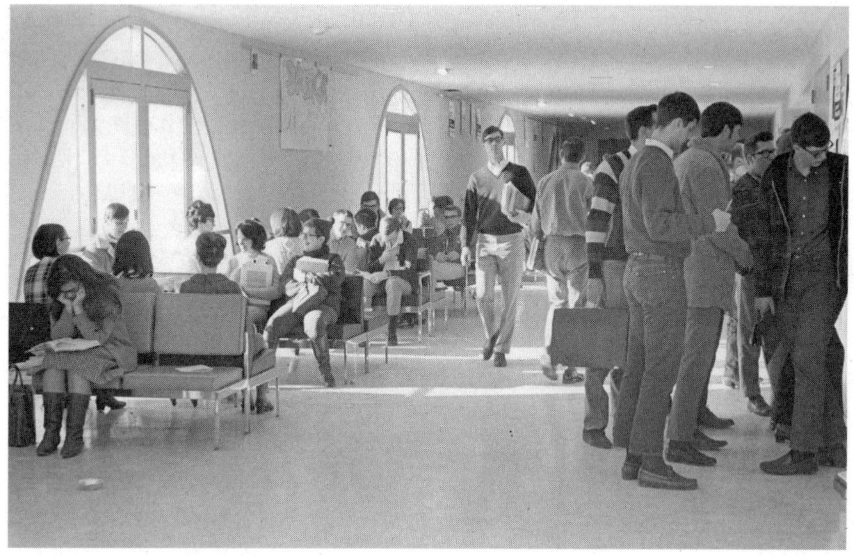

The crowded hallway of the laboratory building in 1968, the year the space shortage on campus was estimated at 275,000 square feet.

The students' union in June 1966 presented a building proposal to the Board of Governors. The proposed structure was to be financed from three sources: student fees, the university capital budget, and revenue from commercial leases.[100] The board appointed a committee to study the plan, but nothing came of it.[101] The project was low on the university's list of planned capital projects, and with the budget cutbacks of the late 1960s and early 1970s it slid even lower. It was now slated for the 1974–80 planning period.

An internal campus study carried out in August 1968 stated that "conditions of overcrowding on the campus have reached a point at which they should be a cause for grave concern, if not alarm." The space shortage was estimated at more than 275,000 square feet, but this gross measurement did not convey the full extent of the problem, since the shortage was most acute in the area of student services – especially cafeteria, lounge, and student office space. "Wherever the students are located for other than purely academic purposes," the report observed, "they exist on sufferance with respect to some other function of the University. That they are fully aware of this fact does nothing to ease current tensions."[102] The SRC offices were moved from the classroom building to make room for the Faculty of Engineering. They were subsequently relocated to the Physical Education Centre, where various other groups encroached upon their space. The cafeteria facilities had been designed to accommodate 1,200 students, not the 3,300 enrolled by

The laboratory building cafeteria in the late 1960s; lunchtime seats were at a premium.

the fall of 1967. Between classes students sprawled on the foyer floor at the entrance to the library or sat in the small area in front of the elevators. President Spinks nudged Riddell, "Had you thought of having a few more settees in the entrance lobby to the Library? This might help to discourage students from lying full length on the carpet."[103]

The Board of Governors decided in May 1968 that some kind of short-term solution would have to be found, and they authorized the construction of a temporary building for student services.[104] It was described as an "emergency measure" and had a completion date "as close to 1 September 1968 as is humanly possible." The usual building codes were disregarded because the structure was not supposed to last for more than ten years. The plan called for a dining room seating 425 persons; a short-order service providing "hamburgers, hot dogs, French fries, milk shakes and similar delicacies"; lounge space; student offices; a stall selling cigarettes, candy, and newspapers; a barber shop with five chairs; and a bank.[105] When the structure opened in the fall of 1969, the *Carillon* ridiculed it as a "Quonset hut" and a "parody" of a students' union building.[106] It was finally demolished in 1997, when a new students' union facility opened in the W.A. Riddell Centre. The students

Student lounge in the old Regina College building, 1952. The crowded conditions at the new campus contrasted with the relative comfort and genteel atmosphere of the downtown campus.

contributed about $4.5 million towards the new building, the amount they had saved and invested since 1963.

In retrospect, the planning and development of the Regina campus was not as smooth and efficient as it might have been. Part of the problem, as mentioned earlier, was the sudden surge in enrolment through the 1960s followed by an equally sudden halt in growth at the end of the decade. This threw the best-laid plans into confusion and forced a major revision of expectations. A second serious difficulty was the sudden shift in late 1965 from the Yamasaki plan to the college system – it was very hard to change direction in midstream. By the time the details of the college system had been worked out, the period of rapid enrolment growth had come to an end, and the window of opportunity for implementing the college plan had closed. It did not help that the provincial government intervened in the process, causing additional delays and confusion. This led to the botched job of College West, which was not a college at all, but a residence with undifferentiated space attached.

Underlying all of these problems was inadequate planning capacity at the Regina campus. The amount of capital expenditure in 1969–70 per planning staff member was $1 million at the Saskatoon campus and $900,000 at the Regina campus. By comparison, the figure for York was $500,000; Carleton, $400,000; Calgary, $800,000; and Victoria, $800,000. These numbers alone did not tell the full story, since Regina, as a brand new campus, required a larger amount of time for master and site planning, utilities development, and so on than did the Saskatoon campus. Calgary and Victoria, which came closest to Regina in terms of load, made extensive use of consultants in planning work. In addition, the overall productivity of the planning staff depended to a degree on the ratio of sub-professionals (technicians, supervisors, draftsmen) to professionals (directors, architects, engineers, and their equivalents). For York University the ratio of sub-professionals to professionals in 1969–70 was 1:1, as it was for Carleton, Calgary, and Victoria; for Saskatoon, it was 6:1, and for Regina it was 9:1.[107] The Regina ratio diverged sharply from the norm, and the discrepancy showed in the campus's slow and somewhat disorganized planning and building program.

The most telling criticism of the planning and development process was that the Regina campus during the period 1968–72 was not able to spend its entire capital budget. The amount appropriated by the Board of Governors in 1968–69 for capital programs at the Regina campus was $4,986,000. The amount actually spent in that year was $4,492,000. The figures for 1969–70 were, respectively, $4,787,000 and $3,180,000; for 1970–71, $3,261,000 and $2,378,000; and for 1971–72, $7,735,000 and $6,350,000.[108] This was unfortunate because after 1972 capital funds dried up, leading to the cancellation of the engineering/physics complex and many other buildings. The result for Regina was no residence on campus until 1972 (except for the Luther College residence, completed in 1971), no students' union building worthy of the name until 1997, and many projects left on the drawing board.

But all was not doom and gloom. Despite the frustrations, delays, and dead ends, the new campus took shape. The development of the Wascana Centre Authority in conjunction with the campus not only enhanced the quality of life for Reginans but also placed the university in an attractive natural setting. It effectively enlarged the campus by connecting it to a park area. Yamasaki's library was a success, and most of the other buildings were harmonious and serviceable. President Spinks took pride in what had been achieved. In his convocation address in May 1974 he spoke of bright prospects for the new university: "Its future as an institution of quality is not in doubt. It will be the jewel of the Southern Plains."[109]

9 Art and Music

Clement Greenberg, one of the most influential art critics of the twentieth century – some say *the* most influential, because he "furnished the terms in which Modernism came to be defined"[1] – visited Regina in 1962. After viewing the paintings of Ronald Bloore, Art McKay, Ken Lochhead, Ted Godwin, and Douglas Morton, collectively known as the Regina Five, he assessed their work in the March-April issue of *Canadian Art* magazine: "The specialness of art in Regina consists most of all in a state of mind, of awareness, and of ambition on the part of five abstract painters who live there, and whose activity is centred on the Norman MacKenzie Art Gallery, of which one of them is the director ... I find something wonderful going on in Regina art." Greenberg said of McKay, he "sets rounded squares, blunted ovals, or trued discs, sometimes solid, sometimes open, but always pale, against very dark grounds that are infused with luminous blues, or greens. Where McKay's originality declares itself as much as anywhere is in the curiously spacious way in which his central motifs are related to the shape of the support ... These new pictures of McKay's would be as new in Paris or New York as they are in Regina."[2] Where did the outburst of artistic creativity associated with the Regina Five come from? The answer lies to a large extent in the unique ambience of the Regina campus in the early 1960s.

Regina College had a long and well-established tradition of instruction in the visual arts. As early as 1914 the calendar advertised classes in oil, watercolour, pastel, and china painting, as well as pen, pencil, and charcoal drawing.[3] The art program received a boost in 1936, when Regina lawyer Norman

MacKenzie left his art collection to the college along with a sum of money for the construction of a gallery. Also in that year the university appointed Gus Kenderdine director of the School of Art.[4] After he died, in 1947, he was not immediately replaced, and there was a lull in the program. William Riddell, on assuming the deanship of the college in 1950, was shocked to find many pictures from the MacKenzie collection carelessly deposited in a storeroom and in an office used by the drama league. A number of canvases had been loaned around town and no adequate record kept of their location.[5] Riddell set out to revive the art school and build a gallery. This was one of the main elements of his strategy for the revitalization of the college – a strategy that had the backing of President Thompson. Riddell set out to hire a young, dynamic director to lead the school. He chose Ken Lochhead, a twenty-four-year-old artist from Ottawa who had studied for four years at the Pennsylvania Academy of Fine Arts and at the Barnes Foundation[6] and had just been awarded the $1,000 O'Keefe Prize for young Canadian painters.[7]

Lochhead eagerly took on the task of building up the School of Art. In 1952 he hired Art McKay, who was the same age as he was. Born in Nipawin, Saskatchewan, McKay had studied for two years at the Provincial Institute of Technology and Art in Calgary and for one year at the Académie de la Grande Chaumier in Paris. His work was included in the Progressive Painters of Western Canada exhibition in 1953, the Western Art Circuit in 1954, and the Ten Artists of Saskatchewan show in 1955.[8] Although Lochhead and McKay had very few students in the early 1950s, Riddell believed strongly in the program and gave it his full backing. He helped arrange funding for McKay to spend a sabbatical year in New York in 1956–57, an experience that proved to be of great value to McKay's development as an artist. He wrote to Riddell on 18 October 1956: "Things are going well at present, increased excitement resulting in increased output. The Barnes Foundation lectures are extremely interesting and open up new avenues towards meaningful teaching in art, where, as you know, truths are most elusive. The only complaint I have about Columbia [University] is regarding some frivolous classmates who noisily while away their time. I suppose they are found everywhere."[9]

Also of signal importance for the future development of the Regina Five was the construction of a small gallery in 1953;[10] an extension was added in 1957. It was the only A gallery in the province, which meant that it was the only one equipped with the facilities required to host major travelling exhibitions.[11] Thus, with the establishment of the gallery and the art school, the basic infrastructure was in place to support the outpouring of artistic creativity that occurred in the late 1950s and early 1960s.

Douglas Morton, the third member of the Regina Five, came to the city from Winnipeg in 1956 to work as a sales representative in the family business. He painted in his spare time, sketching on a pad balanced across the

Regina lawyer Norman MacKenzie on one of his art-collecting tours. He died in 1936, bequeathing to Regina College his art collection and funds to construct an art gallery.

steering wheel of his Oldsmobile as he travelled the arrow-straight roads of rural Saskatchewan. Although not formally attached to the college, he maintained close ties with Lochhead and McKay. They met frequently to discuss painting and constantly critiqued each other's work. Ronald Bloore, born in Brampton, Ontario, in 1925, joined the group in 1958, when he was appointed director of the Norman MacKenzie Gallery, replacing Richard Simmins, who left to join the staff of the National Gallery in Ottawa. Bloore shared an inexpensive basement studio in the seedier part of town with twenty-six-year-old Ted Godwin, who had moved to Regina from Calgary in 1958 to take a job designing neon signs. Chance brought these five young artists to Regina in the 1950s. Although they did not all paint in the same style, they shared an outlook and, even more important, an intense desire to express themselves in a bold and original way.

The university owned a facility at Emma Lake, where summer art classes had been offered for several years. Lochhead came up with the idea of holding an advanced two-week workshop led by a prominent artist from outside the province. "We felt so isolated," he recalled; "we asked ourselves what would create a more lively scene."[12] Vancouver artist Jack Shadbolt led the first workshop in 1955, followed by Joe Plaskett, also of Vancouver, in 1956, and Wil-

Students at the Regina College School of Art in 1951. Regina Five member Art McKay described the art scene in Regina in the early 1950s as the domain of "a few hobby Sunday painters."

liam Barnet of New York in 1957. The breakthrough came in 1959, when Barnett Newman agreed to be guest instructor. Newman, one of the foremost abstract expressionists of the twentieth century,[13] had just arrived at a pivotal moment in his career. His March 1959 exhibition in New York had met with critical acclaim, establishing him as a major force in the art world. According to critic Michael Kimmelman, Newman did more than any other painter in the history of modern art – with the possible exception of Jackson Pollock – "to change the nature of what painting is. It was not just that a painting no longer had to depict an image or simulate a window. It became an object unto itself, a physical entity in a room, of a certain size and with stretches of color that had their own palpable auras. Newman's mature paintings no longer depicted anything except themselves. They were what they were."[14]

Newman did no painting at Emma Lake, nor did he show slides. He just talked. After viewing one of McKay's canvases, he commented, "That's a beautiful painting, Art. Is that all you want to do?" This was an epiphany for McKay. "I realized," McKay later said, "that I was playing around with design rather than expressing myself. So I switched over, dumped my oil paintings, got into black and white, blackboard paint on paper, and started to make abstract painting. They were really abstract, not just contrived."[15] Newman emphasized the spiritual aspect of painting; the studio for him was a sacred place. He advised McKay not to let anyone he did not like into the space where he did his painting. At times, he said, it was necessary to let *no one* in.

Newman did not create the Regina Five. Rather, he galvanized the talent and adventurous spirit that was already there. Lochhead, in Italy on sabbatical, missed the 1959 workshop, but his letters brimmed with the same insights that energized Emma Lake that summer. "This period abroad not only opened a renewed appreciative eye to tradition," he confided to Riddell in April 1959, "but also provided a fresh perspective to life in Canada and particularly the prairies. We have something in Regina that Rome could use. Vitality." Lochhead believed that Regina and the prairies gave those who lived there "a chance to breathe" and the "opportunity to 'break through' and clear new horizons for man." It was the same spirit that had animated Woodrow Lloyd's cornerstone-laying speech in September 1963, when he proclaimed, "Something different can be done here – different and worthwhile and needed." And it was the same spirit that motivated the faculty members who gathered at Regina Beach in December 1963 to affirm a liberal arts program involving "a kind of intellectual slum-clearance, a breaking up of those conventional myths which are frequently identified with reality." The artists did not exist in isolation from the main currents of Regina campus life. They caught the spirit that was in the air and gave visual expression to the ideas and feelings that were circulating within the community.

But while the Regina painters believed they could trust themselves to try something new, they were not parochial in their approach to their work. As Lochhead insisted, "Our approach to self-confident pride should never be shallow or lacking insight ... In order to recognize quality we must continue to rely upon the expert from near and far."[16] This was why he invited creative people from New York to Emma Lake. The Regina artists were self-confident, but not self-satisfied. They knew that it was not necessary for them to live in New York to be good artists, but at the same time they realized that it was important to know what was going on in metropolitan centres.[17] They were not afraid to play in the big leagues.

Ronald Bloore in 1961 organized the May Show at the Norman MacKenzie Gallery to coincide with the annual meeting of the Canadian Museums Association, which was held in Regina that year. It included paintings by Lochhead, McKay, Morton, Bloore, and Godwin, sculptures by Wolfram Niessen, and architectural models and drawings by Clifford Wiens. Roy Kiyooka, who had been appointed art instructor at the college in 1956 and had been very much a part of the group, was left out because he moved to Vancouver shortly before the exhibition. The show caught the attention of Richard Simmins, director of exhibition extension services at the National Gallery. Simmins wanted the exhibition for the gallery in Ottawa and for

The Regina Five — Ronald Bloore, Art McKay, Douglas Morton, Ken Lochhead, and Ted Godwin — whose exhibition at the National Gallery in November 1961 was hailed as "one of the most significant shows of contemporary Canadian art."

a national tour, but he was not interested in Niessen's sculptures or Wiens's architectural models and drawings. The National Gallery show was to consist of paintings only.[18]

The exhibition titled Five Painters from Regina opened in Ottawa on 30 November 1961. Reviewers hailed it as "a remarkable phenomenon of the Canadian Prairies" and "one of the most significant shows of contemporary Canadian art." One critic announced that "Five young painters [have] put the Prairies on the map."[19] Simmins's exhibition catalogue took particular note of the fact that virtually no relationship existed between the work of the Regina artists and the avant-garde in Montreal or Toronto. Nor did they have anything in common with the "semi-abstractions of the West Coast" or the "pervading realism" of the Maritimes. The connection, if anything, was to New York, but, as Simmins made clear, the influence had not produced "a local imitation of abstract expressionism, but an intellectual upheaval resulting in great experimentation and an artistic milieu favorable to the production of important works of art."[20]

Simmins believed that the Regina Five, despite obvious differences in their styles, had a common aesthetic. They all "look[ed] inward to see the world. And if the eternal questions of when, why, and whither cannot be solved intellectually, then the very fact that they have emotional realization seems sufficient … And many artists, like the rest of mankind, are only too aware of the impermanence of so-called scientific truths. They recognize few universals; one is the undeniability of the worth of the individual personality or soul, and another is that feeling is perhaps a greater guide to truth than demonstrable logic."[21] These ideas, which Simmins drew out of the paintings, paralleled aspects of the liberal arts debate then underway at the Regina campus. Dallas Smythe, Duncan Blewett, and Alwyn Berland also questioned the validity of objective scientific truth and the technological progress that went with it. Regina Beach cast the university in the role of critic – holding society and its institutions to account by constant reference to such essential human values as love, justice, freedom, and beauty. It insisted on the central importance of developing the individual point of view of the student through teaching based on a process of dialogue. The Regina Five, in a sense, put Regina Beach on canvas.

Following the success of the Ottawa show and the national tour, Lochhead invited Clement Greenberg to give the 1962 Emma Lake summer workshop. His visit proved a mixed blessing. While his praise for the Regina Five raised their profile, his intervention was a source of discord. Bloore disapproved of inviting Greenberg to the workshop because he thought it was wrong for a critic who had never painted to tell painters what to do. He accused Greenberg of imposing his own "blinkered, restrictive, inhibited vision" on Saskatchewan artists. "We were doing fine before Greenberg came," Bloore later said. "He came as a colonizer and colonized. You could almost say he cloned some people."[22] Lochhead and McKay saw the matter differently. They thought that it was up to the individual to accept or reject Greenberg's advice. As McKay said, "He did make suggestions to people about their painting. If they took it, okay. If they didn't, okay."[23]

Soon the members of the Regina Five began to go their separate ways. Lochhead accepted a position at the University of Manitoba in 1964, Bloore was appointed to the fine arts faculty at York University in 1966, and Morton went to York in 1969. Godwin stayed in Regina until 1985 and McKay until 1995. Although the five were not together long, they made their mark on the history of Canadian art. William Riddell deserves some of the credit, too, because he helped put in place the supporting infrastructure of the School of Art and the Norman MacKenzie Gallery, enabling the painters to do their work. The Emma Lake workshops were also extremely important in that they exposed the Regina artists to the wider currents of the international art world. And, of course, one cannot overlook the individual talent, training, and dedication of Lochhead, McKay, Morton, Bloore, and Godwin.

There was also another, less tangible, factor. The Regina Five had a vital connection with the local community – not just the campus, but also the city of Regina as a whole. According to art historian Theodore Heinrich, what Regina "uniquely gave, without being conscious that it was doing so, was the opportunity for a group of artists and their students to take natural root in its social fabric. This spared them the alienation that marred the art life and the art of many parts of the world at this time without in the least requiring the dulling of inquiring minds or compromise of adventurous artistic expression or inducing complacence."[24] The Regina Five were part of the community but were not tamed or repressed by it. On the contrary, the community gave them energy and inspiration.

McKay recalled that in the early 1950s the local art scene was dominated by a few "hobby Sunday painters." "Most of them didn't like us," he admitted.[25] In March 1959 Bloore got into trouble for giving a speech titled "So You Wouldn't Be Caught Dead in an Art Gallery?" In his introduction he referred to a letter to the editor that had appeared a few days earlier in the *Leader-Post*, in which a woman had complained about "a considerable number of men and boys trying to be mistaken for intellectuals by growing a beard." Bloore said that in Toronto, where he had previously lived, he had not felt free to have a beard, "so he had come to Regina in search of freedom ... intellectual freedom, artistic freedom, personal freedom." He then turned to his main subject, a defence of modern abstractionist art and the "eggheads" who produced it. "Do the pictures and the statues and modernism and art for art's sake worry you? Do you prefer dull old masters for tired old ladies? Do you want to be numbered with the old biddies taking children on conducted tours to museums looking with affected interest at guff and junk?" Bloore asserted that it was wrong to make artists "conform to the dictates of today's supposed push-button civilization filled with mechanical gadgets, mass entertainment, and streamlined thinking." It was time to accept contemporary art, to have faith in "our own generation and faith in ourselves and our future."[26]

The speech drew censure from C.C. Williams, Regina MLA and minister of labour in the CCF government. "At the risk of being classed as an ignoramus," Williams complained to Riddell, "I can see nothing beautiful in much of this modern art, although I am perfectly willing that those who are interested have every opportunity of creating and showing it, but feel it is not entitled to any preference." He deplored Bloore's reference to "old biddies" who take children on tours of museums. The comment made him wonder whether the director was a fit person to run the gallery: "The whole tone of [Bloore's] remarks is impudent and insulting, to which the general public should not be subjected."[27] Riddell responded tactfully that it was the gallery's policy to have all exhibitions juried by qualified art specialists. As for Bloore's injudicious remarks, Riddell conceded that the gallery director had been "somewhat blunt in the statement of his position, but this should not be considered as rudeness."[28]

The following year Bloore perpetrated a hoax that nearly cost him his job. The provincial government vehicle repair garage was located behind the art school, and next to the garage was a pile of junk, mostly discarded machine parts. Bloore, along with Lochhead and Godwin, collected some pieces and welded them together to create what they called "found object" art. The gallery mounted an exhibit to showcase the work of the brilliant but, alas, unheralded sculptor "Win Hedore" ("win" from Godwin, "hed" from Lochhead, and "ore" from Bloore); her art would finally receive the recognition it so richly deserved. Bloore read a telegram from the artist at the opening in which she explained that she had declined to attend the event because she did not want to be subjected to the personal attacks and vilifications of hostile critics. The entire city was taken in until the hoax was exposed a few days later. The art-loving citizens of Regina were in an uproar, and there were demands for the dismissal of the gallery staff. The story even made *Time* magazine.[29]

But the relationship between the Regina Five and the city cannot be caricatured as avant-garde artists versus middle-class philistines. There was a special atmosphere in Regina in the late 1950s and early 1960s. French art critic Jean Cathelin noticed it when he visited the city in 1961: "The moment the plane landed on the small elegant aerodrome, we liked the atmosphere. The capital of Saskatchewan, with its 100,000 inhabitants ... is certainly one of the most human cities in Canada."[30] Ted Godwin, who arrived in 1958 from Alberta, felt it too: "What a place it was ... the Regina of those days. Quite an experience for a Calgary kid to rub elbows at parties with Spanish Civil War veterans, refugees from the McCarthy Communist witch-hunt south of the border, as well as various assorted brilliant committed socialist intellectuals from all over the globe."[31] The innovative spirit of the Douglas government attracted talented people to Regina – people who came not for the money but because they wanted to do interesting work and make a contribution to society. As one deputy minister put it, "I'm not a CCFer; I'm not even a Saskatchewanian. But I am fully committed to working with this government. I feel so free."[32] Theodore Heinrich, who spent 1964–65 as a visiting art professor at the Regina campus, recalled that "Politics were staples of daily conversation. This created a heavy atmosphere for polemics and debate in which the artists shared."[33]

The 1950s and the early 1960s was a golden time for Saskatchewan. Crops were good and sales of oil, uranium, and potash were on the rise. The CCF government, which had been in power since 1944, announced in 1959 its intention to establish a system of comprehensive, publicly administered health insurance. The legislation was introduced in the fall of 1961 and took effect on 1 July 1962. After a highly rancorous doctors' strike, one that divided the people of the province into two warring camps, a consensus gradually formed in support of the plan. In 1968 the federal government agreed to support medicare across Canada, and it became a national institution. Interestingly, the introduction of medicare legislation in Saskatchewan coincided with the Regina Five show in Ottawa. Both events drew inspiration from the same political and cultural milieu. As Minoru Yamasaki remarked when he got off a plane in Regina to begin designing the new campus, "all I saw was the thin straight line of the horizon. That and the colour of the sky. Nothing else. Then I met with all these vibrant, audacious people – from ministers to officials to educationists to artists – who so believed in the creation of a haven of beauty and enlightenment on the flat prairies. I was caught up by their enthusiasm and I wanted to help."[34] Heinrich, another visitor to Regina in the early 1960s, said of the Regina Five, "There are scores of other towns each with a sprinkling of local artists which have never remotely duplicated the Regina phenomenon." Why did art flourish in Regina at that particular time? Credit must go to the individual artists, but it is necessary also, Heinrich reminds us, to "salute the unusual town which somehow made it possible."[35]

Dennis Reid, in his *Concise History of Canadian Painting*, speculated that LSD and other drugs had something to do with the creativity of the Regina Five. He alleged that Art McKay, "prior to his New York trip [1956–57] had been introduced to the hallucinogenic drug[s] LSD and mescaline through the pioneering controlled experiments then being conducted at the University of Saskatchewan."[36] In his copy of Reid's book, now in the possession of Regina art dealer Susan Whitney, McKay struck out this sentence and wrote in the margin beside it, "LSD April 1961. I took acid in 1961 under A. Hoffer and D. Blewett."[37] Reid also conjectured that McKay's "drug experience intensified an interest in contemplative art and would have opened for him the expanding yet effortlessly contained 'all-over' cosmic images of Jackson Pollock." Next to this sentence McKay wrote "Untrue."[38]

Saskatchewan in the 1950s led the way in LSD research, largely through the efforts of Humphry Osmond (coiner of the word *psychedelic*), chief psychiatrist at the mental hospital in Weyburn, and Abram Hoffer, director of psychiatric research at the University of Saskatchewan. Duncan Blewett of the Regina campus psychology department also participated in the research, which had potential for the treatment of alcoholism and schizophrenia.[39] Blewett became an LSD advocate, not only for its therapeutic value but also for its alleged mind-expanding properties. He believed that the drug offered a path to spiritual growth and enlightenment and that it enhanced artistic creativity. His own use of LSD at times induced, as he freely admitted, bouts of depression: "These experiences let me know how life can seem to lose all purpose, interest, and meaning so that it seems to stretch out like an eternity of despair. Sometimes, too, it can become so jumbled and confused that ideas get twisted together in a frightening mess that seems as though it can never be straightened out and in the awful stretch of time the confusion seems like it will be an eternal nightmare."[40] During such episodes he felt as though he was "being buffeted about like a sock in a washing machine." But he discovered a way to overcome these feelings of hopelessness and alienation. "The answer," he said, "was love. I found it out only in the very bottom of the pit and it always seemed to call for so much effort that I really couldn't do it, but when I looked for other ways of reaching reality I only became more confused and desperate." He arrived at what he regarded as a stunning insight:

> It was through this that I came to feel in the very core of my being that there is direction in the universe and that direction is intelligent and good – that it is, in fact, love itself. I came to know with every cell in my body that no matter where I might venture in the eternity of space and time, no matter how lost or confused or miserable and tiny I might seem, this bond went with me, and though I might deny its existence or my worthiness to be a part of it, it continued to make my body work, to provide me with my intelligence; with the air I breathed, to form within my mind the very images of my senses and to surround me with infinite variety. It existed in the energies of every atom of every object – so near to me that it made up my very structure and my being. The physicist would say that all that exists in the material form is the product of the energies which manifest themselves in particular structures. These energies are simply part of the total cosmic energy from which there can be neither subtraction nor addition. The existence of any single atom implies the whole cosmic energy structure.[41]

As we have seen, McKay took LSD in April 1961 under the supervision of Blewett and Hoffer. He was adamant, however, that the turning point in his artistic development and that of the other members of the Regina Five was not LSD but rather the Barnett Newman workshop at Emma Lake in August 1959. He avowed this in a letter to *Arts Canada* in 1975: "Whatever images that were operative among us, were our own, therefore in 1960 and 1961, before we knew about psychedallia [*sic*]. I'm sure we would have been of the concensus [*sic*] that booze was the only drug worth considering."[42]

Although McKay continued to teach and paint into the 1970s and 1980s, he accomplished his best work in the 1960s. Principal Riddell thought that

LSD had been his downfall, and for this he blamed Duncan Blewett: "I am convinced that [Blewett] wrecked his own mind and should bear much responsibility for the deterioration of others such as Art McKay who tried to let the 'mind-expanding drugs' take the place of natural creativity."[43] Whatever the validity of this assessment, McKay at times had to be hospitalized due to medical and psychological problems. He remained, however, an active painter and an inspiring teacher. Affectionate anecdotes about him abounded. According to one story, he arranged to meet a friend, physicist Len Greenberg, for coffee at a downtown hotel. He told Greenberg that he had some important papers to show him:

> Art arrived at the appointed time with his collected papers in a brief case and ordered some coffee. When Len didn't turn up, he decided to phone him and see if he had remembered. Not wanting to cart the briefcase through the lobby and having a history of being late for meetings himself, he decided to leave the briefcase with the cashier while phoning as proof that he had been there on time. Before proceeding to the lobby he dropped off the briefcase at the cashier's desk with the humorous aside, "Don't worry – there isn't a bomb in here!" By the time he had returned the Manager had thrown the briefcase in the hotel pool and the Regina Police Bomb Squad was on its way. All they found were soggy remnants of 15 years of a man's life. Art is charged with public mischief and sent to the Munro Wing [the mental health ward of the Regina General Hospital] for observation where he is heavily sedated. The Manager saves himself a law suit, and the news is around town that Art has done it again.[44]

In the 1960s drugs such as LSD moved increasingly from medical clinics and laboratories into the streets. They became an integral part of the youth counterculture. The Emma Lake workshop in the summer of 1965 was awash with "booze, grass, and hash." Visiting artist and avant-garde composer John Cage spent much of his time searching the woods for "Amanita Muscaria, a mushroom of the family PSYCHEDELUS EXTREMO!" When he went missing on one of his expeditions, the RCMP organized a search party. Workshop participants combed the area in a grid pattern, while helicopters scanned the site from above. The composer was "eventually found wandering around a lake occasionally yelling, 'WOW!'" The Prince Albert newspaper, not knowing who Cage was, reported that an "art student" had been lost in the forest overnight.[45]

Riddell in May 1961 tried to build on the accomplishments of the art school to secure approval for the establishment of a Bachelor of Fine Arts program at the Regina campus. Saskatoon at this time did not offer the degree. Its teaching in art was confined to one stream of the general Bachelor of Arts.

Riddell argued that the province did not have enough students to support two BFA programs, and, if one were to be established, Regina was the logical place for it. He cited what he considered to be Regina's natural advantages: a well-established art school, an art gallery, and a "moderately extensive art collection." He suggested that Saskatoon concentrate on teaching art history within the College of Arts and Science while Regina introduced the fine arts degree. Ken Lochhead, director of the School of Art, prepared a tentative outline for the program. Its aim was "to bring together the enriching qualities of a liberal education and a high degree of experience in the practice of creative art."[46]

Eli Bornstein of the Department of Art in Saskatoon disagreed with the Regina proposal. Contrary to what Riddell had implied, he said, his department was not solely concerned with teaching the history of art and art appreciation. More than half the courses were practical studio courses in drawing, painting, design, and sculpture. Bornstein was of the opinion that Saskatoon was the proper place to develop an academic degree in fine arts, while "the logical pursuit for the Regina School of Art would be to continue as the professional or technical art school it has always been." He maintained that Regina could perform a very useful service as a training school in the applied and commercial arts, a field of expanding job opportunities.[47]

Regina's campaign for a fine arts degree suffered setbacks in 1964, when Ken Lochhead left for Manitoba, and in 1966, when Ron Bloore accepted a job in Toronto. They resigned to take advantage of better career opportunities and because they were frustrated by the failure to make headway with the BFA program at the Regina campus. The faculty of the Department of Visual Arts (as the School of Art was now called) and the Department of Drama in 1966 prepared a requirements study for the projected fine arts building on the new campus. The plan was to build the facility close to the education building in order to foster close co-operation between the Division of Fine Arts and the Faculty of Education. After the faculty completed the study it learned that because of a lower than anticipated capital budget, the fine arts building had disappeared from the priority list of building projects. The faculty would have to make its home in the normal school building on the College Avenue campus for a period of at least ten years. Ten years stretched into thirty, until finally, in 1997, the Faculty of Fine Arts moved to the Riddell Centre on the main campus.

In the spring of 1969 the fine arts faculty drew up plans and specifications for the renovations to the normal school building, which were to cost in the neighbourhood of $250,000. It submitted its suggestions in May 1969, only to be informed that a mere $80,000 had been allocated for renovations and that the plans would have to be revised accordingly. The renovations, originally scheduled for completion in September 1969, were pushed back to December and then to the spring of 1970. Frank Nulf, associate dean of fine arts, reported to Riddell that there were "deep feelings of frustration and disappointment" among the faculty members. They thought that they had been "shunted off into the position of a third-rate and non-essential part of the University's growth toward maturity."[48]

Regina was scheduled to introduce the Bachelor of Fine Arts degree in the fall of 1969.[49] The faculty learned to its chagrin in April 1969 that the General University Council (a joint body of the two campus councils) had authorized a BFA program for Saskatoon, too. The northern campus was also moving forward with a Master of Fine Arts degree. Although there was as yet no formal program, individual courses of study were being approved on a case-by-case basis. Members of the Regina faculty protested against the duplication of work. They were under the impression that because of the historical advantages associated with the Conservatory of Music and the School of Art, Regina was the preferred place for the development of a fine arts degree program.

The General University Council in October 1969 appointed a subcommittee to consider the issue.[50] The Regina faculty members welcomed this development but were dissatisfied with the slow progress of the subcommittee. They suspected that "the deliberations of the committee [were] being used as an excuse by some colleagues on the Saskatoon Campus to block the development of graduate studies in Fine Arts in Regina, where we are very well qualified to begin them and where we have a strong student demand for them." Edgar Vaughan, the Regina campus dean of arts and science, vented his feelings to the principal in May 1972: "How long must this situation be tolerated and our students be prejudiced? ... I cannot emphasize too much how frustrated we are feeling on this campus in respect of our Fine Arts development. Perhaps you will see fit to transmit the foregoing with your comments to the President."[51]

The Committee on Rationalization of the Fine Arts reported in June 1972. Noting that there were in 1971–72 a total of 550 fine arts majors on the two campuses, almost equally divided between Regina and Saskatoon, it recommended that undergraduate degree programs "in *all* the Fine Arts on *both* campuses" continue. It further advised that graduate work in the fine arts be concentrated at the southern campus. This advice was prompted by the fact that Regina's facilities were "more adequate to handle the expansion of programs that will be necessary" than those in Saskatoon, and that specialization in the fine arts was "consistent with the philosophy established by the University in 1959 for development of the Regina Campus, whereby the Arts, Humanities and Social Sciences would receive special emphasis."[52] The

Darke Hall, which opened in 1929 and served as a venue for the Conservatory of Music and later the Department of Music.

whole episode was but one example of how the university struggled to rationalize its programs and come to grips with the question of which campus should do what.

Music, like the visual arts, had deep roots at Regina College. The music department opened in 1911 under the direction of Dr J.E. Hodgson, "a very short, chunky, rosy-faced Englishman" who had been deputy leader of the Glasgow Choral Union and Scottish Orchestra as well as organist at Landsdowne Church, Glasgow.[53] The department evolved into the Conservatory of Music in 1912 and rapidly established itself as a major focal point for the musical life of the community. The 1913 calendar listed classes in piano, voice, organ, violin, viola, cello, double bass, flute, oboe, clarinet, bassoon, trumpet, trombone, and other orchestral instruments; as well as classes in composition, harmony, counterpoint, form, fugue and orchestration, choral and orchestral conducting, and music history.[54] The University of Saskatchewan, by comparison, did not inaugurate its music department until 1931.[55]

Music educators from Saskatchewan, Manitoba, and Alberta gathered in Regina in 1934 to set up a board to supervise examinations at various grade levels leading to two diplomas: Associate of Music (performance and teaching), and Licentiate of Music (performance). The Western Board of Music (WBM), as it was named in 1936, established a syllabus committee and a uniform standard of music tests, thereby providing an alternative to the Royal

The Conservatory of Music performance of *Faust*, 1952. Richard Watson, director of the conservatory in the early 1950s, specialized in opera production.

Conservatory of Music in Toronto and other eastern Canadian institutions. The Regina conservatory became closely identified with the WBM. Faculty member Dorothy Bee was head of the Piano Syllabus Committee (1968–74) and editor-in-chief of piano-music books for grades one through eight. She and colleague Gordon Wallis published, under WBM auspices, *Explorations* (1969), a set of piano studies designed to help students acquire the skills to overcome specific technical problems. Dan Cameron, head of the voice department from 1923 to 1939 and director of the Regina conservatory from 1939 to 1951, was appointed Saskatchewan director of the WBM in 1951. Howard Leyton-Brown, director of the conservatory from 1955 to 1987, was WBM director through that entire period.[56]

When William Riddell became dean of Regina College in 1950, he had to find a replacement for the seventy-one-year-old Dan Cameron. He selected Richard Watson, an Australian who had studied at the University of Adelaide Conservatory and the Royal Conservatory of Music in London, England. Known for his booming bass voice, he had performed on the opera and concert stage, notably with the D'Oyly Carte Opera Company.[57] As director of the conservatory, Watson specialized in opera production. He founded the Regina Conservatory Opera, which staged one or two operas a season, including *Faust, Così fan tutte, Don Giovanni, Carmen, Amahl and the Night Visitors, Dido and Aeneas,* and *Ruddigore*.[58]

Howard Leyton-Brown, appointed director of the Conservatory of Music in 1955, revitalized the music program. Later he launched the Bachelor of Music degree at Regina campus.

Watson resigned in 1955 and was succeeded by Howard Leyton-Brown, a violinist, born in Melbourne, who had studied in Australia, Germany, Belgium, and at the Guildhall School of Music in London, later obtaining a DMA (Doctor of Musical Arts) from the University of Michigan. During World War II Leyton-Brown had served as a bomber pilot in the Royal Air Force and was awarded the Distinguished Flying Cross. He spent part of the war in western Canada as an instructor for the British Commonwealth Air Training Plan. This brought him to Regina, where he gave a number of concerts, such as the one written up in the *Leader-Post* of 15 March 1943: Knox-Metropolitan United Church "was filled to capacity Sunday night when Flt. Lt. Howard Leyton-Brown, R.A.F., Estevan, Australian violinist, presented an outstanding recital under auspices of the Princess Patricia Club ... Flt. Lt. Leyton-Brown's popularity appears to increase with each of his appearances in Regina and Sunday night each of his program items won many enthusiastic rounds of applause."[59] After the war, Leyton-Brown joined the London Philharmonic Orchestra, first as deputy concertmaster and then, in 1951, as concertmaster.[60] He returned to Canada the next year to become head of the string department at the Regina conservatory, where one of his first projects was to raise the standards of the junior orchestra and string ensemble.[61]

Appointed director in 1955, he introduced reforms in the method by which heads of departments and senior teachers were paid. Instead of earning commissions based on the number of lessons taught, they now received fixed salaries.[62] This provided a measure of financial security and inspired a closer identification with the conservatory. The teachers were no longer just a collection of individuals who happened to be under the same roof, but rather members of an artistic community who were engaged in a common enterprise. Those on salary included Dorothy Bee (piano), Gladys Angley (piano), and Marguerite Buck (piano, organ, and theory). Appointments were made over the next several years to strengthen and diversify the conservatory and to support the Bachelor of Music program that was later introduced. (In the case of those teaching in the degree program, salaries were paid in part by the conservatory and in part by the Faculty of Arts and Science.) Among the new staff members were Gordon McLean (piano), Jan Van der Gucht (voice), Fiona Colquhoun (violin), Mel Carey (brass), Terence Bailey (history), Jack Behrens (theory), Thomas Schudel (woodwinds), Ernest Kassian (viola and Suzuki classes), Raymond Hoffman (cello), Hallgrimur Helgason (theory and composition), H. Bruce Lobaugh (history and clarinet), and Shirley Sproule (voice).[63] Leyton-Brown also encouraged students to participate in ensemble playing, the opera group, the choir, and other group activities, thereby broadening their music education.[64] Conservatory enrolment increased from 600 in 1955–56 to over 900 in 1958–59.[65] Space was at a premium, the shortage only partially alleviated in 1963 by an extension to Darke Hall.[66]

The Regina campus in 1961 submitted a proposal to the Executive of Council for a Bachelor of Music degree program, an idea that had been talked about for many years. A special committee consisting of four members from Saskatoon (President Spinks, Dean Leddy, and Professors Abramson and Adaskin) and three from Regina (F.W. Anderson, Howard Leyton-Brown, and W.A. Riddell) reviewed the submission. Despite meeting four times, the committee was unable to reach a consensus on the proposal, though the "weight of opinion" was against it.[67] As a result, the committee disbanded without preparing a report for the Executive of Council.

Members of the Regina faculty and instructors from the conservatory travelled to Saskatoon for the meeting of University Council on 5 November 1963. They introduced a motion from the floor to approve in principle the introduction of a Bachelor of Music degree at Regina, and, surprisingly, it carried.[68] President Spinks, who chaired the meeting, refrained from mentioning that some of the Reginans in attendance were ineligible to vote, since they were instructors and special lecturers who held ranks below that of assistant professor.[69] The procedure generated a certain amount of ill will in Saskatoon, which did not bode well for the future relationship between the music departments of the two campuses. The Board of Governors gave its approval of the degree program on 8 April 1964.[70]

Howard Leyton-Brown now wore two hats: director of the Conservatory of Music, with its non-credit courses mostly for students under university age; and director of the Bachelor of Music program, which offered credit courses for university students. The two programs had separate budgets, but many faculty members taught in both streams, and their salaries were split between the two. This arrangement was altered in 1968, when the Faculty of Arts and Science adopted a departmental structure. The Departments of Visual Arts and Drama had already been organized, and it seemed logical for music to follow the same pattern. Alwyn Berland, the dean of arts and science, recommended in November 1968 that "the necessary steps be taken to create a Department of Music under a chairman with terms of reference parallel to the other departments of Arts and Science."[71]

The music faculty and instructors in December 1968 voted 16 to 5, with one abstention, to organize themselves into a department as the dean had suggested.[72] They elected as department chairman H. Bruce Lobaugh (PhD, Eastman School of Music, Rochester, New York), who had joined the teaching staff in 1966. The vote was close: 9 to 7 for Lobaugh over Leyton-Brown. The latter continued as director of the conservatory, but he was no longer in charge of the degree program.[73] This responsibility now belonged to Lobaugh as chairman of the Department of Music in the Division of Fine Arts of the Faculty of Arts and Science. Leyton-Brown in April 1969 circulated a memorandum to the members of the Faculty of Arts and Science setting forth the case for the establishment of a college of music that would bring together all music instruction, whether for credit or not, into one administrative unit. He maintained that Regina was too small a place to have a separation between the conservatory and the Department of Music. The enrolment at the conservatory had grown from 500 in 1955 to 1,500 in 1969. "Each year," he said, "visiting examiners comment on the high standards of our students, particularly in piano, strings, and voice. Sir Ernest McMillan has referred to Regina as the string capital of Canada and each year we have many more than our share of members of the National Youth Orchestra."[74] Leyton-Brown warned that all of this was at risk if the conservatory were divorced from the Department of Music.

Although the proposal for the creation of a college of music was not implemented, Leyton-Brown continued to argue the point in a March 1971 memorandum. He claimed that the administrative problems he had foreseen when the Department of Music had been separated from the conservatory had come to pass: "In every respect it is the Conservatory which suffers." He cited a long list of difficulties: the Department of Music received preference in the use of space; instructors with joint appointments were under pressure to reduce their conservatory involvement; university students had been told not to take part in conservatory recitals or performing groups; faculty members had refused to co-operate with community activities, such as festivals and the symphony orchestra; the Western Board of Music examinations, administered by the conservatory, were "actively attacked" by members of the music department; and former conservatory activities, such as the annual opera productions and the baroque orchestra, had been subjected to "unwarranted criticism" and had to be abandoned.[75]

In an attempt to resolve these issues, Principal John Archer, who had succeeded Riddell in early 1970, set up a committee chaired by Judge Fred W. Johnson to examine the relationships among the conservatory, the university, and the community.[76] Bruce Lobaugh, chairman of the music department, presented his views in a brief to the committee. He claimed that the conservatory was systematically undermining the work of the department. "It is regrettable," he observed, "that the Conservatory of Music continues to organize activities, and to encourage University music students to participate in them, somewhat at the expense of departmental activities, creating the feeling that the Department of Music, in a sense, does not have a right of clear access to the students it is serving, and whose services it desperately needs." Equally problematic, he maintained, was what he judged to be the substandard qualifications of instructors with a conservatory background: "Teaching 'lessons' to young children is really something different from being a University professor." Conservatory staff members who had been given university appointments "with rare exceptions have continued their professional lives with the University without change – as if the rules of the University are to be bent to suit those of the Conservatory." He asserted that many of these people did not apply for research grants, engage in professional improvement, or even suggest new library acquisitions. In short, Lobaugh said, the "multiplicity of restraining entanglements" still existing in the department's relationship to the conservatory was handicapping his efforts to build a first-class music department with a good academic reputation.[77]

G. Edgar Vaughan, dean of arts and science, supported Lobaugh in the debate. Vaughan recommended a complete separation of the Department of Music from the conservatory, and he further urged the abolition of the system of joint appointments. In his view, those teaching in the degree program and holding academic rank should be in the Department of Music, their salaries paid from the department's budget. Those primarily involved in teaching conservatory students belonged in the conservatory, their salaries drawn from the conservatory budget. If this clean separation were made, then staff members would "clearly know where they belonged, who was their boss, and what obligations they had entered into." Vaughan did not think that conservatory teachers should have university academic rank, "but rather a hierarchy of their own with a distinct nomenclature." He also perceived an additional benefit. If the music department were firmly placed within the university structure, separate and distinct from the conservatory, then it could more easily enter into co-operative arrangements with other units of the university, such as the Faculty of Education.[78]

Despite Dean Vaughan's unequivocal statement, the Johnson Report recommended grouping the three areas of the music program (the conservatory, the Department of Music, and music education within the Faculty of Education) in one structure under one administrator. Under this arrangement, the conservatory would become the Division of Applied Music; the Department of Music, the more academically oriented division; and music education, the division concerned with teacher training. The concept harked back to the proposal for a college of music that Leyton-Brown had brought forward in 1969 as an alternative to the separation of the Department of Music from the conservatory. The Johnson Report, it is fair to say, reflected the conservatory perspective, as expressed, for example, in the comment that a "narrow academic 'blue-blood' attitude" should not be permitted to inhibit the "development and flowering" of community programs.[79]

Leyton-Brown described the report as "an extremely sensitive analysis of the situation and may well point to a sensible solution."[80] Lobaugh, on the other hand, considered it a document permeated with "emotion-laden terminology." He questioned the assumption that the Department of Music was "academically oriented": "Has no one looked at the Calendar? The *only* concentration in which students are registered in the Bachelor of Music programme at present is PERFORMANCE." He reiterated his view that the Department of Music should be kept separate from the conservatory: "Degree students have no business whatsoever appearing on Conservatory programs, as they now do. Conservatory performing groups must give up the idea of using University students for any purpose. The effects of the tugging and pulling from both sides on degree students is criminal."[81] Lobaugh also opposed the incorporation into the university of the entire conservatory teaching staff. The Department of Music needed "qualified artist-teachers and scholars," not instructors who spent most of their time teaching young children or engaging in "amateurish community music-making."[82] The department managed to quash the Johnson Report, which remained a dead letter. The conservatory reverted to what it had been in the 1950s – namely, a school concerned mainly with giving music lessons to students not enrolled in a degree program. Some lamented the breakup of the unified music program; others failed to see the logic of bringing together in the same administrative structure eight year olds taking violin lessons and advanced university students.

The debate between the conservatory and the university music department was not unique to Regina. The Royal Conservatory of Music in Toronto was involved in a similar conflict in the 1970s and 1980s. Three separate studies were made (1973, 1977, and 1981) in an attempt to sort out administrative arrangements. The university in 1983 appointed a committee to devise a plan "for the integration of the two divisions through which the university offered

Students enrolled in the Regina campus Department of Music, circa 1971.

musical studies." The committee ended up doing the exact opposite of what it had been instructed to do. It recommended a complete separation of the two units, a solution that, after prolonged negotiation, was implemented in 1991.[83] This suggests that there is an inherent tension between conservatory training and university music education. The former focuses on performance (musicianship, skills, technique, and the other practical elements of music making); the latter, while including performance, places more emphasis on history, theory, and academic rigour. This, coupled with the discrepancy in the ages and goals of the students, makes it difficult to combine the two in one unit. Regina ultimately conformed to the dominant North American pattern of keeping non-degree-granting conservatories and music departments academically and administratively distinct.

Despite the conflicts, the music program in the 1960s and 1970s took pride in a record of accomplishment. The 1969–70 calendar for the Bachelor of Music program listed sixteen faculty members and outlined four areas of training: performing, music teaching, school music teaching, and composing. During the first three years of the program general subjects were studied, and in the fourth year the student specialized in one of the four areas.[84] School music teachers received the degree of Bachelor of Music with an education designation and qualified for a professional teaching certificate. Later, this option had to be revised because the Faculty of Education introduced a full semester of teaching internship. This meant that some of the music classes had to be sacrificed to make room for education classes so that students could still complete the degree in four years. With the change in course requirements, the degree was reconstituted as the Bachelor of Music Education, a joint offering of the music department and the Faculty of Education.

A major undertaking of the department was the formation of university ensembles – the concert choir, collegium musicum, chamber orchestra, jazz ensemble, and concert band.[85] Degree students were required to participate in the ensembles as well as give individual recitals for academic credit. These and other revisions to the curriculum, such as new options in music history and theory, as well as graduate studies in several areas, helped bring the department in line with what was expected of a university program and enabled it to attract more students.

Faculty accomplishments included Thomas Schudel's Symphony no. 1, which was awarded first prize at the 1972 International Competition of Symphonic Composition in Trieste, Italy.[86] Jack Behrens, a staff member at the conservatory from 1962–66 and subsequently dean of the Faculty of Music at the University of Western Ontario, composed *The Lay of Thrym* (libretto by conservatory colleague C.K. Cockburn). The chamber opera, based on an Icelandic legend, premiered at Darke Hall on 13 April 1968. Many Regina graduates, among them Brian Boychuk, Gary Kosloski, Darren Lowe, Alanna Deptuch Vagny, and Donald Whyte, were promoted to positions in major orchestras in Canada, the United States, and Europe.[87] Malcolm Lowe took top honours at the CBC Talent Festival in 1972 and was later appointed concertmaster of the Boston Symphony Orchestra.[88]

By 1974 the music program had successfully navigated the transition to the university level of instruction. The conflicts within and between the Conservatory of Music and the Department of Music reflected the need to find a balance between professionalism and liberal education, between academic specialization and community involvement. The same tensions were brought out, on a larger scale, in the debate over the Regina Beach Statement, when the members of the Faculty of Arts and Science discussed the relative merits of specialized training within departmental units and interdisciplinary studies taught through the division system. The ghost of Regina Beach was present too, though in a different way, in the work of the Regina Five, whose paintings marked the most outstanding achievement in the arts at Regina campus during this period. The Regina Five caught the spirit of innovation, challenge to the status quo, and desire for personal authenticity that was in the air in the 1960s and gave it visual representation. They captured what was best about the university in Regina at that moment in history and transformed it into a lasting artistic legacy.

10 Professional Colleges, Graduate Studies, and Research

Even before the Regina faculty gave formal approval to the Regina Beach Statement, the document that was supposed to define the nature of liberal arts education at the Regina campus, it had already passed a resolution approving the establishment of a college of education and the appointment of a dean of education.[1] Regina was never a purely liberal arts college. The third year of the arts and science program was introduced in the fall of 1964, by which time the College of Education had already come into existence. The professional colleges were not an afterthought or aberration from what was supposed to be a liberal arts institution; they were present, if not at the creation, then just after it.

The Board of Governors on 8 April 1964 approved the establishment of a college of education at the Regina campus as recommended by the senate,[2] and Dr Lester Bates was named dean on 1 July 1964. Bates had been an instructor at the teachers' college in Moose Jaw. When the school was moved to Regina, in 1959, he continued as an instructor and later as principal.[3] The Government of Saskatchewan decided in the spring of 1964 that the teachers' colleges, one in Regina and the other in Saskatoon, should be absorbed into the University of Saskatchewan, along with their teaching staffs, who automatically became university faculty.[4] The College of Education in Regina occupied the normal school building on the old campus at the corner of College Avenue and Broad Street until the new education building was opened at the new campus in the fall of 1969.

The college was renamed the Faculty of Education in late 1965 to differentiate it from the residential colleges that were to be built. Thereafter, "faculties" was standard nomenclature on the Regina campus for what in Saskatoon were called "colleges." Thus, the College of Arts and Science became the Faculty of Arts and Science, and the College of Engineering became the Faculty of Engineering, and so on. The Faculty of Education in 1964–65 offered a diploma course, which qualified those who completed it for a professional teaching certificate. Students entered the one-year professional course directly from high school or as transfers from another university program. A student who earned credit for five acceptable university classes (one year's standing) and completed the professional year in the Faculty of Education qualified for the standard A teaching certificate. Those who completed the professional year but did not have at least five university classes outside the Faculty of Education received only an interim standard teaching certificate.[5]

In 1965–66, the second year of operation of the Faculty of Education, the program was expanded to include a full degree course, and the first Bachelor of Education degrees at Regina campus were conferred at convocation in May 1966.[6] By 1968 only about 40 per cent of the students enrolled in the faculty were in the one-year certification program, and the latter was phased out completely in 1969. A two-year course leading to a standard teaching certificate was introduced in the fall of 1967, but this too faded out, and it became the norm for teachers to have a professional degree.[7]

The faculty in 1966–67 launched a four-year Bachelor of Education degree in secondary education, a notable feature of which was a complete semester of internship as part of the total program of eight semesters.[8] This differentiated the Regina program from that of the College of Education in Saskatoon, where the practicum or internship was of much shorter duration – usually two or three weeks. The emphasis on in-classroom experience became one of the hallmarks of the Regina degree. Much of the credit for the innovation belonged to Dr Robert N. Anderson, who was appointed head of the Department of Secondary Education in 1965.[9] A graduate of the University of Saskatchewan and the University of Minnesota, he emerged as one of the leaders of program development during the formative years of the faculty.[10]

Anderson encouraged the faculty members in the Department of Secondary Education to go to professional conferences and keep up with the current literature in their fields. He had each of them put together a committee of the six to eight Saskatchewan high school teachers they considered the most enthusiastic and progressive in their respective subject areas. The faculty members then used the committees to test new education theories in classroom settings and to gather ideas about effective teaching methods. In addition, Anderson held Friday meetings with the members of his department. He asked each to describe one new teaching idea he or she had tried that week and how the innovation had succeeded or failed. In this way, he modelled a basic concept of teacher education. The idea was not for faculty to impose on education students a particular way of teaching, but rather to build on ideas the students already had. Prospective teachers were encouraged to think about what style of instruction worked most effectively for them, not simply to parrot ready-made techniques. The goal was to make the teacher a creative, self-aware professional, not a technician who blindly followed a well-trodden path.

Lester Bates resigned from the deanship on 30 June 1967. His replacement, Norman France, ran into difficulties almost from the start. He had come to Regina from McGill University, where he had been an associate professor of education since 1965. Before that he had held various teaching and supervisory posts in Britain.[11] France was accustomed to a more hierarchical style of administration than he found at the Regina campus, where the atmosphere tended to be democratic and egalitarian. Principal Riddell detected signs of trouble in October 1968: "The situation in the Faculty of Education is extremely serious. It appears that [R.N.] Anderson and his 'satellites' are launching a major drive to get rid of Dean France as Dean. It appears also that this group is making plans to get rid of the Principal as well. The technique is to provoke me in some public meeting so that I will 'blow up' and the claim will be made that I am not stable enough to continue in office."[12] That Riddell should have this perception, whether it was based on fact or not, did not bode well for the Faculty of Education.

Anderson announced his resignation from the university in April 1969, as did a number of other faculty members. At a faculty meeting on 2 April 1969, Evelyn Jonescu moved, and William Otis seconded, a motion of non-confidence in Dean France. The vote, conducted by secret ballot, resulted in a tie, with 23 supporting the motion, 23 opposing, and 2 abstaining.[13] When faculty members who had not been present at the meeting were polled, the tally was 28 for the motion, 32 against, and 3 abstentions.[14] Principal Riddell called a meeting of senior administrators to discuss the situation. According to Riddell's notes, "It was pointed out one of the causes of the difficulty was the authoritarian nature of Dean France's administration and that as new people were recruited, it was more likely that these would be the type that would not accept the authoritarian approach, but would expect the more democratic processes that are being introduced into university procedures."[15]

The controversy spilled over into the public arena. An unnamed faculty member was quoted in the *Leader-Post* saying that France had "never found out how to work in the context of a North American university." Another said that the dean "just doesn't understand today's youth. He feels all activism is Communist inspired." Stan Marsh, who had resigned from the Faculty of Education to take a position as curriculum director for the public school system in Wichita Falls, Texas, commented that France's support "comes mainly from the people who have been here since Teachers' College days. The younger faculty support Dr. Burgess [J. Orrison Burgess, head of the Department of Elementary Education] and Dr. Anderson. It is a fairly even split."[16]

Principal Riddell appointed a committee of inquiry to investigate the turmoil in the faculty and advise him of what remedial measures to take. The committee consisted of Roger Carter, dean of the College of Law in Saskatoon (chair), Les Crossman of the Department of English, Regina campus, and Cam Blachford of the Faculty of Engineering, Regina campus. They reported that there had been "a complete breakdown of the sort of relationship which ought to, and must, exist between academic colleagues in any university, and within any faculty, department or college thereof – a relationship governed by mutual respect, courtesy, confidence and trust." The report noted that Lester Bates, the previous dean, had allowed the heads of the Departments of Elementary Education and Secondary Education considerable latitude in running their departments. The dean had been available for consultation and advice, but he did not impose his will on the department heads, whom he treated more as colleagues than as subordinates.

France had introduced a different pattern of administration. He had failed, in the committee's judgment, "to proceed with sufficient caution and circumspection in his dealings with the faculty and in working out plans which he had in mind for it." Further, he "ought to have been more aware than he apparently was of the implications of the differences between his own administrative experience in the field of teacher education in England and that of his newfound colleagues in Regina." The committee did not lay all the blame on France. They felt that the members of the faculty, especially the department heads, should have tried harder to work with and support the new dean. Nonetheless, the conclusion of the committee was clear: France could not be considered "the permanent occupant of his office." The report recommended that a senior member of the academic community at Regina, but from a faculty other than that of education, be appointed acting dean in 1969–70 and that France be granted a leave of absence.[17]

Against the advice of the committee, Riddell asked France to continue as dean, made W.N. Toombs associate dean, and appointed acting heads for the elementary, secondary, and general education groups. Moreover, Riddell said that since the Faculty of Education was so divided, he himself would select the members of the appointments committee and be "most intimately involved" in recruiting candidates to fill vacant positions.[18] Les Crossman and Cam Blachford, two members of the Committee of Inquiry, privately told Riddell that they were "dismayed that the new organization is almost exactly that proposed by Dean France himself." They felt that Riddell was ignoring the substance of their report and moving in exactly the opposite direction from what they had recommended.[19]

As it turned out, it did not matter what Riddell did, because he, like France, was on his way out. Riddell in March 1969 tendered his resignation to the president and left office at the beginning of January 1970. Arthur Kratzmann took over as dean of education in September 1970.[20] The faculty, under his leadership, undertook a comprehensive review of its internal organization, which led to the adoption of a new administrative structure in the fall of 1971. The traditional elementary/secondary division disappeared and was replaced by subject areas that cut across teaching levels. The Faculty of Education began to operate its program through sixteen departmental units: art, business education, French, health and physical education, language arts, library science and AV education, mathematics, music, early childhood education, reading, science, social studies, and support areas of educational psychology, educational foundations, educational administration, and research. The new organization emphasized faculty involvement in decision making and good communications between all subject areas.[21]

Having reformed its administrative structure, the faculty embarked on a thorough and far-reaching review of the fundamental purposes of the teacher education program. The Program Development Committee, appointed in September 1971, was composed of R.H. Fowler, E. Jonescu, A. McBeath, J.S. Malikail, E.L. Klopoushak, and W.N. Toombs (chair). Its report of July 1972 was a milestone in the development of the faculty. The central idea was to shift from a model based on training teachers to follow set patterns to one based on "producing teachers who are more flexible, self-confident and who view the classroom as an active, problem-centred, experimental place wherein there is an emphasis on intrinsic rather than extrinsic motivation."[22]

This idea had been implicit in many of the innovations that had already been introduced, especially in the secondary school program. Now it was adopted as a guiding principle for the entire faculty. The committee members, canvassing the relevant literature, were particularly impressed with the New Elementary Program (NEP), which had been pioneered at the University of Florida at Gainesville. It seemed to embody most effectively the spirit of the reforms they were looking for. The NEP focused on "humanization," which involved: "(a) developing awareness in each student of his or her potential as a person and a teacher; (b) fostering the development and hopefully the realization in each student of this potential; (c) promoting in students a sensitive perception of the needs, interests, anxieties and concerns of other people." The teacher, according to the NEP, should be "a self-actualized person who will view teaching as a 'helping profession' and will act as a rational decision-maker to effect educational goals." The purpose of teacher education was not to teach others "the right way to teach," but rather "to help the student discover his own best way of operating in whatever school setting he may find himself."[23]

This meant, in concrete terms, that it was more important for education students to learn a few concepts than many facts; learning was more efficient if the learner felt a need to know the material offered; no specific skill was essential for effective teaching; and students had to have a voice in defining and implementing the program. The Program Development Committee did not accept the NEP holus-bolus. Its members believed that it was possible to go overboard with conceptual learning. Information "was not completely irrelevant in methods classes." But the NEP provided the basic philosophy for the reforms in teacher education introduced at the Regina campus.[24] It gave the faculty a renewed sense of purpose and direction and the confidence to see itself as "a dynamic leader in education in Saskatchewan."[25]

These changes occurred at a time when enrolment in education was in flux. It soared to 709 in 1964–65, peaked at 1,793 in the winter semester of 1969–70, then slumped to 996 in the winter semester of 1973–74. This pattern followed that of the entire campus, except that the swings were more extreme because the transition from a one- or two-year teacher-training course to a full degree program occurred while the total number of students was increasing. More students entered the system, and they stayed in the program for a longer period. This created a temporary bulge in enrolment, which disappeared when the degree became the standard qualification required of teachers. Since teaching, especially in elementary schools, was stereotyped as an occupation for women, female students outnumbered male by a large margin. There were, in the fall of 1969–70, 745 men and 1,011 women in a total student population of 1,756.

The development in the Faculty of Education in its formative years conformed in broad terms to the ethos of the sixties. Words like "humanization" and "self-actualization" signified an emphasis on personal meaning over handed-down knowledge, democracy over hierarchical structures, and human values over technology. The idea that there was more than one way to be a good teacher and that following the rules was not always a good thing harmonized with the sixties ideals of authenticity and nonconformity. Even the basic assumption that change is something to be embraced rather than avoided was characteristic of the decade. Hints of the Regina Beach Statement could be detected in the Faculty of Education Program Development Report of 1972. Both emphasized conceptual learning, dialogue, and the student taking responsibility for his or her ideas, actions, and personal development. It is clear that the spirit of Regina Beach was not confined to arts and science – it influenced the professional colleges as well.

TABLE 6: Faculty of Education Enrolment

YEAR	SEMESTER	MEN	WOMEN	TOTAL
1964–65		254	455	709
1965–66		309	518	827
1966–67	fall	395	617	1,012
	winter	386	614	1,000
1967–68	fall	509	763	1,272
	winter	513	737	1,250
1968–69	fall	603	845	1,448
	winter	596	828	1,424
1969–70	fall	745	1,011	1,756
	winter	787	1,006	1,793
1970–71	fall			1,635
	winter			1,609
1971–72	fall			1,246
	winter			1,253
1972–73	fall			1,032
	winter			1,051
1973–74	fall			967
	winter			996

Source: University of Regina Archives, Publications Section, University of Saskatchewan, *Annual Report of the President*, 1965–71; *Principal's Report, 1972–74: University of Saskatchewan, Regina Campus.*

The same was true, though to a lesser degree, of the Faculty of Administration. The faculty grew out of the first-year commerce program that had been offered at Regina College since 1947 and the certificate programs in accounting, business administration, and public administration that had been offered in the 1950s.[26] The pressures of increasing enrolment made expansion to a degree program both logical and necessary. Accordingly, the Regina Campus Council in February 1965 recommended to the senate "that a College of Public and Business Administration be established on Campus [and] that a Dean be appointed by the fall of 1965 with the program of the College to commence by the fall of 1966."[27] The Board of Governors on 5 May 1965 approved the creation of the college, the second year to be offered in 1966–67 and the third and fourth years "as soon thereafter as staff and facilities allow."[28] The Regina Campus Council, however, decided in December 1965 to take the intermediate step of establishing a school of public and business administration within the College of Arts and Science.[29] The name was changed in April 1966 to the School of Administration.[30]

Wes Bolstad was appointed the first director and took office on 1 July 1966. He outlined his ideas in a memo titled "Assumptions about the Philosophy and Objective of the School of Administration." The program, in his opinion, should include the study of both public and business administration, deal with organizations in general (business, government, church, labour, charitable, and so on) rather than any particular type of organization, and consist of two years of general studies followed by two years of more specialized classes. Implicit in this approach was the belief that students should have a solid grounding in the disciplines that formed the foundation of administration, such as economics, political science, sociology, psychology, and mathematics. The accent was on broad, conceptual understanding, not narrow, technical competence. At the same time, the student was supposed to develop by the end of the fourth year "some depth of understanding in at least one Arts discipline (economics, political science, mathematics, sociology, etc.) as well as specialization in an applied area (public finance, business finance, industrial relations, etc.)."[31]

The School of Administration held its inaugural meeting on 7 December 1966. From the beginning, the academic staff conducted their business as though they constituted a separate faculty of administration. They established a committee structure to deal with such matters as curriculum, library resources, and scholarships, and they reported decisions concerning such things as entrance requirements and academic performance standards to the Faculty of Arts and Science, asking for information and advice, not approval. The focus of the School of Administration differed from that of the faculty. It had a more professional, career-preparation orientation, and by its very nature it needed to maintain a close liaison with the business community and the government sector.

The academic staff of the School of Administration on 2 November 1967 passed a motion requesting for their school status as a faculty in its own right.[32] This came about on 1 July 1968, when Ray Harvey became the first dean, succeeding Wes Bolstad. Faculty status, in addition to allowing greater freedom to act, increased the prestige of the program. The fourth and final year of the degree course was introduced in 1968–69, and the first twenty-four graduates of the program received their Bachelor of Administration degrees in May 1969.[33]

Enrolment in the faculty increased from 131 in the fall of 1966–67 to 468 in the winter of 1973–74. Unlike the Faculties of Arts and Science and Education, where enrolment peaked in 1969–70, the administration faculty saw its enrolment grow steadily throughout the period. The program met a specific demand that was not affected by the overall downturn in student numbers. The student body was overwhelmingly male in composition (a ratio of 350 men to 15 women in the 1969–70 fall semester), reflecting the fact that the

TABLE 7: Faculty of Administration Enrolment

YEAR	SEMESTER	MEN	WOMEN	TOTAL
1966–67	fall	123	8	131
	winter	145	9	154
1967–68	fall	233	10	243
	winter	219	11	230
1968–69	fall	283	14	297
	winter	272	14	286
1969–70	fall	350	15	365
	winter	345	13	358
1970–71	fall			383
	winter			381
1971–72	fall			412
	winter			420
1972–73	fall			433
	winter			426
1973–74	fall			457
	winter			468

Source: University of Regina Archives, Publications Section, University of Saskatchewan, *Annual Report of the President*, 1967–71; *Principal's Report, 1972–74: University of Saskatchewan, Regina Campus.*

women's liberation movement was just getting underway and business and management was still predominantly a man's world.

When Ray Harvey resigned as dean to become vice-principal of Regina campus, on 1 July 1970, Wes Bolstad returned as acting dean.[34] He expressed concern that the faculty was drifting away from its original goal of broad, conceptual learning towards narrow, vocational training. He warned against the temptation to stress techniques with an immediate use and application – such as computer languages, interviewing skills, and accounting – at the expense of general education, which would be more useful in the long run. "I feel," Bolstad wrote, "that more attention should be given to policy questions, to problems of goals, to questions of 'what should be done' as opposed to 'how best to do it' ... we can easily drift into the offering of traditional classes in personnel, finance and marketing, etc. (and become indistinguishable from a commerce program)."[35]

The practical, vocational bent of the program was enhanced through the inauguration of the co-operative work/study program in 1973. Students spent as many as four full semesters working in jobs related to their academic studies. Real-world experience complemented classroom instruction so that each reinforced and illuminated the other. Students had the opportunity to develop

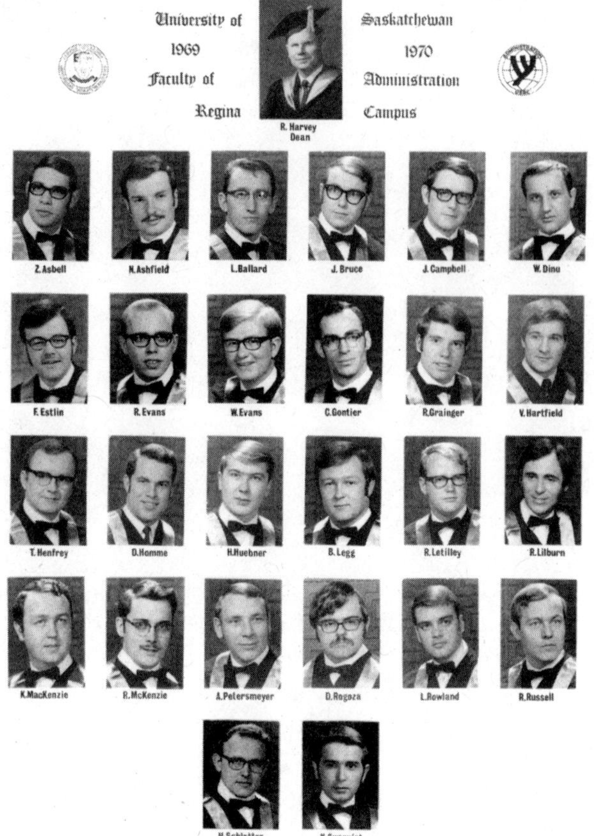

The dean and the graduating class of the Faculty of Administration, 1970. The gender imbalance is striking.

human relations skills, learn how organizations work, and impress potential future employers.[36] Equally important, they were able to "earn while they learned," easing the burden of paying for a university education.[37]

By the late 1970s the Faculty of Administration had evolved in its role of preparing students for professional careers in finance, accounting, human resources, and other facets of administration. The faculty maintained close ties with the business community and the government and sought to respond to their needs and those of their prospective employees.[38] As a result, the program had become less generic and more specialized. It had moved away from the original concept of general education and integration with the social science disciplines to focus more on profession-oriented courses.

The third professional college to be established at Regina campus was the Faculty of Engineering. First-year engineering courses were offered at Regina College in 1945, and by 1965 student demand had risen to the point that a quota of seventy had to be imposed on first-year enrolments. As Regina campus expanded, it seemed natural to build on the first-year programs, such as engineering, that attracted the most students.[39] The Board of Governors on 14 December 1965 approved a senate recommendation to establish a college of engineering in Regina; it also approved the recommendation "that a second year of Engineering be introduced as soon as possible; that course structures in the early years should be such as to permit students to move easily from campus to campus to pursue studies in their chosen fields of specialization; [and] that fields of specialization should be chosen in such a way as to avoid unnecessary duplication of work on the two campuses."[40]

John B. Mantle, the head of the Department of Mechanical Engineering at the College of Engineering in Saskatoon, was appointed the first dean in 1966. He proceeded, in accordance with the policy laid down by the senate, to develop degree programs in chemical, civil, electrical, and mechanical engineering at the Regina campus.[41] In March 1969 he outlined a co-operative education program in which students would spend one semester doing practical work in the engineering field for every two semesters they spent in the classroom. The concept had been implemented at the University of Waterloo and other campuses across North America.[42] Co-op/work study was a feature that differentiated the Regina campus from the College of Engineering in Saskatoon, which embraced the more traditional mode of instruction.

The development of the Faculty of Engineering in Regina fell victim to delays in the planning and construction of the long-awaited engineering/physics building. In the interim, faculty members had to make do with various improvised arrangements. The Chemical Engineering Corrosion-Research Project found space at the old College Avenue campus, while civil engineering won permission in 1970–71 to acquire an engineering field station for its research work. Labs were secured in the maintenance service building for the third-year classes, which were scheduled to begin in September 1972. The dean stated in his annual report for 1970–71 that approximately $180,000 worth of laboratory equipment had been procured, but much of it was still in crates awaiting the arrival of the additional staff members who would put it to use.[43]

Planning for the third and fourth years was suddenly thrown into confusion in March 1972, when the provincial government announced that no more funds would be made available for the engineering/physics building pending a complete review of the engineering programs at the two campuses. The government worried that expansion was proceeding too rapidly, given the downturn in projected student enrolments. In 1965 it had been anticipated that Regina campus would reach 10,000 students by 1975, but now the prediction was closer to 5,000.[44] The Board of Governors was divided over the question of whether Regina should introduce third- and fourth-year courses in engineering while the review was underway. The Saskatoon members of the board wanted to halt development until the review commission had completed its work; the Regina members wanted the scheduled expansions to go ahead. The board in the end agreed to a compromise whereby the third year would go ahead in the fall of 1972 while the fourth year was put on hold.

President Spinks thought that a mistake had been made. He wrote to Principal John Archer, "The original motion approving third *and* fourth years could easily have gone through, and then there would have been a real mess. The compromise resolution leaves a good deal to be desired since it rests mainly on [Deputy Minister of Education] Bergstrom's letter indicating [Minister of Education] MacMurchy's approval of third year, but really doesn't take sufficient account of what I took to be the Premier's very strong objection to any extensive development prior to having a report from a commission."[45] The underlying problem was that the Board of Governors was divided along Regina-Saskatoon lines. The controversy signalled a breakdown of the one-university/two-campus model of university organization and structure. The Engineering Students' Society at Regina campus meanwhile circulated a petition calling for the immediate reinstatement of the decision to proceed with the fourth-year course and the resumption of work on the engineering/physics building. It was signed by 138 students and sent to the Board of Governors.[46]

The university appointed Dr Philip Lapp as chair of the Engineering Review Commission. He had undertaken similar studies in Ontario and the Maritimes and had some knowledge of engineering education at the international level. The other members of the commission were Dean George Ford of Alberta; Dr Alex Corry, former principal of Queen's University; Chief Justice Ted Culliton, former chancellor of the University of Saskatchewan; and Keith Saddlemyer of the Government of Saskatchewan. The Lapp Commission report of December 1972 recommended that the Faculty of Engineering in Regina be closed down after the 1973–74 academic year. The Board of Governors chose not to follow the recommendation, preferring instead to continue the two-year program in Regina for three to five years while a study was undertaken of "alternative developments in the field of applied science and engineering technology for Regina campus."[47]

The Lapp Report triggered a crisis not only for engineering, but also for other programs. As table 8 shows, engineering students made up a significant component of the enrolment in arts and science classes. The loss of engineering would have a ripple effect throughout the entire campus.

TABLE 8: Engineering Students as a Percentage of Registration in Selected Departments of the Faculty of Arts and Science, Regina Campus, 1972–73

DEPARTMENT	ENGINEERING STUDENTS (PERCENTAGE)
Physics and astronomy	31
Mathematics	16
Chemistry (including biochemistry)	14
Geology	9
Biology	0
Computer science	3.5
English	7

Source: University of Regina Archives, Principal's/President's Papers, 80-38, 900.4-1, "Academic Implications for the Regina Campus of the University of Saskatchewan of the Report of the Engineering Review Commission," 4 October 1973.

But of course the blow fell heaviest on the Faculty of Engineering. Two faculty members resigned in late 1972 to take up non-university positions, another accepted a job at the University of Guelph, and a fourth moved to the Saskatoon campus. The co-op/work study program was disrupted because a number of students on work terms transferred to other campuses or left work terms to complete classes prior to transferring out of the Regina program. To compensate for the loss of students, the Faculty of Engineering designed classes to serve the needs of non-engineering students, such as those majoring in geology and computer science. The final sentence in Dean Mantle's 1972–73 annual report summed up the situation: "It is impossible to make an adequate statement of the real feelings of disappointment and frustration of members of this faculty at the developments that have beset us over the past year."[48]

Although the Board of Governors had granted the Faculty of Engineering a reprieve, the uncertainty hanging over the program depressed enrolment, which declined from 235 before the Lapp Report to 147 the following year. Several more faculty members resigned, which meant that last-minute changes had to be made to the class schedule for 1973–74. The dean tried to be optimistic. He said in the annual report for that year that faculty members were working on a new curriculum to replace the cancelled programs in chemical, civil, electrical, and mechanical engineering.[49]

A management consultant firm was hired to conduct a survey of the "marketability of graduates from various suggested programs." After considering the results of the survey, the faculty prepared a program feasibility study report. It recommended that Regina campus be authorized to offer degree

TABLE 9: Faculty of Engineering Enrolment

YEAR	SEMESTER	MEN	WOMEN	TOTAL
1966–67	fall			85
	winter			70
1967–68	fall	111	0	111
	winter	109	0	109
1968–69	fall	183	3	186
	winter	174	3	177
1969–70	fall	210	1	211
	winter	186	1	187
1970–71	fall			202
	winter			210
1971–72	fall			217
	winter			197
1972–73	fall			235
	winter			206
1973–74	fall			147
	winter			143

Source: University of Regina Archives, Publications Section, University of Saskatchewan, *Annual Report of the President*, 1967–71; *Principal's Report, 1972–74: University of Saskatchewan, Regina Campus.*

programs in industrial systems, electronic information systems, and regional systems engineering. The first involved the design of systems such as manufacturing and storage plants; the second related to the design of systems such as telecommunications, television, and library equipment and operations; and the third applied to the design of transportation, waste disposal, water supply, and so on. In each case the overriding goal was to build a system "for human need." The academic philosophy was based on interdisciplinary studies, a systems approach in analysis, extensive use of case studies in classes and laboratories, co-op work/study, and practical applications of mathematical and computer modelling.[50] Senate endorsed the proposal in December 1974, and it received final approval in March 1977.

The Faculty of Engineering emerged from its trials with a distinctive program that set it apart from what was offered in Saskatoon. This was important for the well-being of the campus as a whole. Without the presence of the applied sciences, the university in Regina would have had a truncated and unbalanced development. Engineering helped give the campus a mix of programs that made for a well-rounded institution. Indeed, as we will see later in more detail, the crisis over engineering was a key element in the series of events that led to the creation of the separate and autonomous University of Regina in 1974.

The last of the professional programs to emerge in the pre-1974 period was social work. During the 1950s pressure mounted on the University of Saskatchewan to create such a program. The North Central Regional Hospital Council, meeting in Prince Albert in October 1958, passed a resolution requesting that the university "seriously consider the establishment of a school of social work within the Faculty of Post-Graduate Studies." The matter was referred to the university Forward Planning Committee, which recommended in April 1960 that no plans for a school "be made at this time." Despite the rebuff, the social work community kept up a lobbying effort. The Committee on Education for Social Work of the Saskatchewan Association of Social Workers (SASW), chaired by A.S. Mayotte, in 1963 set up an enlarged study group of representatives of social agencies as well as community leaders who, though not professional social workers, were interested in advancing social welfare issues.[51] SASW president Larry Heinemann asked President Spinks to appoint a university representative to the committee, but he declined on the grounds that to do so would imply university support for the project.[52]

The Regina campus Executive Council recommended to council on 20 October 1966 the establishment of a school of social work in Regina and the appointment of a program advisory committee. Senate endorsed this proposal on 4 November 1966, subject to review by a joint committee of the two campus councils.[53] Finally, in 1967, the senate approved plans for the school, with a target date of fall 1968 for admitting the first students.[54] But nothing happened. Both Spinks and Riddell attributed the delay to the lack of funds in the university budget.

The provincial government began to increase the pressure. Minister of Social Welfare Cy MacDonald wrote to President Spinks in June 1969 indicating that the government was experiencing a severe shortage of trained personnel in social services. Florence Driedger, training coordinator for the department, drafted a letter for the minister's signature pointing out that employees who wanted to upgrade their qualifications could not always enrol in schools of social work in other provinces because these schools had more students than they could handle.[55] It was also difficult to recruit and retain staff from out of province, since competition for trained workers was intense. The problem was not confined to government service alone; it also affected private social service agencies. Sister Stephanie MacNeil, president of the SASW, expressed frustration at not being able to obtain concrete information as to when the university intended to establish a school. The minister of social welfare pressed President Spinks for an answer: "Could you please indicate what priority the School of Social Work has at the University, the date of its expected commencement, and any areas in which we might be of assistance ... We would appreciate an early reply to our inquiry because we believe this has become an urgent matter in the community." As to the university's statement that there was no money for the school, MacDonald added pointedly: "It is my understanding that the Department of National Health and Welfare has an Organizational and Planning Grant to universities who are planning on establishing a professional baccalaureate program in Social Work. Is your University considering the use of this grant at this time?"[56]

The president passed the inquiry along to Principal Riddell, who replied that while a school of social work had been approved in principle in 1967, "the necessary budget in three or four years would be at least $250,000, and it would be quite impossible to find this amount of money in the present budget. Consequently, it was deemed inadvisable to start the program at the present time."[57] John Archer, who succeeded Riddell in January 1970, was able to get things moving. He appointed an ad hoc committee chaired by Dr F. Lester Bates, the former dean of education at Regina campus, to advise on the curriculum. The committee included professional social workers, senior officials at the Department of Social Welfare, and Regina faculty members. It issued a report at the end of September 1970 outlining general principles and emphasizing "the desirability of getting a School started as soon as possible." Dr Harvey Stalwick of the University of Manitoba School of Social Work was appointed director in May 1971. Shortly thereafter, Otto Driedger, director of institutions in the Saskatchewan Department of Social Welfare, became coordinator of field instruction.[58] Art Sihvon, deputy minister of social welfare, was pleased that the program was finally being launched: "This, as you can imagine, is most welcome news to this department, as we have been pressing consistently for such a school for close to ten years."[59]

The General University Council on 9 November 1971 approved curriculum proposals for the four-year Bachelor of Social Work (BSW) degree, the two-year BSW (after BA), and the Certificate of Social Work. A province-wide survey was carried out to obtain information on student needs. The study, conducted by George Maslany, identified the importance of access to education outside Regina and Saskatoon. Although one-quarter of the population of Saskatchewan lived in the two major cities, a large number of potential students lived and worked in smaller centres scattered throughout the province.[60] This led to the adoption of the principle, as expressed by Stalwick, that "the province is essentially the campus."[61] Community education centres were set up in various locales as a means of reaching students, providing a full range of internship options, and strengthening the community-based aspects of the program.

The first students enrolled for the winter semester of 1973, and in the 1972–73 academic year a total of 149 students completed credit classes in North Battleford, Prince Albert, Saskatoon, Regina, and Moose Jaw. Over 80 per cent of them were married, most were over thirty years of age, and 56 per cent were male. Most of the off-campus students came to the program with "extensive life and employment experience touching on most facets of personal social services in the province." Those who enrolled on campus tended to be younger, unmarried, and less likely to have work experience in human services.[62]

A request from the Federation of Saskatchewan Indians (FSI) Cultural College led to a joint program to train counsellors to work on and off Native reserves. It had a full-time enrolment of eighteen Native students in 1974. The School of Social Work and the FSI Cultural College negotiated agreements on admissions policies, administration, and curriculum. The college offered courses in Native history, culture, and treaties, while the school provided instruction in social work and supervised the internship program. The Department of Indian Affairs paid tuition fees and living allowances for Native students and covered some of the overhead costs.[63]

Harvey Stalwick described the year 1973–74 as a time of consolidation. The total enrolment rose to 58 full-time and 256 part-time students living in several locations across the province. Work continued on the development of a "community-focused, problems-specific" curriculum,[64] and requests flowed in for programs ranging from refresher courses for qualified practitioners to training for social services personnel in the criminal justice system. The latter program led to the formation of a joint university-community committee with representatives from the RCMP, the provincial police, the corrections division of the Department of Social Services, and the judiciary. From this developed in 1974–75 the Human Justice Services Program, which later evolved into the School of Human Justice.[65]

The School of Social Work was a good example of Regina campus responding to the expressed needs of the wider community. It was launched at a time when provincial funding for university education was no longer increasing at the pace it had maintained when overall enrolments had been growing by leaps and bounds. From a financial point of view, the circumstances were less than optimal. This explains why fully 50 per cent of the School of Social Work's budget in 1972–73 came from external grants.[66] Its creation was the result not so much of internal university decision-making processes as external pressure from providers of social services in the province. The university responded, albeit belatedly, to the need. Once the decision to proceed was made, Stalwick, Driedger, and others consulted closely with interested persons in the community to ensure that the school served their needs in terms of curriculum, the integration of theory and practice, and province-wide access to the program.

The Faculty of Graduate Studies, though not a professional college per se, organized post-graduate work in all fields of academic and professional study and promoted advanced research at the campus. Its formation was first proposed at a meeting of the Faculty of Arts and Science on 24 March 1964. A graduate studies committee, with A.B. Van Cleave as chair and Dallas Smythe as secretary, was established to draft regulations governing the admission and supervision of graduate students and the granting of graduate degrees. The committee recommended to Campus Council in December 1964 that a school of graduate studies be created. Council accepted the recommendation and the senate approved it on 24 March 1965. Van Cleave was appointed the first director on 1 July 1965.[67]

Graduate work at both campuses was placed under the direction of a university college of graduate studies, which set overall academic policy and approved new graduate programs. Van Cleave endorsed this structure because it facilitated the coordination of graduate programs and ensured uniformity of standards. Even when, in 1968, the school became the Faculty of Graduate Studies and Van Cleave acquired the title of dean, it continued to operate under the supervision of the university college. Van Cleave would not have had it any other way. He thought the arrangement provided a model of efficient coordination and smooth inter-campus relations.[68]

The Regina campus in 1966–67 had seventy-six graduate students, all of them enrolled in master's programs, except for one PhD candidate in psychology. By the fall of 1973 the number had increased to 292. According to Van Cleave, one of the major constraints to growth was the lack of financial support for graduate students. He noted in 1972 that the allocation of funds for teaching assistantships and graduate scholarships had remained unchanged for three years and was not likely to improve in the foreseeable future.[69] This resulted in an increase in the number of part-time graduate students as a proportion of the total. The number of full-time students decreased from 129 in the 1972 winter semester to 113 in the 1973 winter semester, while the number of part-time students increased from 149 to 194.[70]

One way to support more graduate students was to obtain research funding from external agencies such as the National Research Council and the Canada Council. To highlight the link between graduate studies and research, the Faculty of Graduate Studies was renamed on 1 July 1971 the Faculty of Graduate Studies and Research. Regina faculty members received a total of only $455,253 in research grants in 1970–71, and Van Cleave worked tirelessly to increase the amount. He lobbied for the establishment of a properly funded research grants office to assist faculty members in applying for grants, but the proposal was turned down because of a lack of funds. Van Cleave considered this a short-sighted policy. He believed that the office would have more than paid for itself with the revenue generated by a higher success rate on grant applications.[71]

The amount of external research funding for Regina campus rose to $463,885 in 1971–72 and to $564,387 in 1972–73, but the size of the increase was somewhat deceptive. Much of it resulted from one large National Research Council equipment grant to a member of the chemistry department. The total number of awards did not increase significantly over the previous year. The highest success rate occurred among faculty members in the natural sciences and engineering, who won approximately 88 per cent of the grants. According to Van Cleave, "the number of faculty members outside of these areas that apply for financial assistance from external agencies is pitifully small and their success rate is even worse." Support for research and scholarly work in the humanities, social sciences, and fine arts from the Canada Council amounted in 1972–73 to only $18,644, and this was divided among four faculty members.[72]

The Lapp Report recommending the termination of the Faculty of Engineering at the Regina campus had a potentially devastating effect on the research program. Discussions with the National Research Council regarding the possibility of a development grant for "Research and Design in High Voltage and High Current," which was to have been undertaken jointly by the Faculty of Engineering and the Saskatchewan Power Corporation, had to be suspended. The demise of chemical engineering on campus spelled the end of the corrosion research laboratory, where researchers had been studying the effects of corrosion in pipelines and nuclear reactors.[73] On a brighter note, the senate approved in 1973 a proposal to create the Regina Water Research Institute to investigate water quality on the prairies, and the Canadian Plains Research Center was established as a focal point for regional studies that cut across all disciplines.[74]

Another development was the establishment of the Bilingual Centre in 1968. Its origins lay in a proposal from the rector of Collège Mathieu in Gravelbourg, a town located southwest of Regina in an area with a substantial francophone population. The college had for several years offered a BA degree in affiliation with the University of Ottawa. When this arrangement came to an end, the college hoped to find a new partner in the University of Saskatchewan, Regina Campus. However, under the senate statutes of the university, affiliated colleges were allowed to offer only first-year work or theological degrees. The upshot of the negotiations was that Collège Mathieu discontinued its university work, while Regina campus undertook to establish a bilingual college offering classes in both English and French.[75]

Vice-Principal Tommy McLeod presented the proposal to the Board of Governors on 20 January 1966. He argued that the college would serve three purposes: it would provide bilingual instruction for undergraduate students, disseminate French culture, and facilitate post-graduate research.[76] In the wider context, the initiative made good sense, conforming as it did to English Canada's awakening to the Quiet Revolution in Quebec, the threat of separatism, and the federal government's conciliatory embrace of bilingualism as a defining feature of Canada. Beginning in 1968, students who registered in the bilingual program were required to complete at least 30 per cent (later increased to 40 per cent) of their coursework in French if English was their dominant language, or in English if the reverse was the case. The first students graduated with the designation "*mention bilingue*" attached to their degrees in May 1971. By 1973–74 the centre had diversified its programs to include translator training; non-credit language instruction for university faculty and staff, federal and provincial government employees, and members of the judiciary; as well as an English as a second language summer course for visiting students from Quebec.[77]

The academic program at the campus, in both its strengths and weaknesses, reflected the ethos of the sixties. Dallas Smythe, as we have seen, rejected the concept of the ivory-towered academic cloistered from the community and oblivious to its problems. Referring to the Vietnam War teach-in held at the Regina campus in 1965, he wrote, "In a period when international mistrust, misunderstanding and hostility threaten mankind with nuclear war, there is a special burden on us in universities to participate in public discussion of vital public issues."[78] He and his colleagues in the Division of Social Sciences inaugurated the Plain Talk series of public meetings in the fall of 1964. The title was chosen to convey the idea that the talks, though given by experts in their respective fields, were not intended to be "egghead" lectures but rather opportunities for public discussion on matters of general interest. Audience members were given ample opportunity after the formal presentation to ask questions and express their opinions.[79]

The theme of the six talks, held once a month in 1964–65, was "Towards the Future Society." The speakers included Brock Chisholm, former director general of the World Health Organization; Kenneth Boulding, professor of economics at the University of Michigan; Alan Watts, a pre-eminent interpreter of Eastern philosophy and religion, especially Zen Buddhism; Clifford J. Durr, a lawyer and civil rights advocate from Montgomery, Alabama; Kenneth W. Taylor, a former federal deputy minister of finance; and H.H. Wilson, professor of politics at Princeton University. The guest lecturers in subsequent years were equally distinguished. The roster in 1966–67 included Frank Underhill, former professor of history at the University of Toronto; René Hurtubise, professor of law at the University of Montreal and consultant to the Royal Commission on Bilingualism and Biculturalism; Merrill Menzies, a former key adviser to Prime Minister John Diefenbaker; Bishop G. Emmett Carter of Toronto, a participant in Vatican II; Peyton V. Lyon, professor of political science at Carleton University; H.D. Woods, former director of the Industrial Relations Centre at McGill University; and Edmund Carpenter, a prominent anthropologist and expert on the Inuit.[80]

The lectures were often controversial and in some cases led to calls for censorship. The Saskatchewan Chamber of Commerce in April 1966 denounced what it considered to be the "one-sided" nature of some of the presentations, such as a talk on China that the chamber thought was pro-Communist. According to businessman H.A. Purdy, the takeover of Tibet had been portrayed as "a necessary and humanitarian exercise of the Chinese military."[81] Riddell agreed with the criticism and passed it along to Smythe, suggesting that speakers be selected to represent a broader spectrum of opinion. Smythe replied in a lengthy memo, the gist of which was that the speakers were competent social scientists, not ideologues or propagandists. He drew an analogy with physical scientists who analyzed "the causes of disease (revolutionary disturbances in the human body)." They were not blamed for identifying the bacteria that caused the disturbances. "Why then blame the social scientist when his analysis identifies the factors causing a revolutionary disturbance in the body politic?"[82] Woodrow Lloyd, in 1966 the leader of the opposition in the legislative assembly, joined the discussion, reporting to Riddell that he had heard a rumour that the Plain Talk series was to be discontinued. Lloyd said that he placed a high value on the lectures, which he regarded as "a contribution by the University ... of growing importance ... [and] not available from any other source."[83] Riddell quickly assured Lloyd that the rumour was unfounded.[84]

Although Smythe emphasized the responsibility of the academic to become actively involved in public affairs and community activities, he also stressed the importance of research and scholarly writing. His major book *Dependency Road: Communications, Capitalism, Consciousness and Canada* (1981) was published after he left Regina campus in 1973 to take up an appointment as visiting professor of communications at the University of California, San Diego. He joined the faculty of Simon Fraser University in 1974 as the first chairman of the Department of Communication Studies. Over the course of his career he wrote close to 300 journal articles, papers, reports, and briefs. When he died, in 1992, scholars who had been influenced by his pioneering work in the political economy of communications published a festschrift, *Illuminating the Blindspots: Essays Honoring Dallas W. Smythe* (1993). In addition, Thomas Guback, a former student and a professor at the University of Illinois, edited a compendium of Smythe's essays titled *Counterclockwise: Perspectives on Communication* (1994).[85]

Publications of Regina campus faculty members in the 1960s and early 1970s included Saros Cowasjee's *Sean O'Casey: The Man Behind the Plays* (1964), *O'Casey* (1966), and *Goodbye to Elsa* (1975); and Burton Weber's *The Construction of Paradise Lost* (1971) and *Wedges and Wings: The Patterning of Paradise Regained* (1974). Both Cowasjee and Weber were members of the English department. George Arthur (anthropology) published *An Introduction to the Ecology of Early Historic Communal Bison Hunting among the Northern Plains Indians* (1975), while colleague D'Arcy McNickle produced *Indians and Other Americans* (1970), *Indian Man: A Life of Oliver La Farge* (1971), and *Native American Tribalism: Indian Survivals and Renewals* (1973). F.M. Barnard, for a time a member of the Department of Political Science, wrote *Herder's Social and Political Thought from Enlightenment to Nationalism* (1965); B.K. Johnpoll authored *The Politics of Futility: The General Jewish Workers Bund of Poland 1917–1943* (1967); and Evelyn Eager published a standard text on provincial politics, *Saskatchewan Government: Politics and Pragmatism* (1980). To this list may be added *Beyond the New Morality: The Responsibilities of Freedom* (1974) by philosopher Germain G. Grisez (Campion College).

Historian Richard Allen wrote *The Social Passion: Religion and Social Reform in Canada 1914–1928* (1971), and Martin Kovacs, also of the Department of History, became a leading scholar on the subject of Hungarian settlement in Saskatchewan. Others at this time did spadework resulting in later publications. Department of English member Joan Givner worked on *Katherine Anne Porter: A Life* (1982), and colleague Ken Mitchell published *Wandering Rafferty* (1972), one of the first of a series of novels, plays, and short stories. L.W. Brandt, C.K. Knapper, and A.J. Cropley in psychology published a large number of scholarly papers, as did others, such as A.H. Paul (geography), W.D. Chandler (chemistry), Keith Johnson (chemistry), Don Lee (chemistry), Frans Rummens (chemistry), G.A. Papini (physics), S. Hontzeas (physics), J.L. Wolfson (physics), R.Y. Zacharuk (biology), Paul Riegert (biology), D. Sato (mathematics), W.A. Gordon (geology), and P.F. Gross (administration and computer science).

Despite this research and publication productivity, there is little doubt that the campus turmoil of the sixties inhibited scholarly activity. The endless debates about the Regina Beach Statement, the division system, the status of the Regina campus vis-à-vis Saskatoon, student power, and so on, distracted faculty members from their primary duties. In the midst of one particularly heated struggle in October 1972, thirty-two faculty members in the Division of Social Sciences signed a petition calling for the suspension of the operations of the division. They said they needed a break from the continual round of meetings in order to have time for the "reading, reflection, lecture preparation, and research required of them by the university and their consciences."[86]

The Regina full-time faculty in 1959 had numbered twenty-three.[87] The total in 1972–73 was 308, divided as follows: humanities (fifty-one), natural sciences and mathematics (sixty-nine), social sciences (sixty-four), fine arts (twenty-seven), administration (twenty-one), education (fifty-four), engineering (fifteen), and social work (seven).[88] The Regina campus was not simply a liberal arts college, and in a sense it never had been. The original plan had been to establish a strong liberal arts core and then add professional colleges. What happened instead was that the development of the liberal arts program proceeded simultaneously with that of the Faculty of Graduate Studies and Research, the School of Social Work, the Faculty of Engineering, the Faculty of Administration, and the Faculty of Education. By the time the ink was dry on the Regina Beach Statement, the diversification of the campus from its liberal arts base to professional colleges, graduate studies, and research was well underway.

11 Campion and Luther Colleges

In addition to the professional colleges and the Faculty of Arts and Science, the Regina campus included federated colleges, which were administratively distinct but academically integrated into the wider university. Campion College and Luther College were established at the campus before 1974 and therefore fall within the scope of this book, while the Saskatchewan Indian Federated College, later renamed the First Nations University of Canada, came into existence in 1976. The basic concept of a federated college was that it allowed for the formation of a smaller, more intimate community within the larger institutional framework of the university and provided a diversity of viewpoints and values, enriching the academic environment. The Regina campus embraced the principle of federation, entering into agreements with Campion College in 1966 and Luther College in 1971.

Campion College traces its history back to 1917, when the Saskatchewan legislature passed an act to incorporate the "Catholic College of Regina." The act empowered the Archdiocese of Regina "to establish, maintain and conduct at the city of Regina, a College and school where students may obtain a liberal education in the arts and sciences."[1] Regina archbishop O.E. Mathieu, the former rector of Laval University, hoped that the college would form the basis of an independent Roman Catholic university, a dream that was never realized. To counter Mathieu's plans, Walter Murray, president of the University of Saskatchewan, encouraged the establishment of a Catholic college at the Saskatoon campus.[2] This led to the opening in 1936 of St Thomas More College, which had a relationship with the university that could be characterized as something between affiliation and federation. In 1953 the terms of federation were officially codified,[3] establishing the template for the later federation of Campion College with the Regina campus.

Archbishop Mathieu in 1917 decided to entrust the college he had founded to the Jesuits, an order that since its formation in the sixteenth century had been well known for its work in education. Jesuits were already operating Loyola College in Montreal, and it seemed natural for Mathieu to ask them to take charge of the new school.[4] Jesuit Thomas MacMahon arrived in Regina on 13 June 1918, noting in his diary: "Thursday 13 – Arrived in Regina via C.P.R. this a.m. ... Father Daly [a Redemptorist priest and rector of the cathedral] took me in his car through the city. We visited the site of the future college. I find it admirable ... Saw some more of city and surrounding country. I miss the trees – also rivers, lakes, and landscape of the east. There is nothing but the limitless prairies without water or verdure."[5]

Undaunted by the barren landscape, Father MacMahon, with two fellow Jesuits, prepared for the opening of the college. It was placed under the patronage of Blessed Edmund Campion, SJ, an Oxford scholar who in 1581 had given up a promising university career to die a martyr's death for the Catholic cause.[6] The first students arrived in the fall of 1918 and were accommodated in rented houses until the new building was completed in 1921. Enrolment increased from twenty-three in 1918 to nearly 150 by 1926. Although most of the students were registered in high school grades, the college, beginning in 1925, had junior college status with the University of Saskatchewan and offered first-year university courses. In addition it offered a full degree program in scholastic philosophy in conjunction with the University of Manitoba. When the agreement with the University of Manitoba expired in 1936 because of a change in Manitoba legislation limiting the recognition of degree work to in-province institutions, the college negotiated affiliation with the University of Ottawa and subsequently the University of Montreal. All told, from 1926 to 1942 over one hundred students earned BA degrees in philosophy at Campion.[7] In 1942 the program was cancelled, due mainly to the decline in the number of students – many young men had enlisted in the armed forces. Thereafter, the college confined itself to high school and first-year university courses.[8]

On the heels of the announcement in July 1959 that the university planned to establish a full degree program at Regina College, the Jesuit provincial superior asked Dr Gerald Lahey, SJ, to prepare a report on the role that Campion College might play in the development of the new campus. Lahey recommended an expansion to degree work. He noted that Campion had incurred a "great expense of manpower and labs, etc. since 1949 to operate a Junior College with this goal always in view – that the Junior College status would put us in a position to be part of the University that must inevitably come to Regina."[9] Lahey assumed that the university would have no objection to the federation of the college along the same lines as had been arranged for St Thomas More College at the Saskatoon campus.[10] It was also significant that Regina archbishop M.C. O'Neill fully backed the project, which was expected to have the support of the approximately 25 per cent of the population of Regina and southern Saskatchewan that was Roman Catholic.[11]

Campion College on 25 July 1960 formally applied for federation with the Regina campus.[12] The university senate considered the matter and decided that since the second year of the course in arts and science in Regina would not be offered until September 1961 and the third year at some unspecified later date, "no immediate action need be taken concerning your application, and that a complete study concerning conditions for federation should be made before any final applications are considered."[13] A joint committee of the University Council, senate, and Board of Governors reported in March 1961 that while it recognized that the university policy of federation applied to the Regina campus, the time was "not appropriate" for the federation of Campion College, because the campus itself was still in the early stages of formation.[14]

Campion raised the question again early in 1963 with the result that the university reactivated the joint committee. Father Peter W. Nash became rector of the college in July of that year, replacing Father Angus J. Macdougall, who had been appointed provincial superior for the Jesuits in English Canada.[15] Nash had an MA in classics (1940) and a PhD in philosophy (1948) from the University of Toronto. Before coming to Regina as dean of Campion College in 1961, he had taught at Regis College in Toronto and at Mount St Michael's at Gonzaga University in Spokane, Washington.[16] As the new rector of Campion College, he took the lead role in negotiations with the university.

According to the statutes of the senate, a federated college had to satisfy three requirements: it "must be authorized by the University to give classes recognized for credit towards a Bachelor of Arts degree in the subjects of at least four departments of the College of Arts and Science"; "the members of the College staff teaching the above University courses must be recognized as members of the Faculty of Arts and Science"; and "the College must be situated on or adjacent to the main University campus."[17] Campion proposed to satisfy the first requirement by teaching courses in philosophy, sociology, psychology, history, and English, while keeping open the possibility of expanding into other areas. Each professor would possess in the required field at least an MA and, where possible, a PhD. This was in addition to the traditional broad Jesuit formation in the liberal arts, philosophy, and theology. To meet the third requirement, Campion planned to build a structure on the Regina campus costing somewhere between $800,000 and $1,000,000. The building would include a chapel, a student centre, a library, offices, seminar rooms, and residential facilities for the Jesuit staff, but no classrooms. The archdiocesan authorities, through Archbishop O'Neill, had already pledged $500,000 towards the project.[18]

The joint committee of the council, senate, and Board of Governors on 26 September 1963 agreed to support the federation of Campion College with the university. It also resolved that federation would not take effect before 1 July 1966, by which time the complete three-year BA degree program would be offered in Regina. A subcommittee composed of Principal Riddell (chair), two representatives from the Regina campus (H. Jack and L.H. Thomas), and two representatives from Campion (Peter Nash and Gerald Lahey) was appointed to work out the details.[19] By the end of October 1963 the subcommittee had formulated a set of regulations similar to those applying to St Thomas More College in Saskatoon.[20]

All seemed to be going well when the negotiations hit a snag. As Nash explained on 3 November 1963 in a letter to the Jesuit Provincial,

> Everything was just fine. Riddell was to get busy and send out copies of the terms to members of faculty so that they could pass it in Council this coming Wednesday in Saskatoon. He got them out all right and ran into a minor cyclone. The trouble was that a good number of the faculty, being new, had not even heard so much that there was to be a federation! They just hadn't been informed, and, being very touchy at the moment, and more than somewhat neurotic, they proclaimed that they were being railroaded into something they knew nothing about. The scuttlebutt was that if the question came up at the Council meeting they would move to have the whole business tabled. Riddell called me on Friday in quite a state of alarm. I told him that for the sake of peace I would go along with postponing having the matter brought up if the President thought it best. I did say, however, that it was very important that Council at least pass the proposed target date of "not earlier than 1 July 1966" because we needed the time to work with our new architect and with the University.[21]

Because of these complications, all that was presented to University Council on 4 November 1963 was an interim report.[22] The senate on 22 November 1963 voted to approve the federation of Campion College, which was to take place not earlier than 1 July 1966, but it did not consider the specific terms of the federation agreement.[23] Negotiations on the latter resumed, resulting on 28 January 1964 in a second draft. It differed from the first in that the faculty members of Campion College, unlike their counterparts at St Thomas More College, were denied the privilege of membership in the Faculty of Arts and Science at Regina campus.[24] J. Francis Leddy, vice-president (academic) and dean of arts and science at Saskatoon,[25] considered this an "outrage." He urged Lahey not to accept the provision, adding, "Having all these circumstances in mind it is impudent nonsense on the part of the people at the Regina campus to begin to raise objections and new proposals at this date. If it were not for the naïve incompetence and the shallow arrogance which is characteristic of the deplorable proposals from the Regina campus in recent months, I would be disposed to say that it manifested bad faith."[26] Leddy also indicated to Riddell that it was "disappointing to see how your colleagues are complicating and, I think, spoiling negotiations which should have proceeded in a straightforward manner to the mutual advantage of both parties." He added that "so far as the Regina campus is concerned it seemed to me that federation with Campion would be a most helpful stroke in public relations, since to many people in Regina the old traditions of the original Regina College have naturally lingered on, with some undertones of denominational rivalry." "I am frankly concerned," he concluded, "that the earlier delay, now followed by the rather ungracious proposal which is being made is depriving you initially of some of the benefits in public relations which might otherwise have been secured."[27]

The joint committee of the senate, council, and Board of Governors on federation discussed the report of the subcommittee on 10 March 1964. It decided to make the terms of federation for Campion College essentially the same as those for St Thomas More. This meant that, contrary to the recommendation of the subcommittee, faculty of Campion College would have status as members of the Faculty of Arts and Science of Regina campus.[28] The terms of federation, approved by council on 9 April 1964 and by senate in May 1964 were as follows:

(1) The officers and faculty of Campion College are entitled to full membership with power to vote on the following academic bodies: (a) The Senate: The Rector of Campion to be a member; (b) The University Council: The Rector, professors, associate professors, assistant professors and full-time lecturers to be members; (c) the College of Arts and Science: The Rector, professors, associate professors, assistant professors and full-time lecturers to be members.

(2) Students enrolled in the College who have satisfied the University requirements for admission shall be admitted to such University classes as they are qualified to enter and continue therein on the same terms as other University students, provided the fees required for such classes have been paid to the College. Students enrolled in the University ordinarily, with the permission of the College, may take classes in the College recognized for the B.A. degree, provided that the fees required for such classes have been paid to the University. These conditions will apply provided the same annual tuition fee is required by both the College and the University.

(3) The foregoing provision with regard to the tuition fee for the Arts and Science classes applies to the pre-professional classes.

(4) All students enrolled in a professional school or College must pay to the University the full tuition fee required for each year of the professional course; though the University may grant credit for any class or classes taken in the College and accepted by the College of Arts and Science for the corresponding class required in a professional course.

(5) Academic appointments to and promotions within the College shall be made by the Rector but, prior to making such appointments or promotions, the Rector shall secure the approval of the President.

(6) The University will recognize instruction given by the College in Classics, Economics, English, French, History, Philosophy, Psychology and Sociology and such other subjects as may from time to time be agreed upon; Provided that the instruction is given by competent teachers and that the work done in each class is equivalent in extent and standards to that given in the University; This equivalence is to be determined by the Head of the Department in the College and the Head of the Department in the University working out in cooperation the extent of the classes, the standard and all the particulars pertaining to the subjects, including the examinations to their mutual satisfaction or in cases of difficulties to the satisfaction of the President of the University.

(7) The University will confer the B.A. degree on such students of the College as have satisfied the requirements prescribed by the University for admission and for the B.A. curriculum.[29]

The key points, apart from the issue of the membership of Campion faculty in the Faculty of Arts and Science, to which reference has already been made, centred on finances, academic appointments and promotions, and maintenance of academic standards. Campion collected the tuition fees of those students who registered in the college, and the university collected the fees of those who registered through the various faculties in the university. In other words, revenue was linked to the student rather than the specific courses in which he or she was enrolled. Also, the college was responsible for the appointment and promotion of its own faculty members, except that it had to obtain the approval of the president of the university for such appointments and promotions. Finally, courses offered at Campion College had to be "equivalent in extent and standards to [those] given in the University," such equivalence to be worked out co-operatively by "the Head of the Department in the College and the Head of the Department in the University." The agreement was vague about the actual mechanisms by which this co-operation was to occur. It did not specify, for example, whether Campion faculty were members of university departments or even whether they were allowed to attend departmental meetings. This proved to be a source of considerable friction, especially in the departments of philosophy, where there were sharp differences between university faculty members and their Campion counter-

Father Peter Nash, Archbishop M.C. O'Neill, and Mayor Henry Baker turning the sod for the construction of Campion College, 25 May 1966.

parts on a range of issues, from departmental procedures to the selection of textbooks. Finally the difficulties were resolved, and more precise procedural arrangements were spelled out in the 1973 document "Guidelines for a Working Relationship between the Faculty of Arts and Science and the Federated Colleges within the Terms of the Statutes of Senate."[30]

One of the conditions of federation was the construction of a building on the campus. Campion College in 1963 engaged architect Peter Thornton of Vancouver, who had designed several buildings in Canada for the Jesuits. The $1,550,000 structure conceived by Thornton had a spacious chapel, a well-appointed library with space for 80,000 volumes, a theatre/auditorium, a student lounge and cafeteria, clubrooms, offices for faculty and administrators, and a fifth-floor residence for the Jesuit faculty.[31] Peter Nash supervised all the details of planning and construction. For him 1967 was an exhausting year of "fighting contractors' delays and [the] architect's bullheadedness."[32]

The Campion College building at the Regina campus, officially opened on 20 January 1968.

The Jesuits moved into the building in the middle of December 1967. John Deutsch, a Campion graduate and president-elect of Queen's University, officially opened it on 20 January 1968.[33]

The debt incurred to finance the building stood at $830,891.79 in August 1969, which resulted in monthly interest payments of $5,906.59.[34] Nash, who worried constantly about the debt, kept a vigilant eye on interest rate fluctuations. After meeting with the bank manager on 23 October 1969, he concluded that "it's very obvious (a) we *have* to increase enrolments and (b) we haven't a *hope* of paying off the debt without sale of the high school property."[35] Enrolments were important because the college depended on the revenue from tuition fees and because the provincial government tied its grant to the number of students. Nash, as had Ernest Stapleford and Steward Basterfield in the early days of Regina College, travelled throughout southern Saskatchewan trying to recruit high school students. Accompanied by the college public relations officer, he braved a snowstorm in March 1972 to visit the towns of Balgonie and Fort Qu'Appelle. They were supposed to go on to Indian Head, but, as Nash recorded in his journal, "with a blizzard warning out," they headed home instead. They made it, "despite a 40 mph cross-wind blowing snow that at times almost wiped out all visibility."[36] The recruiting efforts yielded results. Enrolment of full-time students increased from 252 in 1966 to 447 in 1973.[37] The financial situation was further allevi-

The coat of arms of Campion College, designed by college president Peter Nash. The motto *Sapienta Regina* ("Wisdom Is Queen") is a pun on the name of the city and the university.

ated in 1974 by the sale of the high school property to the provincial government for $662,500. Half the amount was immediately applied to the debt, reducing it to a manageable $150,000; the other half was invested in a pension fund for retiring Jesuits.[38]

Nash immersed himself in the daily life of the college. He even designed the coat of arms. It featured a gold wheat sheaf on an azure chief (the upper third of the shield); the base presented seven red bands on a gold field. The wheat and the azure signified Saskatchewan, and the red bands were derived from the coat of arms of Ignatius Loyola, the founder of the Jesuit order. The crest above the shield was the original seal of the Society of Jesus; it bore the letters "IHS" – the Greek abbreviation for Jesus – and "C" – which stood for "company" in Spanish. Below the shield on a scroll was the college motto, *Sapienta Regina*, meaning "Wisdom Is Queen," a Latin pun on the city's name. The wreath surrounding the shield bore the words *Collegium Sancti Edmundi Campion* (or "College of the Blessed Edmund Campion"), followed by "MCMXVII," the date of incorporation of the Catholic College of Regina. The college colours, red and gold, replaced the maroon and white of the junior college and high school, symbolizing the change of location and status of Campion as a university college.[39] The design of the coat of arms was later simplified and stylized, but the essential concept remained the same.

Although Nash was a stickler for administrative detail, he also had a broad understanding of the educational purposes of a federated college. He alluded to them in his speech at the Campion cornerstone-laying ceremony on 1 October 1966. He said that the college was small enough to provide students with a sense of community, a home within the larger university where they could be known and appreciated as individuals. Furthermore, as a college with a religious foundation, it offered a different viewpoint from that of the secular university, adding to the variety of the educational life of the campus. Nash believed that the university, in welcoming Campion as a federated college, showed that it was aware of the dangers of "monopoly in education without the foil of diversity, even oddball diversity." The federated college was a sign of the rejection of conformity and the "carbon-copy approach" to education. The university, as a government-funded institution, always ran the risk of too close an identification with the state. The presence of a church college counterbalanced this tendency. Conversely, the college benefited from its exposure to the broader life of the university, which prevented a monopolistic liaison between the church and education.[40]

Nash acknowledged the existence of a certain tension between religious faith and secular learning. He said that scholars who wore Roman collars were sometimes placed in an awkward situation, suspected in the university of not being true scholars and in the church of not being good Catholics. As Nash reminded his audience, one did not have to be a scholar to be a Christian. The gospel message was for everyone, educated and uneducated, rich and poor. Why then was the church in the university at all? Nash gave his fullest answer to this question in a speech he delivered at the Newman Convention in Edmonton, Alberta, in September 1968:

> The Christian community wants to be inserted into that human reality, the University, in order to be enriched by it and to bring to it a new dimension. It has to be in the University in order to learn from the University if it is going to speak to contemporary society in a language it understands. It has to be in the University, which, *par excellence*, is the frontier of new truth and the testing ground of old truths, if it is to live up to its declared devotion to the truth. The Church must at its peril be genuinely involved in scholarship at the University level. Hence, it must seek to attract its members, cleric and lay, into serious scholarship and research and encourage them to become genuine scholars and teachers, dedicated to truth wherever it may be found, freely pursuing truth and proclaiming it responsibly. The Church cannot adequately witness to the Word of God without some of its members committed to scholarship not only in theological investigations but in secular subjects.[41]

In Nash's view, when the priest/scholar interpreted the world to the church, he could do so only by being true to his vocation as a scholar, "which is the pursuit of truth wherever it leads." This meant that he was sometimes cast in the unwelcome role of a prophet and had "to voice disturbing opinions which most often will be appreciated as valid insights or otherwise only after the scholar is dead." The Christian scholar, Nash said, was "between the devil and the deep blue sea, and he would not be elsewhere." He explained that the "devil" in the metaphor is "the very jagged seam made by the ends of the planks on a ship's deck. To be between the seam and the ship's side is indeed a precarious, if thrilling, position!"[42]

Although the discoveries of the scholar could at times unsettle the doctrines of the believer, Nash was convinced that ultimately the two were in harmony. He affirmed that truth is one because God is one. There is continuity, not contradiction, between faith and reason; reason makes faith intelligible, and faith illuminates reason. The latter point was made explicit in the Campion College calendar: "As a Catholic College, Campion is dedicated to the principle that the Christian faith is the crown and surest safeguard of reason and freedom. Campion believes that theology undergirds man's hope of rational solutions to the world's problems, and is a necessary complement to the social sciences, which of themselves cannot fully account for man."[43]

Although Nash was ideologically distant from Dallas Smythe and the other authors of the Regina Beach Statement, there were points of convergence in their approaches to university education. Both questioned the faith of the modern university in the notion that rational free inquiry, scientific investigation, and technological development lead automatically and necessarily to progress. Smythe, following Robert Hutchins, called for the recognition of a hierarchy of truths, a conceptual framework, and a point of view. The Regina Beach Statement asked that the world and the university itself be called to account from the perspective of essential human values. Nash echoed these thoughts in 1968 when he wrote,

> As for bringing to the university a new dimension, the Church has the duty of witnessing therein to its liberating vision of man, a vision known by faith, and of offering to the University the effective means of bringing that vision to fruition. The effective means are Christian hope, counteracting despair of making reasonable solutions work, and Christian charity, repairing the selfishness to which the intellectual is by no means immune. These means, of course, will be effective in the measure in which Christian community is built up among students and professors. They should result in the Church, as present through students and professors, seeking practical ways to work with the University and for the University in its task of preparing students to play their rightful role in society.[44]

Nash the Christian and Smythe the quasi-Marxist both detected inadequacies in the education offered by the modern university. Both challenged the orthodoxies of so-called objective and neutral learning. They sensed that the university, with its fragmentation and compartmentalization of knowledge, unrelenting skepticism, and denial of metaphysical orientation, fell short of what was required of a liberal education. Although the two men did not share a faith or a world view, each perceived shortcomings in the educational status quo. They both attached a high priority to developing within students a capacity for critical thinking and a questioning attitude towards the information placed before them. Nash put it this way: "The prime need of students is to break out of the common-sense pattern of experience into the intellectual pattern in which openness to truth and passion for inquiry is dominant. The student may think that all he has to do is memorize. He doesn't realize the importance of discussion. Yet, if the University is to be more than a degree-mill, he needs to be encouraged to probe, to inquire, and to enjoy having his own bright ideas shot down by his peers."[45] This is virtually a paraphrase of the following portion of the Regina Beach Statement: "The professor is charged with the responsibility of opening and of sustaining a dialogue with the student: the student must be encouraged to see that his relationship to the educational process and to the dialogue, is not that of exposure merely, but of involvement."

Nash did not, however, agree with Smythe's critique of academic freedom or his statement that the function of knowledge is to "provide ways of finding solutions to man's problems."[46] Of course humankind must use its knowledge to solve its problems, but that is not the beginning and the end of it. For the Jesuit, the pursuit and contemplation of truth is always a good in itself. Temperamentally, Nash was the more optimistic of the two men. He did not dwell, as Smythe was apt to do, on the grim realities of the nuclear war threat, environmental pollution, and technology run amuck. But there were moments when Nash allowed himself to stare into the abyss. He wrote in 1980, "I think that Campion has constantly to be addressing itself to the question: Do its programs enable its students to grapple intellectually and maturely with the challenge that Christianity makes to them today in a world that seems increasingly meaningless, selfish, and bent on self-destruction?"[47] The college, he believed, had to concern itself with the problems of the Third World and the global gap between the haves and the have-nots. In the end, what is striking about Nash and Smythe is their common intellectual ground, not the things that divided them.

In one area of educational philosophy, however, Nash was singular. He understood the relationship between liberal education and the physical environment in which it takes place. While others focused on the quantity of building space available for students, he concentrated on the quality of the space. In his educational philosophy faith and reason complemented one another, as did aesthetic appreciation and rational modes of understanding. The calendar stated that one of the goals of Campion College was to introduce students to those experiences by which "we become sensitive to the human condition and to appreciate all that is truly beautiful."[48] Nash believed that students had to be assisted "to break out of the common-sense pattern of

The interior of the Campion College library. Father Nash, who believed in the importance of aesthetics in a liberal arts education, tried to make the library, with its "gold carpet, blue ceiling and soft-toned woods," an oasis of quiet study.

experience into the aesthetic-artistic pattern in which the symbolic imparts to the whole a love of the true, the beautiful, and the good. Without this pattern of experience the intellectual pattern can remain sterile, inoperative. It is a genuine need that is sadly neglected. There may even be much that inhibits such a pattern, for example, a general physical drabness in the buildings and décor, a low cultural level of University radio and newspaper. Where the artistic-aesthetic need of students is not being met, or is being thwarted, surely there is call for a network of appropriate services, a service for music appreciation, and even a service for a more artistically satisfying liturgy."[49] We hear echoes in this passage of Ken Lochhead, who said that art was a means to enable students to see the world in a different way, and of Minoru Yamasaki, who wanted the buildings to have a quiet dignity in keeping with the noble aspirations of education.

Nash, more than any other campus administrator, knew what they were talking about. Liberal education for him developed the spiritual, intellectual, and aesthetic capacities of the student – or, to put it another way, it imparted a love of the good, the true, and the beautiful. He railed against those "factors in University life which militate against the intellectual pattern of expe-

The music room at Campion College.

rience ... poor housing, poor bus service, lack of lounge space or of seminar facilities."[50] He tried to make the Campion library an oasis of quiet scholarly pursuits: "with its gold carpet, blue ceiling and soft-toned woods, [it] encourages students to use these holdings in an atmosphere conducive to study. The library clearly manifests the concern of the college for human values."[51] He ensured that there were good paintings on the walls, and he made the auditorium available for plays, concerts, films, and special lectures.

Nash's only concession to the unaesthetic was rock music at student socials and dances, and he allowed it only because the students insisted on it. The CCSA (Campion College Student Association) had a "beer party in the evening," he noted in his journal on 2 October 1971. "*Why* do they have to have a band that completely discourages all conversation? It was an orderly party otherwise."[52] In this instance his campaign for improving the artistic sensibility of students took second place to the goal of building the Campion College community. He believed that the college would succeed only "in the measure in which Christian community is built up among students and professors." If the members of the college did not feel that they belonged to something bigger than themselves and were not united by a common purpose, the whole enterprise was lost. The Campion College community may be described as a series of concentric circles. At the centre were the Jesuits

Students gathered in the Campion cafeteria to watch the 1972 Canada-Soviet hockey series.

who lived in the residence on the top floor of the building and formed their own religious community. Radiating out from the centre were the members of the non-Jesuit teaching faculty, students, administrative and support staff, alumni, and supporters within and outside the university.

In 1968, the faculty totalled thirteen: five Jesuits and eight non-Jesuits. Nash treated the latter like members of his extended family.[53] His journal entry for 1 February 1973 read, "George [who taught philosophy] and Delia Marshall have a son, the first boy born to Campion professors *after* joining our staff. Up to now there have been *eight girls!*"[54] And he wrote on 18 April 1978, "Dr. Bob Moore [professor of psychology] came in 602nd in the Boston Marathon out of a field of 4,800. His time of 2 hours, 42 minutes, 30 seconds was a personal best. Joe Moran of our advisory board also completed the run in 3 hours, 35 minutes."[55] No detail of college life escaped his notice. Nash also made plenty of time for the students, attending all their social functions, even when he could barely stand the music. At the wind-up party in April 1978 the students presented him with a plaque that read, "To Very Reverend Father Nash. Dear Dad for all of us here. The year was made memorable and special by you – love, the C.C.S.A. and all the Rowdies, '77–78."[56]

The college chaplains played a key role in the formation of Christian community in their capacity as individual counsellors and as facilitators of group events. Religious life centred on the daily Mass (11:30 a.m. and 4:30 p.m.; 8:00 p.m. on Sundays). Sunday Mass had an average attendance in 1973-74 of about 200; on other days the figure averaged about twenty. The chaplains conducted an annual weekend retreat for students, which participants spent in silence and prayer and meetings with their spiritual advisers. There were also special services during Lent and a Seder supper for sixty people on Wednesday of Holy Week.[57] Many of the chapel events were ecumenical, such as the memorial service held the day after Martin Luther King Jr was assassinated in April 1968.[58]

Nash, in his statement of aims for Campion College, emphasized that the college "does not represent fully the riches of every Christian community. Hence it strives to have an openness to other Christian faiths and seeks to work for reunion. It wishes to be open to all manifestations of religious thought in which the seeds of truth are and can be present."[59] This reflected the spirit of renewal of the Roman Catholic Church arising from Vatican II, the second Vatican Council, held from 1962 to 1965, one of the principal concerns of which was "the restoration of unity among all Christians." Nash had good relations with Luther College, built adjacent to Campion on the Regina campus, though he joked in his journal that while Luther was under construction, the "Luther College construction firm tried *smoking* us out with burning straw and coal (to warm up the ground for a trench)."[60] Nash worked closely with both Luther College and St Thomas More College to lobby the provincial government for an improved grant formula from which all the federated colleges would benefit. He also attended Luther events, such as the annual Luther lecture. His diary comment about the inaugural lecture – by Jaroslav Pelikan, entitled "The Irony of the Reformation" – was brief and to the point: "A *super* lecture."[61] His response to the second Luther lecture in February 1978 was equally enthusiastic: "Luther Lecture well attended. Dr. M. Marty tremendous."[62] Together Luther College and Campion College worked to develop a religious studies program at the university, and they saw their efforts rewarded in May 1974 when the Faculty of Arts and Science approved it.[63]

The Lutheran commitment to education can be traced to the teachings of Martin Luther, the leader of the Protestant Reformation in Germany in the early sixteenth century. His firm conviction was that all Christians should be able to read the Bible themselves in order to have a better understanding of the message it contains.[64] It follows that schooling has to be made widely available and that everyone, regardless of status or wealth, should have the benefits of a good education. When German Lutherans immigrated to North America in the eighteenth and nineteenth centuries they brought with them their educational traditions and almost immediately began to establish elementary schools, academies, and colleges. By the early 1900s three main

German Lutheran church groups had emerged. The largest one in western Canada was called the Ohio Synod (renamed in 1930 the American Lutheran Church). Its headquarters was in Columbus, Ohio, site of Capital University, the foremost educational institution of the synod. The Canada district of the Ohio Synod in 1910 approved the founding of a Lutheran academy in Saskatchewan following the practice in the United States. Its purpose was twofold: to offer a secondary education of high quality for those who did not intend to enter university and to provide a thorough academic preparation for those who did.[65]

Pastor Henry Schmidt of Neudorf served as chairman of the board and later as the first principal of the academy. The board debated whether to build the school in Regina or Melville, opting in the end for Melville because it was conveniently located in the middle of a district heavily populated with German Lutherans. A handsome three-storey brick building was constructed one mile west of the centre of town, and the first class – thirty-two boys – enrolled in the fall of 1913. They received instruction in a wide range of academic and practical subjects, including English, mathematics, religion, philosophy, penmanship, agriculture, civics, drawing, music, and commerce. Although the school was at first for males only, girls were admitted in 1920, and the institution was thereafter coeducational. Enrolment increased to fifty-six by 1925, at which time it became apparent that the school had to be enlarged or a new building constructed.[66]

The board, after considerable debate, decided to move the school to Regina. Eighteen acres of land were secured at the western edge of the city between Saskatchewan House (the official residence of the lieutenant-governor) and the RCMP barracks. The Ohio Synod, its Canada district, local congregations, and Regina businessmen together raised $130,000 for the building, which opened in the fall of 1926. Dr Rex Schneider, a graduate of Capital University and the Lutheran Theological Seminary in Columbus, assumed the duties of principal, an office he held for thirty-eight years, until his retirement in 1964.[67] The academy, renamed Luther College, offered, in addition to high school work, first-year courses leading to a BA degree. The latter arrangement was made possible through an affiliation agreement with the University of Saskatchewan similar to the agreements that Regina and Campion Colleges had with the university.

The educational philosophy of Luther College, modelled on that of Capital University, derived from the ideal of service to the broader community, Lutheran and non-Lutheran alike, without abandoning the distinctive features of the Lutheran cultural and intellectual tradition. In the words of Principal Schneider in 1926, the school aimed "to instill the virtues of Christian honor, unselfishness, and good will, a discriminating loyalty of family, state, and church, the ideals of healthful living as a means of participating in the responsibilities of life."[68] It blended high academic standards with a strong sense of community. This community feeling was especially important as increasing numbers of non-Lutherans and day students from Regina enrolled in the college. Lloyd Barber, a graduate of Luther and president of the University of Regina from 1976 to 1990, summed up the Luther ideal in his address to the 1969 graduating class: "good people can only be good if the environment is purposeful. Luther College has been, from the beginning, dedicated to scholarship – purposeful Christian scholarship."[69]

When Rex Schneider retired in 1964, his successor was Morris Anderson, who had taught at Luther since 1955. Anderson took his undergraduate training at the University of Saskatchewan and in 1962 received a master's degree in English and administration from the University of Oregon in Eugene. He also attended St Olaf College in Minnesota, the leading Norwegian Lutheran liberal arts college. A merger of Lutheran churches in 1960 brought together under a single college board the schools of the Ohio Synod and those of the Norwegian Lutheran group. This led to increased contact between Luther in Regina and St Olaf in Minneapolis, so that when Anderson began to think about the issues involved in federation with the Regina campus he sought the advice of Sidney A. Rand, the president of St Olaf College.[70]

The Luther College Board of Regents discussed the possibility of federation as early as 1959, and a formal application was sent to President Spinks in December 1961. As we have seen in the case of Campion, the university deferred consideration of such requests until the development of the Regina campus had reached a more mature stage. In June 1964 the Board of College Education of the American Lutheran Church, with which Luther College was affiliated, carried out a detailed study of the proposed federation. Robert B. Gronlund, vice-president, development and public relations, Capital University, reported strongly in favour of the idea, highlighting especially the need to recruit "an absolutely top faculty, so that whether a particular student takes a class from one of these men or not the reputation of the College would be such as to command approval and attention."[71] He also recommended that the college appoint a development (fundraising) officer and employ a professional agency to assist with the campaign for building funds.

The Board of College Education approved the federation of Luther College in February 1965. The College Board of Regents endorsed the idea and entered into negotiations with the university. The senate and the Board of Governors gave their unanimous approval in May 1965. As had been the case with Campion College, Luther had to fulfill three conditions before the agreement could take effect: it had to appoint faculty who were recognized as members of the Faculty of Arts and Science; it had to offer classes for academic credit in at least four disciplines; and it had to construct a building on the campus or adjacent to it. The third item presented the greatest obstacle, since it involved raising $1.9 million; Luther College would need a building large enough to house classrooms, offices, a library, a chapel/auditorium, a dining area, lounges, games rooms, and a dormitory – it had to accommodate 400 students, 200 of whom would live in residence and 200 off campus.[72] Reverend Don King was appointed development director, professional fund-raising advice was obtained, and the campaign duly launched. Meanwhile, in November 1966 there was a change in the organization of the Lutheran Church in western Canada. The Evangelical Lutheran Church of Canada broke away from the American Lutheran Church and became a separate entity. As a result, Luther College now belonged to the Evangelical Lutheran Church.[73]

The funding gradually fell into place. The college secured a loan of $1,200,000 from the Central Mortgage and Housing Corporation for the dormitory portion of the building, the Government of Saskatchewan contributed 10 per cent of the total capital cost (about $190,000), and the balance came from the contributions of alumni, parents, friends, business corporations, and members of the Lutheran Church.[74] An address given at the groundbreaking ceremony, held on 6 July 1970, aptly summarized the purpose of the project: "We begin the construction of this federated college for the purpose of community where students, staff, and visitors may gather for fellowship and discussion – where the community of learning and the community of faith may meet and interact."[75]

The building, designed by architect Clive Rodham of the firm Kerr, Cullingworth, Riches and Associates, was officially opened on Sunday, 3 October 1971. Regina campus principal John Archer welcomed the college to the university, making the point that universities owed it to their students to deal with moral and spiritual issues: "when students ask crucial questions concerning identity, right and wrong, the good life – and get no response or a stony response, then I think the universities are wrong." Acknowledging that historically there had existed a certain antagonism between the university and the church, especially when the latter tried to control the former, he maintained that relations between the two entities had entered a new era. It was now more widely recognized that secularism was itself a kind of faith, and that "secular establishments and secular methodologies" could be as stifling as religious ones.[76]

Reverend William E. Hordern, president of the Lutheran Theological Seminary in Saskatoon, continued this theme in his dedicatory speech. He defined the Christian college as an institution that demonstrated the "servanthood" of education. It was "the place where we can try to rediscover that the goal of education is not to lord it over others, not to make more money, and get better jobs, but to learn the wisdom of life so that we may serve ... If Luther College becomes merely a small carbon copy of the University of

The Luther College building. It had classrooms, offices, a library, a chapel/auditorium, a dormitory, a dining area, lounges, and games rooms; the building officially opened on 3 October 1971.

Saskatchewan as a whole, then it will serve no real purpose. But here I think there is an opportunity to make experimental thrusts in education for service. Because you are smaller you can create that fellowship among faculty and students, that person-to-person relationship within which education for service can be truly meaningful."[77]

These ideas, summed up in the phrase "quality liberal education in a Christian context," were represented in the college logo. It featured a white capital *L* on a blue background. The *L* held within it a cross, a circle, and the leaves of the tree of knowledge, images that taken together symbolized the reconciliation of faith and reason.[78] The calendar set forth the aims of the college:

1. Provide for the students a broad general education which introduces major fields of human knowledge and makes it possible for them to concentrate in one or more areas of learning, and to equip themselves for further education, for a profession or for life in the contemporary world.

2. Assist students in developing a creative and active integration of faith and learning, of faith and culture, by assisting them to probe the dimensions of the Christian gospel in relation to their own individual lives, the university, and the global community.
3. Develop as much as possible in each student a community concern that extends to others in every dimension of human existence whether in immediate social contexts or in the world at large, and encourage students' individual personal development compatible with dynamic Christian convictions that contribute to responsible leadership and effective community service.[79]

Luther opened its doors in the fall of 1971 with an enrolment of 129, well below the 400 the building had been designed to accommodate.[80] The residence had 181 occupants, 66 of whom were enrolled in Luther arts and science and 115 in other faculties.[81] The baby boom enrolment had peaked, and by the early 1970s it was tapering off. Principal Anderson and other staff members initiated a recruitment drive, taking their message to church groups and high schools in Assiniboia, Swift Current, Hodgeville, Lemberg, Yorkton, Moose Jaw, Outlook, Central Butte, Loreburn, and many other small towns in southern Saskatchewan.[82] The number of students slowly crept upward to 159 in 1972–73, 180 in 1973–74, and 206 in 1975–76.[83] Through concentrated effort the college increased its registration, despite the overall decline in campus enrolment.

Luther College had the advantage of the dormitory, the only one on campus until 1972, when College West opened. Even then dormitory space was in short supply relative to the total size of student population. Out-of-towners, therefore, were drawn to the Luther residence whether or not they enrolled as Luther College students. In planning the residence, the architect tried to design a physical layout that would foster a sense of community and maximize social interaction among the residents. He eliminated the long hallways typical of institutional dormitories and arranged the rooms around central service areas and small lounges. These clusters within the residence were intended to create social groupings, which would combine to form the residence community. The plan to a large extent succeeded. Jim Dale, head resident and dean of students, reported in September 1973 that "the tone of the dorm is exceptionally good already and many student-initiated activities are taking place."[84] The students competed in intramural sports and played hockey and broomball on the outdoor rink next to the residence. There were lessons in "old-time dancing" (waltz, foxtrot, polka, jive, schottische, and cha-cha-cha), film nights, chess tournaments, and every Wednesday night a "talent show" was held.[85]

The Student Life Office organized "explore groups," discussion groups that focused on specific themes. "Explore Our Feelings" was advertised as

The Luther College logo, featuring a large white *L* on a blue background; the *L* contains a cross, a circle, and leaves of the tree of knowledge. Taken together, the symbols suggested the reconciliation of faith and reason.

"Small group interaction dealing with our feelings and emotions. A growth group intended to help us understand ourselves better," while "Explore Our Ideas" centred on issues of faith: "Which idea? Faith? Religion? What can be believed today? What makes sense?" The faculty arranged panel discussions on such topics as "mysticism," "changing roles in changing family structure," and "genetic engineering."[86] The goal was to enrich the total college experience, to make it something more than attending classes and doing assignments. Students were consulted about the topics to be discussed. They vetoed, for example, a proposed seminar on the subject of death: "Area discussions would be good but the topic should be new and different, not something you read about every day in magazines and papers and hear about on TV. Death is not a good topic – too often used and not something you want to take a date to."[87] At a more practical level, the college organized tutorials to help students improve their study skills, to assist them in writing term papers and preparing for examinations.[88] If Luther College faced an obstacle in its efforts to build a sense of community, it was bridging the gap between the day students and those who lived in the residence. The Luther University Students' Association tried to reach out to the off-campus students and get them involved, but with only limited success.[89]

The religious life of the college was generally robust. Reverend Don King, who was appointed part-time pastor in 1972, reported a high level of interest in daily devotions.[90] Since the auditorium was not considered suitable for religious services, the arts and crafts room on the top floor was renovated and carpeted for use as a chapel. Appropriately, it was named the "upper room."[91] Students took an active part in planning the Sunday services, which were attended by about fifty people. The residence newsletter announced in October 1973 that "Many of us experience downers all the time. We've found one positive upper – it's the 'Upper Room' at Luther. We use it for meditation during the week and Sunday mornings we take part in a student orga-

The Luther College residence, which opened in the fall of 1971. It was the only residence on campus until the completion of the College West building in 1972.

nized worship service at 11:15 a.m."[92] In December there was carol singing and an Advent and Christmas celebration held at midnight.[93] The Student Life Office coordinated volunteer work so that students who had some extra time could devote one or two hours per week to reading for the blind, visiting senior citizens, or performing some other community service.[94]

Members of the Luther College Goose Creek Tabernacle Choir. A central goal of the college was to develop a strong sense of community.

The "upper room" at Luther College, a place for meditation and organized worship.

Morris Anderson, the first president of Luther College, in conversation with Jaroslav Pelikan, who inaugurated the Luther lecture series in 1977.

The teaching faculty in 1971–72 consisted of Morris Anderson (English), Bob Ostrem (psychology), Art Krentz (philosophy), and Tom Strutt (English). At first only three disciplines were covered, the university having waived temporarily the requirement that a federated college had to offer classes in a minimum of four areas.[95] Ostrem left and Paul Antrobus was hired to replace him.[96] Gradually, as funds came available, additional academic staff members were hired, notably Roland Miller, who became a key figure in the religious studies program. The college administration encouraged faculty to get to know the students both inside and outside the classroom as part of its initiative to offer a well-rounded education not confined to academic study alone.[97] The chaplain also suggested that faculty members socialize with the maintenance and cafeteria staff in order to "knit relations" and make sure that everyone felt as though they belonged to the college community.[98]

Luther amplified its presence in the university and projected itself outward into the wider community through the Luther College lecture series, inaugurated in 1977. The stated purpose of the series was "to make a distinctive and stimulating intellectual contribution to the life of the university" and "to express, publicly and effectively, a relevant aspect of Luther's goal to educate in a Christian context."[99] The series succeeded in its objective and became a focal point for what the college was trying to accomplish.

By the mid-1970s Luther had established its identity and become a recognized unit within the larger university. The fact that it began operations in 1971, four years after Campion opened its new building, had advantages and disadvantages. In one sense the delay made it easier for Luther, because Campion had to handle the delicate negotiations leading to federated status. Once the terms were in place, Luther had only to sign the template agreement. But the delay also meant that Luther opened at the very moment that the booming enrolments of the sixties, which had justified the building of the new campus, suddenly collapsed. The college had to work hard to find the money and recruit the students it needed to fulfill its educational mission.

Both Campion College and Luther College, each in keeping with its own distinctive traditions, tried to answer the question "What is the best way to give students a liberal education?" This was also at the heart of the debate on the Regina Beach Statement, which preoccupied the campus as a whole. The federated colleges were not peripheral to the discussion but rather vital contributors, because they were able to bring to that discussion ideas and values that were often overlooked or misunderstood in the secular university. In the larger scheme of things, the federation principle added a new dimension to the life of the university. It reconciled diversity of viewpoint with unity of purpose; it combined the intimacy and community feeling of the small college with the academic benefits of participation in the larger university.

12 The Rise of the Citizen Student

The students of the 1960s tended to be vocal and active.[1] They expanded the role of student government and demanded the right to participate at all levels of university decision making. The radicals among them worked for a fundamental transformation not only of the university, but also of society as a whole. An international phenomenon, the movement had an impact on all Westernized countries. An early and dramatic manifestation was the free speech movement at Berkeley in 1964. When the university imposed a campus ban on the distribution of literature and the collection of money for political causes such as civil rights, the students occupied the main administration building. The university called in the police, who dragged the students from the building, arresting 800. Negotiations followed, at the conclusion of which the university administration conceded the right of students to engage in political activities on campus.[2] The free speech movement was a rallying point for students across North America. The *Carillon* published an article in October 1966 citing the Berkeley experience and drawing lessons from it for the Regina campus: "[It] demonstrated that legitimate grievances would receive attention from administrators only if students showed they would not be ignored. They could only show their concern by taking mass action, by striking ... This university is run by the same kind of men who ran Berkeley."[3]

It was estimated that in the spring of 1969 there were demonstrations at three hundred American colleges and universities.[4] In some cases the protests turned violent. Black Power militants armed with guns patrolled the hallways at Cornell University. Students at Columbia took control of the campus for eight days in April 1968 until the police forced them out. Simon Fraser University was the scene of confrontations between students and police, while at Sir George Williams University (now Concordia) in Montreal students set fire to the computer centre, causing millions of dollars' worth of damage.[5] The students at Regina campus were moderate by comparison, yet they were fully engaged in the issues of the sixties. They were not just *in* the sixties; they were *of* the sixties.

In order to appreciate the significance of what happened, it is necessary first to consider student life in the 1950s. Student government at Regina College in 1959–60 was a modest affair, the total annual budget of the Students' Representative Council (SRC) amounting to only $2,860.[6] The council consisted of eleven members: president, vice-president, secretary, treasurer, director of music, director of drama, director of the Men's Athletic Board, director of the Women's Athletic Board, activities director, social director, and yearbook editor. Each had one or more faculty advisers who guided and supervised the student activity to which they had been assigned. Thus the SRC was not an independent entity. It carried out its operations under the watchful eye of the administration and faculty. This point was made explicit in the SRC constitution, which stated that the student president was "responsible to the Dean of the College for the conduct of the SRC and of the Students' Assembly and for the general oversight of all student activities." In addition, student directorates were required to follow, "as well as Council directions, College regulations governing their activities," and cheques had to be "signed by the SRC Treasurer and one member of the faculty appointed by the faculty."[7]

Students in the early 1960s began to grow restless under constraints to their freedom to conduct their affairs as they saw fit. An editorial in the *Sheet* early in 1962 declared, "The SRC should be completely independent. Unadvised actions by the SRC can be checked by the students who elected them. The SRC is responsible to the students and the students are quite capable of checking them."[8] Matters came to a head on 22 February 1962, when the SRC treasurer resigned because of a squabble over the payment of a gas bill. The president, vice-president, and social director also resigned, leaving the student government in a state of confusion.[9] Without these officers the SRC was unable to conduct its business or authorize new elections. Dean W.A. Riddell took it upon himself to call a general meeting of the students in order "to right the capsized ship of student government." Jim Harding, editor of the student newspaper, posted a two-page typewritten statement on the bulletin board denouncing the dean's action as "completely unjustified." He said that it "violated the independence of the student body." Riddell replied that Harding's protest was "stupid," adding, "The SRC derives its authority from the University's board of governors. I'm empowered to step in."[10] The immediate dispute was resolved when the SRC officers who had resigned returned to complete their terms of office, but the larger problem of student discontent continued to fester.

The SRC constitution could be amended by means of a two-thirds majority vote of the student body meeting in a general assembly called by the student president.[11] In the early 1960s a number of changes were made. For example, the clause that made the SRC president accountable to the dean of the college for the administration of student affairs was deleted, as was the provision requiring SRC cheques to be co-signed by a faculty member. Another amendment pertained to student elections. Prior to the fall of 1961, when the second-year degree course was introduced, the college had offered only the first-year program. This meant that student elections had to be held in the early fall for the academic year about to begin. They could not be held the preceding spring because the great majority of students would not be returning for another year. This meant that in September there was no student government in place to take charge of the elections. For this reason the dean asked a faculty member to call for nominations and serve as the returning officer.

When the college began offering second-year arts, it became possible for the students to hold elections in the spring, and the SRC constitution was amended accordingly. It provided for the election of the SRC executive (president, vice-president, secretary, treasurer) in the spring and for the appointment of a student returning officer to organize elections for the other council positions in the fall. The editor of the newspaper was elected at the same time as the executive, but he or she could no longer be a member of the SRC because it was deemed a conflict of interest for the editor to both report on and serve as a member of student government.[12] The first student elections under the amended constitution were a great success. Over 75 per cent of the student body turned out to vote, and they elected Mike Badham (later a long-serving member of Regina City Council) as president.[13]

The faculty in 1962 proposed a change in its relationship with the SRC. Rather than having individual faculty members serve as advisers to the various student directorates (drama, social, yearbook, and so on), it would appoint three faculty committees (athletics, student activities, and SRC) to maintain a liaison with the students.[14] The *Sheet* responded warily that if the committees were to act in an "advisory capacity" and not as "control bodies," then they were acceptable, "but if these committees unnecessarily intervene in student activities, the students will have every right to object."[15]

It did not take long for tensions to develop. A joint faculty-student committee met on 31 October 1962 to discuss regulations governing social events. A second meeting was scheduled for 19 November, but the SRC representatives failed to show up. Nor did they appear at a third meeting, held on 7 December. The faculty members on the committee admitted that "in general there seems to be some feeling among the SRC that the Faculty aspect of this committee is an encroachment on their freedom of action in the running of their affairs."[16] The faculty met as a whole to consider the committee's report and passed a resolution "censuring the SRC very severely for the discourtesy done the members of the Faculty on the Committee."[17]

Dean Riddell rebuked SRC president Mike Badham for failing to take advantage of the offer extended by the faculty to allow the students to "participate in regulating their own affairs." He maintained that "the University does not consist of a series of isolated cells" and that "the students are an integral part of the University and must carry on their activities in ways that are acceptable to the University as a whole. I get the impression from reports of various people who have dealt with the SRC that a number of your members, if not the SRC as a body, take the position that there should be no regulations governing any student activities." Riddell made it clear that if this attitude was not corrected, the faculty and administration would be "forced into the position of imposing regulations on the students." He announced on 18 December 1962 that no student activities would be permitted after the Christmas break until the dates for social events had been cleared by a "suitable committee" and assurances had been received that the events would be conducted "under regulations that are acceptable to the University."[18]

Riddell's position was not altogether consistent. He affirmed, on the one hand, that students were an "integral part of the university," which to him meant that their activities had to be supervised by the faculty and administration; on the other hand, he made no allowance for student participation in the decision making of the university of which they were, by his own admission, an "integral part." There was no student representation on committees or councils other than those concerned exclusively with student government. Riddell portrayed student participation on the committee governing student activities as a generous concession on his part. He wrote to Badham, "I think you and the other members of the SRC have let the student body down by failing to appreciate the real opportunity you had."[19] In reality, student representation on the committee was also useful to Riddell and the faculty because it lent an aura of legitimacy to the authority they exercised.

Badham explained that the student representatives had failed to attend any meetings of the joint committee after the first one because they thought they were a waste of time. The first one turned into "a one-sided chastisement of the students by a faculty member. The meeting lasted for almost two hours, during which time the only thing accomplished was that the Social Director was given some pointers on manners."[20] Since Riddell did not accept this explanation, the joint committee on student activities was replaced by a committee composed entirely of faculty members. It met on 7 January 1963 and

The Regina campus Student Representative Council, 1962–63, a transitional year in the development of a new student culture based on the concept of the student as citizen.

issued a new set of regulations. The SRC was required to submit to the committee chairman in writing and in duplicate prior to 15 January 1963 the dates and places of all planned social and student activities for the remainder of the term. The SRC had also to submit written application in duplicate for permission to hold any student activity ten days before the event was to be held. The names of at least two patrons chosen from the faculty had to be reported to the committee one week in advance of the function. Unless special permission of the committee was obtained, functions and entertainments had to be held on Friday or Saturday evenings, and none could be held after 16 March.[21] The cut-off date ensured that students had a month free of distractions to prepare for their final examinations.

These restrictive measures may have arisen from a vague feeling that the students were getting out of control. Riddell expressed concern in November 1962 when more than eight dozen beer bottles were found outside the gymnasium after a "sox dance." He stated in a memo to the Student Activities Committee that "while there have been a small number of bottles in evidence after any dance on campus, this has got completely out of hand."[22] There were other signs of student unruliness. The *Carillon* ran a banner headline on 26 October 1962: "War Is Declared!" The "war" in question was a campaign to obtain preferential student rates on city buses and at movie theatres. Mike Badham had discussed the issue with Mayor Henry Baker, who had promised his support. The article hinted that some kind of student protest or demonstration was in the offing: "If and when the mobilization occurs, the press and television have tentatively revealed that they will be on hand to cover the situation. Be on hand to put all the legal methods which the BNA Act has bestowed upon us to use to get that to which we are entitled."[23]

On the evening of 31 October 1962, 250 students "marched on the city of Regina." The demonstration began at the college gymnasium and proceeded north on Scarth Street to the Hotel Saskatchewan, where the students spent fifteen minutes parading through the halls. They advanced to the Capitol Theatre and walked up and down the aisles chanting "We want student rates!" Next they invaded National Billiards, making off, according to the police report, with seven balls and three billiard cues – a total value of $59.25. The police challenged the right of the students to assemble in the streets, citing a bylaw that required a special permit to hold a demonstration involving fifty or more persons. When the officers commanded the students to disperse, they refused. Regina police chief Arthur G. Cookson later complained to Riddell that his men were treated with "abuse, ridicule and insults," and that many of the students "showed disrespect and defiance of the police, were rowdy and ill mannered."[24] The students, in turn, alleged that the police had handled them with unnecessary roughness.

The marchers regrouped and formed a conga line, weaving down 11th Avenue to City Hall, where they took up the cry "We want Mayor Baker!" Baker had been victorious in the municipal elections, held that day, and the students, acknowledging the support he had given them in their campaign for cheaper bus fares, cheered his success at the polls. After the demonstration, reported the *Carillon*, "tired feet and dimmed spirits prevailed and the protesters quietly returned to the Campus. An invasion of Sammy's P-Za Palace and the 4D [coffee shop] concluded the evening."[25] The police detained four male students but released them without laying charges.

The *Carillon* headlined its account of the event "The Giant Awakens." It claimed that the "march" would force the SRC, the faculty, and the citizens of Regina "to reassess their appraisal of our student potential. It appears the students are willing to collectively press for some consideration from the business concerns of this city." The SRC apparently had not been involved in planning the event. Vice-President Harvey Walker said that the "student council was against it from the outset."[26] The march seemed to have been the undertaking of a group of students, some of them *Carillon* staff, who portrayed it as a manifestation of the rising consciousness of student power.

The *Leader-Post* was unsure how to interpret the incident. It titled its report "Snake Dance Leads to Police Warning," but in the text of the article "snake dance" was placed in quotation marks as though to indicate that the term did not exactly describe what had happened. Although the terms "march," "parade," "demonstration," "snake dance," and "conga line" were all used, none seemed entirely suitable. The event blended elements of all of them; it represented something new in the history of student culture at Regina campus.

Significantly, the event took place on Halloween, a night associated with revelry, misbehaviour, and the temporary inversion of authority. Historian Keith Walden gives an account of the Halloween rituals of male students at the University of Toronto in the late 1800s and early 1900s. Every year on 31 October they marched from the campus to the downtown area and attended the theatre. Occupying a block of balcony seats, they interrupted the performance with singing, shouting, and college yells. Afterwards they joined in a street parade – which involved more shouting and noise making, as well as property damage and, inevitably, an altercation with the police.[27] The Regina campus demonstration on 31 October 1962 followed an almost identical pattern: a march from the campus to the downtown area, a visit to the theatre (in this case a movie theatre), more marching, and a run-in with police.

There were also local precedents for riotous student activity in public places, though not always on Halloween. The *Leader* (forerunner of the *Leader-Post*) on 4 February 1915 described "a tumultuous mob, shrieking and gesticulating wildly, and garbed in the most grotesque of costumes surg[ing] through the city streets at a late hour last night, rudely disturbing the peaceful occupations of citizens in their vicinity."[28] In the fall of 1923 girls from Regina College, "with great green bows added to their hats," marched from the college to the Capitol Theatre, where they took seats in the front row. The words "Welcome Freshettes of Regina College" appeared on the screen at the end of the movie. A spotlight was turned on the girls, who stood and faced the audience while the orchestra played "The Gang's All Here."[29]

In the 1950s Halloween was typically marked at the college by a night raid on the girls' residence. The student newspaper described the scene in 1951: "Stopping only long enough to barricade the stairs in case of an attack from the rear, [the male students] raced to the washroom and smeared sinks, mirrors, doors, and tubs with corn syrup and thick, black molasses. At the sound of the key turning in the latch of one of the rooms, the vigilantes turned as one man and rushed to that room only to realize that they had been duped; they were met by a shower of ink from the transom above the door. No sooner had they recovered from this surprise than they were confronted with an angry Dean of Women who chased them to the staircase where they met – their own barricade!"[30] The women retaliated the next year with a raid on the men's residence. Dashing wildly from room to room, they tore mattresses from the beds and scattered blankets, sheets, and pillows around the hall. One of the raiders later told the student paper that "the raid was a marvelously timed piece of strategy, and we were safe behind the locked doors of our own rooms within seconds."[31]

Students in the 1950s had snake-danced through the halls of the college as part of the activities associated with the annual fall reception. The snake dance moved outdoors, apparently for the first time, on Halloween night in 1959. The students took their dance into the downtown business district, anticipating what they would do on a larger scale and in a more rowdy manner in 1962. It was no coincidence that 1959 was the year of the announcement that Regina College would expand to a full degree program. As student Elaine Hamilton explained, "The snake dance is a good idea – should become a tradition at Regina College to make everyone realize that Regina College is a university, not just a glorified high school."[32] Students consciously imitated the rituals of older campuses as a means of validating their status as full-fledged university students.

The new element in the 1962 Halloween revelry was politics, as revealed in the chant "We want student rates!" at the theatre and the shouts of support for Mayor Baker at City Hall. What happened in 1962 was neither a snake dance nor a protest demonstration, but a combination of the two. It merged a component of the traditional extracurricular student culture extending back to the late 1800s, if not earlier, with the new culture of student activism emerging in the 1960s. The older style of disorderly behaviour – disruptions at the theatre, street parades, destruction of property, clashes with the police – had a carnival spirit. Such actions did not represent a serious attempt to overthrow the power structure or bring about a revolution. It was well understood that once the students had had their "fun," everything would return to normal. The temporary outburst of mayhem acted as a safety valve; the release of pent-up pressure stabilized and consolidated the hierarchical power structure. The student protests of the 1960s were completely different. Politically motivated, they were intended to bring about fundamental changes in power relationships within the university and in society at large. Thus the Regina campus dance/demonstration of 31 October 1962 simultaneously borrowed from the past and pointed to the future.

The *Carillon* headline "The Giant Awakens" captured the significance of the event. It signalled the arrival of the baby boomers at the university doorstep. Historian Doug Owram argues that the boomers were a generation with a highly developed sense of collective identity and purpose.[33] This arose in large part from the power of their numbers. They had all but overwhelmed elementary and high schools in the 1950s and were about to do the same to universities. The youth market, whether in clothes, records, movies, or automobiles, was of major importance to the economy. It was revealing that the first two issues Regina campus students seized upon – lowering bus fares and movie ticket prices – were bids to exploit baby-boomer buying power.

The University Council, in the aftermath of the march and a similarly rowdy outburst in Saskatoon, decided to ban snake dances. The *Carillon* condemned the prohibition, denouncing it as "gross interference with our right to assemble in protest or to assemble for any reason." This right, the editorial contended, was guaranteed under the Canadian Bill of Rights, recently put in place by the federal government of John Diefenbaker. The university, according to the newspaper, had no authority to regulate the behaviour of students beyond the confines of the campus: "Our actions individually or collectively outside the University area are our business." If disciplinary measures were called for, they should be imposed by students, not by faculty or the university administration. Furthermore, the paper stressed, the discipline committee should be "COMPOSED OF STUDENTS": "If a student acts contrary to rule, let this student be judged by his peers, i.e., other students."[34]

The editorial marked a change in the way many students perceived their role. They no longer saw themselves as subordinates in a hierarchical structure, but rather as members of the university community. As the *Carillon* phrased it, "Let there be close cooperation between students and administration – but cooperation as equals, not as master to slave." The editorial made the broader point that, given the state of the world, the "establishment" had little to be complacent about. The world was a "stinking mess," and if youth were given a chance to run it, they could hardly do worse than the older generation had done. The editorial even hinted that those in authority secretly envied the students. It speculated as to whether the older people who had stood watching the snake dance while vociferously condemning it had subconsciously "wished they had the youth and vitality to take part."[35]

This intergenerational tension was transposed onto the conflict between Regina and Saskatoon. According to the *Carillon*, the Regina campus represented youthful energy and a progressive spirit; Saskatoon represented tired tradition and conservative stuffiness. The paper declared that it was time to sever "the mother-daughter relationship with that northern city."[36] The students saw themselves as active participants in the building of the new campus: "'Iron bars do not a prison make' nor pre-cast concrete a university ... We, the students of this year, must revive the circulation of what can and must be the lifeblood of a great, pulsating university."[37] This led to a march to the legislature in March 1964 in support of autonomy for the Regina campus. The *Carillon* facetiously proposed a name for the new university: "University of Southern Saskatchewan, Regina" – USSR for short.[38]

The rising influence of the student movement led to a major rewriting of the SRC constitution in 1965. The revisions were largely the handiwork of

SRC president Simon de Jong (later an NDP MP for Regina), who explained the basic principles in a message to the student body in September 1964. Whereas the old constitution embodied a concept of the SRC as primarily a coordinator of social and athletic activities, the new version took a much broader view of the role of student government. Its aims now included the advancement of "the cause of higher learning in the Province of Saskatchewan,"[39] involving issues related to tuition fees, student loans, government funding of the university, academic policies, and all other matters relating to the welfare of students.[40] The students' organization was renamed the Students' Union, symbolizing the fact that students regarded themselves as an organized force in society with rights to protect and interests to promote.

A key feature of the new constitution was the incorporation of the Students' Union under the Societies Act (later the Non-profit Corporations Act) of the Province of Saskatchewan. This gave the union independent status and legal authority to own property, issue debentures, and borrow money. However, the university Board of Governors still controlled the purse strings because it collected the student activity fees and made enrolment conditional upon the payment of such fees. The board then handed over the money to the SRC to enable it to finance its operations. Recognizing the power exercised by the board in this matter, the students inserted into the new constitution the clause "The SRC may contract with the Board of Governors of the University of Saskatchewan for the collection of the student fees by the offices of the University."[41] Such a contract would give the Students' Union the financial security and independence it would otherwise lack.

The revised constitution also made changes to the internal structure of student government. The former SRC had consisted of the president, vice-president, treasurer, secretary, and the officers responsible for various directorates, all of whom were chosen in general student elections. Under the new arrangement, the SRC, which functioned as the union's board of directors, was composed of the president, first vice-president, and second vice-president, who were elected by the students at large, and a general council of no less than ten and no more than twenty members elected by students in the various colleges. The SRC then appointed the treasurer, secretary, chairman of the Canadian Union of Students local committee, chairman of the World University Service of Canada local committee, activity director, social director, drama director, music director, public relations officer, publications director (who was responsible for nominating the editor of the newspaper), the Men's Athletic Board director, and the Women's Athletic Board director. The Student Council became a deliberative and policy-setting body rather than an executive authority. Administrative officers, except for the president and vice-presidents, were now appointed, not elected. In addition, the SRC appointed "a committee, consisting of at least three SRC members and any other person the SRC might wish to appoint, to study, investigate and report from time to time to the SRC on all academic matters affecting students."[42] The Students' Union did not restrict its mandate to extracurricular activities. Its concerns extended to academic programs, curricula, and teaching methods, a change that signalled a major shift in the way students thought about themselves and their place in the university.

The student body voted in a plebiscite on 22 February 1965 by a margin of 647 to 154 to approve the new constitution. Turnout at the polls was about 50 per cent.[43] The Board of Governors raised objections to the proposed changes, especially the idea of incorporation, and it informed the students that unless the constitution was revised in accordance with the board's wishes, it would no longer require students to pay activity fees.[44] Such an action would deal a crippling blow to the Students' Union, since it was unlikely that all students, or even a majority of them, would pay the fees voluntarily. The *Carillon* urged the SRC to ignore the board and press ahead with incorporation. It said the SRC's "ace in the hole" was the overwhelming student support for the new constitution: "They won't allow their hands to be slapped with an admonition of 'Naughty, naughty, mustn't touch.'"[45] The SRC went ahead and unilaterally implemented the new constitution, except that it held back on the application for incorporation under the Societies Act. It decided to negotiate this and other key items with the Board of Governors.

A problem surfaced in the meantime with respect to student dances. According to the new constitution, all social functions held by student clubs and organizations had to receive prior approval from the Students' Union social director and were to be conducted "in conformity with the SRC code of regulations." This directly challenged the authority of the Faculty Student Activities Committee and the requirement that all student functions conform to university regulations. The faculty committee met with SRC representatives, and the two parties came to an understanding. They agreed that the SRC would administer the regulations and be responsible for all student social activities. The SRC undertook to prepare a calendar of activities that it planned to sponsor during the academic year and register it with the principal's office by September 15. It also promised to ensure that at least two faculty members were present at all SRC functions (the term "patron" had been dropped). Student social activities were to be open to "students of the University, their spouses, members of the teaching staff and administrative staff of the University, and their guests." They could not be held within fourteen days of the last day of lectures, and "the serving and/or drinking of intoxicating liquors of any sort" on university premises was prohibited.[46]

This agreement resulted in a delegation of responsibility to the SRC, which now drew up the calendar of social events and enforced the regulations that had been agreed to. SRC president Ken Mitchell hailed the arrangement as a breakthrough in faculty-student relations: "the students' council feels that it has to assume responsibility for all Regina campus activities if it is going to be in a position to maintain their rights. This is what was envisaged in the constitution recently adopted by the student union." He commended the faculty committee for its attitude: "If relations between our two respective bodies continue in this fashion throughout the coming year, there is no conceivable limit to the amount of concerted action that the two bodies can carry out. All our goals, regardless of their immediate implications, can be seen to be the same – improvement of university education."[47] Mitchell interpreted the faculty-student relationship as a partnership of two groups in a community dedicated to a common purpose, each group assuming rights and responsibilities for the good of the whole. This was a departure from the traditional *in loco parentis* model of control, which placed the student in the subordinate role of the child.

The new regime suffered a setback in November 1966 when an SRC-sponsored dance disintegrated into drunken mayhem. A janitor reported on what had happened:

> At approximately 11:00 p.m., a washbasin was pulled loose from the wall, allowing water to flood the floor of the washroom on the main floor. While this was being cleaned up, persons unknown opened the water taps in the basement washroom, flooding the floor of the washroom and part of the basement hall. While this was being mopped up, persons unknown pulled the main electrical breaker, shutting off all power in the building. About this time, it appears there had been a disturbance in the Auditorium because of a trail of blood that led from the Auditorium to the washroom and a certain amount of blood was splattered on the walls of the washroom. Sometime during the evening, two soap dispensers were removed from the wall.[48]

The campus administration suspended all dances and social events in university buildings until the SRC came up with a new set of regulations and demonstrated a serious intention to enforce them. The students agreed to fill out a "space order form" at least seven days prior to a social event and include on it the signatures of the faculty "patrons" (the term was back again) and the names of student "supervisors" (that is, bouncers). The latter were paid to enforce orderly behaviour. The SRC also arranged for the Regina police to make periodic checks of the area outside the building where the function was being held.[49] Although the rules were tightened, the university administration did not take away the right of the SRC to control the dances. It merely insisted that the students do a better job.

Theses changes in the role of the student occurred within the context of general social, political, and cultural change. The civil rights movement, women's liberation, the Vietnam War, Aboriginal rights, the Quiet Revolution in Quebec, and the counterculture were all challenging the status quo. Large numbers of Regina campus students, like their counterparts elsewhere, were deeply involved in these movements. They saw themselves not only as citizens of the university but also of the wider society. The two aspects of citizenship went hand in hand. Just as students questioned the paternalistic structure of the university and the limited scope of student government, they began to take an interest in issues external to the university.

The Regina campus branch of the Combined Universities Campaign for Nuclear Disarmament (CUCND) circulated a petition in 1961 against the Soviet Union's testing of a fifty-megaton atomic bomb. About 80 per cent of the students asked to sign it did so.[50] An article in the 5 January 1962 edition of the student newspaper related in vivid terms what would happen if a twenty-megaton bomb were to fall on Regina: "The blast would burn everything in a 400-square-mile area. A person standing 20 miles away would be instantly scorched to death. One thousand square miles would be covered with radioactive fallout."[51]

The supporters of the CUCND did not accept the Cold War ideology of the United States and its allies. They believed that there were two sides to the story, and the Soviet side was not being told. In February 1962 they invited S. Boukine, first secretary to the Soviet ambassador in Ottawa, to give a talk on campus. The talk, entitled "Peaceful Coexistence of Countries with Different Social and Economic Systems," drew 175 students. Boukine argued that capitalists and communists should compete peacefully rather than militarily so that the world could judge which of the two systems best contributed to "brotherhood and happiness."[52] His speech received positive coverage in the student newspaper, which prompted one dissatisfied reader to complain that the paper was "constantly snowed under with the dour 'holier-than-thou' statements of the Ban-the-Bomb movement ... The question is: are the editors of our journal serving the interests of Regina's student body, or are they just using it to publicize the extreme ideas of a minority?"[53] Jim Harding defended the editorial policy, maintaining that "the world, its societies and respective individuals, must undergo change if humanity is to find new and better ways of living ... The *Sheet* has presented many new ideas because of a faith that man's ways will improve; that he will learn to live without war, without hostility, while sharing the produce of the world among all humanity."[54] The editorial had the flavour of something Dallas Smythe might have said, but it was written six months before Smythe arrived at the campus and it predated the Regina Beach Statement by more than a year.

Another insight into student opinion can be gleaned from an informal plebiscite held in March 1962. The paper asked students to fill out a ballot indicating whether they were for or against the medicare plan that the Sas-

Students marching through downtown Regina on 24 October 1962 to protest the Cuban Missile Crisis, an early manifestation of the sixties peace movement.

katchewan government planned to implement on 1 July. The legislation divided the province along ideological lines, those on the left strongly in favour and those on the right strongly opposed. Thirty per cent of the students filled out the ballots: 91 supported medicare, 88 were opposed, and 19 were undecided.[55] The students were split down the middle, reflecting the state of public opinion in the province as a whole. Another indicator of the campus political climate was the election of the student mock parliament in November 1962. With 443 out of 811 students voting, the Progressive Conservatives came first, with 167 votes; the Liberals a close second, with 162; the NDP third, with 97; and there were 17 spoiled ballots.[56]

The divided nature of campus opinion led to controversy surrounding the peace march held at the time of the Cuban Missile Crisis. The Soviet Union in the fall of 1962 secretly placed in Cuba nuclear weapons capable of striking every major city in the United States except Seattle. When President Kennedy demanded that the USSR withdraw the missiles, the world waited anxiously for the Soviet response. After thirteen days the Russians backed down, and nuclear war was averted. Fourteen Regina campus students participated on 24 October 1962 in a noon-hour protest march through downtown Regina. Their placards read "An Atomic War Will Destroy You Too,"

"No More Military Bases," "We Protest against all Military Action," and "Stop Military Action; Talk It Over at the UN." Bystanders generally ignored the marchers, although a few shouted "Better Red than Dead," and "Where's Your Red Flag?" Most of the jeers came from fellow students, who drove cars alongside the marchers and shouted insults.[57] The Young Progressive Conservatives staged a mock invasion of the college cafeteria, during which "armed guerrillas" led by a student dressed as Fidel Castro "abducted" the Tory student leader. The group said that the point of the exercise was to show that democracy did not exist in Cuba.[58]

Although student opinion ranged over the entire political spectrum, the left-wing element was sufficiently vocal to give the campus a radical reputation. Student David Adams in October 1964 published an article titled "Are You a Radical?" He said that "when the Regina campus is mentioned in the presence of one of our big cousins from the Saskatoon campus, the reaction is almost certain to be a scoff accompanied by 'bunch of radicals!' or some such comment. This response is designed to make us country cousins hang our heads shamefacedly." But Adams had no apologies to make. On the contrary, he accepted the radical label as a badge of honour. "Since when," he asked, "has it been shameful for a university student to be a radical?" The world, he claimed, needed radical thinkers to solve the overwhelming problems of poverty, overpopulation, and nuclear arms. "When we are called 'a bunch of radicals out to save the world,'" he declared, "let's not hang our heads. I see nothing wrong with 'trying to save the world' — a phrase which I take here to mean the avoidance of war and the rearrangement of human affairs in accordance with the ideals of human freedom and reason."[59]

The RCMP, as early as 1962, planted informers on the Regina campus and undertook surveillance of radical activity, as they did in Saskatoon and most other universities in Canada.[60] With the Cold War at its height, even relatively innocuous events assumed an exaggerated importance. Kenneth More, the Progressive Conservative MP for Regina, charged in the House of Commons in 1964 that Regina students were being brainwashed. He claimed that Professor A.B. Nicolaev, a visiting lecturer in economics from Moscow University who was spending a year at the campus, was corrupting the minds of the young by teaching them that communism was better than capitalism. More reported that he had received several letters and phone calls from worried parents who did not want their children exposed to subversive ideas. Principal Riddell responded that the university was a place where students should have the opportunity to "criticize and analyze all points of view."[61] The *Leader-Post* also adopted a benign attitude. It editorialized that "Western democratic belief in private enterprise is no political economic theory to be preserved like a delicate flower in the hot-house of protection."[62] It could withstand the lectures of a Marxist professor.

A.B. Nicolaev from Moscow University, who spent 1964–65 at Regina campus as a visiting professor of economics. Regina MP Ken More charged in the House of Commons that Nicolaev was brainwashing students with his subversive ideas.

Nicolaev became a campus celebrity, notorious as much for his habit of throwing open his office window in the middle of winter to perform deep-breathing exercises as for his political views. When he left Regina in April 1965, Jenny Smythe (wife of Dallas) composed a poem:

Nicolaev, Nicolaev
Nothing makes a rhyme.
But we are glad that we have had
You with us for a time.
You've altered all our preconceptions,
Brought us new insight.
On central economic planning
You have shed much light.
Our M.P. feared you would subvert us.
That you never tried.
To foster better understanding,
That has been your guide.
And yet we find you hard to fathom,
For despite winter's winds,
Your window open to Arctic air,
You do your deep knee bends!
We've learned from you and we hope
You have learned from us a bit.
These slippers wear without a care
We hope that they will fit![63]

The CUCND, which had been at the centre of the first phase of student activism, underwent a significant transformation at a national conference held from 28 December to 1 January 1965 in Regina. The 150 delegates in attendance voted to change the name of the organization to the Student Union for Peace Action (SUPA). This reflected a broadening of the agenda from the ban-the-bomb crusade to social action of a more general and comprehensive character. The statement of purpose declared that "poverty, centralized technology, racism and imperialism are primary to the nation state, and are related to the peace issue."[64] SUPA asserted that peace was not possible without justice, and justice could be secured only through a radical overhaul of society. It became the major New Left student organization in Canada, the counterpart to the Students for a Democratic Society (SDS) in the United States. Like the SDS, it supported the civil rights movement, sponsored anti-poverty efforts, and opposed the Vietnam War. In Saskatchewan it launched the Neestow (Cree for "cousin" or "friend") Project, which sent groups of students to live in Indian and Métis settlements and work on community development projects.

The first demonstration against the Vietnam War held in Regina took place in February 1965, just after the United States began its massive Rolling Thunder bombing operation against Hanoi. About fifty members of the Regina branch of SUPA marched under police escort from the old campus to the Legislative Building. According to the organizers the turnout would have been larger if someone had not posted a sign in front of the college building announcing that the march had been cancelled, and if all the placards and protest signs had not been stolen from the trunk of a car. The demonstration went off without incident, except that some bystanders hurled eggs at the marchers from under the Albert Street Bridge.[65] It was the first of many protests that continued until the early 1970s, when the United States finally withdrew its forces from Vietnam.

The *Carillon*, under the editorship of John Conway, began in the fall of 1965 to give more attention to national and international issues. Conway asserted that such matters were of direct concern to students: "We do have a stake in the fact that there is a [federal] election coming at which we can't vote, we do have a stake in the fact that there is a war in Vietnam, we do have a stake in the fact that there is a need for a civil rights struggle in North America, we do have a stake in the fact that poverty exists in such a rampant way in Canada, we do have a stake in the fact that our governments have been unable to answer, let alone confront, the major problems and questions of our time."[66]

The editorial policy was to raise student awareness and devise strategies for social change. Opponents put up a poster that read "Students Arise!! Would you accept 'Izvestia' or 'Pravda' as a publication representative of the student body? NO! Then why the *Carillon*?? Light your cigibutts with it, shine your hides with it, utilize it in a reciprocating motion on the hindmost part of

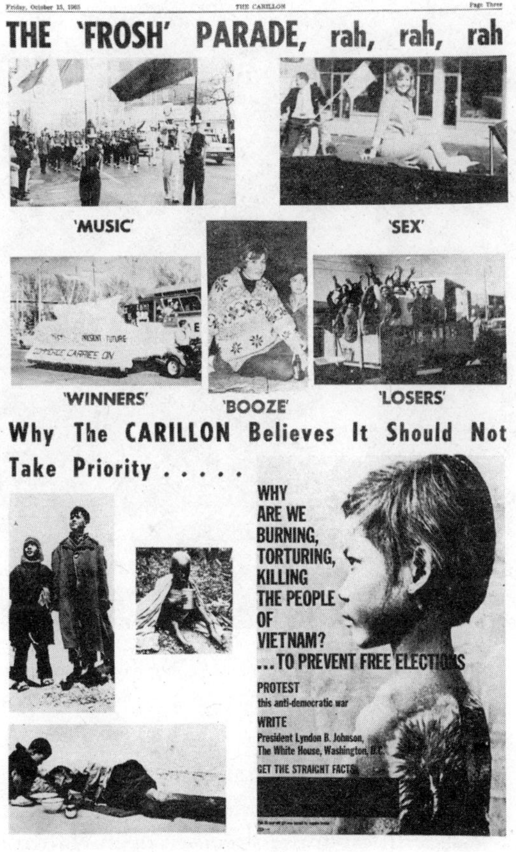

Friday, October 15, 1965 THE CARILLON Page Three

THE 'FROSH' PARADE, rah, rah, rah

'MUSIC' 'SEX'

'WINNERS' 'BOOZE' 'LOSERS'

Why The CARILLON Believes It Should Not Take Priority . . . . .

WHY ARE WE BURNING, TORTURING, KILLING THE PEOPLE OF VIETNAM?

...TO PREVENT FREE ELECTIONS

PROTEST this anti-democratic war

WRITE President Lyndon B. Johnson, The White House, Washington, D.C.

GET THE STRAIGHT FACTS

A page from the *Carillon* of 15 October 1965 juxtaposing images of campus beauty queens with those of starving Third World children in order to raise the level of student political consciousness.

your Body but BOYCOTT NOW!!"[67] Conway and the other *Carillon* staffers withstood the criticism and refused to change the policy. The paper declared its intention not to publish "a column on all new and glorious cars which are swamping the market" or "several pages of the last six playmates of the year for our unsuccessful Romeos on campus."[68] In one issue a page of photos of smiling campus beauty queens was juxtaposed with images of starving Third World children. The SRC intervened in the controversy and fired the editor. The students' council said the first responsibility of the newspaper was to cover campus events, not to give priority to national and global issues.[69]

This outcome reflected the transitional nature of student culture in the early and mid-1960s. It blended elements of the old and the new. Frosh week in the fall of 1963 was celebrated 1950s-style with a parade of floats decorated by students enrolled in various colleges (arts, science, first-year commerce, first-year engineering, and so on). SRC officers and beauty pageant contes-

A go-cart race during frosh week in September 1966. Student culture blended 1950s-style extracurricular activities with the political, social, and countercultural movements of the sixties.

tants rode through the streets in open convertibles, waving at spectators. In the afternoon students went to a Saskatchewan Roughriders football game, and later in the evening they attended a dance at the Wascana Boat Club. Frosh week activities in 1966 included a tug-of-war over a mud pit, a scavenger hunt, Volkswagen-stuffing, and a piano-smashing contest. The campus Bacchus Festival in March 1968 featured snowball fights, pillow fights, log throwing, and chug-a-lugs (beer-drinking relay races). The annual *Carillon* Hotel Inspection Tour (CHIT), inaugurated in the spring of 1965, required contestants to run through the streets of downtown Regina stopping en route at four hotel bars. At each location they had to "inspect" four glasses of beer. The competitor who completed the course first, having guzzled the stipulated quantity of alcohol "without regurgitating," was declared the winner. It was a popular campus event, the teams in 1967 including those from the *Carillon*, the School of Administration, the Men's Athletic Board, the Wascana Housing Co-op, the hockey team, arts and science, and engineering.

These mindless extracurricular activities and stunts coincided with the rise of a student movement that aimed to bring about fundamental social and political change. The two streams of student culture came together in the fall of 1966 at the annual general meeting of the Students' Union. Don Kossick, who chaired the meeting, led the 600 students present in cheers for their respective colleges and warned that there could be police raids at the float-construction sites. The police, it seemed, were on the lookout for illegal drinking. The SRC treasurer then gave the financial report, trying to hold the interest of the engineering students, who were distracted by the five beauty pageant contestants seated in the front row. Former SRC president Simon de Jong gave a speech about the basic concepts underlying the Students' Union, and incumbent president Don Mitchell outlined the agenda for the year: co-op housing, plans for a Students' Union building, the need for psychological counselling services on campus, the importance of student participation in university decision making, and the provincial government's inadequate funding of post-secondary education. After the speeches it was time to select the frosh queen. This apparently was the highlight of the proceedings, since after the queen had been crowned the crowd began to disperse. A number of resolutions were rushed through with little or no debate. These included support of universal accessibility to higher education and opposition to the Vietnam War.[70] The event marked a transitional stage in student culture. Floats and frosh queens mingled with tuition fees and the peace movement.

Mitchell's speech hit a nerve. He appealed for a more personalized, less bureaucratic campus: "Let's for God's sake humanize this place a little bit." As mentioned earlier, cafeterias, lounge space, and student services were in short supply in the early years of campus development. The SRC took matters into its own hands, converting a room in the classroom building into a lounge and lunchroom and furnishing it with second-hand couches, chairs, and cushions.[71] Another group of students organized a coffee house downtown on 11th Avenue between McIntyre and Smith Streets. They called it "the Place" – the place for "talking, reading, putting up of feet, and simply sitting." Patrons were asked to bring their own chairs, a friend, or "one of your professors."[72] As the students explained, "We need a place to sit and have coffee, to talk, to relax, to enjoy ourselves and the company of good friends. A place that removes us from the sterility of the white walls that surround us all day, a place that's warm and stimulating, a place to refresh us, to tire us out ... It can give us a sense of that student community everyone talks about because it's for all of us, because we'll all be there."[73]

The starkly modern space-age aesthetic of the new campus was made worse by dehumanizing registration procedures. Students waited in long lines and were shuffled from pillar to post. They often discovered at the end of this laborious and time-consuming process that the classes they had hoped to sign up for were full.[74] According to the *Carillon* in September 1967, "over three thousand students were virtually herded through a maze of confusion. One student was observed whimpering in the corner of the men's locker

THE CARILLON

Official weekly journal published by the Students' Union, Regina Campus

Postage Paid in Cash at Third Class Rate, Permit No. 6137

Vol 8 No. 14 Friday, September 26, 1969 — 12 Pages

THE UNIVERSITY AS FACTORY

This is the dead land
This is cactus land
Here the stone images
Are raised, here they receive
The supplication of a dead man's hand
Under the twinkle of a fading star.

—"The Hollow Men"
by T. S. Eliot.

The front page of the *Carillon*, 26 September 1969, reflecting disillusionment with the assembly-line methods of mass university education.

room because he had waited in line for two hours only to be turned away at lunch time."[75] "The shuffling lines of subdued, flat-eyed students," wrote John Conway, "make the metaphor of 'knowledge factory' crudely expressive."[76]

Student Ruth Warick described in "Illusions of University" what she had thought the university experience would be like: "I pictured it as an Oxford idyll. There you have distinguished, elderly gentlemen who dress conservatively, and think and talk brilliantly. There you are a very studious person who swallows up tradition with savor and gulps new ideas with relish." She found instead something quite different: a place more akin to a "soup factory." "Like cans of soup, students go through the stages of development, then go out into the world – a product, labelized, etc." She discovered that the "real" university was the unofficial one that operated outside formal classes: "Things like working on the school newspaper, a non-credit theology

A large lecture theatre at the new Regina campus. When baby boomers began attending universities in large numbers in the early 1960s, the intimate, privileged atmosphere of the 1950s college disappeared. Students complained, "I am a student. Do not fold, bend, mutilate, or spindle."

class with supper included, listening to guest speakers like Frank Underhill and Laurier LaPierre, going to an Ecumenical Conference for a weekend, developing your own film and pictures for the first time, going to 'The Place,' reading the odd book at the odd time, meeting new people and listening to people who have something to say."[77] Warick believed that students had to create their own learning experiences and educate themselves.

A turning point occurred in December 1966, when SRC president Don Mitchell led a demonstration of 400 students to protest against the semester system, which had been introduced in the fall of that year. The protesters alleged that professors had failed to adjust their course loads to fit the new system. Some had attempted to cram almost a full year's work into a half-year course. The pressure became more intense as final examinations approached, and students asked for a study period between the last day of lectures and the first day of exams. Waving placards that read "We Like Our Sanity," "A Care

Professor Rex Schneider teaching at Regina College in March 1952. The small classroom and empty desks contrast with the crammed lecture halls that became common in the 1960s.

for Today Is a Cure for Tomorrow," and "Down With the Semester System," they filled the hallways and stairwells leading to the office of Professor Alwyn Berland, chairman of the executive committee of the Campus Council.[78] Berland responded sympathetically to their request for extra study time. It dawned on students that they did not have to accept passively whatever was being handed out.[79]

The students enrolled in Logic 100 in the fall of 1968 were surprised to discover at the front of the classroom not a professor but a tape recorder. The philosophy professor who taught three sections of the same course did not want to give the same lecture three times. He deigned, however, to show up in each class once a week to answer students' questions about what they had learned from the tape recorder. Don Kossick, then a fieldworker for the Canadian Union of Students, entered the classroom and wrote on the blackboard, "Is This Education?" The students applauded, and about one-third of them walked out.[80] According to the chairman of the philosophy department, the taped lectures were an experiment. He said that after a two-week trial period the students would be given an opportunity to vote on this innovation in technologically enhanced instruction.[81]

Two students posing in the starkly modern, space-age surroundings of the new campus. The textbook the girl holds is appropriately titled *Foundations of Euclidean and Non-Euclidean Geometry*.

Students studying on the lawn in front of the main Regina College building. The comfortable, well-treed ambience of the old college differed markedly from the austere aesthetic of the new campus.

President Don Mitchell at the annual meeting of the Students' Union in September 1966 exhorting his fellow students, "Let's for God's sake humanize this place a little bit."

As students became more assertive, Principal Riddell and the campus administration grew more defensive. A skirmish occurred in November 1966, when student president Don Mitchell dropped all of his classes. Riddell advised him of a University Council ruling dated 7 May 1941 requiring that "students holding important student offices must take a substantial year's work." When Mitchell offered his resignation, the SRC refused to accept it. According to one of the bylaws of the Students' Union, "All graduate students and occasional students who have paid the fees of the Union for the current University session shall be considered active members of the Union." Since Mitchell had paid his fees, the SRC deemed him eligible to hold office. Riddell contended that the bylaw had no force because it contravened a university regulation. Moreover, the Board of Governors had not yet officially recognized the Students' Union constitution and bylaws because it did not approve of some of the provisions, including the bylaw defining eligibility for student office.[82]

Riddell laid out his position in a letter to the chairman of the Student Activities Committee of Campus Council. He emphasized that he was

Students in December 1966 protesting against the new semester system. They claimed that some professors had tried to squeeze almost a full year's work into a half-year class. They asked for, and were eventually allowed, more time to study for final examinations.

entirely opposed to "non-students" being on campus and objected strenuously to their holding office in the Students' Union. He added, "I know this is the position of members of the Board of Governors." In his opinion the claim that the demands of student office were too onerous for a full-time student was unfounded. If the president and the other officers of the Students' Union were to concentrate on doing what a student government was supposed to do, the workload would not be heavy. The trouble was, Riddell said, that "too much of the time of the SRC has been devoted to things other than the needs and basic interests of the students on campus." He thought that a student holding senior office should be required to take a minimum of eight semester hours of work (two full classes) in each of the fall and winter semesters.[83]

The faculty did not support Riddell. The Campus Council determined that since the May 1941 ruling applied to the Saskatoon system of a full academic year from September to April, it was ambiguous in its application to the Regina campus semester system. Since Mitchell had registered for three classes in the second semester, he should be allowed to continue as SRC president. Council further advised that the question of eligibility rules for student office should be referred to the Student Activities Committee, and that it would be a good idea to invite SRC representatives to participate in the committee's deliberations.[84] The outcome represented a setback for Riddell and a victory for the students.

The Students' Union on 20 February 1967 acquired legal status as an independent corporation under the Societies Act.[85] The union had wanted to do this in 1965 but had held back because the Board of Governors did not approve. Now the students acted on their own, ignoring the board's objections. The university sought legal advice and was informed that "the authority of the Board would only be required in the event that the applicant for incorporation was a trading company or a commercial company and consequently the Students' Union would not require the authority of the Board of Governors." The lawyer went on to say that the university was not liable other than "morally" for the acts of the Students' Union, since the former was an entity incorporated under the University Act, while the latter, following incorporation, was a separate legal entity.[86]

Although the Board of Governors could not legally prevent the incorporation, there were other ways it could express its displeasure. Riddell informed the students that the board had three possible courses of action: refuse to collect student fees, refuse to designate a site on campus for the proposed Students' Union building, or withhold funds for the building.[87] A joint SRC-Board of Governors committee was set up in the spring of 1967 to discuss the issue, but little progress was made towards a settlement. An uneasy truce prevailed, clouded by the fact that the board had not formally recognized the Students' Union constitution and still reserved the right to take disciplinary action of some sort.

Nevertheless, the student movement clearly had momentum. It had already enlarged the scope of student government, defeated an attempt to force the resignation of the SRC president, and incorporated the Students' Union under the Societies' Act. As Don Mitchell's term in office drew to a close, in March 1967, he speculated in a *Carillon* article about what lay ahead. He thought that students had reached a "fork in the road." Would they continue on the path towards "a more democratic university" and the exercise of "citizenship responsibilities," or would they revert to their former role as organizers of "dances, basketball games and yearbook?"[88] Although Mitchell did not yet realize it, the choice had already been made.

13 Radical Campus

The 1967 fall semester opened with a love-in in the courtyard in front of the classroom building. Four hundred barefoot students danced to the music of the Beatles' most recent album, *Sgt Pepper's Lonely Hearts Club Band*. According to the *Leader-Post* reporter who covered the event, "Girls stood in long velvet dresses alongside a rectangular pool and gazed for endless minutes at its concrete bottom or played with rocks." Three students were "deeply engrossed with stones of a sidewalk." When asked what they were doing, one replied, "We're writing rock poems." David Fairley, an instructor in the English department, had organized the event, which he described as "an outside in for those who are inside out." One onlooker commented, "They look like a rather mixed-up group," and another added, "It's got me stumped as to what is going on. One thing I know is that a university is symbolic of man's highest aspirations. It's a pity they don't realize this yet."[1]

The dreamy sequel to the 1967 Summer of Love was of short duration. Premier Ross Thatcher called a provincial election in October and led his Liberals to a second consecutive term. The premier, in his first major public address after the election, which he delivered at the annual convention of the Potashville Educational Association in Regina on 18 October 1967, stated that the people of the province were becoming "more and more concerned at the staggering annual increases in costs of education." He pointed out that although the provincial government spent $28 million a year on the University of Saskatchewan (out of a total provincial budget of $300 million), "the elected representatives of the people" had virtually no control over university spending: "Year after year, with few details we in fact almost write a blank cheque." To remedy this, the premier announced, "we intend at the next Session, to reform our University Act in a major way. Final details have not been worked out. But, in essence, the University will be obliged to make its financial requests to the Legislature in the same manner as any other spending department. For example, they will have to request so much for salaries, so much for traveling, so much for new buildings, etc. I wish to emphasize that the Government will not interfere with the internal operations of the University. But, from this time forward, there will be direct financial control."[2]

About a week after Thatcher dropped this bombshell, President John Spinks, Vice-President Colb McEown, Chancellor Ted Culliton, and other senior university officials met with Cliff McIsaac, the minister of education, and Davey Steuart, who was both deputy premier and provincial treasurer. Culliton expressed concern about the government's attempt to interfere in the university's internal decision making. Steuart countered with a series of proposals: that the government's budget bureau review the university budget in detail; that the budget be presented to the legislature as a series of itemized sub-votes; that the government manage loan requirements and investments for the university as it would for a Crown corporation; that the university inform the government of its overall staff numbers and proposed increases in those numbers; that the university discuss its top positions with the government and the government approve salary increases; that university purchases, including vehicles, be made through the government purchasing agency; and that the university buildings and grounds department be transferred to the government.[3]

The university representatives responded that the government already received a detailed budgetary submission and that they had no objection to the government's reviewing it. Any items that raised questions could be brought to the attention of the university, but "ultimate responsibility for making detailed budgetary changes within colleges and departments and programs, must remain with the University." The representatives also pointed out that the university Board of Governors, on which the government was well represented, had statutory authority to make all appointments, whether junior or senior, but that "close scrutiny of top positions would be quite unacceptable to the University."[4]

Neither President Spinks nor the Board of Governors made a public rebuttal of the premier's unprecedented attack on the autonomy of the university. This was a mistake, in Riddell's opinion, since it gave the impression that the premier's criticism could be justified and that perhaps something was amiss in the financial administration of the university. Riddell, Principal Robert Begg of the Saskatoon campus, and several board members privately urged

Spinks to make a strong public statement, but both Spinks and Culliton refused to confront the government directly. They thought that more could be accomplished through quiet diplomacy and behind-the-scenes negotiation. According to Riddell, Culliton was under the impression that he had great influence in the Liberal Party and could bring pressure to bear on the premier, but "it was quickly evident to most people that this influence did not exist, although it did not appear to be recognized by the Chancellor."[5]

Riddell's assessment was that Spinks, a "brilliantly clever man," believed he could outmanoeuvre the likes of Thatcher and Steuart, although Riddell doubted it.[6] If the president refused to speak out, other members of the academic community were not as reticent. The *Carillon* on 20 October 1967 published a stop-press bulletin stating that after the paper had gone to press the premier had made an alarming announcement. University decision making, the newspaper warned, was in danger of being removed from educators and placed in the hands of politicians. "And how do you justify to politicians an appropriation for a class in Victorian poetry? ... This is a frontal assault on the university. It cannot be accepted or compromised with. It must be rejected as simply unacceptable." The paper appealed to the administration, faculty, and students to unite in opposition to Thatcher's action: "If we don't, we will not have a university in this province. They may still call it a university, but it won't be one."[7]

The front page of the 17 November 1967 issue of the *Carillon* was blazoned with the headline "Spinks: Don't Rock the Boat; Let Thatcher Torpedo It!"[8] A large billboard was put up at the entrance to the campus that read "University of Sasthatcheran." About 700 students attended a meeting on 3 November 1967 to discuss the crisis; another 200 to 300 had to be turned away because the room was full to overflowing.[9] An "action committee" consisting of Regina campus faculty, students, and support staff coordinated opposition to the government plan.[10] It arranged public meetings, appearances on television and radio open-line programs, and one-on-one visits with MLAs.[11]

The only senior university official to speak out boldly was Alwyn Berland, dean of arts and science at the Regina campus. He said that Thatcher's comments had done serious harm to the university. Contrary to what the premier had implied, the university did in fact submit detailed budget requests to the government "with suitable provisions for explaining and justifying its requests." The university had never asked for or received "a blank cheque," and no one quarrelled with the government's request for information about how the money was spent. The danger lay in the government's seizing the power "to approve or disapprove the budget requests attached to specific academic programs or colleges or courses of study."[12]

Berland also called attention to the fact that a large portion of the provincial government grant came from federal government transfer payments to

A sign posted at the entrance to the campus in October 1967 after Premier Ross Thatcher announced his government's intention to take direct financial control of the university.

the provinces in support of post-secondary education. The financial burden the university represented to the province was much less than Thatcher made it out to be. Since the size of the federal government grant had been increasing annually, the net cost to the provincial treasury was actually declining. An internal analysis prepared by university vice-president Colb McEown confirmed the point. The Government of Saskatchewan's total grant to the university in 1967–68 was $27,700,000; the province contributed approximately $16,100,000 and the rest came from Ottawa. In 1966–67, by contrast, the province had contributed to the university $21,022,000 out of its own tax revenues.[13] The provincial government spent less on the university in 1967–68 than it had in 1966–67 while claiming that out-of-control expenditures made it necessary for it to take direct control of the university's budget.

Deputy Premier Steuart publicly derided Berland as one of a small group of faculty members conducting "a smear campaign" against the government. He compared Berland's irresponsible behaviour with the "responsible position" that the Board of Governors had taken on the budget question.[14] John Gardiner, Liberal MLA for Moosomin, charged that a small minority of staff and students were using the issue "as an excuse to attack the government and the Premier, to get publicity and all in the name of academic freedom." He commended President Spinks and the board "for the fine manner in which they acted in spite of a good deal of provocation from University staff and students and I suspect some provocation from the Government."[15]

Gardiner outlined "two concepts of what a University consists of. We have Group One who says that it is a place to go to meditate, to create, to do research and philosophize. We have Group Two who say that it is a place to train young people to do the professional jobs required in our society and our economy – to provide us with the engineers, the lawyers, doctors and nurses which are so badly needed." He conceded that it was probably acceptable to have a small Group One on campus, "but I can tell you that a Province or a Government who gets a majority of Group One at a University Campus is in trouble."[16] By this reckoning, Berland, as a representative of Group One, was in the government's bad books, but not one member of the senior university administration came to his defence.

A committee of the Board of Governors met with Premier Thatcher and Minister of Education McIsaac on 22 November 1967. They came to an understanding on the general format of the university budget that would be presented to the government. After the meeting, the premier announced that the government had "no intention of amending the University Act or of introducing administrative procedures that will in any way affect the autonomy, independence or internal management of the University." He stated that consultations were continuing as to whether economies could be achieved in the university's building program. To this end, all new building plans would now require the approval of the minister of public works. With respect to the budget itself, new sub-votes were to be placed in the estimates to provide additional information to members of the legislature. Thatcher gave assurances that such changes were "merely in the form of presentation and not in the substance of the University budget and, while important, [were] merely routine in nature."[17] When the budget came before the legislature, on 25 April 1968, there was one vote for operations and another for the capital grant.[18]

Although the government retreated from its attempt to take direct financial control of the university, Premier Thatcher kept a close eye on what was going on at the Regina campus. He questioned Principal Riddell on 22 January 1968 about a proposed field trip to Toronto organized by Professor Jim McCrorie for a class in urban sociology. "This is his privilege, of course," the premier wrote, "as long as no Provincial funds are involved. I would think his time as a professor could be better utilized. Would you be kind enough to make discreet inquiries and then advise me of details?" Riddell supplied the itinerary for the field trip, along with the information that the students had raised $400 through their own efforts and had agreed to pay the balance of the expenses out of their own pockets.[19]

As part of the effort to ease the financial burden of the university on the government, tuition fees were increased from $320 per year in 1967–68 to $400 in 1968–69.[20] In response, about 500 Regina campus students marched to the legislature on 15 February 1968 carrying signs that said "Tax Potash

Not Students," "Autonomy Not Autocracy," and "Education Is Our Birthright, Not a Privilege." A number of dignitaries were on hand for the opening day of the legislative session. Deputy Premier Steuart paused briefly to tell reporters that the only thing the students were proving was that they knew how to skip classes. The demonstrators booed President Spinks and cheered opposition leader Woodrow Lloyd. Premier Thatcher, the *Carillon* reported, "looked grim."[21]

Tuition fees in 1968–69 accounted for 23.5 per cent of the total operating budget of the campus, compared with 19.8 per cent in 1967–68.[22] Student leaders demanded that the fees be abolished altogether because they were a barrier to university education for those from low-income families. A Students' Union brief argued that, quite apart from considerations of social justice, free access to higher education would benefit the economy: "Money spent in developing 'human' resources, like that spent on natural resources or industry, brings direct long-range benefits to the state. The financing of higher education is not a welfare measure, but rather a sound economic investment even if it requires deficit financing."[23] Premier Thatcher replied that he was "unequivocally opposed to any suggestion of eliminating tuition fees." He advised those who could not afford to go to university to take out a federal government student loan.

As tensions escalated between student activists on one side and the provincial government and the university administration on the other, the *Carillon* became a flashpoint. Spinks on 16 November 1967 tersely informed Riddell, "This is to let you know in a formal way that I disapprove extremely strongly of the last number of *The Carillon*, dated November 3."[24] The "number" to which Spinks referred was almost entirely devoted to criticism of his failure to respond publicly to the government's attempt to take direct financial control of the university. Riddell replied on 28 November 1967 that "the situation" had been brought to the attention of the editor of the *Carillon* and the president of the SRC, but there were no signs that his verbal warnings had produced the desired result. Riddell said that he believed that "only drastic action [would] be effective" – namely, the withdrawal of permission for the *Carillon* to use the name of the university, refusal to allow the *Carillon* staff to use university facilities, and discontinuation of the collection of student fees.[25] The Board of Governors discussed Riddell's suggestions at their next meeting but decided not to act on them.[26]

Allan Guy, the minister of public works, told a Liberal gathering in Moose Jaw that he had been "shocked" by what he had read in the *Carillon*. He wrote to Principal Riddell on 4 January 1968, "I, of course, acknowledge their right to write the articles, but I believe I also have the right to criticize their writings should I see fit."[27] Some members of the Board of Governors were also upset. They communicated to Riddell on 1 February 1968 their "very grave concern about the *Carillon* and its editorial policy. It was stressed that they have the right to protest and criticize but that the vulgarity that permeated the paper was very definitely objectionable both to the University and the public."[28]

Riddell learned in the second week of February 1968 that the *Carillon* was about to publish a story that was damaging to Allan Guy's reputation. He telephoned SRC president Ralph Smith and left a message warning him that the article could lead to legal action against the paper. Riddell then got in touch with the printer and delivered the same message. The printer told him that the lawyer for the Students' Union had looked over the article and had given the opinion that the paper was not at legal risk.[29] The story appeared in the 16 February 1968 issue of the *Carillon*. A large photo of Allan Guy dominated the front page over the caption "The Strange Story of One Student's Loan; Or, How a Guy Gets a Loan." In 1966–67, Guy, then a Liberal MLA but not yet appointed to the Cabinet, received a $1,000 federal government student loan, the maximum allowable for one year. This was at a time when many students who considered themselves deserving and eligible had been turned down for loans.[30]

The story was embarrassing for Guy. He had to endure the taunts of NDP MLAs, who draped the front page of the *Carillon* over the fronts of their desks in the legislative assembly.[31] It also created problems for Riddell, who was in the middle of negotiations with Guy over plans for the construction of the College West building. Furthermore, the students attacked Riddell for attempting to kill the story before it made it to press. The *Carillon* denounced his intervention as a "flagrant and intolerable violation of editorial freedom."[32]

Riddell summoned SRC president Ralph Smith and other SRC representatives to a meeting with a committee of the Board of Governors on 27 February 1968. There were two items on the agenda: the Students' Union constitution of 1965, which the board had still not approved; and "the effect of the editorial policy of the *Carillon* upon public opinion about the University." Riddell asked the SRC to show cause why the university should continue to collect fees for the Students' Union, why the union should be allowed to continue using the name of the University of Saskatchewan, and why the university should continue to provide space on campus for the *Carillon*.[33] The university's assumption was that the students had done something wrong and had to demonstrate why they should not be punished.

In the course of the meeting various charges were made. Riddell said that certain people had decided against donating money to the university because of the obscenity of the *Carillon*. E.C. Leslie, chairman of the Board of Governors, described the paper as an "indecent publication." When asked for examples of articles he considered indecent, he answered, "Read the paper yourself." In addition, board members objected to the "tone of criticism" the newspaper had used in discussing those in authority. They said that the Allan Guy story had created difficulties in the university's relationship with the government. They also resented what they considered unwarranted attacks on the university administration. E.C. Leslie took umbrage at the *Carillon*'s reference to the Board of Governors as a bunch of "bumbling buffoons." Editor Don Kossick replied that the description had to be taken in the context of the board's handling of the autonomy crisis.[34]

President Spinks, at a meeting of Regina Campus Council two days later, reiterated many of the charges that had been brought against the *Carillon*. Several faculty members spoke out in the paper's defence. One said that it was moderate compared to newspapers at other universities and that any attempt to impose censorship would create more difficulties than it solved. This statement was greeted with a round of applause, which, Riddell noted, "appeared to be the result of antagonism to the President." Bill Livant, a professor in the psychology department, handed out mimeographed copies of Riddell's letter to SRC president Ralph Smith in which Riddell had asked the SRC to show cause why disciplinary action should not be taken against the *Carillon*. Livant then introduced a motion stating that students should be free to "enjoy all their rights and privileges." Even though the motion was tabled, it was an indication of the increasingly strained relations between the president and members of the Regina faculty.[35] According to Riddell, Spinks was "quite unhappy" about the situation, so much so that in a moment of frustration he told Riddell that he wished that the Regina campus were not part of the University of Saskatchewan.[36]

University presidents at a meeting of the Association of Universities and Colleges of Canada (AUCC) on 10 July 1968 discussed a report on campus unrest prepared by the AUCC secretariat. According to the report, the events at Berkeley, Columbia, and other universities in the United States, and still others in Germany, France, Britain, and Canada left no doubt that "major outbreaks of trouble and violence occur[ed] as a result of carefully planned and carefully timed efforts on the part of non-students who are exceedingly mobile, well-organized and highly dedicated." The technique was to seize upon some small local incident or situation, generate sympathy among the mass of students, and escalate demands until a major confrontation took place. The report contended that the aim of the radicals was not to reform the university but to use the university as a base for revolutionary activities in order to overthrow the established order.[37]

Riddell in the summer of 1968 made contingency plans for a student uprising. According to him, "lack of decision or even firmness" could lead to loss of control. The resort to force, however, could "bring forth the cry of police brutality and cause the conservative students to make common cause with the activists."[38] "If buildings are occupied," Riddell wrote, "the staff should withdraw and set up some headquarters outside the university." It might, as a last resort, be necessary to have the police remove the occupiers from the campus.[39] A meeting was held to discuss the situation in the office of the mayor of Regina on 26 August 1968. In attendance were Mayor Henry Baker; Bruce Smith, city manager; W.L. Johnson, assistant city manager; Arthur G. Cookson, chief of police; President Spinks; Principal Riddell; and J.A. Pringle, university controller. The city officials were apprised of the dangers, and they offered their full co-operation. Riddell and Cookson agreed on a code word to summon police to the campus. This was to guard against student radicals calling in the police in order to provoke a violent confrontation.[40]

Vice-Principal Tom McLeod briefed the local media on 7 August 1968 on how they might "responsibly" cover the topic of student unrest. He stated that extremist radicals did not really want to solve problems or bring about reforms; they were mainly interested in getting publicity and stirring up trouble. It was important, therefore, that the media not play into their hands or give them more attention than they deserved. The journalists were skeptical. One said that the lively campus atmosphere of the sixties was a welcome "relief from the apathy and materialistic approach of the former generation." Another offered the opinion that dissent was healthy, as long as it was nonviolent.[41] The topic of rebellious youth, it might be added, sold newspapers and attracted television audiences. As events were shortly to prove, the *Carillon* generated enormous interest at this time, both on campus and off.

Tensions mounted in the fall of 1968. Regina campus students, including Norm Bolen, John Gallagher, and Gerald Pout-Macdonald, attended a congress of the Canadian Union of Students in Guelph, Ontario, from 28 August to 4 September. The congress passed a series of resolutions blaming "corporate capitalism" for the "repressive instincts in Canadian universities" and demanding that student unions take control of "the learning process and university decision-making."[42] Delegates heard a speech from John Cleveland of Simon Fraser University propounding a theory of student power based on the idea that "power is yours only to the extent to which you seize it." According to Cleveland, the strategy of the politically aware vanguard was to create an incident to attract the attention of the mass of students and then "take advantage of their attention to politicize them. If that fail[ed], create another incident, and another ... "[43]

The *Carillon* on 13 September 1968 published instructions, complete with diagram, for making a Molotov cocktail. Five days later Martin Loney, president-elect of the Canadian Union of Students and a key figure in the disturbances at Simon Fraser University, spoke to a crowd of about 500 on campus. He said that if students did not assert their rights, the university authorities would continue to run roughshod over them.[44] The mood on campus was such that even the Cystic Fibrosis Shinerama campaign came under suspicion. SRC councillor John Gallagher declared that students had better ways to spend their time than shining shoes.[45]

The *Carillon* on 20 September 1968 demanded that students be given "full citizenship" in the university, which meant a "full voice in the university decisions which ultimately shape their social and economic destinies." According to the editorial, the Board of Governors needed to be radically restructured or eliminated altogether and "replaced by a governing body which represents society as a whole, and not just government and corporate interests." There was also a need to change the research agenda of the university so that it was aimed "at finding solutions to problems which affect oppressed groups rather than established interest groups such as corporations and the military." This statement of goals took the student movement beyond the limited objective of securing full control of extracurricular activities. The aims now were to participate in running the university and to use the university as a platform for social change. Although the nature of the change was not precisely spelled out, it was based on the ideal of a more "democratic" and "equal" society.[46]

Don Mitchell developed these ideas further in "What Can We Do about Democracy?" which appeared in the *Carillon* on 27 September 1968. He argued that democracy in the classroom meant student participation in determining course content and teaching methods: "The teacher should serve as a resource for the learning program determined by the class, not a dictator of a program in which they have no say." He believed that students should have equal representation with faculty members in department meetings and that both groups should have veto power over all decisions. Democracy at the higher levels of the university required the abolition of the Board of Governors and the establishment of a "buffer body," consisting of "labor and consumer groups, business, professional groups, etc.," to serve as a liaison between the university and the people of the province. The governing body for the planning and operations of the university would be a reformed senate composed of students and faculty elected through campus-wide elections.[47]

Mitchell drew an analogy between students and workers. Labour unions in capitalist countries had been able to achieve only "peripheral changes" to the economic system, such as wage increases and safer working conditions. They had failed to win control over decision making in the workplace, and corporate bosses still determined what was good for the worker. In like manner, students' unions had made modest gains in securing control over extracurricular activities but had not yet won a share in controlling the university. The Board of Governors was still in charge. Neither workers nor students, Mitchell claimed, "have particularly creative working environments and both of us are controlled by the state of the business community which does not share our interests."[48] Mitchell by this logic expanded the concept of student unionism to embrace "participatory democracy." Just as labour unions needed to have a greater measure of control over the workplace, students' unions needed to have more power within the university.

Student leaders seized upon the resignation of Alywn Berland, the dean of arts and science, as an issue on which they could focus their demands. Berland, who had arrived in Regina from the United States in 1963, was one of the primary authors of the Regina Beach Statement. He was sympathetic to the student movement and had taken a leading role in the successful and well-attended Vietnam War teach-in held on 30 June 1965; it had continued through the night and ended at 6 a.m. the next day. He had even compared academics who fled the United States in the 1960s because of their opposition to the Vietnam War to European scholars persecuted by the Nazis who sought refuge in the United States in the 1930s.[49]

When Berland resigned he cited his lack of confidence in the administration of the university. He referred specifically to the failure of senior administrators to publicly defend the institution during the budget crisis in the fall of 1967. The second reason he gave for his resignation was the lack of autonomy of the Regina campus: "While each Campus has been theoretically self-contained for almost a year – each with its own Principal, Registrar, Deans, etc. – the University administration continues to function, too powerfully, much as before: from Saskatoon. University (as opposed to Campus) administrators spend no time on the Regina campus except when specific meetings of such groups as Council or the Board demand their presence. At the same time, all curricular changes and developments at Regina campus require higher approval. Regina will be hampered in its development as a first-rate university so long as it is treated as a branch or junior auxiliary of the parent company."[50]

Finally, Berland registered a protest against what he called "the shocking inadequacy of the physical facilities available to the Regina campus in relation to its enrolment." There were insufficient cafeteria and lounge-study facilities for students, inadequate office space for faculty, and a shortage of classrooms and laboratories for academic programs – all of this despite the fact that "the present enrolment was anticipated a number of years ago." He pointed out that the most recent brochure in support of the university building campaign projected far more impressive development for Saskatoon than for Regina, even though Saskatoon had almost reached what had previously been stated as its maximum enrolment and Regina was expected to expand from 20 to 30 per cent annually.[51]

Berland submitted his resignation on 6 February 1968. The Board of Governors accepted it on 19 April on the understanding that it would take effect on 31 December 1968. Berland emphasized that he was leaving on a point of principle and did not have a firm job offer in hand. Subsequently, he was appointed executive secretary of the Canadian Association of University Teachers.[52] Student activists considered him an ally and were sorry to see him go. At a general meeting of the Students' Union on 25 September, 850 students passed a resolution demanding a voice in the choice of his successor. They proposed a selection committee composed of three students and three faculty members. The committee would nominate a candidate for the deanship, and its choice would then be submitted to a referendum vote of both the Students' Union and the Faculty Association. The union demanded a response to its proposal no later than 12:30 p.m. on 3 October 1968.

Principal Riddell explained that under the terms of the University Act the Board of Governors had the power to appoint the dean. Under existing regulations the board acted on the advice of an appointments committee consisting of the principal of the campus, a board member, and two deans; the president of the university served as chair. The committee consulted widely and sought the views of department chairmen and other members of the faculty before submitting their recommendation to the board.[53] President Spinks discussed the appointments process in a speech to about 500 Regina campus students on 3 October 1968. He said he did not have confidence in the judgment of students to select candidates for the position of dean of arts and science. On the broader question of student activism, he distinguished between those he called "reformers" and "anarchists." While reformers could make a useful contribution to university life, anarchists were "train-wreckers who wished only to destroy our universities as part of their aim to destroy our western society."[54]

The largest student demonstration of the decade took place on 2 October 1968, when 1,200 students (including two busloads from Saskatoon) gathered at the legislature to protest against the inadequacies of the federal student loan program. Despite the fact that the maximum allowable loan was $1,000, the full amount was given only to "independent" students, defined as those who fell into one of the following categories: students who were over twenty-one years of age and had been working at least one year, students who had completed at least four years of university, or students who were over twenty-one and married. All other applicants had to report their parents' income, and the higher the income, the smaller the loan. The program assumed that parents were willing to help their children pay for their university education, which was not always the case. Students were also upset about long delays in processing loan applications. The government had set 16 October 1968 as the deadline for notification of approval of loans, which meant that students who were denied loans had to drop out of school halfway through the semester.[55]

Premier Ross Thatcher and Prime Minister Pierre Trudeau were at the legislative grounds to unveil a statue of Louis Riel.[56] The students listened politely to the speeches, but, as soon as they were over, the demonstration erupted. Trudeau, standing on the steps of the Legislative Building, deflected the protests with his usual acerbic repartee. As the crowd became more rowdy, the RCMP advised the prime minister to leave the premises via the back door of the building, but he refused to make such a timid and cowardly retreat. He insisted on going down the front steps, protected by a cordon of RCMP officers who guided him to a waiting limousine, which whisked him off to the airport.[57]

The demonstration provoked a backlash from moderate and conservative students, such as Gord Clark, who did not see why taxpayers should have to foot the bill to put the protesters through university. As he stated in the *Carillon*, "There are some students on this campus it seems whose idea of a university is an institution where one comes because it doesn't cost anything in order to study fields (academic or otherwise) which interest them (of course there would be no exams). In general everyone would learn to love everyone else and it would be a real groovy time. In the meantime some poor s.o.b. that flunked out of grade 10 is picking up the tab for this 'ideal institution.'"[58] Another student, W.D. Harvey, divided the activists into two categories: the moderates, who wanted "a sprinkling of student representatives who would be able to air grievances directly"; and a very small New Left group, who laboured under the delusion that "they have been called by John Q. Taxpayer to take over the present Campus administration." The latter, Harvey said, "couldn't care less what a degree is practically worth upon graduation. They won't be looking for a job in present society's mainstream."[59] About seventy-five students, most of them enrolled in either the Faculty of Administration or the Faculty of Engineering, held a meeting on 7 October 1968 to form an association of "moderate" students. They criticized the editorial policy of the *Carillon* and expressed opposition to what they described as the takeover of the SRC by "a group of radicals."[60]

The unsettled mood of the campus carried over into the fall convocation ceremonies, held at Darke Hall on 26 October 1968. During "O Canada" (sung, according to the *Carillon*, with the "usual timidity"), student Ron Thompson stood "with his right arm extended, fist clenched – a symbol of student power." Honorary degree recipient Graham Spry gave a convocation address in which he denounced what he called the "fascist" tendencies in the student movement, and President Spinks delivered a jeremiad against the destructive tendencies of "anarchists," whom he lumped together with train robbers and bandits. When Thompson – black gown open, beads dangling from his neck, long hair, beard, and blue jeans – came forward to receive his degree, he asked the chancellor for the opportunity to address the audience. Thompson believed that the student movement had been slandered, and he wanted to correct what he considered to be the erroneous statements of Spry and Spinks. When the chancellor refused to give him the microphone,

Ron Thompson (wearing beads), who walked out of convocation on 26 October 1968 when platform dignitaries made reference in their speeches to "fascist" tendencies in the student movement.

Thompson strode off the stage without his diploma, removed his gown, and left the hall. The reception that followed the ceremony buzzed with gossip about the incident: "That filthy hippy. If they would have let him speak I would have gotten up and left"; "Three thousand nice kids at the campus, and some like that"; "That's the type of thing they're going to play up on television and the paper."[61]

President Spinks by the fall of 1968 had grown very concerned about the situation. When Lieutenant-Governor Robert L. Hanbidge in October 1968 sent him a newspaper clipping about student power at Carleton, Spinks wrote back, "The whole thing is gradually taking on a nightmarish aspect." He said he hoped to have the opportunity to talk about the problem with the lieutenant-governor "in the next week or so."[62] Spinks gave a number of talks around the province attacking the "anarchists," who, he said, were intent on destroying the university.[63] Student May Archer charged in the *Carillon* that the president was "attempting to consolidate his position against reform in the university by feeding popular prejudice." She alleged that he defined the role of the university too narrowly "as that of servant to a technology which facilitates affluence."[64] Don Mitchell called upon Spinks to supply the names of the anarchists he was talking about: "If the President only thinks they exist, then he should perhaps reserve comment until he has some evidence."[65] An editorial rejected Spinks's contention that the student radicals were having a negative effect on the university's fundraising campaign. The newspaper claimed that it was the president who was doing the damage: "He spends a good deal of time tearing around the province telling people, in his clipped British accent, that anarchists are running rampant on the campus. What straight-thinking businessman would give to a university described this way, as it were, out of the horse's mouth?"[66]

The Board of Governors in January 1968 hired the public relations firm of Duff, Abbott and Associates to conduct a survey of public opinion concerning the university. The consultants reported on the basis of more than 200 confidential interviews that there was widespread concern about the lack of "administrative discipline" and the "irresponsible journalism" of the student newspapers. It was thought that the papers were excessively preoccupied with "booze and sex." Many of those surveyed hoped that "responsible" students would "clean up" the offensive articles, but if they did not, then the university was expected to take remedial action. The consultants reported that the two campus principals, William Riddell in Regina and Robert Begg in Saskatoon, were considered "too gentlemanly" in their approach to discipline.[67]

Riddell in his address to Regina Campus Council on 18 October 1968 made a sweeping indictment of student and faculty behaviour. He scolded faculty members for not working hard enough to build support for the university in the community. Professors had not given generously to the United Appeal and had failed to join service organizations such as the Kiwanis and Rotary Clubs. Faculty members were too quick to "[rush] into print" on subjects they knew little about. "Exasperation reached the boiling point," Riddell said, when some professors told their students there would be no assignments, no examinations, and everybody would pass. Students, too, were giving Regina campus a bad name. Those who applied for summer jobs displayed "unkempt physical and mental attitudes." The *Carillon* was filled with obscenities, protests and demonstrations had become a nuisance, and the cafeteria and library entrance were in "filthy condition." All of this had contributed to a "frightening groundswell of reaction against the University." Riddell predicted that unless students and faculty began to conduct themselves in a more responsible manner, the provincial government would be tempted to take matters into its own hands to restore order and decency to the campus.[68] This hinted at the possibility that the government had quietly said to Riddell, "Clean up the campus or we will do it for you."

The *Carillon* riposte was published on 15 November 1968. The editorial said that the cafeteria was cluttered because "it was serving about three times the number it was designed to serve" and the library entrance was littered "mostly with the bodies of students who have nowhere else to go, because facilities are overcrowded and inadequate on this campus, because there is NOT ONE student lounge, not to mention residences." And perhaps the faculty did not contribute as much to the United Appeal as Riddell thought they should because "they consider it little short of criminal that human-welfare programs must depend upon the whimsy of private donations while the military machine is publicly financed."[69]

The editorial also rejected Riddell's claim that the *Carillon* was obscene. The paper considered itself, on the contrary, "one of the cleanest campus newspapers in Canada." In support of this claim, it cited the way it had dealt with the notorious essay "The Student as Nigger." Written by Jerry Farber, an English professor in California, the essay drew a parallel between the plight of students and that of African American slaves. It had been published in unexpurgated form in college newspapers across North America. The *Carillon* reprinted it, too, but only after deleting most of the sexually explicit language. The editors explained, "We do not consider the obscenity issue of overriding importance, and we do not want to give a politically motivated board the opportunity to scuttle us on a side issue." The *Carillon* believed that the Board of Governors was persecuting the paper for political reasons and that the obscenity charges were just a cover for the suppression of legitimate dissent.[70]

Riddell in November 1968 made a bid to bring the *Carillon* under control. He solicited the assistance of SRC president David Sheard and vice-president Ken Sunquist, conferring with them at off-campus locations so that other students would not know that the meetings had taken place. Sheard and Sunquist said they agreed that something had to be done, but they feared that drastic action "would cause a major uprising among the students and might probably bring about the formation of a group of the SDS" (Students for a Democratic Society, a radical US-based organization). Riddell had reason to hope that the problem would be resolved. A member of the *Carillon* staff had told him that they planned "to change the approach of the paper to make it more objective in reporting news, directing the news to Canadian rather than foreign situations and to limit the editorializing to an editorial page." Riddell, on the basis of these assurances, recommended to the Board of Governors on 13 November 1968 that no disciplinary action be taken against the paper and that the board continue to collect student activity fees for the Students' Union.[71]

The situation changed dramatically on 6 December 1968, when the *Carillon* published a graphic drawing of a woman giving birth. The child emerging from the womb bore a resemblance to Ho Chi Minh, the Communist leader of North Vietnam. Although the image had political overtones, with its allegorical suggestion of the birth of a new political order, it was the alleged obscenity and vulgarity that stirred up controversy. Riddell came under intense pressure to "do something." Angry parents telephoned his office, and he could not attend a cocktail party without being subjected to a barrage of complaints.[72] He wrote to President Spinks on 16 December 1968 calling for firm action. The *Carillon*, Riddell charged, had "continued to attack the University in a most damaging way, it has been extremely biased in its editorial policy and grossly inaccurate in the handling of news. Its general policy appears to be carefully designed to detract from the University, its officials and the Board of Governors and to offend the reader." Although Riddell gave no specific examples to support these allegations, he contended that "a rising tide of public resentment directed against the University as well as *The Carillon*, particularly since the last issue for 1968, makes it essential that some action be taken immediately." He advised, therefore, that the Board of Governors agree to discontinue collecting student activity fees "until such time as the SRC makes arrangements for administering its affairs, including adequate supervision and control of *The Carillon*, completely satisfactory to the Board of Governors."[73]

The Board of Governors decided by a mail vote to accept Riddell's advice and announced on 31 December 1968 that it was suspending the collection of student fees at the Regina campus. While Allan Tubby, the board's chairman, admitted that the paper's criticism of the government and the university administration had been a matter of major concern, he insisted that the university had acted primarily to curb the paper's alleged obscenity. According to Tubby, "the use of offensive and vulgar language became so common that the public became enraged."[74] The *Carillon* countered that the obscenity charge was "patently fraudulent and only a cover for the real intentions of those who wish to silence the *Carillon*," pointing out that the harassment had begun with the publication of the Allan Guy story on 16 February 1968. Since then there had been "an intensive campaign on the part of the provincial government and the university administration to suppress *The Carillon*."[75]

Despite the claims of the students, the Board of Governors was not simply using obscenity to cloak more sinister motives. Many members of the general public were offended, not only by what they regarded as the gratuitous indecency of the *Carillon*, but also by the 1960s sexual revolution in general. A mother whose daughter was enrolled in the Faculty of Education wrote the dean to say that she was ashamed to have her daughter bring the campus newspaper into their home. She claimed that the *Georgia Straight*, the Vancouver hippy newspaper, was positively wholesome compared to the *Carillon*. When the Board of Governors suspended the collection of student fees, twenty-five clergymen signed a petition praising the university for upholding standards of decency and morality.[76] However, while the university was responding to genuine public outrage at the *Carillon*'s alleged obscenity, there is no doubt that it would have had trouble harassing the paper on purely political grounds. Political censorship of anti-establishment views was difficult to justify, especially when the body doing the censoring had been the target of *Carillon* criticism.

The *Carillon* editors must have known when they published the controversial picture on 6 December that they would get a strong reaction. They had already admitted to toning down the Jerry Farber article to avoid giving the university an excuse to clamp down on freedom of the press. The students knew what buttons to push to provoke a confrontation, and it is possible that they deliberately instigated the crisis. All through the fall of 1968 the pressure had been building: the Molotov cocktail diagram, Berland's resignation, the demonstration at the legislature, Ron Thompson's convocation protest, Spinks's anti-anarchist speeches. All it took was one "obscene" picture to push the administration over the edge.

But just as the Board of Governors was "innocent" in its use of the obscenity charge as a weapon against the *Carillon* – in the sense that it was genuinely appalled at the material in question – the students were, in a manner of speaking, also "innocent." They said that they saw nothing wrong with publishing four-letter words and pictures of naked women (all the editors of the *Carillon* during this period were male). The students considered themselves enlightened, progressive, and liberated. They assumed that the Board of Governors was being hypocritical about sex and making a fuss about obscenity in order to disguise a repressive political agenda. Thus, the sexual revolution became mixed up in what was essentially a power struggle between the university administration and the students.

The *Carillon* dispute was framed in such a way that the advantage lay with the students, not the Board of Governors. The SRC staked out its position in a statement to the press on 2 January 1969: "Can we look to a situation in which only students with 'safe' ideas will be permitted to attend university? Will students a few years from now be expected to demonstrate their political and ideological purity?" The press release quoted the Regina Beach Statement: "Above all, the role of critic, of examiner of institutions and ideas, belongs to the modern university functioning as a community of scholars … This constant critique must be applied first to the structure and function of the university itself."[77] The students cast themselves in the role of defenders of free speech and of their right to control the newspaper that they paid for.

Support poured in. Roy Atkinson, president of the Saskatchewan Farmers' Union, expressed "amazement" at the Board of Governors' suspension of student fee collection. W.G. Gilbey, president of the Saskatchewan Federation of Labour, called upon the university to rescind its reprehensible decision.[78] Opposition leader Woodrow Lloyd declared that "when authority resorts to such throttling, it violates the general public right of freedom of speech and freedom of association."[79] Reid Robinson, president of the Regina campus

THE CARILLON

Official weekly journal published by the Students' Union, Regina Campus

Vol. 7 No. 11 Friday, November 29, 1968 — 12 Pages

MADE IN Campion

FREE SPEECH
Reality or Rhetoric

The front page of the *Carillon*, 29 November 1968, which portrayed the university's attempt to censor the student newspaper as a denial of free speech. The words "made in Campion," inscribed on the padlock, allude to the fact that the university administration offices were then located on the fourth floor of Campion College.

Faculty Association, characterized the board's action as "somewhat abhorrent ... a fiscal sledgehammer being used for censorship." Alwyn Berland sent a message from Ontario: "The Board's move opens the door into the internal affairs of the university. If the community should decide it doesn't like the Sociology department, will the Board decide to close that up too?" Even the Regina campus men's and women's athletic boards, hardly bastions of student radicalism, backed the SRC in its battle with the Board of Governors.[80]

The board, too, had its supporters. The president of the Regina Chamber of Commerce congratulated the university on the stand that it had taken. When Deputy Premier Davey Steuart was asked whether the *Carillon* needed reforming, he quipped that it needed disinfecting.[81] The *Leader-Post* claimed that the principle of freedom of the press did not apply in this case because students, as individuals, did not purchase copies of the *Carillon*. If

THE CARILLON

Official weekly journal published by the Students' Union, Regina Campus

Vol. 7 No. 7 — Friday, October 25, 1968 — 14 Pages

THIS UNIVERSITY

BELONGS

TO THE STUDENT!

DIG IT

The front page of the *Carillon*, 25 October 1968, which made a strong statement in support of student power.

the students wanted to have a newspaper, they should pay for it on a per copy basis and not expect the Board of Governors to collect the money for it. The *Carillon* said it regretted the *Leader-Post's* lack of "any sense of fraternity with another newspaper under attack."[82]

The Students' Union held a general meeting on 8 January 1969 to consider what its next move should be. About 1,600 attended what was described as "the largest gathering of students on the Regina campus for a meeting of its kind in the history of the institution."[83] The students voted overwhelmingly to censure the Board of Governors and to hold a referendum to demand a contract with the university for the collection of student fees. Despite the show of support for the Students' Union, opinions about the *Carillon* were mixed. Many students made it clear that while they disagreed with the newspaper's

A *Carillon* cartoon, 13 October 1967, depicting students overpowering the authority of the university Board of Governors.

editorial policy, they thought that it was a matter for students, not the Board of Governors, to deal with. "The issue," SRC president David Sheard stated, "is not *The Carillon*, whether it is good or bad; whether it is obscene, as some have charged, or not obscene, but who has final control of the student newspaper." About 43 per cent of eligible students voted in the referendum; 1,101 were in favour of a contract, 539 were opposed, and 5 spoiled their ballots.[84]

The SRC and the Board of Governors entered into negotiations to settle the dispute. On 3 February 1969 a group of students burst into the room where the discussions were taking place and demanded that the board members present leave the meeting and join a teach-in that was underway in a nearby lecture hall. The board members refused and tried to leave the building. Students linked arms in the hallways and tried to steer them into the room where the teach-in was being held. The board members were able to escape, but they were pursued by students who hung onto their car bumpers and threw snowballs at them.[85] The *Leader-Post* condemned this "mob action," claiming that such behaviour was "indefensible" and would "not be tolerated

THE CARILLON

Official weekly journal published by the Students' Union, Regina Campus

SPECIAL EDITION — Wednesday, January 8, 1969 – 4 Pages

Administration announces Power Play

The Board of Governors of this university has deliberately broken commitments made to your Union. Without consultation with faculty, students or employees, the board announced last week that it would discontinue immediately the collection of Students' Union fees. The board's decision has two aims. The first is to censor the student paper. The second is to kill your Students' Union. The issues are simple – freedom of the press and the right of students to organize and run their own independent union.

THIS IS YOUR UNION

Let's keep it that way

The front page of the *Carillon*, 8 January 1969, during the struggle for control of the paper. Board of Governors chairman E.C. Leslie, arms folded, is on the right.

by the people of Regina and the province."[86] Minister of Public Works Allan Guy hinted ominously that "NDP agitators" and "young Communists" had been behind the incident,[87] and Premier Thatcher let it be known that any attempt to disturb the normal functioning of the university would be "met with a firm hand."[88]

Stan Atkinson, a Regina businessman and a member of the Board of Governors committee negotiating with the SRC, advised against making concessions to the students. He believed that the *Carillon* had to be prevented from doing further damage to the university's reputation. He thought that public opinion would support firm action, citing as evidence a remark that he had overheard at a social function: "Why does the administration permit this filthy rag to carry on?"[89] Atkinson claimed that the root of the problem was "the attempt by a central organization to use the campus for a base to promote the foreign political ideology through the use of indoctrinated students and some of the staff who are indoctrinated and that this purpose to them is of paramount importance above that of education."[90] The "central organization," presumably, was the Communist Party, though he did not actually say so. Atkinson commended the approach to student radicalism that had been taken by Ronald Reagan, governor of California, whose tough, no-nonsense methods had quelled the unrest at Berkeley.[91] And, as he reminded Spinks, Regina had one advantage over California – the subduing effect of thirty-below-zero temperatures on outdoor protests.[92]

The students told their side of the story in a special edition of the *Carillon* published in February 1969. With the aid of the National Farmers' Union and the Saskatchewan Federation of Labour, 100,000 copies of the paper were distributed across the province. Students who came from towns outside Regina took bundles home with them on the weekend and delivered them door to door.[93] The special edition attempted to expand the dispute from the narrow issue of the collection of student fees to a broad discussion of the main purpose and governing structure of the university. It included a table with detailed information about the occupations, business interests, political affiliations, and community activities of the members of the Board of Governors. It pointed out that the board represented business and professional interests, not farmers, workers, or the "ordinary" citizens of the province: "What we NEED on this board are farmers, workers, teachers, students and faculty – the people of Saskatchewan."[94]

The special edition also addressed the inequality of access to university education. It cited statistics showing that while families with an annual income of $7,000 or less paid 53 per cent of taxes in Canada, only 25 per cent of university students came from families in that income bracket. It declared, "We don't think that this is fair. We want the university to be open to farmers, workers, housewives and Indians – open to those who really pay for it." It was also critical of the research being conducted at the university, which it claimed served the needs of big business and the wealthy. The university should instead "[use] its brains to help solve the problems of the people – like grain marketing, housing, wheat and soil conditions, and the problems of the laborers and working people of Saskatchewan."[95]

The Board of Governors and the Students' Union meanwhile continued their negotiations. They reached an agreement on 11 March 1969 to resume student fee collection. The agreement was for one year but would be renewed annually on 31 August unless either party gave notice of cancellation prior to 1 March. This meant that the board could not suspend fee collection without warning as it had done on 31 December 1968. The agreement did not include new measures to regulate the *Carillon*. The Board of Governors had asked for a publications board, but the students rejected the idea. They agreed only to the creation of a Board of Governors-Students' Union liaison committee to discuss matters of common concern. The committee was strictly consultative and had no powers of enforcement. The Students' Union also promised that the *Carillon* would adhere to the Canadian University Press code of ethics, something the *Carillon* claimed already to be doing.[96] The students had won the *Carillon* and fee-collection battle.

Spinks had assumed that the "troublemakers" were a small minority. This was true, but only to a point. There had been a fundamental change in the way the broad mass of students perceived their role in the university and a seismic shift in student expectations. Students now regarded themselves as citizens of the university, not as subordinates who did what they were told. Spinks, who liked to describe situations in scientific terms, characterized student protests not as "earthquakes" but as "explosions." He wrote in August 1968:

> A recent number of *Science* contained a long article on student protests, emphasizing the need for a general study of the phenomenon (July 5, 1968, page 20). The suggestion was made that the present series of student protests "might be compared to a succession of earthquakes." I think this analogy is quite inappropriate and, in fact, dangerous. A much better analogy would be an explosion with its accompanying body of theory. One can think of immediate parallels to the effect to catalysts, inhibitors, temperature, concentration of reactants, the phenomenon of successive explosions, the theory of branching chains. Of particular importance is the triggering off of a latent explosion by some outside agent and it is here particularly that the analogy of an explosion is more appropriate than that of an earthquake. It seems quite clear now that many, if not all of the major campus explosions, have occurred as a result of carefully planned and timed operations by non-students who often mastermind a number of campus upsets in succession. The tactics for countering such operations will obviously differ markedly from those applicable to genuine student protests.[97]

But, contrary to Spinks's analysis, the *Carillon* crisis was more akin to an earthquake than an explosion. The student leaders enjoyed widespread support for their stand in defence of the Students' Union and newspaper. The battle over the *Carillon* symbolized the end of a university system based on paternalism and unchallenged authority. However, the radicals were not successful in their attempts to expand the confrontation and bring about a restructuring of the Board of Governors, the abolition of tuition fees, or a change in the focus of university research. Most students did not support such proposals; they did not want a "revolution" in that sense of the word.

Thus the momentum of the great *Carillon* fight did not continue into the fall of 1969. The SRC tried to make an issue of the tuition fee increase, the fourth in five years (fees were now double what they had been in 1963), but it could not mobilize mass support. Students ignored a request to withhold payment of fees, and two "emergency" meetings failed to achieve significant results. A proposal to occupy the bursar's office was voted down at a general meeting because most thought that there was little support for militant action.[98] Don Mitchell, the "grandfather" of the student movement, lamented, "I miss the wars of the old days." A *Carillon* editorial asked, "Can participatory democracy work without participation?" It conceded in October 1969 that "students on this campus really don't want radical social change in this society, a fact which should have been obvious to us. They want to simply vegetate here for three years, picking up their meal ticket (degree) in the process."[99]

A *Carillon* columnist in September 1969 satirized the tedious ritual into which student politics had degenerated. The predictable cycle began when the "establishment" did something stupid. The *Carillon* ran a banner headline, the SRC held an emergency meeting, and then it called a general meeting of the Students' Union:

> Now begin the interminable speeches, the countless amendments; the mind wanders. The card games to your right and left continue undisturbed, except for the bodies packed in around them. The Mouth finally stops moving, a new speaker approaches ... Three hours have passed, a lot of people have left, and it's hot. They only cool thing is watching the girls, or maybe that card game. God, what a drag ... Whatever the outcome, the losers violently denounce the winners with the appropriate words ... But it's not over yet; 3 or 4 meetings, with a steadily dwindling attendance, will be necessary before the issue is finally beaten to death. A rest comes to pass; orgasm is complete. The hunt begins for another inane action by someone. The cycle is complete; the ritual begins again.[100]

The student movement of the sixties was loosely organized around the vague ideal of "participatory democracy." As the movement faltered and the majority of students lost interest, a dedicated few embraced a hodgepodge of revolutionary dogmas. Some adopted Marxism-Leninism; others, Maoism; and still others, Trotskyism. This led to bitter ideological infighting, which further estranged the radicals from the mass of students. Sloganeering replaced intellectual debate as each faction denounced the errors and perfidy of their opponents.[101] Seven staffers left the *Carillon* in the summer of 1969 to work for *Prairie Fire*, a radical community newspaper inspired by Mao's saying "A single spark can start a prairie fire." Funded by a federal government Opportunities for Youth grant, it collapsed in 1971, a victim of underfunding, staff shortages, and ideological warfare. As one *Prairie Fire* veteran recalled, "We felt as if nobody was reading us anymore; that we could have achieved the same response if we had dumped 500 papers out of our office window into the alley below."[102]

It seems clear in hindsight that the student movement at the Regina campus peaked in 1968–69. The student body resisted the move by the Board of Governors against the Students' Union and the *Carillon*. Thereafter, a split opened between a minority of students who embraced a radical agenda and the majority, who were liberal and moderate in their views. The radicals appeared to be more influential than they actually were because they were active, vocal, and well organized. They dominated the SRC and the *Carillon* mainly because they took the trouble to run for office and work for the paper. As an AUCC "spy" who attended the 1968 Canadian Union of Students congress put it, "the activist students are sincere, likeable, intelligent and determined. As a result, although the radical element is only a small minority of the university student population ... it can force its views through against the apathy of the mass or the opposition of the committed 'liberals.'"[103] After 1969 the university administration, having had its fingers badly burned in the *Carillon* affair, treated student radicals deferentially – perhaps a little too deferentially. The senior officials did not realize that the student movement was past its prime and already in decline.

14 Athletics

Athletics at Regina campus in the 1960s and early 1970s was not only an area of growth and development but also of conflict and turmoil. The Department of Physical Education and the Students' Union had differing visions of what a university athletics program should accomplish. The union put forward a philosophy that emphasized mass participation, general fitness, minimal competition, and attention to the needs of women and disadvantaged groups. The faculty in the physical education department advocated a balanced approach that combined intramural programs for the average student with intercollegiate competition for elite athletes. Apart from the clash of ideals, there was a struggle for control. Students historically had exercised considerable authority over athletics, and they were reluctant to give it up. The raison d'être of the student movement was to gain more power and responsibility, not to surrender what they had already won. When the Department of Physical Education tried to assume greater responsibility for the athletics program, the scene was set for confrontation.

Prior to 1961, the athletics directorate of the Students' Representative Council, with the assistance of faculty advisers, had organized athletic activities at Regina College. When the college evolved into a campus with a full degree program, the students voted in a referendum to replace the athletics directorate with a men's athletic board (MAB) and a women's athletic board (WAB) modelled on those at the Saskatoon campus. The stated purpose of the MAB was "to promote athletics among the male students" and "to control those athletics which enter intercollegiate competition and other sports activities not controlled by an intramural board." The board was composed of two non-voting ex-officio members (the dean of the college and the SRC president, if a male, otherwise a male appointed by the SRC) and seven voting members (the MAB president, elected at the annual student elections; three male students appointed by continuing members of the board to a one-year term; the director of physical education, who was a faculty member; one faculty member appointed by faculty; and one alumni member appointed by the outgoing MAB). The students constituted a majority on the board, which set policy and selected the managers of the various sports teams and the coaches of men's sports.

Operations were financed by a portion of the activity fees paid by the students, an amount fixed under the SRC constitution. The director of physical education drew up a tentative budget, which he submitted to the board for consideration and approval. The MAB president then submitted it to the SRC for final approval. This was an important feature, since it gave the SRC ultimate control over how the money was spent. The college bursar kept a separate set of books for all MAB revenues and expenditures, and any funds earned by the MAB through its own activities were credited to its account. The constitution could be amended by a two-thirds vote of members of the board, with the proviso that the SRC also had to ratify the amendment.[1] The WAB was virtually identical, except that it supervised female sports and the wife of the dean of the college served on the board in place of the dean.[2] According to the SRC president, one argument in favour of setting up two separate boards was to give girls "an equal opportunity with the boys." Given the chance to formulate their own budget and plan their own programs, women were expected to achieve a greater measure of equality.[3]

At the time the MAB and WAB came into existence, annual student activity fees were increased from ten to fifteen dollars, five of which went to athletics programs (previously, two of the ten dollars had gone to athletics). It was hoped that the fee increase would place the program on a sound financial basis. Dean W.A. Riddell readily admitted that this had not been the case in the past, when team trips to out-of-town events had been financed by Coca-Cola sales or sock dances, and "often out of the pockets of people like Sam Stewart," the basketball coach.[4] The MAB financial statement for the fiscal year ending 30 June 1962 indicated that student fees had been allocated to the board in the amount of $2,041.60, and an additional $80.79 had been raised by selling soft drinks from vending machines. Expenditures were as outlined in table 10.

Basketball and hockey received the lion's share of the funds, mainly because of the size of the teams and associated travel costs. The university advanced the money for uniforms, which had to be repaid on a four-year

TABLE 10: Men's Athletic Board, Regina Campus, Expenditures, 1961–62

Badminton	$62.57
Basketball	$878.86
Bowling	$42.57
Cross-country running	$77.00
Curling	$42.57
Fencing	$42.58
Hockey	$233.01
Swimming	$42.57
Volleyball	$52.59
General (awards, dry cleaning, stationery, telephone, banquet, etc.)	$765.48
Total	$2,239.80

Source: University of Regina Archives, Dean's/Principal's Office Files, 75-7, 400.1-2, MAB, financial statement for the year ended 30 June 1962.

TABLE 11: Women's Athletic Board, Regina Campus, Expenditures, 1961–62

Badminton	$40.33
Basketball	$569.98
Bowling	$44.08
Curling	$44.34
Fencing	$40.33
Volleyball	$40.33
General	$428.68
Total	$1,208.07

Source: University of Regina Archives, Dean's/Principal's Office Files, 75-7, 400.1-2, WAB, financial statement for the year ended 30 June 1962.

instalment plan: $35.73 per year for the hockey uniforms and $81.64 for the basketball uniforms.[5] The Women's Athletic Board financial statement for the same year showed that it had received $1,011.63 from students fees, about half of what the men received. The hoped-for equality had not materialized.

Intercollegiate competition in western Canada was organized through the Western Canadian Intervarsity Athletic Union (WCIAU). Although traditionally dominated by the Big Four (the Universities of Manitoba, Saskatchewan, Alberta, and British Columbia), it expanded in the 1960s to include new members: Brandon University and the Universities of Winnipeg, Lethbridge,

Members of the Regina campus fencing team exhibiting their skill at the official opening of the Physical Education Centre, 18 February 1967. The fencers lunged and parried their way to a Western Canadian Intervarsity Athletic Union championship.

Calgary, and Victoria. Regina campus joined as an associate member in 1961, which entitled it to compete in curling, badminton, cross-country running, fencing, and wrestling. The fencers were particularly successful, lunging and parrying their way to a Western Canada Intervarsity Athletic Association (WCIAA) championship in 1966–67.[6]

The men's basketball team competed in the Regina senior men's league and played exhibition games against junior college teams from Montana. Coaches Sam Stewart and Ernie Nicholls made a conscious effort to prepare the Cougars for their entry into WCIAU competition in 1968–69. The men's basketball team that year posted a record of seven wins and thirteen losses.[7] Crowds averaged 800 to 1,200 people per game, and there was extensive newspaper, radio, and television coverage. The Regina *Leader-Post* reported a 69 to 65 win by the Cougars over the University of Saskatchewan Huskies in February 1970: Jim Sekulich "spelled the difference in the game, scoring 28 points. Speedy John Schepers added 10 points and Merv Prier and Don Blackburn each picked up 9." Saskatoon challenged for the lead in the final moments of the game, and with only twelve seconds remaining and the Cou-

The 1976–77 men's wrestling team. Coach Don Clark is in the middle of the back row.

gars ahead by one point, "referee Keith Rever called a technical foul against Jacoby for failing to raise his hand on the foul call. Schepers managed to sink all 3 free shots to put the game out of reach for Saskatoon."[8]

The women's basketball team competed in a league that included a team from the teachers' college, a team of General Hospital nurses, and another sponsored by Regina Western Furs. Coach Jean Waldie in 1963 made two suggestions for improvement: "Push Cougette games more – more publicity – maybe we can get more than the manager and the sports representative of the paper to the games. Work out a way to pay for oranges – $2.00 from each girl at the beginning of the year."[9] The women, like the men, joined the WCIAU in 1968–69. In their first year of league play they won one game and lost eleven.[10]

The WCIAU in 1972–73 split into two parts: Canada West (the Universities of British Columbia, Victoria, Alberta, Calgary, Lethbridge, and Saskatchewan, Saskatoon campus) and the Great Plains Athletic Conference (GPAC) (Lakehead University, Brandon University, and the Universities of Winnipeg, Manitoba, and Saskatchewan, Regina campus). The Cougars had in 1961 traded their traditional green and gold colours for the green and white of the parent university. Now, in 1972, as the teams entered GPAC, Regina reverted to the green and gold,[11] foreshadowing the move to university independence two years later.

The Regina fencers in the first year of GPAC competition took the league championship, and the men's and women's curling teams placed second. Linda Vail of the women's basketball team captured the individual scoring championship, and Brian Johnson did the same in men's basketball. But

The 1972–73 Cougars men's basketball team, with coach Gene Rizak at the right, in its first year of competition in the Great Plains Athletic Conference.

during these years defeats outnumbered victories. One can sense the disappointment and frustration in basketball coach Gene Rizak's open letter to his players in 1974: "We are now 0-6 in league play and any opportunity to win the Conference Championship and go to the Canadian Finals is lost. I'm sure that this is a disappointment to you as it is to me ... Please stick with me. There is not much to look forward to in the remaining 10 games, but if you keep plugging away, I'm sure we will develop into a fine team ... I'm sure that Neil, Merv, and Wayne, who are graduating this year, will help you to become good basketball players with the hope that you new fellows will put the University of Regina on the map as a basketball power as it should be."[12] The most rapid advances were made in women's basketball, due to the coaching of Sue Higgs. She was the first women's coach to encourage her players to lift weights, train hard, and, so to speak, play like men.

The physical education department defined its philosophy in a 1973 promotional publication: "We hold to the position that students are students first and then ought to be given every opportunity to excel in competitive sports."[13] The team policy of the early 1970s was to "work towards a proper attitude in

The 1977–78 Cougettes women's basketball team demonstrating a more athletic style of play than had been characteristic of women's basketball in the 1950s.

defeat and victory. Respect your opponents. Basketball rules do *not* permit *any* player to argue *any* decision of an official. Only the captain may request an interpretation and then it must be made in a courteous manner. The captain must therefore be knowledgeable of the rules, be constantly alert, and a gentleman – not necessarily the biggest, loudest and most volatile!!"[14] The Men's Athletic Board travel and discipline regulations in 1969 reinforced the message: "Team Personnel shall conduct themselves as gentlemen whose actions reflect upon the University of Saskatchewan, Regina Campus."[15]

The emphasis in intramural athletics was on "participation and friendly competition." The program in 1973–74 included the team sports of flag football, basketball, volleyball, curling, hockey, softball, and floor hockey and the individual sports of archery, badminton, bowling, swimming and diving,

Coach Sue Higgs introduced new techniques, including weight training and drills, thereby raising the standard of women's basketball.

table tennis, basketball free throw, skiing, cross-country running, and tennis. Although teams were usually organized according to faculty affiliation, any group of interested individuals could enter a league or event. Points towards the high-point trophy were awarded on the basis of participation level and number of games won.[16]

Lack of funds was the most serious impediment to the development of the athletics program. The university paid the salaries of Department of Physical Education faculty, who coached teams and supervised intramural activities. It also covered the cost of building and maintaining the gymnasiums, swimming pool, and other sports facilities. All other expenses – team travel, purchase of uniforms, payment of referees, rental of off-campus facilities, administrative overhead – had to be paid out of student activity fees. When Regina campus entered WCIAU and then GPAC competition, these costs increased enormously, placing a great strain on the budget. The Department of Physical Education argued that if the athletics program was to be adequately funded, the university would have to take a larger share of the financial responsibility.

The SRC decided what portion of the student activity fee would go to athletics. In 1969 it amounted to $7.00 out of an annual fee of $33.25. The fee could not be increased without the approval of the students, voting in a referendum. This gave the students considerable leverage over the athletics program – he who pays the piper calls the tune. Since the SRC did not want to give up this control, it opposed the Department of Physical Education's push to get the university to pay for the program. According to SRC logic, if the university absorbed more of the cost, the students would end up paying the bill anyway, since the administration would raise tuition fees to obtain the extra money.[17] The student power movement was in decline by the early 1970s, and campus radicalism had lost its momentum. Athletics became the last stand for student activist diehards.

There were also fundamental principles at stake. At the annual Students' Union general meeting in November 1969, first-year student Bruce Shepard was one of many who voiced unhappiness with the sports program. He maintained that in society at large, "the trend was towards participatory sports. Money should be spent to get more people involved in athletics." Ken Black, the president of MAB, defended interuniversity athletics, pointing out that many top athletes volunteered their time to community projects, such as summer sports clinics for primary-school children. "One of the sports types" argued that the campus "would become well known through its sports activities." This view did not sit well with student John Fagan, who asked, "How many people knew who were the university champions in volleyball, water polo, badminton, fencing or any other sport?"[18]

The Students' Union held a referendum on 28 November 1969 to decide whether support for interuniversity sports should be terminated. The ballot presented three options: a combined program of interuniversity and intramural sports funded by at least $7.00 per student out of the total student activity fee of $33.25; a program of intramural sports funded by up to $3.00 per student out of the activity fee; or no sports subsidized by student fees. The first option received 1,194 votes; the second, 215; the third, 45; and 8 ballots were spoiled.[19] It seemed that a large majority of students wanted both intramural and interuniversity sports to continue. Nevertheless, there remained a wide gap between what was required for a comprehensive athletics program and the funds available to pay for it. Athletics director Ernie Nicholls prepared a budget for 1970–71 based on a total expenditure of $50,516 and revenues of $35,350, resulting in a deficit of $15,166. Almost $30,000 of budgeted revenues came from the SRC (estimated on the basis of 4,200 students paying seven dollars each), with lesser amounts from gate receipts and tickets for the awards night dance. The bulk of the expenditures were dedicated to intercollegiate sports ($37,327); intramurals accounted for far less ($2,882). An additional $10,307 was set aside to cover the overhead costs of administering the entire program.

Nicholls called it a "bare bones" budget, since all requests for new sports had been rejected, except for women's junior basketball, and only eighty dollars had been allotted for that. Applications for the introduction of ice hockey, water polo, and rugby had all been turned down. Nicholls thought it was particularly shameful for the campus not to have a team for Canada's "national sport": "We are a 'community' of nearly 5,000 persons and there isn't one community of that dimension in the entire province that can't boast of their arena and hockey team." Even without hockey in the program, the size of the projected deficit was a matter of serious concern. Coaches indicated that there was no room for further cuts to existing programs. If savings had to be made, they said, the elimination of targeted programs was preferable to across-the-board reductions. Nicholls proposed that in the short term the university provide a supplementary grant to cover the deficit; over the long term it should assume half the cost of operating the program.[20] He argued that the traditional method of raising money through student fees could not support the added costs associated with interuniversity competition.

The Students' Union refused to split the financing of athletics equally with the university. Nicholls met in July 1970 with Principal John Archer and SRC president Fred Cuddington. He came away exasperated with "Fred's seeming unbending attitude towards the students having to pay 100 per cent of the operating costs of the program ... We sure don't see eye to eye on what the university community is made up of. I claim it is students, administration, faculty, alumni, etc., etc. – Fred says it's *students* only!"[21] Protracted discussions led in June 1971 to the formation of an athletics council as the policy-making body for athletics.[22] Its voting membership comprised one student member of WAB, one student member of MAB, the SRC president (or his designate), the SRC treasurer (or his designate), the principal of Regina campus (or his designate), the director of physical education, the director of women's athletics, the director of men's athletics, and two students appointed by the SRC. Although students had a majority of six members out of ten, the MAB and WAB students tended to support the faculty. This did not mean much, however, since the SRC retained veto rights over the budget, and "any major changes in expenditures and programming" had to be approved by a referendum vote by members of the Students' Union. The union continued to be the sole source of operating funds for the athletic program, providing annually seven dollars per student (five dollars for interuniversity sports and two for intramural). The creation of the Athletics Council in effect reaffirmed the status quo and did nothing to resolve the underlying difficulties.[23]

The Academic Board of the Department of Physical Education requested in September 1971 that its athletic program subcommittee, chaired by Professor Don Clark, undertake a study of athletics on campus. The subcommittee's report in January 1972 recommended that effective 1 July the university assume full responsibility for the administration and financing of the athletics program. It proposed that the necessary funds come directly out of the university's operating budget and not from student activity fees. The athletics director would prepare the budget and submit it to the Department of Physical Education, which would take full responsibility for spending the funds. The additional annual cost to the university was estimated at about $50,000. The report recognized that if hockey and football were added to the program, operating costs could rise to double that figure. Students would still have a voice in policy making through their participation in the Athletics Council, but their influence would be limited to expressing opinions and giving advice. Decision-making authority would rest firmly with the Department of Physical Education.[24]

The Clark Report argued that these changes were needed because the existing Athletics Council was dysfunctional. As a case in point it cited the hockey referendum fiasco. The council had agreed on 23 September 1971 that a student referendum be held on whether or not the activity fee should be raised by three dollars per student to support a university hockey team. The SRC devised a ballot that presented four options for hockey and basketball combinations to be phased in at different times. As a result, the pro-hockey vote was split and the proposal to fund a hockey team defeated. Several members of the Athletics Council insisted that the students should have been allowed to vote on a simple, direct question. They resented the SRC for complicating and obfuscating the issue.

The Department of Physical Education contended that the Students' Union had neither the expertise nor the continuity of personnel required to make athletics policy and supervise the program. As the Clark Report pointed out, "Membership of the SRC changes through elections each year. New people bring forward new ideas, quite often contrasting severely with the ones of the year before, so that the outlook on athletics changes." Student activity fees did not provide a stable financial base and were insufficient to cover the added expenses resulting from Regina campus participation in GPAC. To be a full member of GPAC the campus had to compete in men's hockey and basketball and four or more additional men's sports, as well as five or more women's sports. Universities that failed to meet this requirement were classified as associate members with reduced voting privileges (three votes, as compared to five for full members). Regina campus could not become a full member unless the athletics budget was substantially increased to support more teams, including a hockey team. GPAC rules stipulated that a member university must give three years' notice before withdrawing from participation in a particular sport. This meant that funding had to be predictable and stable over the long term.

Beyond making these specific recommendations, the Clark Report set forth a philosophical justification for the athletics program in all its dimensions. It asserted that the program operated on three levels, serving, in the first instance, students in the Department of Physical Education, then the university as a whole, and, ultimately, the community beyond the university. At the departmental level, students enrolled in physical education courses were given an opportunity through intervarsity sports to develop their skills in high-level competition, while others gained experience as administrators and officials. Competitive teams in a wide range of sports attracted well-qualified coaches, who brought their expertise to the academic program, thereby enhancing the professional image of the department.

Athletics also contributed to the university at large. It helped students "maintain a balance between mental and physical development," fostered college "spirit," and attracted students to Regina who might otherwise have attended another university. As for the wider community, the coaches of intervarsity teams acted as resource people, lecturing, conducting coaching clinics, and assisting with sports programs for the city's youth. They also organized extension classes and non-credit programs of various kinds. Perhaps most significant of all, a successful sports program raised the profile of the university and generated good publicity. No other aspect of campus life attracted so much media attention and interest from people who otherwise would not have spared a thought for what was going on at the university.[25] The main purpose of the Clark Report was to provide a rationale for an adequately funded, well-balanced, and professionally administered athletics program. The goal was to serve students of all types, from the engineering major who enjoyed a game of floor hockey once a week to the talented basketball player capable of competing with the best university athletes in the country. Such a program would be a source of pride and prestige for the university and a stimulus to the development of sports and recreation in the wider community.

The SRC responded with a brief that challenged the basic premises of the report. It stated that "the essence of athletics in sport is 'fitness' and 'fitness for all,'" principles that the SRC claimed the Department of Physical Education had not accepted: "Programs involving approximately 100 persons consume the major portion (70 per cent) of the students' financial contribution, the majority of time and energy of Physical Education faculty devoted to athletics, and a considerable portion of equipment and facilities made available by the University." The concentration on elite intervarsity sports had relegated the majority of students to the passive role of spectators, "a perversion of the ideal of general popular involvement." According to the SRC, this tendency was linked to the "professionalization" and "commercialization" of sport in North America, aspects of popular culture that were in turn related to "conservatism, authoritarianism, sexism, racism, and chauvinism." Although the precise nature of the links was not explained, the SRC saw the discussion about campus sports as part of a much larger debate. Essentially, it preferred the egalitarianism of broad participation and general fitness to the elitism of select teams involved in high-level competition. The SRC referred specifically to the low participation rate of women in sport. "We object strongly to physical activity being conceived as a 'manly' pursuit. Special attention should be given to the encouragement of female participation."[26]

The SRC debunked the idea of using sport to generate "healthy college spirit." "One is inclined to assume," the brief acidly remarked, "that immature (and often destructive) college rivalry, social and political irresponsibility, undue reverence for the institution, pep rallies such as characterized American colleges during the 1950s are the essence of the argument." It also questioned the use of athletics to burnish the image of the university. "We would regard the development of such an image as harmful to the university. The public image of the university has to be based on substantive service and meaning to the community; the priorities of image must deal with primarily academic concerns." The SRC conceded that competitive sports, including interuniversity athletics, attracted a good deal of mass media attention, and that this coverage, far from being foisted on an unwilling public, was a response to consumer demand. From the SRC's perspective, however, this tendency to transform athletics into entertainment had to be resisted, not indulged. "One must recognize," the brief said, "that the media and most athletic activities relegate the largest majority of people to the role of spectator which does nothing to promote general fitness."[27]

In answer to the Clark Report's claim that students could not give stable leadership to the sports program because of the turnover in SRC membership, the SRC maintained that its general approach to athletics had been very consistent over the years. One-quarter to one-third of the SRC was returned to office from one year to the next, and the veterans tended to exert more influence on policy decisions than did the newcomers. The brief pointed out that some SRC members had been at the university longer than certain members of the committee that had written the Clark Report – a tribute to the longevity of student politicians. The SRC also dismissed the argument that the Regina campus had binding obligations to GPAC. The conference was dominated by larger, wealthier campuses that had little concern for the welfare of smaller institutions. "The suggestion that we have some moral obligation or commitment to them in the face of their callousness and disregard is not legitimate." According to the SRC, the Regina campus was too small to compete with larger universities. "The fact that others of comparable size attempt to do so does not make such expectations, on the part of Department members, any more legitimate."[28]

The SRC advanced an alternative to the Clark Report aimed at "physical fitness for as large a number of persons within the University as possible." In order to give more emphasis to programs in which everyone could participate, it recommended that full-time faculty members be appointed to the positions of men's and the women's intramural directors. Special attention needed to be given to "the development, promotion and operation of women's activities," which had to be carried out "in a much more deliberate and enthusiastic fashion." This implied a more equal distribution of expenditures for men's and women's sports. The SRC also suggested that intramural sports be reorganized to reduce the competitive element. Proposed reforms included eliminating team designation by college or faculty, abandoning the practice of awarding points for winning, and putting an end to the recording of statistics. Such practices promoted "unnecessary rivalry" and unhealthy attitudes. The best athletes should be distributed among various intramural teams and encouraged to do informal coaching, an athletics version of "sharing the wealth." The SRC opposed holding sports clinics to recruit top-quality athletes for university teams and recommended appointing a faculty member with the expertise to develop programs for "the middle-aged, elderly, handicapped, and the socially and economically deprived."[29]

The SRC explicitly rejected the physical education department's concept of "professionalism." (The Clark Report had said that the SRC had neither the time nor the staff to administer the athletics program in a "professional manner.") It said that the program should be directed not by professionals or "technicians" but "on the basis of student interests as the students perceive them." It attributed the "fixation" of physical education faculty members on "professionalism" to their desire to win recognition as academics on a par with their colleagues in other disciplines. These faculty members, the SRC suggested, felt embattled because physical education was regarded in the university as a minor element in teacher training and in society at large as "frivolous, anti-intellectual ... purely as entertainment." The SRC insinuated that rather than confronting this issue directly, physical education faculty members were trying to acquire second-hand prestige by building up a strong intervarsity athletics program.[30]

Here the SRC touched a sore spot. Members of the Department of Physical Education were engaged in a struggle to upgrade the status of their department to that of a school or faculty. They wanted to offer a separate degree in physical education rather than merely teaching classes that counted towards a Bachelor of Education degree with a minor in physical education, but the Campus Council turned down their request. The inferior status of the department led to uncertainty as to where it belonged in the administrative structure of the university. It functioned initially as a stand-alone unit, joined the Faculty of Education in 1968, and then returned to separate departmental status in 1971.[31] Department members were beleaguered on three fronts: they were uncomfortable as a component of the Faculty of Education, unable to gain recognition as a faculty in their own right, and attacked by the Students'

Union for attempting to place the athletics program on a professional footing. The SRC, fully aware of internal university politics, fastened on this point of vulnerability. It accused physical education faculty members of trying to take control of athletics to prove they were professionals. They responded that they deserved to have control *because* they were professionals. Without their knowledge and expertise, the athletics program would function at a less than optimal level.

The debate at the Regina campus was a miniature version of a discussion occurring at the national level. The Association of Universities and Colleges of Canada and the Canadian Intercollegiate Athletic Union in 1972 jointly sponsored a comprehensive study of university athletics that culminated in a 1974 report authored by A.W. Matthews. Its conclusions coincided, for the most part, with the views expressed in the Clark Report.[32] Matthews recommended "that physical education and athletic programs be integrated into a single administrative unit"; "that financial responsibility for the physical education and/or athletic and recreational programs be assumed by the institution"; and "that effort be directed towards providing aggressive and dedicated professional leadership to intramural and recreational activities."[33] This was to avoid the American model in which the athletics department functioned as an independent business and entertainment subsidiary of the university, and its students were, for all intents and purposes, professional athletes.

The Matthews Report also echoed some points that had been made in the SRC brief. It noted that while competition was an important part of intramural activities, "modern intramural programs are making provision for the student in whom the competitive urge, if it exists, is very low key, by grouping teams into a division in which 'winning the game' is de-emphasized and 'play' is the thing." Matthews also highlighted the importance of giving greater encouragement to women in athletics, though he made no specific recommendations in this regard.[34] Neither the Matthews Report nor the Clark Report addressed the needs of the handicapped and the disadvantaged, as the Regina campus SRC had done.

The Canadian Council of University Physical Education Administrators reacted favourably to the Matthews Report, but it pointed out that the report had not addressed certain contentious matters, such as "pressure from government and sports governing bodies to emphasize the training of elite athletes," "the use of athletics by certain Canadian universities to publicize the general university program, with resulting exploitation of athletes and commercializing of the program," and "the need for a balanced program, which provides equal emphasis and resources for all aspects of university athletics programs, that is, intercollegiate, intramural, organized recreational programs, informal recreational activities, and sports skills instructional programs."[35] The Department of Physical Education at Regina campus concurred.[36] Its aim was

Graffiti on the wall of the Physical Education Centre. In the late 1960s and early 1970s the Department of Physical Education and student radicals battled over the direction and philosophy of the university athletic program.

to establish a balanced program, and in its opinion the program in Regina was not tilted in favour of elite athletics. On the contrary, the campus was struggling to fund enough teams to qualify for membership in GPAC. Nor were sports exploited to publicize the university. There was hardly enough money to buy running shoes, let alone pay for advertising or give financial assistance to student athletes. Regina campus, in the view of the Department of Physical Education, had a long way to go before it reached the level of elitism and commercialism of older and more established universities.

The year of reckoning was 1973–74. Student representatives at a meeting of the Athletics Council on 18 September 1973 pushed through a resolution recommending "that within the shortest period possible the Regina campus commitment to select intercollegiate athletics as represented by the Great Plains Athletic Conference be phased out to its final elimination and that we pursue more involvement in local and southern Saskatchewan leagues." They proposed that instead of supporting intervarsity teams the campus sponsor ten or more teams in each sport to compete in various recreational leagues operating in Regina and the surrounding area. Top athletes would be dispersed among the teams as a means of encouraging the less talented and raising the overall quality of play.[37] News of this resolution came as a shock to campus teams preparing for GPAC competition. They continued to train without knowing whether they would have a chance to play in the coming season. The entire program was thrown into confusion.

Neil Sherlock, the acting director of physical education, made a strong protest to Principal John Archer: "Once again, our athletes and coaches have been placed in limbo awaiting the magical results of a referendum which will reinforce or remove the license for them to operate." Sherlock asserted that the very question posed in the referendum proved that the Athletics Council, supposedly an equal partnership between the Students' Union and the Department of Physical Education, was unworkable. The two parties were diametrically opposed in philosophy and attitude; one did everything in its power to destroy what the other was trying to build. Sherlock urged Archer to take a stand. "The ball is in your court. It is time for the senior administration and decision-makers on this campus to climb down off the fence and produce a decision reflecting their judgments and attitudes in regard to athletics at Regina campus." Faculty members wanted to know where they stood. "Do you, the hirers, back and support the very experts you appoint? If you continue to show little positive support for our views by failing to make decisions you are in fact indicating non-confidence in the Department of Physical Education." He concluded with an ultimatum: "We of the Department of Physical Education have advised you of our views and values. Should you move contrary to this viewpoint, we feel our only alternative is to ask to be relieved of all responsibility for any decision made which is contrary to our beliefs. Our professional reputations are at stake and we require that our position in this matter be made general knowledge both to the professionals in the field of education and to the public at large."[38]

The campus administration had allowed the situation to deteriorate into a crisis. The explanation, in part, was that Principal Archer did not want to antagonize the Students' Union. The Government of Saskatchewan had in May 1973 appointed a Royal Commission to look into the structure and organization of university education in the province, including the possibility of independent status for the university in Regina.[39] It was important for Regina campus to maintain a united front at this critical juncture in its history. The last thing Archer wanted to do was pick a fight with the students.[40] He also had a very practical reason for "sitting on the fence." The soaring enrolment of the 1960s had peaked in 1969, causing the provincial government to decelerate the rate of increases to university funding.[41] Facing a budgetary crisis, the campus administration looked for ways to save money. The suggestion that the university absorb the cost of operating the athletics program was not welcome in a climate of fiscal restraint. The students' demand that the university *not* spend any money was much more appealing.

The students on 5 October 1973 voted in a general referendum on the question "Are you in favor of transferring the Students' Union Athletic Fees away from the intervarsity program to fund an expanded program of student participation in intramurals and community athletics?" The result was 316 for and 484 against.[42] The turnout – 810 of a possible 4,013 – was low, indicating that the radicals did not have widespread support. It was equally obvious that students had not rallied in large numbers to uphold intercollegiate sports. Most seemed indifferent, or at least insufficiently motivated to cast a ballot. The athletics program continued to hobble along, severely underfunded and in constant threat of being closed down by a referendum. Its level of financial support (seven dollars per student) had remained unchanged for seven years, and it was barely enough to maintain minimal GPAC requirements. Coaches feared that unless funding was increased, either through a fundraising effort or direct grant from the university's operating budget, they would have to withdraw their teams from competition.[43]

The swim team dropped out of GPAC in 1973–74, mainly because of "a lack of competent and interested swimmers."[44] Since Regina campus no longer fielded teams in at least eight sports, its associate membership status in GPAC was in jeopardy.[45] The Athletics Council decided to limit participation in 1974–75 to men's and women's basketball, women's volleyball, and men's wrestling. Regina delegates (Neil Sherlock, Ernie Nicholls, and Fyola Lorenzen) encountered a rather hostile atmosphere at the annual general meeting of GPAC, held in Brandon on 4–5 April 1974. The first item of business was a question from the floor as to whether Regina campus was in good standing with the conference and had the right to participate in the meeting. After considerable debate, Regina was allowed voting privileges for the rest of that day. It was agreed that the GPAC Board of Governors (the heads of the physical education departments of each participating school) would meet later in the day to review the situation and prepare a recommendation to bring to the plenary session the next morning.

The Regina delegates then introduced a motion to eliminate the distinction between "full members" and "associate members." They argued that all members of GPAC should enjoy equal status and that invidious distinctions should not be made between larger and smaller schools. Under the existing system full members (the Universities of Manitoba and Winnipeg and Lakehead University) had five votes, while associate members (Brandon University and Regina campus) had only three. This meant that three universities dominated the conference to the detriment of the other two. The motion to equalize the situation was resoundingly defeated.

A second motion was put forward that would have allowed Regina campus to retain associate membership in GPAC by participating in four sports in 1974–75, six in 1975–76, and eight in 1976–77. This motion, too, went down to defeat, by a vote of 11 to 9. A third motion proposed that a new category of membership be created to give playing privileges to institutions unable to qualify for associate membership. A university enjoying such privileges would be allowed three votes in matters pertaining to those sports in which it competed and one vote in constitutional matters. The Regina delegates abstained from this vote on the grounds that they did not have permission from their Athletics Council to participate in such a scheme, which represented an obvious downgrading of the status of Regina campus in the organization. When the motion passed unanimously, the Regina representatives left the meeting. It was clear to them that the larger schools in the conference had little concern for the financial problems they faced.

The Academic Board of the Department of Physical Education and the Regina campus Athletics Council agreed to send observers to the annual meeting of the Canada West University Athletic Association in Lethbridge on 6–8 May 1974; they would seek playing privileges in men's and women's basketball and men's wrestling.[46] "Philosophically," Neil Sherlock wrote, "We are a great deal closer to Canada West in our attitude towards University Athletic programs. These should be programs of excellent quality for the elite local athlete, not an attempt at semi-professionalism."[47] Canada West rejected Regina's petition, leaving the campus without a conference to play in. Sherlock then went back to GPAC, asking for playing privileges in men's and women's basketball, women's volleyball, and men's wrestling. The conference replied, "Your request has been denied. The major reason for this is the inability of the University of Saskatchewan, Regina Campus to make a commitment beyond 1974–75."[48] Regina campus now had an athletic program of good quality, particularly in women's basketball and men's wrestling, with no access to intercollegiate competition.[49]

The program was a victim of a combination of adverse circumstances, especially the shortage of funding and the ongoing conflict between the Students' Union and the Department of Physical Education. A truce was finally achieved in an agreement that went into effect on 1 July 1975. The Students' Union continued to allocate five dollars per student for the support of intercollegiate athletics, but in addition, for the first time in the history of the institution, the university promised to provide "at least" an equal amount. The Athletics Council was retained as the policy-making body responsible for "allocating and overseeing all expenditures from the Athletic Fund," but the budget did not have to be ratified by the SRC. Nor did major policy changes have to be approved by student referendum.[50]

If not a permanent solution, the agreement at least provided a modus vivendi. As the more radical phase of the student movement receded, the Students' Union became less confrontational, and intercollegiate athletics, along with intramural sports, were accepted as a normal and desirable feature of campus life. With the University of Regina reinstated in GPAC for the 1976–77 season,[51] the struggles of the late 1960s and early 1970s gradually came to an end. Although the debate took its toll on the participants, it was not entirely futile. Some of the radical students' ideas entered into mainstream discourse and helped shape physical education as an academic discipline. Students led the way in advocating gender equality and asserting that physical education was not just for the young and able-bodied – it was also for the elderly, the handicapped, those recovering from serious illness, and the socially excluded. Some of their other ideas were extreme, if not eccentric, such as the notion that the best athletes should not be allowed to compete against each other but should be required to train their less athletically talented brethren. Similarly, the proposal to eliminate competition from sports was not feasible. It would be like taking the saltiness out of salt.

The athletics debate faintly replicated the discussions over the Regina Beach Statement. Some of the basic questions were the same. Was the university meant to provide professional training or a well-rounded education? Was it meant to serve the general population or a small elite? Student radicals, caught up in the egalitarian and anti-hierarchal social and political movements of the day, accused physical educators of promoting semi-professional competitive sports for the few at the expense of intramural and recreational activities for the many. The physical educators said they were doing no such thing. They argued for a balanced approach; a student was a student first and an athlete second. The student radicals were right to point out the dangers of placing intercollegiate athletics at the service of mass entertainment, institutional chauvinism, and public relations propaganda, but they underestimated the healthy sense of community that can be generated by supporting the home team. At the end of the day, the balanced approach won out.

15 The Unravelling of Regina Beach

The radical, innovative temper of the Regina campus had always been linked to the Regina Beach Statement of 1963. The statement had inspired the formal adoption of the divisional structure for the Faculty of Arts and Science in 1965, and the implementation of the semester system and the new arts and science curriculum in 1966. However, a struggle soon developed between two factions in the Faculty of Arts and Science: one championed Regina Beach, and the other attacked it. The conflict occurred on several levels. It was at once a debate between general education and professionalism; interdisciplinary learning and specialization; community involvement and the ivory tower; applied knowledge and knowledge for its own sake; social activism and traditional academic standards; the community and the individual; human values and technology; conservatives and liberals; left and right – and much else besides.

Dallas Smythe, the chairman of the social sciences division, was the chief proponent of Regina Beach and the division system. He attempted to recruit faculty "whose interests lay more in relating knowledge to the problems of the real world in Saskatchewan and less in the varieties of possible ivory towers." He acknowledged, however, that most faculty members hired in the social sciences division during the 1960s were what he referred to as "conventional academic types" – especially those specializing in history, economics, and geography. Neither humanities nor fine arts made a special effort to recruit faculty sympathetic to the Regina Beach policy. As a result, some professors in these divisions supported it while others did not. As for the Division of

Natural Sciences and Mathematics, almost everyone hired was the conventional type of research scientist with no interest in making the Faculty of Arts and Science a beacon for the principles of Regina Beach. Many of them looked down on Smythe and his group, considering them left-wing activists rather than genuine scholars. According to Smythe, the leaders of the traditionalist group were a few senior people who had come from Saskatoon and wanted to shape the Regina campus in the same pattern as the parent institution.[1] Prominent among them was Allan B. Van Cleave, the chairman of the Division of Natural Sciences and Mathematics, who enjoyed the support of President Spinks and Principal Riddell. The Faculty of Arts and Science from 1964 to 1968 was an arena of struggle between the two camps. Meetings were long, arduous, and invigorating because they dealt with the fundamental issues of liberal education. But as time went by they became increasingly repetitive, stale, and acrimonious. Many faculty members dropped out and stopped attending, choosing instead to concentrate on teaching, conducting research, and staying out of the crossfire.

The Regina Beachers soon lost the battle for "satisfactory introductory 100-level courses," by which they meant courses that provided an overview of the basic conceptual and methodological assumptions of the discipline, as opposed to courses that provided a foundation for further specialized work. Smythe discovered to his chagrin that "the Natural Science faculty simply could not or would not teach [courses] in the way the policy required." Another setback for Regina Beach was the failure to implement effectively the system that offered four types of majors: departmental, divisional, interdivisional, and individual. Most students selected the traditional departmental major rather than an interdisciplinary program of studies. Smythe attributed this to the absence of "an even-handed counselling system" that would inform students of their options. A third defeat was the erosion of the sixteen-class limit imposed on departments to prevent the proliferation of specialized courses with a disciplinary rather than an interdisciplinary orientation. One after the other, departments secured exemptions and were allowed to offer eighteen, or twenty, or even more classes. The externally imposed limits gradually became meaningless.[2]

When the divisional organization was formally adopted in 1965, it was on the understanding that it would be reviewed in three years. As the date for the review approached, in April 1967, the Division of Natural Sciences and Mathematics submitted to Campus Council a request for recognition as a separate faculty. If granted, it would mean not only the end of the division system but also the breakup of the Faculty of Arts and Science. The Senior Academic Committee of Council set up a task force to review the situation and make a recommendation. The brief from the Division of Natural Sciences asserted that nearly all its members believed that they could function more effectively if they were organized as a unit sharing interests and objectives rather than as a component of Arts and Science. They did not want to have to seek approval of course proposals and academic policies from colleagues in the social sciences and humanities, who often seemed hostile to what natural scientists were trying to accomplish. The brief pointed out that on many occasions the split in the Faculty of Arts and Science had run along divisional lines, with the natural sciences in the minority and therefore overruled.

A survey of practices at other universities suggested that once a faculty of arts and science reached a certain size, it tended to break into two parts. There were exceptions to the pattern – for example, the faculties at the University of Toronto and the University of Saskatchewan, Saskatoon Campus – but the organizational structure that the Division of Natural Sciences desired was by no means unprecedented or unusual. Van Cleave argued that when a faculty grew to include 100 to 150 members, the meetings became too large and unwieldy for effective debate. Faculty members did not attend because much of what was discussed had no direct bearing on them and they believed that they could spend their time more profitably doing something else. Van Cleave also reminded his colleagues that in 1967 natural science students constituted 20 to 25 per cent of the total enrolment at Regina campus. He thought they would have more college spirit if they could identify with a distinct faculty that had its own jackets, insignia, and other emblems of esprit de corps. The Faculty of Arts and Science was too large, diverse, and amorphous to generate a sense of loyalty or group identity. The natural scientists claimed that a separate faculty of science would enhance the reputation of the university by giving scientists free rein to exploit their "unique ability" to establish a rapport with the public. They could do this by conducting scientific research of practical value. The brief stated that "one of the student's major functions is to aid in the conversion of new knowledge into the technology which improves the human lot." The scientists at Regina campus had, according to Van Cleave, "already made notable strides in this direction. Creation of a separate faculty will help quicken the pace."[3]

For Dallas Smythe, this represented a direct challenge to the educational policy adopted at Regina Beach. He contended that "scientists should not contract out of the debate on the problems technology creates for human society nor surrender their detachment as scholars to groups who call the tune in technology." The natural scientists in his view were trying to create "a professional school concerned with the success of its students in furthering technological progress but indifferent to and perhaps incapable (by their premature professionalization) of discussing the problems that technological progress creates for human beings, and which are the special pre-occupation of the social scientist." Regina Beach had stood for a concept of liberal education that placed all knowledge in the context of "essential human values" and social responsibility. It had stressed the importance of "critical intelligence" and the dismantling of conventional myths, including those that mainstream society holds most dear. Smythe did not think the scientists should be allowed to march off in their own direction, eyes firmly fixed on the "the conversion of new knowledge into the technology which improves the human lot." He believed that it was a fundamental error to "identify the university with the short-term interests of the technological order." To do so would be to expose the university to pressure from outside groups that wanted to harness scientific research for commercial and military purposes. Smythe said that if this was what it desired, then the Division of Natural Sciences did not go far enough in its brief: "A scientific laboratory for natural scientists and mathematicians attached to some industrial base would be a much more efficient means of training students 'to aid in the conversion of new knowledge into the technology that improves the human lot' than would be the proposed separate professional faculty of Science and Mathematics. But if encounter in a free and open dialogue is the object of the university, the proposed halfway station towards a technical institute or industrial laboratory is incompatible with the nature of the university itself."[4]

It would be an oversimplification to characterize the debate between Smythe and Van Cleave in terms of left versus right. The philosophical currents ran in different and more complicated channels. As Canadian conservative philosopher George Grant cogently argued, the supreme value in liberal society is freedom, which leads to the unlimited use of technology for the conquest of nature, both human and non-human.[5] This is what liberals (in Grant's definition) call progress. Since freedom is accorded the status of the highest good, in practice if not in theory, there are no effective brakes placed upon the discovery and application of new technology. What can be done eventually will be done. Although Smythe described himself as a Marxist,[6] there was also a conservative cast to this thought. He believed in subordinating freedom to a higher good. Van Cleave, who was regarded as a conservative and traditionalist because he took a strong stand against campus radicalism, was actually a small-*l* liberal. He upheld the academic freedom of scientists to pursue truth as they saw fit, unimpeded by those who had a different concept of the purpose of a university.

The task force on the organization of the Faculty of Arts and Science reported in April 1968 to the Senior Academic Committee of the Executive of Council. The majority report stated that the separation of the faculty into two or more autonomous faculties would not be in the best interests of the university. It acknowledged, however, that the natural scientists needed relief from the continual conflict with the social scientists. This could be achieved by setting up distinct councils, each headed by an associate dean, within the wider framework of the arts and science faculty.[7] The faculty would still constitute one unit, but each component would have more autonomy to set policy and look after its own affairs.

Physicist Joseph Wolfson submitted a minority report. As he put it, the majority of task force members recognized that the "present marriage [was] not a happy one, but [recoiled] from the therapy of divorce." Most of the opposition to separation had been prompted by a desire to preserve the liberal arts education policy contained in the Regina Beach Statement. Wolfson commented that while

> no honorable person of good will could possibly find fault with the Policy ... it surely must be realized that it means different things to different people, and it is interpreted by each according to his interests. To some it is a very useful weapon; one simply states that a proposal not to one's liking is in violation of the Policy and forthwith the proposal is defeated. But more than this, the Policy is a magic cloak which provides sure immunity against attack. Like some medieval knight holding out the cross to ward off evil, the wearer presents his own proposals for approval, secure in the knowledge that nobody would be so foolhardy as to attack one manifestly as holy as he. To those skilled in its use the policy is indeed both invincible armament and impenetrable armor.[8]

Regina Beach, according to Wolfson, had acquired a symbolic status beyond its literal meaning. It had become a touchstone and talisman, a receptacle for the hopes and dreams of the campus. When the tape recordings of the discussions that took place at the 1963 Regina Beach retreat went missing, Smythe hinted darkly that they had been deliberately destroyed. Only a conspiracy could account for the disappearance of records that were charged with such value and meaning.[9]

Wolfson claimed that the fragile unity of the Faculty of Arts and Science was doomed. He thought that his colleagues in the social sciences, humanities, and fine arts did not fully accept the natural sciences as a liberal art. As evidence he pointed to the fact that natural science majors were expected to take a number of classes in other divisions, but non-science majors had to take only one science class. Consequently, most BA graduates were, from a scientific point of view, illiterate. The supposedly broad-based education promised in the Regina Beach Statement was, in his estimation, largely a fiction. He said that he favoured breadth and interdisciplinarity in the undergraduate program, but to achieve it he did not think it was necessary to preserve the formal unity of the Faculty of Arts and Science. The objective could be secured though informal dialogue among the various departmental units. Indeed, the forced marriage of arts and science produced more ill will than friendly co-operation. Of one thing Wolfson was certain. The status quo was intolerable, and eventually the scientists would have their own faculty: "It must be written somewhere that those who refuse to face facts eventually face disaster."[10]

Concurrently with the task force, the Faculty of Arts and Science appointed a committee to evaluate the division system. It sent out a questionnaire soliciting the opinions of faculty members on how they thought the system was working. Only three of twenty-six respondents in the natural sciences said that they were satisfied with the divisional structure. This compared with twenty-two of twenty-seven in the social sciences, ten of seventeen in the humanities, and five of eleven in the fine arts. The comments of faculty members reflected a wide range of opinion. In answer to the question "In the Division where you are appointed, what does the Divisional system mean in practical terms to you?" one wrote, "It means closer contact and cooperation between disciplines than would otherwise be the case. It fosters interdisciplinary planning and class development." Another said, "An annoying and unnecessary step in the process of approval of programs and procedures."

Supporters of the division system were effusive in their praise. They regarded it as "the most optimal setting for grass-roots democracy I've yet encountered," and "an indispensable tool for the exploration and implementation of change in the academic field." The critics were harsh: "Give it a decent burial – R.I.P."; it is "the source of a good amount of frustration and irritation." Asked if they favoured "continuing the Divisional system as it now stands," thirty-nine respondents said that they were either "very much in favor" or "on the whole in favor," thirty-six said they were "very much opposed" or "on the whole opposed," and fourteen gave no answer.[11] Judging from this, the Faculty of Arts and Science was split into two factions of almost equal size.

The divisional system committee, chaired by Dallas Smythe, proposed three changes designed to ease the situation. The first was to allow divisions more autonomy and flexibility in how they organized their internal operations. It was acknowledged that some divisions might want to have individual, self-contained departments while others preferred to function in a more integrated fashion. Each division needed the freedom to choose the mode of operations that suited it best. To this end, it was recommended that "subject committees" be officially recognized as "departments." The second change was to provide more autonomy for divisions vis-à-vis the Faculty of Arts and Science. Within a broad policy framework, each division was to "develop its own classes and courses of study, and develop and administer its own budget and recruiting activities" without having to bring these matters to the faculty as a whole. The third change was to strengthen the coordinating capacity of the dean's office by appointing associate deans (formerly division chairmen) to preside over each division and to serve as members of the Dean's Executive Committee. It was hoped that this committee could resolve many matters of concern to the divisions before they came to a full meeting of the Faculty of Arts and Science. This would make the meetings more efficient by eliminating the frustrating work of developing solutions to complex problems in a large group.

The Faculty of Arts and Science adopted the committee's report on 9 July 1968.[12] Although the unity of the faculty had been preserved, the division system had been significantly altered and diluted in order to appease the natural scientists. Departments were now stronger, and divisions had more autonomy. At Van Cleave's insistence, the Division of Natural Sciences and Mathematics was given the right to determine its own curriculum and degree requirements for majors and honours students within the area of science and mathematics and the right to refer such matters directly to Campus Council for approval without going through the Faculty of Arts and Science. In addition, the associate dean of science and mathematics (formerly the chairman of the Division of Natural Sciences and Mathematics) enjoyed full membership in the Committee of Deans and Directors.[13]

Smythe and his supporters had lost the battle to keep the natural sciences closely integrated within a larger arts and science framework. The creation of a separate faculty of science was now just a matter of time. Wolfson summed up the situation on 15 March 1973: "It is true of course that our most serious grievances, viz. those concerned with curricula, were redressed to a large extent by the reorganization of 1968. Nevertheless we do not possess that degree of autonomy which status of a faculty confers, with its attendant rights and responsibilities for determining its own goals, and therefore its organization, operation and curricula, consistent with its obligations to the entire university community."[14] In a referendum held in April 1973 the members of the Division of Natural Sciences and Mathematics voted 52 to 8 for a separate faculty of science,[15] and the final break came in 1974.

From 1968 onward the battle for Regina Beach gradually moved from the larger arena of the Faculty of Arts and Science to the smaller one of the Division of Social Sciences. The factional struggle that had torn apart the Faculty of Arts and Science was reproduced on a smaller scale. The social sciences division had always been the unit of the university most committed to the principles of Regina Beach. It had promoted the idea of divisional, as opposed to departmental, majors, and, more than any other division, it had fostered interdisciplinary studies. Now it was the last holdout. But even there the influence of Smythe and his supporters had begun to diminish. As we shall see in the next chapter, the final denouement coincided with the last hurrah of the radical student movement.

It is evident in hindsight that the radical element at Regina campus was in retreat by 1969, but it did not appear that way at the time. Conservative and moderate groups in the wider community expressed unease about what was going on, or what they thought was going on, at the university. The Regina Chamber of Commerce in 1970 published a report, "The Role of the University in the Community," declaring that some members of the faculty had a left-wing bias. It accused these professors of using "legitimate dissent" as a cover to incite riots and "orgies of destruction."[16] A group called the Responsible Citizens' Committee, organized in 1970 with the assistance of the Saskatchewan Employers' Association, went even further. It reported that faculty members were "counseling the whole spectrum of sexual activity in their classes."[17] As they did during the *Carillon* crisis of 1968–69, political issues became entangled with instinctive reactions against shifting sexual mores and the excesses of the counterculture. The Responsible Citizens' Committee had a strong supporter in Regina police chief Arthur G. Cookson, who attributed student unrest to "an international conspiracy of leftists who operate through the university." He sounded the alarm: "Anything I've heard here – revolution is the only answer – the people will rule – these are stock slogans. I'm satisfied it's an international organization. They're left of the left, Maoists quarreling with Leninists and Marxists, I think it's a matter to be concerned with. They're undermining our youth, clouding their brains with drugs."[18]

Another critic was Roy H. Bailey, a graduate of Regina campus and a school principal in the town of Bengough in southeast Saskatchewan. He posed the question in the *Weyburn Review* in November 1969 "Is the university the right place to send your children?" He said that students at the Regina campus were being told that everything their parents had taught them was "phony," and that parents had no right to place restrictions on the behaviour of young people, "particularly against sexual desires." According to Bailey, one professor had devoted an entire lecture to "ridiculing the sacred institution of marriage," while another had attempted to prove that God is merely the product of man's imagination. He had first-hand evidence of Communist activity: "I watched Maoist students fly the Viet Cong flag. I've seen the left-wing element demonstrate their desires and sing the Communist anthem. Good? Allow them their freedom, but remember they would deny freedom to any one in opposition to their doctrine."[19]

Riddell worried that such articles damaged the image of the university and discouraged parents from sending their children to Regina campus. In November 1969 he asked Edgar Vaughan, dean of arts and science, to take action to correct the situation: "It appears high time that some evidence be forthcoming that the situation in the Social Sciences is being brought under control ... If the Social Sciences cannot put their house in order I think the Faculty as a whole should do so."[20] Vaughan replied cautiously that although the problems could not be solved overnight, "we hope by constant vigilance gradually to reduce if not eliminate irresponsibility in the classroom." At the same time, he said, it was not a good idea to ban from "the classroom the

TABLE 12: Analysis of Regina Campus Faculty by Nationality, 1971

FACULTY	TOTAL	CANADIAN	USA	OTHER (English-speaking	OTHER (non-English speaking
Administration	22	15 (68%)	4 (18%)	1 (5%)	2 (9%)
Arts and science	257	137 (53%)	58 (21%)	38 (15%)	24 (11%)
Engineering	7	6 (85%)	0	1 (15%)	0
Education	73	55 (76%)	12 (16%)	3 (4%)	3 (4%)
Total	369	222 (60%)	73 (20%)	45 (12%)	29 (8%)

Source: University of Regina Archives, Office of the University Secretary Files, 78.5, 307.0, "Analysis of Faculty by Nationality," 15 March 1971.

presentation of radical views of God, Sex [*sic*], marriage, the Church, or any other human concept or institution." It was important, however, that such views be "part of a bona-fide academic treatment of the subject matter of the particular class." It would be improper "to introduce a discussion that was not germane to the content and objectives of the particular class," and controversial topics should be presented in a balanced way, with due attention paid to accepted views. Further, "no instructor should penalize a student for defending the status quo any more than we would expect an instructor to penalize a student for his unorthodoxy."[21]

The general public often linked campus radicalism with the influx of American professors who had left home because they opposed the Vietnam War, some of whom were draft dodgers. Minister of Education J. Clifford McIsaac in November 1970 asked the principal for a report on this matter. McIsaac said that he was repeatedly asked about it, "on two occasions following political meetings and on two occasions by students who approached me."[22] As table 12 indicates, 20 per cent of the Regina faculty in 1971 were American, 20 per cent were of another foreign nationality, and 60 per cent were Canadian. Americans constituted 34 per cent of the Division of Social Sciences faculty, 43 per cent were Canadian, and 23 per cent were of other foreign nationalities.

Most of the hiring at Regina campus occurred at a time when universities across Canada were growing rapidly and qualified professors were in short supply. In the country as a whole, fully 80 per cent of new academic appointments in 1968 went to non-Canadians.[23] But whereas larger and more established universities readily absorbed the newcomers into the existing academic culture, newer institutions, such as Regina campus, were less able to do so. The impact of non-Canadian professors was therefore proportionally greater. That being said, many of the Americans who found employment at Regina campus were neither radical nor left wing in their political beliefs. They came to find jobs and advance their careers, not to make a statement against American government policies. Regina campus radicalism cannot be explained solely, or even primarily, by the presence of academics from the United States. There were other contributing factors, such as the political culture of the province, the rapid growth of the campus, the lack of stabilizing traditions, the high ratio of arts and science students relative to students enrolled in professional colleges, and the rather bleak and overcrowded physical environment. The notion that anti–Vietnam War draft dodgers shaped the radical character of Regina campus was a largely a myth.

Critics of Regina campus radicalism in the 1960s raised questions about a perceived decline in academic standards. Principal Riddell in November 1968 held a small gathering at this home to which he invited Alwyn Berland, Dallas Smythe, and few other senior administrators. He related various rumours that were making the rounds in the city, such as the story about an "instructor in Sociology [who] had announced to her class that there would be no examinations; that they would all get a grade point of 2 (the equivalent of a C) unless they wished a higher grade [in] which case they would have to do one paper." Riddell also reported that "some instructor, I believe in Psychology, had instructed the class to go to some downtown store and steal something in order to see what it feels like to be a thief."[24]

In response to such complaints, the Faculty of Arts and Science in February 1969 set up a committee to look into the grading practices of various departments.[25] The campus at the time used a five-point grade scale in which a two was roughly equivalent to a C, or 65 per cent. The committee assumed that the normal average for an introductory class was in the range of 1.6 to 2.4. It found, however, that grade-point averages in some departments were considerably higher than in others. The average for Anthropology 100 in the 1960 winter semester was 3.6; in Political Science 100, 3.4; and in Social Science 100, 4.8.

The committee acknowledged that there was disagreement among faculty members over what grading should accomplish. Some thought that it should "evaluate individual self-development," while others adopted the more conventional view that it should measure student performance against objective standards of academic achievement. The committee realistically observed, "as long as our society continues to be competitive and selective, faculty members will be asked to make comparative evaluations among students." It recommended that average grades for all large first-year classes fall within the range of 1.6 to 2.4. While there could be no ironclad rule, because there was always the possibility of an exceptionally good or an exceptionally poor class,

TABLE 13: Grading System with Equivalent Values, Regina Campus

SIX-POINT SCALE	VERBAL DESCRIPTION	LETTER GRADE	PERCENTAGE GRADE
5	outstanding	A+	95
4	very good	A	85
3	good	B	75
2	satisfactory	C	65
1	poor	D	55
0	unsatisfactory	F	less than 50

Source: University of Regina Archives, College/Faculty of Arts and Science, University of Saskatchewan, Regina Campus Files, 85-54, 104-13, "Report to Committee on Grading System," 18 April 1966.

TABLE 14: Class Averages in Selected First-Year Courses, Regina Campus, 1969 Winter Semester

COURSE	CLASS AVERAGE
Anthropology 100	3.6
Biology 100	1.5
Chemistry 100	1.5
Economics 100	1.8
History 100	2.0
Physics 100	2.1
Political Science 100	3.4
Psychology 100	2.2
Social Science 100	4.8
Sociology 100	3.6

Source: University of Regina Archives, College/Faculty of Arts and Science, University of Saskatchewan, Regina Campus Files, 85-54, 104-13, "Interim Report of Committee on Grading," 16 April 1969.

the norm was to be adhered to over the long term. The Faculty of Arts and Science adopted the report on 2 June 1969, and the more unconventional grading practices began to be phased out.[26]

By the spring of 1969 the various problems and controversies besetting the campus reached a crescendo. The dispute about grading practices, the *Carillon* crisis, the uproar in the Faculty of Education over the leadership of the dean, the strife between the social sciences division and the natural sciences and mathematics division, the controversy concerning the direction of the athletics program, the tensions between the conservatory and the Department of Music, the delays in launching a school of social work, the derailing of the college system, the obstacles to building a student residence, and the postponement of the construction of an engineering/physics building – all these issues bore down on Riddell and led him to consider resigning as principal. He took the step on 25 March 1969, confessing in a letter to President Spinks that he was "near the point of nervous and physical exhaustion." He hoped that "a younger person might provide more vigorous leadership and might understand the aspirations of younger faculty and students better than I can." His resignation letter, without going into specifics, alluded to areas of conflict within and between departments. It mentioned also "the spectre of student unrest that will arise from time to time in acute form even though the local situation is quiet at present."[27]

Although Riddell was still three years away from normal retirement age, the Board of Governors accepted his resignation at its meeting in Saskatoon on 2 April 1969. He found it disturbing that after the meeting adjourned no one spoke to him or expressed regret that he was stepping down. In Regina the reaction was quite different. As Riddell recorded in his diary, "a number expressed regret and others expressed appreciation for what I had done over the years. All indicated that they understood why I had made the decision and wondered how I had carried on as long as I did."[28] Several faculty members wrote letters expressing their gratitude for the leadership he had given during a crucial phase in the history of the university.[29]

Professor Les Crossman of the Department of English delivered a tribute at a meeting of the Faculty of Arts and Science. He recalled that when Riddell had been appointed dean of Regina College, in 1950, the full-time teaching staff had numbered less than twenty and the students less than two hundred. Faculty members rode the streetcar to work, and even the students "somehow got along without cars." College life was uncomplicated compared to what it would become: "'Square' meant simply honest or having four equal sides and a right angle ... 'hippy' meant thick in the hips, 'grass' a poem by Carl Sandburg, or what grew (if it rained) in Lakeview, 'groovy' had it meant anything, might have meant wrinkled; 'cool' was a word used to describe, with suitable understatement, a day in mid January, or the look you got from Miss Belcher when your French assignment was not done; 'pot' was something you made stew in, or worried about in middle age; or got up at night to set the baby on."[30]

By 1969 Regina campus had over 300 faculty members and over 4,000 students. Riddell had steered the transition from college to university during a period of immense upheaval and social change. He had presided over the recruitment of staff, the development of programs, and the planning and construction of the new campus. Crossman also acknowledged Riddell's personal qualities: "You have not known the man Riddell until you have played golf with him or discussed his stereo set (or yours) with him or borrowed a

The installation of John H. Archer as principal of the University of Saskatchewan, Regina Campus, 15 May 1970.

book from him or chatted with him about a play or a movie or a concert. It is on such informal occasions that the warmth, the sincerity, the humour, and the friendliness of the man are felt."[31]

John Hall Archer, who took over as principal in January 1970, was born in 1914 of English homesteader parents on a farm near Broadview, Saskatchewan. He attended normal school in Regina in 1932–33 and taught in rural schools until 1940, when he enlisted in the Royal Canadian Artillery. Commissioned from the ranks, he graduated at the top of his class in the Officer Training Unit in England.[32] He served in the United Kingdom, Africa, and Italy, rising to the rank of captain. In later years he was made honorary colonel of the Tenth Field Regiment, Royal Canadian Artillery. After the war, he resumed his post-secondary education, earning a BA in 1947, an MA in history in 1948 (both from the University of Saskatchewan), and a degree in library science from McGill University in 1949. He held the posts of Saskatchewan legislative librarian from 1951 to 1964 and assistant clerk of the legislature and provincial archivist from 1956 to 1961. He played a key role in organizing Saskatchewan's highly successful golden jubilee celebrations in 1955. On a visit to Rideau Hall in connection with planning the event, he signed the guest book with characteristic flourish: "Archer of Broadview."[33] In

1964 he became director of libraries at McGill and in 1967 university archivist and associate professor of history at Queen's, where he earned a PhD in history in 1969.[34]

Archer was by nature an optimist, and those who knew him best noticed that he was "very seldom critical and never cynical."[35] He outlined his views on campus unrest in a speech to the Regina Kiwanis Club on 8 June 1970, admonishing those who were "most properly upset and uptight over some non-Scrabble words that get into the *Carillon*" that 85 per cent of the students at the campus "come from Saskatchewan homes and they know the words when they come!" He interpreted the generation gap as a clash of values. His generation had measured progress in terms of material things: "in a debt-free farm or store; in all taxes paid and money in the bank; in education for our children; in better machinery, a car, a radio and good clothes for Sunday." "Isn't it a shocker," he said, "when your own children appraise with candid eyes the things you have earned with hard work and sweat, and find these things unworthy or old-fashioned!" He described the youth of the sixties as "the brightest, best prepared and most sensitive generation that has ever been admitted to our universities," adding that it was a "sad thing, a terrible tragedy that we in the universities have spent so much time trying to produce graduates in our own image, when the world cries out for people conversant with new problems. We have not made so great and glorious a success of solving the problems of war, pollution, racial tensions that we can be complacent." Archer closed the speech on a personal note: "If we must enforce a rigid regimen and forbid free expression, we have all failed – for these are my young people, too. I perhaps know them better than you do. I see them, young and aggressive, better prepared for life than were you or I at their age, more sophisticated, more conscious of the world around them, capable of greater things than we were." The last sentence was almost a prayer: "Grant us understanding of their problems – and grant them compassion as they seek to make worthwhile the society we leave to them."[36]

When Archer had finished speaking, a member of the audience, Justice R.L. Brownridge, stood up and declared that he did not want to see "every hoodlum who parades under a university banner defended by university professors ... Let's not be the first generation to run up the white flag. Let's not defend the indefensible ... Thank God for Spiro Agnew" (vice-president of the United States under Richard Nixon).[37] Archer held his ground. He insisted that the troublemakers – "anarchists, nihilists, and drug pushers" – were a very small minority, and that the vast majority of students were fine people. The *Carillon* took notice of Archer's performance in the lion's den of the Kiwanis Club. An editorial praised his speech and thanked him for putting in a good word for the students.[38]

The key to Archer's success with the student activists was that he genuinely admired their idealism, if not always their tactics. Where Riddell had sometimes reacted defensively to challenges to his authority, Archer adopted a more relaxed, benign attitude. At the same time, he did not allow the students to take advantage of him. A man who had faced German tanks in the Italian campaign was not likely to be intimidated by long-haired teenagers using four-letter words.

Radicalism among students at Regina campus in 1970 was at low ebb. "Take away the SRC types and the *Carillon* staffers," the student newspaper reported on 9 October 1970, "and the turnout at the Annual General meeting became five."[39] The meeting had to be postponed for lack of a quorum. A group of conservative students gave notice of a motion to be discussed at the general meeting rescheduled for 27 October 1970: "Be it resolved that the student body of the University of Saskatchewan, Regina Campus demand a cessation of political activities and expenditures of student funds for partisan political causes by the SRC. We further demand that the SRC operate as a non-partisan, non-political organization having only the students' welfare as their reason for existence."[40]

For the old radicals this was a backward step – they believed that the promotion of the welfare of students was by its very nature a political activity. Student Ed Holgate, in "This Union Is a Political Union," advised those who disagreed with the stands taken by the SRC to elect councillors sympathetic with their own political viewpoint rather than try to turn the clock back to when the SRC did nothing more than "plan dances and college home-comings."[41] The motion was fiercely debated at the general meeting, but before it could be voted on the quorum had disappeared.[42] There was a general feeling on campus that the glory days of the student movement were over. A jaded *Carillon* columnist lamented, "our time was the sixties and they are passed,"[43] while another noted sardonically that in 1970 "even the lefties went back to class determined to get those degrees."[44]

In September 1970 the Regina Beach Statement, the very emblem of dissent from orthodoxy, came under direct attack. Professor Frans Rummens of the chemistry department introduced a motion at a faculty meeting to form a committee "for the purpose of assessing the relevance of the so-called Liberal Arts Education Policy as presently worded in the academic calendar for the Faculty of Arts and Science with a view towards alterations (in clear English!), or removal as dictated by present-day thinking and practices."[45] The motion passed on the condition that it would not go into effect until there had been a full semester of public discussion of the issue "through the medium of *The Carillon* or any other appropriate medium."[46] Lyn Goldman, campus public relations officer, urged the dean of arts and science not to open this "Pandora's Box." She said that it could jeopardize "the small degree of stability we have gained over the past few years." As for the claim that the Regina Beach Statement needed to be rewritten "in clear English," she commented that it was "the only piece of good writing" in the calendar.[47]

The *Carillon* on 30 October 1970 published a letter from Dean Vaughan inviting contributions to a debate on liberal arts policy. He expressed his personal view that the general principles in the Regina Beach Statement were "unexceptional" and harmless, but that the "phraseology" might be improved. Vaughan objected in particular to the term "Liberal Arts Education," which he thought did not do justice to the natural sciences. A title such as "the Educational Policy of the Faculty of Arts and Science" would be more inclusive. He also wanted to replace expressions like "intellectual slum clearance" and "mindless counting" with "more understandable terms," and he hoped to delete the introductory quotation attributed to Socrates ("the unexamined life is not worth living"), though he did not say what was wrong with it.[48]

The invitation to participate in the debate elicited minimal response. Students had little to say, and faculty members only slightly more. Rummens, who had initiated the motion to revise the statement, provided a thorough critique. Like Vaughan, he thought the natural sciences were being slighted. In addition, he wanted more emphasis on "increasing" knowledge, as distinct from merely "preserving" and "transmitting" it. He called for explicit acknowledgment of the mission of faculty members to conduct "scholarly work, research and graduate studies." Rummens characterized the literary style of the Regina Beach Statement as "a quaint hybrid of Jugend-Stil romanticism and hippy-generated jargon of the Sixties." What, he asked, was meant by "essential human values." "Why single out human values? Is the rest of the Universe not equally important?" As far as Rummens was concerned, the talk of "love, justice, freedom and beauty" was just "naïve motherhood rhetoric."[49] Physics professor Jaroslav Pachner could not have agreed more: "It seems to me to be necessary either to define exactly what has to be understood under the nature of love, justice, freedom and beauty (as I see it, there exist only different opinions on those concepts, but no way at all to find out what is their nature) or to omit those unscientific terms."[50]

Dallas Smythe rallied to the defence of Regina Beach. Although willing to modify some of the phrases, he insisted on retaining the essential meaning of the original. He summarized these "essentials" as the obligation of the arts and science faculty "to the larger community and to its students to be a critic of the status quo"; the obligation of the scientist "to be skeptical of received doctrine and 'facts' if he would be more than obedient technologist"; an emphasis on the "study of values"; the need for students and faculty alike to try to "synthesize and give meaning to their intellectual activity"; a constant critique of the "structure and functioning of the University itself";

"a skeptical attitude toward conventional myths about the University, about science and about scholarship"; and the recognition "that education is an active process in which the capacity to evaluate the context and point of view are possibly more important than the capacity to 'absorb' facts."[51]

Smythe no longer had the influence on campus that he had once wielded. His words went unheeded, and in December 1971 the Faculty of Arts and Science approved a new arts and science education policy statement for insertion in the calendar:

I. The members of the Faculty of Arts and Science believe in a university whose purpose is the preservation, transmission, interpretation and enhancement of the cultural heritage of man, and the acquisition and expansion of new knowledge and understanding.

II. They seek to fulfill this purpose by interpreting the past, examining and clarifying contemporary thinking and anticipating the possibilities of the future. Their efforts should be sustained by sensitivity to change, and an enthusiasm for investigation and creativity.

III. The Faculty derives its strength from a unity of purpose combined with a diversity of outlook which requires it to examine every facet of life and uphold the higher human values implicit in the arts, the humanities and the sciences. The Faculty will serve the needs of society but, in so doing, it will also be society's critic, encouraging independent thinking, free discussion and the pursuit of truth.

IV. The Faculty is jealous of its freedom, which it will exercise without fear or favor, promoting in its members and students the spirit of courageous enquiry.

V. The Faculty recognizes that the constitution and function of the university itself should be open to re-examination by the academic community as whole. The Faculty maintains that to serve society best the university must be self-determining in academic matters.[52]

Faint echoes of the original Regina Beach Statement could still be detected, but it was a bland document, a pale version of its former self. It lacked the coherent philosophy and bold spirit of the original. "Examining and clarifying contemporary thinking" was not as strong as "above all, the role of critic, examiner of institutions and ideas, belongs to the modern university functioning as a community of scholars." Upholding "the higher human values implicit in the arts, the humanities and the sciences" was weak in comparison with "a deliberate renewal of the study of the nature of love, of justice, freedom, beauty, science: in fact, all those values which give meaning and substance to life." And such ringing declarations as "above all the idea, the general context, the point of view is what should be transmitted to the student" and "the professor is charged with the responsibility of opening and of sustaining a dialogue with the student; the student must be encouraged to see that his relationship to the educational process, and to the dialogue, is not that of exposure merely, but of involvement" had been dispensed with.

The Regina Beach Statement, though set in the context of the 1960s, was actually part of a much older debate about the nature and purpose of liberal education. Historian Bruce Kimball has developed a typology that helps us sort out what people are saying when they make various claims on this subject. He posits two distinct schools of thought; one he calls the "oratorical" and the other, the "philosophical." Each is an abstract, ideal type, and neither is to be understood as providing a complete description of liberal education in a particular historical setting. Each type represents a general pattern, a cluster of ideas, and a stream of thought. Although this framework does not explain everything, it is useful for analyzing the liberal arts discussions at Regina in the 1960s.[53]

The oratorical tradition emphasizes general education as preparation for the duties of citizenship. It assumes that truth can be known and expressed, and that classical texts provide insight into the nature of truth and goodness. The responsibility of the individual for the well-being of the community is given priority over the freedom of the individual to pursue his or her own goals. The philosophical ideal, however, exalts the freedom to search for truth, an "endeavour that liberates the mind from the chains of its shadowy cave of ignorance." It is characterized by critical skepticism, systematic doubt, tolerance of other viewpoints, and individual fulfillment. The pursuit of truth is valued for its own sake; it is an eternal quest that never attains its goal. Kimball argues that the philosophical ideal (which he also calls the "liberal-free" ideal) has become the ruling paradigm in modern universities. From the late nineteenth century onward, the natural sciences assumed an increasingly dominant position, and scientific techniques were applied to an ever-widening area of investigation, including the social sciences. This led to increasing specialization, departmentalization, and fragmentation of the university curriculum.[54]

The Regina Beach Statement was at heart a revival of the oratorical tradition. It triggered a multi-faceted debate concerning the relative merits of general education and specialization; community service and the ivory tower; academic freedom and relevant research; socially useful knowledge and the pursuit of truth for its own sake; individualism and the common good; essential human values and technological progress; Karl Marx and Adam Smith; conservatives and liberals. The debate was too complicated to be reduced to a simple dichotomy of left and right. It is better understood as a contest between "orators" and "philosophers."

At the root of the debate lies our society's concept of the highest good. Is it knowable truth expressed in active citizenship, as the orators would have it, or is it the freedom to search for truth without necessarily finding it, as the philosophers believe? Each taken by itself as the sole principle guiding liberal education is unsatisfactory. The critical skepticism and open-mindedness of the liberal-free ideal can lead to excessive individualism, unbridled technology, and the dissolution of community standards. The orator's conviction that the truth is known and has only to be taught can give rise to dogmatism, rigidity, and the denial of academic freedom. Nor can the two ideals be happily blended to combine their assets and cancel out their deficiencies, since the strength of each ideal is also the source of its greatest weakness. This is the paradox at the heart of liberal education, and there is no way to resolve the conundrum. The best we can hope to do is maintain a balance between the two, recognizing that this is not a completely satisfactory solution to the problem. The worst situation is the total domination of one ideal over the other. The great value of the Regina Beach Statement was that it reminded us of the importance of general education grounded in essential human values as a preparation for the rights and responsibilities of citizenship. As Dallas Smythe wrote, the death of the liberal arts "will only be inevitable if and because a succession of people make mistaken decisions to identify the university with the short term interests of the technological order."[55]

16 Parity and the Legacy of the 1960s

While most students at Regina campus in the fall of 1972 displayed no symptoms of revolutionary zeal, a radical minority became more extreme in their views. In the Students' Union elections the preceding spring a group calling itself the United Socialists had fielded a full slate of candidates. Its goal was the "revitalization of the student movement on campus," and its platform had three main planks: the creation of a "women's liberation university"; the expulsion of "war makers" from the campus; and the reform of the structures of university government. The first item involved the repeal of abortion laws, the expansion of the facilities of the women's centre, and the creation of a women's studies department. The second plank was aimed at employers such as the Defence Research Board of Canada, which held recruiting drives and conducted job interviews on campus. The United Socialists called for a halt to all university involvement in war-related activities and a refocusing of academic research to "serve the needs of the people: the labor unions, the Farmers' Union, anti-pollution groups, tenants organizations, the women's movements and, most importantly, the organizations of the Indian and Metis people of this province."[1]

Finally, the radicals demanded the abolition of the senate and Board of Governors and their replacement with a governing body controlled by students, faculty, and support staff. The goal was to end the alleged stranglehold of "agri-business and industrial firms" over the university. Running under the slogan "Kick big business off campus!!! Education for the people, not for profit!!!"[2] the entire slate of United Socialists went down in defeat in the elections. Bob Lyons, the leader of the group, contested a by-election in October 1972 for the office of external vice-president and lost to his opponent, Larry Day, by a vote of 625 to 140. Lyons was probably correct in his assessment that the defeat "reflected the political level of the students."[3]

The Students' Union annual general meeting in the fall of 1972 had to be postponed twice for lack of a quorum. As the *Carillon* put it, "Student apathy was alive and well."[4] When the meeting was finally held, on 16 November 1972, a constitutional amendment was approved that did away with the Students' Representative Council and replaced it with a students' council, which would hold meetings every two weeks to deal with the business of the union. All students were welcome to attend the meetings, and everyone had full speaking and voting rights.[5] The stated purpose of the change was to democratize the union by transferring power from the representative council to the entire membership, but since most students were not interested in student politics, the actual effect was quite the opposite. Power shifted to the small group of radicals who were willing to attend meetings. They, together with the elected five-person executive (president, external vice-president, internal vice-president, academics chairman, and secretary-treasurer), ended up running the union.[6]

The constitutional amendment did nothing to revive interest in student politics. Only 665 out of 3,641 registered students (18 per cent) bothered to vote in the annual elections for student offices on 15 February 1974. This compared with 40 per cent in 1967 – which, by the standards of the early 1960s, when participation had been as high as 75 per cent, was a poor turnout.[7] The winner of the Students' Union president vote was Marv Mochoruk, who received 210 votes, followed closely by Tom Turkey (a fictitious candidate) with 174 votes.[8]

As the Students' Union degenerated into a narrow insider group, the *Carillon* came under the control of radicals who were disengaged from the day-to-day concerns of students and caught up in the struggles of a variety of off-campus groups. The paper mounted a campaign against the provincial government's curtailment of the collective bargaining rights of labour unions, and it supported a number of strikes, including those at the Sherwood Co-op and the Parkside Nursing Home in Regina.[9] Many articles were devoted to agricultural issues and the campaign of the National Farmers' Union to boycott Kraft products.[10] There were also exposés of the unethical practices of Regina's slumlords.[11] These issues, however worthy of serious investigation, were not uppermost in the minds of the great majority of *Carillon* readers. On the political front, the paper supported the Waffle, the radical New Left faction that emerged within the NDP in 1969. Don Mitchell, a former Students' Union president, ran as the Waffle candidate for the leadership of the Saskatchewan NDP in 1970.[12] Though he lost to Allan Blakeney, Mitchell did surprisingly well, obtaining 22 per cent of the vote on the first ballot.[13] The *Carillon* relentlessly attacked the right-wing Thatcher government (liberal in name only), which had been elected in 1964 and re-elected in 1967. It celebrated the government's defeat in June 1971 with the headline "Twilight of the Gods: Colonel Thatcher's Storm Troops Reduced to Corporal's Guard."[14]

Students who disliked the *Carillon*'s editorial policy made their views known at the annual meeting of the Students' Union in October 1971.[15] They circulated a petition demanding the impeachment of the editor and obtained over 250 signatures in an hour.[16] The *Carillon* branded its opponents "right-wing freaks from the professional colleges" who were afraid that the radical reputation of the campus would hurt their chances of getting a job when they graduated. The paper scorned such petty motives: "We are out to smash capitalism, and we mean business."[17] *Carillon* staffers in 1973 proclaimed their journalistic creed: "*The Carillon* is a newspaper whose present members share A COMMON interpretation of the weaknesses in their society. We are critical of the all-pervasive influence of the profit motive and its insidious distortion of human values. We believe private profit should be outlawed since it promotes disregard for fellow human beings and creates inequalities that cause unnecessary suffering and hardship given the present technological achievements of humankind."[18]

The radicals' insistence on ideological purity alienated the broad mass of students. Their influence was further weakened as a result of tactical concessions made by the university administration to increase the level of student participation in university decision making. This satisfied most students – those who wanted to have their voices heard but had no wish to run the university. The radicals dismissed the measures as mere tokenism, which only served to widen the gap between the extremist minority and the moderate majority.

The process of increasing student involvement in decision making began as early as January 1965, when the Board of Governors set up a committee to review the relationship of the Student Representative Councils on the two campuses to the university as a whole.[19] When nothing substantial emerged from the review, the Regina campus Students' Union put forward a proposal of its own. It passed a resolution on 15 January 1967 calling for open meetings of the Campus Council, senate, and Board of Governors.[20] SRC president Don Mitchell's presentation to the board in support of the proposal got a cool reception. At one point in the proceedings President Spinks accused the student president of "ungentlemanly behavior." The remark caught Mitchell off guard, and he let it pass. However, a few days later he wrote to Spinks seeking an explanation: "It is one thing to direct allegations towards another person during the course of a private meeting or conversation at which time such remarks can be challenged and refuted, or else evidence produced to back them up. It is quite another thing I suspect to direct remarks of a personal or derogatory nature to a participant in a meeting intended for non-personal business particularly when those present are not familiar with the circumstances or personalities alluded to ... Without questioning your authority to reprimand me (a mere student), I do question the timing of your action and the basis for it."[21] Spinks replied that his choice of words was justified. He said that Mitchell was not a gentleman because he had failed to reprimand the *Carillon* for its criticism of the university administration (that is, Spinks.) Apparently, it was Mitchell's job to control the student newspaper.[22]

Despite this inauspicious beginning, the university administration understood the value of including students in decision making. President Spinks stated in July 1968 that as a matter of policy "the administration should maintain the initiative" in this area. He recommended the establishment of joint faculty-student committees on each campus and in each college. "Such a move on our part," he calculated, "would place the administration in a strong position in dealing with unreasonable student protests and demonstrations."[23] Principal Riddell distributed a memo to the Regina campus faculty on 12 September 1968 urging "that discussions be held with individual students or groups of students to discover how they believe they could effectively participate."[24] In accordance with this general directive, students were invited, in somewhat haphazard fashion, to join a number of committees and councils at various levels of the campus administration.

A June 1970 survey revealed considerable disparity among academic departments with respect to student representation on decision-making bodies. The psychology and sociology departments had implemented full parity – that is, equal numbers of students and faculty with voting privileges attended all departmental meetings. The chairman of the sociology department reported that the system was working very well: "Our experience with the process so far has been productive. The student representatives have displayed considerable imagination in dealing with the Department and University problems. Their sense of honesty and responsibility is beyond reproach."[25] The meetings of the anthropology department were open to all students who wished to participate. Only two students were officially members, but, as the chairman of the department pointed out, "no votes are taken at meetings and we proceed on the basis of consensus [so] formal membership tends to have little meaning."[26] The drama department appointed three student representatives, who were regarded as "an important and vital part of its day-to-day functioning." According to the chairman, they had "accepted the responsibility totally and have done an excellent job in presenting their views and opinions."[27]

At the opposite end of the spectrum were the departments that had virtually no student representation. The Department of Mathematics said that it had received "no response from students to any invitations to discuss formal or informal participation in meetings."[28] The Department of Economics had the same experience,[29] and neither biology nor philosophy and classics had any student representatives.[30] Chemistry allowed four students to attend departmental meetings, but their attendance was sporadic – perhaps, as the department chairman surmised, "because of a conflict with studies."[31] The English department had one student representative, who attended as an observer without voting privileges,[32] while the history department allowed student participation in all matters except the budget and decisions about merit and promotion, hiring, or dismissal.[33] A common difficulty, one that was never fully resolved, was to find a suitable method for the selection of student representatives. While most departments left this up to the students, the modern languages department devised a complicated system involving elections in each class with representation weighted according to course level. Twelve representatives were chosen through a kind of electoral-college mechanism to serve as voting members at department meetings.[34]

Just as the level of student participation varied from department to department, so too did it vary among the four divisions in the Faculty of Arts and Science. The humanities division had no student representatives at all,[35] and in the natural sciences division participation was slight.[36] In fine arts students elected as representatives in individual departments were also eligible to attend divisional meetings.[37] The social sciences division had the most extensive student participation. Each department was permitted to elect student representatives to the division up to the number of full-time teaching faculty in the department. According to the bylaws of the division, membership in a department could be one of three types: A, B, or C. A members were instructors, lecturers, and professors assigned to the department; B members were faculty members from outside the discipline (at least two in number) elected annually by the division to serve as full members of the department; and C members were students no greater in number than the A members. C members were elected annually through procedures acceptable to the students. Members of the social sciences division, who were eligible to vote in meetings of the division, were either A members, C members, or sessional assistants not registered for a course of studies.[38]

The terms of membership in the Campus Council were laid out in the University Act. Since the administration and the SRC could not come to an agreement about how the act should be amended to provide for student participation, students attended council meetings on an informal basis. They were allowed to speak, and if a student wanted to introduce a motion, a faculty member could do so on his or her behalf.[39] The University Act was amended in 1970 to allow two students from each campus to sit on the senate, and in

1971 it was further amended to give one student from each campus a seat on the Board of Governors.[40] In this respect, the students had an advantage over the faculty, who did not have a representative on the board until 1974.

The issue of student participation in university governance became controversial in the social sciences division in 1972. The conflict originated in a motion passed at a meeting of the division on 5 April 1972 to set up a divisional guidelines committee with a mandate to "develop guidelines for program development during the period of budgetary retrenchment." The preamble to the motion stated that in the past, two basic approaches had been taken with respect to the curriculum and the organization of the division. The first was the "promotion of strong, relatively independent departments emphasizing abstract intellectualism"; the second was the "promotion of strong, interdisciplinary programs with a view to attacking concrete local, provincial and Canadian problems." The latter followed the spirit of the Regina Beach Statement; the former did not. The motion made it clear that the proposed divisional guidelines committee was expected to choose the Regina Beach approach and "ensure the further development of the divisional concept."[41]

Budget cutbacks and the prospect of faculty layoffs intensified the battle over the academic program. The more conservative faculty members suspected that the purpose of the guidelines committee was to come up with a rationale for firing professors who did not conform to the divisional concept. They feared an alliance between radical faculty and radical students to take control of the division, an apprehension seemingly borne out by the result of the vote on a motion to reconsider the decision to establish the guidelines committee. The motion failed by a vote of 42 to 36 (3 abstentions), with the student representatives in the division voting 7 in favour of reconsidering the motion and 19 against (4 abstentions).[42] It was obvious that the students had tipped the balance in favour of the pro-Regina Beach faculty.

The struggle resumed in the fall of 1972. On 27 October the division approved a resolution to amend the bylaws of the social science division to require departments to have equal numbers of students and faculty members on department councils. This was known as the parity principle. Up to this time parity had been optional rather than compulsory at the departmental level. The bylaw forced it on all departments in the Division of Social Sciences, whether or not they considered it good policy. The change would have the effect of increasing student representation at divisional meetings, since all students members of departments were also automatically members of the division. Given that most students who became involved in departmental politics had a radical orientation, their attendance at divisional meetings was bound to strengthen the pro-Regina Beach faction. To prevent this from happening, the dean of arts and science, Edgar Vaughan, ruled the motion

G. Edgar Vaughan, dean of arts and science, whose offices were occupied by student protesters from 16 to 22 November 1972.

to amend the division bylaws out of order. He said that departments had the right to determine their own membership, and the division had exceeded its authority in attempting to impose the parity formula on all departments.[43]

Vaughan believed that the drive to force parity on the three departments in the division that did not already have it – economics, history, and geography – was part of a larger plan to extend student power. A student confided to Principal Archer that activists had in their sights the humanities division, especially the large English department, where the faculty was split on the question of student representation.[44] The atmosphere in the social sciences division grew extremely tense, the frequent meetings, constant debate, and strained emotions taking their toll on faculty members.[45]

The crisis escalated when the students took direct action. At the annual general meeting of the Students' Union on 16 November 1972, a motion was approved to "oppose all University cutbacks, oppose cutbacks of faculty positions, sessional lecturers and lab assistants, support those staff members being cut, and oppose all fee increases." In addition, the following resolution was passed: "that the Students' Union demand the right to parity in all departments of the University including Social Sciences and that it censure the ruling of Sir Edgar Vaughan." (The students were not being sarcastic

– Vaughan had in fact been knighted for his services as a British diplomat in South America prior to his coming to Regina.) Finally it was moved and seconded that "this body as a whole go immediately to Sir Edgar Vaughan's office and deliver the motion of censure in person and demand he recind [*sic*] his ruling." The motion was never voted on; rather, as the minutes stated, "by general concensus [*sic*] of the student body (i.e. Student Union) present the motion was implemented and the meeting adjourned to reconvene in Sir Edgar's office at approximately 3 p.m. Thursday, November 16."[46]

About 200 students confronted the dean and demanded that he withdraw his veto.[47] When he refused they occupied the office and announced that if their demands were not met by the next day at noon they would take further action. In the meantime they issued a press release and made plans for a general meeting of students to be held the next day. They also collected money for sandwiches and coffee and arranged for the care and upkeep of the building they were occupying.[48] The general meeting on Friday, 17 November drew a crowd of about 1,000 students. Principal Archer gave a speech explaining that he would not be able to contact the university's lawyers until late afternoon for an opinion on the legality of Dean Vaughan's veto of the parity motion. The students extended their deadline to 7:00 p.m. Friday and then to Monday afternoon. Those attending the general meeting passed a resolution supporting the disruption of administrative services through the occupation of the dean's office, while classes continued as usual. There was no call for a student strike.

Principal Archer received a legal opinion from T.C. Wakeling on Monday, 20 November. The lawyer stated that according to the terms of the University Act, the department chairman had full responsibility for the operation of his department, subject only to the qualification that he "consult with the department in committee." Although the "department in committee" did not have binding authority, the department head almost always followed its recommendations. On the question of who had the right to serve on a department committee, Wakeling said that the framers of the act had probably assumed that only faculty members would serve, but he acknowledged that there was "nothing to clearly indicate this is the only interpretation." He argued that the senate, as the senior academic body, had overriding authority in the event that the department could not adequately resolve a disagreement relating to the membership of its committees, and since the senate had never by regulation or resolution dealt with the issue, Dean Vaughan was entitled to make his ruling. In Wakeling's opinion, it was appropriate to refer the dispute arising from the ruling to the senate, "which would then take the matter out of the hands of both the department and the Dean."[49]

Archer held a press conference the same day, at which he declared:

Students participating in the 1972 sit-in. Their goal was parity – that is, equal representation with faculty on the decision-making bodies of the university.

A student strategy session during the occupation. Principal John Archer defused the crisis by refraining from calling in the police and allowing the protest to fizzle out of its own accord.

> It is now clear that the University Act gives the Chairman of a department the responsibility for making decisions within both the academic and administrative spheres of his department. He may seek advice on all matters coming within his jurisdiction and I expect Chairmen to consult students as well as faculty members. But a Chairman is appointed by the Board and is responsible through the Principal to the Board. That is the situation under the University Act as it is today. Of course the Act can be changed and channels for change have always been, and are still, open. In order to effect such a change, a more adequate definition of parity would certainly be needed. If parity means the sharing of information and responsibility in all areas where students have a deep interest (such as courses, standards and discipline), then I would warmly support this ... If, however, parity means the simple tyranny of numbers where a majority in one department can impose their will upon the members of another department (against the expressed will of a majority of students in that department), then I am not for that. If, in order to achieve parity, it is necessary to contravene the University Act, I am not willing to do that. If those who seek what they regard as more adequate student representation are prepared to press for change through recognized channels, then I support that.[50]

Archer cited the legal opinion selectively and bent it to his own purposes. Wakeling had not claimed that the University Act would have to be changed in order for the students to have parity; he had said that the senate was the appropriate body to settle the matter. Archer framed the issue in such a way that his listeners were led to believe that there was a legal, as distinct from an administrative, barrier to parity. He encouraged students to work through "recognized channels" to have the University Act amended. Finally, he blurred the meaning of "parity," saying that he was all for it if it meant "the sharing of information and responsibility in all areas where students have a deep interest." This, of course, was not what the radicals meant when they used the term. Archer's strategy was to win over the majority of students who supported student participation in decision making but were not asking for equality with faculty on department committees. He reinforced this point in the conclusion to his statement: "But I do not think that students pay their fees and come to Regina campus in order to be given the task of running the university. They come to acquire knowledge and to learn the methods and techniques whereby they may continue to learn ... Regina campus has benefited immeasurably from the good work and sound advice received from the many students who serve on numerous important committees. I hope very much that a high level of cooperation and mutual respect will continue."[51]

The students occupying the dean's office were not satisfied with Archer's response. They passed a motion to "act as if parity for students were in fact the case, and sit in all faculty meetings."[52] Messages of support came in from the SRC at the Saskatoon campus, the National Farmers' Union, the Allied Printing Trades Union, the Saskatchewan Waffle Federation, the Regina campus Young New Democrats, and students at Memorial University in St John's, Newfoundland, who were engaged in a dispute with their own university administration.[53] The message from Allied Printing Trades was particularly forceful: "The university must be made to serve the needs of the people of Saskatchewan, and until real control of the university lies in the hands of students, the community and faculty, this shall not be possible."[54]

The students escalated their protest on the afternoon of Monday, 20 November by occupying the offices of A.B. Van Cleave, the dean of graduate studies. When they tried to force their way into his office, Van Cleave attempted to bar the door, warning that he would bring assault charges against anyone who laid a hand on him. One student managed to slip in, jump over a desk, and remove the window screens, letting others in through the window. At this point Van Cleave gave up. He later recalled, "We left the office about 4:30 p.m. for the curling rink, where I regret to say, I was no more successful than I had previously been in defending my office."[55] As a precautionary measure, the university ordered the early closing of the bookstore, registrar's office, bursar's office, and laboratory building cafeteria. The students criticized the action as an "obvious attempt to smear the students in the eyes of the public. We indicate that we are not the irresponsible people that the administration want the people to believe."[56]

Archer chose not to call in the police, a decision that won praise from political science professor Milnor Alexander, who wrote, "If we react in a hostile or belligerent way, it will only escalate the controversy into a major battle, instead of letting it simmer down, as it soon will."[57] Reid Robinson of the chemistry department concurred: "I greatly appreciate the way in which you have sought to defuse the potentially explosive situation of this last week ... I would like to assure you of support in continuing policies of reason, negotiation, and conciliation."[58] Others demanded that Archer take a tougher stand. Van Cleave, in a statement to council on 24 November 1972, asserted that the time had come to put the radicals – both students and faculty – in their place. He blamed the outbreak of student unrest on the activities of "a group of Faculty members who should have been dismissed from the University with good cause long ago."[59]

Dallas Smythe denounced what he described as Van Cleave's "inflammatory and demagogic public statements." He accused him of "using tactics reminiscent of the late Senator McCarthy of ill fame in the United States – tactics which amount to a witch hunt." Van Cleave's attitude, Smythe said, stood in sharp contrast to the "reasonableness, restraint and responsibility for University property and personnel on the part of the students."[60] Some members of the general public did not share Smythe's assessment of the situation. Radio open-line shows were jammed with calls from citizens expressing disgust at what was going on at the university. Stan Atkinson, a former member of the Board of Governors, urged strong measures, including the abolition of tenure for faculty members and curbs on "academic freedom," which he claimed had degenerated into "academic license."[61]

Archer moved to defuse the crisis with a set of proposals, which he brought to a general meeting of students on Wednesday, 22 November 1972:

(1) I favor the concept of self-determination for the university in Regina and I favor greater participation on the part of faculty, students, and the general public in the governance of the institution;
(2) I believe that faculty and students have a vital role to play in the internal governance of the university. For example, students have a vital concern in matters pertaining to curriculum, student fees, standards and quality of teaching. Faculty members have their specific role in these and other areas. Under the present University Act the level of student participation varies. I am prepared to urge a review of the nature and level of student participation with a view to ensuring that students have opportunity to make their full contribution;
(3) I welcome and urge a review of the University Act and I am prepared to discuss proposed changes with faculty and students, and to take steps to arrange a meeting with the Minister of Continuing Education and his deputy minister to pursue this end;
(4) In return, I expect the students to terminate their occupation of areas in the Classroom Building and return to academic pursuits;
(5) I am further prepared to establish a committee composed of students, faculty members, plus members of the public to move toward the implementation of this position.[62]

The students accepted the proposals and agreed to end their occupation that afternoon. They had gained nothing except a promise from Archer to establish a committee.

The 1972 occupation was just the reverse of the *Carillon* crisis of 1968–69. During the latter crisis the university administration moved aggressively against the students, suspending the collection of student activity fees and trying to shut down the newspaper. The Board of Governors was placed on the defensive, accused of attacking student self-government and freedom of the press. The majority of students, even those who did not agree with much of what they read in the *Carillon*, rallied in support of the Students' Union. Faced with a strong, united opposition, the Board of Governors backed down.

In 1972, by contrast, the students moved aggressively against the university administration, occupying offices in a bid for parity. Archer, by showing restraint and refusing to call in the police, averted an escalation that might have shifted sympathy to the occupiers. Tactically speaking, he kept the administration on the defensive and the students on the offensive (they were the ones breaking the law) and thus held the higher moral ground. Archer knew that the radical group was small relative to the total student population – Dean Vaughan estimated it at no more than 150.[63] The key was to prevent the radical minority from coalescing with the silent majority. Archer accomplished this by making conciliatory noises about the value of student participation without ever conceding the principle of parity and by making sure that the radicals were not able to portray themselves as victims of police brutality. The students' victory of 1969 was a defensive one, in that they preserved what they already had: the independence of the Students' Union and control of the *Carillon*. The defeat of 1972 was a failure to gain something they did not have: equality with faculty in university decision making.

When the occupation ended, Archer appointed a tripartite committee composed equally of students, faculty, and people from outside the university. Its report of 24 April 1973 recommended "that students have the right to membership in a department. A department shall be composed of all faculty who are appointed by the Board to that department, plus a number of student representatives elected by the student electorate of the department. The number of student representatives may be equal to the number of faculty members in the department."[64] The operative word was "may." In the case of a disagreement over the number of student representatives in a department, the principal was to set up a committee composed of an equal number of faculty and students from that department, plus a chairman chosen by the principal from outside the department. This committee would be charged with recommending a resolution to the dispute, but the final decision rested with the principal, who could either accept or reject the recommendation.

Three faculty members on the Tripartite Committee (R.H. Fowler, J.G. Locker, and R.Y. Zacharuk) issued a minority report, which drew a distinction between student input, which they favoured, and parity in decision making, which they did not. Their objections to parity were threefold. First, students did not have the knowledge or experience required to make "long-term quality educational decisions." Second, students could not be held accountable for decisions in the same manner as faculty because they were at the university for a relatively short period. Third, they did not have the time to acquire the knowledge they needed to participate effectively in committee work.[65] The authors of the minority report believed that students had enough to do to keep up with their academic work; there were not enough hours in the day to discharge the added responsibility of helping to run the university.

Janice Moulton of the English department in a brief to the Tripartite Committee pointed out that such terms as "parity," "democracy," and "competing interest groups" belonged more to the realm of the state than they did to that of the university. While the state existed to regulate the exercise of power in society, the academic community had a different purpose. She described the university as "a free and sheltered place" where scholars engaged in the search for truth. Students and teachers in this context were not "opposed interest groups," but rather "sharers in the enterprise of learning." Conflicts over ideas could not be resolved by majority vote, but only in accordance with impersonal standards of logic and judgment, standards that governed both students and teachers. The university in its essential nature was not a democracy, but rather an intellectual community.

Moulton had advice for those who wished to make the university an agency for social reform. She said that political parties existed for this purpose, and, "if they seem inadequate, the procedures for creating new ones are well known and easily followed." If, however, the university were transformed into a political agency, what institution could take its place as the centre of learning and scholarship? Moulton contended that knowledge and power were two different concepts, and therefore the university had to be divorced from politics. Smythe would probably have retorted that everything, including knowledge, is political and that not taking a political stand is in itself a political stand.

The administration delayed action on the Tripartite Committee report because a subcommittee of the Senior Academic Committee of Executive of Council, appointed in May 1972, was also engaged in a study of student participation in university government. The subcommittee, chaired by A.G. McBeath, conducted a survey of faculty views, and, as did the 1970 survey, it uncovered a variety of opinions. Keith Costain, chairman of the English department, considered student representation a non-issue: "There was once some force and verve behind the drive for inclusion in the making of policy decisions, but since most students have come to realize what an utterly boring process the making of policy decisions often is, there seems to me to be little concern outside the Division of Social Sciences for 'student participation.'"[66] J.N. McCrorie, chairman of the sociology department, disagreed, maintaining that students had contributed to "a sharper and more imaginative definition of the seminal issues ... In a period in which young people have become increasingly critical and suspicious of their parents and teachers, the commitment of the Sociology faculty to the principle of student participation has been viewed by students as evidence of our respect for them as human beings, and our recognition that many of the issues they raise for critical examination are worthy of attention and resolution."[67] Chris Knapper, chairman of the psychology department, took a middle-of-the-road approach. While acknowledging that student representatives had been very active on department committees, he said there was no consensus among the faculty as to the value of their contributions. Although harbouring some reservations, he thought that student participation was on the whole a good thing.[68] The committee tried to conduct a similar survey of student opinion but was unable to obtain a response. It seemed that most students were not interested enough to make a comment.

The McBeath committee delivered its report in June 1973. It was more restrained than the Tripartite Committee had been, observing that students were most likely to make "significant contributions to the operation of the University" at the department level, and that each department should "devise its own mode of student participation." Above the department level, it recommended that students comprise up to 20 per cent of the number of faculty members on councils and committees.[69] This represented a reduction in student participation for the Division of Social Sciences, where the proportion of students was already higher than that and, in theory at least, could be equal in number to the faculty representatives.

The McBeath committee presented its report to Campus Council in January 1974. An amendment to allow student representation of "at least 20 per cent" of faculty on councils and committees above the departmental level instead of "up to 20 per cent" was defeated.[70] However, a grandfather clause was inserted that applied to bodies, such as the social sciences division, where students previously had enjoyed more than 20 per cent representation. The existing levels prevailed, provided that two-thirds of the faculty members on the council or committee agreed to their continuation. The vote on the recommendations was 98 in favour, 29 opposed (11 abstentions).[71] The *Carillon* grumbled that the students "had been shafted again," adding, "The faculty and administration seem to have forgotten the occupation which took place here in November 1972. A great many of the students have not."[72] Despite the rhetoric, there was no resumption of student protests or occupation of administrative offices. The Board of Governors on 3 September 1974 approved the formal mechanism for student participation that had been passed by council.[73] The parity issue quietly died.

Archer had handled the issue masterfully and prevented it from escalating into something bigger. An optimist and idealist of a typically pragmatic Saskatchewan variety, he took the student movement in stride. As he said in 1970, "These young people are not plotting to burn down the university. They are much more blasé about so-called leftist plots than are people downtown. They are concerned about the university, and they do want to reform the administration. They are not content to put up with poor teachers, or imposed and unreasonable edicts. They resent being taken for granted."[74] Archer's attitude was epitomized by his response to a delegation of students who showed up at his office in October 1971 asking for classes to be cancelled to protest the nuclear bomb test in the Aleutian Islands. Although he refused the request, he noted in a private memo that "It was really a very good discussion and I must say I have a certain admiration and respect for these young people who find time and energy to be concerned over the future of the world."[75]

The decline of student radicalism was attributable partly to Archer's diplomacy and partly to the expansion of student opportunities to participate in university decision making. But there were also broader economic and demographic factors at work. As the economic boom of the 1960s came to a close, the job market began to shrink. The unemployment rate in Canada climbed from 4.7 per cent in 1969 to 6.3 per cent in 1972, while prices rose at an alarming rate. A dollar in 1975 purchased what 72 cents could buy in 1971.[76] The *Carillon* in the late 1960s had been full of ads for white-collar positions in such fields as education, health care, social work, and administration. Students were able to snap up well-paying jobs without even completing their degrees. Suddenly, in the early 1970s, the situation changed. The *Carillon* published a special edition on unemployment on 13 April 1971, and the next month an article on the spring convocation was tinged with pessimism: "The other cloud that hung over the proceedings was the gloom associated with a rather lean future. No longer do graduates go from Convocation to corporate boardrooms and the suburbs. No more steak barbecues on the patio with the boss – only dreary trips to the unemployment office."[77] Students in the 1960s could take jobs for granted; they were able to give time and energy to idealistic causes because their personal futures were secure. Now they had to worry about getting a job.

The first baby boomers were now approaching thirty, the age at which, by their own admission, they could not be trusted. As they settled into nine-to five work routines, got married, and raised children, they had less time for political activism and protest demonstrations. When the leading edge of the baby boom entered university, in the late 1950s, they strained the capacity of the system to its limits. Now, as they began to graduate in large numbers, they had the reverse effect. The enrolment at Regina campus peaked at 4,345 full-time and 299 part-time day students, for a total of 4,644, in the fall of 1969. In addition there were 1,794 students taking degree, certificate, and non-credit classes through the extension program. In the fall of 1970 the number of full-time and part-time day students (excluding extension students) declined to 4,567. In 1971 it fell to 4,267; in 1972 it was 4,009; and in 1973, 4,013.[78] The student power of the baby boomers had always been based on numbers. As the numbers declined, so did the power.

Although the movements of the sixties gradually subsided, they left an enduring legacy. Students had earned the right to participate in making the decisions that affected the quality of their university education. As William Riddell admitted to the Students' Union internal vice-president, Rob Milen, in January 1970, this represented a major improvement over the 1950s, "when there was almost no interest in student government or in issues that should have been [of] concern to students." Despite the fact that Riddell had borne the brunt of student protests, which may have hastened his retirement as principal, he congratulated the students for having brought about worthwhile reforms: "Some of the changes of the past few years have been the result, to some extent at least, of the pressures exerted by the students for change – many for the better."[79] Without doubt, the students of the sixties were at times self-righteous, self-indulgent, and even obnoxious, but at least they asked important questions and tried to make their mark on the world. They did not, in the words of George Grant, "crawl through the university simply as a guarantee of the slow road to death in the suburbs."[80]

The student movement also helped to transform the role of women at the university. While it is true that the women's liberation movement found inspiration in a variety of sources, students made a significant contribution. In the early and mid-1960s, campus beauty contests were still popular. "Amid tears and cheers, seventeen-year-old, green-eyed Nora Best was crowned [Regina] Campus Queen at the Christmas Prom" in 1963. "'I can't believe it,' exclaimed the young brunette, clutching her 23 victory roses." The *Carillon* described Miss Best as "an active co-ed, a cheerleader and a member of the Cougettes basketball team." She also had a mind of her own: "I believe in college education for women and in a greater role for women in modern society, she said, once she had regained her composure."[81] "Breathtaking Miss Pam Gawley" was chosen in October 1964 as the campus candidate for the Miss Saskatchewan Roughrider contest. Miss Gawley, gushed the *Carillon*, "has wrapped her charm in a 5' 1" 106-pound package, topped with blonde hair and sky-blue eyes."[82]

Women students on campus organized a club called Tap-Way, supposedly after a Cree word for "true." They sponsored a "girls' night out" on 23 September 1964, which featured a fashion show of "sportswear originals." "Ten poised young ladies" modeled their "own favorite outfit."[83] In the fall of 1965 Tap-Way hosted a dance called "Bondage a-Go-Go." The men brought to the dance female "slaves" they had acquired at a "slave auction" held during the noon hour in one of the lecture halls: "Twenty of the most tempting, tantalizing, and fun-loving coeds on campus will be sold for a mere pittance. The rules are simple. The bidding on each of these rarities will start at 5 cents and will not exceed $3.00 (unless by popular demand). The slave you buy (if you should be so lucky), will be yours to do with as you please according to the code of slave ethics from 8:30 a.m. until 12 o'clock midnight Friday, November 5. The code of slave ethics is as follows: (1) The slave cannot be stopped from attending her regular classes (barring unforeseen circumstances); (2) No financial obligation on the part of the slave (barring unforeseen circumstances); (3) Christian moral standards? Must be upheld?"[84]

Nora Best, who was crowned campus queen in 1963. The women's liberation movement did not make a significant impact on the Regina campus until the late 1960s.

An early sign of the women's liberation movement was the publication in September 1968 of the first instalment in a continuing series of *Carillon* articles on the status of women.[85] The author, who wrote under the byline "Wilma Brown," said that she had been inspired by the Royal Commission on the Status of Women, which the federal government had established in 1967. Her articles explored various aspects of discrimination against women in Canadian society. Another important development was the formation by the fall of 1969 of a women's liberation caucus on campus. The members defined themselves as "a group of women who felt limited by the roles we were expected to play and those we expected of ourselves. We had no clear understanding of these very real feelings. Gradually, on talking to one another we began to realize that these were not personal difficulties or deficiencies but instead problems with a common root, social problems."[86]

A *Carillon* editorial in October 1969 recognized women's liberation as "perhaps the single most important new issue that has sprung up on campuses this year." Women were tired of being treated "as objects, as walking vaginas,

A "slave auction," organized by a campus girls' club in November 1966, in which male students bid for ownership of a female slave for a day. A women's liberation group forcibly closed down the auction in 1971.

as cheap labor." The editorial attacked the frosh queen contest and all the other beauty contests in which women were "paraded around like 'cattle' to be ogled at by flesh connoisseurs."[87] Feminists in November 1971 disrupted the "beaver auction" put on by the Engineering Society. The protesters stood on the table that was being used as the auction block, seized the microphone, and informed the audience that the proceedings were degrading and offensive to women. After failing to convince those in attendance to disperse, they collapsed the table and forcibly shut down the event.[88] The women's liberation group, with the support of the Student's Union, established a women's centre in September 1970. Located in the student services building, it was a place for women to get together and talk about issues that concerned them.[89] It also distributed feminist literature, dispensed birth control information, and loaned money to help women obtain legal abortions.[90]

In the fall of 1967 a group of women taking classes at Regina campus asked the university to set up a daycare centre for children. The Principal's Planning Committee expressed sympathy but did nothing.[91] In September 1969

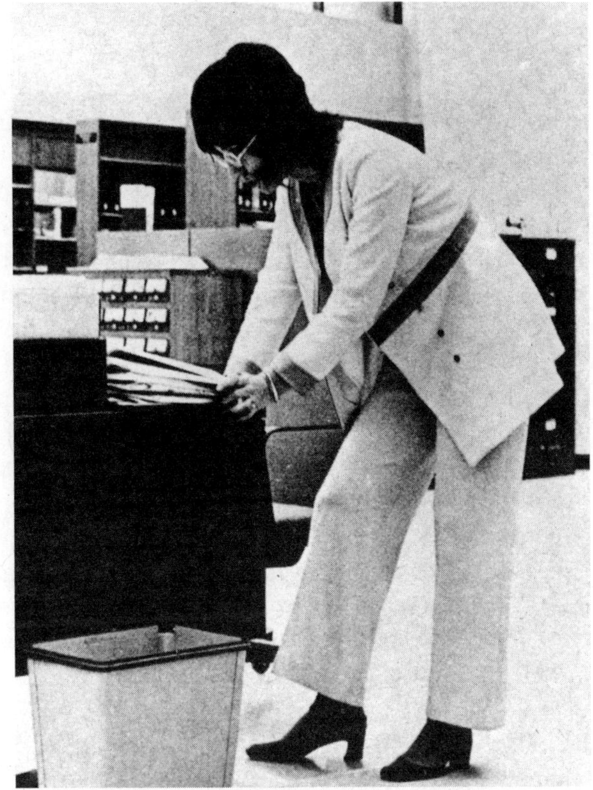

Library assistant Carol Phillips wearing a pantsuit. A fall 1970 personnel office ruling permitted women staffers to wear such outfits as long as they were neat, clean, colour-coordinated, and discreet. Phillips later became director of the MacKenzie Art Gallery.

the Students' Union stepped in and set up a makeshift daycare facility in the lounge of the Students' Union building. Parents subsequently signed a lease with the university for daycare space in the basement of the college building at the downtown campus. A full-time supervisor was hired at a salary of $300 per month, and parents took turns filling in as part-time staff. The centre operated on a tenuous basis, chronically short of funds, but it survived.[92]

Women's liberation also began to have an impact on the university curriculum. Professor Milnor Alexander of the Department of Social Studies pioneered an experimental women's studies class in January 1973.[93] It was well received, adopted as a regular class, and listed in the calendar as Social Studies 220, "Women's Liberation." Offered a second time in the fall of 1973, it was described as "an analysis of the causes, ideological bases, and organized groups in the women's liberation movement in Canada, the United States, Great Britain, France, and the Scandinavian countries. There will also be some discussion of women's rights in China and the Soviet Union and Cuba for comparative purposes."[94] By 1975 the campus was offering six accredited courses on women's issues. However, Dr Alexander opposed the creation of a separate women's studies department, preferring to have the courses taught within existing departments under a loosely coordinated women's studies framework. She did not want the courses to be "ghettoized," because she thought it was important for men, as well as women, to take them.[95]

Principal Archer in the fall of 1974 appointed a committee to review the status of women with Milnor Alexander and budget officer A.J. Ayre serving as co-chairs. Its terms of reference were to "review the status of women in their roles as members of the academic faculty, members of the administration and academic support staff and students. The Committee will make whatever recommendations it deems necessary and appropriate to ensure that all women members of the University community receive equitable and non-discriminatory treatment in every aspect of the University's operations."[96] The committee received a number of briefs and collected data about the rates of pay and the opportunities for promotion of women employees as compared with men. The final report raised campus awareness of gender issues and pointed the university in the direction of greater equality for men and women at every level, from support staff to senior administration.

Another important development of the sixties was the Aboriginal rights movement. The *Carillon* brought the issue to the fore at a time when the mainstream media were ignoring it. An article in March 1963 titled "Racial Prejudice and the Regina Indian" showed that racial discrimination at lunch counters was not something confined to the American South. The *Carillon* reporter recounted an incident that had occurred in a downtown Regina coffee shop. Two Indians entered the restaurant, sat at a table, and waited for someone to take their order. After a long wait they realized that they were not going to be served and quietly left.[97] In September 1967 the *Carillon* devoted its entire front page to an exposé of racial discrimination practised in a hotel beverage room in Montmartre, a small town near Regina. The students were able to prove that there was an unwritten rule requiring Indians to sit on one side of the room.[98] Other articles documented the poverty experienced in First Nations and Métis communities across the province. *Carillon* staffer Barbara Cameron gave a vivid description of living conditions in Sandy Bay, a small town in northern Saskatchewan,[99] and First Nations student Matt Bellegarde wrote "The Indian in Saskatchewan," a comprehensive overview of Native organizations and government programs.[100]

Regina campus students also took practical steps to improve social conditions, volunteering as tutors for Native and Métis high school students. In the summer of 1965 the Student Union for Peace Action (SUPA) organized the Neestow Project, which gave students the opportunity to live on Indian reserves and in Métis settlements, assisting the residents to develop their communities. The Company of Young Canadians, an organization

THE CARILLON

Official weekly journal published by the Students' Union, Regina Campus

Vol. 7 No. 9 Friday, November 15, 1968 — 12 Pages

RIEL
16 NOVEMBRE
1885

on the 83rd Anniversary of the MURDER of LOUIS RIEL by the Canadian government, has anything changed?

The front page of the *Carillon*, 15 November 1968, commemorating Louis Riel and affirming that the struggle for Aboriginal rights had not yet been won.

created by the federal government to channel youthful idealism into constructive social action, also undertook projects in Saskatchewan. When right-wing politicians turned their fire on the so-called "hippies" and "potheads" in the CYC, the *Carillon* came to their defence. In a variety of ways, the paper raised the profile of Aboriginal issues at a time when they were largely ignored in the mainstream media. For example, it included poster inserts of Louis Riel and Gabriel Dumont for students to hang on their walls alongside their pictures of Che Guevara. The *Carillon* front page on 15 November 1968 featured a photo of Riel's grave with the caption "On the 83rd Anniversary of the Murder of Louis Riel by the Canadian Government – Has Anything Changed?"

All this was part of the larger context of an emerging Aboriginal rights movement. The National Indian Council, which was formed in 1961, evolved in 1968 into two separate organizations, one for First Nations and the other for Métis. Provincially, the Federation of Saskatchewan Indians (now the Federation of Saskatchewan Indian Nations) and the Métis Society matured as policy-making and program-delivery organizations. The strong opposition in 1969 to the Trudeau government's *Statement on Indian Policy*, better known as the White Paper, which recommended doing away with Indian status and phasing out treaties, further galvanized Aboriginal activists. As a result, the goal of public policy shifted from assimilation to Aboriginal self-determination. In the sphere of education this meant the adoption of the principle of Indian control of Indian education, which led directly to the establishment in May 1976 of the Saskatchewan Indian Federated College (now the First Nations University of Canada), with its main building at the Regina campus.

The sixties was the crucible for the formation of the University of Regina, the historical context that shaped its identity. Superficially, much of what happened in that decade seems to have failed or left no lasting legacy. The Regina Beach Statement was abandoned, parity defeated, and the "revolution" aborted. Radical politics dissolved in ideological infighting and tiresome sloganeering. Apparently, nothing important was achieved – it was all just a waste of time. But to leave it at this is to sell the sixties short. In 1950 a Chinese Canadian boy was expelled from Regina College because he had brought a case of beer into residence and put his coat in the wrong room, female students were not allowed to run for the office of SRC president, and an Indian could not get a cup of coffee in a Regina restaurant. The movements of the 1960s brought these issues into the open. They helped to create a more equitable society and a more inclusive university. This, in the end, was the true legacy of the sixties.

17 University of Regina

The University of Saskatchewan, Regina Campus became the University of Regina in 1974, when legislation was passed implementing the recommendations of the Royal Commission on University Organization and Structure. When one of the commissioners was asked "Why should there be a university in Regina?" he answered, "Because it's there now."[1] There was a good deal of truth in this remark. The provincial government did not create the University of Regina in 1974; it was already there. As a result of decisions made by the Board of Governors and the senate of the University of Saskatchewan, there existed in Regina a campus of 5,000 students enrolled in the Faculties of Arts and Science, Education, Administration, Engineering, and Graduate Studies and Research, as well as the School of Social Work. The University of Regina was not created in 1974 – that is when it gained independent status.

As Lloyd Barber, who became president of the university in 1976, later maintained, this development "was inevitable in much the same way as the independence of India from Britain was inevitable."[2] The basic problem before 1974 was to find a model of university government that could satisfy the needs of both the Regina and Saskatoon campuses. To this end a joint committee of the senate, Board of Governors, and two councils was established. Its report, which the senate adopted on 4 November 1966, rejected the idea of a separate university in Regina. It said that if separation occurred, the provincial government would be obliged to establish a university grants committee to allocate funds to the universities. Under the existing system, the government set aside a certain amount for university education in the province, and the University of Saskatchewan decided how resources were allocated within the overall budget, including the division of money between Regina and Saskatoon. If there were two universities, then authority to divide the funds would shift from the University of Saskatchewan to the provincial government, resulting in a diminution of the university's ability to coordinate spending on higher education in the province. For this reason, the committee rejected the creation of a second university and endorsed the one-university/two-campus model of organization.

It first outlined the historical background, recalling the decision in 1959 to develop a second campus: "the Saskatoon Council studied projections of university student enrolment in Saskatchewan, and preferred a student body not in excess of 10,000 at Saskatoon. Thus the decision was taken to expand the Regina campus to degree level."[3] In fact, the university Forward Planning Committee in 1959 had targeted the enrolment for Saskatoon at 8,000, a figure that Vice-President Colb McEown was still using as a reference point in 1962. At some point between 1962 and 1966 the enrolment ceiling floated upward from 8,000 to 10,000 students. The report went on to say that "The Regina campus eventually will approximate the Saskatoon campus in size and activity, and the principle of autonomy of both Councils and campuses has been accepted. Therefore the appropriate organization would appear to be one that reflects a 'University group' and two 'campus groups.' The Executive organization of the University group will be referred to as 'The Office of the President,' and of the campus group as 'The Office of the Principal.'"[4]

More specifically, this meant that each campus would have its own principal, who would serve as the senior academic and executive officer, a vice-principal or vice-principals, deans of faculties, a provost, a registrar, a bursar, a planning officer, and any other officials needed in the campus administrative group. The university administration, which was to be known as the University Office, would preside over and coordinate the activities of both campuses. It would consist of the president, a vice-president or vice-presidents, a controller, a university secretary, an officer responsible for the planning and construction of buildings, and "such other officers as may be required from time to time." While the principal and his staff on each campus were responsible for day-to-day operations, they were to work "in consultation with the corresponding officers in the University Office within the policies established for the University." W.A. Riddell continued as principal at Regina, and on 1 July 1967 Robert Begg was appointed principal at Saskatoon.[5]

The basic principles of the report were implemented in amendments to the University Act, proclaimed on 3 June 1968. As before, each campus had a council to make decisions about academic programs, but now there was also a general university council (GUC) "to ensure the effective coordination of the academic programs of the two campuses and to make appropriate recommendations thereon to the Senate."[6] The GUC consisted of the president, vice-presidents, university secretary, principals, and vice-principals of the campuses, the two secretaries of the campuses, and eighteen members elected from each campus council.[7] Although the two campuses had an equal number of elected representatives, the majority of ex officio members were based in Saskatoon.[8]

Another change made in 1968 was the appointment for each campus of a finance and personnel committee, which was essentially a subcommittee of the Board of Governors that dealt with matters specific to the campus. It consisted of the principal as chairman, the vice-principal, two members of council, the business manager, local members of the Board of Governors, along with the university president, controller, and secretary.[9] The Board of Governors continued as the "Board of Management for the whole University," with final responsibility for the "total university budget, allocation of funds to campuses, promotion, tenure, and salaries."[10] The board received advice on these and other matters from the President's Executive Committee, which in October 1968 was renamed the University Executive Committee.[11] Its members were the president, the two principals, the vice-president, the controller and treasurer, the vice-president (research), the director of planning, and the university secretary.[12]

The 1968 reorganization represented a serious attempt to make the one-university system work. Spinks had high hopes for it: "We feel that the transition from a one campus-one University to a two campus-one University situation has taken place reasonably successfully. With good will from all concerned, the present structure should prove adequate to meet the varied needs of the Province for some time to come."[13] The success of the structure hinged on finding a way to resolve differences between the two campuses – especially those relating to the rationalization of academic programs and the distribution of resources – in a manner that both parties perceived as fair and impartial. This was difficult to do when the University Office was located at the Saskatoon campus and staffed by officials who had built their careers at the Saskatoon university.

The meetings of the General University Council were held in Saskatoon or Regina or sometimes in the small town of Davidson, about halfway between the two cities.[14] The problems with the body surfaced at the first meeting, on 30 October 1968.[15] All the faculty and ex officio members from Regina voted together on a critical vote concerning campus authority over curriculum, but they still lost 23 to 21. According to Joe Roberts, a member of the Department of Political Science at Regina campus who attended the meeting, Regina was accused of block voting – "an ad hominem ploy that necessitated an embarrassed defence from our spokesmen and introduced a defensive and recriminatory reaction within our own ranks. But what gall – consider the final vote ... the body is stacked de facto in favor of the 'metropolis.'"[16] By 1971 senior administrators on both campuses had come to the conclusion that the GUC had failed and needed to be replaced with a more effective mechanism for coordinating the academic programs of the two campuses.[17]

Enrolment at the Regina campus reached 4,345 full-time and 299 part-time day students in 1969–70, for a total of 4,644 (excluding students taking degree, certificate, and non-credit classes through the extension program). The number fell to 4,013 in 1973.[18] The student population in Saskatoon peaked at 10,181 in 1969–70 and declined to 9,714 in 1974.[19] As enrolment levelled off, a budget crunch developed, placing increased strain on the relations between the two campuses. It was difficult enough in good times to divvy up the money. When the flow of funds failed to meet expectations, the battles over who should get what became even more intense. Principal Archer told President Spinks on 18 January 1971 that questions about the development of the Regina campus would be clarified "if a firm ceiling was put on the growth of the Saskatoon operation."[20] Spinks replied, "There is, of course, a firm ceiling on the Saskatoon Campus. When I say 'firm,' naturally I do not mean exactly 10,500, but until the Campus and the Board change their mind, that is where the figure is, and I don't think that the present Board would agree to the figure changing very much until Regina has reached something like the same figure."[21] The ceiling was firm at 10,500 (up from 10,000 in 1966), at least for the time being.

The Joint Committee on Organization and Structure was reactivated in May 1971 to carry out a general review of the governing mechanisms of the university.[22] The chairman was W.A. Riddell, who, after resigning as principal, had become a special assistant to the president. Riddell favoured the continuation of the existing system, but he wanted to "devise ways of eliminating or minimizing the weaknesses and cumbersome aspects that can now be identified on the basis of several years experience."[23] The Regina Campus Council appointed a special committee to study the structure and functioning of the university and to prepare a position paper for presentation to the joint committee.[24] As this process got underway, Archer detected a "sharpening of attitudes" on the campus. He informed Spinks on 30 September 1971 that "the campus here is quite willing to go through the regular procedures to bring briefs and views forward through the proper committees, but that these briefs and views will now be firmly for more autonomy on the campus." Archer did not see Spinks as hostile to increased autonomy for the Regina campus. On the contrary, he thought the president was receptive to the idea. "The real point," Archer predicted, "will be to know where to put the stick-point as to the powers left to the central body. I do not think anyone on this campus is so naïve as to think that any government in Saskatchewan will set up two independent universities, vying with each other for programs, funds and people. This just is not in the books so the arrangement may very well revolve around whether or not our campus has its own Board and how our Board might fit under whatever umbrella the support Council develops."[25] Riddell noted in his diary that Spinks was telling people that they should stop talking about "two campuses" and speak rather of two universities working "within a Saskatchewan university system."[26]

Regina Campus Council passed a resolution on 26 January 1972 that approved "in principle that this institution be made an independent university with full authority over its operations, exercised through a simpler structure than the existing one."[27] The entire discussion was taking place in the context of budget restraint, the extent of which Vice-Principal Ray Harvey outlined at a special meeting of the council on 22 March 1972. He told the faculty that the university's anticipated operating grant of $36,686,000 (both campuses) for 1972–73 had been cut back to $35.75 million. Since this was the third lean budget in a row, the university had little room to manoeuvre. As Harvey succinctly put it, "Virtually all the fat had been trimmed from our operation so that further contraction means cutting into the meat and bone."[28]

The financial crisis centred on the future of the Faculty of Engineering at the Regina campus. At a meeting of university and government representatives on 17 February 1972, Premier Allan Blakeney said that he did not fully accept such statements in the university's submission as, "a *university* requires a number of major faculties, say five or six," and, "an engineering type college is a *must* for a modern university." In his view the quality of an institution did not depend on the diversity of its course offerings. Further, he made it clear that the government had serious reservations about the full development of engineering at Regina.[29] The upshot was that on 3 March 1972 the government ordered a halt to all design work on the proposed engineering/physics building at the Regina campus. The university was told there would be no funds for the project in 1972–73. [30]

A special meeting of the Regina Campus Council was held on 1 May 1972. "The view was expressed," reported Archer, "that Regina campus was at a critical stage in its history. It was held that decisions to be taken by the senior bodies in the University and by the Government in the near future would either substantiate the claim of the campus to being a viable, developing institution or would relegate it to a satellite role in the realm of higher education. It was stated that the publicly announced policy of Government and of University was that the Regina campus would grow and develop as a full partner in the University. If present day conditions had led to a change in policy, then this change should be made public and should be debated."[31] The council unanimously passed the following resolution:

Whereas the members of the Council have noted that the resources now available to the Regina campus are inadequate to stimulate the growth and variety originally planned for, and that the Saskatoon Campus, because of its age and size, has superior resources and advantages leading to a pre-emption of new developments in Saskatoon and inhibiting developments in Regina, the said members resolve, through the Principal, to draw the attention of the Chancellor and the President of the University and of the Chairman of the Board of Governors to the failure of the governing bodies of the University to establish policies for a fair and sensible distribution of Colleges, Faculties, Schools and Departments and of new programs between the two campuses and to their view that unless such policies are adopted and implemented the Regina campus will be relegated to an inferior status, which is not in keeping with the intention of the Province when the new Campus was inaugurated, nor with the needs of the Province.[32]

E.C. Leslie, chairman of the Board of Governors and a member of the board since the early 1950s, stated that he very much regretted "the attitude taken by the Faculty on the Saskatoon Campus with regard to Engineering Education." If that attitude continued, it "would do much to make each Campus a separate University." Leslie added that he had "always been of the view that in time the Regina Campus and the Saskatoon Campus would become equal." He endorsed the position taken by the Regina Faculty Council that "the Regina Campus should not be relegated to an inferior status" and that "such a relegation would not be in keeping with the intention of the Province when the new Campus was inaugurated."[33]

Lloyd Barber, who became vice-president of the University of Saskatchewan in 1968 after the death of Colb McEown, later pondered this issue in his "University of Regina: Future Directions Study," dated 26 July 1977. He said that when the Regina campus was being planned, "There were also discussions about whether or not Regina should develop as a liberal arts college only, and the extent to which it should concentrate on Social Sciences while Saskatoon concentrated on Natural Sciences. It would be difficult, short of a thorough search of the University archives, to document many of the assumptions being made at the time and even then conclusive evidence of the approach being taken by the decision-makers of the time could probably not be obtained."[34] Barber gave Spinks a copy of this study, and in the margin next to the quoted paragraph Spinks wrote, "Point was made many times and accepted that Regina was to be a well developed University and not just a Liberal Arts institution."[35] This contention is borne out, for example, in Spinks's convocation address at the Regina campus in May 1972, when he said, "Speaking rather more generally about the development of the Regina Campus, it is essential, from the point of view of the impact of a centre of higher education on the surrounding community, that Regina be a real, full-fledged university and not just a large liberal-arts college."[36]

The issue of the engineering program at the Regina campus became a surrogate for the larger question of whether, as Spinks put it, "Regina was to be a well developed University and not just a Liberal Arts institution." The Board of Governors in March 1972 appointed a commission with Dr Philip Lapp of Ontario as chairman to conduct a study of the future of the engineering programs on the two campuses.[37] John Archer's brief to the commission throws light on the context in which the matter was viewed in Regina. Archer asserted that it had been "the publicly expressed determination of the Senate, Board of Governors, and Government of Saskatchewan ... that the Regina campus would become a co-equal, full partner of the northern sister campus." He added that "The decision to erect Regina College to the status of a full partner signified an unwillingness on the part of Southern Saskatchewan to accept junior status as a permanent policy ... It could be a university with a sufficient range of offerings to give students in the southern part of the province a real alternative to the Saskatoon institution."[38]

As things stood in 1972 Saskatoon had colleges of arts and science, fine arts, education, engineering, law, commerce, nursing, home economics, pharmacy, medicine, dentistry, veterinary medicine, and agriculture. Regina had arts and science, fine arts, engineering, administration, education, and social work. Each campus had a faculty of graduate studies. Archer argued that in order to fulfill the intention of the board, senate, and provincial government to have two equal campuses, a redistribution of professional colleges between the two campuses was required. He listed education, home economics, commerce, and law as possible transfers from Saskatoon to Regina. As for engineering, the students enrolled at Regina constituted "an important element in all assessments of class loads and teaching positions in various areas of Arts and Science." The removal of engineering would have a negative effect on the entire institution, as well as contradict the basic principle that "Regina campus must have a mix of students, a mix of academic disciplines, a number of faculties and schools to provide the substantial base for partnership, for growth, for development of centres of excellence."[39]

The Lapp Commission in December 1972 recommended that all engineering instruction be concentrated in Saskatoon, a recommendation that was not well received in Regina. Archer thought that it had been a mistake to refer the matter "to wise men from Central Canada who come in with the conditioning which much larger universities such as Toronto, or York, or McGill, give them and who then write reports from their experience, purportedly to solve problems which are different in setting, different in size, and different of solution." In his opinion there was room for a faculty of engineering in Regina "doing certain specific things and a larger College on the Saskatoon Campus doing the majority of the older, traditional things." Regina reacted to Lapp Report with shock and dismay. Rumours began to circulate that the Faculty of Education was next on the chopping block, a move, Archer said, that "would indeed be a death blow to this campus and would, in fact, relegate it to a liberal arts college status."[40]

Principal Robert Begg of the Saskatoon campus did not help matters by stating, "I have full sympathy for the dilemma [that falling enrolment] creates for Regina and the dreams that have been shattered. Saskatoon has a drop in registration which has also led to real problems." He made a pitch "for a return to the concept of a University of Saskatchewan in which neither the interests of Regina nor Saskatoon are paramount, but where equal consideration is given to Swift Current, Yorkton, Meadow Lake, and Prince Albert. We are the university of all Saskatchewan and our decisions should be based on what is best for education in all of Saskatchewan."[41] This appeal fell on deaf ears because as far as Regina was concerned, there were already in fact, if not in law, two universities. The clock could not be turned back to the pre-1960s era. As if to bear this out, the Board of Governors split down the middle on the Lapp Report. Individual board members identified with either the Regina campus or the Saskatoon campus, and not, as Begg had hoped, with the university as a whole.[42] Because of Regina's strong opposition to shutting down engineering at the southern campus, the board directed the Regina Faculty of Engineering to revert to a two-year program while conducting an investigation of "alternative developments in the field of applied science and engineering technology for Regina campus."[43] Thus the struggle over engineering foreshadowed the breakdown of the one-university system.

The provincial government gradually came to believe that the university was incapable of resolving its internal problems. The report of the government's Advisory Committee on Reorganization of the University of Saskatchewan, issued on 15 August 1972, sheds light on how the matter was evolving. The document is unsigned, but the author was likely Ray Harvey, who had been appointed deputy minister of continuing education in June 1972.[44] The report asked the key question "Can effective rationalization be done within the one University structure?" It acknowledged that "many of the University's administrators are now working very hard to demonstrate that it can." Largely under the leadership of Vice-President Lloyd Barber and Jim Wedgwood, director of planning, a university planning committee had undertaken three "rationalization" studies: a comprehensive study of space and space utilization on both campuses; a study of enrolment trends; and a study of teacher education in Saskatchewan. In addition, the university's budget committee had begun to use more sophisticated techniques of data analysis to achieve a more rational basis for resource allocation.

Ray Harvey, dean of the Faculty of Administration (1968–70) and vice-principal of the Regina campus (1970–72). He was appointed deputy minister of continuing education at a critical moment, when the government was trying to come to grips with the reorganization of the province's university system.

Given these developments, the report considered whether the university should "be left undisturbed for another couple of years at least to see if it cannot work out its own destiny." Two factors weighed against this option. One was "the very considerable disenchantment with the one-university concept which exists on both campuses, particularly on the Regina Campus. There is no doubt in my mind that 90 per cent at least of Regina faculty and students would even sacrifice a modicum of financial and growth potential to be out from under the burden of poor-relation status which has plagued them in the relationships with Saskatoon. I believe, too, that the majority of Saskatoon Campus people feel that their style is being cramped by the millstone of Regina around their necks."[45] The second factor was the alleged "lack of firm leadership of President Spinks ... [who] still shows no strong indication of putting the firm managerial hand on the helm. But he is a very distinguished Canadian and a very imaginative scholar who has made great contributions to both the University and the nation; any step to enforce his retirement would have to be taken with great sensitivity and diplomacy."[46]

The report recommended dividing the University of Saskatchewan into two separate universities, each with its own board of governors, senate, and faculty council. It would be necessary for the Department of Continuing Education to develop a research and evaluation division with a staff "capable of realistic financial and academic analysis of university operations." The division would have two principal aims: to assist the government in negotiations with each university for the annual grant level; and to help plan rationalization of programs and expenditures between the two universities. The report anticipated that President Spinks and "the people in his Office" would oppose the plan. There might also be opposition from "academics on both campuses" who would interpret the plan as "a sinister plot by the Government to control the University."[47]

Meanwhile, the Joint Committee on Organization and Structure trundled along, working on an internal solution to the university's problems. According to its chairman, W.A. Riddell, the committee started out with a fair degree of enthusiasm. He was troubled, however, by the fact that some members saw no reason to make changes, believing that the "the present system is working." As time passed Riddell detected a slackening of interest on Spinks's part. Although a crucial meeting had been set for 17 August 1972, when decisions were to be made on the basic recommendations of the committee, Spinks arranged a meeting with the minister of continuing education at the same time. This indicated to Riddell that the president "does not consider there is much to do at the Joint Committee." Spinks was apparently worried that some members of the Board of Governors were not in favour of major changes, and he did not want to have a confrontation with them. Believing that this was a major mistake, Riddell wrote in his diary on 11 August 1972, "The campuses might accept [the failure to make changes] at the time, but the whole thing might blow up in six months. Legislators might take this as evidence that the university cannot resolve its own internal difficulties. Public might be upset for same reason."[48] Another possibility is that Spinks already intuited that the government was about to make a move, and for that reason Riddell's committee was irrelevant.

The Joint Committee on Organization and Structure produced an interim report on 10 November 1972, which recommended that each campus have its own board of governors and council. The General University Council would be abolished, and coordination would be achieved through a "Board of the Saskatchewan university system" and a senate exercising authority over both universities.[49] The plan represented a further devolution of authority to the campuses while preserving the essential unity of the system. It did not generate much interest or enthusiasm on either campus. The Board of Governors twice declined the opportunity to debate it.[50]

The government decided to intervene, introducing Bill 90 in early April 1973. It gave each campus its own president, board of governors, and senate but maintained the formal unity of the university through an overarching board of regents that would "regulate costs, allocate resources to each campus, establish salary scales, and adjudicate questions of the powers and rights of other university bodies."[51] Half of its members would be government appointees and the other half non-government appointees (like the existing Board of Governors), and its secretary would be the deputy minister of continuing education. Bill 90 did not go as far as the August 1972 recommendation of the Advisory Committee on Reorganization of the University of Saskatchewan, which called for a complete split between the two campuses and no buffer body between them and the government. Perhaps the government interposed this board of regents as a coordinating and resource-allocation mechanism to forestall charges that it was making a power grab. If so, the ploy failed. Both President Spinks and Vice-President Barber assailed the government's plan. Spinks denounced Bill 90 as the "use of naked and brutal political power ... removing any real autonomy from the university."[52]

Blakeney thought that this criticism was unfair. He underlined the fact that the government would appoint only half the members of the proposed board of regents.[53] As Spinks pointed out, however, the board, unlike the University Office, would have no support staff. It would have to rely on the expertise of Department of Continuing Education bureaucrats channelled to the board through the deputy minister.[54] The existing university administration would be dismantled and its function transferred to the board of regents and its staff. Spinks would be out of a job, as would Barber and all the other officials attached to the University Office, unless they could be absorbed into one or other of the campus administrations.

Norman Ward, a political scientist at the Saskatoon campus, warned the government that it was making a mistake. He considered the University of Saskatchewan to be the best administered major university in Canada; its cost per student was among the lowest in the country. Spinks, he said, was "a stout champion of Regina development who gets no credit whatever for it down there." At the same time Spinks was criticized in Saskatoon for doing too much for Regina. Bill 90, Ward said, would "abolish one of the ablest administrations in the country and replace it with an untested new system which – if it is to operate without people of the caliber and experience of Drs. Spinks and Barber – is going to be behind the eight-ball from the first day."[55]

As a result of the public outcry, the government on 19 April 1973 withdrew the bill[56] and referred the matter to a three-man Royal Commission chaired by Chief Justice Emmett Hall. His credentials were impeccable. A former justice of the Supreme Court of Canada, he had headed the Royal Commission that led to the implementation of medicare across Canada, and he was co-author of the Hall-Dennis Report on education in Ontario. Since his party affiliation was Progressive Conservative, he had no political ties to the provincial NDP government. The other two commissioners, Stewart Nicks and Gordon South, identified respectively with the Liberals and the NDP, had been members of the university Board of Governors.[57] The Royal Commission on University Organization and Structure came into existence on 3 May 1973. Its mandate was to examine the administrative structure of

Gordon South, Chief Justice Emmett Hall, and Stewart Nicks, the members of the Royal Commission on University Organization and Structure, which recommended in December 1973 that the campuses at Saskatoon and Regina become separate universities.

the University of Saskatchewan and "to report to the government suggested changes in the present university system of government and administration which may be better designed to meet current and future needs."[58]

Hearings began at Yorkton on 25 June 1973 and continued in Estevan, Weyburn, Swift Current, Rosetown, North Battleford, Prince Albert, Melfort, and Moose Jaw, concluding with one four-day session in Regina and another in Saskatoon. Eighty individuals and organizations presented briefs or made submissions. There were also private sessions with university officials at Saskatoon and Regina and with government officials at Regina. On 5, 6, and 7 October the commissioners met with educators and university administrators in Toronto, as well as consulting experts in university affairs "from all provinces in Canada and the State of Massachusetts."[59]

Principal Archer tried to ensure that the Regina campus spoke with one voice to the commission. To accomplish this, Vice-Principal Wes Bolstad met on 16 May 1973 with student leaders Fred Cuddington and Bill Wells. According to Bolstad, "Fred and Bill felt that it is possible to develop a proposal for the Hall Commission which would include features which could be actively supported by all groups on Campus (including the Students' Union)." Such a proposal would have to endorse "a separate university in Regina; the addition of professional schools such as law; community involvement in defining program needs; faculty and student involvement in the governing structure." Faculty members suspended their internal conflicts to present a united front. Although the Division of Natural Science and Mathematics had been conducting a campaign to break away from the Faculty of Arts and Science and gain recognition as a separate faculty, Associate Dean J.L. Wolfson consulted the members of his division on 3 May 1973: "Shall we go out of our way to avoid controversy at this time? Is it important that we appear united while the Hall Commission is sitting? I discussed this with the department chairmen yesterday. The question is simply: shall we ask the Principal to defer action on our request to seek means for reconstituting our Division as a Faculty of Science until such time as the Hall Commission has reported?" The scientists consented to a temporary truce. Archer postponed action on contentious matters, such as the appointment of a new dean of arts and science, until the Hall Commission was out of the way.[60]

Bolstad met on 17 May 1973 with a small group (Brian Tinker, Reid Robinson, Jim McCrorie, and Bev Robertson) to develop a strategy for the commission hearings. They agreed that Principal Archer should prepare a statement that would serve as "the flag around which people on campus can rally." It would outline "the kind of institution we want to establish in Regina and the kind of governing structure that could facilitate the achievement of such an institution." The committee also advised Archer to "warn Deans and Directors that the parts of the Campus must stick together, or the campus is in grave danger. For example, the parts should not make statements that provoke statements from other parts (not push selfish causes; we are more important than you are, etc.)."[61]

Archer's brief of 20 June 1973 offered a vision for the development of the University of Regina. It brought together various elements in such a way that everyone – natural scientists, social scientists, those involved in the fine arts, students, administrators, radicals, conservatives, rural people, urban people, Indians, and Métis – could see their interests and concerns reflected in the document. He began by saying that Regina campus was not just a liberal arts college. It aimed to mature as a full-fledged university with "a mix of arts, sciences, and professional schools – the mix to be determined by the overall philosophy of the institution as translated into its function and purpose." In terms of a special focus, he supported interdisciplinary studies, "particularly as they relate to the plains area," and the development of "areas of excellence that stem from the study of the prairie environment and the lives, struggles, literature and society of prairie people."[62]

Archer did not see the University of Regina as an institution isolated from the surrounding community: "We have no yearnings for the ivory tower; our destiny is tied to a more relevant seed bed." The university had to accept its responsibility to develop new knowledge through research, especially research that was "related to the needs and uses of the society about us." He supported "basic research to make for a well-rounded program, but our main thrust should be in the realm of problems associated with the prairie region – rural problems, social problems, economic problems, transportation, local government, water usage, urban growth, environmental well being, educational services, Métis and Indian lifestyles." The professional schools should be people- and service-oriented and might well include "law, education, social work, administration, journalism, local government, recreation, home economics, fine arts, architecture." He had no doubt that "engineering in some form should be a part of our program."

The brief went on to provide a critique of the one-university/two-campus model. It had not, in Archer's view, met the tests of "efficiency, acceptability or adaptability." On matters of broad policy and the rationalization of programs, the members of the Board of Governors were polarized. There was indeed a need for rationalization, "but rationalization and coordination between equal partners is a different matter to rationalization between senior and junior campuses." Each university, in Archer's view, should have its own board of governors and senate. The existing system carried too much of the burden of the past, "a psychological barrier as much a hindrance to understanding in Saskatoon as it is an irritant in Regina." He favoured a board or similar coordinating mechanism interposed between the two universities and the government. This board needed its own support and research staff headed by a ranking academic. It would then have the knowledge base to adjudicate rival claims between Saskatoon and Regina and rationalize programs at the two universities.

With respect to internal governance, Regina wanted to ensure "substantial participation" by the general public, faculty, and students. It wanted to develop in its own way and carve out its own identity: "The end purpose of it all is that we may build and develop here in Regina a university institution true to the best ideals of a university as an academic institution, relevant to this society on the plains, fulfilling the needs and aspirations of Saskatchewan people."[63] The faculty welcomed Archer's statement as a boost to morale. Keith Costain of the English department offered support: "there are obvious battles ahead, and battles in which we shall all be involved whether we like it or not. I should therefore like to know in what way or ways the ordinary faculty member can help and further the interests of the campus vis-à-vis other interested bodies."[64]

While Archer's brief dealt with issues of mission and identity, the City of Regina brief to the Hall Commission had a more pragmatic thrust. It pointed out that the university had become the city's second-largest employer, paying out annually $10 million in wages and salaries. Over half the full-time students who attended the campus were not from Regina, and they spent an average of $1,600 per academic year on food, clothing, shelter, entertainment, and so on. This totalled approximately $6 million annually – a substantial contribution to the local economy.[65]

The brief alleged that each year, from the beginning of the Regina campus in 1961 until 1970, more money had been given to Saskatoon for capital projects than had been allotted to Regina; indeed, Saskatoon often got twice as much.[66] Saskatoon, since 1962, had acquired a new wing for its men's residence, a large new women's residence, and three high-rise apartment towers. Regina did not have its first residence until 1971, and it was operated not by the university but by Luther College. The first university residence was finally built in 1972. In the early days of the development of Regina campus there had been talk of transferring the colleges of law and commerce to Regina, but this discussion had led nowhere, and new buildings for both colleges had been built in Saskatoon. "The door swung around to open in the opposite direction" when the Lapp Commission recommended closing down engineering in Regina and centralizing it at the other campus. According to the City of Regina brief, Saskatoon had been systematically favoured because most of the senior university officials had been "connected with the Saskatoon Campus in some administrative or teaching capacity prior to assuming their present positions." Saskatoon officials held the balance of power in policy-making and decision-making bodies such as the General University Council and the University Executive Committee: "We do not in any way wish to impute bad faith or bias to any of these individuals. But in view of their backgrounds and the location of the University Office in Saskatoon, there is bound to be some degree of built-in prejudice in favor of the Saskatoon Campus, even if we assume all the best intentions." The brief concluded by stating that "the City of Regina deems it vital that a dynamic and fully-developed university be maintained in Regina to reflect and meet the needs of southern Saskatchewan."[67]

The Saskatoon Campus Council brief also promoted the creation of two separate and distinct universities, but its vision of the future role of the university in Regina was quite different from that of its southern counterpart. The Saskatoon Campus Council regarded the Regina institution primarily as an appendage and feeder of Saskatoon: "There should therefore be one university offering a complete range of courses and a second, smaller university, offering pre-professional courses, liberal arts course and community-oriented courses."[68] This implied the dismantling of the professional programs already operating at the Regina campus – education, administration, engineering, and social work. The brief of the Saskatoon Faculty Association followed the same lines as that of the council. It supported "the two-Universities concept ... Saskatoon retaining a core of Arts and Science classes plus professional colleges; Regina having exclusively an Arts and Science program 'complementary' to the Saskatoon University."[69] By contrast, President Spinks, the officials of the University Office, the senate, the alumni association, and the Board of Governors all wanted to maintain the principle of autonomous campuses within the framework of one university. They believed that the problems between the two campuses were best worked out internally without government involvement.

The Hall Commission released its report in December 1973. "We must record," the commissioners said, "that we found animosity, even bitterness, between academics on the two campuses and this caused us great concern. To paraphrase Lord Durham: 'We found two campus groups warring within the bosom of a single University.'"[70] The central recommendation was that the campuses at Saskatoon and Regina be separate universities. The report observed that the Regina campus enrolment in 1973–74 exceeded that of five universities in Ontario, two in Manitoba, one in Alberta, one in British Columbia, five in Nova Scotia, two in New Brunswick, and one in Prince Edward Island. There was no reason to think that the university in Regina could not be viable on its own.

The two universities, the report continued, "must work in harmony subordinating local or regional ambitions and pride for the common good." It proposed the establishment of a Saskatchewan universities commission "to receive, review and rationalize budgets presented by the two universities and having done so to present to government a complete budget for university education in Saskatchewan" and "to allocate and distribute operating and capital funds among those institutions." The commission would have no jurisdiction concerning: the basic right of the universities to formulate academic policies and standards; the independence of the universities in fixing standards of admission or of graduation; or the independence of the universities in the appointment or tenure of staff. It was to consist of nine part-time members, including the chairman, all appointed by the government. The Hall Report suggested that the government, in making the appointments, should strive to make the body "broadly representative of the province as a whole and of the dominant groups both male and female within the province, namely agriculture, labor, management and the professions."[71] The universities commission was to appoint a full-time executive secretary to act as its chief executive officer and "to exercise the function of the Controller and Treasurer, which shall include accounting, systems development, investments and internal audit." There were to be three standing committees to assist the commission in its work: the Universities Coordinating Committee, the Capital Planning and Development Committee, and the Graduate Studies and Research Committee. All three would have substantial representation of academics and administrators from the two universities.

The Hall Report also commented on the recommendation of the Lapp Commission to discontinue engineering at the Regina campus. Lapp had based his finding on the assumption that a viable program had to graduate a minimum of forty to fifty students per year. Hall noted that this overlooked the fact that a significant number of Canadian universities did not attain this standard, but had, nevertheless, developed successful engineering programs. The decision by the Board of Governors to restrict the program in Regina had had "a devastating effect" on morale, not only in the Faculty of Engineering, but also throughout the whole institution. "To a considerable degree the difficulties between the two campuses which had increasingly manifested themselves were accentuated or brought to a head by that decision."[72] The Hall Report accordingly recommended that the full degree program in engineering at Regina, as approved by the senate in 1971, be re-established: "The University of Regina has a right to expect to be something more than just a small liberal arts college, and having embarked upon an Engineering program that was receiving praise and endorsement and was being duplicated elsewhere, it must be permitted to continue with that program as an integral part of its destiny as a university."[73] The statement that the University of Regina had a right to be "something more than just a small liberal arts college" was an attempt to break out of the mindset that had perplexed the discussion of higher education policy in the province. Hall tried to put to rest the formula that went back to 1909 and had been repeated many times since: Regina has the legislature and Saskatoon has the university. He found, however, that his recommendation was not welcome in some quarters. He confided to a friend, "The parochial reaction in Saskatoon has been almost infantile and the editorial comment even of a lower scale."[74] John Diefenbaker, chancellor of the University of Saskatchewan, exploded at Hall: "What are you doing to my university?" Don't you realize, the former prime minister harrumphed, that this issue was settled in 1905?[75]

Spinks believed that the university had been well on its way to solving its own problems without the interference of the government. "While Regina campus doesn't think so," he maintained, "the fact is that the two Campuses are even now equally independent and equally autonomous." The General University Council did not work "mainly because a few people were determined not to make it work." He compared the existing university structure to a "2-division army under one command" and characterized what Hall proposed as "two separate small armies." The philosophy of the former was "to coordinate and strengthen"; of the other, to "divide and conquer."[76]

Lloyd Barber did not think that the proposed universities commission, which had fiscal powers but no academic authority, would wield sufficient clout to function effectively as a coordinating mechanism. He predicted that "strong academics from either Campus would not be long in by-passing

Lloyd Barber, vice-president of the University of Saskatchewan (1968–74) and the second president of the University of Regina (1976–90).

the commission to take issues directly to the Government ... A more logical approach for the operation of two independent Universities might be the elimination of a Commission altogether."[77] Barber was right, and the commission was abolished in 1983. When the Blakeney government announced its intention to implement the Hall Report, Barber resigned as vice-president of the University of Saskatchewan, informing the chairman of the Board of Governors on 6 February 1974, "I have concluded that because it would be least disruptive to a reformed University and satisfactory to me, I should resume my position as Professor of Administration, College of Commerce, Saskatoon Campus. I assume the effective date of this resignation to be 30 June 1974."[78]

Spinks did not offer his resignation. When the Blakeney government first came into power in 1971 he had offered to step aside if the government did not want him,[79] but now he held on to his position. The difficulty was that either Spinks or Saskatoon campus principal Robert Begg was out of a job – Saskatoon did not need both a president and a principal. The Saskatoon Campus Council was divided about what should happen. One faction supported Spinks, a second wanted Begg as president, and a third was "primarily concerned about preventing the establishment of a precedent of the government dismissing university officials and appointing others."[80] The Saskatoon council voted on 30 January 1974 to recommend postponing the change in university structure until 30 June 1975, thereby allowing time for new boards to be appointed and new presidents to be selected at the two universities. This would have permitted Spinks to remain in office for one more year and retire at the age of sixty-seven.[81]

Begg disassociated himself from the council vote. He advised the government not to prolong the uncertainty and instability: "The administration of the University and the campuses has been under a cloud of uncertainty and tension for a year and this will continue until June. The best plans and decisions are not made under these circumstances and a prolongation until mid-1975 would inflict additional damage and I consider the potential gains very dubious."[82] Barber had voiced similar sentiments in September 1973. He had urged Spinks to advise the government to move quickly after the release of the Hall Report: "If the Government is concerned about the future of the University, then it will bring itself to make this kind of firm statement regardless of the political flak it must endure as a result. A wishy-washy course of action at this time can only result in further deterioration in an already badly eroded situation." Reinforcing the point, Barber added: "Much more of the current state of uncertainty and there will be little University left to follow any course of action."[83] Begg and Barber were in agreement: to delay resolution of the issue until July 1975 would be to court disaster. The government followed this counsel, introducing legislation in April 1974 to establish the University of Regina and a universities commission. The legislation also removed Spinks and Barber from office as of 30 June 1974. Barber, of course, had already resigned. The campus principals, Archer and Begg, were made acting presidents of the two universities until such time as two newly constituted boards of governors made permanent appointments.[84]

Regina welcomed the Hall Report and the legislation that flowed from it. The outcome was not that different from what Archer had envisaged in his brief to the commission. A "name the campus" campaign, launched in November 1972, resulted in 340 nominations.[85] These included names based on geographical setting (Prairie Lily University, University of Buffalo Plains); the city of Regina (Capital City University, University of Victoria and Albert); famous people (Trudeau University, Woodrow Lloyd University, Ross Thatcher University); spiritual values (Freedom University, University of New Horizons); and First Nations traditions (Poundmaker University, Oskuna-Kasas-Take University).[86] The committee narrowed these down to five (Wascana University, Qu'Appelle University, University of Regina, University of the Plains, and Gabriel Dumont University) and then down to one.[87]

Spinks, in his address to the final convocation of the University of Saskatchewan, Regina Campus, in May 1974, said that "all developing institutions have their problems, particularly when the development takes place in the middle of a student population explosion and in a period of campus

John Archer, principal of the University of Saskatchewan, Regina Campus (1970–74), and first president of the University of Regina (1974–75).

unrest and indeed world unrest." The growing pains at Regina campus were compounded by the fact that rapid expansion gave way abruptly to a period of declining enrolment and unrealized expectations. Despite the stresses and strains, Spinks remained optimistic: "In a few weeks, we shall have a Regina University, born in travail after what some consider an over-long gestation period ... The academics, students and faculty alike, on both campuses, must realize their common obligations, their common loyalties and *pull together*. In this way we shall emerge from this period of trial with a strengthened system of higher education in the Province of Saskatchewan." As for Regina, Spinks predicted bright prospects: "I have no uncertainties about the future of this campus, this University. Its future as an institution of quality is not in doubt. It will be the jewel of the Southern Plains."[88] The University of Regina now joined, albeit somewhat belatedly, the other new universities that had emerged in western Canada in the sixties: the University of Victoria (1963), Simon Fraser University (1965), the University of Calgary (1966), the University of Lethbridge, the University of Winnipeg, and Brandon University (all in 1967).[89]

John Archer gave his summation at a testimonial dinner held in his honour in November 1975. He recalled that during the years of rapid growth of the campus in the 1960s, "many in the Regina community wondered why their

The University of Regina in 1974, viewed from the northwest.

university wasn't more like the good old University of Saskatchewan!" They were troubled by the radicalism, the student protests, and the "excess of zeal evident in *The Carillon*." But in spite of the difficulties – and thanks "to a solid core of academic staff," the "ultimate good sense of the students," and "the wisdom and concern of the Board of Governors" – Regina campus pulled through. It "conceded to some new ideas; held firm to some valued old ideas," and emerged a little battered, perhaps, but a survivor. In the early 1970s the rapid growth suddenly ended. The campus now faced a whole new set of challenges: cutbacks, retrenchment, and scaled-down expectations. But it had weathered this too. "This gathering tonight," Archer said, "tells me what we are all saying is a 'well done' to the University of Regina – an institution that has won its spurs."

The university was not an overnight creation. Its roots reached back to 1911, when Methodists founded a college for the training of youth to "intellectual mastery and in the principles of Christian citizenship."[90] There had been golden times in the 1920s; hardship in the 1930s; takeover by the University

The University of Regina in 2005.

of Saskatchewan in 1934; the loan of the buildings to the RCAF during World War II; veterans bursting the seams of the college after the war; the university's decision in 1959 to establish a full arts and science degree program in Regina; the adoption of the Regina Beach Statement in 1963; the reinvention of the role of student government in the sixties; the rise of professional programs – education, administration, engineering, and social work; the federation of Campion College and Luther College; and the act establishing the University of Regina on 1 July 1974.

Many people had contributed: Ernest Stapleford, the formative president of Regina College; Maude Stapleford, his able helpmate; William Ramsay, teacher par excellence, who made sure the college was not relegated to obscurity in the war years; George and Ethel Barr, who "carried the torch, even in the darkest hours"; W.A. Riddell, who guided the campus through years of hectic growth; Tommy McLeod, who lent his administrative expertise when it was most needed; Woodrow Lloyd, who dreamed that "something different can be done here – different and worthwhile and needed"; John Spinks, who fostered the development of the Regina campus, but received precious little credit for it in either Regina or Saskatoon; Minoru Yamasaki, who believed that the physical environment of the university should symbolically express "the highest aspirations of man"; Dallas Smythe, who warned against identifying the university with the short-term interests of the technological order; A.B. Van Cleave, proponent of scientific research, both pure and applied; the Regina Five, young painters who put the prairies on the map; Don Mitchell, who forged the path of the "citizen student"; Peter Nash, upholder of the classical ideal that truth, beauty, and goodness are one; Morris Anderson, who aimed for "quality education in a Christian context"; Milnor Alexander, pioneer of women's studies; John Archer, who brought stability in time of turmoil; Alwyn Berland, who wrote the Regina Beach Statement; and many others besides, all of whom gave of themselves to build the University of Regina.

The newly independent university emerged from the crucible of the sixties, a time of social activism, political upheaval, and cultural transformation. The movements of the era – peace, civil rights, women's liberation, Aboriginal rights, student power – had a powerful and transformative impact on the Regina campus. Change was in the air; the time seemed right to build a better world. The Regina campus shared in this spirit of youthful idealism and commitment to social reform. It was fitting, therefore, that the University of Regina in 1974 chose for its motto "As One Who Serves," harking back to the social gospel traditions of the church college from which it sprang. Regina College in 1911 selected a verse from the Bible (Luke 22:27) to express the spirit it hoped to embody. Hearing his disciples quarrelling over which one of them would be acknowledged as the greatest, Jesus said, "No; the greatest among you must behave as if he were the youngest, the leader as if he were the one who serves. For who is the greater: the one at table or the one who serves? The one at table, surely? Yet here I am among you as one who serves."

Appendix
Significant Events in the History of the University of Regina

1911
September: Regina College begins its first year of operations.

1925
September: Regina College is affiliated as a junior college with the University of Saskatchewan.

1934
1 July: Regina College becomes part of the University of Saskatchewan; William Ramsay is appointed dean of Regina College.

1940
May: The RCAF takes occupancy of Regina College buildings and sets up an air training school; the college moves into new quarters in the Regina Trading Company Building.

1944
December: Regina College returns to its former quarters, the RCAF having closed down its air training facility.

1945
September: A first-year program in engineering is introduced.

1947
September: A first-year program in commerce is introduced.

1950
1 July: William A. Riddell is appointed dean of Regina College.

1954
March: The Regina College Citizens' Committee is formed under the leadership of George Herbert Barr.

1955
July: Howard Leyton-Brown is appointed director of the Conservatory of Music.

1959
July: The University of Saskatchewan decides to establish a full BA degree program in Regina.
August: Barnett Newman is visiting instructor at the Emma Lake Workshop.

1961
January: John Spinks, president of the University of Saskatchewan, announces the site of the new Regina campus.
1 July: Regina College is renamed the University of Saskatchewan, Regina Campus; William A. Riddell is named dean of the College of Arts and Science at Regina and acting principal of the Regina campus.
July: Minoru Yamasaki is appointed master planner for Wascana Centre and the Regina campus.
September: A second-year program in arts and science is introduced.
30 November: The National Gallery exhibition Five Painters from Regina opens in Ottawa.

1962
8 April: William Riddell is appointed principal of Regina campus.
1 July: A.B. Van Cleave is appointed chairman of the Division of Natural Sciences.
August: Clement Greenberg is visiting instructor at the Emma Lake Workshop.
October: The *Sheet* is renamed the *Carillon*.

1963
1 July: Faculty member Charles Lightbody resigns from Regina campus and issues a press release calling for the campus to be made fully autonomous; Dallas Smythe is appointed chairman of the Division of Social Sciences.
26 September: Premier Woodrow Lloyd lays the cornerstone for the first building on the new campus, saying, "Something different can be done here – different and worthwhile and needed."
13–15 December: The Regina Beach retreat is held.

1964
10 February: The Regina campus faculty adopts the "Educational Policy for the Liberal Arts," also known as the Regina Beach Statement.
March: About 200 students march to the Legislative Building demanding autonomy for Regina campus.
28 April: The first meeting of Regina Campus Council is held.
May: T.H. (Tommy) McLeod is appointed dean of arts and science.
1 July: The College of Education is officially established, with Dr F. Lester Bates as dean.
September: The third-year program in arts and science is introduced; a Bachelor of Music course is introduced.

1965
May: The first graduates of Regina campus receive their BA degrees.
1 July: T.H. McLeod is appointed vice-principal of the Regina campus while continuing to serve as dean of arts and science; the School of Graduate Studies is established with A.B. Van Cleave as director.
8 October: The classroom and laboratory buildings are officially opened at the new campus.

1966
1 July: Wes Bolstad is appointed director of the School of Administration.
1 September: J.B. Mantle is appointed dean of engineering.
September: Regina campus implements the semester system and the new BA program.

1967
18 February: The physical education centre is officially opened.
1 July: Norman France is appointed dean of education; T.H. McLeod is appointed full-time vice-principal of Regina campus; Alwyn Berland is appointed dean of arts and science.
14 October: The library building is officially opened.

1968
20 January: The Campion College building is officially opened.
6 February: Alwyn Berland resigns as dean of arts and science effective 31 December 1968.
1 July: The Faculty of Administration and the Faculty of Graduate Studies are established.
November: Minoru Yamasaki resigns as master planner for Wascana Centre and the Regina campus.
31 December: The Board of Governors suspends the collection of student activity fees.

1969
1 January: G. Edgar Vaughan is appointed acting dean of arts and science; A.B. Van Cleave is appointed dean of the Faculty of Graduate Studies.
March: The Board of Governors and the Students' Union reach an agreement on the collection of student activity fees; William A. Riddell announces his intention to resign as principal of Regina campus effective 31 December 1969.
1 July: G. Edgar Vaughan is appointed dean of arts and science; H. Bruce Lobaugh is appointed chairman of the Department of Music; Howard Leyton-Brown continues as director of the Conservatory of Music.
24 October: The education building is officially opened.
Fall: The "temporary" student services building is opened.

1970
1 January: John Archer is appointed principal of Regina campus; Ray Harvey is appointed acting vice-principal of Regina campus; William A. Riddell is appointed special assistant to President Spinks.
1 July: Ray Harvey is appointed vice-principal of Regina campus.
1 August: Arthur Kratzmann is appointed dean of education.

1971
May: Harvey Stalwick is appointed director of the School of Social Work.
3 October: The Luther College building is officially opened.
December: The Faculty of Arts and Science replaces the Regina Beach Statement with a new education policy statement.

1972
3 March: The provincial government orders a halt to design work on the engineering/physics building.

16–22 November: Students occupy the offices of the dean of arts and science and the dean of graduate studies and research.
Fall: The College West building is opened.

1973
January: The College West residence is opened; the School of Social Work enrols its first students.
April: The Royal Commission on University Organization and Structure (the Hall Commission) is appointed.
May: The administration/humanities building is opened.
30 June: Dr Dallas Smythe retires from Regina campus.
22 December: The Hall Report is released.

1974
1 July: The University of Saskatchewan, Regina Campus, becomes the University of Regina; John Archer is appointed the first president of the University of Regina.

Notes

INTRODUCTION

1 Doug Owram, *Born at the Right Time: A History of the Baby-Boom Generation* (Toronto: University of Toronto Press, 1996), 218.

2 George Parkin Grant, *Technology and Empire: Perspectives on North America* (Toronto: Anansi, 1969), 65.

3 F.H. Leacy, ed., *Historical Statistics of Canada*, 2nd ed. (Ottawa: Statistics Canada, 1983), series W340-438.

4 Theodore Roszak, *The Making of a Counter Culture: Reflections on the Technocratic Society and Its Youthful Opposition* (New York: Doubleday, 1969).

5 Luther College Archives (LCA), History of Luther College Collection, 2004–L01, A100-25, dedication, 3 October 1971, address by William Hordern.

6 Ibid.

7 James M. Pitsula, *An Act of Faith: The Early Years of Regina College* (Regina: Canadian Plains Research Center, 1988), 30.

8 For the history of the social gospel in Canada, see Richard Allen, *The Social Passion: Religion and Social Reform in Canada, 1914–1928* (Toronto: University of Toronto Press, 1973); Ramsay Cook, *The Regenerators: Social Criticism in Late Victorian Canada* (Toronto: University of Toronto Press, 1985); and Nancy Christie and Michael Gauvreau, *A Full-Orbed Christianity: The Protestant Churches and Social Welfare in Canada, 1900–1940* (Montreal and Kingston: McGill-Queen's University Press, 1996).

9 "The Kingdom of Heaven in Regina," *Leader* (Regina), 5 May 1913.

10 Pitsula, *Act of Faith*, 15–16.

11 University of Regina Archives (URA), Pamphlet File, W.W. Andrews, "Regina College: Its Purpose and Plan."
12 URA, *Regina College Calendar*, 1913–14.
13 *Leader* (Regina), 1 November 1913; 8 November 1913; 1 November 1919; 13 March 1920.
14 *Leader* (Regina), 26 March 1932.
15 URA, "Regina College: A History" Papers, 88-20, Elsie Stapleford, "Ernest William Stapleford and Family."
16 "Regina Beach Statement," University of Saskatchewan, Regina Campus, Calendar, 1964.
17 Avi Akkerman and Bill Barry, "Population," in *Atlas of Saskatchewan*, ed. Ka-iu Fung (Saskatoon: University of Saskatchewan, 1999), 188.
18 John H. Archer, *Saskatchewan: A History* (Saskatoon: Western Producer Prairie Books, 1980), 355.
19 Government of Saskatchewan, the Honourable C.A. Dunning, budget speech, 27 January 1920, 5–6; 6 December 1920, 9–10.
20 Province of Saskatchewan, A *Submission by the Government of Saskatchewan to the Royal Commission on Dominion-Provincial Relations*, 1937, 132, 134, 141.
21 *Leader* (Regina), 2 July 1927.
22 *Leader* (Regina), 22 December 1920.
23 For a thorough discussion of Saskatchewan Liberal machine politics in this period, see David E. Smith, *Prairie Liberalism: The Liberal Party in Saskatchewan* 1905–71 (Toronto: University of Toronto Press, 1975), especially chapter 2, "The Well-Oiled Machine: Liberal Politics, 1905–17."
24 Archer, *Saskatchewan*, 153–4; Clinton O. White, *Power for a Province: A History of Saskatchewan Power* (Regina: Canadian Plains Research Center, 1976), 64–5.
25 For more background on Saskatchewan's approach to economic development, see James M. Pitsula, "Disparate Duo," *Beaver*, August-September 2005.
26 Catherine L. Cleverdon, *The Woman Suffrage Movement in Canada* (Toronto: University of Toronto Press, 1974), 82.
27 Gordon L. Barnhart, *"Peace, Progress and Prosperity": A Biography of Saskatchewan's First Premier, T. Walter Scott* (Regina: Canadian Plains Research Center, 2000), 76.
28 Harold W. Fogt, A *Survey of Education in the Province of Saskatchewan*, 1918, 23.
29 Barnhart, *"Peace,"* 70.
30 Arthur S. Morton, *Saskatchewan: The Making of a University*, rev. and ed. Carlyle King (Toronto: University of Toronto Press, 1959), 51.
31 Quoted in Michael Hayden, *Seeking a Balance: The University of Saskatchewan, 1907–82* (Vancouver: University of British Columbia Press, 1983), 43–4.
32 This is evident from Thomson's correspondence with Premier Scott. A letter to Scott on 28 March 1910 enclosed an application from Mrs C.J. Heazle for a job in the Land Titles Office. C.E. Sheldon Williams applied on 10 October 1910 on behalf of her sister, who is "very anxious to secure a clerkship in the Land

Titles Office by the New Year ... Mr. Levi Thomson has kindly promised to write to either Mr. Scott or Mr. Turgeon [the Attorney General] on her behalf." Saskatchewan Archives Board (SAB), Walter Scott Papers, M1, IV, 15, private secretary to L. Thomson, 30 March 1910; C.E. Sheldon Williams to J.A. Calder, 10 October 1910. Thomson served as crown prosecutor in Wolseley and received an Order-in-Council appointment in October 1910 as "Agent of the Attorney General in and for the Judicial District of Moosomin." SAB, Government of Saskatchewan, Executive Council, O.C. 681/10, 27 October 1910.

33 Quoted in Jean E. Murray, "The Contest for the University of Saskatchewan," *Saskatchewan History* 12, no. 1 (1959): 14–15.

34 Ibid.

35 Hayden, *Seeking a Balance*, 44.

36 Walter P. Thompson, *The University of Saskatchewan: A Personal History* (Toronto: University of Toronto Press, 1970), 219.

37 *Leader* (Regina), 9 April 1909.

38 Morton, *Saskatchewan*, 50–1.

39 Quoted in *Leader* (Regina), 17 April 1909; quoted in Murray, "Contest," 21.

40 *West* (Regina), 14 April 1909.

41 SAB, Walter Scott Papers, M1, I, J.W. McLeod to W. Scott, 17 April 1909.

42 *Leader* (Regina), 12 April 1909.

43 Pitsula, *Act of Faith*, 8.

44 Ibid., 3, 8.

45 *Leader* (Regina), 26 October 1911.

46 Ibid.

47 *Leader* (Regina), 28 October 1911.

48 J. William Brennan, *Regina: An Illustrated History* (Toronto: James Lorimer and Company; Hull, QC: Canadian Museum of Civilization, 1989), 193–4.

49 J. William Brennan, "Development of the City of Regina," in *Atlas of Saskatchewan*, ed. Ka-iu Fung (Saskatoon: University of Saskatchewan, 1999), 281.

50 Barnhart, *"Peace,"* 77–8.

51 Pitsula, *Act of Faith*, 58.

52 Archives of the University of Saskatchewan (AUS), PPI, A74, W. Murray to H.M. Tory, 19 April 1927.

53 Pitsula, *Act of Faith*, 59.

54 Ibid., 132.

55 AUS, J.E. Murray Papers, E. II. B9, *Regina Daily Star* clipping, 11 June 1931; W. Murray to J.T.M. Anderson, 16 June 1931; J.T.M. Anderson to W. Murray, 18 June 1931.

56 W.S. Learned and E.W. Wallace, *Local Provision for Higher Education in Saskatchewan*, 1934.

57 Walter Murray to Henry Suzzallo, 14 June 1932, quoted in *The Prairie Builder: Walter Murray of Saskatchewan*, by David R. and Robert A. Murray (Edmonton: NeWest Publishers, 1984), 191.

58 AUS, J.E. Murray Papers, E. II. C34, E.W. Stapleford to W. Hamilton Fyfe, 5 January 1934.

59 Archer, *Saskatchewan*, 217.

60 Seymour Martin Lipset, *Agrarian Socialism: The Cooperative Commonwealth Federation in Saskatchewan* (Berkeley: University of California Press, 1971), 125.

61 Brennan, *Regina*, 135–7.

62 City of Regina Archives (CORA), City Clerk's Papers, COR-5, 4002a (31), D.J. Thom to the mayor and City Council, 26 January 1932.

63 CORA, City Clerk's Papers, COR-5, 4002d (31b), P.H. P__ to mayor, 12 December 1932.

64 Pitsula, *Act of Faith*, 126.

65 *College Record*, 1 December 1937.

66 Stapleford, "Ernest William Stapleford."

67 Pitsula, *Act of Faith*, 126.

68 URA, Publications Section, Regina College, Executive of the Board of Governors minutes, 16 January 1934, attached letter, P.E. Mackenzie to the Regina College Board of Governors, 13 January 1934.

69 Ibid.

70 URA, Publications Section, Regina College, Executive of the Board of Governors minutes, 22 January 1934.

71 University of Saskatchewan, *Annual Report of the President*, 1936–37, in Hayden, *Seeking a Balance*, 169.

72 "'Great Citizen' Lost in Dr. Stapleford," *Leader-Post* (Regina), 9 June 1937.

73 Pitsula, *Act of Faith*, 160.

74 This idea is explored in James M. Pitsula, "History, Myth and the University of Saskatchewan, 1907–1974," *Saskatchewan History* 55, no. 2 (2003). See also Michael Hayden, James Pitsula, and Raymond Blake, "Saskatchewan's Universities – A Perception of History," Saskatchewan Institute of Public Policy, Policy Paper 15, May 2003.

75 Pitsula, *Act of Faith*, 135.

CHAPTER ONE

1 "I can think of no finer view in Regina than that of the lake from your front porch." University of Regina Archives (URA), Dean's/Principal's Office Files, 75-7, 300.1-1, L. Murray to W.A. Riddell, 2 August 1950.

2 "First Dean Dies," *Leader-Post* (Regina), 27 October 1965.

3 William Ramsay, foreword, *College Record*, 2 November 1939.

4 "First Dean Dies," *Leader-Post* (Regina), 27 October 1965.

5 "Retired Classics Professor Celebrates 80th Birthday," *Leader-Post* (Regina), 3 March 1956.

6 James M. Pitsula, *An Act of Faith: The Early Years of Regina College* (Regina: Canadian Plains Research Center, 1988), 152.

7 URA, Dean's/Principal's Office Files, 75-7, 300.1-6, J.F. Leddy to W.A. Riddell, 21 February 1956.

8 J. Francis Leddy, "Memories of a Canadian Classicist, 1928–1978 (Part I)," *Échos du monde classique/Classical News and Views* 24, no. 1 (1980): 34–5.

9 "Retired Classics Professor Celebrates 80th Birthday," *Leader-Post* (Regina), 3 March 1956.
10 Leddy, "Memories," 34–5.
11 The difficulties attending the transfer of the college to the University of Saskatchewan are dealt with in chapters 7 and 8 of Pitsula, *Act of Faith*.
12 URA, Principal's Papers, 75-2, 800-13, W. Ramsay to J.G. Rempel, 18 May 1938.
13 "First Dean Dies," *Leader-Post* (Regina), 27 October 1965.
14 The university's Board of Governors appointed the Regina College Advisory Board (sometimes referred to as the "Advisory Council" or the "Advisory Committee"). The members had no fixed terms of office. Archives of the University of Saskatchewan (AUS), President's Office Records, series 3, B163, 1951, W.P. Thompson to W.A. Riddell, 6 April 1951.
15 URA, Regina College Minute Books, 75-15, Advisory Council minutes, 13 October 1939.
16 "Air Force Headquarters," *Leader-Post* (Regina), 21 December 1939.
17 URA, Regina College Minute Books, 75-15, Advisory Council minutes, 2 March 1940.
18 URA, Principal's Papers, 75-2, 800-20, J.S. Thomson to W. Ramsay, 4 March 1940.
19 AUS, President's Office Records, series 2, B151, Regina College, January-April 1940, J.S. Thomson to Colonel G. Gibson, 18 March 1940.
20 URA, Principal's Papers, 75-2, 800-20, W. Ramsay to J.S. Thomson, 4 March 1940.
21 Ibid.
22 URA, Principal's Papers, 75-2, 800-20, J.S. Thomson to W. Ramsay, 5 March 1940.
23 Michael Hayden, *Seeking a Balance: The University of Saskatchewan, 1907–82* (Vancouver: University of British Columbia Press, 1983), 194.
24 Ibid., 184.
25 James Sutherland Thomson, *Yesteryears at the University of Saskatchewan, 1937–1949* (Saskatoon: University of Saskatchewan, 1969), 36.
26 S.B. Frost, "James Sutherland Thomson," in *The Church in the Modern World: Essays in Honor of James Sutherland Thomson*, ed. George Johnston and Wolfgang Roth (Toronto: Ryerson Press, 1967), 2; Hayden, *Seeking a Balance*, 184.
27 Hayden, *Seeking a Balance*, 184.
28 URA, Principal's Papers, 75-2, 800-20, W. Ramsay to J.S. Thomson, 5 March 1940.
29 Thomson, *Yesteryears*, 17, 42.
30 URA, Principal's Papers, 75-2, 800-20, W. Ramsay to J.S. Thomson, 13 March 1940.
31 AUS, President's Office Records, series 2, B151, Regina College, January-April 1940, J.S. Thomson to W. Ramsay, 13 March 1940.
32 URA, Principal's Papers, 75-2, 800-20, W. Ramsay to J.S. Thomson, 13 March 1940.

33 URA, Principal's Papers, 75-2, 800-5, J.S. Thomson to S. Basterfield, 23 April 1941.
34 Pitsula, *Act of Faith*, 134–6.
35 URA, Principal's Papers, 75-2, 800-20, W. Ramsay to J.S. Thomson, 10 March 1940.
36 URA, Principal's Papers, 75-2, 800-14, W. Ramsay to J.S. Thomson, 28 September 1938; J.S. Thomson to J.D. Armstrong, 13 October 1938.
37 URA, Principal's Papers, 75-2, 800-14, J.S. Thomson to W. Ramsay, 25 October 1938.
38 "Colleges in Air Scheme?" *Leader-Post* (Regina), 6 March 1940.
39 "With College Appropriated by Militia, Regina in Need of Gallery, Says Kenderdine," *Leader-Post* (Regina), 7 March 1940.
40 "Youth Council Protests Use of College," *Leader-Post* (Regina), 13 March 1940.
41 "College Proposals Condemned," *Leader-Post* (Regina), 15 March 1940.
42 Ibid. D.J. Thom, the acting president of the Board of Trade, was a member of the Regina College Advisory Board.
43 "College for Air Training," *Leader-Post* (Regina), 18 March 1940.
44 "Assurance Is Given to Students," *Leader-Post* (Regina), 18 March 1940.
45 "Regina College's Gift to War," *Leader-Post* (Regina), 19 March 1940.
46 "Will Be Appreciated," *Leader-Post* (Regina), 19 March 1940.
47 AUS, President's Office Records, series 2, B151, Regina College, January-April 1940, J.S. Thomson to Colonel G. Gibson, 18 March 1940.
48 AUS, President's Office Records, series 2, B151, Regina College, January-April 1940, J.S. Thomson to Colonel G. Gibson, 29 March 1940.
49 AUS, President's Office Records, series 2, B151, Regina College, January-April 1940, F.E. Riches to J.S. Thomson, 14 April 1940.
50 AUS, President's Office Records, series 2, B151, Regina College, January-April 1940, P.E. Mackenzie to J.S. Thomson, 16 April 1940.
51 "Shameful to Spoil Spring Day But Examinations on Horizon," *Leader-Post* (Regina), 19 April 1940.
52 "No. 4 Air Chief," *Leader-Post* (Regina), 6 May 1940.
53 "Council against Immediate Step," *Leader-Post* (Regina), 8 May 1940.
54 "Regina College to Occupy Part Office Building," *Leader-Post* (Regina), 14 May 1940.
55 AUS, President's Office Records, series 2, B157, Regina College, 1940, Memorandum of Lease and Agreement; G.W. Forbes to J.S. Thomson, 7 June 1940.
56 AUS, President's Office Records, series 2, B157, Regina College, 1940, W. Ramsay to J.S. Thomson, 20 May 1940.
57 "Retired Classics Professor Celebrates 80th Birthday," *Leader-Post* (Regina), 3 March 1956; URA, Dr W.A. Riddell Papers, 84-31, 45, Dr D.C. Ramsay to W.A. Riddell, 25 October 1965.
58 URA, Principal's Papers, 75-2, 800-20, W. Ramsay to J.S. Thomson, 20 May 1940.
59 URA, Principal's Papers, 75-2, 800-20, J.S. Thomson to W. Ramsay, 21 May 1940.

60 AUS, President's Office Records, series 2, B38, Regina College, 1939–49, P.E. Mackenzie to J.S. Thomson, 10 July 1940.

61 "Terms Made for Use of School," *Leader-Post* (Regina), 12 June 1940; "College Transfer Is Made," *Leader-Post* (Regina), 30 May 1940.

62 "Two Trains of Airmen for Regina," *Leader-Post* (Regina), 2 July 1940.

63 "Air Schools for Regina," *Leader-Post* (Regina), 3 April 1940.

64 Saskatchewan Archives Board (SAB), photo R-B13507, information on back of photo; SAB, R-348, Provincial Secretary, Companies Branch, Defunct Company Files, Regina Trading Company Ltd.

65 The authorized capital of the New Regina Trading Company as of 6 March 1940 was $100,000, divided into 1,000 shares of $100 each. The shareholders and the number of shares they respectively owned were as follows: George H. Barr, 31.5; Clifton P. Church, 50; William H. Duncan, 172; William P. Cumming, 20; Peter S. Stewart, 29; Archibald W. McGregor, 20; Mae Dawson, 10; Robert Martin, 31.5; Hugh MacLean, 50; Susan MacLean, 7; Charles Willoughby Estate, 53; Isabel R. Willoughby, 11; William T. Rogers, 101; Mary F. Rogers Estate, 101; Jessie Stewart, 4; C. Morley Willoughby, 11; Ethel L. Barr, 18; the Saskatchewan Life Insurance Company, 280. Government of Saskatchewan, Department of Justice, Corporations Branch, New Regina Trading Company Ltd, file 008838.

66 "Colonel J.A. Cross Heads Board of Transport," *Leader-Post* (Regina), 21 February 1940.

67 *Henderson's Regina City Directory*, 1941.

68 AUS, President's Office Records, series 2, B157, Regina College, 1940, J.S. Thomson to D.H. Russell, 21 May 1940.

69 URA, Information File, "Steward Basterfield, 1884–1954" (from *The Proceedings of the Royal Society of Canada*, 1954).

70 "Gentleman and Scholar," *Leader-Post* (Regina), 22 February 1954.

71 Thomson, *Yesteryears*, 40.

72 Hayden, *Seeking a Balance*, 194.

73 Thomson, *Yesteryears*, 40.

74 "A Scholar of Many Parts," *Leader-Post* (Regina), 26 February 1954.

75 "Gentleman and Scholar," *Leader-Post* (Regina), 22 February 1954.

76 URA, William Clifford Blight Papers, 80-34, 2, W.C. Blight, "Coming to Regina College, 1945."

77 URA, Dr W.A. Riddell Papers, 75-1, 1203, W.A. Riddell, "How Well I Remember," 43.

78 "Six Hundred Guests Attend Reception at Regina College Honoring Newly Named Dean," *Leader-Post* (Regina), 18 September 1940.

79 URA, Principal's Papers, 75-2, 800.7, "Dean's Report on Regina College," 1940–41.

80 Steward Basterfield, foreword to *College Record*, 8 November 1940.

81 *College Record*, 31 January 1945.

82 *College Record*, 18 May 1942.

83 "Open Letter to Houston, Willoughby and Company, Ltd.," *College Record*, 20 March 1941.
84 AUS, President's Office Records, series 2, B157, Regina College, 1940, F.E. Wagg to J.S. Thomson, 18 September 1940.
85 *College Record*, 5 March 1948.
86 Hilda Neatby, "So Much for the Mind," in *Glimpses of the Last Fifty Years*. SAB, Pamphlet File, Regina College.
87 *College Record*, 31 January 1945.
88 John Bray, letter to the editor, *College Record*, 20 March 1941.
89 "Regina College Entertains Students at Splendid Banquet," *Leader-Post* (Regina), 17 March 1941.
90 Ralph Foster, "A Salute to Regina College," *College Record*, 20 March 1941.
91 "University Platoon in Regina," *Leader-Post* (Regina), 29 October 1940; *College Record*, 8 November 1940.
92 University of Saskatchewan, *Annual Report of the President*, 1943–44.
93 Hayden, *Seeking a Balance*, 184.
94 AUS, President's Office Records, series 2, B151, Regina College, 1941–43, S. Basterfield to J.S. Thomson, 22 July 1942.
95 AUS, President's Office Records, series 2, B151, Regina College, 1941–43, J.S. Thomson to S. Basterfield, 4 August 1942.
96 Up until 1934, it was possible to enter university with junior matriculation, the equivalent of grade 11, and take a four-year arts degree. In 1934 junior matriculation ended. Students now had to pass either the senior matriculation examination or grade 12 examinations in the obligatory subjects set by the Department of Education. This meant that there were now three instead of four years in the university arts and science course. In the earlier years, therefore, what table 1 refers to as "matriculation" was known as first year, and what the table calls "first year" was designated second year. Hayden, *Seeking a Balance*, 178.
97 University of Saskatchewan, *Annual Report of the President*, 1940–41. During the war years approximately 60 to 70 per cent of Regina College students came from Regina, and only 30 to 40 per cent from out of town. University of Saskatchewan, *Annual Report of the President*, 1941–42 to 1944–45.
98 University of Saskatchewan, *Annual Report of the President*, 1941–42 to 1942–43.
99 University of Saskatchewan, *Annual Report of the President*, 1943–44.
100 Walter P. Thompson, *The University of Saskatchewan: A Personal History* (Toronto: University of Toronto Press, 1970), 133.
101 University of Saskatchewan, *Annual Report of the President*, 1944–45.
102 "Officials Urge Students to Bear Responsibility," *Leader-Post* (Regina), 16 March 1942.
103 URA, Regina *College Records*, 79-5, file 34, registrar to F.M. Riches, 21 September 1939.
104 A former Regina College student, conversation with author, 29 December 2002.
105 University of Saskatchewan, *Annual Report of the President*, 1940–41; 1941–42.

106 *College Record*, 4 December 1939.
107 Grant Carscallen, "I Gambled with Death," *College Record*, 1 February 1940.
108 D. Simes, "A Thought," *College Record*, 20 February 1940.
109 Alice Goodfellow, "Tomorrow," *College Record*, 8 November 1940.
110 "Why Not Here?" *College Record*, 8 November 1940.
111 Bob Ellis, letter to the editor, *College Record*, 2 December 1940.
112 *College Record*, 20 March 1941.
113 Editorial, *College Record*, 20 March 1941.
114 Mae King, "Should Girls Wear Silk Stockings to School?" *College Record*, 4 February 1941.
115 Mae King, "The Unknown Legions," *College Record*, 8 November 1940.
116 Editorial, *College Record*, 16 January 1941.
117 Goodfellow, "Tomorrow." Upon completing her studies at Regina College, Alice Goodfellow entered medical school at the University of Toronto in a special accelerated program that was established during the war to overcome the shortage of doctors. She graduated with a specialization in pediatrics.
118 Fran Hyland, "Thoughts on an Exhibition," *College Record*, 1 May 1945.
119 Mose, "How We Like It," *College Record*, 31 January 1945.

CHAPTER TWO

1 L.G. Crossman, "Post-war Bulge," in *Glimpses of the Last Fifty Years*, Saskatchewan Archives Board (SAB), Pamphlet File, Regina College.
2 Peter Neary, "Canadian Universities and Canadian Veterans of World War II," in *The Veterans Charter and Post–World War II Canada*, ed. Peter Neary and J.L. Granatstein (Montreal & Kingston: McGill-Queen's University Press, 1998), 118.
3 Ibid., 118–19.
4 Ibid., 122.
5 University of Saskatchewan, *Annual Report of the President*, 1945–46.
6 *College Record*, 1 May 1945.
7 Crossman, "Post-war Bulge."
8 University of Saskatchewan, *Annual Report of the President*, 1945–46.
9 Crossman, "Post-war Bulge."
10 University of Saskatchewan, *Annual Report of the President*, 1945–46.
11 University of Regina Archives (URA), William Clifford Blight Papers, 80-34, 2, W.C. Blight, "Coming to Regina, 1945."
12 James Sutherland Thomson, *Yesteryears at the University of Saskatchewan* (Saskatoon: University of Saskatchewan, 1969), 73.
13 University of Saskatchewan, *Annual Report of the President*, 1945–46.
14 URA, William Clifford Blight Papers, 80-34, 10, W.C. Blight, "A Teacher's Education Is Not Obtained Solely from His Formal Education."
15 Bob Fuller, "President's Greeting," *College Record*, 4 December 1944.
16 "Social," *College Record*, 31 January 1945.

17 URA, Dr W.A. Riddell Papers, 75-1, 1203, W.A. Riddell, "How Well I Remember," 47.
18 J.D. Herbert, "Grounded," *College Record*, 1 May 1945.
19 URA, Regina College Minute Books, 75-15, Advisory Council minutes, 1 May 1947.
20 J. Herbert, "What Price Education?" *College Record*, 1 May 1945.
21 Neary, "Canadian Universities," 133–4.
22 G.K. Piller, "With the Vets," *College Record*, 19 March 1948.
23 Ibid.
24 URA, Principal's Papers, 75-2, 800.3, "University Matriculation."
25 Regina College, University of Saskatchewan, *Calendar*, 1946–47.
26 Ibid.
27 Ibid.
28 Hilda Neatby, "So Much for the Mind," in *Glimpses of the Last Fifty Years*, SAB, Pamphlet File, Regina College.
29 "Sound Off," *College Record*, November 1955.
30 University of Saskatchewan, *Annual Report of the President*, 1947–48.
31 URA, Dean's/Principal's Office Files, 75-7, 201.8, J.F. Leddy to W.P. Thompson, 18 January 1950.
32 Mose, "Dear Mr. Langley," *College Record*, 1 May 1945.
33 Bob Ellis, "Why I Like Regina College," *College Record*, 8 November 1940.
34 URA, Public Relations Office Files, 84-11, 179, academic faculty minutes, 20 November 1946.
35 URA, Public Relations Office Files, 84-11, 180, academic faculty minutes, "Rules for Eligibility in Extra-curricular Activities."
36 URA, Dean's/Principal's Office Files, 75-7, 401.2-1, W.P. Thompson to W.A. Riddell, 21 April 1952.
37 Regina College, University of Saskatchewan, *Calendar*, 1946–47.
38 Neatby, "So Much for the Mind."
39 Ellis, "Why I Like Regina College."
40 University of Saskatchewan, *Annual Report of the President*, 1947–48.
41 "Future Depends on Individuals," *Leader-Post* (Regina), 18 March 1946.
42 *College Record*, 16 March 1949.
43 *College Record*, 5 March 1940.
44 *College Record*, 14 April 1949.
45 *College Record*, fall 1951 (first issue).
46 *College Record*, 4 December 1944.
47 *College Record*, 30 October 1948.
48 *College Record*, 5 March 1940; 5 March 1948.
49 "End-of-Term Activities at Regina College," *Leader-Post* (Regina), 15 March 1940.
50 This date, 24 March, was late for the banquet, which was usually held around March 15. However, the opening of the January session in 1945 had been delayed due to the move from the Regina Trading Company Building over the Christmas break.

51 "After Dinner Speeches Enjoyed by 175 Guests," *Leader-Post* (Regina), 26 March 1945.

52 Ibid.

53 A.W. Johnson, *Dream No Little Dreams: A Biography of the Douglas Government of Saskatchewan, 1944–1961* (Toronto: University of Toronto Press, 2004), 59–93.

54 *College Record*, 1 May 1945; "After Dinner Speeches Enjoyed by 175 Guests," *Leader-Post* (Regina), 26 March 1945.

55 Neatby, "So Much for the Mind."

56 Archives of the University of Saskatchewan (AUS), President's Office Records, series 2, B151, Regina College, 1939, J.S. Thomson to W. Ramsay, 28 February 1939.

57 "College Life Value Outlined," *Leader-Post* (Regina), 18 March 1940.

58 URA, Principal's Papers, 75-2, 800-18, resolution passed by the academic staff of Regina College, 31 March 1938; 75-2, 800-19, W. Ramsay to J.S. Thomson, 21 March 1939; 75-2, 800-20, J.S. Thomson to W. Ramsay, 22 March 1939.

59 *College Record*, 30 January 1950.

60 *College Record*, 4 December 1939; 30 January 1950.

61 *College Record*, 5 March 1940.

62 *College Record*, 30 January 1950.

63 *College Record*, 4 December 1944.

64 "Needle Work," *College Record*, 19 December 1949.

65 "Data with Don," *College Record* 25 November 1948.

66 URA, Public Relations Office Files, 84-11, 180, academic faculty minutes, "Recommendation of the Special Committee Named by the Dean to Consider Problems Arising out of the Present Regulations Governing Social Activities at Regina College."

67 "College Holds First Dance," *College Record*, 2 November 1939.

68 "Hairless Joe's Hoedown," *College Record*, 5 March 1948; *College Record* 5 March 1940; H. Jones, "Looking Back," *College Record*, 1 May 1945; "Topsy-Turvy College Dance Hawkins Affair," *Leader-Post* (Regina), 26 February 1940.

69 *College Record*, 2 November 1939.

70 *College Record*, 19 March 1948.

71 "Mother and Son Tea," *College Record*, 25 November 1948.

72 *College Record*, 5 March 1940.

73 The name "Cougars" is mentioned in Cam Hetherington, "Sports," *College Record*, 1 May 1945: "Running up to the last two games before a loss the 'Cougars' (which is now the school name for the school team) finally lost out to the experienced players of Bill and Fred's Toilers in a close decision."

74 URA, Public Relations Office Files, 84-11, 180, academic faculty minutes, 11 October 1946.

75 *College Record*, 18 December 1947.

76 *College Record*, 14 April 1949; 16 March 1949.

77 Hetherington, "Sports."

78 *College Record*, 20 February 1940.

79 *College Record*, 5 March 1940.
80 *College Record*, 25 February 1949.
81 *College Record*, 5 March 1948.
82 *College Record*, 25 February 1949.
83 "Shutout in School Puck Loop," *Leader-Post* (Regina), 5 February 1940.
84 *College Record*, 20 February 1948.
85 Letter from the editor, *College Record*, 16 March 1949.
86 *College Record*, 16 March 1949.
87 University of Saskatchewan, *Annual Report of the President*, 1945–46 to 1949–50.
88 University of Saskatchewan, *Annual Report of the President*, 1947–48.
89 University of Saskatchewan, *Annual Report of the President*, 1948–49.
90 URA, Principal's Papers, 75-2, 800-1, J.S. Thomson to Dean Basterfield, 25 February 1949; URA, Principal's Papers, 75-2, 800-1, T. Thorvaldson, chairman of the Faculty Relations Committee, to Dean Basterfield, 9 March 1949.
91 URA, Dean's/Principal's Office Files, 75-7, 201.8, "Statement of the Chancellor Regarding Regina College," 26 March 1949.

CHAPTER THREE

1 University of Regina Archives (URA), Regina College Minute Books, 75-15, Advisory Council of Regina College, 12 March 1949.
2 "Regina College Medical School Urged," *Leader-Post* (Regina), 11 March 1949.
3 "A Bold Student Move," *Leader-Post* (Regina), 12 March 1949.
4 "City Council to Push College Use for Arts," *Leader-Post* (Regina), 16 March 1949.
5 H.F. Thomson was the son of Levi Thomson, the Board of Governors member who cast the deciding vote in 1909 to locate the university in Saskatoon instead of Regina.
6 "Church to Watch College Interests," *Leader-Post* (Regina), 21 March 1949.
7 F.H. Auld, deputy minister in the Department of Agriculture, lived in Regina.
8 URA, Dean's/Principal's Office Files, 75-7, 201.8, "Statement of the Chancellor Regarding Regina College," 26 March 1949.
9 Archives of the University of Saskatchewan (AUS), President's Office Records, series 3, B163, Regina College, 1950, statements of revenues and expenditures, 1946–49.
10 URA, Dean's/Principal's Office Files, 75-7, 201.8, "Statement of the Chancellor Regarding Regina College," 26 March 1949.
11 Ibid.
12 "Regina College Needs Students," *Leader-Post* (Regina), 9 April 1949. The university's understanding of the commitment it had made with respect to Regina College is contained in the minutes of the university Board of Governors meeting of 12 January 1934. See Saskatchewan Archives Board (SAB), W.S. Lloyd Papers, R-61.3, E-25, 15/37.

13 Walter P. Thompson, *The University of Saskatchewan: A Personal History* (Toronto: University of Toronto Press, 1970), 60.
14 Michael Hayden, *Seeking a Balance: The University of Saskatchewan, 1907–82* (Vancouver: University of British Columbia Press, 1983), 202.
15 Ibid., 203–4, 207.
16 James Sutherland Thomson, *Yesteryears at the University of Saskatchewan* (Saskatoon: University of Saskatchewan, 1969), 12.
17 Hayden, *Seeking a Balance*, 206.
18 Thompson, *University of Saskatchewan*, 153–5.
19 URA, Dean's/Principal's Office Files, 75-7, 201.8, "The Future of Regina College."
20 University of Saskatchewan, *Annual Report of the President*, 1949–50.
21 URA, Dean's/Principal's Office Files, 75-7, 201.8, "The Future of Regina College."
22 URA, Dr W.A. Riddell Papers, 84-31, 48, J.G. Rempel to W.A. Riddell, 7 January 1970.
23 URA, Dr W.A. Riddell Papers, 75-1, 1203, W.A. Riddell, "How Well I Remember," 41; AUS, President's Office Records, series 3, B163, Regina College, 1949, H. Auld to W.P. Thompson, 18 October 1949.
24 AUS, President's Office Records, series 3, B163, Regina College, 1949, W.A. Riddell to W.P. Thompson, 1 December 1949.
25 Riddell, "How Well I Remember," 13.
26 Riddell, "How Well I Remember," 1–35; SAB, William A. Riddell Papers, R-487, I 1, curriculum vitae.
27 AUS, President's Office Records, series 3, B163, Regina College, 1949, W.A. Riddell to W.P. Thompson, 1 December 1949.
28 URA, Dr W.A. Riddell Papers, 84-31, 28, W.P. Thompson to W.A. Riddell, n.d.
29 AUS, President's Office Records, series 3, B163, Regina College, 1949, W.A. Riddell to W.P. Thompson, 9 December 1949.
30 SAB, W.S. Lloyd Papers, R-61.3, E-25, 15/37, "Regina College."
31 AUS, President's Office Records, series 2, B151, Regina College, January-April 1940, G.W. Forbes to J.S. Thomson, 19 March 1940.
32 URA, Publications Section, Regina College, Executive of the Board of Governors minutes, 16 January 1934, attached letter, P.E. Mackenzie to the Regina College Board of Governors, 13 January 1934.
33 URA, Dean's/Principal's Office Files, 75-7, 201.8, "Report of the Regina College Committee."
34 Ibid.
35 Riddell, "How Well I Remember," 42.
36 URA, Dr W.A. Riddell Papers, 84-31, 27, W.A. Riddell to father and mother, 7 March 1950.
37 URA, Dr W.A. Riddell Papers, 84-31, 44, C.V. Thackeray to W.A. Riddell, 4 April [1961?].
38 Riddell, "How Well I Remember," 44. E.R. Thackeray described the university's attitude towards Regina College as follows: "Generally speaking Saskatoon staff

are ignorant about it or if they know they are entirely uninterested and consider it an extra burden." AUS, Vice-President (Administration) Office Records, F-10, Regina College, 1934–54, E.R. Thackeray, handwritten notes.

39 SAB, T.C. Douglas Papers, R-33.1 V 224 (5-3), 7/11, W.P. Thompson to W.S. Lloyd, 25 May 1954.

40 Riddell, "How Well I Remember," 44. Freud notwithstanding, sometimes a cigar is just a cigar.

41 University of Saskatchewan, *Annual Report of the President*, 1950–51; 1952–53.

42 University of Saskatchewan, *Annual Report of the President*, 1956–57.

43 University of Saskatchewan, *Annual Report of the President*, 1954–55.

44 This section on courses offered at the college in the 1950s is based on University of Saskatchewan, *Annual Report of the President*, 1950–51 to 1958–59.

45 URA, Regina College Minute Books, 75-15, Advisory Council minutes, 25 February 1953.

46 University of Saskatchewan, *Annual Report of the President*, 1955–56.

47 URA, Dean's/Principal's Office Files, 75-7, 506.1-1, "Space Requirements at Regina College," 12 June 1954.

48 URA, Dean's/Principal's Office Files, 75-7, 506.1-2, "Dean's Report on Regina College," 1 May 1959.

49 URA, Principal's Papers, 75-2, 1300, "Report of the Committee on Admissions," 14 April 1954.

50 URA, Principal's Papers, 75-2, 1300, "Regina College Matriculation Course," September 1958.

51 Riddell, "How Well I Remember," 49.

52 URA, Dean's/Principal's Office Files, 75-7, 506.1-1, "Space Requirements at Regina College," 12 June 1954.

53 AUS, President's Office Records, series 2, B38, Chancellor, 1939–49, J.S. Thomson to P.E. MacKenzie, 10 November 1944.

54 AUS, President's Office Records, series 2, B151, Regina College, 1944–45, J.H. Sturdy to J.S. Thomson, 17 February 1945.

55 URA, Principal's Papers, 75-2, 1500-1, clipping, "Return of Building to College Planned," *Leader-Post* (Regina), October 1954.

56 URA, Regina College Minute Books, 75-15, Advisory Council minutes, 14 September 1950.

57 URA, Regina College Minute Books, 75-15, Advisory Council minutes, 26 November 1951; 14 October 1952; 25 February 1953.

58 URA, Regina College Minute Books, 75-15, Advisory Council minutes, 1 May 1953; 11 August 1955.

59 URA, Dean's/Principal's Office Files, 75-7, 506.1-1, report prepared by W.A.R., April 1954, headed "not submitted to everyone."

60 URA, Principal's Papers, 75-2, 1500-1, clipping, "Return of Building to College Planned," *Leader-Post* (Regina), October 1954.

61 URA, Dean's/Principal's Office Files, 75-7, 506.1-1, report prepared by W.A.R., April 1954.

62 AUS, President's Office Records, series 3, B163, Regina College, 1958–59, W.A. Riddell to C.G. Willis, 30 May 1958.

63 URA, Regina College Minute Books, 75-15, Advisory Council minutes, 2 May 1958; AUS, President's Office Records, series 3, B163, Regina College, 1958–59, C.G. Willis to W.A. Riddell, 5 June 1958.

64 "Government Closing Vehicle Garage," *Leader-Post* (Regina), 5 May 1965.

65 SAB, T.C. Douglas Papers, R-33.1, V 224 (5-3), 7/11, G.H. Barr to C.C. Williams, 20 April 1954.

66 Ibid.

67 URA, Dean's/Principal's Office Files, 75-7, 506.1-1, report prepared by W.A.R., April 1954.

68 URA, Regina College Minute Books, 75-15, Advisory Council minutes, 17 November 1954.

69 URA, Regina College Minute Books, 75-15, Advisory Council minutes, 21 February 1955.

70 URA, Regina College Minute Books, 75-15, Advisory Council minutes, 2 September 1955.

71 "Regina's New Art Gallery," *Leader-Post* (Regina), 29 October 1957.

72 URA, Regina College Minute Books, 75-15, Advisory Council minutes, 1 May 1953.

73 URA, Regina College Minute Books, 75-15, Advisory Council minutes, 11 August 1955.

74 URA, Regina College Minute Books, 75-15, Advisory Council minutes, 25 February 1959.

75 URA, Dean's/Principal's Office Files, 75-7, 506.1-2, "Regina College," 22 May 1959.

76 URA, Regina College Minute Books, 75-15, Advisory Council minutes, 20 December 1955.

77 AUS, Vice-President (Administration) Office Records, F-10, Regina College, 1957–59, Gymnasium.

78 URA, Regina College Minute Books, 75-15, Advisory Council minutes, 2 May 1958.

79 URA, Regina College Minute Books, 75-15, Advisory Council minutes, 30 October 1958.

80 URA, Regina College Minute Books, 75-15, Advisory Council minutes, 15 January 1959; URA, Dean's/Principal's Office Files, 75-7, 506.1–2, "Regina College," 22 May 1959.

81 URA, Dean's/Principal's Office Files, 75-7, 506.1-2, "Regina College," 22 May 1959.

82 URA, Regina College Minute Books, 75-15, Advisory Council minutes, 1 March 1956.

83 W.A. Riddell, "Building Plans for Regina College," *Sheet*, March 1959; University of Saskatchewan, *Annual Report of the President*, 1958–59.

84 Riddell, "Building Plans."

85 New construction at the Saskatoon campus in the post-war period included the Medical College Building (1946–49), the University Hospital (1948–55), an addition to the Engineering Building (1946–48), a students' union building (Memorial Union Building, 1953–55), an agriculture building (Kirk Hall, 1947–49), a soil and dairy science building (John Mitchell Building, 1947–49), a gymnasium (1948–49), a virus laboratory building (Fulton Building, 1947), a library (Walter Murray Memorial Library, 1954–56), St Thomas More College (1954–55), the Department of Agriculture Laboratory Building (1955–57), and, finally, towards the end of the decade, an arts building, an animal husbandry building, and a biology building. Hayden, *Seeking a Balance*, 217.

CHAPTER FOUR

1 *Leader-Post* (Regina), 8 September 1954.
2 *College Record*, fall 1951 (first issue).
3 *College Record*, December 1954.
4 Michael Hayden, *Seeking a Balance: The University of Saskatchewan, 1907–82* (Vancouver: University of British Columbia Press, 1983), 216.
5 *Sheet*, April 1958.
6 Ibid.
7 University of Regina Archives (URA), Office of the University Secretary, 78-5, 191, Sam Stewart, speech given at a testimonial dinner for W.A. Riddell, 27 January 1970.
8 Catherine Gidney, "Poisoning the Student Mind?: The Student Christian Movement at the University of Toronto, 1920–1965," *Journal of the Canadian Historical Association* new series 8 (1997): 149.
9 See Beth L. Bailey, *From Front Porch to Back Seat: Courtship in Twentieth Century America* (Baltimore: Johns Hopkins University Press, 1989).
10 *College Record*, 19 December 1949; fall 1951 (first issue).
11 *College Record*, March 1954.
12 *College Record*, December 1954.
13 URA, Dean's/Principal's Office Files, 75-7, 400.1-1, E. Hawkesworth to W.A. Riddell, 20 April 1951.
14 URA, Dean's/Principal's Office Files, 75-7, 400.1-1, G. Firth to W.A. Riddell, 3 March 1952.
15 Ibid.
16 URA, Dean's/Principal's Office Files, 75-7, 400.3-1, W.A. Riddell to G. Firth, 29 September 1953.
17 *College Record*, fall 1951 (first issue).
18 *College Record*, 15 December 1951.
19 *College Record*, 8 December 1952.
20 *College Record*, January 1955.
21 URA, Dean's/Principal's Office Files, 75-7, 400.1-2, SRC Social Directorate, "Social Functions: Required Procedure," 22 February 1955.
22 *College Record*, 5 April 1950; *Sheet*, April 1958.

23 *College Record*, January 1954; 18 January 1952.
24 *College Record*, 8 December 1952; December 1954; *Sheet*, January 1959.
25 *Sheet*, January 1959.
26 *College Record*, 19 December 1949.
27 *College Record*, 30 January 1950.
28 *Sheet*, March 1959.
29 *Sheet*, January 1959.
30 *Sheet*, April 1958.
31 *College Record*, fall 1951 (first issue).
32 *College Record*, 19 December 1949.
33 *College Record*, fall 1951 (first issue).
34 *Freshman* (Regina College yearbook), 1949, 60.
35 URA, Dean's/Principal's Office Files, 75-7, 400.4, Student Elections; 75-7, 300.1-7, nominees proposed by the nominating committee for standing committees for the year 1958–59, 9 September 1958.
36 URA, Publications Section, Students' Union Ephemerae, "The Constitution of the Students' Representative Council of Regina College of the University of Saskatchewan."
37 Editorial, *Sheet*, February 1962.
38 URA, Dean's/Principal's Office Files, 75-7, 400.1-1, "Re: The *College Record*, March/51 from Kinsman."
39 *College Record*, December 1955.
40 URA, Dean's/Principal's Office Files, 75-7, 400.1-1, "Re: The *College Record*, March/51 from Kinsman."
41 Dean W.A. Riddell, "To All Students," *College Record*, March 1955.
42 Margot Moffat, "Dear Joe College," *College Record*, 30 October 1948.
43 Letter to the editor, *College Record*, February 1955.
44 Bert Promislow, "Presenting True Democracy," *College Record*, 18 November 1947.
45 URA, Dean's/Principal's Office Files, 75-7, 400.1-1, "Re: The *College Record*, March/51 from Kinsman."
46 G.K. Piller, "Food for Thought," *College Record*, 29 January 1948.
47 I. Kreel, "A Real Education," *College Record*, 19 March 1948.
48 "Men's Residence," *Sheet*, April 1958.
49 *College Record*, February 1955.
50 *Sheet*, 1956 (first issue).
51 Doug Owram, *Born at the Right Time: A History of the Baby-Boom Generation* (Toronto: University of Toronto Press, 1996), 178
52 URA, Dean's/Principal's Office Files, 75-7, 401.4, "Regulations, Women's Residence, Regina Campus, University of Saskatchewan," 1962.
53 Beth Bailey, *Sex in the Heartland* (Cambridge: Harvard University Press, 1999), 10–11.
54 URA, Dean's/Principal's Office Files, 75-7, 401.5, J.W. Gibson to W.P. Thompson, 30 November 1950.

55 URA, Dean's/Principal's Office Files, 75-7, 401.5, W.A. Riddell, memo, November 1950.
56 URA, Dean's/Principal's Office Files, 75-7, 401.5, J.W.G. to W.P. Thompson, 30 November 1950.
57 URA, Dean's/Principal's Office Files, 75-7, 401.5, W.A. Riddell to W.P. Thompson, 4 December 1950.
58 URA, Dean's/Principal's Office Files, 75-7, 401.5, W.P. Thompson to W.A. Riddell, 6 December 1950.
59 URA, Dean's/Principal's Office Files, 75-7, 401.5, "Discipline Committee Report," 15 November 1950.
60 *College Record*, 5 March 1940.
61 Letter to the editor, *College Record*, 4 February 1941.
62 *College Record*, 5 March 1948.
63 Joan Hart, Arts and Science, *Sheet*, February 1960.
64 Editorial, *College Record*, November 1955.
65 G.L. Parrott, "We Are, We Are," *College Record*, 23 February 1950.
66 *Sheet*, February 1958.
67 *College Record*, 18 November 1947.
68 Parrott, "We Are, We Are."
69 *College Record*, 5 April 1950.
70 "They Just Think They Are – They Really Ain't," *College Record*, 5 April 1950.
71 "Lab techs," letter to the editor, *College Record*, March 1955.
72 *Sheet*, April 1959.
73 "Catalytic Vapor-Phase Oxidation of Engineers," *Sheet*, January 1959.
74 *Sheet*, November-December 1960.
75 "On Chianti," *Sheet*, December 1961.
76 Editorial, *Sheet*, January 1959.
77 *Sheet*, April 1959.
78 URA, Public Relations Office Files, 84-11, 181, academic faculty minutes, 27 February 1953.
79 URA, Public Relations Office Files, 84-11, 181, academic faculty minutes, 13 November 1956.
80 URA, Dean's/Principal's Office Files, 75-7, 400.4, "Notice from the Dean," 29 September 1954.
81 Gwen Ellis, "J'accuse," *College Record*, 30 January 1950.
82 Editorial, *College Record*, November 1953.
83 Letter to the editor, *College Record*, February 1955.
84 "Another student," letter to the editor, *College Record*, March 1955.
85 "Sound Off," *College Record*, November 1955.
86 University of Saskatchewan, *Annual Report of the President*, 1947–48.
87 URA, Dean's/Principal's Office Files, 75-7, 300.1-2, S. Basterfield to W.A. Riddell, 28 April 1952.
88 URA, Dean's/Principal's Office Files, 75-7, 300.1-6, W.A. Riddell to W.P. Thompson, 17 December 1956.

89 Archives of the University of Saskatchewan (AUS), President's Office Records, series 2, B151, Regina College, 1944–45, E.R. Thackeray to J.S. Thomson, 2 April 1945.
90 AUS, President's Office Records, series 2, B151, Regina College, 1948–49, E.R. Thackeray to J.S. Thomson, 2 December 1948.
91 AUS, President's Office Records, series 2, B151, Regina College, 1948–49, E.R. Thackeray to J.S. Thomson, 6 May 1949.
92 AUS, President's Office Records, series 3, B163, Regina College, 1949, H. Auld to W.P. Thompson, 18 October 1949.
93 AUS, President's Office Records, series 2, B151, Regina College, 1948–49, J.S. Thomson to E.R. Thackeray, 10 May 1949.
94 "Valediction," *Sheet*, April 1958.

CHAPTER FIVE

1 University of Regina Archives (URA), Principal's Papers, 75-2, 800-14, Dean Ramsay to J.S. Thomson, 28 September 1938; 75-2, 800-6, W.P. Thompson to Dean Basterfield, 14 August 1946; 75-2, 800.7, Dean Basterfield to W.P. Thompson, 6 February 1950.
2 URA, Dean's/Principal's Office Files, 75-7, 200.1, W.A. Riddell to W.P. Thompson, 3 April 1951.
3 URA, Dean's/Principal's Office Files, 75-7, 200.1, J.F. Leddy to W.A. Riddell, 18 April 1951.
4 URA, Dean's/Principal's Office Files, 75-7, 200.1, "Report of the Special Committee to Consider the Request from the Faculty of Regina College."
5 URA, Dean's/Principal's Office Files, 75-7, 300.1-2, F.E. Wagg to W.A. Riddell, 27 April 1952.
6 URA, Dean's/Principal's Office Files, 75-7, 506.1-1, report prepared by W.A.R., April 1954, headed "not submitted to everyone."
7 J.R. Bothwell, "Those Who Came Before," *Leader-Post* (Regina), 22 June 1955. The sketch of G.H. Barr is also based on "George Barr, Noted Lawyer, Dies at 82," *Leader-Post* (Regina), 8 February 1960; Andrew Kozma, "Second-Generation City Lawyer Describes Variety of Experiences," *Leader-Post* (Regina), 8 July 1978; Nick Russell, "Barr of the Bar," *Western Living*, July 1986.
8 Mary Ann Fitzgerald, "The Old Order Is Changing," *Leader-Post* (Regina), 7 September 1956; "Pioneer Woman Honored by Club She Founded," *Leader-Post* (Regina), 12 October 1954; "Resident since 1883 Dies at 80," *Leader-Post* (Regina), 6 September 1963.
9 Saskatchewan Archives Board (SAB), G.H. Barr Papers, R-8, 36, ¾, G.H. Barr to E.W. Stapleford, 15 January 1952.
10 Michael Hayden, *Seeking a Balance: The University of Saskatchewan, 1907–82* (Vancouver: University of British Columbia Press, 1983), 44.
11 SAB, Walter Scott Papers, M 1, I, J.W. McLeod to W. Scott, 17 April 1909.
12 SAB, W.S. Lloyd Papers, R-61.3 E-25, 23/37, G.H. Barr to T.C. Douglas, 26 February 1954.

13 Bothwell, "Those Who Came Before."
14 SAB, W.S. Lloyd Papers, R-61.3 E-25, 23/37, G.H. Barr to T.C. Douglas, 26 February 1954.
15 SAB, G.H. Barr Papers, R-8, 36, ¾, G.H. Barr to E.W. Stapleford, 15 January 1952.
16 SAB, G.H. Barr Papers, R-8, 36, ¾, G.H. Barr to E.W. Stapleford, 29 January 1952.
17 SAB, G.H. Barr Papers, R-8, 36, ¾, E.W. Stapleford to G.H. Barr, 27 February 1952.
18 URA, Dean's/Principal's Office Files, 75-7, 200.1, W.A. Riddell to W.P. Thompson, 2 February 1952.
19 URA, Regina College Minute Books, 75-15, Advisory Council special committee minutes, 28 February 1952.
20 URA, Principal's Papers, 75-2, 1500-1, clipping, "Aldermen Voice Objections to Part of College Report," *Leader-Post* (Regina), n.d.
21 Editorial, *Leader-Post* (Regina), 10 February 1953.
22 SAB, G.H. Barr Papers, R-8, 36, ¾, E.W. Stapleford to G.H. Barr, 17 January 1953.
23 "Let Regina College Grow," *Leader-Post* (Regina), 22 February 1954.
24 "Degree Course for Debate," *Leader-Post* (Regina), 12 March 1954.
25 "Regina Committee Seeks Arts Course," *Leader-Post* (Regina), 22 March 1954.
26 SAB, W.S. Lloyd Papers, R-61.3 E-25, 22/37, "Resolution," 19 March 1954.
27 "Regina Committee Seeks Arts Course," *Leader-Post* (Regina), 22 March 1954; the occupations list is based on entries in *Henderson's Regina City Directory*, 1954.
28 Walter P. Thompson, *The University of Saskatchewan: A Personal History* (Toronto: University of Toronto Press, 1970), 33; URA, Dr W.A. Riddell Papers, 75-1, 1203, W.A. Riddell, "How Well I Remember," 49.
29 Fitzgerald, "Old Order."
30 Russell, "Barr of the Bar."
31 "Principals Lukewarm to Arts Course Plan," *Leader-Post* (Regina), 23 March 1954.
32 Reverend Athol Murrary, letter to the editor, *Leader-Post* (Regina), 2 April 1954.
33 Archives of the University of Saskatchewan (AUS), President's Office Records, series 3, B163, Regina College, 1954, E.C. Leslie to W.P. Thompson, 23 March 1954.
34 SAB, W.S. Lloyd Papers, R-61.3 E-25, 23/37, W.S. Lloyd to W.P. Thompson, 9 April 1954.
35 AUS, President's Office Records, series 3, B163, Regina College, 1954, W.S. Lloyd to W.P. Thompson, 9 April 1954.
36 SAB, T.C. Douglas Papers, R-33.1 V 224 (5-3) 7/11, W.P. Thompson to W.S. Lloyd, 25 May 1954.
37 SAB, T.C. Douglas Papers, R-33.1 V 224 (5-3) 7/11, "Statement by the University of Saskatchewan about the Proposal that Regina College Become a College Carrying Students to the Degree in Arts."

38 SAB, T.C. Douglas Papers, R-33.1 V 224 (5-3) 7/11, W.P. Thompson to W.S. Lloyd, 25 May 1954.
39 URA, Principal's Papers, 75-2, 1500-1, "Varsity Rejects Regina Bid for Degree Course," *Leader-Post* (Regina), 28 May 1954; "Something Missing," May 1954.
40 SAB, T.C. Douglas Papers, R-33.1 V 224 (5-3) 7/11, G.H. Barr to T.C. Douglas, 4 June 1954.
41 SAB, T.C. Douglas Papers, R-33.1 V 224 (5-3) 7/11, "Mr. Premier and Gentlemen ..."
42 "Amendment May Pave Way for Arts Course," *Leader-Post* (Regina), 25 February 1955; "Barr Urges MLA's Support for Degree Course at College," *Leader-Post* (Regina), 1 March 1955.
43 "Perseverance Will Be Rewarded," *Leader-Post* (Regina), 28 March 1955.
44 Dean Leddy, letter to the editor, *Leader-Post* (Regina), 20 June 1955.
45 "Varsity Facilities Adequate," *Leader-Post* (Regina), 10 November 1955.
46 University of Saskatchewan, *Annual Report of the President*, 1955–56; 1965–66.
47 "Political Issue Threat Develops from College Degree Status Controversy," *Leader-Post* (Regina), 29 April 1955.
48 SAB, T.C. Douglas Papers, R-33.1 V 224 (5-3) 7/11, J.F. Leddy to J. Foster, 24 May 1955.
49 SAB, T.C. Douglas Papers, R-33.1 V 224 (5-3) 7/11, J. Foster to "Sir or Madam," 11 May 1955.
50 SAB, T.C. Douglas Papers, R-33.1 V 224 (5-3) 7/11, J.F. Leddy to J. Foster, 24 May 1955.
51 AUS, President's Office Records, series 3, B163, Regina College, 1955, E.C. Leslie to W.P. Thompson, 29 April 1955.
52 AUS, President's Office Records, series 3, B163, Regina College, 1955, W.A. Riddell to W.P. Thompson, 2 August 1955.
53 AUS, President's Office Records, series 3, B163, Regina College, 1955, W.P. Thompson to W.A. Riddell, 8 August 1955.
54 SAB, T.C. Douglas Papers, R-33.1 V 224 (5-3) 7/11, "Brief Presented to the Premier of Saskatchewan, Regina Representatives in the Provincial Government, and Regina Members of the Board of Governors of the University of Saskatchewan," 27 June 1955.
55 SAB, W.S. Lloyd Papers, R-61.3 E-25, 26/37, A. Tait to W.S. Lloyd, 13 August 1955; J.A. Klein to T.C. Douglas, 9 March 1955.
56 SAB, T.C. Douglas Papers, R-33.1 V 224 (5-3) 8/11, memorandum of brief to members of the legislature, Premier's Office, 7 February 1956.
57 "McDonald Charged Using Arts Course as 'Football,'" *Leader-Post* (Regina), 18 February 1956.
58 "MLA Says College Hurt," *Leader-Post* (Regina), 3 May 1956.
59 "Far from Invincible," *Leader-Post* (Regina), 16 March 1956.
60 "Suggestions for the Opposition," *Leader-Post* (Regina), 3 March 1956.
61 SAB, T.C. Douglas Papers, R-33.1 V 224 (5-3) 8/11, G.H. Barr, "Wake Up, Regina! A Call to Action," received 28 December 1956.

62 A.W. Johnson, *Dream No Little Dreams: A Biography of the Douglas Government of Saskatchewan, 1944–1961* (Toronto: University of Toronto Press, 2004), 182–3.
63 Government of Saskatchewan, budget speech delivered by the Honourable W.S. Lloyd, 27 February 1961, 7.
64 Johnson, *Dream*, 183.
65 J. William Brennan, *Regina: An Illustrated History* (Toronto: James Lorimer and Company; Hull, QC: Canadian Museum of Civilization, 1989), 191.
66 Paul Axelrod, "Higher Education, Utilitarianism, and the Acquisitive Society: Canada, 1930–1980," in *Modern Canada, 1930–1980s*, ed. Michael S. Cross and Gregory S. Kealey (Toronto: McClelland and Stewart, 1984), 186.
67 Doug Owram, *Born at the Right Time: A History of the Baby Boom Generation* (Toronto: University of Toronto Press, 1996), 179.
68 Ibid., 179–80.
69 AUS, President's Office Records, series 3, B163, Regina College, 1958–59, W.P. Thompson to W.A. Riddell, 4 July 1958.
70 SAB, T.C. Douglas Papers, R-33.1 V 224 (5-3) 10/11, W.S. Lloyd to T.C. Douglas, 30 December 1958.
71 URA, Principal's Papers, 75-2, 1500-3, Clippings File, "University Must Expand: Needs 'Substantial Funds,'" 8 May 1959.
72 According to the University of Saskatchewan *Annual Report of the President*, the enrolment in 1958–59 was 4,114. Double that number would place the upper limit on enrolment at Saskatoon at 8,228.
73 URA, Publications Section, University of Saskatchewan Senate minutes, 8 July 1959.
74 Ibid.
75 Hayden, *Seeking a Balance*, 236.
76 URA, Publications Section, University of Saskatchewan, Board of Governors minutes, 17 June 1959.
77 Riddell, "How Well I Remember," 56.
78 Hayden, *Seeking a Balance*, 237.
79 Riddell, "How Well I Remember," 56.
80 SAB, W.S. Lloyd Papers, R-61.3 E-25 36/37, minutes of a meeting of the university senate, 8 July 1959.
81 Riddell, "How Well I Remember," 57.
82 SAB, W.S. Lloyd Papers, R-61.3 E-25 36/37, minutes of a meeting of the university senate, 8 July 1959.
83 Hayden, *Seeking a Balance*, 238.
84 SAB, T.C. Douglas Papers, R-33.1 V 224 (5-3) 10/11, T.J. Bentley to T.C. Douglas, 20 March 1959.
85 John Spinks, *Two Blades of Grass: An Autobiography* (Saskatoon: Western Producer Prairie Books, 1980), 93.
86 "Degree Status for Regina College," *Star-Phoenix* (Saskatoon), 11 July 1959.
87 "Educators, Officials Welcome Campus," *Leader-Post* (Regina), 10 July 1959.

CHAPTER SIX

1 University of Regina Archives (URA), Publications Section, University of Saskatchewan Senate minutes, 11 May 1960.

2 Ibid.

3 Archives of the University of Saskatchewan (AUS), President's Office Records, series 4, C38, Regina Campus Files, W.A. Riddell, 1959–63, A. Johnson to W.P. Thompson, 4 September 1959.

4 John Spinks, *Two Blades of Grass: An Autobiography* (Saskatoon: Western Producer Prairie Books, 1980), 4, 5, 8, 15, 31, 40, 69–70, 73.

5 AUS, President's Office Records, series 4, C38, Regina Campus Files, W.A. Riddell, 1959–63, W.A. Riddell to J.W.T. Spinks, 13 October 1960.

6 URA, Dr W.A. Riddell Papers, 75-1, 1203, W.A. Riddell, "How Well I Remember," 59–60.

7 AUS, President's Office Records, series 4, C38, Regina Campus Files, W.A. Riddell, 1959–63, W.A. Riddell to J.W.T. Spinks, 13 October 1960.

8 Ibid.

9 URA, Principal's/Dean's Office Files, 78-3, 400.18, report to faculty submitted by the Special Committee on Divisional Organization, April 1963.

10 Riddell, "How Well I Remember," 58–9.

11 URA, Public Relations Office Files, 84-11, faculty of Regina College minutes, 1958–60, proposed arts and science curriculum for the University of Saskatchewan, Regina branch, 8 December 1959.

12 Ibid.

13 URA, Owen Holmes Papers, 84-33, "Planning for the Main Campus, 1962," J.F. Leddy to W.A. Riddell, 11 December 1959.

14 URA, Owen Holmes Papers, 84-33, "Planning for the Main Campus, 1962," Regina Campus Expansion Committee on Course Content and Staff, 16 December 1959.

15 Riddell, "How Well I Remember," 58–9.

16 AUS, President's Office Records, series 4, C38, Regina Campus Files, W.A. Riddell, 1959–63, G. Ledingham to J.W.T. Spinks, with attached memo, 14 October 1960.

17 URA, Public Relations Office Files, 84-11, faculty of Regina College minutes, 11 April 1960.

18 Ron Bloore and Art McKay were members of the Regina Five group of painters, which received national acclaim in 1961.

19 URA, Dean's/Principal's Office Files, 75-7, 102.2, L.H. Greenberg, R.L. Bloore, A.F. McKay, memo concerning the name of the university, April 1960.

20 URA, Dean's/Principal's Office Files, 75-7, 102.2, L.H. Greenberg, "A Name for the New University to be Situated in Regina."

21 URA, Dean's/Principal's Office Files, 75-7, 102.2, L.H. Greenberg, R.L. Bloore, A.F. McKay, memo concerning the name of the university, April 1960.

22 URA, Public Relations Office Files, 84-11, 182, faculty of Regina College minutes, 25 April 1960.

23 URA, Dean's/Principal's Office Files, 75-7, 102.1-7, W.A. Riddell to J.W.T. Spinks, 29 October 1960.
24 URA, Publications Section, University of Saskatchewan, Board of Governors minutes, 3 March 1961.
25 URA, Publications Section, University of Saskatchewan, Board of Governors minutes, 27 June 1961.
26 "Regina Leapfrogs to Status," *Star-Phoenix* (Saskatoon), 3 July 1961.
27 URA, Publications Section, University of Saskatchewan, Board of Governors minutes, 27 June 1961.
28 Riddell, "How Well I Remember," 60.
29 Ibid.
30 URA, Dean's/Principal's Office Files, 75-7, 102.1-7, J.W.T. Spinks to Board of Governors, 16 August 1961. McEown and Leddy were appointed, respectively, vice-president (administration) and vice-president (academic) in 1961.
31 URA, Dean's/Principal's Office Files, 75-7, 102.1-7, W.A. Riddell to J.W.T. Spinks, 29 August 1961.
32 URA, Dean's/Principal's Office Files, 75-7, 102.1-7, J.W.T. Spinks to W.A. Riddell, 1 September 1961.
33 URA, Dean's/Principal's Office Files, 75-7, 102.1-7, J.W.T. Spinks to W.A. Riddell, 11 September 1961.
34 AUS, President's Office Records, series 4, B60, Chancellor F. H. Auld to H.C. Pinder, 27 December 1961.
35 URA, Dean's/Principal's Office Files, 75-7, 102.1-4, A.C. McEown, "Report on the University of Saskatchewan, Regina Campus," September 1961.
36 URA, Dean's/Principal's Office Files, 75-7, 501.1-1, W.A. Riddell to A.C. McEown, with attachment, 23 October 1961.
37 Ibid.
38 URA, Publications Section, University of Saskatchewan, University Council minutes, 11 April 1962.
39 AUS, President's Office Records, series 4, C21, Regina Campus Expansion Committee, J.W.T. Spinks to Board of Governors, with attachment titled "Statement for the Board of Governors Regarding the Regina Campus," 16 April 1962.
40 URA, Publications Section, University of Saskatchewan, University Council minutes, 11 April 1962.
41 AUS, President's Office Records, series 4, C21, Regina Campus Expansion Committee, J.W.T. Spinks to Board of Governors, with attachment titled "Statement for the Board of Governors Regarding the Regina Campus," 16 April 1962.
42 URA, Principal's/Dean's Office Files, 78-3, 102.1-1, Planning Committee minutes, 14 December 1961.
43 URA, Publications Section, University of Saskatchewan, University Council minutes, 11 April 1962; 8 November 1961; University Council executive minutes, 6 February 1962.
44 URA, Dean's/Principal's Office Files, 75-7, 102.1-10, C. French to W.A. Riddell, 24 January 1963; W.A. Riddell to C. French, 2 February 1963.

45 URA, Dean's/Principal's Office Files, 75-7, 503.2-2, W.A. Riddell to J.F. Leddy, 1 February 1963.
46 URA, Dean's/Principal's Office Files, 75-7, 300.6, J.W.T. Spinks to W.A. Riddell, 30 January 1963; W.A. Riddell to A.C. McEown, 13 February 1963.
47 URA, Dean's/Principal's Office Files, 75-7, 503.2-2, L.H. Thomas, "Memo Re: Proposed Establishment of a Council at the Regina Campus," 29 March 1963.
48 James McConica, "Charles Wayland Lightbody," *Green and White*, summer 1983, 7.
49 Saskatchewan Archives Board (SAB), W.S. Lloyd Papers, R61.4, IV, 40 (4-1-1), "Statement of Dr. C.W. Lightbody, Associate Professor, Department of History, University of Saskatchewan, Regina Campus," 10 July 1963.
50 University of Alberta Archives (UAA), L.H. Thomas Papers, 73-138, file 3, C. Lightbody to L.H. Thomas, 10 July 1963.
51 SAB, W.S. Lloyd Papers, R61.4, IV, 40 (4-1-1), Charles Lightbody, "Supplementary Memorandum."
52 "Appendage of Saskatoon," *Leader-Post* (Regina), 12 July 1963.
53 UAA, L.H. Thomas Papers, 73-138, file 3, "Statement of the Executive of the Faculty Association, University of Saskatchewan, Regina Campus," 17 July 1963.
54 Bob Gaudry, letter to the editor, *Leader-Post* (Regina), 24 July 1963; UAA, L.H. Thomas Papers, 73-138, file 3, C. Lightbody to W.A. Riddell, 25 September 1963.
55 UAA, L.H. Thomas Papers, 73-138, file 3, "Senate Inquiry on Campus Academic Freedom Pressed," clipping, 18 July 1963.
56 "Saskatoon-Regina Relations," *Star-Phoenix* (Saskatoon), 17 July 1963.
57 UAA, L.H. Thomas Papers, 73-138, file 3, "Saskatoon Professors Back Regina Autonomy," clipping, 19 July 1963.
58 UAA, L.H. Thomas Papers, 73-138, file 3, C. Lightbody to L.H. Thomas, 14 August 1963.
59 URA, Dean's/Principal's Office Files, 75-7, 201.15, memo to Principal Riddell from L.G. Crossman, L.H. Greenberg, O.G. Holmes, A.M. Kristjanson, G.F. Ledingham, K.C. Lochhead, and L.H. Thomas, July 1963.
60 At the time the appointment committee for Regina faculty included the president and the two vice-presidents, but not the head of the department in Saskatoon. URA, Dean's/Principal's Office Files, 75-7, 201.15, notes on meeting, 29 July 1963.
61 URA, Dean's/Principal's Office Files, 75-7, 201.15, memo to Principal Riddell from L.G. Crossman, L.H. Greenberg, O.G. Holmes, A.M. Kristjanson, G.F. Ledingham, K.C. Lochhead, and L.H. Thomas, July 1963.
62 URA, Dean's/Principal's Office Files, 75-7, 201.15, W.A. Riddell to faculty members, 8 August 1963.
63 The principal of Regina campus was not made a vice-president of the university until 1967. URA, Dr W.A. Riddell Papers, 84-3, 600, J.W.T. Spinks to W.A. Riddell, 28 April 1967.
64 URA, Dean's/Principal's Office Files, 75-7, 503.2-2, J.F. Leddy to W.A. Riddell, 12 September 1963.

65 URA, Principal's/President's Papers, 80-38, 302.11-8, statement of Dallas Smythe to the Hall Commission, 2 August 1973.
66 URA, Principal's/Dean's Office Files, 78-3, 102.6-1, W.A. Riddell, "Discussion with Pres.," 20 February 1964.
67 Ibid.
68 URA, Principal's/President's Papers, 80-38, 302.11-1, "Address by Premier W.S. Lloyd, Laying of Cornerstone," 26 September 1963.
69 Ibid.
70 "Lloyd Lays Cornerstone of First Varsity Building," *Leader-Post* (Regina), 27 September 1963.
71 Brett Quiring, "The Social and Political Philosophy of Woodrow S. Lloyd," *Saskatchewan History* 56 (2004): 1, 7.
72 Ibid., 17.

CHAPTER SEVEN

1 Dallas Smythe, *Counterclockwise: Perspectives on Communication* (Boulder: Westview Press, 1994), 16–25.
2 Ibid., 35–42.
3 Ibid., 57.
4 Simon Fraser University Archives (SFUA), Dallas Smythe Fonds, F-16-1-1-0-5, D. Smythe to J.F. Leddy, 27 November 1962.
5 SFUA, Dallas Smythe Fonds, F-16-1-1-0-5, J.F. Leddy to D. Smythe, 3 December 1962.
6 SFUA, Dallas Smythe Fonds, F-16-1-1-0-5, A.E. Safarian to D. Smythe, 8 January 1963.
7 Smythe, *Counterclockwise*, 57.
8 University of Regina Archives (URA), Principal's/Dean's Office Files, 78-3, 102.1-1, Forward Planning Committee minutes, 4 February 1963.
9 URA, Principal's/Dean's Office Files, 78-3, 102.1-1, Forward Planning Committee minutes, 23 October 1963.
10 URA, Principal's/Dean's Office Files, 78-3, 102.1-1, Forward Planning Committee minutes, 10 October 1963. The Smythe-Hutchins connection supports Kevin Brooks's suggestion that liberal education in the Canadian prairie provinces was influenced as much by midwestern American examples as it was by eastern Canadian university models. Kevin Brooks, "Liberal Education on the Great Plains: American Experiments, Canadian Flirtations, 1930–1950," *Great Plains Quarterly* 17 (1997): 103–17.
11 Robert Maynard Hutchins, *The Higher Learning in America* (New Haven: Yale University Press, 1936), 95.
12 Mary Ann Dzuback, *Robert M. Hutchins: Portrait of an Educator* (Chicago: University of Chicago Press, 1991), 110–34.
13 Ibid., 240, 260.
14 URA, Dean's/Principal's Office Files, 75-7, 102.1-10, D. Smythe to R. Hutchins, 11 October 1963.

15 Dzuback, *Robert M. Hutchins*, 254.
16 Victor S. Navasky, "The Happy Heretic," *Atlantic Monthly*, July 1966.
17 Frank K. Kelly, *Court of Reason: Robert Hutchins and the Fund for the Republic* (New York: Free Press, 1981), 359.
18 Navasky, "Happy Heretic," 54.
19 URA, Principal's/Dean's Office Files, 78-3, 102.7, W.H. Ferry, "Why the College Is Failing" (paper presented to the American Association for Higher Education, Detroit, 1 July 1963).
20 URA, Principal's/President's Papers, 80-38, 600.1-1, W.H. Ferry, "Liberal Education: Reflections and Surmises," 14 December 1963.
21 URA, Dean's/Principal's Office Files, 75-7, 102.1-12, Dallas Smythe, "A Few Comments on the Liberal Arts Situation at Regina." Woodrow Lloyd was invited to the Regina Beach retreat but was unable to attend.
22 URA, Dean's/Principal's Office Files, 75-7, 102.1-12, Duncan Blewett, "Views on a Liberal Arts Programme."
23 URA, Principal's/Dean's Office Files, 78-3, 102.7, K.C. Lochhead, "In Search of a Philosophy for a College of Arts and Science at the University of Saskatchewan, Regina."
24 URA, Dean's/Principal's Office Files, 75-7, 102.1-12, Alwyn Berland, "Some Notes on Education in the University."
25 URA, Publications Section, University of Saskatchewan, Regina Campus News Service, news release, 31 May 1968.
26 URA, Office of the President Files, 87-51, 400.13, J.W.T. Spinks to L. Barber, 29 September 1977.
27 URA, Principal's/Dean's Office Files, 78-3, 102.6-1, A.B. Van Cleave, "Some Thoughts, Problems, and Suggestions Regarding the Development of Regina Campus," November 1963.
28 URA, Principal's/Dean's Office Files, 78-3, 102.7, A.B. Van Cleave, "Professional Training in Relation to the Liberal Arts," 15 December 1963.
29 University of Saskatchewan, Regina Campus, *Calendar*, 1964.
30 URA, Principal's/Dean's Office Files, 78-3, 102.7, J. Mitchell to W.A. Riddell, 3 February 1964.
31 Jack Mitchell, guest editorial, *Carillon*, 13 March 1964.
32 URA, Principal's/Dean's Office Files, 78-3, 600.1, "Resolutions Adopted by the Faculty of Arts and Science Consequent upon the Findings of the Regina Beach Retreat," 8 September 1964; College/Faculty of Arts and Sciences, University of Saskatchewan, Regina Campus Files, 85-54, 104.18, Faculty of Arts and Science minutes, 10 and 11 February 1964.
33 URA, Principal's/Dean's Office Files, 78-3, 102.7, W.A. Riddell to P. Ferry, 8 January 1964.
34 URA, Principal's/Dean's Office Files, 78-3, 102.7, P. Ferry to W.A. Riddell, 17 January 1964.
35 URA, Principal's/Dean's Office Files, 78-3, 102.1-4, "To the Planning Committee."

36 URA, Principal's/Dean's Office Files, 78-3, 201.1, A.F. McKay to W.A. Riddell, "Morale and Trends on the Regina Campus."
37 URA, Principal's/Dean's Office Files, 78-3, 605.1, D. Smythe to faculty, Division of Social Sciences, 17 March 1964.
38 URA, Principal's/Dean's Office Files, 78-3, 102.1-1, Forward Planning Committee minutes, 5 May 1964.
39 URA, Principal's/Dean's Office Files, 78-3, 600.6, Report of the Committee on Divisional Organization (as amended 21 January 1965); URA, Publications Section, Regina Campus Council minutes, 17 February 1965.
40 *University Government in Canada* (Duff Berdahl Report) (Toronto: University of Toronto Press, 1966).
41 URA, Principal's/Dean's Office Files, 78-3, 600.7, W.A. Riddell to T.H. McLeod, 17 December 1964.
42 URA, Publications Section, University of Saskatchewan, Board of Governors minutes, 24 June 1965.
43 URA, Publications Section, Regina Campus Council minutes, 20 and 21 October 1965.
44 URA, Principal's/Dean's Office Files, 78-3, 600.1, "Summary of New Curriculum as Approved by Arts and Sciences Faculty," September 1965.
45 Ibid.
46 Quoted in Paul Axelrod, *Scholars and Dollars: Politics, Economics, and the Universities of Ontario, 1945–1980* (Toronto: University of Toronto Press, 1982), 105.
47 Patricia Jasen, "'In Pursuit of Human Values (Or, Laugh When You Say That)': The Student Critique of the Arts Curriculum in the 1960s," in *Youth, University and Canadian Society: Essays in the Social History of Higher Education*, ed. Paul Axelrod and John G. Reid (Montreal and Kingston: McGill-Queen's University Press, 1989), 254–62.
48 URA, Dr W.A. Riddell Papers, 75-1, 1203, W.A. Riddell, "How Well I Remember," 61–2.
49 T.H. McLeod to the author, 1 May 2004.
50 "PM Becomes First Alumnus," *Leader-Post* (Regina), 18 May 1965.
51 URA, Principal's/Dean's Office Files, 78-3, 100.5-4, "Excerpts from the Prime Minister's Convocation Address at the University of Saskatchewan, Regina Campus," 17 May 1965.
52 "Convocation Ball for Graduates," *Leader-Post* (Regina), 18 May 1965.
53 "The First Convocation," *Leader-Post* (Regina), 18 May 1965.
54 University of Saskatchewan, *Annual Report of the President*, 1958–59.
55 "Hopelessly Inadequate," *Leader-Post* (Regina), 9 April 1965.
56 "Unitary University System Good for Province – Spinks," *Star-Phoenix* (Saskatoon), 18 May 1965.
57 Editorial, *Carillon*, 29 March 1963.
58 URA, Principal's/Dean's Office Files, 78-3, 600.1, "A Brief Prepared by the Students of the University of Saskatchewan, Regina Campus, Requesting a Royal Commission into the Structure of University Government," 19 March 1964.

59 Ron Thompson, "Student Boycott," *Carillon*, 16 September 1964.
60 "Student Protest Gets Support," *Leader-Post* (Regina), 24 March 1964; "Sound Report," *Leader-Post* (Regina), 28 March 1964.
61 "Bonnie Prince Charlie (Over the Border!)," *Star-Phoenix* (Saskatoon), 21 March 1964.
62 "Regina Campus Students Want Royal Commission on Autonomy," *Leader-Post* (Regina), 20 March 1964.
63 URA, Dr W.A. Riddell Papers, 84-31, 17, W.A. Riddell to C. Lightbody, 25 March 1964.
64 URA, Dr W.A. Riddell Papers, 84-31, 17, C. Lightbody to W.A. Riddell, 31 March 1964.
65 URA, Publications Section, Regina Campus Council minutes, 28 April 1964.
66 URA, Principal's/Dean's Office Files, 78-3, 102.1-3, "Report of the Sub-committee on the Resolution Calling for a Royal Commission on Higher Education in Saskatchewan."
67 Ibid.
68 URA, Publications Section, Regina Campus Council minutes, 20 and 21 October 1965.
69 "Do We Want Autonomy?" *Carillon*, 9 October 1964.
70 "The Role of the University," *Carillon*, 20 September 1965; "The New Student," *Carillon*, 20 September 1965.
71 Dave Orr, "The Student as Instrument," *Carillon*, 12 September 1966.

CHAPTER EIGHT

1 University of Regina Archives (URA), Publications Section, University of Saskatchewan, Board of Governors minutes, 11 January 1961.
2 "$2,650,000 Regina College Expansion Plan Mooted," *Leader-Post* (Regina), 19 August 1959.
3 URA, Dean's/Principal's Office Files, 75-7, 102.1-1, faculty meeting minutes, 1 September 1959.
4 URA, Vice-President, University of Saskatchewan Papers, 81-12, 760.1, "Requirement Study for a Campus for the University of Saskatchewan at Regina," 7 March 1960.
5 URA, Vice-President, University of Saskatchewan Papers, 81-12, 760.1, Shore and Moffat, Regina campus site appraisal, supplement to a report dated 30 April 1960, 11 June 1960.
6 URA, Dr W.A. Riddell Papers, 75-1, 1203, W.A. Riddell, "How Well I Remember," 76.
7 A.W. Johnson, *Dream No Little Dreams: A Biography of the Douglas Government of Saskatchewan, 1944–1961* (Toronto: University of Toronto Press, 2004), 230–1.
8 URA, Dean's/Principal's Office Files, 75-7, 102.1-4, "Wascana Center: A Center for Government, Education, Arts, and Recreation in Regina, Saskatchewan."

9 Archives of the University of Saskatchewan (AUS), President's Office Records, series 4, B302, Wascana Centre Authority, 1960–61, memo concerning university campus proposed purchases, 12 October 1960.
10 "A Long Fight Won," *Leader-Post* (Regina), 27 January 1961.
11 "Law, Commerce Colleges May Be Moved to Regina," *Leader-Post* (Regina), 3 March 1961.
12 "Blakeney Said Overlooking Government, Varsity Separation," *Leader-Post* (Regina), 6 March 1961.
13 "Unwarranted Charge – Blakeney," *Leader-Post* (Regina), 7 March 1961.
14 AUS, President's Office Records, series 4, B302, Wascana Centre Authority, 1960–61, A.E. Blakeney, memo concerning Regina campus, 9 January 1961.
15 Riddell, "How Well I Remember," 77–8.
16 "Famous Architect Likely Wascana Center Planner," *Leader-Post* (Regina), 18 July 1961.
17 URA, Dr W.A. Riddell Papers, 84-31, 44, W.A. Riddell to L. Crossman, 21 July 1961.
18 URA, Dean's/Principal's Office Files, 75-7, 103.2, Minoru Yamasaki and Thomas Church, "Report on Wascana Centre."
19 Ibid.
20 URA, Publications Section, University of Saskatchewan, Board of Governors minutes, 5 February 1964.
21 "Regina Campus Master Plan Passed," *Leader-Post* (Regina), 4 January 1962.
22 URA, Publications Section, University of Saskatchewan, Board of Governors minutes, 4 January 1962.
23 URA, Publications Section, University of Saskatchewan, Board of Governors minutes, 19 December 1961.
24 "Regina Campus Master Plan Passed," *Leader-Post* (Regina), 4 January 1962.
25 URA, Dean's/Principal's Office Files, 75-7, 501.4-2, Building and Grounds Committee (Regina Campus) minutes, 6 February 1962; AUS, President's Office Records, series 4, C21, Regina Campus Expansion Committee, W.A. Riddell, "Problems of Expansion – Regina Campus," 2 November 1964.
26 URA, Publications Section, University of Saskatchewan, Board of Governors minutes, 1 November 1962.
27 AUS, President's Office Records, series 4, B302, Wascana Centre Authority, March-November 1962, J.W.T. Spinks to M. Yamasaki, 27 November 1962.
28 AUS, President's Office Records, series 4, B302, Wascana Centre Authority, March-November 1962, M. Yamasaki to J.W.T. Spinks, 21 November 1962.
29 URA, Dean's/Principal's Office Files, 75-7, 501.4-1, W.A. Riddell to J.A. Wedgwood, 10 December 1962.
30 URA, Publications Section, University of Saskatchewan, Board of Governors minutes, 27 February 1963.
31 AUS, President's Office Records, series 4, C21, Regina Campus Expansion Committee, W.A. Riddell to J.W.T. Spinks, 3 November 1964.
32 AUS, President's Office Records, series 4, C21, Regina Campus Expansion Committee, W.A. Riddell, "Problems of Expansion – Regina Campus," 2 November 1964.

33 URA, Principal's/Dean's Office Files, 78-3, 101.8-2, "Concrete, Aggregate Form Exteriors," *Western Construction and Building,* June 1965.
34 "Campus Open for Business," *Leader-Post* (Regina), 17 July 1965.
35 "Grow Vines!" *Carillon,* 20 September 1965.
36 Letter to the editor, *Carillon,* 13 September 1968.
37 URA, Principal's/Dean's Office Files, 78-3, 302.5-2, "Student Service Center," 6 May 1968.
38 "Realization of Visions of Many for 60 Years," *Leader-Post* (Regina), 9 October 1965.
39 URA, Principal's/Dean's Office Files, 78-3, 101.10-2, A.C. McEown to W.A. Riddell, 30 June 1967.
40 URA, Principal's/Dean's Office Files, 78-3, 102.4-1, "University Library, Regina Campus: Summary of Requirements," 13 August 1964.
41 URA, Principal's/Dean's Office Files, 78-3, 100.5-6, "Formal Opening of New Library, Tentative Program," 14 October 1967.
42 URA, John Archer Speeches and Reports, 80-35, FP 80-004, v. 1, John H. Archer, "Address Delivered at the Opening of the Library Building," 14 October 1967.
43 URA, Principal's/Dean's Office Files, 78-3, 102.4-3, "Physical Education Centre, Summary of Requirement Study," 22 October 1963.
44 URA, Publications Section, University of Saskatchewan, Board of Governors minutes, 27 February 1963.
45 URA, Publications Section, University of Saskatchewan News Service, news release, 18 February 1967.
46 URA, Publications Section, University of Saskatchewan, Board of Governors minutes, 7 October 1964.
47 URA, Publications Section, University of Saskatchewan, Board of Governors minutes, 17 March 1965.
48 URA, Principal's/Dean's Office Files, 78-3, 101.13-1, F.L. Bates to W.A. Riddell, 5 October 1965.
49 URA, Principal's/Dean's Office Files, 78-3, 101.13-1, J.W.T. Spinks to W.A. Riddell, 14 October 1965.
50 URA, Principal's/Dean's Office Files, 78-3, 101.13-1, College of Education Building Committee minutes, 18 August 1966.
51 URA, Principal's/Dean's Office Files, 78-3, 101.13-3, W.A. Riddell to H.T. Coutts, 26 September 1969.
52 URA, Principal's/Dean's Office Files, 78-3, 100.14-1, T.H. McLeod to W.A. Riddell, 16 November 1964.
53 URA, Principal's/Dean's Office Files, 78-3, 100.14-1, Principal's Planning Committee minutes, 30 April 1965.
54 URA, Publications Section, Regina Campus Council minutes, 14 May 1965.
55 URA, Principal's/Dean's Office Files, 78-3, 101.16-1, W.A. Riddell to T.H. McLeod, 28 June 1965.
56 URA, Principal's/Dean's Office Files, 78-3, 100.14-1, Principal's Planning Committee, "Proposal for Organization of the University," 6 July 1965.
57 Ibid.

58 URA, Principal's/Dean's Office Files, 78-3, 100.14-1, "Proposal for Organization of the University, Memo No. 2," 29 July 1965.
59 URA, Publications Section, Regina Campus Council minutes, 20 and 21 October 1965.
60 URA, Publications Section, University of Saskatchewan, Board of Governors minutes, 2 June 1966.
61 URA, Principal's/Dean's Office Files, 78-3, 101.8-3, W.A. Riddell to M. Yamasaki, 2 August 1966.
62 URA, Principal's/Dean's Office Files, 78-3, 101.16-1, J.A. Wedgwood to M. Yamasaki, 23 June 1966.
63 URA, Principal's/Dean's Office Files, 78-3, 101.8-3, W.A. Riddell to M. Yamasaki, 2 August 1966.
64 URA, Principal's/Dean's Office Files, 78-3, 400.1-1, "Principal's Remarks to Council," 20 October 1966.
65 URA, Principal's/Dean's Office Files, 78-3, 101.1, M. Yamasaki to J.W.T. Spinks, 7 November 1968.
66 URA, Principal's/Dean's Office Files, 78-3, 101.1, J.A. Wedgwood to W.A. Riddell, 28 October 1968.
67 URA, Principal's/Dean's Office Files, 78-3, 101.16-2, "Report of the Building Subcommittee for College Buildings."
68 URA, Principal's/Dean's Office Files, 78-3, 101.16-2, R. Thatcher to J.W.T. Spinks, 23 December 1966.
69 URA, Principal's/Dean's Office Files, 78-3, 101.16-2, R. Thatcher to J.W.T. Spinks, 11 January 1967.
70 URA, Principal's/Dean's Office Files, 78-3, 101.16-2, W.A. Riddell to R. Thatcher, 26 January 1967.
71 URA, Principal's/Dean's Office Files, 78-3, 101.16-2, J.W.T. Spinks to R. Thatcher, 28 January 1967.
72 URA, Principal's/Dean's Office Files, 78-3, 101.16-2, W.A. Riddell, record of a telephone call to R. Thatcher, 2 February 1967.
73 URA, Principal's/Dean's Office Files, 78-3, 101.16-2, W.A. Riddell to J.W.T. Spinks, 2 February 1967.
74 URA, Principal's/Dean's Office Files, 78-3, 302.2-3, A.C. McEown to A. Guy, 19 January 1968.
75 URA, Principal's/Dean's Office Files, 78-3, 302.2-3, W.A. Riddell to A.C. McEown, 5 February 1968.
76 URA, Principal's/Dean's Office Files, 78-3, 102.1-4, T.H. McLeod to members of the planning committee, 26 February 1968.
77 URA, Principal's/Dean's Office Files, 78-3, 101.16-3, A. Guy to J. Pringle, 2 April 1968.
78 URA, Publications Section, University of Saskatchewan, Board of Governors Executive Committee minutes, 8 August 1968.
79 URA, Principal's/Dean's Office Files, 78-3, 101.16-3, A. Guy to J.A.E. Bardwell, 21 February 1969.

80 URA, Publications Section, University of Saskatchewan, Board of Governors minutes, 27 August 1970.
81 URA, Vice-Principal/President's Office Files, 78-4, 152, "Project Report, College West," 17 December 1970.
82 URA, College/Faculty of Arts and Sciences, University of Saskatchewan, Regina Campus Files, 85-54, 102.3, R.F.E. Harvey, "College West," 25 October 1971.
83 URA, University Secretary's Office Papers, 85-34, 304.0, Long-Range Planning Committee minutes, 29 November 1971.
84 URA, University Secretary's Office Papers, 85-34, 304.0, Long-Range Planning Committee minutes, 25 April 1972.
85 URA, Publications Section, University of Saskatchewan, Board of Governors minutes, 7 September 1972.
86 URA, Publications Section, University of Saskatchewan, Board of Governors minutes, 6 October 1966.
87 URA, Principal's/Dean's Office Files, 78-3, 101.15, "Requirement Study for the Faculty of Engineering, Regina Campus," June 1967.
88 URA, Principal's/Dean's Office Files, 78-3, 101.15, "Engineering-Physics Complex, Regina Campus," 29 August 1969.
89 The Prestressed Concrete Institute gave the award in 1967. The awards jury commented that "A substantial challenge is the design of a good-looking power plant on a university campus. Here the problem has been solved with eminent success. What might have been a jarring anachronism becomes a handsome feature consistent with the environment and landscaping." *Leader-Post* (Regina), 22 July 1967.
90 URA, Principal's/Dean's Office Files, 78-3, 101.2-2, "Brief on the Engineering Building, University of Saskatchewan, Regina Campus," 11 March 1969.
91 URA, Principal's/Dean's Office Files, 78-3, 101.15, J.A. Wedgwood, "Regina Engineering-Physics Project," 30 January 1970.
92 URA, Vice-Principal/President's Office Files, 78-4, 157, D.A. Larmour to D. Rew, 9 March 1972.
93 URA, Principal's/Dean's Office Files, 78-3, 101.17, Biology-Geology Building Committee minutes, 11 September 1968.
94 URA, Publications Section, University of Saskatchewan, Board of Governors minutes, 4 August 1966.
95 URA, Publications Section, University of Saskatchewan, Board of Governors minutes, 6 May 1964.
96 URA, Publications Section, University of Saskatchewan, Board of Governors minutes, 8 August 1968.
97 University of Saskatchewan, *Annual Report of the President*, "Regina Campus, Principal's Report," 1973, 2.
98 URA, Dean's/Principal's Office Files, 75-7, 501.1-2, M. Badham to W.A. Riddell, 25 April 1963.
99 URA, Publications Section, University of Saskatchewan, Board of Governors minutes, 24 June 1965.

100 URA, Principal's/Dean's Office Files, 78-3, 302.2-2, "The Proposed Students' Union Building," June 1966.
101 URA, Publications Section, University of Saskatchewan, Board of Governors minutes, 6 October 1966.
102 URA, Principal's/Dean's Office Files, 78-3, 200.2, statement concerning the Students' Union Building, 6 August 1968.
103 URA, Principal's/Dean's Office Files, 78-3, 101.10-2, J.W.T. Spinks to W.A. Riddell, 8 October 1968.
104 URA, Publications Section, University of Saskatchewan, Board of Governors minutes, 2 May 1968.
105 URA, Principal's/Dean's Office Files, 78-3, 302.5-2, "Student Service Centre," 6 May 1968.
106 "Quonset Hut," *Carillon*, 29 November 1968.
107 URA, Principal's/Dean's Office Files, 78-3, 101.1, J.A. Wedgwood to J.W.T. Spinks, 28 November 1969.
108 AUS, J.W.T. Spinks Fonds, unprocessed accession, Hall Commission, excerpt from a memo from J.A. Wedgwood, 21 September 1971, with figures updated to 1 January 1973.
109 Saskatchewan Archives Board, A.E. Blakeney Papers, R-565 III 158a, John Spinks, address to Regina convocation, May 1974.

CHAPTER NINE

1 Charles Harrison, introduction to *Homemade Esthetics: Observations on Art and Taste*, by Clement Greenberg (Oxford: Oxford University Press, 1999), xiii.
2 Clement Greenberg, "Painting and Sculpture in Prairie Canada Today," in *Clement Greenberg: The Collected Essays and Criticism*, vol. 4, ed. John O'Brian (Chicago: University of Chicago Press, 1993), 155–8. Previously published in *Canadian Art*, March-April 1963.
3 James M. Pitsula, *An Act of Faith: The Early Years of Regina College* (Regina: Canadian Plains Research Center, 1988), 79.
4 Ibid., 159.
5 Archives of the University of Saskatchewan (AUS), President's Office Records, series 3, B163, Regina College, 1950, W.A. Riddell to W.P. Thompson, 4 July 1950.
6 Mark Reynolds, "The Emma Lake Encounters," *Beaver*, December 2001-January 2002.
7 AUS, President's Office Records, series 3, B163, Regina College, 1950, "Candidates for Art Director."
8 AUS, President's Office Records, series 3, B-163, Regina College, 1956–57, W.A. Riddell to W.P. Thompson, 11 January 1956.
9 University of Regina Archives (URA), Dean's/Principal's Office Files, 75-7, 300.1-6, A. McKay to W.A. Riddell, 18 October 1956.
10 AUS, President's Office Records, series 3, B163, Regina College, 1954, W.P. Thompson to F.H. Auld, 26 May 1954.

11 John O'Brian, *The Flat Side of the Landscape: The Emma Lake Artists' Workshops* (Saskatoon: Mendel Art Gallery, 1989), 33.
12 Reynolds, "Emma Lake Encounters."
13 Thomas B. Hess, *Barnett Newman* (New York: Museum of Modern Art, 1971), 15.
14 Michael Kimmelman, "Epiphany in a Vibrant Universe Depicting Nothing but Itself," *New York Times*, 12 April 2002.
15 Art McKay in *A World Away: Stories from the Regina Five*, produced and directed by Mark Wihak (Chat Perdue!, MGR: 2001). See also John D.H. King, *The Emma Lake Workshops 1955–1970* (Brandon, MB: 1972), 89–91.
16 URA, Dr W.A. Riddell Papers, 84-31, 20, K. Lochhead to W.A. Riddell, 16 April 1959.
17 URA, Theodore A. Heinrich Papers, 89-44, box 112, file 1385, Theodore Allan Heinrich, "Of Five Painters and When They Were the Five of Regina," 6 July–5 August 1980.
18 Ronald Bloore in *A World Away*.
19 Newspaper clippings in *A World Away*.
20 URA, Ronald Bloore Papers, 86-72, 1961, Richard B. Simmins, "'Five Painters from Regina,' an Exhibition Organized and Circulated by the National Gallery of Canada," 30 November 1961.
21 Ibid.
22 Ronald Bloore in *A World Away*; see also King, *Emma Lake Workshops*, 124.
23 Art McKay in *A World Away*.
24 Heinrich, "Of Five Painters."
25 Art McKay in *A World Away*.
26 "Director Defends Right to Grow Beard," *Leader-Post* (Regina), 14 March 1959.
27 AUS, President's Office Records, series 3, B163, Regina College, 1958–59, C.C. Williams to W.A. Riddell, 20 March 1959.
28 AUS, President's Office Records, series 3, B163, Regina College, 1958–59, W.A. Riddell to C.C. Williams, 1 April 1959.
29 *A World Away*.
30 Quoted in Simmins, "Five Painters."
31 URA, Ken Lochhead Papers, 86-29, Correspondence, Ted Godwin, Art McKay, 1974–85, Ted Godwin, "Ancient Days of Yore."
32 A.W. Johnson, *Dream No Little Dreams: A Biography of the Douglas Government of Saskatchewan, 1944–1961* (Toronto: University of Toronto Press, 2004), 187.
33 Heinrich, "Of Five Painters."
34 Johnson, *Dream*, 232.
35 Ibid.
36 Dennis Reid, *A Concise History of Canadian Painting* (Toronto: Oxford University Press, 1973), 270.
37 I am grateful to Susan Whitney for showing me the copy of the book with McKay's annotations.

38 McKay also tried to set the record straight in a letter to *Arts Canada*. URA, Ronald Bloore Papers, 86-72, Correspondence, Artists, 1966–86, A.F. McKay to the editor, *Arts Canada*, 5 February 1975.
39 URA, Principal's/Dean's Office Files, 78-3, 605.5, D. Blewett to W.A. Riddell, 8 August 1967.
40 URA, Duncan Blewett Papers, 88-29, Correspondence, 1965, DBB, 26 January 1965.
41 Ibid.
42 URA, Ronald Bloore Papers, 86-72, Correspondence, Artists, 1966–86, A.F. McKay to the editor, *Arts Canada*, 9 February 1975.
43 URA, Dr W.A. Riddell Papers, 75-1, 1203, W.A. Riddell, "How Well I Remember," 67.
44 Godwin, "Ancient Days."
45 Ibid.
46 URA, Owen Holmes Papers, 84-33, School of Art, 1959–63, W.A. Riddell, brief submitted to A.C. McEown, assistant to the president, 12 May 1961, appendix A, BFA course (tentative), prepared by K. Lochhead.
47 URA, Owen Holmes Papers, 84-33, School of Art, 1959–63, Eli Bornstein, "Future Development of Art Program at University of Saskatchewan in Saskatoon and at Regina Campus," 4 August 1961.
48 URA, Principal's/Dean's Office Files, 78-3, 602.1, F.A. Nulf to W.A. Riddell, 2 December 1969.
49 URA, College/Faculty of Arts and Science, University of Saskatchewan, Regina Campus Files, 85-54, 301, statement by J. Sures, October 1970.
50 URA, College/Faculty of Arts and Science, University of Saskatchewan, Regina Campus Files, 85-54, 301, G.E. Vaughan to F.W. Anderson, 27 October 1970.
51 URA, Principal's/President's Papers, 80-38, 403.21, G. Edgar Vaughan to J.H. Archer, 19 May 1972.
52 URA, Vice-President, University of Saskatchewan Papers, 81-12, 800.1, "Report of the Committee on Rationalization of the Fine Arts," 9 June 1972.
53 Pitsula, *Act of Faith*, 64.
54 Ibid., 65.
55 Ibid., 64.
56 *Encyclopedia of Music in Canada*, 2nd ed., ed. Helmut Kallmann (Toronto: University of Toronto Press, 1992), 1396, 102, 751.
57 AUS, President's Office Records, series 3, B163, Regina College, 1951, press release, 16 April 1951.
58 University of Saskatchewan, *Annual Report of the President*, 1952–53, W.A. Riddell, "Regina College," 68; *Encyclopedia of Music in Canada*, 1120.
59 "Violinist Gives Excellent Program," *Leader-Post* (Regina), 15 March 1943.
60 *Encyclopedia of Music in Canada*, 751.
61 AUS, President's Office Records, series 3, B163, Regina College, 1952, W.A. Riddell to W.P. Thompson, 18 September 1952.
62 William A. Riddell and Howard Leyton-Brown, *The Regina Conservatory of Music: Seventy-five Years of Growth and Service, 1912 to 1987* (n.p.: Regina, 1988), 24.

63 Ibid.
64 URA, Conservatory of Music Records, 80-17, "Regina Conservatory of Music, Interim Report of Review Committee," 28 March 1956.
65 University of Saskatchewan, *Annual Report of the President*, Regina College, 1955–56; 1958–59.
66 Riddell and Leyton-Brown, *Regina Conservatory*, 11.
67 URA, Publications Section, University of Saskatchewan, University Council minutes and agendas, November 1963, "Report of the Special Committee on the Bachelor of Music, Regina Campus."
68 Ibid.
69 W.A. Riddell, *The First Decade: A History of the University of Saskatchewan, Regina Campus* (Regina: University of Regina, 1974), 46.
70 URA, Publications Section, University of Saskatchewan, Board of Governors minutes, 8 April 1964.
71 URA, College/Faculty of Arts and Science, University of Saskatchewan, Regina Campus Files, 85-54, 301.3, A. Berland to W.A. Riddell and T.H. McLeod, 12 November 1968.
72 URA, Principal's/Dean's Office Files, 78-3, 602.6, acting dean of arts and science to the Board of Governors, n.d.
73 Ibid.; URA, Conservatory of Music Files, 87-14 Correspondence, Faculty, Leyton-Brown, Howard, 1968–69, W.A. Riddell to H. Leyton-Brown, 7 January 1969.
74 URA, Principal's/Dean's Office Files, 78-3, 602.4, H. Leyton-Brown to members of the Faculty of Arts and Science, 16 April 1969.
75 URA, Principal's/President's Papers, 80-38, 103.1, Howard Leyton-Brown, "The Conservatory of Music," 11 March 1971.
76 URA, College/Faculty of Arts and Science, University of Saskatchewan, Regina Campus Files, 85-54, 301.3, memo from Roy Borrowman, 29 November 1971.
77 URA, College/Faculty of Arts and Science, University of Saskatchewan, Regina Campus Files, 85-54, 301.3, H.B. Lobaugh to R. Borrowman, 9 December 1971.
78 URA, College/Faculty of Arts and Science, University of Saskatchewan, Regina Campus Files, 85-54, 301.3, G.E. Vaughan to R. Borrowman, 16 December 1971.
79 URA, Principal's/President's Papers, 80-38, 404.19, "Report to the University of Saskatchewan Regarding Music at Regina Campus" (Johnson Report).
80 URA, Conservatory of Music Files, 87-14, "Relationship between Conservatory and Faculty of Music," H. Leyton-Brown to E.B. Tinker, 20 November 1972.
81 URA, College/Faculty of Arts and Science, University of Saskatchewan, Regina Campus Files, 85-54, 301.3, H.B. Lobaugh to J. Archer, 20 June 1972.
82 URA, College/Faculty of Arts and Science, University of Saskatchewan, Regina Campus Files, 85-54, 301.3, H.B. Lobaugh to J. Archer, 26 June 1972.
83 *Encyclopedia of Music in Canada*, 1156.
84 University of Saskatchewan, Regina Campus, *Bachelor of Music Calendar*, 1969–70.
85 *Encyclopedia of Music in Canada*, 1345.

86 Ibid., 1201.
87 Ibid., 751.
88 Ibid., 776.

CHAPTER TEN

1 University of Regina Archives (URA), Publications Section, University of Saskatchewan, University Council minutes and agendas, executive committee report, February 1964.
2 URA, Publications Section, University of Saskatchewan, Board of Governors minutes, 8 April 1964.
3 URA, Principal's Papers, 75-2, 1500.8, "Dr. Bates Named Dean of Education," *Saskatchewan Bulletin*, June 1964.
4 Michael Hayden, *Seeking a Balance: The University of Saskatchewan, 1907–82* (Vancouver: University of British Columbia Press, 1983), 219.
5 URA, Dean's/Principal's Office Files, 75-7, 503.2.2, "The Diploma Course in Education"; University of Saskatchewan, *Annual Report of the President*, 1965, 37–8.
6 University of Saskatchewan, *Annual Report of the President*, 1966, 31.
7 University of Saskatchewan, *Annual Report of the President*, 1968, 60.
8 University of Saskatchewan, *Annual Report of the President*, 1967, 31.
9 University of Saskatchewan, *Annual Report of the President*, 1965, 37–8.
10 URA, Principal's/Dean's Office Files, 78-3, 803.2, "Dr. Robert Newton Anderson."
11 "Education Dean Named for Campus," *Leader-Post* (Regina), 28 February 1967.
12 URA, Dr W.A. Riddell Papers, 84-31, 40, Diary, 7 October 1968.
13 URA, Principal's/Dean's Office Files, 78-3, 800.1-4, W.C. Blight to W.A. Riddell, 2 April 1969.
14 URA, Principal's/Dean's Office Files, 78-3, 800.1-4, "Official Results of Mail Vote in Faculty of Education."
15 URA, Dr W.A. Riddell Papers, 84-31, 40, Diary, 28 April 1969.
16 Katie Fitzrandolph, "Regina Campus Faculty Investigation Rumored," *Leader-Post* (Regina), 30 April 1969.
17 URA, Principal's/President's Papers, 80-38, 801.1-1, "Report of the Principal's Committee of Inquiry into the Faculty of Education, Regina Campus," 6 June 1969.
18 URA, Principal's/Dean's Office Files, 78-3, 800.1-6, W.A. Riddell, "Report of Committee on Inquiry," 4 July 1969.
19 URA, Principal's/Dean's Office Files, 78-3, 800.1-6, L. Crossman and C. Blachford to W.A. Riddell, 9 July 1969.
20 URA, Publications Section, *Principal's Report, 1971: University of Saskatchewan, Regina Campus*, 23–4.
21 URA, Publications Section, *Principal's Report, 1972: University of Saskatchewan, Regina Campus*, 15–17.

22 URA, Principal's/President's Papers, 80-38, 800.1-1, "Report of the Program Development Committee," July 1972.

23 Ibid.

24 Ibid.

25 URA, Publications Section, *Principal's Report, 1972: University of Saskatchewan, Regina Campus*, 15–17.

26 URA, Principal's/Dean's Office Files, 78-3, 302.1-1, "College of Public and Business Administration."

27 URA, Publications Section, University of Saskatchewan, Regina Campus Council minutes, 17 February 1965.

28 URA, Publications Section, University of Saskatchewan, Board of Governors minutes, 5 May 1965.

29 URA, Publications Section, University of Saskatchewan, Regina Campus Council minutes, 13 December 1965.

30 URA, College/Faculty of Arts and Science, University of Saskatchewan, Regina Campus Files, 85-54, 106, W.G. Bolstad, "Proposal to Establish a Faculty of Administration," 4 January 1968.

31 URA, College/Faculty of Arts and Science, University of Saskatchewan, Regina Campus Files, 85-54, 107, W.G. Bolstad, "Assumptions about the Philosophy and Objectives of the School of Administration," 1 July 1966.

32 URA, College/Faculty of Arts and Science, University of Saskatchewan, Regina Campus Files, 85-54, 106, W.G. Bolstad, "Proposal to Establish a Faculty of Administration," 4 January 1968.

33 URA, Vice-Principal/President's Office Files, 78-4, 262, "Faculty of Administration Annual Report," 1968–69.

34 URA, Publications Section, *Principal's Report, 1971: University of Saskatchewan, Regina Campus*, 12–13.

35 URA, Principal's/Dean's Office Files, 78-3, 700.1, W.G. Bolstad, "Comments about the Philosophy and Direction of the Bachelor of Administration Program," 14 September 1970.

36 URA, Principal's/President's Papers, 80-38, 700.1, R.H. Anderson to members of the Faculty of Administration, 4 December 1972.

37 URA, Publications Section, *Principal's Report, 1973: University of Saskatchewan, Regina Campus*, 8.

38 URA, Publications Section, *Principal's Report, 1974: University of Saskatchewan, Regina Campus*, 10.

39 URA, Principal's/Dean's Office Files, 78-3, 302.1-1, Regina campus, "Proposal to Establish a College of Engineering," 31 March 1965.

40 URA, Publications Section, University of Saskatchewan, Board of Governors minutes, 14 December 1965.

41 University of Saskatchewan, *Annual Report of the President*, 1967, 32.

42 URA, Principal's/Dean's Office Files, 78-3, 900.2, J.B. Mantle, "Regina Campus and Co-op Education," March 1969.

43 URA, Publications Section, *Principal's Report, 1971: University of Saskatchewan, Regina Campus*, 25.

44 URA, Principal's/President's Papers, 80-38, 900.1-1, University of Saskatchewan, press release, 16 March 1972.
45 URA, Principal's/President's Papers, 80-38, 900.1-1, J.W.T. Spinks to J.H. Archer, 20 March 1972.
46 URA, Publications Section, University of Saskatchewan, Board of Governors minutes and agendas, 3 April 1972.
47 URA, Principal's/President's Papers, 80-38, 900.1-1, Faculty of Engineering, "Proposal for Change in Program," 5 November 1973.
48 URA, Publications Section, *Principal's Report, 1973: University of Saskatchewan, Regina Campus*, 14–16.
49 URA, Publications Section, *Principal's Report, 1974: University of Saskatchewan, Regina Campus*, 17–18.
50 URA, Principal's/President's Papers, 80-38, 900.1-1, Faculty of Engineering, "Proposal for Change in Program," 5 November 1973.
51 URA, Dean's/Principal's Office Files, 75-7, 102.1-10, "Preliminary Report on Need of Social Work Educational Facilities in Saskatchewan," 8 February 1963.
52 Karl Henry Stange, "A Short Season of Reform: The Regina School of Social Work 1971–1978" (PhD diss., University of Wisconsin-Madison, 1979), 100, 102, 118–19.
53 Ibid., 128, 130.
54 URA, Principal's/Dean's Office Files, 78-3, 802.1-1, C.P. MacDonald, minister of social welfare, to J.W.T. Spinks, 9 June 1969.
55 Stange, "Short Season," 132.
56 URA, Principal's/Dean's Office Files, 78-3, 802.1-1, C.P. MacDonald, minister of social welfare, to J.W.T. Spinks, 9 June 1969.
57 URA, Principal's/Dean's Office Files, 78-3, 802.1-1, J.W.T. Spinks to C.P. MacDonald, 4 July 1969.
58 Stange, "Short Season," 139, 143, 146–7.
59 URA, Principal's/Dean's Office Files, 78-3, 802.1-1, A.W. Sihvon to J. Archer, 9 June 1970.
60 Stange, "Short Season," 153–4, 156.
61 URA, *Publications Section, Principal's Report, 1973: University of Saskatchewan, Regina Campus*, 35–6.
62 Ibid.
63 URA, University Secretary's Office Papers, 85-34, 1701.0, School of Social Work, 1973–74, "Otto Driedger to File on the Indian Social Work Education Program," 29 November 1973.
64 URA, Publications Section, *Principal's Report, 1974: University of Saskatchewan, Regina Campus*, 41–2.
65 Otto Driedger, letter to author, 27 August 2003.
66 URA, Publications Section, *Principal's Report, 1973: University of Saskatchewan, Regina Campus*, 35.
67 URA, Principal's/Dean's Office Files, 78-3, 1000.1-4, A.B. Van Cleave, "History of the Establishment and Growth of Graduate Studies Programs at the University of Saskatchewan, Regina Campus, 1964–1969," February 1969.

68 Ibid.

69 URA, Publications Section, *Principal's Report, 1972: University of Saskatchewan, Regina Campus*, 19.

70 URA, Publications Section, *Principal's Report, 1973: University of Saskatchewan, Regina Campus*, 16.

71 URA, Publications Section, *Principal's Report, 1971: University of Saskatchewan, Regina Campus*, 26–8.

72 URA, Publications Section, *Principal's Report, 1973: University of Saskatchewan, Regina Campus*, 6–18.

73 Ibid.

74 URA, Publications Section, *Principal's Report, 1974: University of Saskatchewan, Regina Campus*, 19–20.

75 W.A. Riddell, *The First Decade: A History of the University of Saskatchewan, Regina Campus, 1960–1970* (Regina: University of Regina, 1974), 50.

76 URA, Publications Section, University of Saskatchewan, Board of Governors minutes, 20 January 1966, T.H. McLeod, "Proposal for the Creation of a Bilingual and a French Cultural Institute on the Regina Campus."

77 URA, Publications Section, *Principal's Reports, 1972, 1973 and 1974: University of Saskatchewan, Regina Campus*.

78 URA, Principal's/Dean's Office Files, 78-3, 605.13, D. Smythe to W.A. Riddell, 11 June 1965.

79 URA, College/Faculty of Arts and Science, University of Saskatchewan, Regina Campus Files, 85-54, 502.1, D. Smythe to the faculty of the University of Saskatchewan, Regina Campus, 25 September 1964.

80 URA, Plain Talk Series Files, 75-11, 27, Plain Talk publicity posters.

81 URA, Principal's/Dean's Office Files, 78-3, 606.3, H.A. Purdy to W.A. Riddell, 6 April 1966.

82 URA, Principal's/Dean's Office Files, 78-3, 606.3, W.A. Riddell to D. Smythe, 20 April 1966; Plain Talk Series Files, 75-11, 3, Dallas Smythe, "Some Observations on the 1965–66 Plain Talk Series," 15 April 1966.

83 URA, Principal's/Dean's Office Files, 78-3. 606.3, W. Lloyd to W.A. Riddell, 3 May 1966.

84 URA, Principal's/Dean's Office Files, 78-3, 606.3, W.A. Riddell to W. Lloyd, 9 May 1966.

85 Robert E. Babe, "Paeans to Dallas Smythe," *Journal of Communications* 46, no. 1 (1996); Bill Melody, "Dallas Smythe: A Lifetime at the Frontier of Communications," *Canadian Journal of Communications* 17, no. 4 (1992).

86 URA, College/Faculty of Arts and Science, University of Saskatchewan, Regina Campus Files, 85-54, 303, petition, 30 October 1972.

87 URA, *Regina College Calendar*, 1959–60.

88 URA, Publications Section, University of Saskatchewan, Regina Campus, "Summary Expenditure Establishment and Student Class Registration, November 1973."

CHAPTER ELEVEN

1 Archives of Campion College (ACC), Federation File, B42a, Reverend Gerald F. Lahey, SJ, "Report on University Status for Campion College," 9 September 1959.
2 Alphonse de Valk, "Independent University or Federated College?: The Debate among Roman Catholics during the Years 1918–1921," *Saskatchewan History* 30, no. 1 (1977): 18–19.
3 Michael Hayden, *Seeking a Balance: The University of Saskatchewan, 1907–82* (Vancouver: University of British Columbia Press, 1983), 173.
4 Joseph G. Schner, SJ, "Campion College: A History," in *Heritage and Hope: The University of Regina into the 21st Century*, ed. K. Murray Knuttila (Regina: Canadian Plains Research Center, 2004), 66.
5 Quoted in Schner, "Campion College," 66.
6 Edmund Campion, SJ, was canonized on 25 October 1970.
7 Schner, "Campion College," 67.
8 Ibid., 68.
9 Lahey, "Report on University Status."
10 Hayden, *Seeking a Balance*, 173.
11 Lahey, "Report on University Status."
12 ACC, Federation File, B42a, Reverend J.J. Farrell, SJ, to J.W.T. Spinks, 25 July 1960.
13 ACC, Federation File, B42a, N.K. Cram, registrar, to Reverend A.J. MacDougall, SJ, 10 January 1961.
14 University of Regina Archives (URA), Publications Section, University of Saskatchewan, Board of Governors minutes, 12 June 1963.
15 ACC, Federation File, B42b, P.W. Nash, SJ, to J.W.T. Spinks, 31 July 1963.
16 ACC, Nash, Rev. E.P.W. (Peter) SJ File, B98c, "Peter Nash, S.J."
17 URA, Principal's/Dean's Office Files, 78-3, 106.1, Joint Committee Regarding Federation and Affiliation minutes, 26 September 1963, A.J. Macdougall, SJ, to J.W.T. Spinks, 29 April 1963.
18 Ibid.
19 URA, Principal's/Dean's Office Files, 78-3, 106.1, Joint Committee Regarding Federation and Affiliation minutes, 26 September 1963.
20 URA, Dean's/Principal's Office Files, 75-7, 207.4, Federated Colleges, 31 October 1963.
21 ACC, Federation File, B42b, P. Nash to Father Provincial, 3 November 1963.
22 ACC, Federation File, B42b, P. Nash to Chief Justice E.M. Culliton, 12 November 1963.
23 ACC, Federation File, B42b, J.W.T. Spinks to P. Nash, 17 December 1963.
24 URA, Principal's/Dean's Office Files, 78-3, 106.1, "Proposed Terms and Conditions for the Federation of Campion College," 28 January 1964.
25 J. Francis Leddy's father, J.J. Leddy, had been the leader of a group of Catholic laity who had lobbied for the federation of St Thomas More College with the University of Saskatchewan in 1936. Hayden, *Seeking a Balance*, 171–3.

26 ACC, Federation File, B42b, J.F. Leddy to G.J. Lahey, SJ, 6 January 1964.
27 URA, Principal's/Dean's Office Files, 78-3, 106.1, J.F. Leddy to W.A. Riddell, 9 March 1964.
28 URA, Principal's/Dean's Office Files, 78-3, 106.1, Joint Committee Regarding Federation and Affiliation minutes (meeting held at the Regina campus), 10 March 1964.
29 URA, Publications Section, University of Saskatchewan, University Council minutes, 9 April 1964.
30 URA, College/Faculty of Arts and Science, University of Saskatchewan, Regina Campus Files, 85-54, 107, annex III, "Guidelines for a Working Relationship between the Faculty of Arts and Science and the Federated Colleges within the Terms of the Statutes of Senate," 25 April 1973.
31 URA, Principal's/Dean's Office Files, 78-3, 106.2-2, J.L. Allard and E.J. Monahan, "Report on Campion College," October 1969.
32 ACC, History of Campion College File, B65f, Peter Nash, "Campion College Journal," 10 September 1968.
33 Ibid.
34 ACC, History of Campion College File, B65f, Peter Nash, "Campion College Journal," 25 August 1969.
35 ACC, History of Campion College File, B65f, Peter Nash, "Campion College Journal," 23 October 1969.
36 ACC, History of Campion College File, B65f, Peter Nash, "Campion College Journal," 6 March 1972.
37 University of Saskatchewan, *Annual Report of the President*, 1967; *Principal's Report, 1974: University of Saskatchewan, Regina Campus.*
38 ACC, Advisory Board File, B1d, "Principal's Report," 1973–74.
39 URA, Principal's/Dean's Office Files, 78-3, 106.2-1, program of the official cornerstone-laying ceremony, 1 October 1966.
40 URA, Principal's/Dean's Office Files, 78-3, 106.2-1, Reverend P.W. Nash, address, 1 October 1966.
41 ACC, Newman Club File, B101a, P.W. Nash, "The Newman Apostolate and the Catholic College on a Secular Campus" (paper presented to the National Newman Convention, Edmonton, September 1968).
42 URA, Principal's/Dean's Office Files, 78-3, 106.2-1, Reverend P.W. Nash, address, 1 October 1966.
43 ACC, Calendars File, B11b, *Campion College Calendar*, 1972–73.
44 Nash, "Newman Apostolate."
45 Ibid.
46 URA, Dean's/Principal's Office Files, 75-7, 102.1-12, Dallas Smythe, "A Few Comments on the Liberal Arts Situation at Regina."
47 ACC, Long Range Planning Committee File, B81b, P. Nash to T. Rendall, 7 August 1980.
48 ACC, Calendars File, B11b, *Campion College Calendar*, 1972–73.
49 Nash, "Newman Apostolate."
50 Ibid.

51 ACC, Commission of Inquiry File, B19a, "Campion College: Statement of Aims," 2 October 1971.
52 ACC, History of Campion College File, B65f, Peter Nash, "Campion College Journal," 2 October 1971.
53 Samira McCarthy, "Peter W. Nash, S.J.," *Globe and Mail*, 12 November 1997.
54 ACC, History of Campion College File, B65f, Peter Nash, "Campion College Journal," 1 February 1973.
55 ACC, History of Campion College File, B65f, Peter Nash, "Campion College Journal," 18 April 1978.
56 ACC, History of Campion College File, B65f, Peter Nash, "Campion College Journal," 26 April 1978.
57 ACC, Chaplaincy File, B17b, "Report on Campion Chaplaincy, April 1973 to April 1974."
58 ACC, Commission of Inquiry File, B19a, "Campion College: Statement of Aims," 2 October 1971.
59 Ibid.
60 ACC, History of Campion College File, B65f, Peter Nash, "Campion College Journal," 23 February 1971.
61 ACC, History of Campion College File, B65f, Peter Nash, "Campion College Journal," 3 March 1977.
62 ACC, History of Campion College File, B65f, Peter Nash, "Campion College Journal," 28 February 1978.
63 ACC, History of Campion College File, B65f, Peter Nash, "Campion College Journal," 15 May 1974.
64 Richard Hordern, "The Heritage and Hope of Luther College: Quality Education in a Christian Context," in *Heritage and Hope: The University of Regina into the 21st Century*, ed. K. Murray Knuttila (Regina: Canadian Plains Research Center, 2004), 40.
65 Ibid., 43–4.
66 Ken Mitchell, *Luther: The History of a College* (Regina: Luther College, 1981), 6–8.
67 Hordern, "Heritage and Hope," 48–50; Mitchell, *Luther*, 34.
68 Hordern, "Heritage and Hope," 50.
69 Quoted in Mitchell, *Luther*, 33.
70 Hordern, "Heritage and Hope," 53.
71 Luther College Archives (LCA), Miscellaneous Reports File, 1955–85, 2300-30, Robert B. Gronlund, "Analysis and Recommendations in Regard to a Development Program for Luther College," 1965.
72 LCA, Buildings, University, Central Mortgage and Housing Corporation Loan File, 350-20, B. Don-Bernard to M. Anderson, 5 June 1970.
73 LCA, Principal's Reports File, 2300-50-15, "Principal's Report to the Board of Regents," 21 November 1966.
74 LCA, Buildings, University, Central Mortgage and Housing Corporation Loan File, 350-20, B. Don-Bernard to M. Anderson, 5 June 1970; Building, 350-100, M. Anderson to R. Thatcher, 4 November 1969.

75 LCA, Buildings File, Scrapbook, 350-110, "Luther College Groundbreaking Ceremony," 6 July 1970.
76 LCA, Events, University Files, 750-20, John Archer, "The Call of Duty," 2 October 1971.
77 LCA, History of Luther College Collection, 2004-L01, A100-25, dedication, 3 October 1971, address by Dr William Hordern.
78 The colours blue and white were chosen to differentiate the university college from the high school (both called Luther College), which continued to use the gold and white.
79 LCA, Publications, University Calendars File, 1976–84, 2275-10, *Luther College Calendar*, 1976–77.
80 LCA, Minutes, Faculty Meetings, University File, 1800-25, 23 September 1971.
81 LCA, Principal's Reports File, 2300-50-20, "Principal's Report to the Board of Regents," 17 April 1972.
82 LCA, Minutes, Faculty Meetings, University File, 1800-25, 15 December 1971; 24 January 1973.
83 LCA, Minutes, Faculty Meetings, University File, 1800-25, 21 September 1972; LCA, Lutheran Church File, ELCC Yearbook and Convention Reports, 1600-10-5, Evangelical Lutheran Church of Canada, *1975/76 Yearbook and Fourth Convention Report*, 88; ELCC Yearbook and Convention Reports, 1600-10-5, Evangelical Lutheran Church of Canada, *1976/77 Yearbook and Fifth Convention Report*, 78.
84 LCA, Minutes, Faculty Meetings, University File, 1800-25, 27 September 1973.
85 LCA, Events, University File, 1971–79, 750-20, "Welcome to Luther," 1974.
86 LCA, Minutes, Faculty Meetings, University File, 1800-25, 15 December 1971.
87 LCA, Minutes, Faculty Meetings, University File, 1800-25, "Notes from Faculty-Student BBQ," 3 May 1972.
88 LCA, Events, University File, 1971–77, 750-20, "Fresh Ideas," October 1973.
89 LCA, Minutes, Faculty Meetings, University File, 1800-25, 1 May 1974.
90 LCA, Minutes, Faculty Meetings, University File, 1800-25, 8 December 1972.
91 LCA, Minutes, Faculty Meetings, University File, 1800-25, 28 April 1972.
92 LCA, Events, University File, 1971–79, 750-20, "Fresh Ideas," October 1973.
93 LCA, Events, University File, 1971-79, 750-20, "Ho, Ho," December 1973.
94 LCA, Events, University File, 1971-79, 750-20, "Welcome to Luther," 1974.
95 LCA, Lutheran Church File, ELCC Yearbook and Convention Reports, 1600-10-1, Evangelical Lutheran Church of Canada, *1973/74 Yearbook and Third General Convention Report*, 79.
96 LCA, Lutheran Church File, ELCC Yearbook and Convention Reports, 1600-10-5, Evangelical Lutheran Church of Canada, *1975/76 Yearbook and Fourth Convention Report*, 88.
97 LCA, Minutes, Faculty Meetings, University File, 1800-25, 16 September 1971.
98 LCA, Minutes, Faculty Meetings, University File, 1800-25, 14 October 1971.
99 LCA, Luther Lecture Series File, 1400-10, R.E. Miller to J. Pelikan, 8 December 1976.

CHAPTER TWELVE

1 Martin L. Friedland, *The University of Toronto: A History* (Toronto: University of Toronto Press, 2002), 525.
2 Carl Singleton, *The Sixties in America* (Pasadena, CA: Salem Press, 1999), 294–5.
3 "Berkeley Approach Seems Answer to Student Problems," *Carillon*, 4 October 1966.
4 Doug Owram, *Born at the Right Time: A History of the Baby-Boom Generation* (Toronto: University of Toronto Press, 1996), 291.
5 Ibid., 287.
6 *Sheet*, November 1959. The breakdown was SRC general expenses, $125; yearbook, $1,125; newspaper, $550; debating, $45; social committee, $275; sports, $550; music, $85; drama, $105.
7 University of Regina Archives (URA), Dean's/Principal's Office Files, 75-7, 400.1-2, "Constitution of the Students' Representative Council of Regina College of the University of Saskatchewan, Regina, Saskatchewan."
8 Editorial, *Sheet*, 16 February 1962.
9 "Resignations Cause Uproar," *Sheet*, 2 March 1962.
10 "Editor of '*Sheet*' Charges Riddell with Interfering," *Leader-Post* (Regina), 28 February 1962.
11 URA, Dean's/Principal's Office Files, 75-7, 400.1-2, "Constitution of the Students' Representative Council of Regina College of the University of Saskatchewan, Regina, Saskatchewan."
12 Ibid.
13 "M. Badham Wins SRC Election," *Leader-Post* (Regina), 17 March 1962.
14 URA, Dean's/Principal's Office Files, 75-7, 400.1-2, "Report of the Special Committee on the SRC."
15 "SRC Report," *Sheet*, 12 October 1962.
16 URA, Dean's/Principal's Office Files, 75-7, 400.1-2, "Report of the Student Activities Committee."
17 URA, Dean's/Principal's Office Files, 75-7, 400.1-2, W.A. Riddell to M. Badham, 18 December 1962.
18 Ibid.
19 URA, Dean's/Principal's Office Files, 75-7, 401.1, W.A. Riddell to M. Badham, 7 January 1963.
20 URA, Dean's/Principal's Office Files, 75-7, 400.1-2, M. Badham to W.A. Riddell, 18 January 1963.
21 URA, Dean's/Principal's Office Files, 75-7, 401.1, Faculty Committee on Student Activities to SRC, 8 January 1963.
22 URA, Dean's/Principal's Office Files, 75-7, 400.1-2, W.A. Riddell to the Student Activities Committee, 16 November 1962.
23 "War Is Declared!" *Carillon*, 26 October 1962.
24 URA, Dean's/Principal's Office Files, 75-7, 400.1-2, A.G. Cookson to W.A. Riddell, 5 November 1962.

25 "The Giant Awakens," *Carillon*, 9 November 1962.

26 "Snake Dance Leads to Police Warning," *Leader-Post* (Regina), 1 November 1962.

27 Keith Walden, "Respectable Hooligans: Male Toronto College Students Celebrate Halloween, 1884–1910," *Canadian Historical Review* 68, no. 1 (1987): 10–16.

28 *Leader* (Regina), 4 February 1915.

29 URA, Publications Section, Regina College Register, December 1923.

30 "Hijinx," *College Record*, fall 1951 (first issue).

31 *College Record*, 8 December 1952.

32 Elaine Hamilton, "Arts and Science," *Sheet*, November 1959.

33 Owram, *Born at the Right Time*, 159–61.

34 Editorial, *Carillon*, 23 November 1962.

35 Ibid.

36 Editorial, *Carillon*, 29 March 1963.

37 "Here We Go?" editorial, *Carillon*, 25 September 1963.

38 "Why Not?" *Carillon*, 25 September 1963.

39 "The Proposed Constitution and Bylaws," *Carillon*, 22 January 1965.

40 "Welcoming Message," *Carillon*, 17 September 1964.

41 "The Proposed Constitution and Bylaws," *Carillon*, 22 January 1965.

42 Ibid.

43 "Students Adopt New Constitution," *Leader-Post* (Regina), 23 February 1965.

44 URA, Publications Section, University of Regina, Board of Governors minutes, 17 March 1965.

45 Ron Thompson, "The Waiting Game – Its Fact and Failure," *Carillon*, 2 March 1965.

46 URA, Principal's/Dean's Office Files, 78-3, 400.2-1, "Regulations of the University Council, Regina Campus, Student Social Functions."

47 URA, Principal's/Dean's Office Files, 78-3, 400.2-1, K. Mitchell to R. Bain, 7 April 1965.

48 URA, College/Faculty of Arts and Science, University of Saskatchewan, Regina Campus Files, 85-54, S. Mein to A. Berland, 8 November 1966.

49 URA, Principal's/Dean's Office Files, 78-3, 400.10, A.G. Lowenberger to A. Berland, 11 January 1967.

50 "Announces November 11 March," *Sheet*, 3 November 1961.

51 "It's a Fact," *Sheet*, 5 January 1962.

52 "Peaceful Coexistence Brings out 175," *Sheet*, 16 February 1962.

53 "Reprint from 'Action Press,'" *Sheet*, 2 February 1962.

54 "Editorial Policy," *Sheet*, 30 March 1962.

55 "Referendum Supports Medicare," *Sheet*, 2 March 1962.

56 "Tories Win Campus Vote with Stand on Weapons," *Leader-Post* (Regina), 24 November 1962.

57 "Varsity Students March 'Protesting Everything,'" *Leader-Post* (Regina), 25 October 1962.

58 "Not from Cuba," *Leader-Post* (Regina), 20 November 1962.

59 David Adams, "Are You a Radical?" *Carillon*, 16 October 1964.
60 Steven Hewitt, "'Information Believed True': RCMP Security Intelligence Activities on Canadian University Campuses and the Controversy Surrounding Them, 1961–1971," *Canadian Historical Review* 81, no. 2 (2000): 191–228.
61 "More Is Enough!" *Carillon*, 2 October 1964.
62 "Visiting Russian Professor," *Leader-Post* (Regina), 30 September 1964.
63 URA, College/Faculty of Arts and Science, University of Saskatchewan, Regina Campus Files, 85-54, 502.1, Jennie N. Smythe, "Warm Heats, Cold Winter, and a World 'First.'"
64 "CUCND Changes Name, States Purpose," *Carillon*, 15 January 1965.
65 "SUPA Marches on Gov't," *Carillon*, 19 February 1965.
66 "Editorial Policy," *Carillon*, 20 September 1965.
67 "Ag Club Witchhunts and Redbaits *Carillon*," *Carillon*, 15 October 1965.
68 "Answer to *Carillon* Critics," *Carillon*, 15 October 1965.
69 "Editor Fired," *Carillon*, 22 October 1965.
70 "Student Unionism Boosted, Becomes Campus Priority," *Carillon*, 30 September 1966.
71 "Lounge for Students," *Carillon*, 15 September 1967.
72 "'The Place' Opens Tuesday," *Carillon*, 30 September 1966.
73 "The Place??" *Carillon*, 27 January 1967.
74 John Conway, "University of the Absurd," *Carillon*, 23 September 1966. See also "Rampant Bureaucracy," 24 September 1965; Ron Thompson, "Registration Frustration," 16 September 1966; "Discontent," 15 September 1967; "Registration," 17 November 1967; "The Legend of Reggie Strarr," 24 November 1967.
75 "Discontent," *Carillon*, 15 September 1967.
76 John Conway, "University of the Absurd," *Carillon*, 23 September 1966.
77 Ruth Warick, "Illusions of University," *Carillon*, 28 October 1966.
78 "Demonstration Airs Student Grievances," *Carillon*, 20 January 1967.
79 Saskatchewan Archives Board (SAB), Oral History Project no. 87, "Student Unrest at the University of Saskatchewan, Regina Campus in the 1960s and 1970s," tape R-10, 319, Michael Edge, interview with Don Mitchell, 8 April 1987.
80 "Tapes Substituted for Teachers," *Carillon*, 15 November 1968.
81 "Students to Vote on Tape Recorder Teaching," *Carillon*, 22 November 1968.
82 URA, Principal's/Dean's Office Files, 78-3, 400.2-2, Executive Committee of Council, agenda item, 28 November 1966.
83 URA, Principal's/Dean's Office Files, 78-3, 400.10, W.A. Riddell to A.G. Lowenberger, 23 December 1966.
84 URA, Principal's/Dean's Office Files, 78-3, 400.2-2, "Supplementary Report of the Executive Committee of Council," 5 December 1966.
85 Province of Saskatchewan, Corporations Branch, Students' Union File, University of Saskatchewan, Regina Campus, file 063488.
86 URA, Principal's/Dean's Office Files, 78-3, 302.1-2, F. Alexander to S. Mann, 27 February 1967.
87 "Students' Union Incorporated," *Carillon*, 27 February 1967.

88 Don Mitchell, "Past ..." *Carillon*, 6 March 1967.

CHAPTER THIRTEEN

1 "City's Flower Children Bloom at Campus Courtyard Love-In," *Leader-Post* (Regina), September 1967.
2 University of Regina Archives (URA), Principal's/Dean's Office Files, 78-3, 302.7, Ross Thatcher (speech presented at the annual convention of the Potashville Educational Association, Regina, 18 October 1967).
3 URA, Publications Section, University of Saskatchewan, Board of Governors minutes, 2 November 1967.
4 Ibid.
5 URA, Dr W.A. Riddell Papers, 84-31, 40, W.A. Riddell, memo on university-government relations, 16 March 1971.
6 Ibid.
7 "Stop Press Bulletin," *Carillon*, 20 October 1967.
8 *Carillon*, 17 November 1967.
9 "Mass Meeting Oppose Thatcher," *Carillon*, 10 November 1967.
10 URA, Principal's/Dean's Office Files, 78-3, 302.7, Action Committee to all administrative staff, 1 December 1967.
11 URA, Principal's/Dean's Office Files, 78-3, 302.7, R. Swales, acting vice-chairman of the Faculty Association, to all faculty members.
12 URA, Vice-Principal/President's Office Files, 78-4, 266, Alwyn Berland, press release, 23 October 1967.
13 URA, Principal's/Dean's Office Files, 78-3, 302.7, A.C. McEown, "The Federal Contribution to University Finance."
14 URA, Principal's/Dean's Office Files, 78-3, 302.7, press release, 5 January 1968.
15 URA, Principal's/Dean's Office Files, 78-3, 302.7, John Gardiner, "Debate on Throne Speech," 26 February 1968.
16 Ibid.
17 URA, Publications Section, University of Saskatchewan, Board of Governors minutes, 19 December 1967, W. Ross Thatcher, "Statement re University Following a Meeting with the President, Chancellor and Board Members," 22 November 1967.
18 URA, Publications Section, University of Saskatchewan, Board of Governors minutes, 2 May 1968.
19 URA, Principal's/Dean's Office Files, 78-3, 605.1, R. Thatcher to W.A. Riddell, 22 January 1968; J. McCrorie to W.A. Riddell, 22 January 1968.
20 The tuition fees for first-year arts and science were $300 per year in 1967–68 and $385 in 1968–69. This did not include the student activity fee, which remained unchanged at $33.25.
21 "Students Marched – February 15th," *Carillon*, 1 March 1968.
22 URA, Principal's/Dean's Office Files, 78-3, 302.1-2, "Fees as a Per Cent of Operating Expenditure and of Non-ancillary Revenue."

23 URA, Principal's/Dean's Office Files, 78-3, 2000.1-1, Don Mitchell, "Brief Presented to the Saskatchewan Government, Department of Education," 9 May 1966.
24 Archives of the University of Saskatchewan (AUS), President's Office Records, series 4, C38, Regina campus, W.A. Riddell, 1964–69, J.W.T. Spinks to W.A. Riddell, 16 November 1967.
25 AUS, President's Office Records, series 4, C38, Regina campus, W.A. Riddell, 1964-69, W.A. Riddell to J.W.T. Spinks, 28 November 1967.
26 AUS, President's Office Records, series 4, C38, Regina campus, W.A. Riddell, 1964-69, J.W.T. Spinks to W.A. Riddell, 3 January 1968.
27 URA, Principal's/Dean's Office Files, 78-3, 302.7, A. Guy to W.A. Riddell, 4 January 1968.
28 URA, Dr W.A. Riddell Papers, 84-31, 40, W.A. Riddell, memo, 1 February 1968.
29 URA, Principal's/Dean's Office Files, 78-3, 2000.3, note to file, W.A. Riddell, 15 February 1968.
30 "The Strange Story of One Student's Loan; Or, How a Guy Gets a Loan," *Carillon*, 16 February 1968.
31 "Guy Claims NDP Tool of Campus Protesters," *Leader-Post* (Regina), 6 February 1969.
32 "Principal Concerned about Guy Story," *Carillon*, 1 March 1968.
33 "Copy of Letter Sent from Principal Riddell to Ralph Smith, President SRC," *Carillon*, 8 March 1968.
34 "Students' Union Threatened," *Carillon*, 8 March 1968.
35 URA, Dr W.A. Riddell Papers, 84-31, 40, W.A. Riddell, notes on council meeting, 29 February 1968.
36 URA, Dr W.A. Riddell Papers, 84-31, 40, W.A. Riddell, diary, 15 April 1968.
37 URA, Principal's/Dean's Office Files, 78-3, 400.20, AUCC Board of Directors meeting, 10 July 1968.
38 URA, Principal's/Dean's Office Files, 78-3, 2001.9, W.A. Riddell to J.W.T. Spinks, 17 June 1968.
39 AUS, J.W.T. Spinks Fonds, unprocessed accession, Student Unrest, W.A. Riddell, "Student Activism," 17 June 1968.
40 URA, Principal's/Dean's Office Files, 78-3, 400.20, meeting with city officials to discuss university unrest held in the office of Mayor Henry Baker, 26 August 1968; "Police Have Codeword," *Carillon*, 31 January 1969.
41 URA, Principal's/Dean's Office Files, 78-3, 400.20, press conference, 7 August 1968.
42 "CUS Congress Mounts Attack on Society," *Carillon*, 13 September 1968.
43 AUS, J.W.T. Spinks Fonds, unprocessed accession, Student Unrest, notes on the Canadian Union of Students' congress, Guelph.
44 "Loney Outlines Student Power Philosophy," *Carillon*, 20 September 1968.
45 "SRC Holds First Regular Meeting," *Carillon*, 13 September 1968.
46 Editorial, *Carillon*, 20 September 1968.
47 Don Mitchell, "What Can We Do about Democracy," *Carillon*, 27 September 1968.

48 Ibid.
49 Eric Malling, "Anti-American Bias Discounted on Campus," *Leader-Post* (Regina), 19 December 1968.
50 AUS, President's Office Records, series 4, C5, Arts and Science, 1963–69, statement by Alwyn Berland, 18 September 1968.
51 Ibid.
52 Ibid.
53 URA, Principal's/Dean's Office Files, 78-3, 302.1-4, W.A. Riddell to D. Sheard, 3 October 1968.
54 URA, Publications Section, University of Saskatchewan, Board of Governors agendas and minutes, 12 November 1968, exhibit D.
55 URA, Principal's/Dean's Office Files, 78.3, 2000.1-2, "Why We Are Demonstrating," 7 October 1968; "An Open Letter to Premier Ross Thatcher."
56 Many people thought the statue did not do justice to the Métis *leader*, and it was later removed.
57 National Archives of Canada, Canadian Security Intelligence Service, Record Group 146, vol. 2774, part 4, W.L. Higgett to D.B. Beavis, 19 November 1968.
58 "Admin Student in Vanguard," *Carillon*, 11 October 1968.
59 "Demonstrators Attacked," *Carillon*, 11 October 1968.
60 "Moderates Organize," *Carillon*, 11 October 1968.
61 "Thompson Challenges Convocation," *Carillon*, 8 November 1968.
62 AUS, J.W.T. Spinks Fonds, unprocessed accession, Student Unrest, J.W.T. Spinks to R.L. Hanbidge, 15 October 1968.
63 "Spinks: Plagiarist or Lackey of Outside Agitator?" *Carillon*, 27 September 1968.
64 May Archer, "Spinks – Anarchists," *Carillon*, 29 November 1968.
65 URA, Principal's/Dean's Office Files, 78-3, 2000.1-3, D. Mitchell to W.A. Riddell, 24 February 1969.
66 "Images of Fund Raising," *Carillon*, 22 November 1968.
67 URA, Principal's/Dean's Office Files, 78-3, 100.37-1, public relations report, January 1969.
68 URA, Principal's/Dean's Office Files, 78-3, 2000.3, W.A. Riddell, "Statement to Council," 18 October 1968.
69 "Censor *The Carillion*...? Scold the Faculty...? Develop a 'Good Public Image'...?" *Carillon*, 15 November 1968.
70 Ibid.
71 URA, Principal's/Dean's Office Files, 78-3, 302.1-4, "Statement re: Students' Representative Council," W.A. Riddell, 13 November 1968.
72 URA, Principal's/Dean's Office Files, 78-3, 2000.3, W.A. Riddell, note to file, 10 December 1968.
73 AUS, J.W.T. Spinks Fonds, unprocessed accession, Student Unrest, W.A. Riddell to J.W.T. Spinks, 16 December 1968.
74 URA, Principal's/Dean's Office Files, 78-3, 302.1-4, Allan Tubby, statement.
75 "The Strange Story of Political Obscenities in the *Carillon*; Or, How to Suppress a Paper without Appearing to Try," *Carillon*, 24 January 1969.

76 URA, Principal's/Dean's Office Files, 78-3, 2000.3, letter signed by twenty-five clergymen.
77 URA, Principal's/Dean's Office Files, 78-3, 2000.1-3, SRC, press release, 2 January 1969.
78 "Labor, SFU Rap Governors," *Leader-Post* (Regina), 6 January 1969.
79 "No Right to Throttle Criticism, Lloyd Says," *Leader-Post* (Regina), 3 January 1969.
80 "Union Supporters," *Carillon*, 8 January 1969.
81 URA, Principal's/Dean's Office Files, 78-3, 2000.1-2, G.E. Ross Sneath to A. Tubby, 31 December 1968; "Board Decision Only – Steuart," *Leader-Post* (Regina), 4 January 1969.
82 Editorial, *Carillon*, 8 January 1969.
83 "Referendum Supports Union," *Carillon*, 13 January 1969.
84 Ibid.
85 URA, Principal's/Dean's Office Files, 78-3, 2000.1-3, notes on negotiations between the Board of Governors Committee and the SRC Committee, 3 February 1969; "Students Take Story to Public," *Carillon*, 14 February 1969.
86 "Public Won't Stand for Outrageous Acts," *Leader-Post* (Regina), 6 February 1969.
87 "Guy Claims NDP Tool of Campus Protesters," *Leader-Post* (Regina), 6 February 1969.
88 "Thatcher Attacks Students," *Carillon*, 7 February 1969.
89 URA, Principal's/Dean's Office Files, 78-3, 2000.1-4, S.C. Atkinson to the Board of Governors, 6 December 1968.
90 URA, Principal's/Dean's Office Files, 78-3, 2000.1-3, S.C. Atkinson to J.W.T. Spinks, 6 January 1969.
91 URA, Principal's/Dean's Office Files, 78-3, 2000.1-4, S.C. Atkinson to the Board of Governors, 7 January 1969.
92 URA, Principal's/Dean's Office Files, 78-3, 400.20, S.C. Atkinson to J.W.T. Spinks, 17 January 1969.
93 Saskatchewan Archives Board (SAB), Oral History Project no. 87, "Student Unrest at the University of Saskatchewan, Regina Campus in the 1960s and 1970s," tape R-10, 319, Michael Edge, interview with Don Mitchell, 8 April 1987.
94 *Carillon*, special edition, February 1969.
95 Ibid.
96 "Union Agreement Expected Wednesday," *Carillon*, 3 March 1969.
97 AUS, J.W.T. Spinks Fonds, unprocessed accession, Student Unrest, J.W.T. Spinks to P.H. Abelson, 2 August 1968.
98 "Students Defeat Occupation Motion," *Carillon*, 26 September 1969.
99 "Can Participatory Democracy Work without Participation?" *Carillon*, 24 October 1969.
100 Tamerlane, "Machiavelli's Manor," *Carillon*, 8 September 1969.
101 "Caged Conformity," *Carillon*, 2 December 1969. See also "Chapter 12 of Quotations from Chairman Mao Tse-Tung Says," *Carillon*, 23 October 1970.

102 Barry Lipton, "Prairie Fire History Illustrates Struggles of the Alternate Press," *Briarpatch*, May 1980, 35.

103 AUS, J.W.T. Spinks Fonds, unprocessed accession, Student Unrest, Jeff Holmes, "Notes on Canadian Union of Students' Congress, Guelph."

CHAPTER FOURTEEN

1 University of Regina Archives (URA), Dean's/Principal's Office Files, 75-7, 400.1-2, "Constitution of the Men's Athletic Board, Regina College."

2 URA, Dean's/Principal's Office Files, 75-7, 400.1-2, "Constitution of the Women's Athletic Board," Regina College.

3 Donald H. Amichand, "Views on Forthcoming Referendum," *Sheet*, "Extra, Extra, Extra" edition, 1960.

4 URA, Dean's/Principal's Office Files, 75-7, 501.1-1, W.A. Riddell to A.C. McEown, 28 February 1961.

5 According to Mel Kartusch, the men's hockey coach in the early years, the university supplied only the sweaters and socks. The players had to pay for the rest of their gear out of their own pockets. They even brought their own pucks to practice. This may explain why the basketball uniforms were more expensive than the hockey uniforms.

6 URA, Faculty of Physical Activity Studies/Department of Physical Education Files, 87-60, "Faculty of Physical Activity Studies, Athletics, University of Saskatchewan, Regina Campus, Men's Intercollegiate Athletics, Annual Report," 16 May 1967.

7 URA, Faculty of Physical Activity Studies/Department of Physical Education Files, 87-60, Faculty of Physical Activity Studies, Athletics, University of Saskatchewan, Regina Campus, "Men's Intercollegiate Athletics, Annual Report," 29 May 1969.

8 URA, Faculty of Physical Activity Studies/Department of Physical Education Files, 87-60, Athletics, Cougars, Basketball, 1968–70, Larry Schwentke, "Regina Cougars Upset Huskies," 19 February 1970.

9 URA, Faculty of Physical Activity Studies/Department of Physical Education Files, 87-60, Athletics, Cougettes, Basketball, 1962–68, "Basketball Team Report," 1962–63.

10 URA, Faculty of Physical Activity Studies/Department of Physical Education Files, 87-60, Athletics, Cougettes, Basketball, 1962–68, "Women's WCIAA Basketball, Summary of Results," 1968–69.

11 URA, Faculty of Physical Activity Studies/Department of Physical Education Files, 87-60, Athletics, Cougars, Basketball, 1971–74, E.A. Nicholls to H. Jansen, 19 November 1972.

12 URA, Faculty of Physical Activity Studies/Department of Physical Education Files, 87-60, Athletics, Cougars and Cougettes, 1973–74, Coach Rizak, "Open Letter to Cougars."

13 URA, Faculty of Physical Activity Studies/Department of Physical Education Files, 87-60, Athletics, Ephemerae, 1973–74, pamphlet.

14 URA, Faculty of Physical Activity Studies/Department of Physical Education Files, 87-60, Athletics, Cougars, Basketball, 1971–74, "Cougar Basketball Policy."

15 URA, Faculty of Physical Activity Studies/Department of Physical Education Files, 87-60, Athletics, Cougars, Basketball, 1968–70, Men's Athletic Board, "Team Travel and Discipline Regulations," 3 October 1969.

16 URA, Faculty of Physical Activity Studies/Department of Physical Education Files, 87-60, Athletics, Ephemerae, 1973–74, pamphlet.

17 "Sports Controversy Heating Up," *Carillon*, 2 October 1970.

18 Don Humphries, "Annual General Meeting Held," *Carillon*, 2 December 1969.

19 "Results on the Referendum," *Carillon*, 2 December 1969.

20 URA, President's Office Files, 84-32, 801.3-1, E.A. Nicholls to J.H. Archer, S.G. Mann, and F. Cuddington, 3 July 1970; E.A. Nicholls, "Proposed Athletics Budget for 1970–71," presented to SRC, 30 June 1970.

21 URA, President's Office Files, 84-32, 801.3-1, E. Nicholls to P. Ventre, 17 July 1970.

22 In time it became apparent that the Athletics Council had made the Men's Athletic Board and the Women's Athletic Board redundant. By 1973–74 MAB and WAB were not functioning. URA, Faculty of Physical Activity Studies/Department of Physical Education Files, 87-60, Athletics, University of Saskatchewan, Regina campus, "Annual Report on Intercollegiate Athletics," 1973–74.

23 URA, President's Office Files, 84-32, 801.3-2, "Constitution of the Athletics Council," University of Saskatchewan, Regina campus, 27 June 1971.

24 URA, President's Office Files, 84-32, 801.3-2, "A Report from the Athletic Subcommittee to the Academic Board of the Department of Physical Education concerning the Administration and Financing of the Athletic Program at the Regina Campus, University of Saskatchewan," January 1972.

25 Ibid.

26 URA, President's Office Files, 84-32, 801.3-2, SRC Regina campus, "A Report on Physical Activity Programming," June 1972.

27 Ibid.

28 Ibid.

29 Ibid.

30 Ibid.

31 URA, University Secretary's Office Papers, 85-34, 304.0, "Report from the Subcommittee on the Status of Physical Education on Regina Campus to the Long Range Planning Committee," 18 June 1971.

32 URA, Faculty of Physical Activity Studies/Department of Physical Education Files, 87-60, Athletics, Matthews Report, 1975, N.B. Sherlock to E.B. Tinker, 24 October 1975.

33 A.W. Matthews, *Athletics in Canadian Universities: The Report on the AUCC/CIAU Study of Athletic Programs in Canadian Universities* (Ottawa: Association of Universities and Colleges of Canada, 1974), 38, 69.

34 Ibid., 66.

35 URA, Faculty of Physical Activity Studies/Department of Physical Education Files, 87-60, Athletics, Matthews Report, 1975, "A Response to the Matthews Report on Athletics in Canadian Universities by the Canadian Council of University Physical Education Administrators," June 1975.

36 URA, Faculty of Physical Activity Studies/Department of Physical Education Files, 87-60, Athletics, Matthews Report, 1975, N.B. Sherlock to E.B. Tinker, 24 October 1975.

37 URA, Vice-Principal/President's Office Files, 78-4, 340, N. Sherlock to faculty, 19 September 1973.

38 URA, Vice-Principal/President's Office Files, 78-4, 340, N. Sherlock to J. Archer, 5 October 1973.

39 Government of Saskatchewan, Report of the Royal Commission on Organization and Structure, 22 December 1973.

40 URA, Principal's/President's Papers, 80-38, 302.11-1, W. Bolstad to J. Archer, 23 May 1973.

41 URA, Publications Section, University of Saskatchewan, Board of Governors minutes, 14 November 1968.

42 URA, Faculty of Physical Activity Studies/Department of Physical Education Files, 87-60, Athletics, Intercollegiate Athletics, Annual Reports, Fyola Lorenzen and Ernest Nicholls, "Annual Report on Intercollegiate Athletics," 1973–74.

43 URA, President's Office Files, 84-32, 801.3-3, R. Robinson to J. Archer and E.B. Tinker, 11 October 1973.

44 URA, President's Office Files, 84-32, 801.3-3, R. Robinson to E.B. Tinker, 9 January 1974.

45 URA, Faculty of Physical Activity Studies/Department of Physical Education Files, 87-60, Athletics, University of Saskatchewan, Regina campus, "Annual Report on Intercollegiate Athletics," 1973–74.

46 URA, Faculty of Physical Activity Studies/Department of Physical Education Files, 87-60, Correspondence, Negotiations with Great Plains Athletic Conference and Canada West for Playing Privileges, 1974, N.B. Sherlock to E.B. Tinker, 2 May 1974.

47 URA, Faculty of Physical Activity Studies/Department of Physical Education Files, 87-60, Correspondence, Negotiations with Great Plains Athletic Conference and Canada West for Playing Privileges, 1974, University of Saskatchewan, Regina Campus to Canada West University Athletic Association, 3 May 1974.

48 URA, Faculty of Physical Activity Studies/Department of Physical Education Files, 87-60, Correspondence, Negotiations with Great Plains Athletic Conference and Canada West for Playing Privileges, 1974, V.W. Pruden to N. Sherlock, 17 May 1974.

49 URA, Faculty of Physical Activity Studies/Department of Physical Education Files, 87-60, Correspondence, Negotiations with Great Plains Athletic Conference and Canada West for Playing Privileges, 1974, F. Lorenzen to M. Keyes, 27 May 1974.

50 URA, President's Office Files, 84-32, 801.3-4, "Agreement between the Students' Union and the University of Regina concerning Intervarsity Athletics," 28 April 1975.

51 URA, President's Office Files, 84-32, 801.3-4, R.W. Higgs to L. Barber, E.B. Tinker, and A.J. Ayre, 20 April 1976.

CHAPTER FIFTEEN

1 University of Regina Archives (URA), Principal's/President's Papers, 80-38, 302.11-8, Hall Commission, statement of Dallas Smythe, 2 August 1973.

2 Ibid.

3 URA, Principal's/Dean's Office Files, 78-3, 400.18, "Analysis of the Briefs Received by the Task Force Enquiring into the Desirability of Establishing a Faculty of Science and Mathematics"; A.B. Van Cleave, "Re: Proposed Faculty of Science and Mathematics," 30 January 1968.

4 URA, Principal's/Dean's Office Files, 78-3, 400.18, "Analysis of the Briefs Received by the Task Force Enquiring into the Desirability of Establishing a Faculty of Science and Mathematics"; D. Smythe to the faculty of the Division of Social Sciences, draft brief to the Senior Academic Committee, 26 January 1968.

5 George Grant, *Lament for a Nation: The Defeat of Canadian Nationalism* (Ottawa: Carleton University Press, 1982), 94.

6 At the time of his death, in 1992, Smythe was writing his autobiography. He did not complete the chapter on the Regina years (1963–73), but he left a few notes, including the cryptic comment that one of the themes of the chapter would be "the emergence of my Marxism in theory and practice." Simon Fraser University Archives, Dallas Smythe Fonds, F-16-1-6-1, notes for autobiography.

7 URA, Principal's/Dean's Office Files, 78-3, 400.18, "A Report to the Senior Academic Committee of the Executive of Council, Regina Campus by the Task Force Enquiring into a Recommendation at the Regina Campus for a Separate Faculty of Science and Mathematics," 12 April 1968.

8 URA, College/Faculty of Arts and Science, University of Saskatchewan, Regina Campus Files, 85-54, 102.1, J.L. Wolfson, "Concerning the Proposal to Form a Faculty of Natural Sciences and Mathematics: A Minority Report."

9 URA, Principal's/President's Papers, 80-38, 302.11-8, Hall Commission, statement of Dallas Smythe, 2 August 1973. The fate of the tapes remains a mystery.

10 URA, College/Faculty of Arts and Science, University of Saskatchewan, Regina Campus Files, 85-54, 102.1, J.L. Wolfson, "Concerning the Proposal to Form a Faculty of Natural Sciences and Mathematics: A Minority Report."

11 URA, College/Faculty of Arts and Science, University of Saskatchewan, Regina Campus Files, 85-54, 104.10, Committee to Study the Divisional Structure, analysis of questionnaires, 27 March 1968.

12 URA, Publications Section, University of Saskatchewan, Regina Campus, Faculty of Arts and Science minutes, 9 July 1968.

13 URA, College/Faculty of Arts and Science, University of Saskatchewan, Regina Campus Files, 85-54, 102.1, Senior Academic Committee minutes, 9 May 1968.

14 URA, College/Faculty of Arts and Science, University of Saskatchewan, Regina Campus Files, 85-54, 102.1, J.L. Wolfson, "A Review of Considerations concerning a Separate Faculty of Natural Sciences and Mathematics," 15 March 1973.

15 URA, College/Faculty of Arts and Science, University of Saskatchewan, Regina Campus Files, 85-54, 304, J.L. Wolfson to the faculty of the Division of Natural Sciences and Mathematics, 12 April 1973.

16 "Half Truths in Brief," *Carillon*, 20 March 1970.

17 Keith Reynolds, "Responsible to Whom?" *Carillon*, 23 January 1970.

18 "Cookie on Commies," *Carillon*, 18 June 1970.

19 URA, Principal's/Dean's Office Files, 78-3, 605.1, Roy H. Bailey, "University: Is It the Right Place to Send Your Children?" *Weyburn Review*, 13 November 1969.

20 URA, Principal's/Dean's Office Files, 78-3, 605.1, W.A. Riddell to G.E. Vaughan, 14 November 1969.

21 URA, Principal's/Dean's Office Files, 78-3, 605.1, G.E. Vaughan to W.A. Riddell, 25 November 1969.

22 Saskatchewan Archives Board (SAB), J. Clifford McIsaac Papers, R-66, 137b, J.C. McIsaac to J. Archer, 9 November 1970.

23 Patricia Jasen, "'In Pursuit of Human Values (Or, Laugh When You Say That)': The Student Critique of the Arts Curriculum in the 1960s," in *Youth, University, and Canadian Society: Essays in the Social History of Higher Education*, ed. Paul Axelrod and John G. Reid (Kingston and Montreal: McGill-Queen's University Press, 1989), 258.

24 URA, Dr W.A. Riddell Papers, 84-31, 40, W.A. Riddell, diary, 28 November 1968.

25 URA, College/Faculty of Arts and Science, University of Saskatchewan, Regina Campus Files, 85-54, 104-13, G.E. Vaughan to members of the Committee on Conventional and Unconventional Programs and Grading, 21 February 1969.

26 URA, College/Faculty of Arts and Science, University of Saskatchewan, Regina Campus Files, 85-54, 104-13, "Report to the Faculty of Arts and Science from the Committee on Programs and Grading," 9 May 1969.

27 URA, Dr W.A. Riddell Papers, 84-3, 600, W.A. Riddell to J.W.T. Spinks, 25 March 1969.

28 URA, Dr W.A. Riddell Papers, 84-31, 40, W.A. Riddell, diary, 29 April 1969.

29 URA, Dr W.A. Riddell Papers, 84-31, 47. This file contains a number of letters of appreciation to Riddell from faculty members.

30 URA, Vice-Principal/President's Office Files, 78-4, 268, Les Crossman, address to the Faculty of Arts and Science, 12 December 1969.

31 Ibid.

32 Information provided by Lieutenant Colonel Gerry Carline, CD.

33 Ian Wilson, "John H. Archer, 1914–2004," funeral service, St Luke's Anglican Church, Regina, 10 April 2004.

34 URA, Office of the President, Administrative Assistant (Shirley Wenger) Files, 92-15, 5, John Archer biography.

35 Ian Wilson, "John H. Archer, 1914–2004," funeral service, St Luke's Anglican Church, Regina, 10 April 2004.

36 URA, John Archer Speeches and Reports, 80-35, 7, John Archer, "Speech to Kiwanis Club," 8 June 1970.

37 "Archer's Defence of Students Hit by Judge Brownridge," *Carillon*, 18 June 1970.

38 "Principal Archer Does Well," *Carillon*, 18 June 1970.

39 "Great Turn Out," *Carillon*, 9 October 1970.

40 URA, Principal's/Dean's Office Files, 78-3, 2000.1-4, "Resolutions to Be Brought Up for Discussion at the Annual General Meeting to Be Held Tuesday October 27 at 12:30 in the Education Auditorium."

41 Ed Holgate, "This Union Is a Political Union," *Carillon*, 30 October 1970.

42 "At the General Meeting Roberts Rules Rides Again," *Carillon*, 13 November 1970.

43 "Machiavelli's Manor," *Carillon*, 20 March 1970.

44 Ron Thompson, "Foot and a Half," *Carillon*, 27 November 1970.

45 URA, College/Faculty of Arts and Science, University of Saskatchewan, Regina Campus Files, 85-54, 104-18, F.H.A. Rummens to the Faculty of Arts and Science, notice of motion, 8 September 1970.

46 URA, College/Faculty of Arts and Science, University of Saskatchewan, Regina Campus Files, 85-54, 104-18, G.E. Vaughan to F.H.A. Rummens, 17 September 1970.

47 URA, College/Faculty of Arts and Science, University of Saskatchewan, Regina Campus Files, 85-54, 104-18, L. Goldman to G.E. Vaughan, 17 September 1970.

48 G. Edgar Vaughan, letter to the editor, *Carillon*, 30 October 1970.

49 URA, College/Faculty of Arts and Science, University of Saskatchewan, Regina Campus Files, 85-54, 104-18, F.H.A. Rummens, "Report on the 'Liberal Arts Education Policy,'" 15 January 1971.

50 URA, College/Faculty of Arts and Science, University of Saskatchewan, Regina Campus Files, 85-54, 104-18, J. Pachner to M. Scholar, 29 September 1971.

51 URA, College/Faculty of Arts and Science, University of Saskatchewan, Regina Campus Files, 85-54, 104-18, D. Smythe to M. Scholar, 5 February 1971.

52 URA, College/Faculty of Arts and Science, University of Saskatchewan, Regina Campus Files, 85-54, 104-18, G.E. Vaughan to D. Pogany, 4 January 1972.

53 Bruce A. Kimball, *Orators and Philosophers: A History of the Idea of Liberal Education* (New York: Teachers' College Press, 1986).

54 Ibid., 37–8, 119–22, 161–7.

55 URA, Principal's/Dean's Office Files, 78-3, 400.18, D. Smythe to the Division of Social Sciences, 26 January 1968.

CHAPTER SIXTEEN

1 "Socialist Students Platform," *Carillon*, 11 February 1972.

2 Ibid.

3 "Students Elected," *Carillon*, 27 October 1972.

4 "Student Apathy Alive and Well," *Carillon*, 27 October 1972.

5 Government of Saskatchewan, Corporations Branch, Students' Union, University of Saskatchewan, Regina campus, file 063488, annual general meeting, 16 November 1972.

6 "Solidarity against Bureaucracy," *Carillon*, 30 March 1973.

7 Editorial, *Carillon*, 27 February 1967.

8 "Student Elections Flop," *Carillon*, 22 February 1974.

9 "Students' Union to Support Saskatchewan Workers," *Carillon*, 13 March 1970; "Another T. Eaton Branch in Regina," *Carillon*, 3 October 1969; "A Worker-Student Alliance," *Carillon*, 20 March 1970; "Government Moves to Place Construction Workers under Bill 2," *Carillon*, 2 July 1970; "Colonel Thatcher Attacks Labour," *Carillon*, 4 December 1970; "Strike at Parkside Nursing Home Goes into Third Week," *Carillon*, 30 July 1970.

10 "Farmers' Bust," *Carillon*, 21 November, 2 December 1969; "Farmers' Union: Opposition to Thatcher," *Carillon*, 14 May 1971; "NFU Informs Consumers about Kraft Boycott," *Carillon*, 26 November 1971.

11 "Aftermath: Regina Court Fire," *Carillon*, 29 October 1971; "Groups Organizing to Protect Tenants," *Carillon*, 23 March 1973; "NDP MLA Owns Apartment Fire Hazard," *Carillon*, 23 March 1973.

12 "NDP Leadership Race," *Carillon*, 4 June 1970.

13 Dennis Gruending, *Promises to Keep: A Political Biography of Allan Blakeney* (Saskatoon: Western Producer Prairie Books, 1990), 75.

14 "Twilight of the Gods: Colonel Thatcher's Storm Troops Reduced to Corporal's Guard," *Carillon*, 25 June 1971.

15 "All Hell Breaks Loose at General Meeting," *Carillon*, 8 October 1971.

16 "More on Administration Backlash," *Carillon*, 29 October 1971.

17 Heintz, "Grafitti," *Carillon*, 15 October 1971.

18 "Editor's Note," *Carillon*, 19 October 1973.

19 University of Regina Archives (URA), Publications Section, University of Saskatchewan, Board of Governors minutes, 13 January 1965.

20 URA, Principal's/Dean's Office Files, 78-3, 2000.1-2, Students' Union, open letter to the Board of Governors.

21 URA, Principal's/Dean's Office Files, 78-3, 2000.1-2, D. Mitchell to J.W.T. Spinks, n.d.

22 URA, Principal's/Dean's Office Files, 78-3, 2000.1-2, J.W.T. Spinks to D. Mitchell, 24 February 1967; Archives of the University of Saskatchewan (AUS), President's Office Records, series 4, C45, Regina campus, Students' Union, D. Mitchell to J.W.T. Spinks, 14 March 1967.

23 URA, Principal's/Dean's Office Files, 78-3, 400.9, J.W.T. Spinks to W.A. Riddell, 2 July 1968.

24 URA, Principal's/Dean's Office Files, 78-3, 400.9, W.A. Riddell to all members of faculty, 12 September 1968.

25 URA, College/Faculty of Arts and Science, University of Saskatchewan, Regina Campus Files, 85-54, 104-11, J.N. McCrorie to G.E. Vaughan, 10 June 1970.

26 URA, College/Faculty of Arts and Science, University of Saskatchewan, Regina Campus Files, 85-54, 104-11, R. Pope to G.E. Vaughan, 25 June 1970.

27 URA, College/Faculty of Arts and Science, University of Saskatchewan, Regina Campus Files, 85-54, 104-11, W. Dixon to G.E. Vaughan, 17 June 1970.

28 URA, College/Faculty of Arts and Science, University of Saskatchewan, Regina Campus Files, 85-54, 104-11, C.L. Kaller to G.E. Vaughan, 8 June 1970.

29 URA, College/Faculty of Arts and Science, University of Saskatchewan, Regina Campus Files, 85-54, 104-11, A.B. Hillabold to G.E. Vaughan, 9 June 1970.

30 URA, College/Faculty of Arts and Science, University of Saskatchewan, Regina Campus Files, 85-54, 104-11, G.F. Ledingham to G.E. Vaughan, 8 June 1970; H.H. Jack to G.E. Vaughan, 16 June 1970.

31 URA, College/Faculty of Arts and Science, University of Saskatchewan, Regina Campus Files, 85-54, 104-11, W.B. McConnell to G.E. Vaughan, 10 June 1970.

32 URA, College/Faculty of Arts and Science, University of Saskatchewan, Regina Campus Files, 85-54, 104-11, L.G. Crossman to G.E. Vaughan, 17 June 1970.

33 URA, College/Faculty of Arts and Science, University of Saskatchewan, Regina Campus Files, 85-54, 104-11, B. Zagorin to G.E. Vaughan, 8 June 1970.

34 URA, College/Faculty of Arts and Science, University of Saskatchewan, Regina Campus Files, 85-54, 104-11, R.C. Cosbey to G.E. Vaughan, 17 June 1970.

35 URA, College/Faculty of Arts and Science, University of Saskatchewan, Regina Campus Files, 85-54, 104-11, R.C. Cosbey to G.E. Vaughan, 18 June 1970.

36 URA, College/Faculty of Arts and Science, University of Saskatchewan, Regina Campus Files, 85-54, 104-11, J.L. Wolfson to G.E. Vaughan, 8 June 1970.

37 URA, College/Faculty of Arts and Science, University of Saskatchewan, Regina Campus Files, 85-54, 104-11, B. Lobaugh to G.E. Vaughan, 17 June 1970.

38 URA, College/Faculty of Arts and Science, University of Saskatchewan, Regina Campus Files, 85-54, 303, Division of Social Sciences, bylaws, 23 November 1970.

39 URA, College/Faculty of Arts and Science, University of Saskatchewan, Regina Campus Files, 85-54, 104-1, W.A. Riddell, "Student Participation in University Government, University of Saskatchewan," 28 September 1970.

40 "Student on Senate," *Carillon*, 6 March 1970; *Carillon*, "Students to Sit on BOG," 9 October 1970.

41 URA, College/Faculty of Arts and Science, University of Saskatchewan, Regina Campus Files, 85-54, 303, P. Hemingway to G.E. Vaughan, 10 April 1972.

42 URA, College/Faculty of Arts and Science, University of Saskatchewan, Regina Campus Files, 85-54, 303, summary of the student vote to reconsider the motion to set up a divisional guidelines committee.

43 URA, College/Faculty of Arts and Science, University of Saskatchewan, Regina Campus Files, 85-54, 303, G.E. Vaughan to F.W. Anderson, 9 November 1972.

44 URA, Publications Section, University of Saskatchewan, Board of Governors agenda, 30 November 1972, Dean Edgar Vaughan, confidential report, 19 November 1972.

45 URA, College/Faculty of Arts and Science, University of Saskatchewan, Regina Campus Files, 85-54, 303, petition, 30 October 1972.

46 Government of Saskatchewan, Corporations Branch, Students' Union, University of Saskatchewan, Regina campus, file 063488, annual general meeting, 16 November 1972.

47 "Democratic University," *Carillon*, 21 November 1972.
48 URA, Dr W.A. Riddell Papers, 83-19, 206-1, author unknown, "A History of the Occupation."
49 URA, College/Faculty of Arts and Science, University of Saskatchewan, Regina Campus Files, 85-54, 303, T.C. Wakeling to J. Archer, 20 November 1972.
50 URA, Principal's/President's Papers, 80-38, 4000.6, statement by John Archer, 20 November 1972.
51 Ibid.
52 URA, Jack Boan Papers, 83-8, Youth/Students, Student Participation Issues, mimeograph, 21 November 1972.
53 URA, Jack Boan Papers, 83-8, Youth/Students, Student Participation Issues, Students' Union, University of Saskatchewan, Regina campus, press release, 20 November 1972.
54 "Archer Refuses to Support Students' Struggle for Parity," *Carillon*, 21 November 1972.
55 URA, Principal's/President's Papers, 80-38, 4000.6, statement by A.B. Van Cleave to the Regina Campus Council, 24 November 1972.
56 URA, Jack Boan Papers, 83-8, Youth/Students, Student Participation Issues, mimeograph, 21 November 1972.
57 URA, Principal's/President's Papers, 80-38, 4000.6, M. Alexander to J. Archer, 22 November 1972.
58 URA, Principal's/President's Papers, 80-38, 4000.6, R. Robinson to J. Archer, 23 November 1972.
59 URA, Principal's/President's Papers, 80-38, 4000.6, statement by A.B. Van Cleave to the Regina Campus Council, 24 November 1972.
60 URA, Principal's/President's Papers, 80-38, 4000.6, D. Smythe to J. Archer, 22 November 1972.
61 URA, Vice-President, University of Saskatchewan Papers, 81-12, 5017.1, S.C. Atkinson to J.W.T. Spinks, 21 December 1972.
62 URA, Principal's/President's Papers, 80-38, 4000.6, statement by John Archer, 22 November 1972.
63 URA, Publications Section, University of Saskatchewan, Board of Governors agenda, 30 November 1972, confidential report by Dean Edgar Vaughan, 19 November 1972.
64 URA, Jack Boan Papers, 83-8, Youth/Students, Student Participation Issues, "Recommendations of the Tripartite Committee re Student Participation on Departmental Committees," 24 April 1973.
65 URA, Jack Boan Papers, 83-8. Youth/Students, Student Participation Issues, R.H. Fowler, J.G. Locker, and R.Y. Zacharuk, "Recommendations Concerning Student Involvement in University Government: A Report of a Minority of the Tripartite Committee."
66 URA, College/Faculty of Arts and Science, University of Saskatchewan, Regina Campus Files, 85-54, 103.5-1, K.M. Costain to G.E. Vaughan, 31 July 1972.
67 URA, College/Faculty of Arts and Science, University of Saskatchewan, Regina Campus Files, 85-54, 103.5.1, J.N. McCrorie to G.E. Vaughan, 25 September 1972.

68 URA, College/Faculty of Arts and Science, University of Saskatchewan, Regina Campus Files, 85-54, 103.5-1, C. Knapper to G.E. Vaughan, 2 August 1972.
69 URA, Jack Boan Papers, 83-8, Youth/Students, Student Participation Issues, subcommittee of the Senior Academic Committee, "A Report on Student Participation in University Government, Regina Campus, University of Saskatchewan," June 1973.
70 "Students Shafted Again," *Carillon*, 1 February 1974.
71 URA, Publications Section, University of Saskatchewan, Regina Campus, News and Information Services, news release, 15 February 1974.
72 "Soft Chairs, Soft Heads," *Carillon*, 1 February 1974.
73 URA, College/Faculty of Arts and Science, University of Saskatchewan, Regina Campus Files, 85-54, 102.1, D.T. Lowery to the Board of Governors, 3 September 1974.
74 URA, John Archer Speeches and Reports, 80-35, 24, John Archer, "The University and the Community," 1 December 1970.
75 URA, Principal's/President's Papers, 80-38, 4000.1-1, J.H. Archer, memo to file, 29 October 1971.
76 Doug Owram, *Born at the Right Time: A History of the Baby-Boom Generation* (Toronto: University of Toronto Press, 1996), 306; see also "Annual Inflation Rate – Canada, 1971 to 2004," http://www.oia.ucalgary.ca/cpi/tables/Canada.pdf
77 "That's Not Performance," *Carillon*, 28 May 1971.
78 University of Saskatchewan, *Annual Report of the President*, 1970–71; 1972–73; 1973–74.
79 URA, Dr W.A. Riddell Papers, 84-31, 48, W.A. Riddell to R. Milen, 23 January 1970.
80 George Grant, "A Critique of the New Left," in *Canada and Radical Change*, edited by Dimitrios I. Roussopoulus (Montreal: Black Rose Books, 1973), 59.
81 "Queen Is Best," *Carillon*, 17 January 1964.
82 Caption under the photo of Pam Gawley, *Carillon*, 2 October 1964.
83 "Tap-Way," *Carillon*, 2 October 1964.
84 "Bondage a-Go-Go," *Carillon*, 29 October 1965.
85 Wilma Brown, "Status of Women," *Carillon*, 13 September 1968.
86 "Women's Caucus and the Birth Control Pamphlet," *Carillon*, 19 September 1969.
87 Ibid.
88 Untitled, *Carillon*, 19 November 1971.
89 "Women's Centre on Campus," *Carillon*, 14 May 1971.
90 URA, Principal's/Dean's Office Files, 78-3, 2000.1-4, F.H. Cuddington to J. Archer, 21 September 1970.
91 URA, Principal's/Dean's Office Files, 78-3, 100.14-2, Principal's Planning Committee minutes, 8 November 1967.
92 URA, Principal's/Dean's Office Files, 78-3, 2001.11, Barb Cameron and Maija Crane, "University of Saskatchewan, Regina Campus, Day Care Centre," September 1969; URA, 78-3, 2001.11, Roy Borrowman, report on the daycare centre, 1 May 1970.

93 URA, College/Faculty of Arts and Science, University of Saskatchewan, Regina Campus Files, 85-54, 303.8-1, Department of Social Studies minutes, meeting 11, 2 March 1973.
94 URA, College/Faculty of Arts and Science, University of Saskatchewan, Regina Campus Files, 85-54, 303.8, Department of Social Studies to all faculty members in arts and science and education, 28 May 1973.
95 URA, Budget Office Files, 86-10, 98, minutes of a meeting of the Committee to Review the Status of Women at the University of Regina, 9 June 1975.
96 URA, Budget Office Files, 86-10, 96, minutes of a meeting of the Committee to Review the Status of Women at the Regina campus, 22 October 1974.
97 "Racial Prejudice and the Regina Indian," *Carillon*, 15 March 1963.
98 "Civil Rights Tested in Montmartre," *Carillon*, 29 September 1967.
99 Barbara Cameron, "A Study in Frustration," *Carillon*, 13 September 1968.
100 Matt Bellegarde, "The Indian in Saskatchewan," *Carillon*, 8 March 1968.

CHAPTER SEVENTEEN

1 Archives of the University of Saskatchewan (AUS), Emmett Hall Fonds, MG 70, VI E, University Organization and Structure, Correspondence, 1973, E. Hall to S. Nicks, 23 November 1973.
2 University of Regina Archives (URA), University Secretary's Office Papers, 85-34, 82.0, chairman's remarks to council, 27 April 1977.
3 URA, Publications Section, University of Saskatchewan: Organization and Structure: Report of a Committee on the Organization and Structure of the University, as Amended and Adopted by the Senate of the University of Saskatchewan, 4 November 1966, 9.
4 Ibid., 14.
5 Michael Hayden, *Seeking a Balance: The University of Saskatchewan, 1907–82* (Vancouver: University of British Columbia Press, 1983), 245.
6 University of Saskatchewan, *Annual Report of the President*, 1968, 1.
7 An Act Respecting the University of Saskatchewan, 1968, ch. 80.
8 URA, University Secretary's Office Papers, 85-34, 62.0, members of the GUC, 2 November 1972.
9 URA, Principal's/Dean's Office Files, 78-3, 400.1-2, J.W.T. Spinks, remarks to Regina Campus Council, 12 December 1968.
10 Hayden, *Seeking a Balance*, 247.
11 URA, Publications Section, University of Saskatchewan, Board of Governors minutes and agendas, 14 November 1968.
12 URA, Principal's/Dean's Office Files, 78-3, 400.1-2, president's report to Regina Campus Council, 19 April 1969.
13 Quoted in Hayden, *Seeking a Balance*, 247.
14 Ibid., 248.
15 URA, Principal's/Dean's Office Files, 78-3, 400.1-2, J.W.T. Spinks, remarks to Regina Campus Council, 12 December 1968.
16 URA, College/Faculty of Arts and Science, University of Saskatchewan, Regina Campus Files, 85-54, 103.1-1, J.K. Roberts to members of council, n.d.

17 URA, Office of the President, 83-16, Emma Lake Workshop, 13–15 June 1971, audiotape 3, sides 1 and 2. President Spinks acknowledged in a letter to John Archer concerning the rationalization of fine arts programs that "the G.U.C. method is not working very well." AUS, President's Office Records, series 4, B127, General University Council, J.W.T. Spinks to J. Archer, 7 June 1972.
18 University of Saskatchewan, *Annual Report of the President*, 1969–70 to 1973–74.
19 Hayden, *Seeking a Balance*, 250.
20 AUS, President's Office Records, series 4, C4, Archer, J.H., J.H. Archer to J.W.T. Spinks, 18 January 1971.
21 AUS, President's Office Records, series 4, C4, Archer, J.H., J.W.T. Spinks to J.H. Archer, 27 January 1971.
22 URA, University Secretary's Office Papers, 85-34, 408.0, J.A.E. Bardwell to the Joint Committee on Organization and Structure, 10 September 1971.
23 URA, Publications Section, University of Saskatchewan, Regina Campus Council minutes and agendas, 2 March 1971, W.A. Riddell, "University Organization for Rational and Cooperative Development," 3 February 1971.
24 URA, Publications Section, University of Saskatchewan, Regina Campus Council minutes, 4 May 1971.
25 AUS, President's Office Records, series 4, C4, Archer, J.H., J.H. Archer to J.W.T. Spinks, 30 September 1971.
26 URA, Dr W.A. Riddell Papers, 84-31, 40, W.A. Riddell, diary, 11 August 1972.
27 URA, Publications Section, University of Saskatchewan, Regina Campus Council minutes, 26 January 1972.
28 URA, Publications Section, University of Saskatchewan, Regina Campus Council minutes, 22 March 1972.
29 Saskatchewan Archives Board (SAB), A.E. Blakeney Papers, R-565, III, 159, "Report to the Board of a Meeting of University and Government Representatives," 17 February 1972.
30 URA, Vice-Principal/President's Office Files, 78-4, 157, D.A. Larmour to D. Rew, 9 March 1972.
31 AUS, President's Office Records, series 4, C4, Archer, J.H., J.H. Archer to J.W.T. Spinks, 12 May 1972.
32 AUS, President's Office Records, series 4, C4, Archer, J.H., J.H. Archer to J.W.T. Spinks, 12 May 1972, attached resolution.
33 URA, College/Faculty of Arts and Science, University of Saskatchewan, Regina Campus Files, 85-54, 102.1, E.C. Leslie to J. Archer, 16 May 1972.
34 URA, President's Office Files, 84-32, 302.1, Lloyd Barber, "University of Regina: Future Directions Study," 26 July 1977.
35 URA, Office of the President Files, 87-51, 400.13, J.W.T. Spinks to L. Barber, 29 September 1977.
36 URA, Principal's/President's Papers, 80-38, 100-5.4, convocation, spring 1972, address by President J.W.T. Spinks.
37 URA, Principal's/President's Papers, 80-38, 900.1-1, press release, 16 March 1972.

38 URA, Principal's/President's Papers, 80-38, 900.4-1, J.H. Archer, brief to the Lapp Commission, July 1972.
39 Ibid.
40 AUS, President's Office Records, series 4, C4, Archer, J.H., J.H. Archer to J. Diefenbaker, 27 April 1973.
41 URA, Principal's/President's Papers, 80-38, 900.4-1, R.W. Begg, "The Lapp Report and the University of Saskatchewan."
42 SAB, A.E. Blakeney Papers, R-565, III 159, R.A. Walker to G. McMurchy, 11 December 1972.
43 URA, Principal's/President's Papers, 80-38, 900.1-1, Faculty of Engineering, "Proposal for Change in Program," 5 November 1973.
44 Hayden, *Seeking a Balance*, 275.
45 SAB, A.E. Blakeney Papers, R-565, III 132a, "Report of Advisory Committee on Reorganization of the University of Saskatchewan," 15 August 1972.
46 Ibid.
47 Ibid.
48 URA, Dr W.A. Riddell Papers, 84-31, 40, W.A. Riddell, diary, 11 August 1972.
49 URA, University Secretary's Office Papers, 85-34, 62.0, "Interim Report of the Joint Committee on Organization and Structure," 10 November 1972.
50 AUS, President's Office Records, series 4, C4, Archer, J.H., J. Archer to J. Diefenbaker, 27 April 1973.
51 Hayden, *Seeking a Balance*, 279–80.
52 "Spinks Says Gov't Aim to Control University," *Leader-Post* (Regina), 11 April 1973.
53 SAB, A.E. Blakeney Papers, R-565, III 162 2/2, Allan Blakeney, "The University Act."
54 "Spinks Says Gov't Aim to Control University," *Leader-Post* (Regina), 11 April 1973.
55 SAB, A.E. Blakeney Papers, R-565, III 162 ½, N. Ward to R. Romanow, 5 April 1973.
56 SAB, A.E. Blakeney Papers, R-565, III 137a, Saskatchewan Government Information Services, "Bill 90 Withdrawn from Consideration," 19 April 1973.
57 Hayden, *Seeking a Balance*, 281.
58 Report of the Royal Commission on Organization and Structure, 22 December 1973.
59 Ibid.
60 URA, College/Faculty of Arts and Science, University of Saskatchewan, Regina Campus Files, 85-54, 304, J.L. Wolfson to all members of the Division of Natural Sciences and Mathematics, 3 May 1973.
61 URA, Principal's/President's Papers, 80-38, 302.11-1, W. Bolstad to J. Archer, 23 May 1973.
62 URA, Principal's/President's Papers, 80-38, 302.11-2, John Archer, "Submission to the Commission on University Structure," 20 June 1973.
63 Ibid.

64 URA, Principal's/President's Papers, 80-38, 302.11-1, K.M. Costain to J. Archer, 22 June 1973.

65 URA, Principal's/President's Papers, 80-38, 302.11-8, City of Regina, brief to the University Organization and Structure Commission, 19 July 1973.

66 Ibid.

67 Ibid.

68 SAB, A.E. Blakeney Papers, R-565, III 137a, "Summary of Saskatoon Campus Council Brief re: Administrative Structure of the University."

69 SAB, A.E. Blakeney Papers, R-565, III 137a, "Summary of Brief from Saskatoon Faculty Association re: Administrative Structure of the University."

70 Report of the Royal Commission on Organization and Structure, 22 December 1973.

71 Ibid.

72 Ibid.

73 Ibid.

74 AUS, E.M. Hall Fonds, MG 70 IA, Personal Correspondence, 1974, E. Hall to P.F. Pocock, 25 January 1974.

75 Frederick Vaughan, *Aggressive in Pursuit: The Life of Justice Emmett Hall* (Toronto: University of Toronto Press; Osgoode Society for Canadian Legal History, 2004), 232.

76 SAB, A.E. Blakeney Papers, R-565, III 137b, J.W.T. Spinks to G. MacMurchy, 16 January 1974, comments on the Hall Report.

77 SAB, A.E. Blakeney Papers, R-565, III 137b, L.I. Barber, "Comments on Hall Commission Report," 9 January 1974.

78 URA, Dr W.A. Riddell Papers, 84-3, 600, L. Barber to J.Y. McFaull, 6 February 1974.

79 John Spinks, *Two Blades of Grass: An Autobiography* (Saskatoon: Western Producer Prairie Books, 1980), 144.

80 Hayden, *Seeking a Balance*, 283.

81 SAB, A.E. Blakeney Papers, R-565, III 158a, J.W.T. Spinks to A.E. Blakeney, 11 July 1974.

82 SAB, A.E. Blakeney Papers, R-565, III 137b, R.W. Begg to G. MacMurchy, 1 February 1974.

83 AUS, J.W.T. Spinks Fonds, unprocessed accession, L.I. Barber to J.W.T. Spinks, 5 September 1973.

84 Hayden, *Seeking a Balance*, 284.

85 URA, Principal's/President's Papers, 80-38, 403.22, "Report of the Committee for Naming the Regina Campus," 22 November 1972. As early as July 1971 Spinks had written to Archer urging that "we change the name of our University." He could "foresee the day when we will have our own Board of Governors on this campus," and he wondered whether there would be "a council or commission or some other body that will look after the coordination and rationalization of programs and finances." URA, Principal's/President's Papers, 80-38, 403.22, John Archer, memo to file, 28 July 1971.

86 URA, Principal's/President's Papers, 80-38, 403.22, "Variations of Names with Frequency Count."

87 URA, Principal's/President's Papers, 80-38, 403.22, "Revised Report of the Committee for Naming the Regina Campus," 15 December 1972.

88 SAB, A.E. Blakeney Papers, R-565, III 158a, J.W.T. Spinks, address to the Regina campus convocation, May 1974.

89 James M. Pitsula, "Higher Education Policy in Saskatchewan and the Legacy of Myth," SIPP Public Policy Paper 12 (Regina: Saskatchewan Institute of Public Policy, February 2003), 24.

90 "Lieut Governor Brown Lays Corner Stone of the New Regina Methodist College," *Leader* (Regina), 26 October 1911.

Index

Illustration Credits

PAGE

25 Regina Central Collegiate Staff about 1915. Saskatchewan Archives Board, R-B3001

27 Regina College, 1947. Saskatchewan Archives Board, R-B4244

28 Panorama of Regina looking north from the dome of the Legislative Building. Saskatchewan Archives Board, R-B9678

34 William Ramsay. University of Regina Archives, 80-2, #93

36 Regina Trading Company Building. Saskatchewan Archives Board, R-B13507

38 Steward Basterfield. Saskatchewan Archives Board, R-A10891

42 Regina College faculty and full-time students, 1939–40. University of Regina Archives, 88-28 #1 oversize

52 Second World War veterans at Regina College, 1945. University of Regina Archives, 80-2, #107

62 The 1948–49 Regina College Cougar basketball team. *Freshman*, 1949, p. 50, University of Regina Archives

63 The 1948–49 Regina College Cougette basketball team. *Freshman*, 1949, p. 48, University of Regina Archives

64 The 1948–49 Regina College hockey team. *Freshman*, 1949, p. 54, University of Regina Archives

65 The 1948–49 Regina College debating club. *Freshman*, 1949, p. 43, University of Regina Archives

71 William A. Riddell. University of Regina Archives, 84-3, #4

76 Laboratory technician students at Regina College in 1954. Saskatchewan Archives Board, R-B6248-2

77 Student nurses at Regina College in 1954. Saskatchewan Archives Board, R-B6681

82 Norman MacKenzie Art Gallery, 1953. University of Regina Archives, 80-2, #76

84 Students studying in the Regina College library, 1952. University of Regina Archives, 80-2, #75

89 Student Christian Movement, 1950–51. *Freshman*, 1951, p. 50, University of Regina Archives

90 Regina College students at the prom, 1952–53. University of Regina Archives, 85-67, #29

91 Two Regina College students, 1953. University of Regina Archives, 85-67, #35

92 The French club, 1950–51. *Freshman*, 1951, p. 51, University of Regina Archives

92 Students at Regina College, 1952–53. University of Regina Archives, 85-67, #5

96 Regina College faculty members, 1952. University of Regina Archives, 80-2, #98

111 George Herbert Barr. Saskatchewan Archives Board, R-A6517-2

112 Ethel Laureen Barr. Saskatchewan Archives Board, R-B740

136 Crest of the University of Saskatchewan, Regina Campus. University of Regina Archives, 78-3, #3

137 Installation of William Riddell as principal of University of Saskatchewan, Regina Campus. University of Regina Archives, 80-6, #73

147 Premier Woodrow Lloyd laying the cornerstone for the first buildings at the Regina campus. University of Regina Archives, 80-22, #132

151 Dallas Smythe , University of Regina Archives, 89-49, #37

158 Alwyn Berland. University of Regina Archives, Info File Berland

160 Allan B. Van Cleave. University of Regina Archives, 77-2, #1

169 T.H. McLeod. *Tower*, 1966, p. 15, University of Regina Archives

171 Prime Minister Lester B. Pearson receiving an honorary degree, 17 May 1965, University of Regina Archives, 84-11, #224

173 Student protest demonstration, March 1964. *Carillon*, 16 September 1964, University of Regina Archives

178 Dominion Experimental Farm. University of Regina Archives, 84-11, #69

179 Dominion Experimental Farm, aerial view, University of Regina Archives, 75-18, #36 oversize

180 Minoru Yamasaki. Saskatchewan Archives Board, R-B5716-1

183 Yamasaki presenting the master plan for Regina campus. University of Regina Archives, 84-11, #128

184 Model of the master plan for Regina campus. University of Regina Archives, 84-11, #130

188 Premier Ross Thatcher at the official opening of the Classroom and Laboratory Buildings. University of Regina Archives, 80-20, #1110

189 The Library, the Laboratory Building and the Classroom Building. University of Regina Archives, 87-32, #10,

190 Library, main floor. University of Regina Archives, 80-38, #4

191 William Riddell, John Archer and Minoru Yamasaki. University of Regina Archives, 80-20, #1155

200 Laboratory Building hallway. University of Regina Archives, 84-11, #935

201 Laboratory Building cafeteria. University of Regina Archives, 80-20, #834

202 Regina College student lounge. Saskatchewan Archives Board, R-B5890

206 Norman MacKenzie. University of Regina Archives, 85-42, #2 oversize

207 Regina College School of Art. University of Regina Archives, 80-2, #101

209 Regina Five. University of Regina Archives, 80-20, #847

218 Darke Hall. University of Regina Archives, 87-14, #28

219 Conservatory of Music production of *Faust*. University of Regina Archives, 89-3, #1

220 Howard Leyton-Brown. University of Regina Archives, 87-14, #1

225 Department of Music students. University of Regina Archives, 80-25, #95

236 Faculty of Administration graduates. University of Regina Archives, 82-10, #1

256 Father Peter Nash, Archbishop M.C. O'Neill, and Mayor Henry Baker. Campion College Archives

257 Campion College. Campion College Archives

258 Campion College coat of arms. Campion College Archives

262 Campion College library. Campion College Archives

263 Campion College music room. Campion College Archives

264 Campion College students. University of Regina Archives, 84-11, #921

269 Luther College. University of Regina Archives, 80-20, #504

271 Luther College logo. Luther College Archives

272 Luther College residence. University of Regina Archives, 87-65, #8

273 Goose Creek Tabernacle Choir. Luther College Archives

273 Luther College "upper room." Luther College Archives

274 Morris Anderson and Jaroslav Pelikan. Luther College Archives

280 Student Representative Council, 1962–63. *Tower,* pp. 64-65, University of Regina Archives

289 Student protest march, 24 October 1962. *Carillon,* 29 March 1963, University of Regina Archives

291 A.B. Nicolaev. University of Regina Archives, 91-73, #3

293 *Carillon,* 15 October 1965, University of Regina Archives

294 Frosh week go-cart race. *Carillon,* 30 September 1966, University of Regina Archives

296 *Carillon,* 26 September 1969. University of Regina Archives

297 Regina campus lecture theatre. University of Regina Archives, 85-78, #1

298 Regina College classroom. Saskatchewan Archives Board, R-B6488

299 Students at the new Regina campus. Photography Department, University of Regina

299 Students at the old Regina College campus. Photography Department, University of Regina

300 Don Mitchell. *Carillon,* 30 September 1966, University of Regina Archives

301 Student protest, December 1966. *Carillon,* 20 January 1967, University of Regina Archives

306 "University of Sasthatcheran" sign *Carillon,* 3 November 1967, University of Regina Archives

316 Ron Thompson. *Carillon,* 8 November 1968, University of Regina Archives

321 *Carillon,* 29 November 1968. University of Regina Archives

322 *Carillon,* 25 October 1968. University of Regina Archives

323 Student power cartoon. *Carillon*, 13 October 1967, University of Regina Archives

324 *Carillon*, 8 January 1969. University of Regina Archives

332 Regina campus fencing team, 1967. University of Regina Archives, 80-20, #57

333 Cougar men's wrestling team, 1976–77. University of Regina Archives, 89-25, #3

334 Cougar men's basketball team, 1972–73. University of Regina Archives, 85-32, #64

335 Cougar women's basketball team, 1977–78. University of Regina Archives, 92-8, #7

336 Sue Higgs., University of Regina Archives, 87-60, #492

344 "Revolution Now" graffiti. Photography Department, University of Regina

361 Installation of John H. Archer as principal of University of Saskatchewan, Regina Campus. University of Regina Archives, 84-11, #301

374 G. Edgar Vaughan. Photography Department, University of Regina

376 Student sit-in. *Carillon*, 24 November 1972, University of Regina Archives

376 Student strategy session. *Carillon*, 24 November 1972, University of Regina Archives

385 Nora Best crowned campus queen. *Carillon*, 17 January 1964, University of Regina Archives

386 "Slave" auction *Carillon*, 10 November 1966, University of Regina Archives

387 Library assistant wearing pantsuit. *Carillon*, 9 October 1970, University of Regina Archives

389 *Carillon*, 15 November 1968. University of Regina Archives

399 Ray Harvey. University of Regina Archives, 84-11, #6

402 Hall Commission. University of Regina Archives, 87-54, #268

408 Lloyd Barber. University of Regina Archives, 81-12, #1

410 John ArcherPhotography Department, University of Regina

411 University of Regina in 1974. University of Regina Archives, 84-11, #1179 oversize

412 The University of Regina in 2005. Photography Department, University of Regina (Don Hall)